THE BLACKWELL
BIOGRAPHICAL DICTIONARY OF
BRITISH POLITICAL LIFE IN
THE TWENTIETH CENTURY

THE BLACKWELL
BIOGRAPHICAL
DICTIONARY OF
BRITISH
POLITICAL
LIFE
· IN THE ·
TWENTIETH CENTURY

——

Edited by
KEITH ROBBINS

——

BLACKWELL REFERENCE

Copyright © Basil Blackwell 1990
© Editorial organization Keith Robbins 1990

First published 1990

Basil Blackwell Ltd
108 Cowley Road, Oxford OX4 1JF, UK

Basil Blackwell Inc.
3 Cambridge Center
Cambridge, MA 02142, USA

British Library Cataloguing in Publication Data

The Blackwell biographical dictionary of British
political life in the twentieth century.
1. Great Britain. Politics. Biographies.
Collections
I. Robbins, Keith
320'.092'2
ISBN 0–631–15768–9

Library of Congress Cataloging-in-Publication Data

The Blackwell biographical dictionary of British
political life in the twentieth century.
edited by Keith Robbins.
p.   cm.
Includes bibliographical references.
ISBN 0–631–15768–9
1. Politicians—Great Britain—Biography—Dictionaries.
2. Great Britain—Politics and government—20th century—Dictionaries.
3. Great Britain—Biography—Dictionaries.
I. Robbins, Keith.
II. Title: Biographical dictionary of British
political life in the twentieth century.
DA566.9.A1B57   1990
920.041—dc20   89–48260   CIP

Typeset in 9.5 on 11pt Ehrhardt
by Wyvern Typesetting Ltd
Printed in Great Britain at the Alden Press,
Oxford

CONTENTS

EDITOR'S INTRODUCTION

THIS biographical dictionary is designed to provide succinct summaries of the careers of leading figures in twentieth-century British political life, together with concise estimates of their stature and significance. Front-rank politicians who have held the traditional major offices of state – Prime Minister, Chancellor of the Exchequer, Foreign Secretary, Home Secretary – largely select themselves and receive the most substantial allocation of words. Thereafter, choices have to be made, since complete coverage of every MP is not attempted. Party leaders have been included, for example, even though they have not in some cases reached cabinet rank, while some cabinet members have been left out. Some 'characters' have forced their way in, occasionally elbowing aside more worthy but more pedestrian figures.

'Political life' has not been restricted to politicians in a narrow 'professional sense', though; in extending the net, coverage is more 'representative' than fully comprehensive. Newspaper proprietors and editors jostle with men of war, and spies neighbour with archbishops. Trade union leaders sit alongside cartoonists. There are some prominent civil servants and scientists. There is a place for some political theorists and even the occasional historian.

Some men and women have played a part in British political life even though they have not been British. Some politicians from Northern Ireland have been included, whether or not they conceived themselves to be 'British', and so have certain politicians from the Irish Free State/Republic of Ireland whose careers were largely spent seeking to extricate themselves from British political life.

In short, there are no hard and fast rules for inclusion. The editor can only apologize to those men and women whose political prizes no longer seem to glitter as brightly as once they might seem to have done. There is, however, a rule which all authors have attempted to follow. They have tried to give basic biographical information in a crisp form, but at the same time to criticize and even amuse.

The editor wishes to express his gratitude to all the authors – drawn from the diverse worlds of journalism, the universities, business and politics – who have put their expertise at his disposal, accepted with relish the task of cramming the essence of a career into tight word limits and tolerated his occasional amendments. The brief guide for further reading which normally accompanies each entry enables the reader to take matters further, as does the selective list of writings offered with some articles. The editor is also grateful for the advice and guidance constantly available from various members of the staff of Basil Blackwell, with whom it has been a pleasure to work.

KEITH ROBBINS
University of Glasgow

CONTRIBUTORS

MARTIN ADENEY
London

JOHN BARNES
London School of Economics and Political Science

DAVID BEBBINGTON
University of Stirling

IAN BECKETT
Royal Military Academy, Sandhurst

MICHAEL BENTLEY
University of Sheffield

PAUL A. E. BEW
Queen's University of Belfast

MICHAEL BIDDISS
University of Reading

BRIAN BOND
King's College, University of London

ANTHONY BOTTOMS
Institute of Criminology, Cambridge

TOM BOWER
London

ANDREW BOYLE
London

MICHAEL BROCK
Windsor

JUDITH BROWN
University of Manchester

K. D. BROWN
Queen's University of Belfast

A. CALDER
The Open University in Scotland

JOHN CAMPBELL
London

DAVID CARLTON
University of Warwick

MARTIN CEADEL
New College, Oxford

RICHARD A. CHAPMAN
University of Durham

JOHN CHARMLEY
University of East Anglia

P. F. CLARKE
St John's College, Cambridge

PATRICK COSGRAVE
London

JULIAN CRITCHLEY
London

†J. A. CROSS

M. A. CROWTHER
University of Glasgow

G. DE GROOT
University of St Andrews

DAVID DUTTON
University of Liverpool

O. D. EDWARDS
University of Edinburgh

DEREK EZRA
London

GEOFFREY FINLAYSON
University of Glasgow

M. R. D. FOOT
London

D. W. FRENCH
University College, London

GEOFFREY FRY
University of Leeds

ANTHONY GANDY
London School of Economics and Political Science

JOHN GOLBY
The Open University

ADRIAN HASTINGS
University of Leeds

STEPHEN HOWE
Ruskin College, Oxford

KEITH JEFFERY
University of Ulster

KEVIN JEFFERYS
Polytechnic South West

CONTRIBUTORS

DAVID JEREMY
Manchester Polytechnic

D. JUDD
Polytechnic of North London

DENNIS KAVANAGH
University of Nottingham

MICHAEL LEAPMAN
London

ANDREW MCNEILLIE
Oxford

DAVID MARQUAND
University of Salford

C. M. MASON
University of Glasgow

K. N. MEDHURST
University of Bradford

KEITH MIDDLEMAS
University of Sussex

KENNETH O. MORGAN
University College of Wales, Aberystwyth

A. J. A. MORRIS
University of Ulster

LIZ OTTAWAY
Cartoon Study Centre, University of Kent at Canterbury

G. C. PEDEN
University of Bristol

BEN PIMLOTT
Birkbeck College, University of London

ANDREW PORTER
King's College, University of London

MARTIN PUGH
University of Newcastle upon Tyne

WILLIAM PURCELL
Oxford

WILLIAM PURDUE
The Open University

JOHN RAMSDEN
Queen Mary College, University of London

DONALD READ
University of Kent at Canterbury

DEREK ROBBINS
Polytechnic of East London

KEITH ROBBINS
University of Glasgow

JOHN ROWETT
Brasenose College, Oxford

G. R. SEARLE
University of East Anglia

ANTHONY SELDON
Institute of Contemporary British History, University of London

COLIN SEYMOUR-URE
University of Kent at Canterbury

MAURICE SHOCK
Lincoln College, Oxford

ADRIAN SMITH
La Sainte Union College of Higher Education, Southampton

IAIN SMITH
University of Warwick

MALCOLM SMITH
St David's University College, Lampeter

ZARA STEINER
New Hall, Cambridge

A. J. STOCKWELL
Royal Holloway and Bedford New College, University of London

GERALD STUDDERT-KENNEDY
University of Birmingham

RICHARD TAYLOR
University of Leeds

A. P. THIRLWALL
University of Kent at Canterbury

RICHARD THORPE
Charterhouse

DAVID M. WALKER
University of Glasgow

ALLEN WARREN
University of York

TIM WHISLER
London School of Economics and Political Science

JEREMY WILSON
Fording Bridge

A. W. WRIGHT
University of Birmingham

C. J. WRIGLEY
University of Nottingham

ABBREVIATIONS

ADC	aide-de-camp
AEI	Associated Electrical Industries
BAC	British Aerospace Corporation
BALPA	British Air Line Pilots' Association
Bart.	Baronet
BBC	British Broadcasting Corporation
B. Comm.	Bachelor of Commerce
BOAC	British Overseas Airways Corporation
B.Sc.	Bachelor of Science
Capt.	Captain
CEGB	Central Electricity Generating Board
CH	Companion of Honour
CIA	Central Intelligence Agency
CND	Campaign for Nuclear Disarmament
Co.	Company, County
CVO	Commander of the Royal Victorian Order
DCL	Doctor of Civil Law
DHSS	Department of Health and Social Security
D. Litt.	Doctor of Letters
DSO	(Companion of the) Distinguished Service Order
EEC	European Economic Community
FBI	Federal Bureau of Investigation
FRS	Fellow of the Royal Society
GCB	Knight Grand Cross of the Order of the Bath
GCHQ	Government Communications Headquarters
GCIE	Knight Grand Commander of the Order of the Indian Empire
GCMG	Knight Grand Cross of the Order of St Michael and St George
GCSI	Knight Grand Commander of the Order of the Star of India
GCVO	Knight Grand Cross of the Royal Victorian Order
GEC	General Electric Company
GOC	General Officer Commanding
GSO	General Staff Officer
Hon.	Honorary
ICI	Imperial Chemical Industries
ICL	International Computers Limited
IMF	International Monetary Fund
IRA	Irish Republican Army
JP	Justice of the Peace
KBE	Knight Commander of the Order of the British Empire
KC	King's Counsel

KCB	Knight Commander of the Order of the Bath
KCMG	Knight Commander of the Order of St Michael and St George
KCVO	Knight Commander of the Royal Victorian Order
KG	Knight of the Order of the Garter
KGB	USSR 'Committee of State Security'
KT	Knight of the Order of the Thistle
LCC	London County Council
LL B	Legum Baccalaureus (Bachelor of Laws)
LL D	Legum Doctor (Doctor of Laws)
Lt.-Col.	Lieutenant-Colonel
Ltd	Limited
MA	Master of Arts
MC	Military Cross
MEP	Member of the European Parliament
MP	Member of Parliament
NATO	North Atlantic Treaty Organization
OM	(Member of the) Order of Merit
PAYE	pay-as-you-earn
Ph.D.	Doctor of Philosophy
QC	Queen's Counsel
RAF	Royal Air Force
R. & D.	research and development
Rev.	reverend
RNVR	Royal Naval Volunteer Reserve
SHAEF	Supreme Headquarters Allied Expeditionary Force
TUC	Trades Union Congress
UK	United Kingdom
UN	United Nations
UNESCO	United Nations Educational, Scientific and Cultural Organization
USA	United States of America
USSR	Union of Soviet Socialist Republics
v.	versus
VAT	value added tax

ILLUSTRATION ACKNOWLEDGEMENTS

The Editor and Publishers gratefully acknowledge the following for supplying illustrations and granting permission for their use. Acknowledgements are due to the collections by whose permission the illustrations are reproduced and to the following sources of photographs. Ander McIntyre and Lucy Reford undertook the work of picture research.

While every effort has been made to trace and clear copyright for illustrations that appear in this book, should anyone inadvertently have been overlooked we shall be pleased to make proper acknowledgement in future editions.

Acknowledgements are listed alphabetically by source; references are to page numbers.

Hulton Deutsch Collection: 8, 11, 14, 21, 27, 32, 35, 40, 47, 51, 74, 90, 93, 100, 109, 119, 125, 134, 137, 141, 145, 160, 164, 166, 168, 172, 177, 180, 183, 193, 205, 208, 211, 216, 241, 247, 252, 256, 266, 272, 279, 282, 289, 296, 305, 309, 312, 315, 322, 330, 342, 357, 364, 380, 403, 412

© **Rob Judges, Oxford:** 426

The Raymond Mander & Joe Mitchenson Theatre Collection: 371

Popperfoto: 5, 66, 83, 97, 139, 142, 157, 196, 218, 230, 234, 245, 260, 298, 300, 319, 321, 336, 345, 391, 393, 396, 415, 421

© **Billett Potter, Oxford:** 80, 409

© **Vernon Richards/UCL Orwell Archive:** 334

A

Abbott, Diane (Julie) (*b.* London, 27 September 1953). Labour politician. Born in London of Jamaican parents, Abbott became Britain's first black woman MP in June 1987, holding Hackney North and Stoke Newington for Labour. She was educated at Harrow County Girls' Grammar School and at Newnham College, Cambridge, where she read history, and first worked as a Home Office Administrative Trainee. In rapid succession she then served as Race Relations Officer for the National Council for Civil Liberties, as a television researcher and reporter, as Equality Officer for a trade union and as a press officer for the Greater London Council and Lambeth Borough Council. A Labour Party member since 1971, she sat on Westminster City Council from 1982 to 1986 and stood unsuccessfully for Labour's National Executive Committee. She had early joined the Black Sections movement within the party, whose demands for greater representation and for the right to separatist organization within decision-making bodies led to clashes with Labour leaders.

In Parliament Abbott became secretary of the small Black Caucus, and was strongly associated with the dissident left wing within the Parliamentary Labour Party. While she and other black MPs rejected claims that such activities produced a conflict of interests between partisan and ethnic loyalties, there was evident potential for tension among the black members between their party ties, their local representative functions and the role inevitably thrust upon them of being spokespeople for black causes on a national level. Representing one of Britain's most ethnically diverse constituencies and vocal in support both of Labour's 'hard left' and of specific black causes, Abbott found herself at the heart of these tensions.

STEPHEN HOWE

Adams, Gerry (*b.* Belfast, 6 October 1948). President of Sinn Fein. The Troubles which erupted in Northern Ireland in 1969 threw up one substantial leader on the northern Republican side – Gerry Adams. Irish republicanism tends towards a kind of military élitism and fanaticism, but Adams displays a consistent capacity to think politically. Although despised by the British media, he has made Sinn Fein the dominant party of Catholic Belfast. He did not want IRA violence to cease, however; rather, he wished to avoid civilian casualties, and he also hoped to keep a certain distance from it. IRA terrorism was thus intended to continue, almost as inevitably as the fall of rain – a disruptive factor which could be ended only by negotiations with Adams leading to British withdrawal from Northern Ireland.

Adams's early life contained much that was unexceptional later: a remarkably quiet child at St Finian's school on the Falls Road, he afterwards attended St Mary's and then worked as a barman. In 1964, however, as a teenager, he had joined the Republican movement, and with the onset of the Troubles his involvement intensified. He was interned in 1971 as a suspected IRA leader in the tough Ballymurphy area, and the following year was released to take part in secret London talks between the IRA leadership and William Whitelaw which led to a brief ceasefire. A series of such contacts, culminating in a meeting with Douglas Hurd in 1979, helped to convince Adams that Britain would eventually meet the IRA's demand for withdrawal.

In February 1978 Adams was charged with membership of the IRA, but after being remanded in custody for seven months he was freed by the Lord Chief Justice, Sir Robert Lowry. By this stage, Adams's career had taken a more political bent; in June 1979, as Vice-President of Sinn Fein, he told a Wolfe Tone Commemoration ceremony at Bodenstown, Co.

Kildare, that the aims of the Republican movement could not be achieved simply by military means. The upsurge of nationalist sentiment which followed the IRA hunger strikes of 1981 aided Adams enormously; in 1983, as a Sinn Fein abstentionist, he won the West Belfast seat in Parliament and in 1987, despite the Anglo-Irish Agreement which was designed to reduce his support base, he increased his vote. Adams, who had become President of Sinn Fein in 1984, easily outmanoeuvred the slow-witted English politicians in the Northern Ireland Office, but he had much less success in persuading the electorate in the Republic of Ireland to take his party seriously and thus to broaden his base of support in a way which he himself had declared to be necessary. In 1989 Adams and his aides increasingly concentrated on the notion of a nationalist broad front (involving the Catholic Church, the Social Democratic and Labour Party and Fianna Fail): much would depend on the future of this problematical concept.

FURTHER READING

Bew, P., Hazellhorn, E. and Patterson, H., *The Dynamics of Irish Politics* (London: Lawrence and Wishart, 1989).

Patterson, H., *The Politics of Illusion: Republicanism and Socialism in Modern Ireland* (London: Radius/Century Hutchinson, 1989).

PAUL A. E. BEW

Addison, Christopher [Viscount Addison of Stallingborough] (*b.* Hogsthorpe, Lincolnshire, 19 June 1869; *d.* Radnage, Buckinghamshire, 11 December 1951). Statesman and social reformer. He was a major figure in British Liberal and Labour politics in the early twentieth century, and was unique in serving as a cabinet minister in both postwar governments, that of 1918 and that of 1945.

The son of a Lincolnshire tenant farmer, he embarked on a distinguished medical career and became an eminent professor of anatomy, first at Sheffield University, then at Charing Cross and St Bartholomew's hospitals. However, his strong social conscience took him into radical politics and he became Liberal Member for Hoxton, in London's East End, in

January 1910. He soon became deeply involved in the drafting and passage of Lloyd George's National Insurance Bill of 1911, as a progressive backbencher who was also an authority on medical matters. This episode began an alliance with Lloyd George which shaped Addison's life for over a decade. He remained closely connected with Lloyd George's social welfare programmes for health, and also pioneered the establishment of what later became the Medical Research Council. Just after the outbreak of war, he became parliamentary secretary to the Board of Education. Then in May 1915 he went with Lloyd George to the newly formed Ministry of Munitions, as his undersecretary. Here he was most energetic in stimulating and costing arms production. More controversially, perhaps, he was caught up in the union troubles among the engineering workers on the Clyde.

Addison played an important role in promoting Liberal support for Lloyd George during the ministerial arguments over military conscription. In December 1916 he strongly backed Lloyd George's succession to the premiership in place of Asquith. His reward was to become Minister of Munitions in the new coalition government. Again much of his time was taken up in union troubles concerning the direction of skilled labour, but his reputation as a vigorous minister was generally enhanced. He became a reforming Minister of Reconstruction in July 1917 and was a key figure in building up Lloyd George's Coalition Liberal Party, which resulted from the decision to hold a 'Coupon' Election and remain in postwar alliance with the Conservatives.

After the war, Addison was the major symbol of the government's professed commitment to social reform and building 'homes for heroes'. He became President of the Local Government Board in January 1919 and, five months later, the first Minister of Health. His main achievement here – if a controversial one – was his Housing and Town Planning Act of 1919, which enshrined the principle of making housing a social service through a treasury subsidy to the local authorities. More than 200,000 houses were thus built between 1919 and 1922, the first-ever council housing programme. However, the inflationary costs of the project, plus difficulties with the unions and private builders, meant that Addison's bold schemes were dogged by criticism. Conservatives attacked him as a wasteful spender and a crypto-socialist. In April 1921 he was removed from the Ministry of Health to become Minister without Portfolio. In July 1921, amid a furious public row with Lloyd George, he resigned from the government, bitterly attacking the Prime Minister for reversing his housing drive. His career as a Coalition Liberal was at an end and his future in politics uncertain.

However, after defeat at Hoxton in the 1922 election, Addison forged a new career in the Labour Party. He was the only major Coalition Liberal to join Labour and he now emerged as its leading expert in the very different field of agriculture. In 1929 he was elected for Swindon and became junior minister at Agriculture in Ramsay MacDonald's second Labour Government. In June 1930 he became Minister of Agriculture and here pursued a bold quasi-protectionist policy of marketing schemes with guaranteed prices for farm producers. His Marketing Act of 1931 launched a new policy of state support for the farmer. However, he was defeated at Swindon in the 1931 election after attacking MacDonald's new National Government, and, although returned again for Swindon in a by-election in 1934, was defeated in 1935. In 1937 he went to the Lords as a baron; in 1945 he became a viscount.

For a second time, his career seemed to be over. But Addison was now an important Labour policy-maker, and also a close confidant of the new Labour leader, Clement Attlee. After the 1945 general election, Addison possessed considerable influence in the new Attlee government, as leader of the Lords, an important chairman of cabinet inter-departmental committees, and honoured elder statesman. He was also Dominions Secretary until October 1947 where he helped build up important trade and defence links with the Commonwealth and formed a close friendship with the Canadian premier, Mackenzie King. Addison's voice was influential in cabinet on issues ranging from the National Health Service (which he strongly backed) to steel nationalization (where he had grave doubts).

He also led the largely Tory House of Lords with much skill and defused possible clashes with the Labour Government. He remained a prominent cabinet minister after the 1950 election, as Lord Privy Seal, then Lord President of the Council, and was still in office when the government fell in October 1951. Two months later, he died of cancer. He married twice, and was survived by a widow and four children.

An uncharismatic figure, Addison left a major mark on the Liberal and Labour parties, and the British progressive tradition. He promoted innovative policies in various key departments over a lengthy span of years. He is also the most important doctor ever to have played a significant part in British politics.

WRITINGS

Politics from Within, 2 vols. (London: Herbert Jenkins, 1924).
Four and a Half Years, 2 vols. (London: Hutchinson, 1934).

FURTHER READING

Morgan, Kenneth O., *Consensus and Disunity: the Lloyd George Coalition Government, 1918–1922* (Oxford: Clarendon Press, 1979).
Morgan, Kenneth and Jane, *Portrait of a Progressive: the Political Career of Christopher, Viscount Addison* (Oxford: Clarendon Press, 1980).
Morgan, Kenneth O., *Labour in Power, 1945–1951* (Oxford: Oxford University Press, 1984).

KENNETH O. MORGAN

Aitken, Max. See BEAVERBROOK, LORD.

Alanbrooke, Viscount. See BROOKE, ALAN.

Alexander, Harold (Rupert Leofric George) [Earl Alexander of Tunis] (*b.* London, 10 December 1891; *d.* Wexham, Buckinghamshire, 16 June 1969). General, Commander-in-Chief and Minister of Defence. He did not really come to public notice until he was appointed Commander-in-Chief in the Middle East in August 1942, and, in a sense, he remained an enigmatic figure throughout his public career. Indeed, it has been suggested that he rose beyond his real level of capability as a commander, although he was an ideal military figurehead for Allied coalition warfare in the Mediterranean theatre during World War II.

The third of four sons of the 4th Earl of Caledon, Alexander was always conscious of his Ulster origins. As a young subaltern in the Irish Guards he had threatened to resign his commission at the time of the Curragh Incident in March 1914. Most of his early childhood was spent at Caledon in County Tyrone, as were holidays from his preparatory school at Westgate in Kent and from Harrow, where he excelled in games. Alexander would have preferred to make his way as a professional painter, and passing through the Royal Military College to a commission in 1911 was therefore intended only as a temporary career. However, although painting remained a lifelong preoccupation, World War I committed him to the army.

In the war Alexander advanced from the rank of Lieutenant to that of acting Lieutenant Colonel commanding the 2nd Battalion of his regiment. In the process he was twice wounded and won both the MC at Loos in 1915 and the DSO on the Somme in 1916. Despite a faint air of dandyism that clung to him throughout his life, his courage was undoubted and the war confirmed his reputation for imperturbability and leadership qualities. Seeking further active service at the end of the war, he joined the Allied Relief Commission in Poland in 1919 and went on to the British Military Mission in the Baltic, commanding the locally raised Baltic *Landwehr*, which campaigned against Bolshevik forces in Latvia and Estonia, until it was incorporated into the new Latvian Army in March 1920. Alexander then returned to regimental service with the Irish Guards, commanding his battalion at Constantinople and on Gibraltar.

Alexander went to the Staff College as a student in 1926 at the relatively advanced age of 34 and, as a full Colonel, was senior in rank to many of his instructors, including Alan Brooke and Montgomery. Further regimental duties were followed by study at the Imperial Defence College in 1930, and he was then posted to the Directorate of Military Training

in the War Office. Having married the daughter of the Earl of Lucan in 1931, Alexander was appointed GSO 1 in Northern Command and remained there until given command of the Nowshera Brigade on the Indian North-West Frontier in 1934. He led his brigade capably in two campaigns against warring tribesmen, and it has been suggested that he reached a professional peak as a brigadier. Certainly, he lacked a wider imagination. He was also little interested in administration, having delegated such matters as logistics to his subordinates ever since becoming a battalion commander. However, as his most recent biographer has remarked, promotion 'generates its own momentum' and in 1937 Alexander became the youngest Major-General in the army upon assuming command of the 1st Division at Aldershot.

Alexander's composure was of considerable account when, in common with the rest of the British Expeditionary Force (BEF), his division was driven back on the beaches of Dunkirk in May 1940. Indeed, Alexander was chosen to command the rearguard when it was judged that his superior commanding I Corps (although expendable in a way that Alexander was not) was not up to the task. Alexander fully put into effect the meagre and somewhat conflicting orders given him and did not leave Dunkirk until the early morning of 3 June – having personally travelled along the shoreline in a small boat looking for additional British troops to take off. After assuming command of I Corps on 31 May, Alexander was retained in his appointment and was responsible for the defence of the northern coasts, with headquarters at Doncaster, through the difficult months of the summer. In December 1940 he was promoted to Lieutenant-General upon taking over as GOC of Southern Command.

Alexander had already come to the notice of the new Prime Minister. Churchill appears always to have been immensely drawn to him. As a result, Alexander figured in a number of stillborn Churchillian projects until, recently knighted, he was sent out to Burma in February 1942 with the forlorn mission of trying to save the country from the Japanese onslaught; he replaced Lieutenant-General Hutton, who had lost the confidence of both Delhi and London.

General Alexander,
Commander-in-Chief,
Middle East, at the wheel of
his own jeep, Benghazi,
December 1942

In particular, Hutton's plan to abandon Rangoon had damned him in the eyes of the Commander-in-Chief in the Far East, Wavell, and the latter expected Alexander to fight for the city. In fact, Wavell greatly underestimated the Japanese and, having arrived in Rangoon on 5 March with the intention of complying with instructions, Alexander quickly grasped the realities of the situation. Accordingly, the city was abandoned on the 6–7 March and Alexander and his forces only just managed to escape encirclement. Thereafter, he ensured that Mandalay did not also become a trap for British troops, and he resisted pressure from both London and the nationalist Chinese by withdrawing his whole force towards India rather than some falling back on China.

Recalled to Britain in May 1942, Alexander first took over command of the 1st Army designated for the Allied invasion of North Africa ('Torch') but on 15 August the shake-up in the Middle East command saw him translated to Commander-in-Chief in the Middle East, with Montgomery commanding the 8th Army. It was a partnership ALAN BROOKE had urged on Churchill precisely because he felt that Alexander would not interfere with Montgomery's tactical handling of the desert battle, and as much as anything Alexander was there to interpose himself between Montgomery and Churchill's impatience for

action. While his responsibilities obviously extended beyond the Western Desert, Alexander's low profile in the campaign was assumed deliberately and accorded with his personal preference. At times he might well have interfered with profit in Montgomery's tactical decisions but invariably chose to make concessions to his difficult subordinate's stronger will. Consequently, Montgomery tended to display an increasingly off-hand attitude in dealings with Alexander.

In many ways Alexander resembled the American, Eisenhower. The latter was delighted when Alexander was suggested as Deputy Supreme Commander to himself for the conclusion of the North African campaign, Alexander taking over the 18th Army Group comprising the 1st and 8th Armies and the US II Corps in February 1943. It was a role that admirably suited Alexander's personality and he ensured that all nationalities shared the victory won in Tunisia. He endeavoured to achieve the same when the Allies invaded Sicily in July 1943, by which time the 18th Army Group had been renamed the 15th Army Group and the American presence had been increased to army strength. However, the Sicilian campaign was a more unhappy experience. Alexander was often caught between Montgomery and the equally difficult George Patton commanding the US 7th Army. Nevertheless, the escape of German forces to Italy owed far more to the fact that the Allies were entirely undecided as to their future strategic plans.

In fact, Alexander was constantly subjected for the remainder of the war to decisions taken elsewhere, as his army group was committed to an invasion of Italy in September 1943. Planning in advance was frequently bedevilled by Allied disagreements, and Alexander was never able to exploit the campaign in the way he wished. The most notable examples were the virtual closing down of the theatre as a result of the decision to effect a landing in the South of France in August 1944 and the failure to push on to Vienna in 1944–5, although this last was probably beyond attainment. As in North Africa, Alexander remained an executor rather than an originator, and much credit for the success of the campaign at a strategic level is usually accorded to Alexander's chief of staff, John Harding. However, Alexander should be commended for saving the Salerno bridgehead by prompt despatch of reinforcements and provision of supporting aerial and naval fire-power in September 1943. He also won Allied approval for a final push in northern Italy in April 1945, which resulted in complete German capitulation there a month later.

Alexander might have become Eisenhower's Deputy Supreme Commander in North-West Europe and he was also considered for the supreme command in the Mediterranean, but it was felt that he was more valuable in Italy. However, when Sir Henry Maitland Wilson was appointed to replace Sir John Dill as head of the British Military Mission in Washington in December 1944, Alexander was elevated to the rank of Field Marshal and to the supreme command in the Mediterranean, which gave him the additional responsibility of handling relations with the Yugoslav partisans and for the Allied attitude towards the emerging civil war between monarchists and communists in Greece. He remained supreme commander until October 1945. Alan Brooke apparently proposed that Alexander should succeed him as Chief of the Imperial General Staff, but instead Alexander, who was made a Viscount in January 1946, went to Canada as Governor-General. He proved extremely popular and travelled widely before being recalled by Churchill in January 1952 to join his government as Minister of Defence.

Alexander was elevated to an earldom on his retirement from Canada. He disliked politics but felt it his duty to accept the office offered him. Indeed, he could never adjust to the attributes required of a politician, and a criticism he uttered at a private function concerning the positioning of United Nations reserves in Korea, in the belief that it would go unreported, illustrated his lack of political acumen. In fact, his role was undefined and he made no attempt to exert authority, leaving the service ministers largely alone to run their departments while Churchill, who no doubt appointed him for precisely this reason, retained effective control of defence policy. Retiring in October 1954, Alexander took on a number of directorships. He was Constable of the Tower from 1960 to 1965 and Lord Lieutenant of the County of London from 1957 to 1965 and of Greater London from 1965 to 1966. He also turned more and more to his painting.

Success seemed to come easily to Alexander and he never actually failed in anything he did. Moreover, he had the right attributes to weld effective teams from disparate individuals of varying nationalities, but there is a distinct impression that he rose to high command in spite of himself. Few ever penetrated his detached reticence and his most recent biographer has aptly commented that Alexander 'did not wish to be known too well and perhaps there was not a great deal more to know.'

FURTHER READING

Alexander of Tunis, Field Marshal Earl, *Memoirs, 1939–1945*, ed. John North (London: Cassell, 1962).

Jackson, W. G. F., *Alexander as Military Commander* (London: Batsford, 1971).

Nicolson, Nigel, *Alex* (London: Weidenfeld and Nicolson, 1973).

Seago, Edward, *The Paintings of Earl Alexander of Tunis* (London: Collins, 1973).

I. F. W. BECKETT

Allenby, Viscount [Edmund Henry Hynman; Viscount Allenby of Felixstowe and Megiddo]

('The Bull') (*b*. Brackenhurst, Nottinghamshire, 23 April 1861; *d*. London, 14 May 1936).   General and statesman. Allenby was a notable military figure in the history of British rule in the Middle East.

He was educated at Haileybury and entered Sandhurst only after having first failed to pass the entrance examination for the Indian Civil Service. He was commissioned into the Inniskillings (6th Dragoons) in 1882 and saw active service in Bechuanaland (1884–5) and Zululand (1888). Unlike most of his contemporaries, he never served in India. He attended the Staff College at Camberley, where he was a contemporary of Sir DOUGLAS HAIG, between 1896 and 1898. Allenby was more popular than Haig with his fellow students and they elected him master of the Staff College drag hounds even though Haig was the better horseman. This may have soured relations between the two men and Allenby never felt at ease when serving under Haig during World War I.

During the Boer War Allenby gained a reputation as a capable cavalry leader, first as a squadron commander in Sir John French's Cavalry Division during the advance to Pretoria and subsequently as a column commander hunting down Boer commandos during the guerrilla phase of the war. He spent the entire period between the end of the Boer War in 1902 and the outbreak of World War I serving at home, first as a regimental and then as a brigade commander and finally, shortly after being promoted to Major General in 1909, as Inspector General of Cavalry. It was at this point in his career that he began to acquire a reputation for possessing a seemingly uncontrollable temper. He did not suffer fools or sycophants gladly.

As Inspector General, Allenby was rigorous in the pursuit of efficiency. But when he took the Cavalry Division to France in August 1914 as its commander, it still suffered from serious defects. The division had no permanent peacetime staff and one had to be improvised on mobilization. Before the war, regiments had been scattered throughout the United Kingdom and came together only twice as a division between 1910 and 1914. Even so, the cavalry succeeded in covering the flanks and rear of the British Expeditionary Force (BEF) during the retreat from Mons. During the first battle of Ypres (October–November 1914) Allenby's dismounted troopers played a vital role in plugging gaps in the fragile British line.

Allenby's career on the Western Front in 1915–16 was relatively undistinguished. In May 1915 he took command of V Corps and in October he was promoted to command the newly formed Third Army. His outstanding achievement in France was at the battle of Arras, which began in April 1917. Determined to restore an element of surprise to operations on the Western Front, he insisted that his assault should be preceded by a short but very intense artillery bombardment rather than by a very lengthy one, such as that which had heralded the start of the battle of the Somme in July 1916 and had served to warn the Germans of the British intention to attack. Haig's headquarters objected to this revolutionary feature of his plan and he was forced to lengthen the preliminary bombardment somewhat, but the operation was still a distinct, if strictly limited, success. The British advanced three and a half miles on the first day of the battle. That was the longest advance carried out by any army on the Western Front since the start of trench warfare at the end of 1914.

Allenby and Haig had never been comfortable in each other's company and Haig was probably glad to release him to take over command of the Egyptian Expeditionary Force (EEF) in Palestine in June 1917. In April, Allenby's predecessor, Sir Archibald Murray, had failed to break through the Turkish lines at Gaza and advance to Jerusalem. Immediately on his arrival, Allenby conducted a personal tour of inspection of his troops, designed to restore their confidence and to familiarize himself with their problems. He did both. He demanded and received reinforcements from Britain, and at the very end of October his army began an advance which took them to the gates of Jerusalem before Christmas.

In January 1918 the government in London wanted Allenby to advance still further north and to knock the Turks out of the war. However, in March the Germans began a major offensive on the Western Front and Allenby's army had to be milked for reinforce-

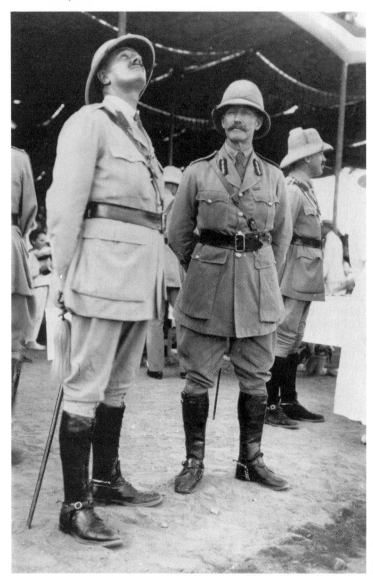

Viscount Allenby as British
High Commissioner in
Egypt, early 1920s

ments to sustain Haig's troops. Thus it was not until mid-September 1918, when many of Allenby's British troops had been replaced by Indians, that he could resume his advance. Allenby possessed a considerable advantage over the Turks in infantry, artillery, aircraft and cavalry and in addition he was assisted by the Arabs in the Hejaz, whose revolt against the Turks had been organized by a group of British officers, the most outstanding of whom was Colonel T. E. Lawrence. Allenby's attack began on 19 September and by 30 October, when the armistice with the Turks was signed, he had destroyed the Turkish army in Palestine and Syria. He had captured nearly 75,000 prisoners, 360 guns and occupied Damascus and Aleppo.

Allenby's active career did not finish at the end of the war. Between 1919 and 1925 he was British High Commissioner in Egypt. In this post he demonstrated qualities of statesmanship which had been lost to the Indian Civil Service when he failed their entrance examination nearly 40 years before. Confronted by a violent nationalist revolt against the British Protectorate, he persuaded the Foreign Office to release the main nationalist leader, Saad Zaghlul, from internment in Malta. He was soon convinced that the continuation of the Protectorate was impossible and in 1922 he finally persuaded the British Government that it should be abolished. It was replaced by an Anglo-Egyptian treaty which granted Egypt sovereign status but reserved for the British control of what they deemed most valuable to their imperial interests – control of the Suez Canal, the right to station troops in the Canal Zone, and a continued condominium over the Sudan.

Allenby's reputation continues to puzzle historians. He was notoriously bad-tempered – hence his nickname 'The Bull' – and his outward appearance seemed to typify a generation of British generals who were baffled by the tactical conundrums of World War I. But as commander of the EEF in 1917–18 he showed himself to be a master of mobile warfare. By meticulous planning, he was able to orchestrate the operations of his infantry, artillery, cavalry and aircraft, to defeat a succession of Turkish armies and to advance over 350 miles from Gaza to Aleppo. After the war, as British High Commissioner in Egypt, he showed himself to be a politically astute and far-sighted imperial pro-consul. As a young man he developed a passion for travel, he was a skilled artist and he was passionately fond of rose-growing and ornithology. He retired in 1925 and died in 1936.

FURTHER READING

Gardner, B., *Allenby* (London: Cassell, 1965).
Wavell, A. P., *The Palestine Campaigns* (London: Constable, 1928).
Wavell, Lord, *Allenby: Soldier and Statesman* (London: Harrap, 1940).

DAVID FRENCH

Amery, Leo(pold Charles Maurice Stennett) (*b.* Gorakhpur, India, 22 November 1873; *d.* London, 16 September 1955). Conservative politician and author. It was said of Leo Amery that had he been half a head taller and had his speeches been half an hour shorter he might have been Prime Minister. Baldwin's private secretary spoke of his 'alpinising energy', but it tended to stun rather than inspire colleagues.

Born in the North-Western provinces of India, Amery was brought up in England by his Hungarian mother (his father had thrown up his job in the Indian Civil Service for a new life in the USA); he inherited his gift for languages from her. Educated at Harrow and Balliol College, Oxford, he took Firsts in classical moderations and classics and philosophy and won his half blue for cross country. He was awarded the Ouseley scholarship in Turkish by the Imperial Institute in 1895 and at the second attempt secured a Fellowship at All Souls in 1897. He had spent the interim period as private secretary to the Liberal Unionist politician Leonard Courtney. An assignment in the Balkans writing for the *Manchester Guardian* attracted the attention of *The Times* correspondent in Vienna, and to this Amery owed his appointment as assistant to the paper's foreign editor, Sir Valentine Chirol. He spent the next decade on *The Times*. His activities in arranging the coverage of the Boer War led to a major assignment as editor and in large part author of the seven-volume *Times History of the War*. He was also called to the Bar in 1902, but increasingly saw his future in politics.

In South Africa Amery had fallen under the spell of Lord Milner, who became a close friend and patron. He remained a lifelong advocate of the virtues of the British Empire. When Joseph Chamberlain took up the cause of tariff reform, Amery compared his action to Luther's pinning up the Wittenberg theses; it had a profound impact on his own thinking. He also advocated army reform, publishing *The Problem of the Army* in 1903, and he drafted much of Arnold-Forster's White Paper in 1904. Later he gave support to the National Service League. As one of the founders of a cross-party dining club, the Coefficients, he was portrayed in H. G. Wells's novel *The New Machiavelli* as Crupp. Although he was offered the editorship of *The Observer* in 1908 and of

The Times in 1912, he turned both offers down: after four unsuccessful attempts, he had finally entered Parliament in 1911. He held South Birmingham (later named Sparkbrook) until it was taken by Labour in 1945.

Amery sided with the diehards in their last-ditch opposition to the Parliament Bill and wrote a polemic, *Case Against Home Rule*. He was frustrated by his leader's decision to abandon food taxes as part of party policy in 1913 since he saw these as key to any effective policy of Imperial Preference. In 1914, when it seemed that the Liberals were likely to decide on neutrality, he helped ensure that they knew the Conservative Party was for war, and he subsequently helped Kitchener to organize the earliest recruiting drives. However, he continued to advocate conscription. He saw service as an intelligence officer in Flanders, the Balkans, at Gallipoli and Salonika, and was lucky to escape with his life when the *Caledonian* was torpedoed in 1916. Milner suggested him as deputy secretary for the War Cabinet, and he was appointed, despite Hankey's reluctance, as one of the two political secretaries. His experience of the workings of the War Cabinet turned him into a lifelong advocate of a small non-departmental policy cabinet. He was a major advocate of an 'eastern' strategy for winning the war, and he also envisaged a homeland for the Jews as a potential bastion of empire in the Middle East. He helped draft the Balfour Declaration. In 1918 he was dispatched to serve the Supreme War Council at Versailles, but the job did not develop as he had hoped.

In 1919 Amery became Parliamentary Under Secretary to Milner at the Colonial Office, and then in 1921 Parliamentary and Financial Secretary to the Admiralty. Although used by Lloyd George to help devise policy towards empire development, he became increasingly unhappy at the negative policies pursued by the Coalition Government, nor did he like the 1921 Irish Treaty. He was active therefore in the moves which led to the Carlton Club meeting, although vainly trying for a compromise to allow Austen Chamberlain to retain the leadership. In Bonar Law's Conservative government, Amery was considered for the Colonial Office but appointed First

Lord of the Admiralty. He furthered the choice of Singapore as Britain's Far Eastern naval base, attempted in vain to recover control of the Fleet Air Arm for the navy, and developed a major cruiser building programme. He believed – probably wrongly – that he had played a key part in Baldwin's appointment as Prime Minister when Bonar Law resigned in May 1923, and he was one of the major influences on Baldwin's decision to go to the country on a tariff reform platform in December.

Amery became Colonial Secretary in November 1924 and played a major role in the revolution which transformed the empire into a commonwealth of freestanding dominions, linked by their common allegiance to the Crown. Although he had little to do with the actual drafting of the Balfour formula, the concept of using the 1926 Imperial Conference to redefine relationships within the empire was Amery's, and, if anything, it strengthened his determination to draw the economic ties of empire closer. He created an Empire Marketing Board with an annual grant of a million pounds, but it was never popular with the Treasury and was abolished in 1933. While his wish to use the Crown Agents as a general staff never came to fruition, his appointment of the Fisher Committee in 1928 laid the foundations for a more unified colonial service. In his earlier spell at the Colonial Office he had put the Empire Settlement Act on the statute book, subsequently coined the phrase which summed up the creed of the 'Imperial visionaries' – 'men, money and markets' – and argued that empire development would resolve Britain's unemployment problem. Despite Treasury resistance, Amery secured the passage of the East African Loans Act 1926 and laid the foundations of the seminal Colonial Development Act of 1929. He made a successful tour of the dominions in 1927–8, but felt later that he would have been better engaged in arguing for a more advanced tariff policy at home. After the Conservative defeat in 1929, he was impatient with the slowness with which Baldwin adjusted the tariff policy of the party, but his personal affection for his leader prevented him from taking charge of Beaverbrook's Empire Crusade. Eventually in October 1930 he and

Neville Chamberlain persuaded Baldwin to adopt the policy of the 'free hand'. On the question of moves towards the self government of India, he was in full support of the line pursued by Baldwin and often operated in its defence against Churchillian acolytes in the party's India Committee. He was less enthusiastic about Baldwin's decision to join in a temporary national combination to deal with the 1931 economic crisis, prophesying rightly that the party would find it difficult to disentangle itself from this 'tar baby'. Baldwin's efforts to secure him office in the subsequent National Government were baulked by MacDonald, and Amery became critical of the tariff policies actually adopted. His open disappointment with the agreements reached at the Ottawa Conference in 1932 made him unpopular with his former colleagues and destroyed any chance of a return to office.

Instead Amery pursued an active business career, and in 1935 he published his most considerable work, *The Forward View*, which sketched his vision of a world made up of regional economic entities and explained why he thought this a better base for successful international organization than mechanical schemes like the League of Nations and illusory dreams of world disarmament. He was,

with Churchill, an advocate of British re-armament, but this did not prevent him from helping frustrate Churchill's onslaught on the Government of India Bill. Subsequently he found himself at odds with the government over its support for League of Nations sanctions against Italy. This probably cost him the new Ministry for the Coordination of Defence in March 1936, and he was further disappointed when Neville Chamberlain would not give him office in 1937. In the late 1930s Amery led the opposition to any attempt at the colonial 'appeasement' of Germany, supported a sensible partition of Palestine, and was a bitter critic of the way in which policy towards the Jews subsequently developed. He could not stomach the stratagem which led to Munich and was a leading member of the so-called Amery–Eden group which from that moment united most Conservative critics of the government's foreign policy.

When war came, he became the leading Conservative critic of Chamberlain's government, not least for its inability to get its economic act together. When the government was forced to abandon its intervention in Norway, Amery made a devastating parliamentary attack, quoting Cromwell: 'You have sat too long here for any good you have been doing.

Leo Amery, June 1940

Depart, I say, and let us have done with you. In the name of God, go.' Although canvassed himself as a possible Prime Minister, he warmly welcomed Churchill's appointment and continued to do so even when he was denied the defence post or the economic over-lordship for which he thought himself well qualified. He considered himself side-tracked at the India Office to which Churchill sent him, but with his usual energy strove to win Indian nationalist support for the war by a guarantee of constitutional progress after it ended. Church-ill emasculated his efforts and the declaration made in August 1940 fell well short of what he wished to offer. A disappointed Congress embarked on civil resistance and persisted in their demands to have immediate control of the government of India and its defence, even in the face of the Japanese onslaught. Gradual Indianization of the Viceroy's Council and a revised version of Amery's earlier offer of a constituent assembly could not prevent them from embarking on the Quit India campaign in July 1942. Their leaders were arrested and order restored with surprising ease. Amery continued to search for ways of achieving a partial transfer of power and he found an ally in Wavell, who was appointed Viceroy in August 1943. Churchill, however, proved resistant to any conciliatory moves and it was not until October 1944 that Amery suggested a dramatic possibility: to grant India independence on the existing constitution and then let those con-cerned develop a new constitution. It was perhaps too simple and imaginative a plan to carry conviction and neither the Viceroy nor Amery's colleagues were persuaded. Amery subsequently put his weight behind Wavell's plan for a provisional government on a 50–50 communal basis, but was not able to secure cabinet agreement until 31 May 1945. The Simla Conference which followed broke down before the Conservative Government left office. Defeated himself in the 1945 election, Amery was left to reflect on the end of his hopes of maintaining a united subcontinent.

Within the wartime government Amery had contributed to the making of strategy on the Middle East Committee, particularly in 1941, and he had also been the major critic of US efforts to secure the end of Imperial Preference as part of the Lend Lease agreement. Later he worked with Beaverbrook in a vain attempt to prevent British adhesion to the Bretton Woods agreement. Despite his absence from the post-war House of Commons, he remained politi-cally active, a staunch opponent of the Washington loan and of all schemes which seemed to further American economic domination of the postwar world; an equally strong supporter of the European movement, envisaging links between Europe and the Com-monwealth; and a last-ditch defender of Imperial Preference against the 1951 Con-servative Government's support of GATT (General Agreement on Tariffs and Trade). The Suez Group was formed at his house in 1954. He also found time to write three volumes of memoirs, which have been well described as 'a vivid historical chronicle as well as a testimony of faith', and to publish his classic *Thoughts on the Constitution*. He remained to the end remarkably catholic in his range of interests and political contacts; his knowledge of men and places, his profound learning and his kindly humanity made his house a mecca for many of the younger gener-ation in politics.

WRITINGS

My Political Life, 3 vols. (London: Hutchinson, 1953, 1953, 1955).

FURTHER READING

Barnes, John and Nicholson, David (eds.), *The Leo Amery Diaries*, i: *1896–1929*; ii: *The Empire at Bay* (London: Hutchinson, 1981, 1988).

JOHN BARNES

Amory, Derick (Heathcoat) [Viscount Amory] (*b.* Tiverton, Devon, 26 December 1899; *d.* 20 January 1981). Conservative Chancellor of the Exchequer. Amory was appointed Chancellor in January 1958 and resigned in April 1960. Had he not done so, he might well have been considered as a possible successor to the Prime Minister, Harold Mac-millan. That at least was the opinion of a good many close to the centre of things. He was a successful Chancellor presiding over an expansionary phase of the economy, but contemporary opinion in retrospect felt that he had 'given too much away' in his 1959 budget and had put the balance of payments under strain. He would seem to have been in agreement with his critics, warning the Prime Minister before he retired of the need for greater restriction. However, there is some evidence that the boom accentuated by the Conservatives' third successive election victory would have burnt itself out without necessitating further deflationary action. Amory's chancellorship saw a remarkable combination of price stability, economic growth and balance of payments surpluses, while unemployment in all but two months was below 500,000.

Amory was educated at Eton and Christ Church, Oxford, and when he went down in 1923 he joined the accountants Price Waterhouse. His father arranged that he should spend a year touring the world; he returned homesick after only a few months and together with his elder brother took over the family silk manufacturing business, John Heathcoat and Co., in his native Tiverton. He proved to be an excellent businessman and as managing director successfully steered the firm through some difficult times. Originally a Liberal, he took little interest in politics and found his way on to the Devon County Council in 1932 because of his interest in education. He was elected to the chair of the Education Committee. He also took a keen interest in the scouting movement, serving as County Commissioner from 1930 to 1945.

Amory was involved in the Territorial Army from 1919 until the outbreak of World War II, in which he served in the Royal Artillery. He saw action at Salerno and later took up various staff appointments in France. He trained paratroops for the Arnhem operation and insisted on participating in the action. He broke his thigh in the jump and was taken prisoner. At the end of the war he took the place of a cousin killed in action as the Conservative candidate for Tiverton. Elected in 1945, he held the seat until he retired from politics in 1960.

As a backbencher Amory was well regarded for his diligence and ability, and his moderate Toryism fitted in well with the new look Butler was giving the Conservative Party. When

Churchill won the 1951 election, he asked Amory to become Minister of Pensions: Amory's modesty was such that he is said to have asked whether the invitation was intended for Julian Amery. His firm recommendation, after only a short time in the post, that his department should be amalgamated with the Ministry of National Insurance was characteristic of his lack of personal vanity. The merger was carried through in 1953, and Amory became Minister of State at the Board of Trade. His reward for ten months' successful work was promotion to the cabinet as Minister of Agriculture and Fisheries in July 1954.

His first task was to preside over the merger of his ministry with the Ministry of Food. During the Suez Crisis Amory was among those who were unhappy with the way that government policy developed, and in cabinet he voted against going ahead with the landings on 4 November; having decided not to resign, Amory loyally defended the policy and his attitude did him no harm with either his leader or his colleagues. Eden had considered him for promotion in 1955 and Amory actually refused Macmillan's offer of another post in January 1957, preferring to remain at the Ministry of Agriculture, where he successfully introduced the Agriculture Act 1957.

In January 1958 Peter Thorneycroft resigned as Chancellor of the Exchequer in protest against his colleagues' reluctance to cut public expenditure, and Macmillan asked Amory to take his place. In retrospect the deft way in which Macmillan handled this crisis can be seen as the turning point in the government's fortunes. At the time its stock was low and the new Chancellor's role unenviable. He speedily made it clear that he had no intention of departing substantially from the disinflationary policies Thorneycroft had pursued. A slow relaxation of the credit squeeze followed. Towards the end of the year Macmillan became more insistent on reflation and chaired a cabinet committee created, it would seem, to spur the Chancellor on. Amory offered an expansionist budget for 1959 with cuts in the rates of both income tax and purchase tax. However the decision to reduce the former by as much as 9d had to be urged on the Chancellor from Number Ten. The budget laid the

Derick Amory, as Minister of Agriculture, auctioning the first pen of sheep after opening the new cattle market at Canterbury, March 1955

foundations for the Conservatives' third successive election victory, but that in turn accelerated the economic boom which was already in train. Amory's 1960 budget therefore aimed at slowing the rate of expansion, and his final advice to Macmillan before he resigned was a counsel of caution.

Amory's insistence on returning to private life in July 1960 disappointed Macmillan and he persuaded him to take up the post of High Commissioner in Canada the following year. After his retirement from this appointment in 1963, Amory returned to his earlier interests, serving as a director of ICI (1964–70), chairman of John Heathcoat and Co. (1966–72), president of the Association of County Councils (until his death) and president of the London Federation of Boys Clubs. He served as chairman of the Medical Research Council (1960–1, 1965–9) and the Voluntary Services

Overseas (1964–75), and in his native Devon was successively pro-Chancellor (1966–72) and then Chancellor of the University of Exeter. Among his final legacies to his native county was the successful Exeter Cathedral Appeal which he headed.

FURTHER READING

Allen, W. Gore, *The Reluctant Politician* (London: C. Johnson, 1958).
Brittan, Samuel, *The Treasury Under the Tories* (Harmondsworth: Penguin, 1964).
Seldon, Anthony, *Churchill's Indian Summer* (London: Hodder and Stoughton, 1981).

JOHN BARNES

Anderson, Sir **John** [Viscount Waverley] (*b.* Edinburgh, 8 July 1882; *d.* London, 4 January 1958). Leading civil servant and politician.

The range of his career – official, proconsular, and ministerial – was probably unique in the British system of government, as his contemporary, Lord Salter, once observed. He was well described by his official biographer, Sir John Wheeler-Bennett, as 'one who made his way from humble origins by fierce and honest competition through his own tremendous efforts of intellect and character to the highest positions and honours in the land.'

Born the son of an Edinburgh stationer and his wife in 1882, Anderson made remorselessly successful academic progress through George Watson's School, followed by the University of Edinburgh, excelling even his first class degree in mathematics and natural philosophy obtained there by his achievement in finishing first in the Class I open competitive examination for the Civil Service in 1905. Shortly afterwards, he was appointed as a Second Class Clerk (Higher Division) at the Colonial Office and then embarked on a remarkable Civil Service career, which, in 1912, saw him involved in Lloyd George's National Health Insurance adventure, along with administrative exotics such as Sir Robert Morant and Sir Warren Fisher. Morant ensured that Anderson was promoted above his seniors to become Secretary to the Insurance Commissioners in 1913. Anderson became Secretary of the Ministry of Shipping in 1917 and, after a brief period at the Local Government Board, Second Secretary at the Ministry of Health in 1919 (again being associated with Morant); the same year he was appointed Chairman of the Board of Inland Revenue, and spent a brief and dangerous spell in Dublin Castle serving the Lord Lieutenant of Ireland before becoming Permanent Under Secretary at the Home Office in 1922 at the age of 40. He retained that post until 1932, when he became Governor of Bengal.

Relinquishing that office in 1937, Anderson embarked on a political career in March 1938 as an Independent MP for the Scottish Universities. From November 1938 to July 1945 he was a cabinet minister being, initially, Lord Privy Seal with special responsibilities for civil defence, then Home Secretary and Minister for Home Security, both in Neville Chamberlain's government, before becoming succes-

sively Lord President of the Council (1940–3) and Chancellor of the Exchequer (1943–5) under Winston Churchill's prime ministership. Anderson then served on the opposition front bench until 1950, when the abolition of university seats removed him from the House of Commons. He declined Churchill's offer to take part in his short-lived 'Overlords' experiment in 1951, believing that supervising ministers located in the House of Lords had no place in peacetime politics. He accepted a peerage as Lord Waverley in 1952, one of the many honours awarded him, including the Order of Merit in 1957. Anderson's latter years, before his death in 1958 at the age of 75, involved business activity with prominent companies such as ICI and Vickers.

Anderson thus had a remarkable career within the machinery of British government, first as a career civil servant, then as a proconsul in India, and finally, as a politician. Wheeler-Bennett wrote that, from the outset, Anderson's contemporaries believed that he would go to the top of the Civil Service. Anderson, for all his ability, was fortunate to enter the service just before the reforming Liberal Government of 1906 enlarged the state bureaucracy and then World War I expanded it further, and his political career prospered too from being conducted in the period of and around World War II – when his lack of political acumen mattered less. As it was, a man nicknamed 'Jehovah' by his Home Office colleagues for his tendency to speak like an official minute even in ordinary conversation had the aura of the ideal conventional civil servant, even of a man born to play such a role in the British machinery of central government.

FURTHER READING

Wheeler-Bennett, J., *John Anderson: Viscount Waverley* (London: Macmillan, 1962).

GEOFFREY K. FRY

Angell, Sir **Norman** [Lane, Ralph Norman Angell] (*b.* Holbeach, Lincolnshire, 26 December 1872; *d.* Croydon, Surrey, 7 October 1967). Author and internationalist. A freelance peace campaigner, he served as

Labour MP for Bradford North (1929–31), and won the 1933 Nobel Peace Prize. Although he wrote about 40 books, he was famous primarily for his much up-dated million-seller, *The Great Illusion* (1910), which argued that (aggressive) war does not pay.

Although in some respects a donnish figure, Angell lacked a conventional education. The precocious seventh son of a prosperous Lincolnshire draper and grocer, he had attended the Lycée de St Omer in France, a business school in London, and (while working as a teenage journalist) a year's classes at the University of Geneva. And at the age of 17 he had abandoned formal education altogether in favour of travelling, ranching and (eventually) journalism in the USA. Late in 1897 he headed back to Europe, and spent the next 16 years in Paris. From 1904 to 1912 he was general manager of the continental edition of Northcliffe's *Daily Mail*, and this responsibility forced him to take a pen-name – his middle names – for his independent writings.

Angell's international and journalistic experience, combined with his reading of J. S. Mill, had converted him to the liberal view popularized above all by Richard Cobden: that there were no real causes of war between advanced states. But Cobden had implied that free trade and popular education would automatically produce a growing awareness of the possibilities of international cooperation – a prediction which seemed by the end of the nineteenth century to have been falsified by imperialism. British radicals explained the latter in terms of the selfish vested interests of international finance; but Angell pointed out that in other countries (notably France) the forces of finance were opposed to jingoism, and even where this was not the case the financiers needed to be able to exploit public emotions in support of their machinations. Influenced by the French social psychologist Gustav Le Bon, Angell believed that it was the emotionalism to which the mass-mind was prone which constituted the real danger to peace. His first book, *Patriotism under Three Flags: a Plea for Rationalism in Politics* (1903), examined nationalism in the USA, Britain and France, and argued that 'sentimentalism' and not material interests constituted the main threat to peace.

Mounting Anglo-German tension made Angell feel obliged to explain his assumption that material interests could no longer be furthered by conquest. In a short book, *Europe's Optical Illusion* (1909), he argued that 'the complex financial interdependence of the capitals of the world' which had developed during the previous 30 years meant that war would disrupt the system of international credit and make everyone poorer. When the following year the book was republished in an expanded version as *The Great Illusion*, it became a huge success. Angell deliberately contrasted his 'New Pacifism' with the emotionalism of the 'Old' variety, and courted 'realists' in Whitehall and the City who appreciated his defence of financiers. In 1912, through the good offices of Lord Esher and A. J. Balfour, the industrialist Sir Richard Garton established a foundation under whose auspices Norman Angell Leagues, International Polity Clubs and a journal, *War and Peace*, were all established; and efforts were also made to spread 'Norman Angellism' in Germany.

As early as the Balkan wars of 1912–13, however, Angell was accused of having said war was impossible; and when World War I broke out the same accusation was renewed. Angell was a convinced neutralist (largely because of dislike of fighting alongside Russia), and helped to found the Union of Democratic Control. Having thus become too controversial for the Garton Foundation, and finding himself associated with a political left and a peace movement from both of which he had previously tried to distance himself, Angell struggled, while keeping up a stream of books and articles on international issues, to work out how socialist and pacifist he really was. In October 1915 he had contemplated advocating 'non-resistance', and sometimes thereafter implied that pacifism was his preferred policy. Yet in 1916 he had volunteered (unsuccessfully) for military service; and after 1933 he emerged as a strong supporter of collective security, being associated after 1937 with the 'Focus' group of Churchillian 'anti-appeasers'. The former isolationist had thus become an interventionist; but at the same time his political views were reverting to their pre-1914 condition. He had joined the Labour Party in

1920, contesting the Rushcliffe division of Nottinghamshire in 1922 and Rossendale in 1923 before his success at Bradford North. But in the 1931 political crisis he came close to supporting Ramsay MacDonald (from whom he had accepted a knighthood the previous year), and declined to seek re-election in that year's general election. Although he stood for Labour in the London University seat in 1935, he had broken with socialism. In July 1940 he explained to Gilbert Murray: 'I have been pushed more and more to the conclusion that it is your type of Liberalism which alone can save us.'

Apart from a brief early marriage, about which he was reticent, Angell lived alone, spending much of his time in the USA. He continued to write prolifically on issues of war and peace in his old age, and received a warm 90th-birthday tribute from Prime Minister Harold Macmillan.

WRITINGS

After All (London: Hamish Hamilton, 1951).

FURTHER READING

Miller, J. D. B., *Norman Angell and the Futility of War* (London: Macmillan, 1986).

Weinroth, Howard, 'Norman Angell and *The Great Illusion*: an episode in pre-1914 pacifism', *Historical Journal*, 17 (1974), pp. 551–74.

MARTIN CEADEL

Armstrong, Sir **Robert (Temple)** [Lord Armstrong of Ilminster] (*b.* Exeter, Devon, 30 March 1927). Leading civil servant. Not all holders of the post of Head of the Home Civil Service, or, before that, of the Civil Service, have become politically controversial figures, but, despite their being drawn from a career bureaucracy, a surprising number of them have done so, and none more than Sir Robert Armstrong. He was successively Permanent Under Secretary of State, Home Office (1977–9), Secretary of the Cabinet (1979–87), Joint Head of the Home Civil Service (1981–3) and Head of the Home Civil Service (1983–7).

Armstrong was educated at the Dragon School, Oxford, as a King's Scholar at Eton, and as a Scholar at Christ Church, Oxford, where he secured a second class honours degree in Greats, before success in the Administrative Class open competitive examination enabled him to enter the Treasury as an Assistant Principal in 1950. He then served as Private Secretary to the Economic Secretary to the Treasury (1953–4) and to the Chancellor of the Exchequer (1954–5), being promoted to Principal in 1955. Duties that followed involved being Secretary to the Radcliffe Committee on the Working of the Monetary System (1957–9) and being seconded as an Assistant Secretary to the Cabinet Office (1964–6); he returned to the Treasury at the same level to serve eventually as Principal Private Secretary to the Chancellor of the Exchequer in 1968. In October of that year, Armstrong was promoted Under Secretary in charge of the Home Finance Division of the Treasury, and in July 1970 he was appointed Principal Private Secretary to the Prime Minister. He retained that post until April 1975, when he was appointed Deputy Under Secretary of State at the Home Office, in charge of the Police and Broadcasting Departments, becoming Permanent Under Secretary there in July 1977. In October 1979 Armstrong was appointed Secretary of the Cabinet. In November 1981 he was additionally appointed Head of the Home Civil Service, holding that post at first jointly with Sir Douglas Wass, and, from 1983, on his own. He retired from the Civil Service at the end of December 1987, to be created Baron Armstrong of Ilminster the following year, when he was also appointed Chairman of the Board of Trustees at the Victoria and Albert Museum.

There can have been few more politically contentious periods in which to be Head of the Home Civil Service than the years 1981 to 1987, remembering that the previous holder of the post, Sir Ian Bancroft, had been in effect dismissed by the Prime Minister, Mrs Thatcher. Relations between a heavily unionized career Civil Service with a vested interest in bureaucratic expansion and a Conservative government committed to economic liberal goals were bound to be antagonistic in tone; and it was this running conflict rather than, as most observers seemed to consider,

Armstrong's dual role as Secretary of the Cabinet and Head of the Civil Service that made for his difficulties. That the government felt no need to come to terms with the unions was made evident in 1984 when it expelled them from GCHQ, having the right to override any objections that Armstrong may have had. Similarly, official secrets legislation did give the government the right to prosecute civil servants such as Clive Ponting caught leaking confidential information as a means of embarrassing it. In the wake of the settlement of the Ponting case in 1985, Armstrong published a statement about the constitutional relationship between ministers and civil servants which led to him being accused of an excess of traditionalism by critics, none of whom was able to demonstrate on what alternative basis a career Civil Service could be organized within the British system of government. Operating within that system, Armstrong was impressive in giving evidence to the House of Commons Defence Committee in 1986 when it investigated the Westland affair. When, later in 1986, the *Spycatcher* case made him subject to different rules in an Australian court, Armstrong's sophistications, of being 'economical with the truth' and so forth, were less widely admired.

Sir Robert Armstrong was a higher civil servant in the classic British style, by common consent possessing outstanding capacities as an administrator that took him to the top of his demanding profession.

GEOFFREY K. FRY

Ashdown, Paddy [John Jeremy Durham] (*b.* New Delhi, 27 February 1941). First Leader of the Social and Liberal Democrats. After serving in the Royal Marine Commandos (1959–71), including a spell in the Special Boat Squadron and a course in Mandarin Chinese, he joined the Diplomatic Service, being listed as a member of the UK Mission to the United Nations in Geneva (1971–6). His work in industrial management (1976–81) was followed by a period of unemployment while he concentrated on his parliamentary candidacy. Ashdown entered the Commons as a Liberal MP when he won Yeovil from the Conservatives in the 1983 general election. Almost from the start of his parliamentary career he was seen as a potentially important figure, but was difficult to place. His election victory had come about through a classic campaign of community politics, sustained over several years, which brought him into sympathy with those Liberals who were most uneasy about the leadership style of David Steel. When Ashdown declared his support for British nuclear disarmament he was seen by some as the challenging, charismatic star of radical Liberalism. Unilateralism was totally unacceptable to the Social Democratic wing of the Alliance, but when Ashdown switched his support to the multilateral policy favoured by Steel and the SDP, radical Liberals felt let down, while SDP suspicions were not completely laid to rest.

The bitter dispute within the Conservative Government over the sale of Westland Helicopters to an American company gave Ashdown his opportunity to win recognition from a wider political audience: his constituency included the Westland factory; he was the Liberal parliamentary spokesman for Trade and Industry; and he had a service background. A further opportunity to consolidate his reputation came when the Liberal/SDP Alliance agreed on joint parliamentary portfolios in the run-up to the 1987 general election, and he became the Alliance spokesman for Education and Science.

Ashdown took no part in the difficult negotiations to merge the Liberal parties and the SDP after the 1987 general election. His preparations to win the leadership of the merged party were, however, meticulous and effective, and the ballot of members in 1988 gave him a substantial victory over Alan Beith, the former Deputy Leader of the Liberal Party.

Ashdown's first year of leadership was not a success. The SDP minority continuing under David Owen's separate leadership made it seem that the Alliance had split rather than merged. Ashdown, oversensitive perhaps to his need to hold the confidence of Social Democrats in the merged party, emphasized the newness, and played down the Liberal roots, of the Social and Liberal Democrats, laying down an agenda which laid stress on the environment and the quality of life rather than the liberty and responsibility of the individual citizen. The party survived local government elections in England and Wales in May 1989 relatively well, but fared badly in the European elections a month later. The continuing dispute over whether the party should campaign as the Democrats or the Liberal Democrats was symptomatic of the underlying debate about its purpose, and of dissatisfaction with Ashdown's leadership. Ashdown's difficulties within the party were resolved by his personal performance at the party conference in September 1989 and a ballot of party members the following month which fixed Liberal Democrats as the campaigning title; but the party itself still trailed in the opinion polls as strife in the government focused public attention on the Labour and Conservative parties.

C. M. MASON

Asquith, H(erbert) H(enry) [Earl of Oxford and Asquith] (*b.* Morley, Yorkshire, 12 September 1852; *d.* Sutton Courtenay, Oxfordshire, 15 February 1928). Liberal Prime Minister. He was Prime Minister from April 1908 until December 1916, and his premiership included massive achievements. Under his guidance his country, then at the height of its power, became a 'welfare state' and intervened decisively at the outset of World War I. By curbing the House of Lords he established a modern parliamentary regime in Britain. However, his Irish policy was less successful, and he failed to supply, or at least to display, the dynamic leadership demanded in war.

Asquith owed nothing to hereditary privilege. Orphaned at the age of eight, he made his way, via the City of London School and four successful years at Balliol College, Oxford, to the Bar. He was returned for East Fife in 1886 as a Gladstonian Liberal and soon became recognized as a debater of 'front bench' calibre. In 1889 a brilliant cross-examination which he had conducted for the Irish leader, Charles Stewart Parnell, brought him a reputation beyond Westminster and enhanced his legal standing.

Asquith's first wife died of typhoid in 1891 and in 1894 he married Margot (Margaret) Tennant (see ASQUITH, MARGOT), the gifted and wilful youngest daughter of a rich Scottish manufacturer whom Gladstone had made a baronet. The more intellectual part of London society to which Margot belonged was much to Asquith's taste. As a young man he had called John Bright 'the only man in public life who has risen to eminence without being corrupted by London society.' By 1894 he had left that attitude behind. The gap between him and the nonconformist Liberals of the provinces had begun to widen.

Asquith became Gladstone's Home Secretary in 1892, and he retained the post under Rosebery. He soon showed a capacity for administration which matched his power in debate; his handling of the Irish dynamiters, of Trafalgar Square meetings, and of rioting Yorkshire miners at Featherstone was firm and sensible. By 1894 he was regarded as the coming Liberal leader: his long ascendancy in the Commons had begun. In February 1895 the Leader of the House told his son that on the Address Asquith had 'knocked Joe [Chamberlain] into a cocked hat.'

In December 1898 Asquith refused the Liberal leadership for financial reasons. In the Liberal dissensions engendered by the Boer War he found himself at odds with his leader, Campbell-Bannerman, and somewhat alienated from the larger section of his party. He had no affinity of temperament with such small national groups as Kruger's Boers and the Irish Nationalists. This was politically a difficult time for him; but in 1901 his father-in-law provided the resources to make him less dependent on his earnings at the Bar.

When the tariff reform issue was raised by Joseph Chamberlain in May 1903 Asquith was presented with a golden opportunity to regain a central position in the Liberal Party. He made the most of it. The defence of free trade brought his remarkable platform powers into full play; his dissection of the weaknesses and inconsistencies in tariff reform doctrine was devastating. During the last months of Balfour's government Asquith, Grey, and Haldane made an effort, which quickly collapsed, to drive Campbell-Bannerman to the Lords (see also GREY, EDWARD, and HALDANE, R. B.). The failure of this 'Relugas compact' between the three (named after the meeting place in Morayshire where Grey had been fishing) was fortunate for Asquith. The inexperienced idealists who were swept into the Commons by the Liberal landslide in the 1906 election might not have responded to him as readily as they did to 'CB'. His position as Chancellor of the Exchequer and Deputy Leader of the House was enough to mark him out as heir apparent to the premiership. He was an undisputed success at the Exchequer. In his 1907 budget he introduced differential tax rates for earned and unearned incomes. In the next year he established means-tested non-contributory old-age pensions from the age of 70: these applied to about half a million people. Before that budget – his third – could be introduced he had become Prime Minister.

Asquith succeeded the dying 'CB' in April 1908, but the strong administration which he formed was shackled by the Conservative majority in the Lords. The Liberals could enact the Old Age Pensions measure because that was a money bill with which the peers could not tamper, but in most areas of legislation they were impotent. Trade was not good in 1908; by-elections were going against the Liberals, and tax rises were needed to pay for a dreadnought programme to match the growth of the German navy. In Lloyd George's budget of 1909 the government broke free: when it was rejected by the Lords, Asquith dissolved and won the election (January 1910), though with a reduced majority. After some uncertain weeks the cabinet decided not to reform the upper house, but to limit the peers' veto on bills, other than money bills, to two years. By the end of April 1910 the Parliament Bill embodying this limitation had been introduced and the Lords had passed the budget.

Edward VII's death (6 May 1910) led to an effort at compromise in a Constitutional Conference. When that failed, in November 1910 Asquith secured the new King's promise that, if a creation of peers should be needed to pass

H. H. Asquith (third from left) at the great Liberal rally at Queen's Hall, London, October 1924; to his left are Earl Beauchamp, Lloyd George and Sir John Simon, and on his right is Sir Alfred Mond

the Parliament Bill, this would be authorized. After the existence of the promise had become known in July 1911 he was much vilified, and was indeed shouted down by the Conservatives in the Commons. Yet in 1910, as in 1832, the demand for a promise was unavoidable and Asquith always denied that he had bullied the King. GEORGE V seems to have resented the stipulation that the pledge should remain secret. Whether this was stipulated in the belief that the Lords might accept the electorate's verdict so that the secret would be kept for good, or in order to give the Liberals an electoral advantage, remains in doubt.

Asquith dominated the election which followed in December 1910. It produced little change in the government's majority. In the end a creation of peers was not needed. The threat of one proved just sufficient and in August 1911 the Parliament Act became law. Asquith's prestige now stood at its height. He found more difficulty in dealing with the problems outside Parliament – the 'great strikes', suffragette violence and Ulster's resistance to Home Rule – during the three years which followed. The Liberals had been pledged to the policy of Home Rule for Ireland since Gladstone's day, and the 1910 elections gave them both the inducement and the opportunity to put this policy into effect. They had become dependent for their Commons majority on the Irish Nationalists; and the Home Rule Bill which the Nationalists required as the condition of their continued support could no longer be killed in the Lords. Between 1912 and 1914 this Bill was duly passed three times by the Commons (and rejected by the Lords) as the provisions of the Parliament Act required. Asquith has been blamed for failing to exclude Ulster from its operation at an early stage. The charge is hardly sustainable. The Conservatives were more concerned with stopping Home Rule than with saving Ulster, while many Liberals, as well as all the Nationalists, believed that a Home Rule regime would not be viable should Ulster be excluded. Characteristically Asquith failed to appreciate the extent to which the Ulster Protestants, faced with the threat of being ruled from Dublin, were prepared for armed resistance. In March 1915 he referred to the outbreak of the Great War, which had prevented this clash, as the greatest stroke of luck of his political life.

Contemporaries singled out Asquith's feat in taking a united country into the Great War for particular praise. Though considerable, the achievement owed much to the German Government, since their ultimatum to Belgium solved the British Prime Minister's problem for him. Until the end of March 1915 Asquith's position remained strong, but thereafter his leadership was heavily criticized. Although much of the criticism was misdirected, his talents were not those of a war premier. His dominance of the party battle in the Commons was no longer of use. He was reluctant to adapt the machinery of government to meet wartime needs, and carried on with a cabinet of normal size unsupported by a secretariat. His habits, which he characterized as 'energy under the guise of lethargy', were not the right ones for the hour. As Bonar Law told him in February 1916, 'in war it is necessary not only to be active, but to seem active.'

In May 1915 the quarrel at the Admiralty over the Dardanelles between Winston Churchill and John Fisher (First Lord and First Sea Lord), and the news of shell shortages on the Western Front, forced Asquith to reconstruct the government as a coalition. He did so at a bitter moment in his personal life, when Venetia Stanley had ended his romantic friendship with her by telling him of her engagement to one of his cabinet colleagues. His relations with Bonar Law never became close; and on the conscription issue there was a wide divergence of opinion between the Conservatives and most of the active Liberals. At the beginning of December 1916 Asquith was faced with a demand that he should appoint a small war committee of which he would not be chairman. He resigned rather than accept such a relegation and DAVID LLOYD GEORGE became Prime Minister.

Asquith lost his seat in the election of December 1918, but won a remarkable by-election at Paisley in February 1920 and kept that seat until defeated in the 1924 election. But his postwar political experiences were not happy. The Liberals were divided between his followers and Lloyd George's, and in his reluctance to work with Lloyd George he did little to help in healing the split. The two leaders came together when Baldwin declared for tariff reform in 1923, but parted finally over the general strike less than three years later.

Asquith was not strong in political imagination, and he lacked some of the habits and political arts which keep a leader close to his followers. But in intellectual mastery and dominance of debate he has had few equals among British prime ministers. In their private comments his leading opponents were not sparing in admiration. In December 1911 Bonar Law told his Chief Whip, 'Asquith drunk can make a better speech than any one of us, sober.' Nearly six years later F. E. Smith said to a supporter, 'That old man [Asquith] has got more brains in his little finger than you and I possess in the whole of our two heads.'

See also BONHAM CARTER, VIOLET.

FURTHER READING

Brock, M. and E. (eds.), *H. H. Asquith: Letters to Venetia Stanley* (Oxford: Oxford University Press, 1982).

Jenkins, R., *Asquith*, 3rd edn (London: Collins, 1986).

Koss, S., *Asquith* (London: Allen Lane, 1976).

Spender, J. A. and Asquith, C., *Asquith*, 2 vols. (London: Hutchinson, 1932).

MICHAEL BROCK

Asquith [née Tennant], **Margot** [Emma Alice Margaret; Countess of Oxford and Asquith] (*b.* The Glen, Peebles-shire, 2 February 1864; *d.* London, 28 July 1945). Wife of H. H. Asquith, and prominent in society and in political circles. She was the daughter of a rich Glasgow industrialist, Charles Tennant, who had bought and greatly extended The Glen, Peebles-shire, a few years before she was born. Her father became a Liberal MP in 1879 and a Baronet in 1885. He entertained a great deal at Glen and his younger daughters, Laura and Margot, were launched into London society with striking success. After Laura's death in 1886 Margot was at the centre of a group of friends known as 'The Souls', which included A. J. Balfour and George Curzon. She first met H. H. Asquith in 1890 (not 1891, the date

given in her *Autobiography*; her standards of factual accuracy, never high, had fallen by 1920, its year of publication). Asquith's first wife died in September 1891, leaving him with five children, and in May 1894 he married Margot. He was thought imprudent to have done so.

This contemporary judgement is readily understandable. Margot was undisciplined, outspoken, and accustomed to the centre of the stage. Warmth of heart and generosity were hers in abundance, and she always remained a loyal and devoted wife; but her misfortunes and short-comings involved her husband in many troubles. Her health was often poor, and of her five children only two survived infancy (Elizabeth, *b.* 1897; Anthony, *b.* 1902). She was not, as she often remarked, cut out to be a step-mother; and her relations with Violet until the latter married Maurice Bonham Carter in 1915 did not help to give the Prime Minister a tranquil domestic life.

Margot's extravagance intensified Asquith's money troubles; and there were limits to Sir Charles Tennant's generosity to his son-in-law. Sir Charles declined in 1898 to provide what would have enabled Asquith to accept the Liberal leadership in the Commons; and when he had given Margot a settlement in 1901 to provide an income of £5,000 a year he took that to be sufficient and left her nothing substantial in his will. Even apart from the worry involved, these financial uncertainties harmed Asquith. They detracted from his reputation for integrity by giving the impression that he could not afford to embark on any policy which might jeopardize his hold on office.

The best of Margot's *bons mots* were inimitable. 'F. E. Smith is very clever', she said, 'but his brains sometimes go to his head.' Her heedless use of this sharp tongue gave much offence. 'It is rather sad', a young man wrote in 1913, 'that she, who must once have had more friends than she could count, should now have so many enemies.' Her political interventions were mostly ill-judged. Lloyd George had to be pacified by the Chief Whip after Margot had advised him, during the second election of 1910, to stop abusing the Lords. Asquith sought rest and distraction in romantic friendships with a number of younger women. His *amitié amoureuse* with Venetia Stanley became intense during the early months of the war, until it was ended, to his great distress, in May 1915 by her engagement to a member of his cabinet, E. S. Montagu.

After Asquith's loss of office in December 1916 Margot grew embittered. Lady Horner, who had known the Asquiths well, told Harold Nicolson in 1930: 'Margot never really made Asquith happy. She allowed him no private life at all; and under the strain the finer fibres of his nature became worn away.' Though perhaps over-severe, this judgement cannot be disregarded.

WRITINGS

Autobiography, 2 vols. (London: Thornton Butterworth, 1920, 1922).

FURTHER READING

Bennett, Daphne, *Margot* (London: Gollancz, 1984).
Brock, M. and E. (eds.), *H. H. Asquith: Letters to Venetia Stanley* (Oxford: Oxford University Press, 1982).

MICHAEL BROCK

Astor [née Langhorne], **Nancy (Witcher)** [Viscountess Astor] (*b.* Danville, Virginia, 19 May 1879; *d.* Grimsthorpe, Lincolnshire, 2 May 1964). Feminist, wit and Conservative MP. She was the first woman to sit in the House of Commons, where she represented Plymouth (Sutton) from 1919 to 1945. Famous for her repartee, she became a celebrated hostess at Cliveden in Buckinghamshire; but during the 1930s her prominence in the 'Cliveden Set' led to her being pilloried for allegedly pro-Nazi sympathies.

Born into a family of 11 children, she grew up among the gentry of Virginia, imbued with the Confederate cause and militant Protestantism. Her strict moral and religious upbringing left lifelong marks in the shape of her campaigns for temperance and moral hygiene, and in her dislike of physical relationships. She conducted a series of safe, platonic affairs with Julian Grenfell, Philip Kerr, T. E. Lawrence and Bernard Shaw. In 1897, at the age of 18,

she married Robert Shaw, but was rapidly repulsed by his drinking and sexual demands and obtained a divorce in 1903. She met her second husband, Waldorf Astor, son of the eccentric millionaire William Waldorf Astor, in 1905. 'I married beneath me', she quipped, 'all women do.' In spite of her wilful, possessive and domineering personality, they made a devoted couple.

From 1909 Astor took an active role in promoting her husband's candidature in Plymouth, where he was elected in 1910. From 1912 until the end of her life she became increasingly absorbed by Christian Science. In spite of her charitable work during the Great War there were no indications of a more public career until October 1919, when Waldorf reluctantly succeeded to his father's peerage. Initially Nancy was regarded as a stop-gap candidate. She stood as a Conservative Coalitionist with the blessing of Lloyd George. Presenting herself as a great lady with the common touch, she relied upon her humour in responding to the hecklers, whom she deliberately provoked. In a three-cornered contest she triumphed by the surprisingly large majority of 5000. As an MP, Astor campaigned on a variety of issues, including temperance, moral hygiene, women police, the Royal Navy, the school-leaving age and nursery schools. Generally popular in Parliament, she was regarded as a colourful character rather than as a serious politician, largely because she lacked the pomposity of the typical male politician. Her major success came in 1923, when she successfully piloted through the Commons a bill to prevent the sale of alcohol to persons under 18. However, her opponents dubbed her a prohibitionist, and at the 1922 election she was opposed by an unofficial Unionist.

Astor had played no part in the women's movement before 1918, and her support for feminist causes was uneven. In 1920 she spoke against a bill to equalize the terms of divorce for the two sexes, despite having taken advantage of similar legislation to obtain her own divorce. After the 1929 election she attempted to recruit the 14 women MPs into a women's party under her leadership; but her credentials for such a role were inadequate, and the idea was firmly rejected by the Labour members. As a result of her independence and strident support for social reform Astor became increasingly isolated: 'Sometimes I wonder whether I am in the right party.' However, her unorthodox creed probably helped her retain her working-class seat against a growing Labour challenge. By 1930 her career appeared to be in decline. From 1936 Claude Cockburn launched his damaging attacks on the 'Cliveden Set' which, he claimed, was subverting government policy in order to appease Hitler. Though unfair to Nancy, these charges had made her a liability to her party by 1939. But the war prolonged her career, and she recovered some of her popularity as Mayoress of Plymouth. In 1944 Waldorf insisted that she avoid the inevitable defeat by retiring at the next general election. She remained in the public eye in the postwar world but her formal political career was at an end.

FURTHER READING

Astor, M., *Tribal Feeling* (London: John Murray, 1963).
Collis, M. S., *Nancy Astor* (London: Faber, 1960).
Masters, A., *Nancy Astor: a Life* (London: Weidenfeld and Nicolson, 1981).

MARTIN PUGH

Atholl [née Ramsay], **Katharine (Marjory)** [Duchess of Atholl] **('Kitty')** (*b.* Edinburgh, 6 November 1874; *d.* Edinburgh, 21 October 1960). Conservative MP and junior minister. She was one of the earliest women MPs and the first Conservative woman to hold government office as Parliamentary Secretary at the Board of Education (1924–9). Her career effectively ended in 1938 when she was defeated in a famous by-election fought on the issue of 'appeasement'.

The daughter of Sir James Ramsay of Banff, she showed scholastic and musical talent, and was educated at the Royal College of Music. A shy, serious-minded girl, she married in 1899 'Bardie', John George Stewart-Murray, Marquess of Tullibardine, heir to the seventh Duke of Atholl. He was a soldier, outward-going and intellectually lightweight. They had no children. Though not a feminist, she soon turned to public work, and gained experience

of canvassing and public speaking when helping her husband, who was MP for West Perthshire (1910–17). While he was more witty and spontaneous, he was 'not as interested in political speaking as I was', she wrote. Kitty became President of the Perthshire Red Cross Society, and served on the Scottish Office Committee enquiring into medical and nursing services in the Highlands. During the Great War she undertook charitable work for the Scots regiments and ran Blair Castle, the family home, as a convalescent hospital. After 1918 she sat on the Perthshire County Education Authority.

In 1917 'Bardie' inherited the dukedom, and in 1921 Lloyd George urged the duchess to enter parliament herself. By 1922 the Conservatives of Kinross and West Perthshire were anxious to repudiate coalitionism and invited her to become their candidate. Standing in 1923 as a tariff reformer, she was narrowly elected over a Liberal free trader. In parliament her cool and intellectual speeches favourably impressed her colleagues, as did her outspoken opposition to equal suffrage for women; Harold Macmillan described her, approvingly, as having 'a masculine mind'. When the Conservatives returned to power in 1924 they wished to emulate Labour by giving a woman junior office. The duchess appeared much the most suitable candidate, and served at Education under Lord Eustace Percy. However, the experience was not entirely happy. She resisted expenditure cuts in 1926, even to the extent of going over Percy's head to the Prime Minister, Baldwin. In 1925 she was appointed the only female member of the British delegation to the League of Nations.

After the Conservative defeat in 1929 the duchess never returned to office. During the 1930s she became a critic of the National Government's policy of constitutional reform in India, assisted Churchill in his rebellion on that issue, and briefly renounced the party whip in 1935. She also grew disillusioned over 'appeasement' and apprehensive about the rise of Fascism. In 1936 she participated in the All-Party Committee for Spanish Relief, which evacuated children from areas bombed during the civil war. As a result of a visit to Spain she wrote a defence of the republican cause, *Searchlight on Spain* (1938), which sold 100,000 copies in a week. However, her rebellious stance provoked criticism in her constituency party, where she was accused of supporting atheism, anarchism and communism. The dissatisfaction reached a head in 1938 when she again resigned the whip; her local association pointedly expressed its confidence in the government's foreign policy and decided to select a new candidate. Thereupon the duchess resigned her seat and fought a by-election in December. While she attacked the recent Munich Settlement, her opponents condemned her as a warmonger, and in a low poll she was narrowly defeated by an official Conservative. During 1939 she made preparations to contest a Scottish University seat as an Independent, but the postponement of the general election led to the abandonment of this plan and to her virtual retirement from politics.

FURTHER READING

Hetherington, S. J., *Katharine Atholl* (Aberdeen: Aberdeen University Press, 1989).

MARTIN PUGH

Attlee, Clement (Richard) [Earl Attlee] (*b.* London, 3 January 1883; *d.* London, 8 October 1967). Labour Prime Minister. Attlee was able to be a great Prime Minister because he did not appear to be a great man. In 1945 he handsomely defeated the great man whose deputy he had been since 1942 – Winston Churchill – and went on to shape the foundations, as he believed, of a socialist Britain. He remained in office for six years. After the general election of 1951, however, he was again Leader of the Opposition, and by the time he retired in 1955 he had been leader of the Labour Party for 20 years. He accepted an earldom on retirement.

At first sight, Attlee's successful career appears mysterious. He was not a great orator capable of dominating his colleagues by force of delivery or power of words. His speaking style was clear, but clipped and unembroidered. His economy with words made ordinary men appear garrulous in his presence. King George VI, who could himself find conversation difficult, referred to his Prime Minister as Clem the Clam. Attlee's autobiography

rigorously excluded any sparkle; its title – *As It Happened* – could not be more matter of fact. His exposition of socialism seemed pedestrian alongside other contemporary treatises on socialist theory. He had not risen inexorably through the party organization. He had never been the boss of a powerful trade union. Everything about Attlee seemed to be so straightforward that journalists were reduced to writing about his wife's car-driving problems in order to create excitement.

This record of conspicuous modesty appears puzzling in a major political leader only if considered in the abstract; Attlee's relative success can be explained only in terms of the relative failure of the Labour Party. When he became leader of the party in 1935, leadership was one of its major problems. Even before 1914 it had not proved easy for the nascent party to agree on the role and function of a leader; personal rivalry between Hardie, MacDonald, Henderson and Snowden had complicated the picture. The first two Labour governments of 1924 and 1929–31 had owed a great deal to Ramsay MacDonald's personal stature, but the crisis of 1931 appeared to show how fateful that degree of dependence had been. Most Labour supporters believed that their erstwhile leader had betrayed them, and MacDonald was expelled from the party. Arthur Henderson lost his parliamentary seat in the general election of 1931 in which Labour as a whole performed disastrously, and the leadership of Labour's parliamentary rump devolved upon George Lansbury. Attlee was his deputy and was the sole candidate for the leadership in 1935, shortly before the general election, when Lansbury resigned. Labour somewhat improved its position in comparison with the 1931 result but the National Government was impregnable in the House of Commons. In the new parliament, Attlee defeated Arthur Greenwood and HERBERT MORRISON in a contested election for the leadership. He obtained less than half of the total vote on the first ballot, and few at the time would have supposed that Attlee would last for 20 years in this uncomfortable position. They seriously underestimated their man.

The Major Attlee who began to lead Labour was the solid product of professional England.

He continued to use in peacetime the military rank he had achieved during World War I, somewhat to the dismay of pacifist opinion within the party. His father was a successful solicitor in the City and he was sent to Haileybury, the school founded originally by the East India Company, where he was caned – even at such a school with a strong military tradition – for the patriotic indiscipline which broke out in 1900 when news of the relief of Ladysmith was received. Subsequently, at University College, Oxford, he read history, obtained a second-class honours degree and was captivated by his surroundings. He never spoke at the Oxford Union. He was not enthusiastic about any career, though accepted that he would probably become a barrister.

It was when he was in London, working in chambers, that Attlee set out on a voyage of discovery. Dressed in silk hat and tail coat, he visited Stepney. That was the beginning of a diligent re-examination of his assumptions and political beliefs. He joined the Fabian Society in 1907 and the Independent Labour Party a year later, though his social work retained priority. He lived in Haileybury House and was responsible for the organization of its activities. He wrote poetry about Limehouse. In 1912 he was appointed to a post in the Department of Social Science and Administration at the London School of Economics. He is best thought of as a 'social worker' and in 1920 was to publish a book with this title.

It was still unclear in 1914 whether these activities were going to constitute a career or whether they were an interlude before embarking on a more lucrative profession. When war came, however, Attlee had no hesitation in volunteering to fight. Not for him the Christian pacifism of one of his brothers or the fulminations against a 'capitalist war' indulged in by many members of the Independent Labour Party. He saw service at Gallipoli, in Mesopotamia and on the Western Front. He missed the smell of the fried-fish shops down Limehouse way. He was wounded on several occasions, and was in hospital in Wandsworth when the armistice came. On his discharge, in January 1919, he returned to Stepney and to Labour politics. He was adopted as prospective parliamentary candidate for Limehouse and

quickly became Mayor of Stepney. He gained his first experience of reconciling differing views on the nature of socialism and the contrasting temperaments of Irishmen and Jews. He was cautious and sensible – too punctilious and sensible for ardent revolutionaries to take seriously. In other words, he had already achieved that reputation for balance which was to make him apparently indispensable to Labour.

In October 1922 Attlee was able to persuade the electors of Limehouse that the contest in the general election was between capital and labour rather than between Tory and Liberal. He was to represent this constituency until 1950 when it disappeared, and he represented West Walthamstow for the remainder of his years in the Commons. He immediately became one of Ramsay MacDonald's Parliamentary Private Secretaries. A Labour Party which contained a major was less vulnerable to the charge of irresponsibility. Attlee was to learn that MacDonald did not invariably respond to the views of Labour MPs, even when dutifully relayed to him. By this time Attlee had married and was living in the suburbs. When the first Labour Government was formed in January 1924, albeit without an overall majority, it was evident that he expected a post in the new administration. He was rewarded by being made Under-Secretary at the War Office. Army legislation was not high on Labour's priorities but he again impressed observers by his diligence. Even though the parliamentary circumstances were difficult, Attlee concluded that the Labour Party did not in fact know what it wanted to achieve. He also realized that trade unionists would not automatically support a Labour government if they believed the interests of their members were at stake.

In the years between the end of 1924 and 1929, when Labour was again in opposition, Attlee spoke increasingly frequently on a wide variety of issues. He was saddened by the failure of the General Strike but at the same time not displeased that its ineffectiveness as a political weapon had been made clear. In November 1927 he accepted appointment on a Commission of Enquiry to examine developments in India since the implementation of the

Clement Attlee (centre) with
Herbert Morrison (left) and
Morgan Phillips at the
Labour Party Conference,
Margate, October 1955

1919 Government of India Act. His visits to
India over the next couple of years were
stimulating. He believed that further political
change was necessary, though he did not
underestimate the extent to which 'India' was a
British creation. His preoccupation with the
Indian Commission meant that when the
second Labour Government was formed in
June 1929 there was initially no place for him. It
was only in November 1930 that Attlee was
appointed Chancellor of the Duchy of Lancaster. In this capacity his special concerns were
supposed to be industrial reconstruction and
agriculture. His experience in this post proved
to be brief since he was made Postmaster-
General in March 1931; it was his only experience of running a specific department before
he became Prime Minister in 1945. After
nearly a decade in the Commons, Attlee had
made a modest mark, but his name was still not
very familiar to Labour voters outside London.

It was undoubtedly the landslide defeat of
1931 – he held on to Stepney by a narrow
majority – which pushed Attlee forward. His
competence was acknowledged even by those
who found him colourless. After 1935 he
developed his own particular emphases within
the party. It seemed vital to assert that socialism
was not exotic. The Labour Party would take
note of British circumstances in implementing
it, but voters should be aware that there would
be a profound change when capitalism was

abolished. He buttressed his position by stressing both points and explained that Labour's
parliamentary votes against both defence
estimates and peacetime conscription were to
be understood primarily as expressions of lack
of trust in government policy.

When war came in 1939 Attlee was recovering from a bout of ill-health, but his support for
the British war effort was clear; a Nazi victory
would 'destroy all our hopes'. Nevertheless,
Attlee did not give Chamberlain uncritical support and indeed came to press for his removal.
When WINSTON CHURCHILL succeeded
Chamberlain in May 1940 Attlee accepted the
new Prime Minister's invitation to serve in a
War Cabinet, together with some of his Labour
colleagues. Attlee remained in this cabinet
until the end of the war in Europe. His role was
a vital but not very public one. He mediated and
conciliated not only between the parties but
between ministers and backbenchers. He had
the task of serving faithfully a Prime Minister
who was regarded by some Labour backbenchers with hatred. His status was enhanced in
1942 when he was formally designated Deputy
Prime Minister. He also had specific responsibility for Dominion affairs. Later in the war,
however, it proved increasingly difficult for
Attlee to balance his responsibilities to the
government as a whole and his specific obligations to the Labour Party. The issues posed on
the one hand by Beveridge, and on the other by

debate about the aspirations of the Soviet Union and about the future of both Germany and Greece, led to increasing strain. Attlee contrived to remain calm in almost all circumstances. He might not be so well known to the public as Cripps, Morrison or ERNEST BEVIN, but in practice he outshone them all in his business-like manner and grasp of issues across the board.

These qualities were displayed to the full after 1945. Labour had an overall parliamentary majority for the first time in its history. Attlee's East End experience made him well aware of what a National Health Service might do for 'his people'. Nationalization of central industries was not only ethically necessary, it would bring increased efficiency too. Yet he was only too aware of the economic circumstances that prevailed. The onset of the cold war increased the difficulties, since a proportion of Labour MPs resented Attlee's apparent 'capitulation' to the USA. There was talk that he would have to go, but would-be plotters could make little progress so long as Bevin's loyalty to the Prime Minister was not in doubt. One area which gave Attlee satisfaction was the ending of the British raj in the Indian subcontinent and the willingness (under some pressure) of India and Pakistan to remain within a Commonwealth of Nations which would be multiracial in character.

Attlee was at the head of a team of powerful ministers but his own controlling role was central to their collective success. It becomes more evident, however, that the man who presided over the 'new dawn' of British socialism after 1945 had a cast of mind which was fundamentally late-Victorian. It is not so much the massive endorsement of Attlee and his team in 1945 that seems significant as his loss of power in 1951 and inability to fashion a coherent opposition thereafter. Attlee lived on for a dozen years after his retirement and tended to spend time thinking about world government. He liked to believe that he was the first Oxford graduate to become a Labour MP and he was the first Labour leader to accept a hereditary earldom. In other respects, too, he united unlikely combinations and attributes. He brought a bourgeois, lapsed-Anglican rectitude to an embattled and somewhat bewildered working-class movement. He was a southern English gentleman who was never at home in the 'industrial North' or in Scotland and Wales – heartlands of his party's strength. He was essentially the middle man.

WRITINGS

As It Happened (London: Heinemann, 1954).

FURTHER READING

Burridge, T., *Clement Attlee* (London: Jonathan Cape, 1985).
Harris, K., *Attlee* (London: Weidenfeld and Nicolson, 1985).
Williams, F., *A Prime Minister Remembers* (London: Heinemann, 1961).

KEITH ROBBINS

B

Baden-Powell, Robert (Stephenson Smyth) [Baron Baden-Powell of Gilwell] **('B-P')** (*b.* London, 22 February 1857; *d.* Nyeri, Kenya, 8 January 1941). General and founder of the Boy Scouts and the Girl Guides. Educated at Charterhouse, Baden-Powell joined the 13th Hussars in 1876 and served in India, Africa and the Mediterranean, often undertaking special duties. Promoted to command the 5th Dragoon Guards in 1897, he acquired international fame two years later for master-minding the defence of the border town of Mafeking in the North-West Transvaal at the beginning of the Boer War (1899–1902), a siege lasting 217 days. After setting up the South African Constabulary he returned to England and took up the post of Inspector-General of Cavalry (1903–7) and later a Territorial Command, before retiring from the army in 1910 with the rank of Lieutenant-General.

While in England, Baden-Powell became interested in adapting his individual (some thought eccentric) ideas on cavalry training for use by civilian workers with boys. He held an experimental 'Scout' camp on Brownsea Island in Dorset in the summer of 1907 and published *Scouting for Boys* in early 1908. The response was so enthusiastic that Baden-Powell quickly found himself organizing a new movement for boys, the Boy Scouts (1908), and a parallel association for girls, the Girl Guides (1909). Both spread rapidly, nationally and internationally, becoming the largest movements of their kind worldwide. Baden-Powell devoted the rest of his life to furthering the Scouts and Guides, along with his wife, Olave (1889–1977), whom he married in 1912. He became Chief Scout of the World in 1920, was ennobled in 1929 and received many honours.

Baden-Powell was very much an individualist, with a strong sense of his own destiny. He was sharp-witted without being systematic intellectually, and his personality combined qualities of imagination, eccentricity and charisma in equal portions. A skilled actor, a competent water-colourist and drawer, and an easy, if at times careless writer, he deployed all his talents in the two halves of his life. A modernizer in cavalry matters, he used his field experience to develop training methods which emphasized individual responsibility, health and the use of the outdoors as well as the more traditional *esprit de corps*. When adapted for use with boys, these ideas were widely adopted in the fields of education and youth work. More specifically, the training provided for Scouts and Guides laid great stress on the camp as the best environment in which to develop the whole character in terms of self-respect, personal discipline, fitness and a commitment to public service. With the expansion of the two movements internationally, Scouting and Guiding came to be seen as agents of racial and religious harmony between peoples, an ideal symbolized by the great international camps or Jamborees held after 1920. In Britain Baden-Powell's two movements acquired an established place in national life, contributing significantly to the increased popularity of outdoor recreation during the inter-war period, and continue to play an important role in the partnership between the voluntary and statutory sectors of the youth service as established under the 1944 Education Act. Even though he remains a controversial figure among historians, Baden-Powell's most lasting memorial remains the many millions of members of his two movements worldwide.

FURTHER READING

Jeal, Tim, *Baden-Powell* (London: Century Hutchinson, 1989).

Warren, Allen, 'Sir Robert Baden-Powell, the Scout Movement and Citizen Training in Great Britain, 1900–1920', *English Historical Review*, ci, no. 399 (April 1986).

ALLEN WARREN

Baldwin, Stanley [Earl Baldwin of Bewdley] (*b.* Bewdley, Worcestershire, 3 August 1867; *d.* Astley Hall, Warwickshire, 14 December 1947). Conservative Prime Minister. He was leader of the Conservative Party for 14 years and during that time three times Prime Minister. He played a key role in adjusting the stance of his party to the onset of democracy and in helping it to maintain a leading role in British political life. Without ever being so dominant a figure in the evolution of policy or actual political issues, Baldwin dominated the political mood of his times and possessed a remarkable gift for understanding instinctively what popular opinion would and would not stand for. He could fairly claim to be, in his own words, 'an interpreter of England'.

He was born into an upper-middle-class family in Worcestershire, the son of a well-to-do ironmaster, Alfred Baldwin. The family firm was of the old-fashioned type, a paternalist employer, and early experience of this was to leave on him a lasting impression for his later political career; insofar as he ever became a specialist on any one policy area, it was industrial relations, where his aim was to foster at the national level the harmony that he remembered from Baldwin's in his youth. His father was also actively involved politically, as a Liberal during Baldwin's youth, though as a Liberal Unionist when many men of his class and occupation changed sides in 1886 – especially in the West Midlands. Stanley Baldwin claimed, though, to have been a Conservative almost from birth, and his outlook later in life certainly indicated a deeply conservative affiliation which contrasted sharply with the Fabian reformism that colleagues such as Neville Chamberlain had brought to their party through Liberal Unionism.

Baldwin was the only son of a dominating father and, as such, there were high expectations of his career. He seems to have continually disappointed his father as a young man, failing to shine at Harrow and at Cambridge, though there was much in this that misled. If he neglected to carry off prizes, he did acquire an understanding particularly of literature that was to make him one of the more articulate of British Prime Ministers in such matters, if never a man who could shine by the brilliance

of his conversation. Disappointment in education was the prelude to two decades in which he immersed himself in local affairs, in the family firm, but also in the roles of county councillor and magistrate, and as a farmer. He acquired in these years a deep knowledge and love of the English countryside, and a gradually developing sense that his position imposed duties and obligations as well as privileges. From his mother, who came from Celtic and Wesleyan stock, he drew a further sense of obligation and even of vocation as his interest in politics developed. In 1906 he stood unsuccessfully as Conservative candidate for Kidderminster, characteristically blaming his defeat on trade-union suspicion of a party which had allowed the Taff Vale judgement to stand. But his father, who had been MP for Bewdley since 1892, died in 1908; Baldwin was returned unopposed at the by-election that followed and represented this safe Conservative seat, often without the necessity of a contest, until he went to the Lords in 1937.

Baldwin made very little impact during the first third of his parliamentary career, speaking but little and then usually on industrial questions on which he could claim a direct knowledge. He remained an inconspicuous backbencher even in the early years of World War I, though he did join the Unionist Business Committee and played a part in its work to bring down first Asquith and then Lloyd George. Perhaps more significantly, he was a member, though equally inactive, of the Unionist Social Reform Committee, which sought to develop a progressive stance for the party between 1911 and 1914. His political career began to move only in 1916, when Bonar Law made Baldwin his Parliamentary Private Secretary. In June 1917 he became joint Financial Secretary to the Treasury; with Bonar Law heavily involved in the War Cabinet as Deputy Prime Minister, and with his joint Financial Secretary often absent on war duty in the USA, Baldwin had to carry much of the weight of explaining the Treasury's case in the Commons. He quickly proved that his long apprenticeship on the back benches had taught him much of the ways of the House, and he was an effective junior minister in a key office for the next four years. Even at this point, few would have predicted that Baldwin was destined to go much further; he talked of the chancellorship, just one step up, as the limit of his own ambitions, and in 1921 he was being seriously considered for the vacant speakership, a testament both to his general popularity with MPs and to his own limited ambition. All of this changed when in April 1921 he joined the cabinet, though still in the junior and relatively technical post of President of the Board of Trade. Baldwin had always been a convinced tariff reformer and his new post brought him into regular conflict with Lloyd George and his colleagues, first over the general issues relating to the safeguarding of industry from the dumping of cheap foreign goods, and in 1922 over the specific case of protection for the fabric goods industry, over which he almost resigned.

More importantly, close association with Lloyd George made Baldwin re-examine his own political and party attitudes. He strongly resented what he saw as the Prime Minister's lack of principle, especially over the sale of honours, and he became one of the key links between Conservatives in the country and the junior Conservative ministers who were each working for the return to normal party government. The Chanak Crisis of October 1922 prompted him again to consider resignation, convinced as he was that Lloyd George was risking a war for domestic political reasons. He spoke briefly but most effectively at the Carlton Club meeting which brought down the coalition, recognizing that Lloyd George was 'a dynamic force' but pointing out that such a force could well end by destroying the Conservative Party. It is clear that Baldwin expected that this speech, opposed to his own leader and to the Prime Minister, would end his career; when instead the meeting ensured a Conservative government which most existing ministers would not join, it made him instead a key figure for the next 15 years. With little talent from which to select, Bonar Law made Baldwin Chancellor of the Exchequer, and in effect second minister in the Commons. His tenure of the Exchequer did not enhance his reputation so far as policy went, for its highlight was a cabinet crisis over the settlement of war debts, which demonstrated his lack of experience and almost broke up the government. Nonetheless, with inevitable press attention on a key post-holder, that period did see his national identity emerging. When ill-health forced Bonar Law's resignation in May 1923, Baldwin was the party choice to succeed him. The only serious alternative from within the government was GEORGE CURZON, ruled out by being in the Lords, and many other party frontbenchers were still sulking in their tents after Lloyd George's fall. Baldwin as Prime Minister was a guarantee to his party against a return to coalition.

As Prime Minister in 1923, Baldwin did not cover himself with glory; he presided over a lacklustre team which watched helplessly as unemployment rose, and he ended by bringing his government down in an unnecessary election, fought on a tariff policy for which the public was not prepared, which produced an inconclusive result. All the same, the year in high office established him as a major national figure and as a huge electioneering asset to his party within the new enlarged electorate. In the aftermath of his defeat he determined to give Labour the chance of minority office rather than construct a new anti-Labour combination, partly no doubt from the calculation that a minority government could do little harm, but partly also because he recognized Labour's essential moderation and saw clearly that office would strengthen that moderation. He was not, though, a very effective leader in opposition, and 1924 was not therefore a happy year. The real work of reconstructing party organization and policy was undertaken by more energetic colleagues, though Baldwin supplied an essential component in a series of reflective speeches which the Conservative press dignified with the tag 'the New Conservatism'. Then, as always, his thinking was not greatly profound or his argument original, but he conveyed the impression that his party was sensible and open-minded after almost two decades of reaction and division. He also saw it as his role to heal splits: he welcomed ex-coalitionists back to the shadow cabinet, and, when returned to office by a landslide in the election of November 1924, even brought in Winston Churchill, returning from 20 years with the Liberals.

Baldwin's government team from 1924 to 1929 was remarkably strong, and contained

Stanley Baldwin leaving the back entrance of Kingsway Hall, London, after a Conservative Party meeting, August 1931

besides himself four past and future party leaders as well as powerful personalities such as Curzon and Birkenhead. Baldwin presided with unspectacular geniality, and with what a junior colleague called 'moral authority', over his cleverer and more turbulent colleagues. Attlee must have learned much from watching Baldwin as Prime Minister, and both Harold Macmillan and Harold Wilson later admitted their debt to him. In extreme circumstances, however, Baldwin's role in cabinet became much less passive, as for example when he forced through a non-provocative policy on trade unions, then a continuing coal subsidy, both in the teeth of party hostility. He came to the fore in rallying both party and middle-class opinion during the General Strike of 1926, making most effective use of the radio; he also ensured that more bellicose ministers such as WINSTON CHURCHILL were unable to escalate the conflict, though Baldwin himself was absolutely steadfast on the main issue – his earlier promise 'not to fire the first shot' did not preclude a determination to win once the firing actually started. The defeat of the General Strike brought his reputation to a height, but it also left him morally and physically exhausted, and there is little doubt that his government lost its way in the aftermath, first with a retaliatory

trade-union bill which went quite against Baldwin's instincts, and then with a wider policy of reaction. To this, along with the rising tide of unemployment which Baldwin felt powerless to stem without recourse to the tariff policy which the electorate had rejected in 1923, can be attributed the Conservative defeat of 1929.

Baldwin's second period as Opposition Leader was more stormy even than the first, for the record of his recent government was now open to criticism from the right. The growing support for tariffs as unemployment rocketed after the Wall Street Crash prompted further divisions; Baldwin added to his difficulties by courageously sticking to the cross-party policy of promoting Indian self-government which he had begun in office, determined that India's future should not, like Ireland's, fall victim to the dictates of party expediency. Between them these issues caused a final breach with Churchill, who never served with Baldwin again. Most of all, Baldwin was ill-fitted for opposition because he could not bring himself to oppose that which he really agreed with, a view that did little to cheer up supporters in the drive for power. His difficulties were compounded by attacks from the outside, by the maverick owners of the popular press, who were denounced by Baldwin in his cousin Kipling's phrase as 'aiming at power without responsibility'. These problems had, however, been surmounted, mainly because it is so difficult actually to unseat a Conservative leader who wishes to stay, but partly because opponents overreached themselves, before the collapse of the Labour government in August 1931 changed the political landscape.

Baldwin was initially unhappy about the re-emergence of coalition, but soon saw a National Government as an ideal vehicle for the centrist politics that he had aimed for over the previous decade, especially if Lloyd George were excluded. He also found, as Tom Jones noted, that being second in command of a government was more congenial than being first, for it enabled him to influence and intervene where appropriate without carrying the great weight of supreme office. In that way he was crucial in forcing through the Government of India Bill by 1935 with cross-party support but without the support of the Tory right. He was also instrumental behind the scenes in pressing for re-armament after Hitler took office, though his public admission that 'the Bomber will always get through' probably did as much to alarm the public as any statesman's utterance could.

Ramsay MacDonald's eventual retirement from the premiership in June 1935 left Baldwin, by then tired and feeling the strain of age, to undertake once again 'the heaviest burden that can fall on the shoulders of an Englishman'. He manoeuvred carefully to achieve a mandate for re-armament in the general election of 1935, while at the same time promising 'no great armaments', and relied heavily on the trust that he had built up over years past – 'and I think you can trust me by now'. Once again the aftermath disappointed, for the Abyssinian crisis, the re-occupation of the Rhineland and the speed of re-armament were inadequately handled, and for this Baldwin's third administration has been roughly treated, deservedly, by both contemporaries and historians. The reason, at least in part, lies in the extent to which Baldwin's own energies were committed, as in 1926, to constitutional issues. The death of George V brought a young and popular Prince of Wales to the throne; at first Baldwin saw it as his prime duty to preside

in a fatherly way over the change of monarch, but, as King Edward's intentions with regard to Mrs Simpson emerged over the summer of 1936, it became Baldwin's painful duty to tell his King some severe home truths, and eventually to stage-manage the first abdication since 1688 (see also EDWARD VIII). His political judgement proved to be superb as he quietly lined up the Labour Party and the Empire behind his firm disapproval of the King's plans; in all this he was helped by a total silence from the press until the event was almost over. As things turned out, the change was managed without much of a disturbance, but this can easily lead to an underestimate of how serious it might have been, risking even the monarchy itself, and for this Baldwin deserves much credit. It was again the cause of a mental and physical collapse, and he waited only for George VI's coronation in May 1937 before retiring, going at the same time to the House of Lords.

In retirement Baldwin came under increasing attack, especially when the outbreak of war and the early British military failures led to his identification as one of the 'guilty men' of the 1930s. He lived a lonely last few years, much hated by a public which had in his prime held him in a remarkable regard. That regard owed as much to his personality as to anything he actually did, a personality that was particularly fitted for radio broadcasts and newsreel appearances in a generation to which both were novelties. He was in fact the first British Prime Minister actually to be familiar in word, voice and gesture to the public. In that lay the secret of his political appeal; on that he built the reputation of 'the man you can trust'.

WRITINGS

On England, and other Speeches (London: Philip Allan, 1926).

FURTHER READING

Ball, Stuart, *Baldwin and the Conservative Party* (London: Yale University Press, 1988).
Hyde, H. Montgomery, *Baldwin* (London: Hart Davis, 1973).
Middlemas, K. and Barnes, J., *Baldwin: a Biography* (London: Weidenfeld and Nicolson, 1969).

JOHN RAMSDEN

Balfour, Arthur (James) [Earl of Balfour and Viscount Traprain] (*b.* Whittingehame, East Lothian, 25 July 1848; *d.* near Woking, Surrey, 19 March 1930). Conservative Prime Minister and elder statesman. He played a major role in British Toryism between the death of his uncle, the third Marquess of Salisbury, in 1902 and the consolidation of the power of Stanley Baldwin in the 1920s. MP for Hertford (1874–85), East Manchester (1885–1906) and the City of London (1906–22), he held the following positions: Parliamentary Private Secretary to Salisbury (1878–80), President of the Local Government Board (1885), Secretary of State for Scotland (1886), Chief Secretary for Ireland (1887–91), Leader of the House of Commons and First Lord of the Treasury (1891–2, 1895–1902), Prime Minister (1902–5), Leader of the Conservative Party (1902–11), First Lord of the Admiralty (1915–16), Foreign Secretary (1916–19) and Lord President of the Council (1919–22, 1925–9).

Balfour appears in retrospect as a crucial transition-figure in the history of twentieth-century political life – overshadowed in his earlier years by Salisbury and Joseph Chamberlain and effaced in his later ones by Baldwin and Lloyd George. Yet his ministerial career lasted longer than theirs and his covert power (as confidant and adviser to the increasingly beleaguered governing classes of Britain) proved more than a match for their superiority on the public platform. He was the last Conservative leader before Sir Alec Douglas-Home to be drawn from circles associated with the landed aristocracy; he was the first whom cabinet colleagues addressed by his Christian name. He figured among the politicians who predicted revolution from the rise of Labour; he ministered to the attenuation of both and died during a Labour government that had shown itself as unrevolutionary as any to which he had contributed. Perhaps this function as a human bridge between divergent eras makes the middle period of Balfour's political career – from 1902 to 1918 – seem the most significant, despite his having held first place for less than four of those years. Two other phases of his life nevertheless demand attention: his political apprenticeship under the tutelage of Salisbury in the 1880s and 1890s, and his later years as an elder statesman respected by politicians across the party spectrum.

Most important in his family background was his sense of isolation outside it. Close friends remained few; he never married. The family supplied brilliance enough, to be sure, and the remarkable atmosphere of superior seclusion created at Whittingehame, wonderfully caught in her memoirs by Balfour's sister-in-law Frances, provided a secure intellectual location for the son of a former Tory MP whose wife had the future Lord Salisbury for a father. The isolation persisted nonetheless. Following the death in 1875 of May Lyttelton, whom he had hoped to marry, Balfour retreated further into a shell, which opened a little at Whittingehame but rarely elsewhere and certainly not among political acquaintances. Indeed the family (in the person of Lord Salisbury) took the initiative in suggesting that Balfour enter the House for the seat of Hertford at the 1874 general election. His undistinguished profile at Eton and Cambridge hardly fitted him for what followed. It prepared him better, perhaps, for his first book, *A Defence of Philosophic Doubt* (1879), than for the sword-lines of party politics which he immediately contrived to cross. During those early years he would appear as frequently in the company of Liberals as of Tories, and the latter, especially Lord Randolph Churchill, were often of the kind to win him little credit among the 'Old Gang' of the party.

His association with a group of rebellious Tories who liked to call themselves the Fourth Party went less deep than many contemporaries and historians have believed. But a certain notoriety helped him compensate for his signal failures as a speaker and kept him in touch with both back bench and leadership. Balfour had no doubt (despite the cartoons provoked by the title of his first book) to which team he belonged and where his ambitions ultimately lay. From 1886, when his uncle entered his stable period of ascendency as a statesman, Balfour became an apprentice prime minister and was seen as such by 1891 when Salisbury made him Leader of the Commons. Oddly, he rose by the route that had led so many nineteenth-century politicians to disaster: he made a success of Ireland. He demonstrated there that a disposition which had often made all forms of action seem dangerously dynamic – observers' most hackneyed description of him was 'languid' – could nevertheless harbour an iron will to do the things that Tory logic said should be done. In Ireland this was novel and could have proved explosive. But Balfour's winning of a second adjective, 'bloody', did him immeasurable good away from the Irish who bestowed it and suggested possibilities no one had anticipated in the halting backbencher of the 1870s.

A future development also escaped expectation. For just as Balfour's career began its upward thrust in the 1890s, so did the revival of Joseph Chamberlain's fortunes after his resignation from the Liberal Party in 1886. These trajectories converged after the Boer War of 1899–1902 by giving rise to an issue that lacerated Balfour's premiership and critically affected the course of Conservative politics in the twentieth century.

When Salisbury's stamina collapsed under the strain of his third government after 1895 and the events that led to war in South Africa, Balfour's succession seemed assured. But controversy followed almost at once. Initially the problems arose in the field of education, where the government was committed to pressing through a reform of educational finance and administration. The 'Balfour Act' of 1902 owed more, in fact, to the Duke of Devonshire than to the Prime Minister, though Balfour's laurels were tattered by nonconformists who loathed the idea of paying an education rate that would finance Anglican schools. Far more serious for Balfour's leadership, however, was the launching by his colonial minister, Chamberlain, of a programme of tariff reform intended, in the wake of the South African war, to strengthen imperial connections and provide a solid base of economic protection for the domestic economy by building around it a tariff wall that would keep out cheap imported materials. From the summer of 1903 to the resignation of his government at the end of 1905, Balfour's administration failed either to squash or to divert the protectionist programme. The Prime Minister operated astutely in coping with Chamberlain's resignation in 1903, less so in the battle of speeches that

ensued when Chamberlain took his campaign to the country. Other issues supervened and eased the pressure from time to time: fighting the nonconformists (again) over licensing laws, battling with the Irish Protestants over the need to reform Irish land purchase, or basking momentarily in the glory of the *entente cordiale* with France negotiated by Foreign Secretary Lansdowne in 1904. Yet, behind and beyond all these lay tariffs and Chamberlain, sapping the government's vitality and exposing the emptiness of Balfour's tortured protestations of sympathy with everyone's case. Balfour's government was not brought down by the Liberals in the House of Commons: it rather wasted away.

In living memory perhaps only Rosebery had left office under so black a cloud as that darkening Balfour in 1905. When the new Liberal Government called an immediate election in January 1906, Conservative candidates knew that the central issue would become the one that Tories did not wish to discuss – the 'Big Loaf versus the Little Loaf', free trade against food taxes. Balfour watched his party fall apart as the results came in; his own loss of East Manchester, to which constituency he had moved in 1885, symbolized the greater destruction of the party as a whole. His overreaction to a humiliating defeat seems understandable. He blamed a new socialist tide that had swept through the country. The sweeper was not, in truth, a socialist force but rather a calculating and powerful imperialist one; and had not Chamberlain helped Balfour by falling victim to a paralysing stroke in 1906, it looks likely that Balfour's leadership of the Tory party would have terminated more quickly than it did. In the short term Balfour recovered. His new constituency in the City of London gave him a secure platform until he went to the House of Lords in 1922. He worked to cool the tariff issue and divert attention elsewhere. He asserted a policy for the conduct of the House of Lords which was enlightened, if ignored. Yet his inability to create a positive style of leadership left him easy meat. He sensibly kept the party out of Lloyd George's coalition-scheming in 1910, but his conduct of the constitutional crisis as a whole brought strong criticism from within the party. It confirmed his

Arthur Balfour playing
tennis

direction of the party since 1903 as a form of rearguard action, and Balfour, more dispirited than unnerved, chose to abandon it. He resigned the leadership of the Conservative Party in November 1911 and never resumed it.

Having lost, within the space of six years, the two major positions to which politicians normally aspire, what remains striking about Balfour is the degree to which he did recover major aspects of his political career over the next decade. The coming of the war played a central role in his resurrection by breaking down traditional methods of government and almost compelling some form of non-party administration. Asquith brought in Balfour when he formed his coalition of May 1915 – ironically placing him at the Admiralty in succession to the disgraced Churchill, despite Balfour's having supported the principle of an attack through the Dardanelles. Lloyd George, similarly, pressed Balfour to take the Foreign Office in the new coalition of December 1916, for all the Prime Minister's previous zest in trying to remove Balfour from the Admiralty. Indeed by 1916 Balfour had become an intellectual ornament to virtually any possible government – valuable for his clear-headedness and coolness of mind more than for any administrative acumen. Not that he eschewed all causes. The Balfour Declaration of November 1917, reporting to Lord Rothschild the government's sympathy for the idea of establishing a national home for the Jewish people in Palestine, owed more to Balfour than had the Balfour Education Act, and commented visibly on his width of thought. But evangelism came unnaturally to him and colleagues sought instead speculative papers about issues of the moment or a lucid rehearsal of possible lines of action. He had always been good at that. It was in the carrying out of any of his courses of action that Balfour had proved wanting.

Lloyd George's attempt at a cross-party government that would organize the peace (just as it had won the war) suited Balfour the elder statesman (just as it had nettled Balfour the prewar party leader). Ultimately his party judgement turned out once more to be flimsy; he wound up on the wrong side of the Carlton Club meeting of October 1922 that terminated the Lloyd George coalition, and then walked the wilderness until Baldwin, in whose appointment as Conservative leader Balfour had played a considerable part in advice he had tendered to the King, brought him back again as a symbol of party togetherness in 1925. But then, many other senior Tory politicians made the same mistake and most of them recovered. What was distinctive about Balfour's longevity was its relation to his membership of a small and strange class of British politician: the brilliant subordinate. As with Neville Chamberlain, a colleague in the Baldwin government of 1924–9, the qualities that made Balfour's rise near-inevitable made his success at the summit most implausible. As with R. B. Haldane, a friend for many years, intellectual concerns made Balfour an able analyst but one often devoid of antennae. Balfour escaped Haldane's fate because his charm made him better-liked. He escaped Neville Chamberlain's because he lacked mission. When it mattered, however, Balfour showed himself unable to escape the conversation of pro with con, the tyranny of argument that lesser men throw off with an executive shrug or miss altogether through a blessed insensitivity. From this point of view, Baldwin knew things that Balfour never fathomed.

WRITINGS

Chapters of Autobiography, ed. Blanche Dugdale (London: Cassell, 1930).

FURTHER READING

Dugdale, Blanche E. C., *Arthur James Balfour, First Earl of Balfour*, 2 vols. (London: Hutchinson, 1936).

Egremont, Max, *Balfour: a Life of Arthur James Balfour* (London: Collins, 1980).

Mackay, Ruddock, *Balfour: Intellectual Statesman* (Oxford: Oxford University Press, 1985).

Young, Kenneth, *Arthur James Balfour* (London: Bell, 1963).

MICHAEL BENTLEY

Barrington-Ward, Robert (McGowan) ('B-W'; 'Robin') (*b.* Worcester, 23 February 1891; *d.* Dar-es-Salaam, Tanganyika [now Tanzania], 29 February 1948). Journalist and editor of *The Times*. Known as 'B-W' to his colleagues, he was editor of *The Times* from 1941 to 1948, in succession to the formidable Geoffrey Dawson. As Dawson's assistant from 1927, he wrote most of the leading articles elaborating the paper's policy of 'appeasing' the European dictators in the 1930s. His own editorship was marked by a radical attitude to postwar reconstruction that was heavily influenced by his chosen assistant, E. H. Carr, and brought accusations from traditionalists that he was turning the paper 'pink'. He died a few days after his 57th birthday while on a cruise intended as a rest cure.

'B-W' was a classic product of the late Victorian professional middle class, wholly suited to the service of a paper which still thought itself virtually an estate of the realm. Fourth son of five in a large and talented family, he was a Scholar of Westminster and of Balliol, where he compensated for a third class degree by being President of the Union. He survived three years in the trenches and won the MC and DSO. He was a devout Anglican, upright, fair, conscientious to a fault. He married in 1927 and had three children.

Barely a week after getting his degree, 'B-W' wrote his first leader for *The Times*, with a job as editorial secretary to Dawson. After World War I he became J. L. Garvin's assistant editor on *The Observer*, where he learnt how to run a newspaper office and had a base from which to widen his circle of acquaintance. Back at *The Times*, he was Dawson's effective deputy by 1934. Dawson delegated to him much administrative work, and what he himself described as a 'wearing sense of responsibility' inclined him to continue writing a good deal too. In due course, as editor, he delegated too little, to the detriment of the paper and of his health.

'Appeasement', to 'B-W', was 'an endeavour to secure by negotiation the removal of the causes of war', not, as it came to seem, the pursuit of peace at almost any price. 'People who decry honest peace efforts', he once wrote to his mother, 'should be made to spend a night in a shell-hole.' That personal experience, with the survivor's sense of obligation to the dead, underpinned his conviction that if only the injustices of the peace settlement were removed, the German threat to peace would dissolve. His argument was essentially moral – and reasoned with a cogency difficult to counter except by starting from less generous premises. He was disabused finally when Hitler broke the Munich settlement in March 1939.

Not long before succeeding Dawson, 'B-W' was pressed by Sir John Reith to follow him as Director-General of the BBC. Though tempted, he concluded (rightly for those days) that editor of *The Times* was 'the bigger job'. Like his predecessors, he moved easily among statesmen on a more or less equal footing. To his proprietor, Colonel Astor, 'B-W' said he thought it 'the duty and opportunity of *The Times* to prepare for the great social changes inevitable after the war'. His mentor for this purpose was the academic and former civil servant E. H. Carr, appointed assistant editor and leader-writer in 1941, whose radicalism became a constant spur. By 1946, when Carr left, 'B-W' was in declining health from what proved to be Parkinson's disease. But his editorship, though brief – and in a period when papers were rationed to only a few pages – was long enough to give *The Times* a firm concern for social and economic issues that outlasted the specific left-of-centre viewpoint of his years.

FURTHER READING

History of 'The Times', vol. IV, part 2 (London: The Times, 1952).

McLachlan, D., *In the Chair: Barrington-Ward of 'The Times'* (London: Weidenfeld and Nicolson, 1971).

Woods, O. and Bishop, J., *Story of 'The Times'* (London: Michael Joseph, 1985).

COLIN K. SEYMOUR-URE

Beatty, David [Earl Beatty] (*b*. Stapeley, Cheshire, 17 January 1871; *d*. London, 12 March 1936). Admiral of the Fleet. Beatty was the youngest British admiral since Nelson. Gallantry in battle, recklessness in hunting and a partiality for women were among the qualities he inherited from his Anglo-Irish ancestors. His biographer rightly regards him as England's last naval hero. His memorial lies close to Nelson's in the crypt of St Paul's Cathedral, though it is a more modest one.

Beatty himself was not modest. He was allowed the title 'Baron Beatty of the North Sea' in recognition of his naval activities in this rather substantial area. The Battle of Jutland on 31 May–1 June 1916 was his greatest test and it is in that connection that his name is chiefly remembered. As a young man he had emerged from *Britannia* somewhat bruised but then moved on to a variety of appointments, which included time on the royal yacht during a summer cruise as well as rather more taxing experiences on the Upper Nile. In the year immediately before the war his experience was with the Battle Cruiser Squadron. On 5 August 1914 he wrote to his wife to say that he could see no reason for the war that was starting but, fortunately, it ought to be all over before the dark nights of winter came on. That turned out not to be the case, but it was widely believed that it was the Royal Navy that might lose the war in an afternoon. By the early months of 1916 a condition of stalemate seemed to have been reached at sea. Beatty was looking for advice from a well-known 'palmist' and she obligingly predicted that a great success lay ahead of her client. Whether the Battle of Jutland was such a success has been much debated ever since. The comparative performances of the British and German battle cruisers in this engagement have been meticulously scrutinized by naval historians – with varying conclusions. The respective roles of both Beatty and Sir JOHN JELLICOE have their admirers and detractors.

Beatty succeeded Jellicoe at the end of 1916 as Commander-in-Chief, and for the remainder of the war wrestled, more or less successfully, with problems of supply and the threat posed by submarines. The 'big thing' – a decisive naval encounter – never came. The Royal Navy could be said to have achieved a kind of victory, or at least to have avoided a defeat. After the war Beatty served as First Sea Lord until 1927 – a period during which he helped to scale down the Royal Navy due both to domestic constraints and international pressure, particularly from the Americans.

The possession of charisma and a romantic aura are not now thought in themselves sufficient qualities for successful command. Beatty would not have agreed – nor, at the time, did a substantial section of the British public which wanted to have a dashing heir to a great tradition. Beatty did his best to oblige.

FURTHER READING

Ranft, B. McL., *The Beatty Papers: Selections from the Private and Official Correspondence of Admiral of the Fleet Earl Beatty* (London: Naval Records Society, 1989).

Roskill, Stephen, *Admiral of the Fleet Earl Beatty: the Last Naval Hero* (London: Collins, 1980).

KEITH ROBBINS

Beaverbrook, Lord [Aitken, (William) Max-(well)] (*b.* Maple, Ontario, Canada, 25 May 1879; *d.* Cherkley, Surrey, 9 June 1964). Proprietor of Express Newspapers, Conservative politician and senior minister. As the proprietor of Express Newspapers from December 1916 until his death, he exercised full editorial control over the *Daily Express*, the *Sunday Express*, and the (London) *Evening Standard*. The commercial success of all three newspapers derived from his rare blend of business acumen and journalistic flair. In Fleet Street and the financial world his achievements were unquestionable, but in Westminster and Whitehall the statesman *manqué* always

remained a colonial conspirator with a direct line to popular opinion. 'The Beaver' pursued a highly individual brand of Conservatism, rooted firmly in the Empire and invariably at odds with his party's leaders. Two notable exceptions were Bonar Law and Winston Churchill, thus facilitating his ministerial appointments in coalitions formed during both World Wars. Beaverbrook accepted a peerage in 1917 and proved an innovative and highly effective propagandist when he became Minister of Information in 1918, but his greatest achievement in office was as Minister of Aircraft Production during the Battle of Britain in 1940. Along with Lords Northcliffe and Rothermere, Beaverbrook was a 'press baron' of almost legendary proportions and a founding father of modern, mass-circulation popular journalism.

Beaverbrook was a son of the Manse, and all his life he remained close to his Presbyterian and New Brunswick roots, peppering his language with biblical allusions and forever consolidating his diverse Canadian interests. He never lost his accent, proved a generous patron of his native province, and in later life insisted that, 'My last home will be where my heart has always been.' If his newspapers were not averse to indulging in sustained malice, witness their owner's public antipathy towards a Stanley Baldwin or a Lord Louis Mountbatten, they abhorred smut and sensationalism. Beaverbrook's firm but characteristically unorthodox faith sustained him through a succession of personal and public reversals, fuelling his wisdom, wit, determination and generosity. Paradoxically, it also underpinned a career of ruthless commercial endeavour and relentless political machination. Similarly, his staunch and naïve belief in the values of empire sustained an illusion that colonial success would ensure his welcome by and acceptance into the very highest circles of power in the mother country. The repeated thwartings of Beaverbrook's political aims and ambitions suggest that this never truly occurred – that he rarely overcame the suspicion of a narrowly English political, business and social élite, especially when he continued to espouse such maverick views and surround himself with fellow outsiders and *arrivistes*.

The then plain Max Aitken was already a proven financier when he arrived in London in 1910 intent on carving out a political career. In the general election of December 1910 he narrowly gained Ashton-under-Lyne from the Liberals. On the Unionist backbenches he rarely spoke, already preferring to exercise influence behind the scenes. Close friendship and financial links with fellow Canadian Bonar Law brought a knighthood in the 1911 coronation honours and the ear of his party's next leader. While still focusing upon business interests on both sides of the Atlantic, Aitken assiduously cultivated powerful friends and contacts. He established a lifelong reputation for generous hospitality and good living, invariably pursued at his Surrey country house, Cherkley Court. Bonar Law's trust in him was confirmed by his intermediary role during the constitutional conference on the future of Ulster in July 1914. Both men retained close contact while Lt.-Col. Sir Max Aitken (Bart., as of January 1916) represented Canadian interests in wartime France and at the War Office; typically, he secured a room close to that of Lloyd George, with whom he now became intimate.

During 1916 Aitken acquired the *Daily Express*, a flagging but potentially profitable challenger to the *Daily Mail*. The focus of his interest for the remainder of his life and a platform for his views, the paper benefited from the very best editorial and managerial staff Aitken could buy, his own commercial expertise, and a proprietorial involvement that stimulated rather than smothered exciting journalism. Scarcely a day passed without the chief shareholder querying editorial decisions, or injecting informed gossip and controversy. By 1936 the *Daily Express* had a world-record circulation of two and a quarter million, and nearly doubled sales again over the next two decades. The *Sunday Express* reached a parallel audience after December 1918, and the *Evening Standard* in the 1920s built up a deserved reputation for quality features and uncompromising leaders. However great the distractions, the fortunes of Express Newspapers were paramount in the owner's daily affairs from December 1916 to his death 48 years later.

Also in December 1916, Aitken actively connived in Asquith's downfall and replacement by Lloyd George. Denied the cabinet post he judged due reward, the now Lord Beaverbrook finally found his *métier* at the Ministry of Information. Throughout 1918 he thrived on a propaganda battle with the Germans and a personnel struggle with the Foreign Office. Out of office, he relished Lloyd George's peacetime travails, taking care to ensure Bonar Law's presence at the historic meeting of the Carlton Club in October 1922. Stanley Baldwin's speech effectively destroyed the coalition and unintentionally secured his accession to the premiership after Bonar Law's death. A formidable and unforgiving enemy, the predominant figure in the inter-war Conservative Party responded to criticism from ostensibly sympathetic newspapers by banishing Beaverbrook from the innermost circles of power.

Between 1929 and 1931 Express Newspapers promoted the 'Empire Crusade', the most serious challenge to Baldwin's party leadership. Beaverbrook sought a firm adherence to 'Empire Free Trade', a system of imperial preference. Early success, including by-election defeats of official Tory candidates, failed to prevent ultimate humiliation. Baldwin's accusation of exercising 'power without responsibility, the prerogative of the harlot throughout the ages' was to haunt Beaverbrook throughout the 1930s. Excluded from involvement in the formation of the 1931 National Government, and thwarted in his efforts to rally support for Edward VIII five years later, he seemed irrelevant to the current Conservative leadership. Beaverbrook's account of the Abdication appeared posthumously, complementing his three highly regarded accounts of high politics between 1916 and 1922. Death prevented the full story of his repeated humiliations at Baldwin's hands.

Imperialist and isolationist, the *Daily Express*'s suspicion of any Continental commitment ensured support for 'appeasement'. However, an unapologetic Beaverbrook threw himself wholeheartedly into the war effort. Renewed intimacy with Churchill brought a place in the War Cabinet in May 1940. His energy and endeavours in servicing the urgent needs of RAF Fighter Command made Beaverbrook's year as Minister of Aircraft Production the culmination of a tempestuous and eventful career. He was back in the limelight, enjoying real power, and offering his leader support during critical moments of doubt and ill-health.

Subsequent appointments at the ministries of Supply and Production and as Lord Privy Seal proved tedious and anti-climactic, relieved only by an absence of office during 1942–3. For 18 months Stalin's most unexpected admirer campaigned vocally for an early Second Front; an unholy alliance of Express Newspapers and the British Communist Party led a brief yet genuine challenge to Churchill's conduct of the war.

Heavy criticism of his role in the Conservatives' 1945 election campaign encouraged a final withdrawal from active party politics, if not from public life. Beaverbrook still controlled his newspapers, and in the course of a lengthy but hectic 'retirement' retained the smug satisfaction that he could still sway public opinion: he died convinced that Macmillan's

Lord Beaverbrook leaving 10 Downing Street after a cabinet meeting, 15 May 1940

failure to enter Europe was largely thanks to Express Newspapers.

FURTHER READING

Taylor, A. J. P., *Beaverbrook* (London: Hamish Hamilton, 1972).

ADRIAN SMITH

Beeching, Richard [Lord Beeching] (*b.* Sheerness, Kent, 21 April 1913; *d.* East Grinstead, Sussex, 23 March 1985).   Industrialist and Chairman of British Rail. Dr Beeching (as he then was) achieved fame as Chairman of the British Transport Commission and subsequently, from 1961 to 1965, of the newly created British Railways Board. He was appointed by Ernest Marples, the Minister of Transport, from within the senior ranks of ICI to carry out a major restructuring of the railways. He set about the task with great skill and determination, and was undeterred by often emotional public objections to the closure of under-used railway lines and stations. This short period will be remembered as a momentous one in railway history.

Beeching was educated at Maidstone Grammar School and then went on to Imperial College, London, where he obtained a first class honours degree in physics, followed by a Ph.D. Throughout his life he regarded himself primarily as a physicist and considered that this gave him the analytical skills needed to tackle the many crucial tasks which came his way.

He first worked at the Fuel Research Station at Greenwich in 1937, but soon moved to the Mond Nickel Company in Birmingham. During the war he was seconded to the Ministry of Supply and in due course served as deputy to Sir Ewart Smith of ICI in the Armaments Design Department. Through Smith, in 1948 he joined ICI, where he remained, with interruptions, until 1968. His career in ICI was impressive. He started as a member of the team which developed terylene and in 1953 was sent out to Canada to supervise the building of a terylene plant in Ontario. Two years later he returned to Britain and was appointed Chairman of ICI's metals division. In 1957, at the age of 44, he was promoted to the main board of ICI as technical director.

Three years after this Beeching's life took a momentous turn. He was appointed a member of the committee of enquiry, under the chairmanship of Sir Ivan Stedford, which was set up by Ernest Marples to look into the management and operation of the railways. Beeching so impressed Marples that he was invited to join the board of the Transport Commission, of which Sir Brian Robertson was then chairman, with a view to succeeding the latter and becoming the first chairman of the newly created British Railways Board. Thus started the historic Beeching era, when more was done to change the railway system than at any other time in the twentieth century. The objective was to reshape the railways into a modern, economically run service. The details were fully set out in a published report which identified 5,000 miles of track and 2,000 stations for closure on grounds of under-utilization. At the same time there was a major staff rationalization and reduction. The reasoning in support of these massive changes, which were quickly carried out, was impressive and revealed to the full Beeching's unique powers of analysis.

In 1965, after a change of government, Beeching left the railways, received a life peerage and became a deputy chairman of ICI. His talents were again put to use in the public service when he was appointed President of the Royal Commission on Assize Courts and Quarter Sessions, which led to major changes in the structure of the courts. He was also asked to prepare a report on Gibraltar and its relations with Spain. His industrial career took a further significant turn in 1970 when (having left ICI two years previously) he became chairman of Redland, the important building materials firm located in Reigate. Under his guidance – he remained chairman until 1977 and on the board until 1983 – the company substantially increased its operations both at home and overseas, progress which has been maintained by his close associate and successor, Sir Colin Corness.

Beeching was a man of considerable intellectual gifts. He was calm in manner, with a quiet sense of humour, friendly and affable. But underlying all was a firm determination to achieve those objectives which his exceptional mental prowess identified in any task with which he was faced. He was undoubtedly one of the most remarkable industrial personalities of his generation.

FURTHER READING

Ferris, Paul, 'The Beeching Revolution', *The Observer* (24 March 1963).

DEREK EZRA

Benn, Tony [Wedgwood Benn, Anthony Neil; formerly Viscount Stansgate] (*b.* London, 3 April 1925). Labour politician. One of the Labour Party's longest-serving cabinet ministers in the 1960s and 1970s, he was from 1979 to the late 1980s the most prominent leader of Labour's left wing in the internal quarrels which wracked the party during those years.

The son of a Labour peer, Anthony Wedgwood Benn – he later shortened his name in what opponents derided as a spurious populist gesture – attended Westminster School and New College, Oxford. He served in the Royal Air Force and Fleet Air Arm from 1943 to 1946, returned to Oxford to complete his degree, and married Caroline Middleton De Camp in 1949. She is a prominent educationist, and three of their four children have become active in politics. Benn entered Parliament at the age of 25 in 1950, sitting for Bristol South-East. His main early interest was in colonial affairs, and he was active in the Movement for Colonial Freedom and the Fabian Colonial Bureau. He also soon became both a frequent broadcaster and one of his party's early experts on media presentation.

Benn was not at this time particularly identified with the left wing of his party, and was personally close to Anthony Crosland, its leading 'revisionist' thinker. He joined Labour's National Executive in 1959 and was widely tipped for future office. However, his political career was interrupted by his father's death in 1960. As the inheritor of the Viscountcy – he had already tried unsuccessfully to renounce the inheritance in 1955 – he was forced to resign his Commons seat. There followed a three-year battle for the right to disclaim his title, which eventually succeeded in 1963.

After Labour entered government in

1964, Benn's promotion was rapid: he was Postmaster-General (1964–6) and Minister of Technology (1966–70). He later claimed that it was ministerial experience that 'really made me into a socialist, in middle age', though at the time he was still generally seen within his party as more technocrat than ideologue. He was opposition spokesman on Trade and Industry from 1970 to 1974, and held successively the Industry and Energy portfolios in the Wilson and Callaghan governments of 1974–9. At the same time he became an ever more active member of the party's National Executive, and was party Chairman in 1971–2. His regular topping of the poll in elections to the Constituency section of the Executive showed how popular he now was with party activists; this support was to be his power base in the inner-party conflicts to come.

From about 1970, and more publicly and dramatically in opposition after 1979, Benn's thinking moved to the left. He became the most prominent exponent of such causes as unilateral nuclear disarmament, greatly extended public ownership and sweeping constitutional reform both within the British state and in Labour's own structures. It was on this last ground that the party's internal battles – perhaps the fiercest any major British party had seen since at least 1945 – were primarily fought out between 1979 and 1983. Benn, and a Labour left now usually dubbed by journalists 'Bennite', won a series of victories both on policy issues and on reforming the party's constitution. He became a sharp critic of Labour's record in government, articulating the aspirations not only of discontented radicals within the party but of those further left who had previously always distrusted Labour politicians. His bid for the party's deputy leadership in 1981, when he came within a hair's breadth of ousting DENIS HEALEY, was the high-water mark of the left's campaigns. Yet many of his parliamentary colleagues and successive Labour leaders now thought him a divisive and destructive influence. They blamed his activities for the public image of disunity and extremism which they felt Labour had acquired. This image, they felt, was responsible for the party's precipitous electoral decline and especially the debacle of 1983.

Benn himself lost his Bristol seat in that defeat, but soon returned to Parliament in a by-election at Chesterfield in March 1984.

Many former supporters now distanced themselves from him: the news media dubbed these the 'soft left' as against the Bennite 'hard left'. After Neil Kinnock's accession to the party leadership in October 1983 the influence of the hard left, and of Benn himself, diminished sharply. Yet although, by the late 1980s, Benn had become an increasingly isolated critic from the left of the party's direction – an isolation underlined by his crushing defeat when contesting the party leadership in 1988 – he remained one of the most compelling orators, and one of the most iconoclastic thinkers, among senior British politicians. All except his bitterest critics (and these were usually to be found within his own party) recognized his qualities of incorruptibility, imagination and infectious enthusiasm for the causes and traditions he held dear. With the publication of his multi-volume diaries, commencing in 1987, he also looks likely to provide future historians of modern British politics with one of their richest sources.

WRITINGS

Out of the Wilderness: Diaries 1963–67 (London: Hutchinson, 1987).
Office without Power: Diaries 1968–72 (London: Hutchinson, 1988).
Against the Tide: Diaries 1973–76 (London: Hutchinson, 1989).

FURTHER READING

Jenkins, R., *Tony Benn: a Political Biography* (London: Writers and Readers, 1980).
Seyd, P., *The Rise & Fall of the Labour Left* (London: Macmillan, 1987).

STEPHEN HOWE

Berlin, Sir Isaiah (*b.* Riga, Latvia [now Latvian SSR], 6 June 1909). Political philosopher and historian of ideas. His contribution to public life has been made as teacher and author, as an historian of political ideas and a philosophical champion of pluralistic liberalism, and as one of the most distinguished of those twentieth-century exiles from Eastern and Central Europe who have become pillars of the British intellectual establishment even while eroding its elements of insular complacency. During World War II he was a diplomat in Washington and (more briefly) in Moscow, but the rest of his long career since the early 1930s has had its roots in Oxford. There he has been a Fellow at New College and at All Souls; Chichele Professor of Social and Political Theory (1957–67); and first President of Wolfson College (1966–75). He was awarded the Order of Merit in 1971, and served as President of the British Academy from 1974 to 1978. As for the most notable acknowledgements of his endeavour to promote better international understanding, he was joint winner of the Erasmus Prize in 1983 and recipient of the Fiat Award for 1987. His lifelong support for Zionism (hardly a stance congenial to many of his wartime Foreign Office colleagues) has been reflected, for example, in writing about Chaim Weizmann and in service as Honorary President of the British Friends of the University of Jerusalem.

Having left St Petersburg at the age of ten in the aftermath of the Bolshevik Revolution, Berlin went to school at St Paul's in London before entering Oxford. By the time of his first book (*Karl Marx*, 1939), he was already more clearly anxious than many of his colleagues to use his philosophical training (as well as his cosmopolitan range and his intimacy with the Jewish and Russian cultures in particular) to illuminate some of the great historical and political themes of modern times. Here the nature of freedom, and the threats to it stemming from extremist bigotry, whether of left or right, have been Berlin's most pivotal and recurrent concerns. He has sought to defend versions of liberty that are flexibly sensitive to the variable needs of different societies according to the contingencies of time and place. Thus he has drawn on the legacies of Vico, Montesquieu and Herder from the eighteenth century, and on their later development by figures such as J. S. Mill in the British liberal tradition and Alexander Herzen in the Russian radical one. Conversely, he has warned against the application to politics not only of mystical irrationalism but also of quasi-scientific, total, and monistic systems of deterministic explana-

tion (epitomized by the more vulgar versions of Marxism). How could formulae of that sort properly accommodate, for instance, the inspired 'agency' of a Weizmann or a Churchill, such seeming improbabilities as the foundation of modern Israel or the survival of Britain after Dunkirk? Berlin's distrust of determinism has been related to his conviction that 'the ends of life' are indeed plural; that we must strive to maximize the individual's freedom to select his own principal goals for himself rather than allow the terms of his fulfilment to be externally dictated either by the postulation of certain impersonal 'laws' deemed to govern history or by the kind of leaders who claim some superior insight into what he 'really' wishes or needs; and that such liberty of personal choice, especially as between competing and even contradictory objectives, also entails the exercise of moral responsibility.

Berlin's best and most characteristic work comes in the genre of the extended essay, good examples being *Four Essays on Liberty* (1969) and *Vico and Herder* (1976).

FURTHER READING

Hausheer, R., 'Isaiah Berlin', in *European Liberty*, ed. P. Manent et al. (The Hague: Martinus Nijhoff, 1983), pp. 49–81.

MICHAEL BIDDISS

Bernal, J(ohn) D(esmond) (*b.* Nenagh, Co. Tipperary, Ireland, 10 May 1901; *d.* London, 15 September 1971). Scientist and politician. Bernal was a polymath and publicist. His early scientific work was undertaken in his own university, Cambridge, and at the Royal Institution, before he went in 1938 to Birkbeck College, University of London, as Professor of Physics. He was Professor of Crystallography from 1965 to 1968, by which time his health had suffered severely as a result of a series of strokes. He became a Fellow of the Royal Society in 1937 and received many other scientific prizes and honours. He was one of the founding fathers of modern crystallography and molecular biology, and he made particular contributions to the study of the crystal structures of the sex hormones and of the structure of protein crystals. His *The Origin of Life* (1967) was the culmination of a long preoccupation with this problem.

Bernal's scientific distinction was undoubted, but what brought his name before a wider public was his political beliefs and his convictions about the social responsibility of scientists. The son of an Irish Catholic gentleman farmer and an American Presbyterian mother, he was sent to Bedford School in 1914 and proceeded to Emmanuel College, Cambridge, at the end of the war. His rebellious instincts were already well developed, and an early immersion in Marxist classics led him to the conclusion that his Catholicism was antiscientific and reactionary and had to be abandoned. So, too, did conventional sexual morals. Bernal felt himself completely liberated to speculate extravagantly on the possibilities of a greatly lengthened human lifespan. There would be an initial 'larval' century or so during which there would be gratifying time for dancing, poetry and lovemaking before the 'chrysalis' stage was reached.

More immediately relevant, however, was the Soviet Union, which he first visited in 1931: what he saw was 'grim but great'. Science and socialism were walking hand in hand. The encounter led him to engage more actively in politics on behalf of the Communist Party as the 1930s progressed, though its leaders were a little suspicious of middle-class intellectuals. In turn, the 'Scientific Establishment' was more than a little suspicious of radical scientists. Bernal's solution was formally to leave the Communist Party but to give it all the support he could as an 'independent' intellectual. He was at least nominally active in some 60 committees devoted to peace, anti-Fascism and friendship with the Soviet Union. His *The Social Function of Science* (1939) was enormously influential: in its endeavour, science was communism. The existing economic system and the advance of science could not for much longer go on together. The vision of the future elaborated by Bernal in numerous writings was splendid, but it took no account of an existing Stalin, and could find a defence of the activities of the Soviet agriculturalist Lysenko.

The advent of war took Bernal into another sphere of activity. His over-fertile mind was employed in various capacities initially in the Home Office and then with Bomber Command; eventually, with Solly Zuckerman, he served as scientific adviser in Combined Operations. He also played a major part in the scientific planning for the invasion of Europe. This work led to the award of the American Medal of Freedom (with palms) in 1945. However, it remained the Soviet Union which excited Bernal and he used his position in the Association of Scientific Workers to reinforce his pre-1939 themes. The advent of the cold war did not cause him to modify his views either about the Soviet Union in general or Lysenko's work in particular, but it did lead to his being frozen out of various British organizations. His eulogies of Stalin were glowingly fulsome and resulted in the award of the Stalin Peace Prize in 1953. He was a founder member of the World Peace Council and was its president from 1958 to 1965. In the course of a somewhat frenzied life, Bernal had come a long way from Tipperary, but he maintained his rebellious indiscipline intact until the end.

FURTHER READING

Hodgkin, Dorothy, 'Bernal, John Desmond', *Biographical Memoirs of Fellows of the Royal Society*, vol. xxvi (1980).
Werskey, Gary, *The Visible College* (London: Allen Lane, 1978).

KEITH ROBBINS

Besant [née Wood], **Annie** (*b.* London, 1 October 1847; *d.* Adyar, near Madras, India, 20 September 1933). Feminist, socialist and theosophist. She was an outstanding propagandist, a compelling orator and a prolific pamphleteer for a multitude of radical causes over half a century. Originally an evangelical Christian, she became an atheist and ended as President of the Theosophical Society. She is best known for her role in promoting the causes of birth control, the London Match Girls' Strike and Indian self-government.

Her father, William Persse Wood, a businessman, died when she was five, leaving the family in financial difficulties. Consequently she was brought up and educated to the age of sixteen by a relative, the highly evangelical Ellen Marryat. She emerged as a pious, emotional, impressionable girl who was repeatedly to fall under the spell of dominant personalities; above all, she desired to sacrifice herself for a cause. At the age of 18 she rushed into a disastrous marriage with the Reverend Frank Besant. Before long she developed doubts about Christianity, which culminated in her refusal to attend Communion and led her husband to insist on a separation in 1873. Already attracted to free thought, Besant rapidly gravitated towards the radical leader Charles Bradlaugh; she joined his National Secular Society in 1874 and was employed on his journal, *The National Reformer*. In 1877, largely at her instigation, they reprinted a 40-year old pamphlet on methods of birth control, *The Fruits of Philosophy*. As a result they were prosecuted for producing an obscene publication and found guilty, but succeeded in having the verdict quashed on appeal. Besant wrote her own tract on birth control, *The Laws of Population* (1877), which sold 110,000 copies in ten years.

However, during the 1880s Besant became occupied in a study of science at London University, and fell increasingly under the influence of socialists, including Edward Aveling, Herbert Burrows and Bernard Shaw. Consequently she drifted away from Bradlaugh's individualist radicalism and by 1885 had joined both the Fabian Society and the Social Democratic Federation. She helped to lead the Trafalgar Square demonstrations by unemployed workers in 1887, and the following year espoused the cause of the poorly-paid women employed at Bryant and May's match factory. Her success as a strike leader coincided with her election to the London School Board, of which she remained a member until 1891. In this capacity she proved to be instrumental in persuading the board to pay trade-union rates, waive fees for poor children and provide free meals. She owed her triumphs to the warm, practical and undoctrinaire manner in which she articulated her case.

However, Besant's career as a social reformer soon faded when she discovered theosophy after reviewing a book by Madame Helena Blavatsky. The explanation is that she remained inherently a religious person whose spiritual needs were not entirely satisfied by socialism. Fascinated by the occult and awed by Blavatsky, she proved to be a great catch for the Theosophical Society, and she served as its president from 1907 until her death. Theosophy took her in 1893 to India, a country which became her home and her last great cause. Attracted by the idea of reincarnation, she devoted much effort to demonstrating the compatibility of Hinduism and theosophy, and in 1898 she founded the Central Hindu College, which later became Benares Hindu University.

It was not until 1913 that Besant took up political work again. Essentially a moderate whose chief appeal was to educated Indians, she wanted Home Rule for India within the British Empire. However, during the war she grew impatient with the cautious Indian National Congress and lined up with B. G. Tilak to launch the Home Rule Leagues. This well-timed initiative brought reforms from London, but in July 1917 the Madras Government foolishly arrested her. Her 94 days in internment made her a martyr. On her release she received a hero's welcome from Indians and in December was appointed President of Congress. Her triumph proved to be short-lived, however, for she was already being outflanked by M. K. Gandhi. Though she lost influence among nationalists, she continued during the 1920s to produce draft constitutions for a self-governing India.

WRITINGS

An Autobiography (London: T. Fisher Unwin, 1893).

FURTHER READING

Nethercott, A. H., *The First Five Lives of Annie Besant* (London: Hart Davis, 1961).
——, *The Last Four Lives of Annie Besant* (London: Hart Davis, 1963).

MARTIN PUGH

Bevan, Aneurin ('Nye') (*b.* Tredegar, Monmouthshire, 15 November 1897; *d.* Asheridge, Buckinghamshire, 6 July 1960). Labour left-winger and creator of the

National Health Service. He was the only leader of genius the British Labour movement has ever produced; yet he never became leader of the Labour Party. For most of his life he was fundamentally at odds with the party establishment, contending passionately but largely in vain for true socialism as he understood it. His greatest achievement, as Minister of Health (1945–51) in Clement Attlee's postwar government, was the creation of the National Health Service. But in 1951 he resigned rather than accept any dilution of the principle of an entirely free service. The consequent split in the party helped to keep Labour out of office for 13 years, and Bevan died in 1960 disillusioned by the unexpected recovery of capitalism and the inexorable fading of the socialist dream.

He was born in Tredegar in the South Wales coalfield, the son and grandson of miners, and went down the pit himself at the age of 13. A voracious autodidact, he quickly graduated from Jack London to Marx and the American syndicalists. Overcoming a severe stammer – of which traces nevertheless remained in his explosive speaking style – he became chairman of his local lodge of the South Wales Miners' Federation and a Tredegar Councillor. Abandoning the delusions of syndicalism after the failure of the General Strike, he was lucky to be elected to Parliament in 1929 when the sitting Member for Ebbw Vale was unprecedentedly deselected. Through all the crises of his subsequent career he retained the seat until his death. But he never departed from his fundamentally Marxist vision of social evolution, by which the capitalist order of society was to be transformed – peacefully and democratically – into a socialist order.

In the 1929–31 parliament Bevan was so frustrated by the helpless defeatism of Ramsay Macdonald's minority Labour Government that he flirted briefly with Oswald Mosley, but dropped him the moment he left the Labour Party. From 1931 to 1939 he fought the class war uncompromisingly both in Parliament and outside, inveighing bitterly against unemployment and the family means test, and joining with communists and others, in defiance of the Labour leadership, in the hunger marches and other demonstrations. Unlike Jennie Lee,

however, whom he married in 1934, Bevan never doubted that the Labour Party, for all its bureaucratic caution, was the only possible vehicle for achieving British socialism. In 1939, with Stafford Cripps, he was expelled from the party for advocating the strategy of the Popular Front; but he was re-admitted in 1940.

During the war Bevan achieved notoriety as the most uncompromising critic of Churchill's leadership. He supported Labour joining the Coalition Government in May 1940, but opposed the electoral truce and condemned what he saw as the Labour leadership's tame subordination to Churchill. He saw the war as Labour's opportunity and confidently predicted the result of the 1945 general election, which he took to be Britain's decisive and irreversible moment of transition towards socialism.

It was a bold stroke on Attlee's part to appoint Bevan straight into the cabinet as Minister of Health. In fact, Bevan surprised his critics by proving an effective and constructive minister. The department's responsibilities then included housing: the acute housing shortage, arising from war damage and the scarcity of building materials, thrust Bevan into a political minefield. Despite deliberately favouring council housing over private building, he eventually succeeded in getting a substantial building programme under way. It was to his credit that housing was no longer a liability for Labour at the 1950 general election.

Bevan's major monument, however, was the National Health Service. Planning for a health service had been going on throughout the war; even had the Tories won the election there would probably have been some form of service established. But in the event it was Bevan who shaped the NHS. His key decision was to unify the ramshackle network of local authority and voluntary hospitals in a single national system. Secondly he overcame the resistance of the medical profession by allowing the continuation of private practice alongside the NHS. The British Medical Association continued to resist, alleging that Bevan intended to make doctors salaried employees of the state. But in July 1948 the service came into operation and was an immediate popular success.

Aneurin Bevan at the
Labour Party Conference,
Margate, October 1955

Subsequently, however, Bevan became increasingly disillusioned with the government's flagging commitment to advancing socialism, which he identified with the growing influence of HUGH GAITSKELL. He was disappointed to be passed over for both the Foreign Office and the Treasury; instead Attlee moved him in January 1951 to the Ministry of Labour. When Gaitskell, as Chancellor of the Exchequer, imposed charges on NHS false teeth and spectacles to help pay for rearmament required by the Korean War, he resigned out of a mixture of socialist principle and pique. Immediately he became the somewhat reluctant leader of a variegated coterie of left-wing rebels, known as the Bevanites, in persistent and often bitter conflict with the party leadership which helped to make Labour unelectable from 1951 to 1964.

Bevan was not a happy rebel; he wanted to be loyal, but his anger, frustration and vanity kept breaking through his good intentions. He was intellectually bewildered by the slowing of what he had taken to be the inevitable progress of mankind towards socialism; his personal testament, *In Place of Fear* (1952), was an eloquent restatement of his fundamentalist faith, but disappointingly bankrupt of new ideas with which to counter the spreading 'affluence' of welfare capitalism. In 1955 he stood for the

party leadership but won only the 70 votes of the committed left.

He reconciled himself unenthusiastically to Gaitskell's leadership, and in 1956 became Shadow Foreign Secretary. Concentrating on foreign and defence policy, he accepted quietly the abandonment of any commitment to further wholesale nationalization but agonized over the British nuclear deterrent, torn between the emotional instinct to get rid of it unilaterally and pragmatic realization of its value as a bargaining counter. At the 1957 party conference he provoked a painful breach with the unilateralist left – hitherto his most devoted supporters – by declaring that they should not send the next Labour Foreign Secretary 'naked into the conference chamber'. But he was not to be that Foreign Secretary. Labour lost the general election in October 1959. Two months later Bevan underwent surgery for cancer. He died in July 1960.

By the end of his life Bevan was revered as a great parliamentarian, a great orator and a great man. During most of his career he had been loathed and vilified even more bitterly by the majority of his own party than by his opponents. After his death he was virtually canonized as the embodiment of Labour's socialist idealism, even as the party – under the former Bevanite HAROLD WILSON – moved ever further to the right. His legacy is mixed: the NHS, the memory of an inspiring personality, some wonderful speeches – but also a sentimental attachment to an outdated fundamentalism which has been a fatal drag on Labour's efforts to modernize its electoral appeal.

WRITINGS

In Place of Fear (London: MacGibbon and Kee, 1952).

FURTHER READING

Campbell, John, *Nye · Bevan and the Mirage of British Socialism* (London: Weidenfeld and Nicolson, 1987).
Foot, Michael, *Aneurin Bevan, 1897–1945* (London: MacGibbon and Kee, 1962).
——, *Aneurin Bevan, 1945–1960* (London: Davis Poynter, 1973).
Lee, Jennie, *My Life With Nye* (London: Jonathan Cape, 1960).

JOHN CAMPBELL

Beveridge, William (Henry) [Baron Beveridge of Tuggal] (*b.* Rangpur, Bengal, 5 March 1879; *d.* Oxford, 16 March 1963). Civil servant, social administrator, academic, and social reformer. While his public career spanned a number of areas, each important in its own right, he was associated primarily with the production of the Beveridge Report (1942), which drew together many strands of social policy. One of these was a collectivist strand, and the report helped to lay the basis of the welfare state as it developed in the 1940s. However, Beveridge retained a belief in individual responsibility and in the importance of the citizen making a contribution to his own welfare and to that of others; he did not, therefore, ignore the long-standing voluntarist tradition in social policy. There were, then, somewhat paradoxical elements in his public career, and his personality and private conduct likewise displayed a mixture of self-centredness and generosity.

The eldest son of a judge in the Indian Civil Service, Beveridge seemed destined to enter the law after taking the degree of Bachelor of Civil Law at Oxford in 1903. This followed an outstanding career as an exhibitioner from Charterhouse to Balliol, where he obtained firsts in Mathematical and Classical Moderations (1898 and 1899) and in Greats (1901). In 1902 he was awarded the non-residential Stowell Civil Law Fellowship at University College, Oxford, which he held until 1909. However, Beveridge decided to devote himself to social issues and – much to his father's displeasure – in 1903 became sub-warden of the Oxford Settlement in East London, Toynbee Hall, where he remained until the end of 1905. From 1906 until 1908 he was leader-writer on the *Morning Post*, and then entered the Civil Service as personal assistant to the President of the Board of Trade, Winston Churchill. He became a permanent civil servant in 1909, reaching, in 1913, the rank of Assistant Secretary. In 1915 Beveridge was drafted to the Ministry of Munitions, returning in 1916 to the Board of Trade. The same year he moved to the new Ministry of Food as Second Secretary, and in 1918 went as British representative on the Inter-Allied Food Mission to Central and Eastern Europe. In 1919 he became Permanent Secretary to the Ministry of Food and was appointed KCB.

The next phase in Beveridge's career led him back to academic life. Resigning in 1919 from the Civil Service, he accepted the invitation of Sidney Webb to become director of the London School of Economics, where he remained until 1937. He was Vice-Chancellor of London University from 1926 to 1928. In 1937 he moved to Oxford as Master of University College. However, he retained his public connections. He served on the Royal Commission on the Coal Industry in 1925–6 and was chairman of the Unemployment Insurance Statutory Committee from 1934 to 1944. When war broke out he expected a summons to the Civil Service and in December 1940 was appointed Under-Secretary at the Ministry of Labour. He became chairman of the Manpower Requirements Committee of the Production Council and of the Committee on Skilled Men in the Services.

After disagreements with Ernest Bevin, in 1941 Beveridge moved – to his chagrin – into a somewhat obscure post: chairman of an Interdepartmental Committee on Social Insurance and Allied Services. The committee was not thought likely to report until after the war was over, but it produced the Report on Social Insurance and Allied Services, the Beveridge Report, in 1942. This was a comprehensive review of the social services, and outlined proposals which aroused great public interest. It sold well over half a million copies. To press the case for the report's implementation, Beveridge resigned as Master of University College in 1944 and became Liberal MP for Berwick-upon-Tweed. He lost the seat the following year and, having been created first Baron Beveridge in 1946, entered the Lords as a Liberal peer. Thereafter he undertook various public roles – he was chairman of Aycliffe Development Corporation (1947–53), Peterlee Development Corporation (1949–51) and the Broadcasting Committee (1949–50) – but devoted these years largely to writing.

Not that writing was a feature only of Beveridge's late career; he wrote throughout his life. His first book, *Unemployment: a Problem of Industry* (1909), was a work of seminal importance. It was matched in significance by his later *Full Employment in a Free Society* (1944). Other works of a scholarly nature included *British Food Control* (1928), the first volume of *Prices and Wages in England from the Twelfth to the Nineteenth Century* (1939), *Voluntary Action* (1948) and, as joint-editor with A. F. Wells, *Evidence for Voluntary Action* (1949). There was also a considerable journalistic output of essays and addresses in the 1930s and 1940s. Other publications dealt with the academic side of Beveridge's career: *A Defence of Free Learning* (1959) and *The London School of Economics and its Problems* (1960). Others again were more personal: a biography of his parents, *India Called Them* (1947), *Antipodes Notebook* (with Janet Beveridge, 1949) and his autobiography, *Power and Influence* (1957). In addition, Beveridge published more than a thousand pamphlets and reports, of which that of 1942 was clearly the most important.

The foregoing selection of Beveridge's publications illustrates not only his prolific output, but also its characteristic subject matter: social and economic issues. His interests departed from the broad nature of his undergraduate studies, supplemented by wide reading of novels, plays, poetry and general science.

He came to have little patience with speculative and abstract matters and admitted that many of the main intellectual issues of his day did not interest him. He was, he wrote, a 'broadminded Philistine', and, significantly, accepted a Fellowship of the British Academy in 1937 only with hesitation, since he thought it might identify him too much with the humanities. His approach was empirical – and none of his work could be said to have possessed the originality of his contemporary J. M. Keynes.

Judged by these standards, Beveridge may be said to have been somewhat pedestrian and derivative as a scholar and writer, one whose particular talent lay in packaging and synthesizing the ideas of others rather than originating ideas himself. Similarly, at the LSE in the 1920s and 1930s, he built up a group of scholars – such as R. H. Tawney, H. J. Laski, L. C. Robbins, F. A. Hayek and Bronislaw Malinowski – who were, arguably, of greater intellectual distinction than the director himself.

This criticism is, however, rather severe, and, moreover, difficult to reconcile with another criticism sometimes made of Beveridge: his marked tendency, as a social reformer, to use evidence to support predetermined positions. The evidence, much of it of a statistical nature, was, indeed, massively constructed. But, despite his painstaking empirical approach, Beveridge emphasized the importance of action rather than pure research – or, rather, used the research to justify action. The Beveridge Report did, indeed, draw on many ideas already in existence – but Beveridge selected them to justify his own ideas. The report was compiled quickly, before the examination of many of the witnesses and discussion with members of the committee, and this was partly because Beveridge himself had already decided on its outlines. This does not suggest a lack of ideas – rather the possession of very fixed ideas. Yet Beveridge also realized that a long delay might have resulted from a more open-ended approach. Like earlier social reformers, such as Edwin Chadwick, Beveridge's particular strength lay in an ability to select ideas to support his own point of view – and to do so quickly and cogently.

If these points are important in relation to

the style and manner of Beveridge's approach, of greater substance is the approach itself. At first sight, Beveridge seems to be a classic case of a retreat from the world of voluntary social action to that of statutory policy. Toynbee Hall, with its philanthropic and paternalistic overtones, was, at least in origin, part of the voluntary tradition. Beveridge's father called his son's involvement with it 'sentimental philanthropy'. Beveridge himself did not see it in that light, since he used his time there to gather information about social issues, such as unemployment in the docks. Yet he did show signs of impatience with voluntarism, with its tendency to see poverty in personal rather than social terms. He wanted to explore environmental issues – 'simply the question', he wrote, 'of under what conditions it is possible and worthwhile for men to live.' And he soon moved into areas which were to be lifelong concerns: malnutrition, old age, unemployment. The report of 1942 has been called 'Bunyanesque' in its identification of five 'Giants', and the parallel is apt; but it has less to do with spiritual and moral obstacles than with environmental ones: want, disease, ignorance, squalor, idleness.

If Beveridge moved from a 'personal' to a 'structural' explanation of poverty, he also saw the limitations of the 'personal' solutions of voluntarism as compared with the 'professional' solutions of statism. At Toynbee Hall, he came to doubt the value of settlements. They tended, he felt, to become patronizing to the inhabitants of their district and he doubted if their indulgence in good works was especially helpful. He was critical of charity and religious enthusiasm, and wrote that he wanted to abandon lecturing to 'ethical and self-improvement societies' and become a 'scientific economist'. When he joined the *Morning Post* he wished to 'stick to social questions, formulate a policy [and] bring a scientific understanding of this question home to the ordinary comfortable public.' He argued for a 'strong centralised bureaucratic state' with a far-reaching programme of 'social organisation'. As a civil servant in this period, he was closely associated with the establishment of labour exchanges in 1909–10 and National Insurance in 1911.

Thus Beveridge's career may be seen as the making of a collectivist and a bureaucrat. It is open to question whether this was an uninterrupted process, and it has been suggested that, in the 1920s, he came to question his earlier enthusiasm for collectivist solutions. Yet even this qualification does not alter the argument which has been put forward that, by the late 1930s and 1940s, Beveridge was a convinced collectivist, calling for widespread state provision of welfare. The proposals of the Beveridge Report for a free national health service, family allowances, government-maintained full employment and a universal subsistence level of social insurance were far-reaching – and became broadly the blueprint for the welfare state, although the legislation after 1945 did not follow all of Beveridge's recommendations. Certainly, too, virtually his whole life was spent in public or academic administration. In 1934 he told the LSE that his ideal society would be run, not by dictators, nor by parliamentary democracy, but by professional administrators.

Yet to see Beveridge's career in such terms has its dangers, for Beveridge never entirely abandoned voluntarism. He retained a belief in the importance of personal and moral qualities and in the desirability for retaining agencies other than the state for their expression. His pre-1914 activities were designed to assist the deserving poor – but not to the extent of making them wholly dependent on the state. Labour exchanges would make the labour market more efficient and help to eliminate casual employment, and would enable the welfare agencies to differentiate between those who were seeking work and those who were not. Beveridge's ideas on social insurance were quite compatible with self-help; and under the 1911 Act, the right to benefit was linked to contributions. Beveridge deplored the extension of insurance beyond contributions in the 1920s, and this attitude persisted in the 1940s. Insurance did, indeed, have wide social implications, but the contributory principle was very important to Beveridge. The encouragement of full employment by Keynesian methods – developed in *Full Employment* – would help to keep state welfare at a minimum and planning within limits. In 1944 Beveridge wrote that society

William Beveridge
addressing a Liberal Party
meeting at Caxton Hall,
London, 1943

existed for the individual; that he put it in this order is significant. If he helped to inspire the welfare state, he himself disliked the term, arguing that it implied over-generous state largesse.

Moreover, Beveridge never lost a belief in the value of voluntary organizations, with their traditions of mutual aid and philanthropy. He was especially attracted to the mutual-aid friendly societies, which, he wrote in *Voluntary Action*, were 'a democratic movement . . . sprung from the working classes.' He argued in his report that they should retain a place in the administration of national insurance, and much regretted that, after 1946, the Labour Govern-

ment denied them any role in this respect, and dissolved their partnership with the state (established in 1911). Nevertheless, he retained his belief in the part which voluntary movements could play in offsetting excessive bureaucracy and affording opportunities for personal service.

Beveridge thus displayed an ambivalence between individualism and collectivism, voluntarism and statism. That some historians have seen him – by the 1940s – as virtually indistinguishable from a socialist and an arch-prophet and proponent of postwar 'New Jerusalemism', and others as a liberal collectivist in the mould of Harold Macmillan's *Middle*

Way (1937), is a mark of the complexity of his position. He never entirely succeeded in reconciling the ambiguities, and sometimes seemed almost unaware of them; and yet he was, in a sense, an embodiment of the varying traditions which have gone into the making of British social policy.

In personal terms, Beveridge also displayed characteristics which were seen differently by different people. To some, he was aloof and abrasive, self-centred, pedantic, opinionated, lacking in sensitivity and consideration for others. He was often inept at handling people, and it might well be said that, notwithstanding his commitment to social causes, he lacked warmth in personal relationships. His administrative methods could verge on the autocratic and dictatorial – and were often resented by the staff of the LSE while he was director. He was sometimes regarded as a lonely and unhappy man who had little in his life except his work. He did not marry until 1942, when he was 63; his wife was his second cousin, Mrs Janet Mair, with whom he had worked in the Civil Service during World War I and who had accompanied him as an administrator to the LSE – where her influence was resented and added considerably to Beveridge's own unpopularity.

Yet, again, there was another side to Beveridge, which others saw. He had a strong belief in family life and was a devoted son to his parents in their (difficult) old age; they lived with him virtually without interruption from 1918 to 1929, which imposed a considerable strain on him. His late marriage was very happy and his wife's death a deep sorrow. He could be emotional and generous, gregarious and companionable; he could enter the world of children and immensely enjoyed such unlikely places as Disneyland. He did much good by stealth with over a third of his income. In personal – as in public – life, Beveridge was something of a paradox.

FURTHER READING

Barnett, C., *The Audit of War: the Illusion and Reality of Britain as a Great Nation* (London: Macmillan, 1986).

Cutler, T., Williams, K. and Williams, J., *Keynes,*

Beveridge and Beyond (London: Routledge and Kegan Paul, 1986).

Freeden, M., *The New Liberalism: an Ideology of Social Reform* (Oxford: Clarendon Press, 1978).

George, V., *Social Security: Beveridge and After* (London: Routledge and Kegan Paul, 1968).

Harris, J., *William Beveridge: a Biography* (Oxford: Clarendon Press, 1977).

Williams, K. and Williams, J. (eds.), *A Beveridge Reader* (London: Allen and Unwin, 1987).

GEOFFREY B. A. M. FINLAYSON

Bevin, Ernest (*b.* Winsford, Somerset, 7 March 1881; *d.* London, 14 April 1951). Trade-union leader, Labour Party minister and international statesman. The most prominent trade-union leader of his generation, he was nearing retirement when, at the age of 59, he first entered the House of Commons as Minister of Labour (1940–45) in the wartime coalition government. His successful organization of manpower was a major element in Britain's victory. Between 1945 and 1951 he was Foreign Secretary under Clement Attlee, doing much to shape the pattern of postwar international relations, especially in Europe.

Bevin was the illegitimate son of Diana Bevin and never knew his father. He was reared in considerable poverty by his mother until her death in 1889, when he went to live with a halfsister. After leaving school in 1892 he had a number of jobs before becoming a van driver. He was an active Baptist until 1905 and even considered a ministerial career. But the Church's failure to concern itself with the social problems which he had encountered in the course of his work diverted his zeal into the Labour movement. He joined the Bristol Socialist Society and was elected chairman of the Bristol carters branch of the Dock, Wharf, Riverside, and General Workers Union. His obvious recruiting and negotiating skills prompted his appointment as a national organizer in 1914. His subsequent involvement in the complex negotiations arising from the government's labour requirements during World War I further hastened his rise through the union's ranks. In 1920 he was elected assistant general secretary.

His national reputation as a union leader was

made in that same year. First, the indictment he made before the Shaw Inquiry of the appalling working conditions in Britain's docks earned him the nickname of the 'dockers' K.C.' Second, it was Bevin who proposed the formation of councils of action as a way of preventing further British intervention in Russia. This success confirmed his opinion that the better organization of industrial labour was the most effective way to exert pressure for change. To this end he planned, argued for, and finally organized the amalgamation of 18 unions into the Transport and General Workers Union in 1922. As its first general secretary he enjoyed enormous powers, partly because of the TGWU's sheer size, partly because of its federal structure. He was often accused of being dictatorial, particularly by communist activists in his own union. Certainly he could be crude and brutal in debate, and was an unforgiving enemy, but only such qualities enabled him to hold together such an initially disparate body. Furthermore, his public intransigence often obscured his commitment to conciliation, albeit from a position of strength. It was this which led him, as a member of the TUC General Council, to favour a negotiated settlement to the General Strike of 1926. It continued to inspire his TUC work thereafter. Together with Walter Citrine, he did much to strengthen the TUC's organization and participated in the Mond-Turner talks of 1927.

Bevin's emphasis on the importance of industrial organization inevitably led him to view politics as a subordinate means of social progress. The events of 1929–31, however, did much to alter this perspective. His intuitive belief that unemployment could be countered by an expansion of public expenditure had been given theoretical substance by J. M. Keynes, with whom Bevin served on the Macmillan Committee. Bevin was sure that the economic crisis of 1931 was artificially engineered by the City and he opposed Ramsay MacDonald's economy package. He had never really trusted the Labour leader, believing he was overly influenced by middle-class theorists. From 1931 onwards Bevin became increasingly influential in the party, taking full advantage of the independence conferred by the fact that he was not an MP. In particular he fought for a realistic re-armament policy in the face of the growing Fascist threat in Europe.

Public life took a heavy toll on his health. He had had a couple of earlier breakdowns when in the mid-1930s he began to suffer from heart strain. He was contemplating retirement with his wife and married daughter when, despite earlier animosities, Churchill invited him to join the wartime coalition. As Minister of Labour, Bevin's contribution to Britain's victory was as important as the Prime Minister's own. His ability to achieve objectives through mastery of detail, personal forcefulness, skilled negotiation, and an essential humanity, were decisive elements in a war ultimately decided by manpower allocation. Following a speedy reorganization of his department, he greatly expanded the labour force, persuaded the unions to accept dilution, and brought workers and employers into top-level consultation – all without deploying the dictatorial legal powers at his disposal.

Bevin's powerful, but often rough-hewn, oratory did not always fit comfortably into the House of Commons (he entered in 1940 as member for Central Wandsworth), but as Foreign Secretary he was the major figure in Attlee's Labour administrations from 1945 to 1951. It was not an obvious appointment, but Attlee believed that Bevin's temperament was ideal for coping with the diplomatic aggression which he was anticipating from the Russians (see also ATTLEE, CLEMENT). Bevin had his failures, notably in the Middle East where he found the Palestinian problem intractable. On the other hand, he built up a series of alliances in Western Europe that culminated in the NATO agreements. He, more than anyone, turned the promise of Marshall Aid into an economic reality, and drew the Americans back into European affairs after the war.

Bevin never lost the common touch that endeared him equally to the working classes and his civil servants. He was a loyal colleague, a demanding chief, a bad enemy and a bruising public speaker. His genius for organization and forcefulness led often to accusations of autocracy and self-seeking. Yet these abilities served the trade-union movement well, charting its more positive course after the setbacks of the 1920s; they did much to influence the Labour Party after the debacle of 1931; and ultimately, they benefited the nation, too, in the testing times of war and cold war between 1940 and 1951.

FURTHER READING

Bullock, A., *The Life and Times of Ernest Bevin*, 3 vols. (London: Heinemann, 1960, 1967, 1983).
Williams, F., *Ernest Bevin* (London: Hutchinson, 1952).

KENNETH D. BROWN

Birkenhead, Lord. See SMITH, F. E.

Birkett, (William) Norman [Baron Birkett of Ulverston] (*b.* Ulverston, Lancashire, 6 September 1883; *d.* London, 10 February 1962). Judge, orator and conservationist. He was a member of the last generation of the great courtroom orators and made his reputation by his eloquence rather than by prowess as an expositor or developer of the law. Birkett studied first for the Wesleyan ministry, but changed to law and was called to the Bar by the Inner Temple in 1913. He practised first in Birmingham, then in 1920 moved to Marshall Hall's chambers in London; he took silk in 1924. Until 1939 Birkett was a leading figure in the courts and outstanding for his oratory and capacity to move juries; he appeared in such notable cases as the defence of Clarence Hatry for fraud (1930), of Maundy Gregory for selling honours (1933) and in the murder cases of A. A. Rouse (1931) and Dr Buck Ruxton (1936). In October 1936 he represented the petitioner at Ipswich Assizes in the undefended divorce case of Wallis Simpson v. Ernest Simpson, decree in which opened the door to Mrs Simpson's marriage with the Duke of Windsor. Birkett also served as a Liberal MP in 1923–4 and 1929–31, but made no mark as a politician.

In 1941 he was made a judge of the King's Bench Division and in 1945–6 sat as the second British judge (the senior was Lord Justice Lawrence, later Lord Oaksey) at the major German War Crimes Trial at Nuremberg. He was promoted to the Court of Appeal in 1950, but was ill-suited to appellate work as he was not a scholarly lawyer with the capacity or interest to expound law and reshape principles in seminal cases.

Birkett retired in 1956 and in 1958 accepted a peerage (he was not a Lord of Appeal in Ordinary). Thereafter he travelled extensively, speaking on any subject to a great variety of audiences, from local organizations to vast American Bar Association meetings, charming everyone by his eloquence. He cared passionately about the English countryside, especially the Lake District, and his last speech in the House of Lords persuaded the House to reject a Manchester Corporation Water Supply Bill which, it was urged, would have spoiled Ullswater. A fell above Ullswater was renamed Birkett Fell after him. He also gave good service to London University, serving as chairman of its Court from 1948 to 1962.

FURTHER READING

Devlin, Lord, 'Birkett, William Norman', *Dictionary of National Biography, 1961–1970*, ed. E. T. Williams and C. S. Nicholls (Oxford: Oxford University Press, 1981).
Hyde, H. Montgomery, *Norman Birkett* (London: Hamish Hamilton, 1964).

DAVID M. WALKER

Blake [Behar], **George** (*b.* Rotterdam, 11 November 1922). Soviet spy. He was largely brought up in Cairo by his uncle Henri Curiel, a banker and communist. His father, Albert Behar, an Egyptian Jew naturalized British in 1919, died in 1936. When the Germans occupied Holland in May 1940, his mother, née Catherine Beijderwellen, and his sisters escaped to England; he stayed to work at Rotterdam University, however, and was denounced as British, arrested and imprisoned, though he escaped to work with the nascent Dutch resistance. In 1943 he got out, through Belgium, France and Spain, to rejoin his family; that year, they changed their surname to Blake.

Blake joined the navy, was commissioned sub-lieutenant RNVR in 1944, and – being fluent in German and Dutch – worked as a translator at SHAEF. In 1945–7 he was a

Control Commission intelligence officer, based at Hamburg. He then took a short Russian course at Downing College, Cambridge, and entered the foreign service as a vice-consul – cover for work for the Secret Intelligence Service. His first foreign posting was to Seoul, where he was captured at the outbreak of the Korean War in June 1950. For nearly three years he was in the hands of a communist regime; thereafter he worked for the Soviet secret police. Whether he had earlier converted to communism remains conjectural.

On release Blake rejoined the staff of the Secret Intelligence Service. He married his secretary, Gillian Allan, who bore him three children, in 1954. From 1955 to 1959 they were in Berlin, where he betrayed numerous agents and an expensive telephone-tapping tunnel to the Russians. After a further year's office work in London, Blake was sent to improve his Arabic in Lebanon, whence he was withdrawn to London in March 1961 and confronted with denunciations of himself by defectors from the USSR. He at once confessed and was sentenced to 42 years' imprisonment, but served only five of them; an Irish friend, Sean Bourke, arranged his escape from Wormwood Scrubbs. He then slipped away to Moscow, where he remarried and appears to live a life of ease.

FURTHER READING

Hyde, H. Montgomery, *George Blake: Superspy* (London: Constable, 1987).

M. R. D. FOOT

Blunt, Anthony (Frederick) (*b.* Bournemouth, Hampshire, 26 September 1907; *d.* London, 24 March 1983). Art historian and Soviet spy. A distinguished art historian of international repute, he was highly regarded for his work at the Courtauld Institute of Art (he was appointed deputy director in 1939 and served as director from 1947 to 1972) and with the royal collections (he was Surveyor of the King's/Queen's Pictures from 1945 to 1972). He was also the author of many scholarly works, including a monumental study of Nicholas Poussin – 'my first love even as a youth at school'. Simultaneously, from his

Cambridge postgraduate days onwards, he lived a double life as a cultivated Soviet 'mole'.

Blunt was the third son of the Rev. A. S. V. Blunt, later vicar of the English Church and Embassy Chaplain in Paris, and Hilda Master, both from respectably upper-middle-class backgrounds with a scattering of aristocratic forbears (so it was claimed). He spent his boyhood in the rarified atmosphere of the British diplomatic community in Paris, before and after World War I, and through his elder brother Wilfred he learned and thoroughly absorbed the Parisian art world. Already well travelled and sophisticated beyond his years, his French was so good at Marlborough that the master would sometimes hand over the class to him. Brilliant and spoiled, he had, in the words of his best friend, Louis MacNeice, a 'flair for bigotry'. At Trinity College, Cambridge, he became one of the youngest and most gifted Fellows (1932). A homosexual and a member of the Apostles, the exclusive debating club, he shared the ferment of communist beliefs, becoming friendly with Guy Burgess, Kim Philby and Donald Maclean. Recruited by Burgess, the ring-leader, he acted as 'talent-spotter', giving names of likely recruits. One of his friends, much influenced by him, was an American, Michael Straight, who, in the end, proved to be his undoing.

During his war service in MI5 (1940–5), Blunt was in a position to pass on secret information to the Russians. Though his espionage activities thereafter seemed to have ceased, he was nevertheless able to assist in the defection of Burgess and Maclean in May 1951. At once suspected by British intelligence, he was interrogated no less than a dozen times during the next 13 years, but lack of direct evidence, apart from his own repeated denials of complicity, frustrated his counter-intelligence examiners. In 1964 fresh evidence from the USA, by way of the FBI and Michael Straight, at last proved his guilt. He was somewhat overhastily granted immunity from prosecution in return for his confession and information about his activities and contacts, about which, incidentally, he gave less than appeared reasonable to British security. Following the publication in late 1979 of *The Climate of Treason* by Andrew Boyle, the Prime Minister, Margaret Thatcher, stated unequivocally in the House of Commons that Blunt had been a Soviet spy. Exposed and stripped of his honours (CVO 1947, KCVO 1956), he pleaded that he had never 'betrayed his conscience'.

FURTHER READING

Boyle, Andrew, *The Climate of Treason* (London: Hutchinson, 1979).

Costello, John, *The Mask of Treachery* (London: Collins, 1988).

MacNeice, Louis, *The Strings are False* (London: Faber, 1965).

Penrose, Barrie and Freeman, Simon, *Conspiracy of Silence* (London: Grafton Books, 1986).

Straight, Michael, *After a Long Silence* (London: Collins, 1983).

Waterhouse, Ellis, Personal Preface to *Studies in Renaissance and Baroque Art, presented to Anthony Blunt on his 60th birthday* (London: Phaidon, 1967).

ANDREW BOYLE

Boateng, Paul (Yaw) (*b.* Gold Coast [now Ghana], 14 June 1951). Labour politician. He became one of Britain's four black MPs – the first since the 1920s – in 1987, after a career in the law and local government.

Boateng was educated at Apsley Grammar School and Bristol University in England. (His father had been Minister of the Interior in Ghana's First Republic, overthrown by a military coup in 1966.) After qualifying as a solicitor in 1976 he became active in civil liberties cases, especially concerning the much-strained relations between police and young black Londoners. He was elected for Labour to the Greater London Council in 1981 and chaired its Police Committee until the abolition of the GLC in 1986. The committee, although lacking real power (London's police are directly responsible to the Home Secretary), produced a series of much publicized and contentious reports, especially on the role of the police in race relations. As a sharp critic of much police practice, Boateng was also prominent in the National Council for Civil Liberties and several pressure groups – but also on the Police Training Council.

He contested West Hertfordshire, the constituency where he had been brought up after moving to Britain, in the 1983 election, but lost the seat. This defeat may have been partially attributable to prejudice among white voters, but also probably owed something to a damaging controversy about Boateng's selection against sitting Labour MP Robin Corbett. In 1987 he stood for Brent South with its large black electorate (around 46 per cent) and was successful. In the Commons he seemed to become a less outspoken figure than hitherto, generally supporting Labour's leaders and mainstream policies. Alone of the new black MPs, he refused to join the parliamentary Black Caucus. In 1989 he became a junior member of Labour's Treasury team. If the party again forms a majority government, many would tip Boateng to become Britain's first black minister.

STEPHEN HOWE

Bonar Law, Andrew. See LAW, BONAR.

Bondfield, Margaret (Grace) (*b.* Chard, Somerset, 17 March 1873; *d.* Sanderstead, Surrey, 16 June 1953). Trade unionist and first woman cabinet minister. She crowned a long career in the trade-union movement when she became Minister of Labour in Ramsay MacDonald's Labour Government of 1929–31.

Bondfield was the tenth child of a foreman lacemaker. From her father she inherited political radicalism and also a deep Christian commitment, which found its expression in public service. After a limited education, she was apprenticed to a draper. Working conditions in the trade were such as to fire her indignation and she joined the National Union of Shop Assistants, Warehousemen, and Clerks. In 1898 she became the union's assistant general secretary and over the next four decades was involved in most trade-union initiatives towards women. She did valuable investigative work for the Women's Industrial Council, was associated with the Women's Trade Union League, and helped Mary Macarthur found the National Federation of Women Workers in 1906. Hers was the dominant force behind the Cooperative Women's Guild efforts to improve maternity provision. During the war she served on several official bodies designed to monitor women's working conditions and in 1921 became chief woman officer of the National Union of General and Municipal Workers.

It was inevitable that such an active trade unionist should become involved in the wider Labour movement. Bondfield seconded the motion calling on the 1899 TUC to support the establishment of the Labour Representation Committee and was twice an unsuccessful Labour candidate in London County Council elections. She was an active lecturer on behalf of the Independent Labour Party, being elected in 1913 to its National Administrative Council. In 1920 she failed to win the Northampton by-election for Labour. She was defeated there again in 1922, but triumphed the following year. As Parliamentary Secretary to the Minister of Labour she was implicated in the failure of the first Labour Government to deal with unemployment. When the 1924 election was called she was leading an official government delegation in Canada, and returned too late to save her seat.

Bondfield re-entered parliament after winning a by-election at Wallsend in 1926. She made many enemies, particularly on the left, by signing the Blanesburgh Report on unemployment insurance. The report rejected most of the proposals jointly put forward by the Labour Party and the TUC, of whose General Council she was currently a member. She defended herself competently at special conferences and, later, in her autobiography. She also beat off the ensuing communist challenge for her seat in the 1929 general election. Appointed Minister of Labour in Ramsay MacDonald's second administration, however, she was unable to redeem her standing. The rapidly mounting cost of unemployment relief exposed her intellectual limitations and she displayed the same economic naïveté and orthodoxy as most of her colleagues. In view of her many achievements on behalf of women workers, it was ironic that in her attempts to reduce expenditure she should have effectively disqualified many married women from receiving unemployment benefit. Although she sided with MacDonald

in voting for economies in August 1931, she did not enter the National Government. Defeated at the general election of that year and again in 1935, spurned in her attempts to return to the General Council of the TUC, she retired from trade-union activity in 1938. Thereafter, Bondfield occupied herself with various women's welfare groups until her death in 1953.

WRITINGS

A Life's Work (London: Hutchinson, 1949).

FURTHER READING

Hamilton, M., *Margaret Bondfield* (London: Parsons, 1924).
Lewenhak, S., *Women and the Trade Unions* (London: Benn, 1977).
Miliband, M., 'Margaret Grace Bondfield', in *Dictionary of Labour Biography*, vol. ii, ed. J. Bellamy and J. Saville (London: Macmillan, 1974), pp. 39–45.

KENNETH D. BROWN

Bonham Carter [née Asquith], **(Helen) Violet** [Baroness Asquith of Yarnbury] (*b.* Hampstead, 15 April 1887; *d.* London, 19 February 1969). Daughter of H. H. Asquith, and upholder of Liberalism. She was the fourth of five children, and the only daughter, of H. H. Asquith and his wife Helen (who died in 1891). Even as a child she talked politics with her father, to whom she remained deeply devoted. She did not undergo the social discipline which schools provide; but she read widely and became a competent linguist.

Her girlhood was privileged but troubled. When she was 18 and a debutante her father's political standing was at its peak. Within a few months he had become Chancellor of the Exchequer, and heir presumptive to the premiership. 'Happy child!' remarked Henry James, 'you are seeing life from the stage box.' Violet's relations with her step-mother, Margot, whom Asquith had married in 1894, were often strained, however. 'It is a grief to me', Asquith wrote to Margot in December 1909, 'that the two women I care for most should be on terms of chronic misunderstanding.' This phase ended in 1915 when Violet married Maurice Bonham Carter, her father's principal private secretary (knighted, 1916).

Violet Bonham Carter became a fine platform speaker, and gave her father notable help during his election campaigns at Paisley. 'In the two or three years when her father's need required it', wrote Churchill, 'she displayed force and talent equalled by no woman in British politics.' Ardent and emphatic, she was not noted for the coolness of her judgement.

Violet Bonham Carter's devotion to liberal principles and to the Liberal Party never faltered. In the 1930s she opposed 'appeasement' from the earliest days and campaigned on behalf of German Jews. She was president of the Women's Liberal Federation (1923–5 and 1939–45) and the first woman to be president of the Liberal Party Organisation (1945–7) (the party was led by her son-in-law, Jo Grimond, from 1956 to 1967). She stood twice for Parliament, for Wells in 1945 and for Colne Valley in 1951. At Colne Valley she was one of the only three Liberal candidates not to be confronted with a Conservative opponent; and Churchill came there to speak in her support.

Disillusionment with the Attlee government had brought her nearer to the Conservatives. 'Until now', Harold Nicolson recorded in October 1947 after talking with her, 'she had believed that the Liberal Party were closer to the socialists than to any other party. Now she doubts it.' As her book, *Winston Churchill as I Knew Him* (1965), was to reveal, she had been a strong Churchillian in youth, and the struggle against 'appeasement' had renewed the bonds between them. In the summer of 1950 R. A. Butler had conducted an abortive negotiation with her for a Conservative–Liberal electoral pact on the basis of what he termed his 'Overlap Prospectus of Principles'.

Lady Violet was a Governor of the BBC from 1940 to 1946 and of the Old Vic from 1945, and a trustee of Glyndebourne Arts from 1955. She was made a DBE in 1963, and entered Parliament at last with a life peerage, as Baroness Asquith of Yarnbury, in 1964. When her son Mark (now Lord Bonham Carter) won the Torrington by-election in 1958 she was interviewed by three journalists on television. 'Considering', Harold Nicolson noted, 'that

she is not ... young ..., has been electioneering for a fortnight, and has had an exciting and strained day, this is pretty sporting of her. She is excellent, and makes not one single foolish remark.'

WRITINGS

Winston Churchill as I Knew Him (London: Eyre and Spottiswoode and Collins, 1965).

FURTHER READING

Churchill, W. S., *Great Contemporaries* (London: Thornton Butterworth, 1937).
Howard, Anthony, *R. A. Butler* (London: Cape, 1987).
Nicolson, Nigel (ed.), *Harold Nicolson: Diaries and Letters, 1945/62* (London: Collins, 1968).

MICHAEL BROCK

Boothby, Robert (John Graham) [Baron Boothby of Buchan and Rattray Head] (*b.* Edinburgh, 12 February 1900; *d.* London, 16 July 1986). Conservative MP, lecturer, author and television personality. Boothby was a sparkling figure with a rich sub-Churchillian voice. In his early youthful years at Westminster he stood out as a 'coming man' of infinite promise, but in the event he was a total failure in politics. He retained the conviction, however, that he had been uniformly right.

Boothby's background was the *haute bourgeoisie* of Edinburgh in the comfortable years before 1914. His father was prominent in banking and insurance. After Eton, Robert went to Magdalen, Oxford, and shone in social, literary and political circles. Self-realization was Boothby's aim, and this included pig-sticking in Morocco. He unsuccessfully fought Orkney and Shetland in 1923 but reached Westminster in 1924, representing East Aberdeenshire. He knew nothing about farming or fishing, but went off like an alarm clock as a speaker. His constituents remained loyal to him for 35 years, though it took him five to understand their speech. His allegiance to that part of Aberdeenshire counter-balanced the life in high society that he otherwise led.

Boothby was never conventional. He was one of the few Conservative MPs in Moscow during the 1926 General Strike. The wife of Harold Macmillan conceived an enduring passion for him. He enjoyed being Churchill's Parliamentary Private Secretary at the Treasury (1926–9), but he had no ministerial office in the 1930s and concentrated instead upon oats, beef and herring, together with economic policy, Russia and Germany. He was a conspicuous traveller. He opposed the return to the Gold Standard and 'appeasement'. In 1940, in the Churchill restoration, he became Parliamentary Secretary at the Ministry of Food, but later the same year the 'Boothby case' erupted. Alleged impropriety in the complex matter of the Czechoslovak gold reserves brought about his resignation. He never again held office but was a trenchant commentator on economic issues. He was a critic of the Yalta agreement and was an enthusiast for European unity. He attacked the Bretton Woods agreement, the postwar American loan and, subsequently, the Suez expedition in 1956. Radio and then television gave him a substantial audience for many years. Boothby had come to see himself as an inveterate critic of 'the Establishment'. He played a considerable part in gaining homosexual law reform. From 1958 he was an Independent life peer. His own explanation for his exciting 'failure' was that he had never really wanted to exercise power.

WRITINGS

I Fight to Live (London: Gollancz, 1947).
My Yesterday, Your Tomorrow (London: Hutchinson, 1962).
Recollections of a Rebel (London: Hutchinson, 1978).

KEITH ROBBINS

Braddock [née Bamber], **Bessie** (*b.* Liverpool, 24 September 1899; *d.* Liverpool, 13 November 1970). Labour politician. She was MP for Liverpool Exchange from 1945 to 1970. With her husband she was a dominant figure in Liverpool politics for more than three decades, and latterly became one of the most colourful and best-known women politicians of her day at national level.

Her mother, Mary 'Ma' Bamber, was one of Liverpool's earliest Independent Labour Party leaders, a trade-union organizer and a prominent suffragette. Bessie followed Mary into intense local political activity from her teens, worked as clerk for the Warehouse Workers' Union, and moved with her from the ILP into the infant Communist Party. She married a fellow activist, Jack Braddock, in 1922. Two years later both left the party: Bessie was to become one of Labour's most vehement critics of communism. Jack was elected to Liverpool City Council for Labour in 1929, Bessie in 1930. In 1945 she won Liverpool Exchange from the Conservatives.

In the 1950s and 1960s the Braddocks dominated Liverpool politics, with Jack as council leader until his death in 1963 and Bessie the city's best-known MP. Their rule was far from universally liked: the *New Statesman* once referred to Liverpool under them as 'Cook County U.K.', implying comparison with the notoriously corrupt regime of Mayor Richard Daley in Chicago. Undoubtedly there was patronage and malpractise. Local Labour organization atrophied, and the Braddocks, who had moved far from their ILP and communist past to a position on Labour's right wing, were deeply disliked by Liverpool left-wingers. Bessie's bitter and vocal criticisms of the Labour left, and especially of its figurehead Aneurin Bevan, brought her into conflict with her local party, which in 1955 actually voted to oust her; but she was saved by intervention from national party headquarters.

Within Parliament, though never occupying governmental or high party office other than membership of Labour's National Executive, Bessie Braddock was constantly a prominent figure. This owed something to her striking appearance and often abrasive manner and her regular involvement in controversy and litigation, but much also to a deceptively sharp political intelligence.

WRITINGS
The Braddocks (London: MacDonald, 1963).

FURTHER READING

Baxter, R., 'The Liverpool Labour Party, 1918–1963', Unpublished D. Phil thesis, University of Oxford, 1969.
Toole, M., *Mrs. Bessie Braddock M.P.* (London: Robert Hale, 1957).

STEPHEN HOWE

Bridges, Edward (Ettingdene) [Baron Bridges] (*b.* Yattendon, Berkshire, 4 August 1892; *d.* Winterford Heath, Surrey, 27 August 1969). Secretary to the Cabinet (1938–46), and Permanent Secretary, HM Treasury, and Head of the Civil Service (1945–56). He was largely responsible for the civil operations of government during World War II and made a major contribution to planning the structure and functions of the machinery of government for the postwar period. Churchill wrote of Bridges as Secretary to the War Cabinet that 'he was an extremely competent and tireless worker . . . a man of exceptional force, ability and personal charm, without a trace of jealousy in his nature.' After the war, Bridges had much influence, if not power, in making appointments to numerous top positions in the public services; he continued to have control of the machinery of government; and he acted as constitutional adviser to prime ministers and other senior ministers. No other official has had so much influence on the British Civil Service since World War II. Bridges made a lasting contribution to its ethos and traditions and set a high standard by his own example of how a civil servant ought to behave.

Edward Bridges was the third child and only son of Robert Seymour Bridges, the Poet Laureate. He was educated at Eton and Oxford, where he graduated with a First in Greats in 1914. In 1920 he was awarded an All Souls Fellowship – a non-stipendiary Prize Fellowship with no prescribed duties except attending college meetings – which he held until 1927; he became a Fellow of All Souls again in 1954. In 1914 he joined the 4th Battalion Oxfordshire and Buckinghamshire Light Infantry and was awarded the MC in January 1917. Later in 1917, after he had been seriously wounded in France, he returned to England and served as a temporary Administrative Assistant in the Treasury. When he was fit again he rejoined his battalion, then stationed in Italy.

After World War I Bridges was successful in the reconstruction competition for Class I Clerkships in the Civil Service and was appointed to the Treasury. In 1920 he was promoted to Principal. His early years in the Treasury were spent on establishment work and on the public expenditure of other departments. He also spent a period on attachment to the Estimates Committee of the House of Commons. In addition to being secretary to numerous departmental committees, he was appointed, uniquely, as secretary to three royal commissions. Immediately before he became Secretary to the Cabinet he was primarily concerned, in the Treasury, with re-armament.

Bridges was promoted to Assistant Secretary in 1934 and Principal Assistant Secretary in 1937. When Sir Maurice Hankey retired from his post as Secretary to the Cabinet in 1938, Bridges was chosen to succeed him. In the Cabinet office he focused his personal attention on the civil and political side of its work, leaving the military side to his deputy, Colonel H. L. (later Lord) Ismay. As a result of this and his previous experience Bridges acquired an unrivalled knowledge of the government machine, and that knowledge and his personal qualities gave him a position of key importance during World War II and in redesigning the organization of government for the postwar period.

From February 1945, when Sir Richard Hopkins retired as Permanent Secretary to the Treasury and Head of the Civil Service, Bridges was appointed to succeed him while also continuing as Secretary to the Cabinet (until Sir Norman Brook, later Lord Normanbrook, assumed that post in 1947). Because he had such a great interest in the machinery of government, Bridges continued to make a major contribution to the design of its structure and functions until his retirement in 1956. He also influenced many other aspects of government through the way he coordinated, enthused and directed his colleagues, operating by example rather than precept. His style of leadership depended more on influence than on public or official statements. He was highly respected and inspired loyalty and affection from his colleagues, though he was also a shy and rather austere person who had few close friends and who valued his privacy.

In his private life, and especially after his retirement from the Civil Service, he had numerous interests. For example, in his youth he played the clarinet well; he was a good draughtsman and at one time toyed with the idea of becoming an architect; he enjoyed literature and felt that a house without books was very dead and soulless; he also had a great love of the country. He pursued his many interests in numerous capacities, both voluntary and official. These included All Souls College, the British Council, Eton College, the National Trust, the Pilgrim Trust, the Royal Fine Art Commission, the Royal Institution of British Architects, and the Royal Institute of Public Administration. He gave many lectures and broadcasts and wrote more for publication than any other top civil servant of the twentieth century.

Numerous honours were conferred on him. In 1952 he was elected to a Fellowship of the Royal Society. He was knighted in 1938, appointed GCB in 1944, GCVO in 1946, made a Privy Councillor in 1953, raised to the peerage in 1957, and appointed Knight of the Garter in 1965. He received honorary degrees from the universities of Oxford, Cambridge, London, Bristol, Leicester, Liverpool, Reading and Hong Kong.

Bridges was one of two great architects of the British Civil Service in the twentieth century (the other was Sir Warren Fisher). His career was an outstanding example of a successful generalist administrator. His role in influencing the machinery of government is still apparent today. He worked behind the scenes to ensure that British government functioned according to the highest principles. His personal qualities impressed and inspired those who worked with him. In 1950 *The Times* said that Bridges possessed that combination of personal modesty and intellectual power which makes the born civil servant. Nevertheless, unless there are fundamental changes in the British system of government it is unlikely that anyone will again assume the significant position of authority occupied by Bridges.

WRITINGS

Portrait of a Profession (Cambridge: Cambridge University Press, 1950).
The Treasury (London: George Allen and Unwin, 1964).

FURTHER READING

Chapman, Richard A., *Ethics in the British Civil Service* (London: Routledge, 1988).

RICHARD A. CHAPMAN

Brittain, Vera (Mary) (*b.* Newcastle under Lyme, Staffordshire, 29 December 1893; *d.* London, 29 March 1970). Author, pacifist and feminist. She was a prominent writer and propagandist, principally for the causes of pacifism and feminism. The author of 29 books, she won an enduring reputation with *Testament of Youth* (1933), a moving autobiographical portrayal of the devastating impact of World War I on her generation.

Her father, Thomas Brittain, ran a family paper-making business in Staffordshire. Although their life in Macclesfield and Buxton was comfortable, she felt trapped by the dull, unintellectual, provincial society; her resentment deepened as she realized that her younger brother, Edward, enjoyed a choice of careers, while she, despite her intelligence, was expected to remain at home until a suitable husband appeared. Yet she exaggerated the restrictions upon her. Well educated at a boarding school, she attended University Extension lectures and won an exhibition to Somerville College, Oxford, at the age of 20. If incipiently feminist, Brittain was always very feminine, taking considerable pride in her appearance and devoting much attention to dress; she certainly wished to marry, but not in Buxton. Her reaction to the outbreak of war in 1914 also suggests that she was more conventional than she would have admitted. Thrilled and excited, she urged her brother to enlist despite their father's opposition: 'Daddy does not care about Edward's honour and courage', she complained. She herself went up to Oxford in 1914 but left in June 1915 to work as a nursing auxiliary; by October she had been accepted as a nurse in the Voluntary Aid Detachments, and subsequently worked in London, Malta and Étaples in Normandy. Her unofficial fiancé, Roland Leighton, died in action in 1915, and her brother in 1918. Depressed and lonely, she returned to Oxford in 1919 to complete a degree in history. Aged 26, she became worried that she might never marry. On the other hand, her friendship with Winifred Holtby strengthened her ambition to carve out a career for herself. In 1921 they left Oxford to establish themselves as writers in London.

Brittain soon enjoyed a modest success as a novelist with works such as *The Dark Tide* (1923), *Not Without Honour* (1924) and *Honourable Estate* (1936), which at the end of the twentieth century are regarded as typical of the school of social, provincial novelists. From the 1920s she supported the Six Point Group, a new feminist organization, and regularly contributed to its journal, *Time and Tide*, founded by Lady Rhondda. Brittain's chief contribution to feminism was to demonstrate what she called the 'semi-detached marriage'. Despite her insistence that the career and interests of a married man should not take precedence over those of his wife, she interrupted her own career in 1925 to marry George Catlin, then a politics lecturer at Cornell University. After an unhappy year with him in the United States she returned to Britain, took up residence with Winifred Holtby again, and saw George only during vacations. She had two children, but managed to keep her career alive by heavy reliance on servants and on Holtby in the role of spinster aunt.

Brittain's name became indelibly linked with the indictment of the Great War and the idea of the 'Lost Generation' by the publication of *Testament of Youth*. Begun in 1929, when the book appeared in 1933 it enjoyed a market already stimulated by similar works by Robert Graves, E. M. Remarque and others; by 1939 it had sold 120,000 copies in Britain. Though written through a woman's eyes, *Testament of Youth* was far from being a feminist work; rather it dramatized the conventional role of women.

The war had turned Brittain towards politics and pacifism. In the 1920s she worked for both the Liberal and Labour parties, joined the Women's International League for Peace and Freedom, and in 1937 became a sponsor of the Peace Pledge Union. During World War II she denounced the saturation bombing of German cities and wrote several pacifist works, including *Humiliation With Honour* (1942) and *Seeds of Chaos* (1944). A prominent supporter of the Campaign for Nuclear Disarmament, she was chairman of *Peace News* from 1958 to 1964. Her daughter, Shirley Williams, served in Labour governments (1964–70, 1974–9) and was a co-founder of the Social Democratic Party.

WRITINGS

Chronicle of Youth: War Diary, 1913–17, ed. Alan Bishop (London: Gollancz, 1981).
Chronicle of Friendship: Diaries of the Thirties, 1932–39, ed. Alan Bishop (London: Gollancz, 1986).

FURTHER READING

Bailey, Hilary, *Vera Brittain* (London: Penguin, 1987).
Berry, Paul and Bishop, Alan (eds.), *Testament of a Generation: the Journalism of Vera Brittain and Winifred Holtby* (London: Virago, 1985).

MARTIN PUGH

Brockway, (Archibald) Fenner [Baron Brockway] (*b.* Calcutta, 1 November 1888; *d.* London, 28 April 1988). Labour MP, journalist, writer and campaigner for socialist causes. Brockway was born in India, where his parents were Christian missionaries, and was educated at what became Eltham College. He concluded that the British Empire was evil and for more than half a century he devoted himself to undermining it. He began work as a journalist, and in 1911 became editor of the Independent Labour Party weekly the *Labour Leader*. After 1914 he threw himself into opposition to the war; his conscientious objection was absolute and resulted in a prison term of increasing severity. This experience led him to write *English Prisons Today* (1922), with Stephen Hobhouse, which had considerable influence on subsequent penal thinking.

The emergence of Gandhi in India inspired Brockway to organize support for him in Britain. He was also active as a 'war resister'. In 1929, the year in which he became Labour MP for Leyton, he became secretary of the League against Imperialism. He was out of parliament throughout the 1930s, but was very active in the Independent Labour Party, serving as its chairman and then its general secretary. Although he had reservations about the Soviet Union, his opposition to Fascism was intense. His background therefore made it difficult for him to develop a consistent line concerning World War II. In 1950 he became Labour MP for Eton and Slough. However, he remained an individualist and had no ministerial aspirations. He became identified in the public mind with the Movement for Colonial Freedom and was an early opponent of nuclear weaponry. On his election defeat in 1964 he took a seat in the Lords, though he was sorely tempted to spend his remaining days planting trees in the Sahara. He continued to campaign for peace in Vietnam and for world disarmament. Throughout his life he was always writing – pamphlets, plays and biographies of fellow-socialists – but his greatest satisfaction came from seeing the end of the British Empire.

WRITINGS

Inside the Left (London: Allen and Unwin, 1942).
Not Out (London: Quartet, 1986).

KEITH ROBBINS

Brook, Sir **Norman (Craven)** [Lord Normanbrook] (*b.* Bristol, 29 April 1902; *d.* London, 15 June 1967). Leading civil servant. 'The outstanding exponent of public administration of his time' was the verdict of *The Times* on Sir Norman Brook at the time of his death in 1967. An official who spent a decade and a half as Secretary of the Cabinet, from 1947 to 1962, and who, towards the end of his career, from 1956 to 1962, combined that demanding role not only with a jointly held post as Permanent Secretary to the Treasury but also with that of Head of the Home Civil Service plainly possessed outstanding administrative capacities of the kind that the British career Civil Service demands of its leading members.

Born the son of an inspector of schools, Brook was educated at Wolverhampton School and then at Wadham College, Oxford, where he obtained a second class honours degree in Greats in 1925. Had he secured the First that his peers believed he merited, Brook would have become an academic, but the verdict of the university examiners meant that he had to embark upon a Civil Service career. Brook passed the Administrative Class open competitive examination in 1925, joining the Home Office as an Assistant Principal.

Brook's administrative abilities were soon recognized in the Home Office, not least by Sir John Anderson, the Permanent Under Secretary there when Brook began his career. Brook was promoted to Principal in 1933, to Assistant Secretary in 1938, and to Principal Assistant Secretary in 1940. Once Sir John Anderson had joined the National Government in 1938, Brook was appointed to work closely with him, initially as Principal Private Secretary when Anderson was Lord Privy Seal, and as Personal Assistant when Anderson was translated to the post of Lord President of the Council in 1940. In 1942 Brook was made Deputy Secretary of the War Cabinet, before becoming Permanent Secretary in the Office of the Minister of Reconstruction from 1943 to 1945. He was then transferred to be an additional Secretary to the Cabinet in the period 1945–6 to assist Sir Edward Bridges, then from 1947 to 1962 held the post of Secretary of the Cabinet. Winston Churchill's return to office delayed Brook's advancement to the headship of the Home Civil Service because Churchill insisted that Bridges stay on in that post. Brook attained the headship in 1956, combining it with a post as Permanent Secretary at the Treasury, with responsibility for Establishments, and the continuing role of Secretary of the Cabinet. He retained all these positions until his retirement in 1962, being awarded a peerage as Lord Normanbrook the following year. Between 1964 and his death in 1967 he served as Chairman of the Board of Governors of the BBC.

Unlike some of his predecessors who had reached the top of the Civil Service, Sir Norman Brook had not sought the limelight. This fact made it ironic that he attracted controversy later. What was clear at the time of the Profumo Affair in 1963, which gravely damaged the Conservative Government of the day, was that in 1961 Brook had withheld information about the errant Secretary of State from the Prime Minister, and had taken it upon himself to issue a warning to the minister, giving an impression, some thought not dispelled by the official inquiry, that Brook had both exceeded his authority and displayed political naïveté.

Sir Norman Brook, of course, was involved in many thousands of decisions, and Lord Trend seemed to speak for those who had worked closely with him in describing him as a highly skilled administrative craftsman.

FURTHER READING

Obituary, *The Times* (16 June 1967).
Trend, Lord, 'Brook, Norman Craven, Baron Normanbrook', in *Dictionary of National Biography 1961–1970*, ed. E. T. Williams and C. S. Nicholls (Oxford: Oxford University Press, 1981).

GEOFFREY K. FRY

Brooke, Sir Alan (Francis) [Viscount Alanbrooke of Brookeborough] (*b.* Bagnères-de-Bigorre, France, 23 July 1883; *d.* Hartley Wintney, Hampshire, 17 June 1963). General and Chief of Staff. He became Chief of the Imperial General Staff in November 1941 at a still dark moment for Britain during World War II. Four months later he also became Chairman of the Chiefs of Staff Committee, and he continued to hold these appointments until June 1946. To the machinery of the Chiefs of Staff Committee he brought cohesion and, with it, influence sufficient to moderate the often excessive strategic imagination of Prime Minister Winston Churchill. Moreover, he also brought a realism and firmness of purpose to Allied decision-making that was not always welcomed by the United States Chiefs of Staff, who frequently failed to match his own strategic vision.

The ninth child (and sixth son) of Sir Victor Brooke, Bart., Brooke was of Ulster stock but born and brought up in the French Pyrenees, where his parents had settled. As a result he became a capable linguist and, after he had been commissioned in the Royal Artillery in 1902, quickly qualified as an interpreter. The family had a distinguished military record and Brooke appears to have decided on a military career at an early stage. He first served in Ireland and India, and it was with the Indian Corps that he reached France in 1914. His progress in war service was impressive, his professionalism and capability as an artilleryman bringing him successive appointments as Brigade-Major, Royal Artillery to 18th Division in 1915, chief of staff to the artillery commander of the Canadian Corps in 1917 and GSO 1, Royal Artillery at First Army Headquarters in 1918.

Brooke had thought deeply about the war's lessons with respect to artillery and his intellectual qualities marked him out for steady promotion in the inter-war army, a positive immersion in professional duties compensating him to some extent for the tragic death in a motor accident in 1925 of his first wife, whom he had married just before the outbreak of the Great War. At that time he was an instructor at the Staff College, having passed through the establishment as a student in 1919 before posting to the regular staff of the 50th Northumbrian Territorial Division. From the instructing staff at Camberley, Brooke reverted to student status in 1927 at the Imperial Defence College, then two years later became Commandant of the School of Artillery at Larkhill. In that same year of 1929 Brooke, who had been left with two young children after the death of his first wife, remarried. His second wife, Benita, herself a widow, was to bear him three more children and provide him with an outstandingly happy marriage for the remainder of his life.

Returning to the Imperial Defence College as an instructor in 1932, Brooke was then unusually chosen as an artilleryman to command the 8th Infantry Brigade in 1934. This emphasized his bright future and he became Inspector of Artillery in 1935 and Director of Military Training at the War Office in 1936. The upheaval in the army's higher command occasioned by Leslie Hore-Belisha as Secretary of State for War saw Brooke chosen to command the experimental Mobile Division on the recommendation of the Chief of the Imperial General Staff, Lord Gort, and the journalist, Captain Basil Liddell Hart, who had Hore-Belisha's ear. However, after only a brief period he was elevated to Lieutenant-General in July 1938 and tasked with organizing an anti-aircraft corps for the air defence of Britain against aerial attack. Brooke was designated to succeed Archibald Wavell as GOC, Southern

Command, in August 1939 but the imminence of hostilities saw him translated to command II Corps in the British Expeditionary Force (BEF).

Whatever his personal feelings, Brooke was always outwardly imperturbable, and this fortified his colleagues and subordinates when the BEF was driven back to the Channel Coast by the German onslaught in May 1940. Ordered home from Dunkirk on 29 May to help reform the army in Britain, he was knighted on 11 June and then promptly sent back to France to command those British forces remaining in the field south of the Somme. This occasioned his first real contact with Britain's new Prime Minister, with whom he was compelled to argue over the desirability or otherwise of endeavouring to fight on (as Churchill deman-

ded) or withdrawing British forces before they were destroyed. Brooke got his way and was able to extract three divisions which Churchill's option would have condemned to capitulation. Subsequently as GOC, Southern Command, and, from July 1940 onwards, as Commander-in-Chief of Home Forces, Brooke was to come into even more frequent proximity to Churchill, while being responsible in the former capacity for the defence of the South Coast from Sussex to Wales and in the latter for the conduct of any land battle following a German invasion of Britain.

By late 1941 the nature of Churchill's character and working methods had exhausted two successive Chiefs of the Imperial General Staff, and, with Sir John Dill's retirement to the calmer waters of the British Military Mission in

Viscount Alanbrooke inspecting men of the London Auxiliary Fire Service on the Horse Guards Parade, November 1950

Washington, Brooke inherited the poisoned chalice on 16 November 1941. The following month he found himself acting as Chairman of the Chiefs of Staff Committee when his naval and air-force colleagues accompanied Churchill to Washington. It proved an invaluable introduction for when he succeeded Admiral Pound as chairman on a permanent basis on 5 March 1942. Simultaneously, Brooke was now professional head of the army and responsible for presenting collective service advice to the Prime Minister and War Cabinet. In practice he delegated much of the routine administration of the army to his subordinates Sir Archibald Nye and Sir Ronald Weeks to free himself for the conduct of higher strategy, but it remained Brooke who selected army commanders and defended those selections under the pressure of events. Moreover, he established his authority over army commanders to the extent that he was able to ensure that his control was not circumvented by private communications between them and the Prime Minister, who was not averse to attempting to bypass him. Twice Brooke was offered a field command himself. In August 1942 Churchill proposed to make him either commander of the 8th Army or Commander-in-Chief in the Middle East, but Brooke declined on the grounds that 'after working with the PM for close on 9 months I do feel at last that I can exercise a limited amount of control on some of his activities, and that at last he is beginning to take my advice.' Accordingly, he pressed the appointment of Montgomery to the 8th Army and Alexander to the Middle East command, although it was only the death of Lieutenant-General Gott in an aircrash that saw Montgomery translated to the 8th Army. In the summer of the following year Churchill again offered the possibility of field command by suggesting that Brooke direct the Allied invasion of Normandy, but this was vetoed by the USA, who insisted on an American in supreme command.

It was fortunate that Brooke remained with the Chiefs of Staff Committee, for he was admirably suited to the complex requirements of reviewing long-term strategic options while simultaneously dealing with current operations and the normal functioning of the machinery of war direction. He did not generally originate ideas but he had the capability of absorbing and pronouncing on arguments with amazing speed. In Allied counsels his mastery of detail was formidable, although the cold lucidity with which he brought harsh reality to bear on decision-making induced considerable suspicion of him among the Americans. However, in this regard he was well served by the diplomatic skills of Dill, who as permanent British member of the Combined Chiefs of Staff Committee in Washington established a rapport with the chairman of the US Chiefs of Staff, George Marshall, which did much to smooth ruffled feelings. For Brooke, Marshall simply lacked strategic vision, and he regarded the US naval chief of staff, Admiral King, and his air-force counterpart, General Arnold, as obsessed with the Pacific and aerial issues respectively.

Brooke's struggle to impose reality on Allied strategy was fought out principally at the great wartime conferences and revolved mainly around the respective merits of exploiting opportunities in the Mediterranean or concentrating upon a cross-Channel assault upon German-occupied Western Europe. He was convinced that it was essential to clear Axis forces from North Africa and Southern Europe before attempting a cross-Channel invasion. This would not only free the Mediterranean sea lanes for Allied shipping but divert German resources away from the Channel Coast. He believed that seizing the opportunities presented by the expulsion of German forces from North Africa in May 1943 and from Sicily in July 1943, and from the Italian capitulation to the Allies in September of that year, could shorten the war. However, it can be noted that his belief in what might be termed a Mediterranean strategy did not extend to Churchill's desire for adventures in the Balkans nor for Alexander's vision of a drive on Vienna from Northern Italy in 1945.

Essentially, Brooke won the argument at the Casablanca conference in January 1943 with the postponement of any cross-Channel operation until 1944, but he was then compelled to fight at succeeding conferences to ensure that the Americans did not renege on the agreements. In particular he disliked the American proposal for a landing in Southern France (codenamed first 'Anvil' then 'Dragoon'), since it would divert resources from the Italian campaign, the continuation of which was itself dependent upon the timing of any cross-Channel invasion (successively codenamed 'Sledgehammer', 'Roundup' and 'Overlord'). Not unexpectedly, the Americans believed that Brooke opposed any Second Front, but it was an insistence that it should be undertaken only at the appropriate moment. Similarly, he recognized earlier than many contemporaries the future threat posed to the West from the Soviet advance into Eastern and Central Europe.

Disagreements with the Americans went hand in hand with a stormy relationship with Churchill, Brooke remarking on one occasion that, 'Never have I admired and despised a man simultaneously to the same extent.' Above all, he stood up to the Prime Minister, again remarking that, 'the first time I tell him I agree with him when I don't will be the time to get rid of me, for then I will be no more use to him.' Thus, Brooke opposed a Churchillian scheme to land in Portugal rather than Normandy, while a particularly acrimonious debate arose between January and March 1944 over Churchill's preference for an Allied operation against Japanese-occupied Sumatra, an issue bringing the Chiefs of Staff perilously close to resignation. Again the service chiefs had to fight Churchill's desire to make Alexander both Supreme Commander in the Mediterranean and land commander in Italy in November 1944, and, while they had their internal differences, one of Brooke's undoubted achievements was to weld unity in the Chiefs of Staff Committee.

Brooke's exhausting wartime regime, alleviated only by an attempt to ensure one day off each week, did not cease with peace, for he then faced the need to re-organize the army for its extended peacetime responsibilities. Promoted Field Marshal in January 1944, he was made Baron in September 1945, at which point he took the title of Alanbrooke, then elevated to Viscount in January 1946. After retiring in June 1946 he held a number of directorships, but was also able to indulge in his lifetime hobby of ornithology.

FURTHER READING

Bryant, Arthur, *The Turn of the Tide* (London: Collins, 1957).

——, *Triumph in the West* (London: Collins, 1959).

Fraser, David, *Alanbrooke* (London: Collins, 1982).

I. F. W. BECKETT

Brooke, Sir **Basil (Stanlake)** [Viscount Brookeborough] (*b.* Colebrooke, Co. Fermanagh, 9 June 1888; *d.* Co. Fermanagh, 18 August 1973). Prime Minister of Northern Ireland. Educated at Winchester and Sandhurst, he was a scion of the 'fighting Brookes', a Fermanagh land-owning family. The first war cost him his religious faith, the second took away two of his sons. Although his considerable political skills did not desert him until his last years in office, he was a man of narrow and even shrewish political temperament, who was haunted always by the bitter anti-nationalist rhetoric that flowed from his involvement in the Ulster Special Constabulary in the 1920s.

Craigavon's replacement as Prime Minister of Northern Ireland in 1940, J. M. Andrews, presided over a geriatric cabinet composed largely of survivors from Craig's first cabinet, established in 1921. Unsurprisingly, this government's response to the problems of wartime industrial mobilization (which included a more radical mood within the Protestant working class) was unimpressive. The result was dissatisfaction both in London and Belfast. Brooke, who was Minister of Commerce, having been Craigavon's Minister of Agriculture since 1931, took advantage of this, and in May 1943 – having formed a shrewd tactical alliance with Sir Wilfrid Spender, head of the Northern Ireland Civil Service – replaced Andrews as Prime Minister. Brooke rapidly modernized by restructuring the cabinet, going so far as to include a Labourist politician, Harry Midgely.

With the election of the Attlee government, the Unionist regime was much exercised by the emergence of the welfare state and the problem of 'creeping socialism'. A strong 'dominion status' lobby emerged within the Unionist Party and cabinet, which was anxious to erect a barrier between left-wing legislation emanating from Westminster and the Ulster scene. Brooke shrewdly rejected this proposal in a key speech in Larne in May 1947: 'To attempt a fundamental change in our constitutional position is to reopen the whole Irish question ... the backbone of Unionism is the Unionist Labour Party. Are these going to be satisfied if we reject the social services and other benefits we had by going step by step with Britain?'

The 1950s was the golden age of Ulster Unionism. Dublin's neutrality in World War II had made the British Government much more keenly aware of the strategic advantages of 'loyal Ulster'. Northern Ireland enjoyed the benefits of relative economic expansion and the welfare state; the Republic, on the other hand, experienced severe economic contraction leading to higher rates of emigration than in the days of British rule, while the Catholic hierarchy successfully stigmatized welfarism as incipient totalitarianism. Not surprisingly the IRA campaign launched in 1956 was a complete failure, but worryingly, more than 150,000 Northern Irish Catholics expressed their alienation by voting for Sinn Fein. The collapse of the IRA's campaign provided Brooke with the best possible opportunity to adopt a more conciliatory stance towards Ulster's Catholic minority. In 1959, however, Brooke shortsightedly endorsed Orange Order opposition to the selection of Catholics as Unionist parliamentary candidates. The apparent strength of Unionism's position had led to a certain ossification and a mistaken belief that concession would never be a necessary or prudent course. Brooke's last years (1960–3) were dominated by various sporadic and ineffectual stratagems designed to curtail the growth of support for the Northern Ireland Labour Party. His successor, Terence O'Neill, observed sourly of Brooke in this period: 'Those who met him imagined that he was relaxing away from his desk. What they didn't realise was that there was no desk.'

FURTHER READING

Barton, Brian, *Brookeborough: the Making of a Prime Minister* (Belfast: Institute of Irish Studies, Queen's University, 1988).
Bew, Paul, Gibbon, Peter and Patterson, Henry, *The State in Northern Ireland 1921–72: Political Forces and Social Classes* (Manchester: Manchester University Press, 1979).
Buckland, P., *A History of Northern Ireland* (Dublin: Gill and Macmillan, 1981).

PAUL A. E. BEW

Brown, George [Lord George-Brown of Jevington] (*b.* London, 2 September 1914; *d.* London, 2 June 1985). Labour Foreign Secretary. He was a prominent Labour politician of the 1960s, serving as deputy leader of the party and then at the Department of Economic Affairs (1964–6) and the Foreign Office (1966–8).

From the landing of his boyhood tenement flat Brown could see the light shining over Big Ben when he went out to wash, but he could have had little expectation that he would spend the greater part of his life in the Houses of Parliament. He was the son of a van driver and was of mixed English, Irish and Scottish descent; a typical Londoner. He left school at the age of 15 and sold furs for the John Lewis Partnership. In 1936 he tried for a full-time post in the Transport Workers Union in which his father was very active. Initially, Ernest Bevin turned this 'whippersnapper' down, though shortly afterwards Brown did become a youthful district organizer. Neither man could have envisaged that they would both become Foreign Secretary in Labour governments.

Brown was bright, industrious and ambitious. Besides his trade-union work, he was active in local Labour politics in Hertfordshire and was making speeches. He remained in trade-union work throughout the war in both industry and agriculture, and his experience was such that in due time he might well have risen to the general secretaryship of his union. However, he already felt the lure of the House of Commons and in 1945 was elected MP for Belper in Derbyshire, the constituency he was to represent until his defeat in 1970. He was immediately made Parliamentary Private Secretary to the then Minister of Labour, before going briefly to the Treasury in the same capacity to Hugh Dalton in 1947. He then became Under-Secretary at the Ministry of Agriculture. His rapid advancement was completed by his appointment as Minister of Works in 1951. He was making a name for himself as one of the coming men. He was not a middle-class, university-educated intellectual and neither was he a 'Bevanite'. His time would surely come as the Labour old guard faded from the scene.

Loss of office in 1951 was particularly difficult for Brown, not least in financial terms, but he supplemented his income by extensive journalism and remained in parliament. He preferred Gaitskell as Labour's new leader to Bevan, though he did not have any fundamental affinity with either man. He shadowed for Labour on defence questions in this period. His approach to East–West relations was robust. When the Soviet leaders Khrushchev and Bulganin visited London in 1956, Brown captured the headlines when he refused to accept as just certain remarks by Khrushchev about Britain's role during World War II. The episode confirmed, among other things, that Brown did not invariably seek to control his emotions. However, in 1960 he had sufficient support in the party to succeed Aneurin Bevan as deputy leader, and this partnership with Gaitskell survived a little uneasily until Gaitskell's death in 1963. There were three candidates for the succession, of whom Callaghan dropped out after the first ballot. In the decisive round HAROLD WILSON defeated Brown by 144 votes to 103. After some hesitation, Brown agreed to continue as deputy leader, though he remained uncertain whether he would be able to work effectively with the new leader.

After Labour's victory in 1964 Brown achieved the creation of the separate Department of Economic Affairs for which he had hankered latterly in opposition. He became its first Secretary of State, and he was also styled First Secretary of State – an indication that he was in effect Deputy Prime Minister. It was a departmental innovation that was supposed to shake off the dead hand of the Treasury. A Planning Department would stimulate plans both national and regional. Brown charged energetically around seeking new men and new ideas at all hours of the day and night. His enthusiasm never waned, but he was upset by the broad lines of government economic policy and the harm which he believed it was doing. Resignation seemed likely on more than one occasion. In the event he stayed on until August 1966, when he was offered the Foreign Office. The change was welcome, but Brown never ceased to believe that his beloved Department of Economic Affairs had been sabotaged by the actions both of some of his ministerial colleagues and of officials. It was the dash for growth that did not happen.

Brown survived at the Foreign Office from August 1966 until March 1968. He was not overawed and indeed set in train a major enquiry into how the Diplomatic Service should be organized. His personal interest in trying to resolve the problems of the Middle East was very high. He was also a convinced believer in British membership of the EEC and accompanied Wilson on the tour round European capitals in 1967. The application, however, did not succeed. Brown's resignation in 1968 was even more spectacular than Anthony Eden's had been in 1938. It was allegedly in protest against the way decisions were being taken in cabinet and reflected the strained relationship between him and Wilson over many years.

After his electoral defeat in 1970 Brown took a peerage. He remained in the public eye but grew increasingly disenchanted with the Labour Party, a disenchantment that was reciprocated. At his best, his common sense was much admired, but it was combined with a mercurial temperament which caused him to lose support. He was almost the Ernest Bevin of the next generation, but that was not enough to bring enduring success. His love–hate relationship with the boss of his old union stemmed from a reluctant recognition of this fact. Like Herbert Morrison, another Londoner, he had to accept that he had not quite made it. And he did not like it.

WRITINGS

In my Way (London: Gollancz, 1971).

KEITH ROBBINS

Buchan, John [Baron Tweedsmuir] (*b.* Perth, 26 August 1875; *d.* Montreal, Canada, 11 February 1940). Novelist and politician.

Buchan was a boy from the Borders whose career straddled the borders of politics and literature. The British Empire was his ideal stage. He grew up through the years of its expansion, played his modest part in its administration, and he died far away from his homeland at a date when its survival was in doubt. Important though his political career was, however, it is on his work as a novelist, historian and biographer that his reputation chiefly rests. Buchan himself would probably not have been satisfied with such a segmented fame: his life was a whole.

The Parable of the Talents, expounded in Glasgow by the young Buchan's father, a Free Church minister, probably informed all his subsequent career. Much would be expected from one to whom much had been given. After school and university in Glasgow he went up to Brasenose College, Oxford, in 1895. His ambition was firm and concentrated. There were goals to be achieved and he would achieve them. The strong inner direction of his life could not be denied. It seemed to some of his contemporaries that he was an intolerable prig, but they knew little about the Scottish world from which he came. He duly gained a First in Greats but failed to become a Prize Fellow in history at All Souls. In 1901 he accepted an offer from Lord Milner of a post in his South African Secretariat. The years there toughened and changed the young would-be barrister and man of letters. He married into an English noble family and took a partnership in Nelsons the publishers. In 1911 he was adopted as Conservative candidate for the Liberal-held constituency of Peebles and Selkirk. The physical strain of his energetic existence was already beginning to tell.

In 1914 Buchan wanted to go to France and fight, but his health made that impossible. Instead, he wrote *The Thirty-nine Steps* (1915) and began *Nelson's History of the War*. His talents then found an opening as director of the new Department of Information – essentially a propaganda agency. More novels rapidly formed in his mind and he wrote with speed and great concentration. He established himself in the Oxfordshire countryside, but his heart was still in the Borders. Despite the fame and income which his writing brought, however, he still aspired to a public role. He had good political contacts, and in 1929 and 1931 was elected unopposed as MP for the Scottish Universities, but no office came his way. He was made a Companion of Honour in 1932 and derived great satisfaction from his appointment as Lord High Commissioner to the General Assembly of the newly re-united Church of Scotland in 1933 and 1934. 'Old ghosts came out of secret places' at dinners in the Palace of Holyroodhouse.

At length, one office did come his way. In March 1935 Buchan was appointed Governor-General of Canada and took the title of Baron Tweedsmuir. It was to be his next great adventure, but he was never to see Scotland or Oxfordshire again. In February 1940 he suffered cerebral thrombosis and died in Montreal. The goals he had so precisely set himself as an undergraduate had only partially been realized. His son is surely right in suggesting that he did not make the kind of mark in British politics which he must once have assumed to be probable. Even so, there can be no full appreciation of Buchan as man of letters which does not grasp that he was also a man of action whose career can be understood only in terms of an empire that has since disappeared.

WRITINGS

Memory Hold-the-Door (London: Hodder and Stoughton, 1940).

FURTHER READING

Adam Smith, Janet, *John Buchan: a Biography* (London: Hart Davis, 1965).
Buchan, William, *John Buchan: a Memoir* (London: Buchan and Enright, 1982).

KEITH ROBBINS

Burgess, Guy (Francis de Moncy) (*b.* Devonport, Devon, 16 April 1911; *d.* Moscow, 30 August 1963). Member of the Foreign Office and Soviet spy. Of all the Cambridge quartet of Soviet agents, he was the most improbable and certainly the most strident, behaving frequently, throughout his subsequent career in the BBC and the Foreign Office, in a thoroughly outrageous and offensive manner, offset, however, by considerable charm and wit. Yet, according to the Soviet defector Vladimir Petrov, who had known his spymaster in Britain, 'the volume of material which Burgess supplied was so colossal that the cipher clerks at the Soviet Embassy were often fully employed in enciphering it.'

Poor eyesight, discovered soon after Burgess entered the Royal Naval College, Dartmouth, put an end to family hopes of the naval career for which he had been groomed from an early age (his father had been a naval commander). Instead he was sent to Eton, where he quickly became an 'all-rounder'. His peers found him witty, high-spirited and 'too clever by half'. Already wayward and homosexual, he won prizes and awards before going in 1931 to Cambridge, where he was soon 'talent-spotted' by senior Marxist dons. He joined the Communist Party and became a Soviet agent. Like Donald Maclean, Kim Philby and Anthony Blunt, his fellow 'Cambridge spies', he was directed by his Soviet controller to lie low, and, by way of camouflage, joined the Anglo-German Fellowship, a thinly disguised Fascist front.

Burgess was a talks producer at the BBC from 1936 to 1939 and was seconded to write war propaganda from 1939 to 1941. From 1941 to 1944 he combined work at the BBC with an alleged freelance role in British intelligence. He then entered the Foreign Office and was appointed one of the personal secretaries to Hector MacNeil, Minister of State for Foreign Affairs in Attlee's government. In 1950 he was transferred to the British Embassy in Washington as Second Secretary under Philby. By early 1951 British counter-espionage had firm evidence that their fellow spy Donald Maclean, who was now in London as head of the American desk at the Foreign Office, was a Soviet agent. Philby learned of this, and plans to warn Maclean of the danger were set in motion. Burgess, having deliberately committed a number of speeding offences, was recalled to London for 'serious misconduct' and was thus able to help Maclean in his escape to Moscow on Friday, 25 May 1951, three days before the interrogation planned by MI5 for the following Monday. Burgess hired a car and drove Maclean to Southampton to catch the cross-channel ferry. He had certainly not planned to accompany his fellow-spy to Moscow; he later explained his spur-of-the-moment decision to do so by the lame excuse that Maclean 'couldn't be trusted to go alone'. Although the latter enjoyed life and work in Moscow, Burgess never settled there happily, dying prematurely in 1963 of severe alcoholic poisoning and kidney failure.

FURTHER READING

Boyle, Andrew, *The Climate of Treason* (London: Hutchinson, 1979).
Connolly, Cyril, *The Missing Diplomats* (London: Queen Anne Press, 1953).
Driberg, Tom, *Guy Burgess: a Portrait with Background* (London: Weidenfeld and Nicolson, 1956).
Rees, Goronwy, *A Chapter of Accidents* (London: Chatto and Windus, 1977).

ANDREW BOYLE

Butler, David (Edgeworth) (*b*. London, 17 October 1924). Political scientist and broadcaster, pioneering authority on British parliamentary elections. Since 1952 he has been a Fellow of Nuffield College, Oxford. He spent a year at Washington as Personal Assistant to HM Ambassador in 1955–6, but Oxford has been his base for a wide-ranging interest in parliamentary democracies and federal systems, particularly those of Great Britain, the USA, Australia and Europe. Without the political partisanship of the Victorian constitutional authority A. V. Dicey or of Dicey's critic Sir Ivor Jennings, he has sustained the preoccupations of the British political science they established, while responding to an inter-disciplinary range of perspectives that have been brought to bear on the study of politics in the last four decades.

Dicey and Jennings concentrated on institutions and the principles behind them, on intended and unintended consequences of structural change, the motivations of politicians, the conventions governing their behaviour, and the mysterious nature of democratic electorates. Butler has encouraged a generation of students to draw on quantitative techniques, social psychology, sociology and media studies in the systematic comparative analysis of all these elements. His essays on Australian government, *The Canberra Model* (1973), express an almost breathless excitement about virgin territory as yet uncolonized by the comparative analyst of parliamentary and federal processes. Characteristically, he takes the Australian academic community to task for neglecting the intrinsic interest and importance of their own institutions and politicians. Democratic systems can be protected and improved only through scholarly understanding, disciplined by a sharp curiosity about particular circumstances and conventions.

Butler's missionary enthusiasm for significant political facts is familiar through radio and television to many who have no professional interest in politics. From the earliest days of the BBC election night and by-election programmes, he has been on hand to place the aggregate movements of voters in constituencies into the context of previous elections, regional and national 'swings', boundary changes and special circumstances, personalities and issues.

Justifying a study of the 1984 European elections, an event that passed largely unnoticed, he observes that it was nonetheless 'a political phenomenon of notable interest to the connoisseur'. The word aptly suggests a refinement of response that stimulates interest without necessarily compelling imitation. However, since 1951, his collaboratively written series of 'British General Election' studies, sponsored by Nuffield, has been followed by journalists, politicians and general readers as well as academic connoisseurs. They are a mine of information, drawing on extensive interviewing and debriefing of politicians, and throwing light, for instance, on the myths and misperceptions of the electoral game.

Inevitably, they venture interpretations of immensely complex occasions which can be belied by subsequent events. Thus, Butler and Kavanagh's account of the 1979 election seems to have underestimated the watershed it represents. However, the critical response to work less crowded by campaign confusions has stimulated debate with serious implications for the British political system. In *Political Change in Britain*, in 1969, Butler and his co-author Donald Stokes of the Michigan Survey

Research Centre developed a general framework for interpreting electoral change from survey evidence. It adapts the 'Michigan model', which emphasizes the social-psychological processes behind party identification. Critics, notably Ivor Crewe of Essex University, turning more to demographic, sociological and historical evidence in conjunction with the surveys, have emerged with a different and disturbing interpretation of change, which distinguishes Britain from comparable Western societies. This emphasizes the increasingly volatile and tenuous identification of British voters with political parties and leaders, and a growing indifference to participation in elections.

GERALD STUDDERT-KENNEDY

Butler, R(ichard) A(usten) [Baron Butler of Saffron Walden] (**'Rab'**) (*b.* Attock, Punjab, 9 December 1902; *d.* Great Yeldham, Essex, 8 March 1982). Conservative Chancellor of the Exchequer. *The Times* called him 'one of the most accomplished and influential statesmen of the century', and the scale of his political achievement seems as remarkable as its range. He was the creator of the modern educational system, the key figure in the revival of postwar Conservatism, arguably one of the most successful Chancellors of the twentieth century and a Home Secretary of reforming zeal. He worked hard for the successful evolution of Empire into Commonwealth, positively in the case of India, more defensively where the break-up of the Federation of Rhodesia and Nyasaland was concerned. He held each of the three main offices of state and three times had a chance to become Prime Minister. It is possible that Macmillan was right to think that he lacked the political ruthlessness which must form part of a leader's make-up, and Butler's failure to fight for the leadership in 1963, when it is believed that he had a majority of the cabinet behind him, supports Macmillan's case. 'We put the gun in his hands and he refused to fire it,' Enoch Powell recalled, but 'Rab' was perhaps the more lovable for not taking that chance. His periods acting as Prime Minister suggest that he was in fact *capax imperii* had he resolved to put it to the touch, and it is just possible that as leader of the Conservative Party he might have won the 1964 election.

Butler was born in India, the son of a distinguished member of the Indian Civil Service, but returned to England at the age of eight to attend preparatory school. While riding in India he fell and broke his arm in three places. He never thereafter had the full use of his right hand. Although only moderately successful at Marlborough, he blossomed at Pembroke College, Cambridge, emerging with Firsts in both French and history. He was immediately elected into a Fellowship at Corpus Christi. He had intended originally to join the Diplomatic Service, but the Cambridge Union gave him a taste for politics. Marriage to Sydney Courtauld the textile heiress, herself a Cambridge graduate, gave him the means to pursue a parliamentary career and the stimulus of an ambitious, forceful and gifted wife. It also brought him a parliamentary seat at Saffron Walden, which he held for 36 years.

In his youth he enjoyed the patronage of Sir Samuel Hoare, a friend of his uncle, Sir Geoffrey Butler, MP for Cambridge. Butler acted as Hoare's private secretary before his own election to the House in 1929, and then as his Parliamentary Private Secretary when Hoare became Secretary of State for India in 1931. In 1932 Butler was appointed Under Secretary of State for India and helped pilot through the Government of India Bill. As a result, he was involved in many clashes with Churchill but attracted favourable attention from the leaders of his party. After a brief spell as a junior minister at the Ministry of Labour, he became Under Secretary of State at the Foreign Office in February 1938, staunchly defending the policy of 'appeasement'. Nevertheless, when Churchill became Prime Minister in 1940 he chose to continue Butler in office and to appoint him a year later both to the presidency of the Board of Education and to the chairmanship of the Conservative Postwar Problems Committee.

Although Churchill was against the thought of legislation in wartime, Butler decided to go ahead with the negotiations with the Churches, whose support was essential to any major educational reform. As a result of the successful completion of these talks he was able to put the 1944 Education Act on to the statute book. It has provided the framework of state education from that day to this. His work for the party was equally prescient but less successful, and after a brief spell as Minister of Labour in Churchill's caretaker administration in 1945 he found himself in opposition. Although he took a full part in parliament, his major contribution to the Conservative revival which followed was made as Chairman of the Conservative Research Department. He was responsible for adjusting Conservative policies to the postwar consensus and chaired the body which produced the Industrial Charter in 1947, the first and still the most famous of the policy documents which signalized his success in that role.

When the Conservatives returned to power in October 1951, faced with a major balance of payments crisis, Butler was asked to be Chancellor. He had no particular qualifications for the job, but he showed great flair and political judgement in his conduct of policy, and he had a remarkable knack for living with a tentative decision overnight before confirming next day that he still felt comfortable with it. Initially he was attracted by the idea of dealing with the crisis by adopting a scheme known as 'Robot'. This would have allowed the pound to float. Although he had the backing of the Prime Minister, his only possible rival for the Exchequer, Oliver Lyttelton, and most of his key advisers in the Treasury (the Economic Adviser was a major exception), the scheme was opposed by the Minister of Economic Affairs and by Churchill's close political adviser, Lord Cherwell. It had few supporters in cabinet and the Party Chairman, Lord Woolton, no friend to Butler, suggested a postponement until the Foreign Secretary had been consulted. Eden was in Lisbon. He indicated serious doubts about the scheme and it was decided to put it on one side until the summer. Butler went ahead with a more orthodox but nonetheless brave response to the government's economic difficulties, refusing to overindulge in deflation and creating a political theme to sustain the logic of what he was doing. The heavy cuts in food subsidies were unpopular, but they were balanced by cuts in taxation, and the opposition was routed politically. Subsequent attempts to revive 'Robot' failed.

R. A. Butler addressing delegates at the Conservative Party Conference, Margate, October 1953

It was the start of a remarkable spell in the Treasury when Butler master-minded the process of decontrol and derationing and introduced a series of expansionist budgets which culminated in a 6d cut in income tax just before the 1955 election. Butler was able to claim in 1954 that Britain was on course to double her standard of living over the next 25 years. In 1953, when Eden was convalescing after a major operation and Churchill suffered a stroke, Butler successfully presided over the government but refused to press his claims to the prime ministership (see also EDEN, ANTHONY). His reward at Eden's hands was dismissal from the Treasury in the autumn of 1955 at a moment when his stewardship of the economy had hit a temporary squall. Rumours that the pound was about to be floated led to a small-scale sterling crisis and the decision to have an autumn budget. Butler was condemned by the opposition for having won the Conservatives the election on a fraudulent economic prospectus, and his subsequent resignation from the Treasury lent some

credence to the charge. A spell as Lord Privy Seal and Leader of the House saw some weakening of his general political influence: he was not in good health and had lost his wife from cancer in 1954. Since she was widely regarded as a crucial influence on his career this was a particular blow.

Eden's prime ministership was dominated by the Suez Crisis. Butler's position on this issue has been generally misunderstood, not least by Conservative backbenchers at the time. He favoured the internationalization of the Suez Canal and was prepared to admit the use of force in the last resort so long as Britain was seen to have tried all other measures first. He would have preferred to have avoided the covert arrangement with the Israelis, but did not oppose it. However, when the pretence of separating the combatants began to collapse in the face of Israeli success, he opposed the landing of troops on 4 November and was among those who insisted that an end had to be put to the operation two days later. It fell to Butler to preside over the government while

Eden was away ill, and both he and Macmillan reluctantly accepted the need to withdraw British forces from the Canal in the face of strong US pressure. But it was Butler who was blamed, and when Eden resigned in January 1957 Conservative cabinet and backbench feeling gave the succession to Macmillan (see also MACMILLAN, HAROLD).

Denied the Foreign Office, Butler chose to make his period at the Home Office memorable as that of a reformer. It cannot be said that he was altogether successful, although he was largely responsible for the White Paper 'Penal Practice' and extracted considerable sums from the Treasury for prison building. He was also responsible for statutes reforming the law on prostitution, betting and gaming, and charities, and had to see through the unsatisfactory Homicide Act of 1957.

After the election Butler became Chairman of the Party Organization and Leader of the House, but he lost both posts to Macleod in October 1961, and his chances of succeeding Macmillan seemed to be receding. He was given charge of the cabinet committee overseeing the negotiations for Britain's entry into the EEC, but the move was tactical, designed to tie a rather lukewarm supporter of the policy to its success. Reluctantly he was compelled to put the first legislation restricting commonwealth immigration on to the statute book in 1962, a step which he had resisted four years earlier; and, with a better grace, he bent his efforts to attempting a solution to the problems of the Central African federation. In the summer of 1962, he lost the Home Office also in Macmillan's 'Night of the Long Knives', and was scarcely compensated with the title of First Secretary of State. Compelled to put an end to the federation, he gained credit for the way in which it was done, and in the wake of the Profumo scandal it looked as if he might yet attain Number Ten.

It was not to be. Macmillan was determined to prevent Butler from succeeding, and when a prostate illness put an end to his own efforts to continue he persuaded first Hailsham, and then Home to put their hats in the ring. The consultations which he set in train pointed to the latter, although there was considerable doubt as to their validity. Almost half the cabinet refused to accept the verdict, but Butler declined to put the matter to the test. He agreed to serve under Home as Foreign Secretary. 'He lacked the last six inches of steel', was Macmillan's brutal verdict. 'Rab' spent an agreeable but not very productive year at the Foreign Office. The major issue which confronted him, Cyprus, he left largely to the Commonwealth Secretary, and his efforts to get on terms with Khrushchev were doomed to disappointment. Shrewdly he advised Home to delay the election to the last moment, but it was characteristic that, when he sensed that a successful result was slipping away, he should have said as much during the campaign.

After the defeat he refused an earldom, but, when he realized how little use would be made of his talents in opposition, he accepted the Mastership of Trinity College, Cambridge, and a life peerage from Wilson. His time at Trinity was rendered memorable because Prince Charles was placed in his care. He made few forays into politics, but he helped inflict defeats on successive governments, first repelling Labour's assault on the ports, and more remarkably defeating the transport clauses of his own party's 1980 Education Bill. He also wrote some laconic memoirs, deliberately keeping them brief to accentuate the contrast with his great rival's six massive volumes, and delighted in the renewed fame they brought him.

WRITINGS

The Art of the Possible (London: Hamish Hamilton, 1971).

FURTHER READING

Brittan, Samuel, *The Treasury Under the Tories* (Harmondsworth: Penguin, 1964).

Dow, Christopher, *The Management of the British Economy 1945–64* (Cambridge: Cambridge University Press, 1964).

Harris, Ralph, *Politics Without Prejudice* (London: Staples Press, 1956).

Howard, Anthony, *Rab: the Life of R. A. Butler* (London: Jonathan Cape, 1987).

Seldon, Anthony, *Churchill's Indian Summer* (London: Hodder and Stoughton, 1981).

Thompson, Alan, *The Day Before Yesterday* (London: Sidgwick and Jackson, 1971).

JOHN BARNES

C

Cadogan, Sir **Alexander ('Alec')** (*b.* London, 24 November 1884; *d.* London, 9 July 1968). Diplomat. Cadogan was appointed Permanent Under-Secretary of State at the Foreign Office in January 1938 when Sir Robert Vansittart was 'promoted' to the post of Chief Diplomatic Adviser. He remained in that position until the end of World War II, and it is in his closeness to the heart of British politics during these vital years that his importance rests.

Cadogan was the youngest child of the fifth Earl Cadogan. His father had occupied minor posts under both Disraeli and Salisbury, and the latter appointed him Viceroy of Ireland in 1895. Chelsea House, the family home in London, was substantial and entertainment was lavish; there was also a large estate in Suffolk. Nevertheless, his upbringing was fairly Spartan and, as the youngest of seven surviving children, Cadogan must have appreciated that he had a career to make. After Eton he went on to Balliol, where he was disappointed not to get a First in history in 1906. He entered the Diplomatic Service (then still separate from the Foreign Office) in 1908 and set off for Constantinople. After a couple of years he moved to Vienna, where he happened to be in charge of the embassy over the weekend of 27–8 June 1914, when the assassination of the Archduke Francis Ferdinand took place. During the war he served in the Foreign Office in London, and at its conclusion in Paris, during the peace conference. His particular responsibility in the 1920s and early 1930s was for League of Nations affairs and disarmament questions. Cadogan was somewhat unusual among his peers in believing that the League of Nations, despite its flaws, was a worthwhile institution, though he did not share the opinions of some extra-mural enthusiasts. He worked well with Sir Austen Chamberlain, and took Arthur Henderson seriously, despite their very different social backgrounds. His involvement with the League of Nations was unusually lengthy and he was glad to have very different responsibilities as British Minister in China in 1933. He was already apprehensive about Europe at the time of his departure, and what he found in East Asia was equally disconcerting. He became increasingly apprehensive about Japanese intentions as time passed. He believed that China would resist but that Japan had little respect for Britain – unless and until Britain became stronger.

Cadogan returned to London as Deputy Under-Secretary of State in early 1936; his succession to Vansittart was likely (see also VANSITTART, ROBERT). He admired Sir Robert but regretted his tendency to dance 'literary hornpipes'. By contrast, in the years that followed, Cadogan composed his minutes clearly and cogently but without flourish. His social background made him at ease in the highest circles but he was neither starchy nor ostentatious. He was also an individual of great discretion, serving men of very different stamp with apparently complete composure. His irritation and impatience he largely reserved for the diary which he meticulously wrote despite all his other responsibilities. He was not greatly in the public eye but his calm experience was invaluable in contexts where he was often surrounded by more volatile men.

His early involvement in the League of Nations made Cadogan an obvious choice in 1946 as the British permanent representative to the new United Nations. It was impossible at that juncture to tell just how significant the new organization would prove to be. The incoming Labour Government attached weight to its success and Cadogan again eschewed both exaggerated optimism and unproductive cynicism. He came back to London in 1950. Perhaps because he knew very little about either radio or television, in 1952 Churchill made him Chairman of the Governors of the BBC, where his previous diplomatic experience proved invaluable in trying to steer an independent path in the difficult circumstances of the Suez Crisis of 1956 in particular.

Cadogan would recognize that he had been born with many advantages. Nevertheless, the particular career which he carved for himself had been his own doing. Few of the guests who graced the great social occasions in Chelsea House before 1914 would have guessed that such a person as Ernest Bevin would be Foreign Secretary in 1945. Cadogan, however, took such developments in his stride. Whatever might happen in the future, he knew that he had played an important role in England's finest hour.

FURTHER READING

Dilks, David (ed.), *The Diaries of Sir Alexander Cadogan* (London: Cassell, 1971).

KEITH ROBBINS

Callaghan, (Leonard) James [Baron Callaghan of Cardiff] (*b.* Portsmouth, 27 March 1912). Labour Prime Minister. Callaghan served as Prime Minister from the resignation of Harold Wilson in March 1976 until his defeat in the general election of May 1979. It was a surprising turn of events. He himself must have supposed, being several years older than Wilson, that he would never reach 10 Downing Street. Wilson's decision meant that 'everything would be in the melting pot', and this unexpected development revived Callaghan's enthusiasm for politics.

Callaghan was the only British Prime Minister born in the twentieth century not to have attended a university, but his modest education was a reflection of his home circumstances rather than a lack of intellectual ability. Confronted by purely ratiocinative ability, however, he emphasized his own earthy commonsense. He read quite widely and knew what questions to ask, but felt that lack of youthful intellectual discipline. He reached 10 Downing Street with a background of experience of the traditional great offices of state unmatched by any of his twentieth-century predecessors. He was Chancellor of the Exchequer from 1964 to 1967, Home Secretary from 1967 to 1970 and

Foreign Secretary from 1974 to 1976. By the time he became Prime Minister he knew the problems and opportunities presented by these major departments from the inside. He had a common touch, but he did not interrupt business to find out football results. His health, carefully husbanded, was sound and he might easily still be a Prime Minister in his seventies.

Callaghan's father (born in Birmingham of Irish descent) served in the Royal Navy in Portsmouth and had been a member of the ship's company of the former Royal Yacht; his pay was sufficient to give James and his sister a warm home and a good basic diet, but he died in 1921. Callaghan went to school largely in Portsmouth. Times were hard, but he never starved. His mother was a Baptist and the family was assisted by other members of the Baptist community, both in Brixham and Portsmouth. Growing up beside the sea was important to Callaghan. Its hazards – his mother's first husband had died at sea – and the necessity for discipline and order were part of his environment. It was almost inevitable that when he came to serve in the war it should be in the Royal Navy, though in fact tuberculosis limited his service. It was chapel, too, that moulded his mind, though at an unspecified date he moved away from the theology he had been taught. In career terms, what his mother wanted for him was a safe and steady job. The Civil Service was the obvious answer because it would give him a pension at 60. However, he had to move to Maidstone to join the Inland Revenue in 1929. He was given some socialist books by colleagues and plunged into the world of G. D. H. Cole and Harold Laski. He went to evening classes on social history and economics, and was an active member of the Association of Tax Officers. After moving to London a few years later, he was drawn into its affairs ever more deeply. Harold Laski arranged for him to use the library at the London School of Economics. When the war came, he initially remained with the union – officials were in 'reserved occupations' – and divided his time between London and Llandudno in North Wales, the new home of the Inland Revenue.

He was adopted as prospective parliamentary candidate for Cardiff South in 1943. Labour carried off all three Cardiff seats in

1945 and Callaghan began an association with his constituency that was to last for more than 40 years. He was not a Welshman, but that did not seem greatly to matter at that juncture. He speedily became Parliamentary Private Secretary to the Parliamentary Under-Secretary at the Dominions Office. By 1947 he had been appointed Parliamentary Secretary at the Ministry of Transport. He duly grappled with the problems of the docks in particular, but the mysteries of transport interested him less than the broader currents in international relations. Shortly before the outbreak of the Korean War in 1950 Callaghan became Parliamentary and Financial Secretary to the Admiralty. He was also selected as a British delegate to the newly formed Council of Europe and acquired some feel for (and taste of) the new Europe that was emerging. Earlier, he had visited Eastern Europe and the Soviet Union. His broad stance on the vexed issues of the cold war during this period can be categorized as 'middle of the road'.

Callaghan was proud of what had been achieved by his seniors but he also recognized that many of them were tired and lacked new ideas. A period in opposition after 1951, if short, would enable Labour to pick up steam again and his generation would come steadily to the fore. Inevitably, Callaghan was not a major figure in the shaping of policy in the early years of opposition. He knew Gaitskell and Bevan reasonably well but he did not link his destiny with either. He was probably closer in spirit to Gaitskell, but his background marked him off from the closet intellectuals who so admired Gaitskell. On the other hand, he respected Bevan's fitful brilliance and shared an opposition to West German re-armament. It is perhaps significant that in his autobiography he passes over the years between 1951 and 1956 in silence.

In 1956 Callaghan accepted Gaitskell's invitation to shadow the government on Commonwealth and Colonial matters, a concern that Bevan was shedding on taking over responsibility for Foreign Affairs as a whole. The issue on which he had to make immediate observations concerned the future of the Central African Federation, and he visited the region. He was sceptical about the federation's future but agreed to reserve judgement until 1960. He enjoyed his extensive travel, both within the Commonwealth and outside it, and he gained an understanding at first hand of the drift of world events which stood him in good stead subsequently. Labour was largely united on Commonwealth and Colonial issues, and Callaghan was not required to take stands which would alienate one section or another of an increasingly divided party. He was a sound man and discreetly made it clear that this should be recognized. The defeat of 1959 was depressing, but Callaghan distrusted the notion that the party's problems could be dealt with by a direct assault on 'Clause Four'. He was not a unilateralist.

Gaitskell invited Harold Wilson to switch from Treasury matters to Foreign Affairs on the death of Bevan in 1960 and asked Callaghan to become Treasury spokesman. In this new role, Callaghan played himself in assiduously, seeking the best advice from academic and other quarters, and he came steadily more confident. When Gaitskell died, Wilson appeared to be the front-runner to succeed him, but he was regarded as a man of the left, at least in some respects, and, speaking generally, 'the Gaitskellites' wanted a fight. George Brown was the leading opponent but he had his weaknesses. Callaghan, backed by Crosland and George Thomson, detected enough support to make standing worthwhile. In the first ballot Wilson gained 115 votes, Brown 88 and Callaghan 44. It was a respectable showing. Nevertheless, it was Wilson's moment and he talked enthusiastically about dynamic, technologically led change. Callaghan played upon the same theme in a more modest manner.

In the event, however, Wilson only scraped home in 1964. There was no doubt that Callaghan would be Chancellor and thus be in a position, in theory, to implement the ideas on which he had been working in his shadow capacity over the previous few years. In practice, no such smooth transition was possible. In the first place, there was Wilson's decision to create a new Department of Economic Affairs, headed by Brown. Brown and Callaghan attempted to achieve a 'Concordat' which defined their respective personal and departmental roles, but they were never able to do so

James Callaghan, on opening a new building for Ruskin College, Oxford, encountering a demonstration against cuts in education spending, October 1976

satisfactorily. The conflict that ensued was not uniformly creative. Secondly, the speculation against sterling, in an era of fixed exchange rates, proved more fundamental and protracted than had at first been envisaged. The preparation of a traditional budget had to take place alongside the formulation of a new 'National Plan'. Great hopes were placed in a Prices and Incomes Board and attendant legislation. By the time Wilson decided to go to the country again after the indecisive result of 1964, sterling was under less pressure, and a certain optimism helped the Labour Party to a handsome victory. Callaghan was able to contemplate a new Selective Employment Tax in relative peace.

The calm was short-lived. In July 1966 devaluation of sterling was considered. Callaghan was with the cabinet majority in opposing it. Brown's subsequent elevation to the Foreign Office and his replacement by Michael Stewart somewhat eased the problems of cooperation between the Department of Economic Affairs and the Treasury, but the pressure on sterling was seemingly constant. By the autumn of 1967 relevant opinion seemed to be shifting in favour of devaluation, but Callaghan still resisted until finally, on 17 November, he accepted that there was no alternative. The new exchange value would be $2.40 instead of $4.80. Callaghan insisted that he should leave the Treasury, and a direct swop with Roy Jenkins was arranged. Callaghan became Home Secretary. He had 'lost', but retained the belief that the devaluation which had been at least discussed three years earlier would not then have been opportune. In his judgement, much would now depend on how devaluation was presented and handled, and for that he was no longer directly responsible.

As Home Secretary, Callaghan had to deal with two major issues alongside the normal routine concerns of the office: immigration and Northern Ireland. Africanization in East Africa meant that the entry of East African Asians into Britain became a contentious issue. Callaghan recognized the serious public concern in the measures that he took, but he did not pander to the more extreme expressions of alarm. Interethnic anxieties were also a major facet of the Northern Ireland problem. There were times in the late 1960s when the province dominated the concerns of the Home Office. Callaghan subsequently wrote his own account of his experiences in this regard in *A House Divided*. He took the bold step in August 1969 of sending in the British Army, with the primary purpose of defending the non-Unionist population. However, such goodwill as this step engendered was lost in the subsequent twists and turns of Ulster politics.

These two issues were contentious enough, but in 1968–9 it was also known that Callaghan was fundamentally opposed to the way in which Wilson and Castle contemplated implementing various legal sanctions as a way of dealing with unofficial strikes. This was but one aspect of the wider issue of trade-union legislation. It was undoubtedly Callaghan's opposition that scuppered the proposals, and his stand increased his influence with trade unionists, though he was by no means unaware of public dissatisfaction with the unions. He expressed the pious wish that trade unionists would take the necessary action themselves; that would be far better than invoking the law. The Prime Minister was not pleased.

In opposition, Callaghan was Foreign Affairs spokesman after 1972, and in 1974, when Labour returned to office without an overall majority, was appointed Foreign Secretary. Britain became a full member of the European Community on 1 January 1973, but the terms of membership had provoked an open split within the Labour Party which neither Wilson nor Callaghan could contain. The majority of Labour MPs voted against membership, or at least claimed that the terms were unacceptable, but a substantial minority voted with the Conservative Government or abstained. The new Labour Cabinet was sharply divided on the issue and there was talk of a referendum of the British people as the only way in which to resolve it. Meanwhile, the somewhat tepid new Foreign Secretary was charged with trying to renegotiate the terms and embarked on a round of visits to European capitals. The referendum was held in June 1975 after the second general election of 1974. It resulted in a large majority for continued membership. 'Europe' dominated most of Callaghan's time while he was at the Foreign Office, though he also struggled to little effect with the problems of Cyprus and Rhodesia.

When Callaghan became Prime Minister his prospects were not rosy, but he brought to the task a genial avuncularity which initially contrasted favourably with the jaded cleverness of his predecessor. Inflation was rampant and the government lacked an effective majority. Surely Callaghan was merely a stop-gap? He did not behave as though this were the case. He tried to inject a new realism, hitting out at the belief that it was possible to spend your way out of a recession by cutting taxes and boosting government expenditure. His remarks were made in the context of a falling pound in September 1976 which led the government to apply to the International Monetary Fund for a stand-by credit of some £2.3 billion. The application divided the cabinet and the future of the government was in doubt on more than one occasion before a package was finally agreed. Perhaps it was the tiny majority which, paradoxically, enabled Callaghan to keep his colleagues in line. Even this situation did not last long. For the remainder of his term of office Callaghan always needed the support of other parties to get his legislation through. By the spring of 1977 a formal pact with the Liberals proved necessary for survival. Legislation for devolution was to be one outcome, but that proved a deceptively simple phrase. The complications inherent in any scheme of devolution for Wales and Scotland swiftly emerged.

By the autumn of 1978 pressure for a general election mounted but Callaghan resisted it. He concluded that the prospects of victory would be better in the spring of 1979. Such a calculation took no account of the way in which the industrial situation deteriorated. Callaghan's dismissive rejection of the notion that there was a crisis on his return from the West Indies in January 1979 did not ring true. The label 'Winter of Discontent' stuck. However, it was the adverse results of the devolution referendums in Scotland and Wales in March which sank the government. It lost a vote of confidence by one vote. In the May general election Mrs Thatcher secured an overall majority. There was little prospect that Callaghan would ever return to office, but it was not until October 1980 that he resigned the leadership. He stayed on long enough to know that the bitterness felt on the left against his 'betrayal' would not disappear.

Throughout his long career Callaghan had been a middle man both by temperament and conviction. He had achieved something, but not enough, in extraordinarily adverse parliamentary circumstances. He prided himself on being a 'bridge' between the conflicting elements in the party, but even the best bridges collapse under conflicting strains.

WRITINGS

Time and Chance (London: Collins, 1987).

FURTHER READING

Donoughue, B., *Prime Minister: the Conduct of Policy under Harold Wilson and James Callaghan* (London: Jonathan Cape, 1987).

KEITH ROBBINS

Campbell-Bannerman, Sir **Henry ('C-B')**
(*b.* Glasgow, 7 September 1836; *d.* London, 22
April 1908). Radical Liberal politician, Secretary of State for War, party leader and Prime
Minister. Following a series of junior appointments, Campbell-Bannerman – or 'C-B' as he
was almost invariably called – entered the
cabinet in Gladstone's last two administrations
as Secretary of State for War, retaining the
same portfolio in Rosebery's short-lived
ministry. He had hoped to be elected Speaker,
a post for which he was well suited by temperament and experience, but was chosen instead to
lead the Liberals in the Commons, an unenviable task made more so by individual and
factional animosity and deceit. His invariably
good-tempered and modest disposition persuaded some to think him no more than a
caretaker easily replaced by a more brilliant
figure. This was an illusion. Despite the disloyalty of faithless followers and execration by
Unionist parliamentarians and press, he
secured the growing support, even affection, of
the electorate, who perceived him to be a
genuine democrat, untouched by society's
enervating influence, a leader qualified to
reconcile politics with morality. In six years he
converted the divided, demoralized shambles
he inherited into an effective, revitalized political party that won a crushing electoral victory.
A brief, triumphant premiership was ended by
illness in April 1908. The paradox, that
someone so lacking in ambition should, after
years of respectable obscurity, achieve supreme
political office, was more apparent than real.
Brave, shrewd, neither indifferent nor indolent
as some supposed, 'C-B', once determined in
his purpose, was adamantine. An unusually
popular Prime Minister, his stature grew in the
memories of his radical supporters, who exaggerated his personal contribution and
influence, insisting that had he lived he would
have stifled the bellicose initiatives of Liberal
imperialist ministers in foreign affairs, with
their advocacy not of a concert but a balance of
power in Europe, friendship with the Tsar's
despotic regime, and secret naval and military
obligations. Their sentimental estimate is con-
founded by the evidence.

Educated at Glasgow and Cambridge
universities, 'C-B' then joined his family's
business, becoming a partner in 1860. That
same year he married Charlotte Bruce; it was
an exceptionally happy marriage marred by
Charlotte's chronic ill-health. They were
devoted to each other, shared the same tastes,
were good linguists and enjoyed travel in
Europe, where they invariably spent part of the
autumn parliamentary recess. Elected MP for
Stirling Burghs in 1868, 'C-B' represented the
constituency without interruption until his
death. He sustained a reputation as an
independent, advanced Gladstonian. In
opposition he spoke rarely; in government he
adopted a relaxed attitude towards his responsibilities. He was loyal, solid, methodical and,
unlike most politicians, was not disposed to
interfere constantly in everything to claim
credit for himself. A thorough Scot, at every
opportunity he returned to what he considered
'the better side of the Tweed'. He was an
informed speaker on Scottish issues and supported devolution for Scotland's domestic
affairs. He voted for the disestablishment and
disendowment of the Church of Scotland, had
a typical Lowlander's distrust of Highlanders,
disliked 'Wee Frees' and preferred claret to
whisky.

In Gladstone's first two administrations
'C-B' served as a junior minister, twice at the
War Office and once at the Admiralty. From
October 1884 to June 1885 he was Chief
Secretary for Ireland. A staunch Home Ruler,
in Gladstone's third administration he was
promoted to the cabinet as Secretary of State
for War. He was a competent administrator
content to play a modest part, relaxed,
courteous, tactful and patient, ready to listen to
advisers but not afraid to pursue an
independent line. As a War Minister 'C-B' is
best remembered for his attachment to the
principles of his mentor in that office, Edward
Cardwell; for securing the retirement of the
Duke of Cambridge; and as the subject of a
censure vote in June 1895, when the government was narrowly defeated in a small House
and the pusillanimous Rosebery resigned. As a
member of the Hartington Commission in
1890, 'C-B' had opposed replacing the
Commander-in-Chief with a Chief of Staff
and Council, arguing that it would be
dangerous and militaristic – an apprehension

Sir Henry Campbell-Bannerman

justified by the later decision of the army's General Staff to pursue an independent continental strategy.

Rosebery's resignation as party leader in October 1896 exacerbated Liberal internal conflict. Events in the Transvaal had dominated political discussion, and radical and imperialist Liberal factions were divided as to whether Joseph Chamberlain, Colonial Secretary, had been implicated in the plot that culminated in the fiasco of the Jameson Raid. Appointed a member of the select committee of enquiry, 'C-B' earned the sharp criticism of radicals for signing the majority report that exonerated Chamberlain. After little more than two years, marred by constant inter-factional squabbling, a thoroughly disillusioned Sir William Harcourt surrendered the leadership. John Morley refused to serve, two Liberal

imperialist candidates withdrew and, almost by default, 'C-B' was elected to lead the Liberals in the Commons.

Even to begin to create an effective opposition posed enormous problems. There was no practical alternative other than to counsel sedulous attention to public affairs and deny any need for immediate innovation. With the nation at war, 'C-B' considered national as much as party imperatives dictated he should swallow his pride and conciliate rebellious Roseberyites. Thus the cracks of schism were first thinly papered over. Some supposed his moderation inspired by moral spinelessness, and there were times, in private, when he wondered whether too high a price was paid not to alienate the Liberal imperialists. The 1900 'Khaki' election intervened. With Liberal organization in disarray, funds and morale alike low, 'C-B' chose to husband resources, minimize the extent of inevitable defeat and live to fight another day. Unionists greeted victory as a mandate for their policies but failed to perceive an overwhelming majority of the electorate no longer favoured war, and wanted, above all else, its swift conclusion.

Emily Hobhouse's account of conditions in the concentration camps so angered and moved 'C-B' that he publicly condemned the army employing 'methods of barbarism' to fight the Boers. He was denounced as a traitor by the Tory press, but the unforeseen, fortuitous consequence of his emotional outburst was that political debate switched from the war's causes (the subject that most divided Liberals) to its conduct. The Liberal imperialists continued to show undisguised animosity towards 'C-B', which was clearly revealed as inspired as much by personal as political differences. As his grip upon party and electorate tightened, so the Liberal imperialists were increasingly isolated. Political debate embraced subjects that promoted Unionist division and enhanced Liberal unity. Yet some of Campbell-Bannerman's younger, more impatient, progressive colleagues were heard to complain that their leader showed insufficient adventurousness in responding to social and economic ills. 'C-B', all his life an unswerving Gladstonian, opposed any collectivist tendency. His heart might regret Labour having few representatives in the

Commons, but his head dictated that the electoral pact he sought was designed first and foremost to serve Liberal not Labour interests. Later criticism of the parties' electoral pact does not reflect informed contemporary assessment.

The Unionists, embarrassed by their own differences on the issue of imperial preference, tried to exploit continued Liberal quarrels on defence and foreign policy. Campbell-Bannerman's views on the army had not changed since he had served at the War Office. On foreign affairs, he found little to complain about in Lord Lansdowne's stewardship: he welcomed the Anglo-French *entente* and remained a committed supporter despite radical complaints of its deleterious effect upon Anglo-German relations. He passively accepted a dangerous extension of the terms of the Anglo-Japanese Treaty in 1905. His opposition to the Committee of Imperial Defence he subsequently abandoned in office. In the last year of Balfour's administration, Campbell-Bannerman's overriding concern was to avoid areas of potential discord in his party. He refused to make detailed declarations of alternative policies that might fuel Liberal schism or distract the electorate's attention from Unionist failures. On Ireland, the most obvious source of Liberal embarrassment, he acknowledged the virtues of Home Rule but argued that, for the moment, it was not practical politics. He persuaded the Liberal imperialists to accept a step-by-step policy, effectively removing Ireland from the immediate political agenda. All accepted save Rosebery, who advertised his disagreement in a public speech. Hoping to make capital from Rosebery's indiscretion and embarrass 'C-B', Balfour resigned. Encouraged by his wife, 'C-B' remained steadfast in the crisis. He cleverly outmanoeuvred the Relugas conspirators who had sought to banish him to the Lords as nominal party leader, created a cabinet representative of all elements within the Liberal Party – not excluding the three conspirators, who were given key appointments at the Exchequer, Foreign and War Offices – and then sought dissolution and the electorate's verdict.

Campbell-Bannerman's short premiership was accurately described by a contemporary parliamentarian as 'the splendid sunset of his career', an apotheosis when he enjoyed ascendancy and authority over Commons and cabinet alike. Accounts of how 'C-B' conducted cabinet business vary, from R. B. Haldane's critical estimate to Lord Crewe's unqualified praise. Perhaps too much was left to individual ministerial initiative, too little to systematic consultation and team work. 'C-B' grew increasingly reluctant to master detail, though he was never afraid to pursue his own line if he judged it proper, even in the face of stiff opposition. His achievements as Prime Minister were all the more remarkable, because he was distracted in his first year by Charlotte's illness then death, and in the second year undermined by his own failing health. Invariably loyal, sensible, solid, never rattled, equable and good-humoured, 'C-B' was constantly underrated because he had no great oratorical gifts. A small voice and an undramatic mode of presentation were compensated for by stamina, good sense and a pawky humour.

The three domestic measures that occupied the Commons during Campbell-Bannerman's premiership all passed the House after prolonged debate. The Trades Disputes Bill was amended by the Lords but became law because the Upper House did not consider it politic to pursue their opposition to the extreme. A Plural Voting Bill was completely lost and an Education Bill so badly mauled that it had to be abandoned, prompting a strong attack on the hereditary chamber by 'C-B'. He warned that the will of the electorate would not be thwarted indefinitely by Tory peers who, at the behest of Balfour, had turned their House into an annexe of the Unionist Party. Resisting more radical suggestions, 'C-B' proposed not changing the membership of the Lords but restricting the Lords' powers so that, within the limits of a single Parliament, the opinion of the elected House would prevail. This proposal, subsequently embodied in the 1911 Parliament Act, was similar to that made earlier by James Mill and then John Bright.

'C-B' demonstrated his sense of equity as well as determination in resolving the South African problem. He jettisoned the Unionists' timid plans for a limited scheme of representative government, never wavering in his conviction that the correct way to treat South Africa was to offer trust and self-government. This bold initiative upon which he insisted paved the way for the eventual Union of South Africa in 1910.

Radical Liberals believed the Prime Minister, whom they counted one of themselves, controlled his Liberal imperialist ministers. But Edward Grey virtually excluded 'C-B' from the conduct of foreign policy. Twice 'C-B' stated his concern at the diplomatic implications of the military conversations between the French and British staffs, then acquiesced in their continuing. He firmly supported Haldane's army reforms. He overrode the powerful objections of the economists in his cabinet rejecting any reduction of the 1908–9 naval estimates. Radicals considered 'C-B' their 'most powerful and convinced statesman'. They remembered the Opposition Leader who had denounced 'methods of barbarism'; the Prime Minister who proclaimed his vision of a 'League of Peace'; the advocate of arbitration rather than force to settle international disputes, who sought armament limitation by negotiation, as in his March 1907 article on The Hague Conference and Disarmament in the *Nation*; the democrat who supported the enfranchisement of women; the parliamentarian whose rejoinder to the news that the Tsar had dissolved the Duma was the bold assertion, 'La duma est morte; vive la duma.' They loved his heroic idealism and, for this reason, disapproved of J. A. Spender's official *Life* (1924), which emphasized his practical wisdom. Campbell-Bannerman's character was a shrewd blend of idealism and practicality. Idealism inspired his principles, practicality tempered his decision-making.

FURTHER READING

Harris, J. and Hazlehurst, C., 'Campbell-Bannerman as Prime Minister', *History* (1970), pp. 360–83.
Hirst, F. W., *In the Golden Days* (London: Frederick Muller, 1947).
Wilson, John, *CB: a Life of Sir Henry Campbell-Bannerman* (London: Constable, 1973).

A. J. A. MORRIS

Carr, E(dward) H(allett) (*b.* London, 28 June 1892; *d.* Cambridge, 3 November 1982). Historian, journalist and diplomat. His career had three main facets. After classical studies at Cambridge, he pursued between 1916 and 1936 a first profession as diplomat, serving the Foreign Office on the Russian desk and at the Paris Peace Conference, then in Riga, and latterly on League of Nations business. For much of World War II he was occupied with journalism, writing influential leaders for *The Times* while acting as assistant editor to Robert Barrington-Ward. In the intervening years he had also launched himself as an academic, obtaining the Woodrow Wilson professorship of international relations at Aberystwyth. It was indeed to scholarship (and eventually to his old college, Trinity) that he returned during the final decades of his long life, when he developed his reputation as one of the world's leading authorities on the early history of the Soviet regime.

Carr's determination to make the experiences of Russians more comprehensible in the West – 'theirs was not really the same world as ours' – was already discernible in his early books, starting with a study of Dostoevsky (1931). The task became increasingly urgent as his enthusiasm for the Soviet 'planned economy' grew at the expense of his allegiance to the liberal-capitalist values which had prevailed during his comfortable middle-class Highgate upbringing. In the early 1940s he was even branded as 'the red professor of Printing House Square' – someone who (according to Randolph Churchill) made *The Times* read like the *Daily Worker*. His editorials championed the emerging welfare state at home, as well as the closest possible cooperation with Moscow in defeating Hitler (whose menace he had appeased and underestimated until 1939) and in settling the postwar international order broadly along the lines followed at Yalta.

Admiration for the achievements of Lenin and Stalin was certainly evident in *A History of Soviet Russia*, which Carr first conceived around 1944. By the time of its completion in 1978, this project had grown into one of the great monuments of twentieth-century British political scholarship. Carr's 14-volume survey of the years from 1917 to 1929 undeniably broke new ground in its indefatigable detailing of the Soviet leaders' efforts to gain supreme control over the mechanisms for a total transformation in the backward economic, social, and political structure of the former Russian Empire, as well as their endeavours to dominate the Communist International. He was, however, understandably criticized for viewing these processes too exclusively from the standpoint of those revolutionaries who had ruthlessly managed to get and maintain power, and for paying scant attention to the alternative strategies proposed by their crushed opponents or to the fate of still more innocent victims. Much of the *History* was attacked for a certain linear predictability, and for its unduly complacent interpretation – now less Whig than Bolshevik – of the unavoidable and progressive fitness of what had indeed come to pass. Only as 'de-Stalinization' gained ground in the USSR did the author's enthusiasm for the policies of Lenin's successor weaken, albeit somewhat ambivalently. (The material in *A History of Soviet Russia* is usefully summarized in *The Russian Revolution: From Lenin to Stalin (1917–1929)*, 1979; and the story is extended via *The Twilight of the Comintern, 1930–1935*, 1982.) The philosophical naivety underlying Carr's brand of determinism was most starkly revealed in his lively and polemical *What is History?* (a book based on his 1961 Trevelyan Lectures at Cambridge, and one much prized by the more callow kind of student), and was most acutely dissected by Isaiah Berlin as the product of someone who was 'essentially a late positivist, in the tradition of Auguste Comte, Herbert Spencer, and H. G. Wells'.

FURTHER READING

Davies, R. W., 'Edward Hallett Carr', *Proceedings of the British Academy*, 69 (1983), pp. 473–511.

MICHAEL BIDDISS

Carrington, Peter (Alexander Rupert) [Baron Carington] (*b.* London, 6 June 1919). Foreign Secretary and Secretary General of NATO. A glittering career awaited the young Sandhurst cadet (who had come thence from Eton), and he won a Military Cross during World War II. In due course he became

KG, KCMG, GCMG and a Privy Councillor. After the war he became an opposition Whip in the House of Lords in 1947. He was, thereafter, a Parliamentary Secretary at both the Ministry of Agriculture and the Ministry of Defence. He served as High Commissioner in Australia from 1956 to 1959, then became First Lord of the Admiralty. When the Conservative Party lost the general election of October 1964 he became Leader of the Opposition in the House of Lords. In 1970 he was appointed Secretary of State for Defence in the Conservative Government headed by Edward Heath. Carrington was Chairman of the Conservative Party from 1972 to 1974 and, between the unhappy months of January and February 1974, the first ever Secretary of State for Energy under Heath. Having thought his political career was over when Margaret Thatcher succeeded Heath as Leader of the Conservative Party in February 1975, he became Foreign Secretary in her first administration in 1979. In 1982 he resigned when his conduct of British relations with Argentina was judged to have led to war in the South Atlantic over possession of the Falkland Islands. However, he became Secretary General of NATO in 1984, and retired from that post and public life only in 1988.

Between moments of government service Carrington became a Fellow of Eton College in 1966 and of St Antony's College, Oxford, in 1982. He has served as chairman of GEC (Britain's second largest industrial company), chairman of the trustees of the Victoria and Albert Museum, and chairman or trustee of various other organizations, including those devoted to the memories of Sir Winston Churchill and Sir Robert Menzies (for many years Prime Minister of Australia).

Withal, Carrington has never been a stuffy man. His self-deprecating humour has passed into political legend. That his family name (changed from 'Smith' by the first Baron in 1796, the title having been created as a result of money lent to George III) lacks the second 'r' is the result 'of my ancestor being drunk at the time'. When asked who would succeed Mrs Thatcher should a bus run over her, he replied, 'The bus wouldn't dare.' When, in 1963, Lord Hailsham and Lord Home resigned their peerages (under legislation introduced by Macmillan's government), he observed that he could not understand why anybody in their right mind could give up a title of nobility for the vulgarity of the House of Commons.

In spite of all this, failure and lack of judgement attended Carrington in many of his high posts. As Parliamentary Secretary at the Ministry of Agriculture he was involved in the Crichel Down affair (when the ministry declined to return property appropriated during World War II). His minister resigned, but he did not. His was the most influential voice in persuading Heath to embark on the (for the government) disastrous general election of February 1974. In spite of detailed advice he failed to foresee the Argentinian attack on the Falkland Islands in 1982. He claimed more credit than he deserved for the settlement of the Rhodesian rebellion (which settlement led to the creation of the state of Zimbabwe in 1980). His affable manner left him untouched by many failures over which he presided, perhaps most notably that of the Vassall espionage scandal, which occurred when he was First Lord of the Admiralty. The record of his service as Secretary General of NATO has yet to be written.

Carrington married, on 25 April 1942, Iona, the daughter of Sir Francis McClean, 'the most beautiful woman I have ever met'. He enjoys himself by writing limericks and collecting walking sticks. He has said that 'I simply cannot understand politics.'

For illustration, see HEATH, EDWARD.

WRITINGS

Reflect on Things Past (London: Collins, 1988).

FURTHER READING

Cosgrave, Patrick, *Carrington: a Life and a Policy* (London: Dent, 1985).
Butler, David and Kavanagh, Dennis, *The British General Election of February 1974* (London: Macmillan, 1974).

PATRICK COSGRAVE

Castle [née Betts], **Barbara** (*b.* Bradford, Yorkshire, 6 October 1910). Labour MP and senior minister. She served in a variety of posts during the Wilson governments of the 1960s and 1970s, achieving particular prominence as Secretary of State for Employment. She later went on to become a leading member of the Socialist Group at the European Assembly.

She was educated at Bradford Girls' Grammar School and St Hugh's College, Oxford. Her route into left-wing politics, to which she soon became committed, was provided mainly through local government and journalism. In the 1930s she served briefly on St Pancras Borough Council, and she later became a member of the Metropolitan Water Board. During World War II she served as a temporary civil servant at the Ministry of Food, but left this post in 1944 to join the staff of the *Daily Mirror*. As housing correspondent and adviser on service issues, she was well placed to observe the swing to the left in public opinion that produced Labour's landslide victory in 1945. Mrs Castle, as she was known after her marriage in 1944, herself played a part in this victory. She successfully contested the seat at Blackburn, an area she was to represent for Labour until 1979.

In the 1950s Castle came to the forefront of Labour politics as a leading 'Bevanite'. She was elected to the National Executive Committee and chaired the party in 1958–9, but like other left-wingers had to wait for promotion until Harold Wilson's election to the Labour leadership (see also WILSON, HAROLD). Wilson's victory in the 1964 general election provided the first opportunity for Castle to demonstrate her administrative abilities at government level. After a brief spell as Minister of Overseas Development, she spent three years as Minister of Transport. In this capacity, she tackled head on a variety of controversial issues, notably the introduction of breathalyser tests in order to combat drunken driving. But it was as Secretary of State for Employment and Productivity from 1968 to 1970 that she faced the greatest controversy of her career. The cabinet had become convinced that the success of its economic policy depended upon wholesale reform of industrial law. Castle foreshadowed this in her White Paper of 1969, *In Place of Strife*. The reaction of the trade-union movement and the Labour Party, however, forced the government to retreat. As the prospect of voluntary modernization of the unions receded, the minister responsible came under bitter attack, in many cases from her erstwhile supporters.

Castle's political reputation was damaged by the whole episode. She was nevertheless able to return to high office after Labour's election victory in 1974; Wilson now offered her the post of Secretary of State for Social Services. She was not re-appointed, however, when James Callaghan became Prime Minister in 1976, and she decided to stand down as MP for Blackburn at the forthcoming election in order to make way for a younger candidate. But Castle's active political career was still far from over. Following in the footsteps of her friend Richard Crossman, she decided to publish her political diaries, highlighting what she saw as some of the failings of the Wilson governments. And in 1979 she found a new outlet for her relentless energy by becoming a member of the European Parliament, representing Greater Manchester. In subsequent years, as head of the British Labour Group, she worked hard to temper the party's traditional hostility to the EEC. She also became a prominent member of the Socialist Group at the European Assembly, thus finding a wider stage on which vigorously to promote her socialist principles.

WRITINGS

The Castle Diaries, 1974–76 (London: Weidenfeld and Nicolson, 1980).
The Castle Diaries 1964–70 (London: Weidenfeld and Nicolson, 1984).

FURTHER READING

De'ath, W. (ed.), *Barbara Castle: a Portrait from Life* (Brighton: Clifton Books, 1970).

KEVIN JEFFERYS

Cecil, Lord (Edward Algernon) Robert (Gascoyne-) [Viscount Cecil of Chelwood] (*b.* London, 14 September 1864; *d.* Tunbridge Wells, Kent, 24 November 1958). Conservative politician and architect of the League of Nations. A high-born but maverick Conservative politician, he devoted the last 40 years of a long life to the ideals of the organization he had

played such an important role in creating. He was Parliamentary Under-Secretary of State for Foreign Affairs from May 1915 to July 1918 (being in the cabinet from February to December 1916), with responsibility for the blockade against Germany, and was then promoted to Assistant Secretary of State – official deputy to his cousin Balfour. His resignation in November 1918 in protest against the disestablishment of the Welsh Church made little immediate difference, as he was at once made head of the Foreign Office's League of Nations section, and played a role second only to President Wilson in the drafting of the League's Covenant at the Congress of Paris. For the next four years he devoted himself to the League of Nations Union (LNU) as chairman of its executive committee (1919–23). Bitterly distrustful of Lloyd George, he also campaigned for the formation of an alternative coalition under Grey. Reconciled to his party by Baldwin, he was cabinet minister in charge of League affairs (as Lord Privy Seal in the first Baldwin government and Chancellor of the Duchy of Lancaster in the second) until frustration with Conservative reluctance to disarm caused his final resignation in 1927. In 1929 the Labour Government made him a League adviser with a room in the Foreign Office, and he also served as a delegate at Geneva for the National Government; but his energies were above all devoted to the LNU, of which he was the undisputed leader, being its president from 1923 to 1938 and thereafter joint president with his close associate and moderating influence GILBERT MURRAY. Cecil's boldest stroke was the 'Peace Ballot', a referendum organized mainly by the LNU from November 1934 to June 1935 in which over 38 per cent of the population took part. Particularly after 1936, he campaigned vigorously for collective security. His pre-eminence as an internationalist was recognized by the award of the Nobel Peace Prize in 1937 and by his appointment as Honorary Life President of the United Nations Association at its inception in 1945.

The third son of the third Marquess of Salisbury, Cecil was educated by private tutors at Hatfield House, then at Eton and University College, Oxford. A successful barrister, he became Conservative MP for Marylebone East in January 1906. But, despite his family background and high-church Anglicanism, he was ill-suited to membership of an increasingly business-dominated party. He was not only a supporter of votes for women but a (moderate) free trader; and it was fear of opposition from tariff reformers in his local party that caused him to seek a different seat in the next general election. After losing at Blackburn in January 1910 and in the Wisbech division of Cambridgeshire the following December, he was successful at a by-election in the Hitchin division of Hertfordshire in November 1911. (He held the seat until 1923, when he was elevated to the House of Lords to avoid having to stand on a protectionist platform.)

It was World War I that gave Cecil a political cause which transcended Conservatism. His support for a League of Nations, first expressed in a Foreign Office paper of September 1916, had three sources: he believed it to be in line with his father's belief in a Concert of Europe; he was upset by the suffering he saw while working in France for the Red Cross in the first nine months of the war; and his blockade work had alerted him to the possibility of economic sanctions as a non-military means of enforcing justice. Though in some respects a political innocent, he showed great skill and resilience both in preventing his colleagues insisting on a League that was simply a continuation of the Supreme War Council and in mobilizing public opinion in support of the League when American refusal to join put its future in jeopardy. He had a long and happy (though childless) marriage to Lady Eleanor Lambton.

WRITINGS

A Great Experiment: an Autobiography (London: Jonathan Cape, 1941).
All the Way (London: Hodder and Stoughton, 1949).

FURTHER READING

Egerton, George W., *Great Britain and the Creation of the League of Nations* (London: Scolar Press, 1979).

MARTIN CEADEL

Chamberlain, Sir **(Joseph) Austen** (*b.* Birmingham, 16 October 1863; *d.* London, 16 March 1937). Conservative and Unionist politician and party leader. The elder son of Joseph Chamberlain and half-brother of Neville Chamberlain, he was a major political figure in his own right. For three decades he was at or near the very centre of the British political stage, and he held an array of senior posts, including the Exchequer (twice) and the Foreign Office, where his most celebrated achievement was to negotiate the Treaties of Locarno in 1925. Despite a distinguished political career, Chamberlain has tended to be remembered for what he did not do. He has been portrayed as a born loser. He remains the only leader of the Conservative Party in the twentieth century who failed to rise to the premiership. In the rather unkind but often repeated words of Churchill (or possibly Birkenhead), Chamberlain 'always played the game and always lost it'.

If ever a man were destined to follow a career in politics, that man was Austen Chamberlain. His father Joseph, a prosperous industrialist, was 27 years of age at Austen's birth and about to embark on a celebrated political adventure which would take him from municipal affairs in Birmingham to the cabinet table in Whitehall. From an early date Austen's education and training were shaped with a view to his eventual succession to the family's political inheritance; from the beginning he was marked out to carry the Chamberlain name into a second generation of political affairs.

Chamberlain's mother died at his birth – a tragedy which left a lasting scar upon his father and upon the relationship between father and son. Brought up at first by his maternal grandparents and then by Joseph's second wife (Neville's mother, who also died in childbirth), Austen attended preparatory school in Brighton before moving to Rugby shortly before his fifteenth birthday. Here he became prominent in the school's debating society, loyally supporting the advanced radical causes which his father was beginning to champion on the national stage. After Rugby, Chamberlain read history at Trinity, Cambridge, where he became Vice-President of the Union. Continuing the careful education of the future statesman, Joseph Chamberlain next ensured that his son should gain experience of contemporary Europe. In September 1885 the young Chamberlain went for nine months to France, where he formed a lasting affection for the country and its people. An extended visit to Germany in 1887 left him with an altogether less favourable impression.

Parliament was obviously the next step for the aspiring politician, and Chamberlain entered the House of Commons unopposed as member for East Worcestershire in March 1892. The constituency was close enough to Birmingham to fall within the orbit of his father's political sway. By this stage, Joseph Chamberlain had broken with the Liberal Party over Ireland and, as a Liberal Unionist, was moving towards alliance with the Conservatives. It was a political journey which Austen easily and readily followed. His radicalism had always been a matter of birth and inheritance rather than conviction and temperament. Although he made a good initial impression in the House of Commons, particularly with the veteran Gladstone, his first taste of governmental office doubtless owed much to his father's influence. When Joseph became Colonial Secretary in Lord Salisbury's Unionist Government in 1895, Austen entered the administration as Civil Lord of the Admiralty. Five years in this post introduced him to the problems of governmental administration rather than political decision-making. In 1900, during the course of the Boer War, he was promoted to be Financial Secretary to the Treasury, and less than two years later entered Balfour's cabinet as Postmaster General. He was still under 40 years of age.

Success and advancement had come easily to Chamberlain, perhaps too easily. So determined was Joseph Chamberlain that his son and heir should not have to overcome the same impediments on the greasy pole of political advancement that he himself had confronted, that Austen's early career lacked that toughening experience out of which the most successful political talents are usually forged. Austen Chamberlain was not a fighter; he had never needed to be. But at critical stages of his later career this flaw in his political make-up was to cost him dear.

Sir Austen Chamberlain, October 1912

Chamberlain's fortunes were still very closely tied to those of his father, indeed very much a function of them. Joseph's celebrated crusade for tariff reform, beginning with his Birmingham speech of May 1903, was to dominate and shape his son's career at least until World War I. When the elder man struck a bargain with Balfour by which he would retire to the back benches to campaign for his cause, part of the arrangement was that Austen should be promoted to the Exchequer to represent his father's interests in the highest reaches of the government. Yet, despite the seniority of the office which he now held, Chamberlain's first period as Chancellor (1903–5) was an uneasy one. Balfour's studied evasion and ambiguity over the central issue of tariff reform left Chamberlain confused and frustrated. The fall of the Unionist Government in December 1905 was a matter of little regret to him.

The events of the next few months brought about a marked change in Chamberlain's position. The scale of the Unionists' defeat in the general election of January 1906 was unprecedented; yet the rump of the surviving parliamentary party seemed more favourable to the Chamberlainite brand of Unionism than its Balfourian alternative. By the summer of 1906, however, a paralysing stroke had removed Joseph Chamberlain permanently from the political landscape and left Austen as the loyal but somewhat inadequate standard-bearer of his father's crusade. For the younger man it was a no-win situation. To Joseph Chamberlain's acolytes and disciples Austen lacked the fire and passion which had won them as unquestioning adherents to his father's cause. To those who stood by the more traditional concept of Conservatism, Austen was tarred with his father's brush – a symbol of the vulgar intrusion into their ranks of 'Birmingham' and all it stood for. These factors help to explain Chamberlain's failure to secure the succession to Balfour as party leader in 1911, but deeper currents were also in play. Had he possessed half of his father's determination and ambition, Chamberlain could probably have secured the leadership on a majority vote. As it was, both he and his rival, Walter Long, withdrew their names from the contest and allowed Bonar Law to emerge as the compromise candidate. Chamberlain's motivation was a combination of not wishing to split the party and an inner lack of conviction about his own potential for leadership.

Chamberlain was never fully committed to the Unionist campaign of opposition to Irish Home Rule after 1912, and in 1913 felt bitterly Bonar Law's effective abandonment of tariff reform as a policy option for the foreseeable future (see also LAW, BONAR). His career revived with the coming of European war in 1914 and he entered Asquith's coalition the following May as Secretary of State for India, remaining in the post when Lloyd George took over as Prime Minister. With the failure of the Mesopotamian campaign, Chamberlain accepted fully – and many thought unnecessarily – the doctrine of ministerial responsibility, and resigned his office in July 1917. In April 1918 Lloyd George recalled him to the government as Minister without Portfolio with a seat in the War Cabinet, and he retained office under Lloyd George after the 'Coupon' Election, becoming Chancellor again in January 1919. Chamberlain played an increasingly

important role inside the postwar coalition, developing a growing appreciation of Lloyd George's qualities and succeeding an ailing Bonar Law as Conservative leader in March 1921. He clearly favoured a realignment of the non-socialist parties to resist the growing advance of Labour, but he failed to take the majority of Conservatives with him in this strategy. As party leader, he remained unwisely aloof from the rank and file of his followers, largely unaware of the reluctance with which the average backbench Conservative continued to submerge his identity inside the coalition headed by an increasingly unpopular premier.

In February 1922 Lloyd George made a formal and apparently sincere offer to resign the premiership in Chamberlain's favour. But the latter declined the offer and paid dearly for his continuing loyalty to the Prime Minister when a revolt of backbench Conservatives, meeting at the Carlton Club that October, broke up the coalition. Chamberlain immediately resigned as party leader. Out of office for the duration of Bonar Law's premiership and excluded from the upper reaches of the Conservative Party for a sufficient time for Stanley Baldwin to establish his ascendancy, Chamberlain returned to government as Foreign Secretary in 1924. Here he enjoyed the most conspicuous, if perhaps overrated, success of his long career. Chamberlain recognized that the question of French security was central to European peace. Abandoning the proposals of the outgoing Labour Government for a wide-ranging security pact, Chamberlain successfully negotiated an agreement with France and Germany, restricted to a guarantee of Germany's western frontiers and the demilitarized status of the Rhineland. Rewarded with the Garter and the Nobel Prize for Peace, Chamberlain's success at Locarno was not followed up in the remaining years of his office. Determined to limit Britain's obligations to a carefully circumscribed area of Europe, he would not take the lead in helping to arrange further security agreements elsewhere on the Continent. His own preoccupations as Foreign Secretary became increasingly imperial rather than continental, and little more was achieved towards a lasting European peace by the time that the Conservatives lost office in 1929. The 'Locarno Era' was widely praised as indicative of a new mood of international cooperation, but was heavily dependent on the personal rapport that existed between Chamberlain, Aristide Briand and Gustav Stresemann, and it failed to survive the changes in personnel which began in 1929. Any lasting optimism was blown away by the chill winds of economic depression in the 1930s, while Locarno itself was revealed as a dead letter when Hitler re-occupied the Rhineland with impunity in 1936.

Chamberlain served briefly as First Lord of the Admiralty in Ramsay MacDonald's National Government in 1931, facing the emergency of the Invergordon Mutiny, but he resigned after the general election to make way for younger men. It was a decision which he later regretted, especially as he became increasingly contemptuous of Sir John Simon's conduct of foreign policy in the years 1931–5. Yet in many ways his final years, as a backbench MP, were the most distinguished of his career. Achieving a considerable following and respect among fellow Conservatives – which had largely eluded him earlier in his life – Chamberlain was among the few British parliamentarians who consistently warned of the Nazi danger after Hitler's rise to power in January 1933. His speeches in the Commons were balanced and reasoned, and always commanded the attention of the House. He probably had it in his power to bring down Baldwin's government over the Hoare–Laval Pact in 1935, had he chosen to do so. Had he lived beyond 1937, Chamberlain would not have emerged, as did Churchill, as a great war leader, but his record in the 1930s – a decade which destroyed so many reputations – will stand comparison with those of most contemporaries.

For almost all of his long career Chamberlain was overshadowed by the more powerful personality either of his father or of his brother. A striking physical similarity to his father, which Chamberlain exaggerated by wearing both a monocle and an orchid, made it difficult for him to carve out an independent identity. In later years it was hard for him to accept being overtaken by his brother. Neville's late advent into national politics was a constant reminder that this was not the way in which Joseph had planned out the careers of his two sons. Rising to high office at a comparatively early age, Austen Chamberlain developed an exaggerated sense of his own dignity which made him a difficult colleague to work with and quick to take offence. The concept of loyalty became an obsession for him, though it did not stop him being highly critical in private of the party leaders under whom he served. His formal stiffness was in part a reaction to the conviction that his father – a self-made man – had never been fully accepted as a gentleman. In part it reflected his innate sensitivity and inner self-doubt, which on more than one occasion stood in the way of his political advancement.

WRITINGS

Down the Years (London: Cassell, 1935).
Politics from Inside: an Epistolary Chronicle, 1906–1914 (London: Cassell, 1936).

FURTHER READING

Dutton, D. J., *Austen Chamberlain: Gentleman in Politics* (Bolton: Ross Anderson, 1985).
Petrie, Sir C., *The Life and Letters of the Right Hon Sir Austen Chamberlain*, 2 vols. (London: Cassell, 1939–40)
Thorpe, R. D., *The Uncrowned Prime Ministers* (London: Darkhorse, 1980).

DAVID DUTTON

Chamberlain, (Arthur) Neville (*b.* Edgbaston, Birmingham, 18 March 1869; *d.* Heckfield, Reading, 9 November 1940). Conservative politician and National Prime Minister. He served as Prime Minister for only three years, from May 1937 to May 1940, but they happened to be momentous years. Consequently, despite the brevity of his period in office, his record has been controversial. His numerous critics have despised him as the 'villain of appeasement', while his supporters have praised his valiant struggle for peace and clear-sighted appraisal of what war, even 'successful' war, would mean for Britain. At the time of his death, when Britain's future survival was still in great doubt, Chamberlain's reputation stood at a very low point. Subsequently, as historians have looked at his career in the round, it has revived somewhat. Even so, Chamberlain was a 'failure', not least in his own eyes. His 'struggle for peace' had led to a war which other policies might or might not have prevented. His conduct of that war seemed so uninspiring that parliamentary support began to ebb away. In May 1940 he reluctantly came to the conclusion that he ought to resign. Six months later, he was dead. Yet, in September 1938, when he apparently brought back 'peace in our time' from the Munich conference, his general popularity could scarcely have been higher. Triumph and disaster, however, were not concentrated for Chamberlain in three dramatic years. His achievement of the premiership at the age of 68 was not the straightforward accomplishment that a simple consideration of his record might suggest.

He seemed to start in life with many advantages. During his youth and early manhood, his father, Joseph Chamberlain, was one of the best-known public men in Britain. At the time of the South African War at the turn of the century, when he was Colonial Secretary in a Unionist government, Joseph Chamberlain was at the height of his influence. Here was the latest extraordinary twist in the career of an erstwhile Liberal/Radical former businessman who had broken with his party because of his opposition to Home Rule for Ireland. But in 1906 he was struck down by paralysis and played no further part in national politics. In the preceding few years, however, his strong advocacy of Tariff Reform caused as many problems for the Conservatives as his earlier opposition to Home Rule had caused for the Liberals. Joseph Chamberlain had not himself become Prime Minister, but he had split two major political parties. It was not a record which necessarily commended his offspring to their political contemporaries.

However, for the first 30 years of his life, the possibility that Neville would carry on the political reputation of his family seemed remote. It was his elder half-brother, Austen, who had been groomed by Joseph for this task. It was Austen who went to Cambridge and who had then spent time in France and Germany, before becoming a youthful MP and later, in 1903, a youthful Chancellor of the Exchequer.

The omens for Austen's future advancement looked good, though it was already clear that he did not find it easy to be his father's son.

Neville, by contrast, seemed destined for obscurity. His father – more someone to be admired from a distance than an intimate associate – sent him to Rugby, but he did not then go on to Cambridge or embark on a period of continental residence cultivating languages and political connections. Instead he went to Mason College (forerunner of the University of Birmingham) to study metallurgy and science, which he did competently. Then, at the age of 21, he was dispatched by his father to manage a sisal plantation in the Bahamas. There were hopes that it could be a considerable financial success; but seven years later, in 1897, Neville came home and the project was abandoned. Neville insisted that failure was due to his own poor business sense – an unnecessary assumption on his part. Still uncertain of his ultimate goals, he settled into Birmingham life, and his involvement in business brought him some personal confidence. He was elected to the city council, and within a short time found himself Lord Mayor. At the age of 42 he also married and seemed to grow in social confidence. In 1914 his father died and Neville seemed to be rapidly becoming the new 'Birmingham' Chamberlain, while Austen operated as the 'national' Chamberlain.

Still without a parliamentary seat, Chamberlain was summoned by Lloyd George, the new Prime Minister, to be director-general of National Service. His career appeared to have changed dramatically. However, having served for only seven months, he resigned in August 1917. He did not find it possible to work with Lloyd George and Lloyd George did not find it possible to work with him. Personal incompatibility was made worse by the fact that it was not clear what the newcomer was precisely expected to do. Critics suggested that Chamberlain ought to go back to Birmingham where his talents were more appropriately exercised: he was out of his depth in London. For his part, in his blacker moments, he rued the day in which he had allowed himself to leave the Midlands. Over the past decade he had rescued himself from failure and obscurity; in 1917 it looked as though he had to start all

Neville Chamberlain addressing the crowd at Heston after his return from Munich, September 1938

over again. Despair was not far away, particularly since his cousin Norman, to whom he was very close, had been killed in France.

In December 1918 Chamberlain was elected MP for Birmingham, Ladywood, and continued to represent this constituency until 1929. He then sat for Edgbaston until his death. It was late to start a Westminster career, but he had something to prove, at least to himself. It was only after the fall of Lloyd George in October 1922 that any serious possibility of advancement existed. Matters were complicated by the fact that Austen remained a coalitionist. However, Neville became Paymaster-General in the Bonar Law government. Governments came and went rapidly in these few years and there was little opportunity for legislative achievement, but Chamberlain's work in bringing about increased Conservative Party unity did not go unnoticed. When the

Conservatives won the general election in late 1924 with a clear majority, the way was at last open for him to show that 1917 had not been a true test of his ability. He could have become Chancellor of the Exchequer, but instead became Minister of Health and remained in that office until the end of the government in 1929. It was his tenure of this post that made his reputation with his colleagues. His personal knowledge of the workings of local government aided the important measures which he introduced in this area. It was typical that he drew up a full list at the outset of the measures he wished to introduce – and that he was to achieve almost all of them. His efficiency was formidable, but he did not seek to ingratiate himself. His attitude towards the Labour opposition was generally dismissive. He was a man who got things done. In private, he loved music and butterflies, but he kept such matters to himself. In opposition after 1929, his serious intentions were confirmed by his chairmanship of the Conservative Research Department.

In 1931 Chamberlain played a leading part in the negotiations that led to the establishment of the National Government, and in November he became Chancellor under Ramsay Mac-Donald. It was in this office that he consolidated his reputation as an administrator. He showed a gift for exposition, but displayed no tendency to be seduced by 'Keynesian' solutions to Britain's economic and financial difficulties in these years. He derived pleasure in 1932 from introducing measures of protection which he claimed would have gladdened his father's heart. At a time of international dislocation it was inevitable that the Chancellor would be drawn into areas of policy and cabinet discussion beyond what might be thought to be 'normal'. Chamberlain did not appear to be averse to enlarging his store of knowledge and his reputation at the same time. He therefore had views on all the international issues with which his colleagues wrestled – ranging from the Far East, to the Mediterranean, to Germany. He was widely believed to be the 'powerhouse' of the National Governments. After 1935, Stanley Baldwin could supply public comfort, while Chamberlain worked at the papers. Chamberlain had come to have great confidence in his own forensic powers. He also came to believe that his own insights and judgements were almost invariably right. Such a conviction is not without parallel among prominent politicians and need cause no surprise. What marked hm out was his belief that he could tackle the domestic and international difficulties which threatened to jeopardize the survival of the British Empire. Nobody of any consequence doubted that he was the logical choice to succeed Baldwin.

'Appeasement', which is so closely linked with the Chamberlain premiership, is a complex phenomenon. He did not invent it in 1937. However, he did bring the conviction of an elderly man that time was short. Viewed from any perspective, war would be a disaster; every effort should be made to avoid it by intelligent anticipation. The promotion of 'peaceful change' was not, in Chamberlain's mind, 'crawling to the dictators'; it was a sensible

programme which rational men, and even those who appeared to be irrational, would accept. In cabinet the Prime Minister was clearly in charge and was also determined not to permit bureaucratic opposition to his plans. He was prepared to take daring and dramatic initiatives – most notably in his flying visits to Germany in September 1938. There had to be 'rearmament' but it must not be allowed to upset the financial stability which Chamberlain himself had so assiduously achieved. His selfconfidence appeared not to waver, though it remains extremely difficult to judge what he really thought about Hitler's personality and intentions. When Chamberlain did appear to have 'won' peace in 1938, public opinion appeared to be behind him and be willing to overlook the price that others had paid for that achievement. In March 1939, however, the public mood began to change in the light of the German invasion of the remainder of Czecho-Slovakia. Chamberlain also changed, but still wished to avoid war. But there were apparently greater grounds for confidence that, if Hitler did march against Poland, Britain was in a better position to defend herself in any general war that ensued them than had been the case in 1938. Whether that claim is justified remains contentious. In any event, it was Chamberlain who in the end took Britain to war in September 1939 and who guided the country through the initial 'Phoney War'. It seemed increasingly apparent that he was not a natural 'war leader'. The debacle of the Norwegian campaign seemed to make that evident. He was not defeated in the House of Commons but suffered such a loss of support that he was persuaded that he could not continue.

Very unusually, therefore, Neville Chamberlain was a Prime Minister who neither won nor lost a general election. He remained a leader of the Conservative Party and gave Churchill loyal support for the last months of his life. More than that, some have argued that it was his stewardship of Britain's resources that enabled Churchill to keep up the fight over the subsequent 18 months. That is a large claim, but it may at least be suggested that the qualities of both Chamberlain and Churchill were appropriate to the particular difficulties that confronted them. Churchill was the only man of the hour in 1940. The victory he helped to achieve was a necessary one, but Chamberlain's assessment of the price of victory was perhaps shrewder.

FURTHER READING

Charmley, John, *Chamberlain and the Lost Peace* (London: John Curtis/Hodder and Stoughton, 1989).

Dilks, David, *Neville Chamberlain*, vol. 1: *Pioneering and Reform, 1869–1929* (Cambridge: Cambridge University Press, 1984).

Feiling, Keith, *The Life of Neville Chamberlain* (London: Macmillan, 1946).

Macleod, Iain, *Neville Chamberlain* (London: Muller, 1961).

KEITH ROBBINS

Chapple, Frank [Francis Joseph; Baron Chapple of Hoxton] (*b*. London, 8 August 1921). Trade-union leader. He was General Secretary of the Electrical, Electronic, Telecommunications and Plumbing Union (a merger of the Electrical Trades Union and the Plumbers' Union) from 1966 to 1984 and a member of the General Council of the TUC from 1971 to 1982 (he was Chairman in his final year). From 1965 to 1971 he served on the National Committee of the Labour Party.

Chapple's father was invalided out of World War I and made his living as a shoe repairer in Hoxton. He could neither read nor write. Frank left school at the age of 14 with a well-developed enthusiasm for racing pigeons. He started work as an apprentice electrician and joined the ETU and the Communist Party. It was not until 1943 that he was called up, serving in the Royal Electrical and Mechanical Engineers. Through the late 1940s and early 1950s he did a variety of electrical contracting jobs and was a keen union member, taking a vigorous part in its internal battles. Although puzzled by Hungary in 1956, he was still a communist. However, a subsequent trip to the Soviet Union helped persuade him to join the Labour Party. He became heavily involved in the struggle against communist control of the ETU; this finally came to the Courts and ballot-rigging was disclosed.

Two years later, in 1963, Chapple became Assistant Secretary of the ETU and in 1966 was appointed Secretary. In this capacity he played a major part in the 'cleansing' of the ETU and emerged as a major force on the right of the trade-union movement. On the General Council he became an exponent of 'realism' and was uninhibited in the expression of his views. In his autobiography, published in 1984, he described himself as a reluctant Labour Party member, in disagreement with the leadership on almost every major policy issue. On retiring from the EETPU he received a life peerage in 1985 and served as a director of Inner City Enterprises and other bodies. He also found himself with a little more time for his first love, racing pigeons.

WRITINGS

Sparks Fly! A Trade Union Life (London: Michael Joseph, 1984).

KEITH ROBBINS

Charles, Prince of Wales [Charles Philip Arthur George] (*b*. London, 14 November 1948). The dilemma facing Prince Charles, eldest son to Queen Elizabeth II and Prince Philip, Duke of Edinburgh, as with most previous male heirs to the throne, is one of finding a fitting and useful role in public life while waiting to succeed as monarch. In the 1980s he has partly resolved this problem by involving himself especially in youth development projects and taking a close interest in and speaking out forcefully on such issues as deprivation in the inner cities, conservation, ecology and modern architecture.

On the death of George VI in 1952, Charles became heir apparent and Duke of Cornwall. Since that time, as the second most important member of the royal family, a deep sense of duty has been instilled in him. Meanwhile, there have been determined attempts to present him as a modern prince. He is the first heir to the throne to have gone to a school, obtained a university degree, and, during his training in the armed services, been in command of his own ship, flown a supersonic jet and made a parachute jump.

In her essential but sometimes fraught relationship with the media, the Queen made

The Prince of Wales laying mortar on a commemorative brick during the inauguration of the first private self-build housing initiative in Tower Hamlets, London, September 1988

determined efforts to prevent the young Charles from being exposed to the press to the extent that she and her sister were in the 1930s. She was not always successful. During his first term at Cheam preparatory school, there were press stories concerning the nine-year-old prince on 68 of the 88 days. His next school, Gordonstoun, which Charles attended from 1962 to 1967, was far from Fleet Street and so, for some brief periods, he was out of the public gaze. Nevertheless in 1968, in response to growing criticisms of the royal family appearing too stuffy and remote, a deliberate decision was made by the Queen and her advisers to reshape their presentation to the public. Charles played a key role in this repackaging exercise. A television film, *Royal Family*, depicting the informal and domestic side of their life, was transmitted on the eve of Charles's Investiture as Prince of Wales. Charles was shown as a hard-working but unpompous prince. The Investiture itself, at Caernarfon Castle on 1 July 1969, was viewed worldwide by a television audience of some 200 million.

As well as affording splendid commercial opportunities and boosting tourism, grand royal occasions provide the few instances now when the world turns its eyes on Britain. The intense international interest in the activities of the royal family was best manifested on 29 July 1981, when Charles married Lady Diana Spencer. The wedding attracted the largest worldwide viewing audience ever: 109 companies were involved in transmitting the processions and ceremony to 750 million people in 74 countries.

The marriage of Charles was long awaited; no Prince of Wales, apart from his uncle (Edward VIII), had remained a bachelor for so long. There are two children from the marriage, Prince William (*b.* 1982) and Prince Harry (Henry) (*b.* 1984). The youth and beauty of Diana, Princess of Wales, who is 13 years younger than her husband, made her an immediate attraction for the media. She has become a leader of fashion, and very often a speech or a visit by Charles is overshadowed by the concentration of the press on his wife's dress or hair-style. This has resulted in a certain embarrassment for the Prince, who wishes to be seen as a serious and influential contributor to a number of contemporary social issues.

For 20 years there has been talk of what

job the Prince of Wales should undertake. Suggestions have ranged from his becoming Governor-General of Australia to taking a non-political post in the civil service. All have been considered and discarded. This does not mean that the Prince has been inactive. His concern for the disadvantaged was central to the setting up of the Prince's Trust. Officially launched in 1976, it aims at helping disadvantaged young people to help themselves by the provision of small, one-off grants. In the following year Charles became chairman of his mother's Silver Jubilee Appeal; £16 million was raised, which is used to fund young people who wish to carry out viable community projects. In 1985 he took over the presidency of BiC (Business in the Community), a body which looks to industry to provide money for community projects, with a special emphasis on the black community. It was estimated in 1987 that BiC was responsible for the creation of some 70,000 jobs. The Prince was also connected with the Youth Business Initiative which, in 1986, was merged into the Prince's Youth Business Trust, an organization established to help young people to set up businesses of their own.

These activities, together with his deep interest in architecture, the development of the inner cities, organic farming, and homeopathic medicine, have driven him in the direction of being part royal social worker, educationalist, ecologist and philosopher. In this respect, his career has been quite different from that of any previous Prince of Wales. If any comparison is to be made with an earlier member of the royal family, it is not with his father or grandfather but with his high-minded and serious great-great-great-grandfather, Albert, Prince Consort.

FURTHER READING

Hamilton, A., *The Real Charles* (London: Collins, 1988).
Holden, A., *Charles: a Biography* (London: Weidenfeld and Nicolson, 1988).

J. M. GOLBY

Cherwell, Lord. See LINDEMANN, F. A.

Churchill, Sir **Winston (Leonard Spencer)** (*b.* Woodstock, Oxfordshire, 30 November 1874; *d.* London, 24 January 1965). Coalition and Conservative Prime Minister and author. Churchill became Prime Minister in May 1940 at the age of 65. His appointment was the unexpected climax to a patchy career. He had been in the limelight from an early age and he had always bubbled with activity. He had known moments of triumph, but latterly he seemed to be spluttering inconsequentially against the tides of his age. The youthful Churchill, who had once sparkled so brightly, appeared to many of his contemporaries in the 1930s to have become an irascible and erratic failure. Then came the national disaster of 1940. Churchill himself sensed that he was walking with destiny. Suddenly, the setbacks and successes of previous decades fell into place. Everything in the past was now but a prelude to the future. He had written an account of his early life in 1930, but now 'my early life' extended to his mid-sixties. He would be the man who won the war. He would be the saviour of his country. And, defeated in 1945, he would again become Prime Minister between October 1951 and April 1955. He would be 90 when he died. He would be the greatest Englishman of his age.

Churchill was born at Blenheim Palace in Oxfordshire, the elder son of Lord Randolph Churchill, who was himself the third son of the 7th Duke of Marlborough. From an early age, Winston could not fail to be conscious of his family. To be a descendant of the great Marlborough gave a certain confidence approaching battle or confronting generals. In the person of his father, however, there was a more ambiguous inheritance. Lord Randolph had shone brightly in the mid-1880s. He was a Conservative Chancellor of the Exchequer in his mid-thirties but then his career collapsed. Ten years later, he was dead. Winston was 20. Even before syphilis had captured Randolph, his relationship with his son had been distant. Winston had not shone at Harrow and had only scraped into Sandhurst. It is not surprising, against this background, that he needed to grapple with his father's strange life. He wrote a two-volume biography which was published in 1906 and was a way of dealing publicly with a private puzzle. More generally, Winston tried to show that his father's low estimate of his own ability was wrong. Here, perhaps, the American strain in his background, with its impatient desire to be up and doing, showed. The English-speaking union which produced Winston blended uneasily English aristocratic arrogance with a Frenchified American unconventionality. The growling tone of voice, only occasionally accompanied by a scowling face, incompletely expressed an impious puckishness that lurked within. Churchill's career was to advance very rapidly, but he grew up very slowly.

He thirsted for excitement and went out of his way to find it. However, even when he saw action at the Battle of Omdurman and elsewhere, he was searching for words to describe it and newspapers to print them. His description of *The River War* (1899) filled two large volumes. Having resigned his commission in 1899, he went to South Africa as a war correspondent. It did no harm both to have been captured and to have escaped by the time he successfully presented himself to the electors of Oldham in the general election of 1900. Only in his mid-twenties, he was already a national figure of whom much was expected. Yet, in May 1904, he caused much astonishment by switching his allegiance to the Liberals. His belief in Free Trade was the ostensible issue, but also, allegedly, the Conservatism of his colleagues was not the Conservatism his father had espoused. Was Churchillian 'instability' showing itself?

His rise up the Liberal hierarchy was rapid. When Campbell-Bannerman formed his government at the end of 1905, Churchill became Under-Secretary for the Colonies. He had to speak in the Commons on behalf of the Colonial Secretary, who sat in the Lords. In public speeches, however, he by no means restricted himself to colonial matters. In 1908 he succeeded Lloyd George, with whom he was seen by Tories as on friendly terms, as President of the Board of Trade. He bombarded the Prime Minister with innovative proposals for social reform. He was not an 'intellectual' but he was adept at grasping the legislative possibilities in other men's ideas: labour exchanges and unemployment insurance. Still only 35, he was moved to the Home Office in 1910. He believed that the government should stand firm in the face of industrial unrest. In October 1911 he was transferred to the Admiralty, where he carried further the reforms initiated by Fisher. The enthusiasm which he brought to the Admiralty was regarded with suspicion in some Liberal circles, where it was taken as evidence that the Tory-soldier had not really changed his spots. On the other hand, the zeal with which he ordered the despatch of a battle squadron to take station off the Isle of Arran during the Ulster crisis in the spring of 1914 was seen by Tories as an unforgivable betrayal by a son whose father had proclaimed that the Orange card was the one to play.

When war came in 1914 Churchill responded eagerly to the challenge. His position was powerful and he was fertile with suggestions. However, it was his role in the Dardanelles expedition and the Gallipoli fiasco which proved his undoing. The amount of blame to be attributed to Churchill for shortcomings in planning and execution remains contentious, but he had to leave the Admiralty. The post of Chancellor of the Duchy of Lancaster was not an adequate substitute, and in 1915 he set off for France in command of a battalion of the Royal Scots Fusiliers. He thus became one of four British Prime Ministers to see active service in the Great War (the others were Attlee, Eden and Macmillan). It was Lloyd George who brought him back from France and appointed him Minister of Munitions in his new Coalition Government. Churchill ended the war quietly. The part he had played in its direction must have disappointed him. The Dardanelles failure continued to hang over him.

Churchill remained in the postwar Coalition, with varying responsibilities for War, Air, and the Colonies, until the government fell in October 1922. During this period he saw in the consolidation of Bolshevism a grave danger to civilization as he understood it. However, his pleas for full-scale intervention to defeat it were not successful in cabinet. No doubt his firm anti-Bolshevism played some part in his electoral defeat at Dundee in 1922. He used the time to write a five-volume history of the

Sir Winston and Lady Churchill with one of Sir Winston's lion cubs at London Zoo, July 1943

war under the title *The World Crisis*. Even if he was never re-elected to parliament, Churchill could earn money and a reputation from his pen. Return to parliament, at least as a Liberal, began to look problematic and, after several setbacks, it was not until 1924 that he was elected as a 'Constitutionalist' MP for Epping.

His return to the Conservative Party looked to be complete when, mysteriously, STANLEY BALDWIN appointed him Chancellor of the Exchequer. Three things stand out concerning his performance in this post. Firstly, he returned the country to the Gold Standard at its prewar parity. This decision was not mere caprice on his part. He took advice, though now it is normally thought to have been wrong. Secondly, he rigorously pruned the defence estimates, with particularly serious consequences for the navy. Thirdly, he played a prominent part in the defeat of the 1926 General Strike. He edited the official *British Gazette* and helped to organize the government's effective counter-measures. Churchill's allegedly provocative role in 1926 was linked by Labour with his role as Home Sec-

retary in 1911 to reinforce the notion that Churchill was not merely conservative, he was a reactionary.

The Conservatives left office in 1929, but, unlike many of his late colleagues, Churchill was not to return until 1939, and then only because of the outbreak of war. In opposition, the Conservatives ran into many personal and policy problems. Churchill had difficulties about Free Trade and was manifestly discontented. His rift with Baldwin occurred because the latter was willing to give support to the Labour Government's proposed constitutional reform in India. Such a course was anathema to Churchill. He knew India, at least the India of the late 1890s, and other people did not. He resigned from the party's Business Committee and tried, without much success, to mobilize backbench opinion in his support. After the formation of the National Government in 1931 there was no place for Churchill and he did not appear to want one. Instead, he wrote articles, travelled, was knocked down in an accident and occasionally appeared in the House of Commons. Like Lloyd George, who behaved similarly, he increasingly appeared to be a survivor from another era. It was unfortunate for Lloyd George that he did not have Marlborough as an ancestor. Churchill settled down to write a four-volume life, the last volume of which appeared in 1938. He surfaced politically only to campaign, again unsuccessfully, against the National Government's massive Government of India Bill. Baldwin, who had earlier described Churchill as a George III endowed with the eloquence of Edmund Burke, appeared to have the measure of the man. Churchill's support for Edward VIII during the 1936 Abdication Crisis looked quixotic. In this light, it is not perhaps surprising that his warnings about German rearmament and intentions could easily appear similarly ill-judged and exaggerated.

When war did come in September 1939 the prophet did receive some honour in his own country, at least to the extent of accepting an invitation to become again First Lord of the Admiralty. He threw himself into his work with characteristic energy, though there is a certain irony in the fact that the Norwegian fiasco in April 1940, which precipitated the downfall of Chamberlain and his own elevation to the premiership, was essentially a naval failure for which Churchill had ultimate responsibility. He became Prime Minister at a time of impending disaster. He used all his mental and physical resources to create a sense of common purpose. Every word and every gesture mattered. Labour was persuaded to join the government and a good working relationship was established with Attlee (see also ATTLEE, CLEMENT). Yet the government was not so much a formal inter-party coalition as a group of men revolving around Churchill. Such a situation had both advantages and disadvantages for the conduct of affairs and the despatch of business. Not everybody could work in the way Churchill worked. There is room for argument, too, about the scale and extent of prime ministerial intervention. It remains true, however, whatever legitimate criticisms in detail may be made, that extraordinary circumstances require extraordinary men.

In retrospect it appears that the 18 months after May 1940 constituted Churchill's finest hour. He galvanized a country to avoid defeat but he could not win the war. It was a fact he only reluctantly recognized. He extolled the merits of the English-speaking peoples. He encouraged the Atlantic partnership in every way, yet he had no wish to preside over the liquidation of the British Empire, even if that was what the Americans wanted. He realized, by the end of the war, that the Americans and the Russians might wish to deal directly with each other. Perhaps he had placed too much weight on his own extraordinarily intimate relationship with Roosevelt. During the war, too, he had praised and supported the Soviet Union, despite his own ideological preconceptions, but by its close he had become deeply apprehensive about Stalin's intentions. Could the Americans be made to see the danger in time?

Sadly for him, Churchill was not to guide British policy in the postwar era. The nation may have been grateful, but the mood of the time suggested that a new political direction was required. Churchill could not adapt to the new expectations. The legacy of his own career in the 1920s hindered him in a world which had come to believe that Beveridge was best. His defeat, therefore, is not as surprising as it appeared to many foreign observers.

It might have been better had he retired from day-to-day politics at this juncture. His reputation was at its height. He could have settled down to the major task of writing his history of the war untroubled by the need to revive a demoralized party. Churchill had never led a political party in his life and he was not going to change his habits in his early seventies merely because he was Leader of the Opposition. It would be up to younger men to devise strategies to roll back the tide of socialism. In the short term, given the government's majority, there was little prospect that any of its major legislation could be defeated in the Commons. Churchill did travel to the USA and detected the descent of an Iron Curtain in Europe. He also encouraged the notion of a United States of Europe, though Britain could not join. He knew that, even without power, he was still a world statesman. That was what he liked being.

His other enjoyment came from presiding over the writing of *The Second World War*, the first volume of which appeared in 1948 and the sixth and last in 1954. This work contributed to the award of the Nobel Prize for Literature in 1953. It was said of *The World Crisis* that Churchill had written an enormous book about himself and given it a strange title. The same remark applied less to the new history, though it was another strongly personal account. Despite its defects, it remains essential reading for any student of the war, and for anyone seeking to understand Churchill himself. He was the only one of the major wartime leaders to give a view from the inside. He never purported to be a philosopher or supposed that consistency was an absolute political virtue. Rather, he expressed his view of himself and, he believed, his country's view of itself, in his attempt to write history. Churchill was perhaps the last British Prime Minister to believe that history mattered. His *A History of the English-Speaking Peoples* appeared after his retirement.

In 1951 the Conservatives had a small but manageable majority, though Labour had obtained more votes. Churchill was not minded to set about dismantling the National Health Service or to restore the newly nationalized industries to private ownership. Opinions differ on his health and vitality during this Indian summer but, while some accounts of his decrepitude may be discounted, it was not to be expected that he would display boundless energy. Some of his younger colleagues grew restive. What kept him going was not mere obstinacy, though there was obstinacy, but the conviction that he could still be useful on the world stage, particularly in East–West relations where, he believed, he could be an effective broker. In the end, he had reluctantly to accept that neither Moscow nor Washington needed him.

In extreme old age, as honours were heaped upon him – though he declined a peerage to the end – he passed beyond the triumph and tragedy that he chronicled in the last volume of his war history. In retrospect, however, it appears that the country he saved was not the country he would have liked to have saved. He did not preside over the liquidation of the British Empire, but his successors did. The span of his life encompassed both the final phase of British imperial expansion and the empire's virtual disappearance. It is difficult, therefore, to decide in the last analysis whether the story of Winston Churchill is the story of success or failure.

FURTHER READING

Churchill, R. S., *Winston S. Churchill* (London: Heinemann): i: *Youth, 1874–1900* (1966); ii: *The Young Statesman, 1901–14* (1967).

Gilbert, Martin, *Winston S. Churchill* (London: Heinemann): iii: *1914–16* (1971); iv: *1917–22* (1975); v: *1922–39* (1976); vi: *Finest Hour* (1983); vii: *Road to Victory* (1986); viii: *Never Despair, 1945–65* (1988).

Pelling, H., *Winston Churchill* (London: Macmillan, 1974).

Taylor, A. J. P. et al., *Churchill: Four Faces and the Man* (London: Allen Lane, 1969).

KEITH ROBBINS

Citrine, Walter (McLennan) [Baron Citrine of Wembley] (*b.* Liverpool, 22 August 1897; *d.* Brixham, Devon, 22 January 1983). Trade unionist and public servant. He was General Secretary of the TUC from 1926 to 1946. He then accepted membership of the newly established National Coal Board and served until 1947. He was chairman of the British Electricity Authority for ten years and a director of the *Daily Herald* for more than 20 years. His administrative abilities were highly prized and he was a central figure in his two careers. Citrine's success stemmed from his extravagant capacity for self-discipline. He mastered shorthand at an early stage, because it might come in useful, and late in life was to be seen running down the stairs of the buildings in which he worked. He feared the corrupting influences of lifts and alcohol in equal measure. He kept full diaries, wrote books about his travels and about trade unionism, and published two volumes of autobiography.

Citrine's early life was spent on Merseyside. He was one of six children. His father's family were all seafarers, who were rather given to drink and to dying around the age of 85. His mother was a Scot from Arbroath who had come south to nurse the infant Duke of Westminster. He was educated only at an elementary school and left at the age of twelve and a half, but he had already become fascinated by words. His early jobs were in electrical contracting, including spells with Pilkingtons in St Helens and Cammel Laird in Birkenhead. In 1911, during the period of industrial upheaval on Merseyside, Citrine joined the Electrical Trades Union. He was already reading books on trade unionism and taking meticulous notes. In 1914 he was elected the first full-time district secretary of the ETU, and he picked up a great deal of experience of industrial relations on Merseyside throughout the war. In the 1918 general election he stood for Labour in Wallasey but the experience put him off the idea of a parliamentary career. Promotion followed fast. In 1920 he was elected Assistant General Secretary of his union and worked in Manchester. Four years later he moved to London as Assistant General Secretary of the TUC, and in 1926, having already acted in this capacity for some months, he became General Secretary.

It was Citrine's tenure of the position that gave it significance in the Labour movement and beyond. Until 1923 it had been a part-time appointment, usually held by a prominent trade unionist. Citrine's immediate predecessor had begun to argue that the TUC needed a full-time official of proven administrative capacity. Citrine fitted that bill admirably, and over the next 20 years he sought to equip the trade-union movement with an effective central administration capable of servicing its needs in its dealings with employers and with government. To take over in the year of the General Strike was perhaps fortunate. After that shattering experience – Citrine kept a record of events from his perspective in his diary – there was a need to reconsider the role and structure of the TUC altogether. What was the function of the General Council and what, if any, was its authority in relation to individual unions? Citrine put forward suggestions, though he was well aware that he could be said to be seeking to increase the authority of his office. As the years passed, his authority did grow because he was always well prepared and conducted meetings calmly. Such efficiency suggested that he was a man of the right and so, in general terms, he was. He eschewed rhetoric and sought to establish personal relations both with employers and with the National Government throughout the 1930s. He accepted a knighthood – though he declined a peerage – from Ramsay MacDonald. He found Neville Chamberlain open and frank in private conversation and quite unlike the general image of him accepted in the Labour movement. In 1938 Citrine accepted an invitation to serve on the Royal Commission investigating social and economic conditions in the West Indies and this took him away from Britain at a time of increasing international tension.

Citrine's perspective had never been narrowly national. He liked travelling and paid a number of visits to continental Europe and the USA. He accepted the chairmanship of the World Anti-Nazi Council, a body less impressive than its name suggests, but one which nevertheless played some part in Britain in alerting public opinion to what was going on in Germany. His greatest foreign interest, however, was in the Soviet Union. He paid his first visit there in 1925 with a TUC delegation, and over the years, in rather different circumstances, he was to pay six visits altogether. As his published impressions make clear, he was sympathetic to the Soviet experiment but by no means uncritical of what was actually happening.

During World War II his accumulated experience and contacts both in Britain and abroad meant that he was frequently employed on important missions – to the USA and the Soviet Union. His cooperation with Ernest Bevin, who had become Minister of Labour, was reasonably harmonious and productive. He declined to join the government but accepted an invitation to become a Privy Councillor. In the latter stages of the war he began, domestically, to prepare the TUC for the 'full employment' which could be anticipated in peacetime and, internationally, for a new World Federation of Trades Unions which, it was hoped, would give the workers of the world a new opportunity to unite. Before this latter project came to grief, however, Citrine left the TUC and began his new career in nationalized industries.

Given his background and sympathies, Citrine was an ideal person from the standpoint of the Labour Government to serve both the coal and the electricity industry. His role in his new capacities was inevitably less public, but he brought to it a determination to inject notions of partnership in working procedures. Although he was now on the other side of the table, he tried still to understand and respect trade-union perspectives. His postwar experience led him to reflect in print again on the role of the TUC and trade unionism generally in a world rather different from that which he had entered 50 years earlier. Citrine had accepted a peerage in 1946, but it was only in the latter years that he played any significant part in the proceedings of the House of Lords. The primary focus of his attention remained what it had been throughout his life – the world of industry, seen from both sides. Not for nothing was he the author of *The ABC of Chairmanship* (1939).

WRITINGS

Men and Work (London: Hutchinson, 1964).
Two Careers (London: Hutchinson, 1967).

KEITH ROBBINS

Coggan, (Frederick) Donald [Lord Coggan of Canterbury] (*b.* London, 9 October 1909). Archbishop of Canterbury. Coggan, an advocate of evangelism and a champion of ecumenicism, was Archbishop from January 1974 to January 1980. His family came from Somerset and was involved in commerce. His ecclesiastical roots lay in the Church of England's evangelical wing but his education at St John's College, Cambridge (1928–31), where he studied oriental languages, and experience gained as an assistant lecturer in Semitic languages and literature at Manchester University (1931–4) encouraged a broadening of his theological sympathies which marked him out as a potential national Church leader. In 1934 he moved to Wycliffe Hall, Oxford, in preparation for ordination. During 1935, while serving as a curate in Islington, he was both ordained and married, and his career from 1936 to 1954 lay in theological college teaching and administration.

Coggan's appointment to the bishopric of Bradford in 1955 was part of a subsequently more general trend whereby the Anglican Church increasingly recruited leaders from among its own theological college teachers. Service in Bradford further developed exceptional pastoral, teaching and administrative skills which, together with widening ecclesiastical concerns, accounted for his translation to the Archbishopric of York (1961) and succession to Michael Ramsey as Archbishop of Canterbury. This primacy was particularly characterized by a continuing preoccupation with evangelism, support for the ordaining of women, the strengthening of links with the leaders of other Christian communities, resistance to increasing partisanship within his own communion, and a concern for the reaffirmation of Christian values in family and public life. The last underlay his 'Call to the Nation' (1975), which fostered some debate about Christian responses to contemporary materialism. Critics maintained that 'the Call' revealed an unduly simplistic and individualistic approach to public issues which betrayed a characteristic lack of prior consultation and preparation. But it also pointed to some re-awakening of political awareness among Anglican evangelicals who, in the twentieth century, had largely eschewed such concerns.

FURTHER READING

Medhurst, K. N. and Moyser, G. H., *The Church and Politics in a Secular Age* (Oxford: Oxford University Press, 1988).
Pawley, M., *Donald Coggan* (London: SPCK, 1987).

K. N. MEDHURST

Cole, G(eorge) D(ouglas) H(oward) (*b.* Cambridge, 25 September 1889; *d.* London, 14 January 1959). Leading left-wing intellectual and prolific author. He came to prominence during the second decade of the century as the theorist of guild socialism, a doctrine of industrial and social self-government as an alternative to either capitalism or state socialism. He remained prominent thereafter as a leading, if maverick, intellectual of the Labour movement. A polymath, he wrote widely, and held academic posts, in several disciplines.

If the young Cole had gone into the family

business, he would have become an estate agent in Ealing. From the first, though, he set his own course. After St Paul's School, where a reading of William Morris took him straight from Toryism to socialism, he went to Balliol College, Oxford, and into undergraduate Fabianism (which he redefined in William Morris terms). Then, in the period just before World War I, Cole's 'Oxford group' tried to win over the Fabian Society from its Webbian state socialism to its own version of industrial democracy and political pluralism known as guild socialism. Having failed, Cole resigned from the Fabian Society in 1915, but in a stream of books, as well as in his work for the Fabian (later Labour) Research Department, continued to press the guild socialist case.

This case won many converts, and influenced the reorganized Labour Party (of which Cole was research secretary for a period), but lost momentum from the early 1920s. Cole remained a guild socialist in essentials, but turned his attention to servicing the needs of the developing Labour Party from the perspective of what he once described as a 'loyal grouser'. As Reader in Economics at Oxford after 1925, he offered a continuous stream of economic advice of a proto-Keynesian kind on the slump and unemployment, while his 'Cole Group' at Oxford established itself as a focus for young left-wing intellectuals. The decline and fall of the second Labour Government spurred him into a new burst of activity, founding the Society for Socialist Inquiry and Propaganda (soon translated into the Socialist League) and then the New Fabian Research Bureau, designed to equip Labour with new thinking and new policies. During the 1930s his prodigious output included a series of massive 'Guides for the Intelligent Man' on contemporary issues. At the end of the 1930s he resurrected the moribund Fabian Society, and during the war directed the Nuffield Social Reconstruction Survey. In 1944 he was appointed as the first Chichele Professor of Social and Political Theory at Oxford, a post he held until retirement in 1957.

Cole's influence was felt in every institution of the Labour movement: Labour Party, trade unions, Fabian Society, *New Statesman* and Workers' Educational Association. He was also a socialist gadfly who irritated these institutions with a series of ginger groups. His wider influence came through his teaching and many books, from his early guild socialist writings, through his historical studies (for example, of William Cobbett and of English social history) and commentaries on current social problems, to the multi-volumed history of socialist thought which he produced in the 1950s. Through all this work he was the persistent advocate of a decentralist, pluralist socialism, a vision which made Cole seem eccentric during most of his lifetime but which has made him a source of renewed interest subsequently.

Cole was a cold fish with warm human passions (though these were reserved for humanity in general rather than human beings in particular, as the biographical study by his wife, Margaret, makes disarmingly clear). He combined poetry with politics and, for diversion, wrote detective stories with his wife. His energy was the more remarkable because of persistent ill-health associated with diabetes. 'With a Bolshevik soul in a Fabian muzzle / Mr G. D. H. Cole is a bit of a puzzle': this was Maurice Reckitt's early verdict in verse on this 'sensible extremist' (Cole's own phrase), who was clearly a simple, complex man of enduring commitments.

FURTHER READING

Carpenter, L. P., *G. D. H. Cole: an Intellectual Biography* (Cambridge: Cambridge University Press, 1973).
Cole, M., *The Life of G. D. H. Cole* (London: Macmillan, 1971).
Wright, A. W., *G. D. H. Cole and Socialist Democracy* (Oxford: Clarendon Press, 1979).

ANTHONY WRIGHT

Cooper, (Alfred) Duff [Lord Norwich] (*b.* London, 22 February 1890; *d.* at sea, 1 January 1954). Conservative politician and Ambassador to France. His chief claims to fame are that in 1931 he saved Baldwin's career by winning the St George's by-election, and in 1938 he destroyed his own by resigning from Chamberlain's cabinet in protest at the Munich agreement.

The son of a surgeon and a duke's déclassé sister, Cooper entered the Foreign Office after a conventional career at Eton and Oxford. Ambition led him towards a political career, from which his own profligacy seemed to bar him. His wife, the fabulously beautiful Lady Diana Manners, provided from her stage career the wherewithal to overcome this obstacle, and election to the Commons in 1924 was followed by a brilliant maiden speech which marked him out as a 'coming man'. But, as so often with Cooper's career, initial promise was not sustained by hard work. Losing his seat in 1929, he made a spectacular come-back in the St George's by-election in 1931, which saved Baldwin.

As Minister for War and First Lord of the Admiralty between 1935 and 1938, Cooper strove to equip Britain for the war against Germany which he was sure would come. His combative political manner and his hedonistic life style told against his political effectiveness, but unable 'to swallow' the Munich agreement he resigned from the government, making a brilliant resignation speech; he had neither the energy nor the ambition to follow this up. Churchill brought him back into the cabinet in 1940, but after successive failures at the Ministry of Information and in Singapore he returned to diplomacy.

As Ambassador to France from 1944 to 1947 Cooper sought not only to mend the fences broken by the bad relations between Churchill and de Gaulle, but also to argue for an Anglo-French alliance as the cornerstone of a Western European alliance. His efforts produced the treaty of Dunkirk in 1947. Cooper's grand seigneurial manner and Lady Diana's social life brought to the embassy a touch of the eighteenth century, which was Cooper's spiritual home. He did not repine, finding in literature and pretty women ample consolations. He died suddenly, at sea, in 1954, but not before producing *Old Men Forget* (1953), one of the best-written volumes of memoirs to come from a modern politician.

FURTHER READING

Charmley, John, *Duff Cooper* (London: Weidenfeld and Nicolson, 1986).

JOHN CHARMLEY

Cousins, Frank (*b.* Bulwell, Nottinghamshire, 6 September 1904; *d.* 11 June 1986). Trade-union leader. He was General Secretary of the Transport and General Workers Union from 1956 to 1969. He was also, briefly, Minister of Technology in the 1964 Labour Government, and a prominent advocate of nuclear disarmament.

Cousins grew up in Doncaster and followed his father into the mines in September 1918 after a wartime elementary schooling. A few years later he left the pit and drifted from job to job throughout the 1920s. He then became a long-distance lorry driver. His increasing involvement in union affairs led to his appointment as a full-time official of the TGWU in July 1938. His work was in South Yorkshire but in 1944 he came to London as national officer for the Road Transport Commercial group within the union. Demobilization, the expansion of road transport and Cousins's own energy combined to boost the union's road-haulage membership. Cousins became that group's national secretary in 1948, but he was regarded by Arthur Deakin, the General Secretary, with suspicion. Deakin did not like communists and thought that Cousins did not dislike them sufficiently. However, a series of deaths in the mid-1950s unexpectedly opened the way for Cousins's rapid promotion and election to the general secretaryship in May 1956.

Cousins's triumph was more than personal. It was taken to symbolize a new impatience and militancy in the trade-union movement as a whole. The domination of the TGWU by Bevin and then by Deakin was at an end. Cousins also had views about international affairs which did not accord with the orthodoxy established in the postwar decade under Tewson as TUC General Secretary. In 1958 he found himself conducting a bus strike in a more 'confrontational' atmosphere than had accompanied other strikes under Conservative governments. He was deeply disappointed by Labour's third election defeat in October 1959 but refused to believe that his 'militancy' had been a contributory cause.

Cousins played a leading part in defeating 'revisionism' within the Labour Party. His espousal of nuclear disarmament added to his prominence. The TGWU, under his leadership, declared itself firmly opposed to any idea of basing British defence policy on nuclear strategy. His critics believed that he was tearing Labour asunder. Whatever they felt about him, in 1960–1 Cousins was the man of the moment. However, he lost the vote in 1961 at Blackpool on the nuclear issue. Thereafter, slowly, it was time to rescue Labour before the next election. Under Woodcock's prompting, though against Cousins's wishes, the TUC did join the National Economic Development Council when it was set up in 1962. Some, including Woodcock, believed that a more 'statesmanlike' Cousins was emerging. It was the Cousins who was offered the new post of Minister of Technology by Harold Wilson in 1964. He was in two minds about accepting, but in the end agreed. He remained in office until July 1966. It was an unhappy and unsuccessful period. Cousins was always uncomfortable in the Commons and that mattered. Equally, he was uneasy about the general tone of the government and found collective responsibility difficult to accept. He had never resigned from the TGWU. In the years of Wilson government that remained, Cousins re-emerged with something of his old fire as a critic of its wages policy and of the proposals for trade-union reform embodied in 'In Place of Strife' (1969). After leaving the TGWU in 1969 Cousins became full-time chairman of the Community Relations Commission, but that did not work out happily and in November 1970 he resigned.

Cousins was the most dynamic trade-union leader to emerge in Britain after 1945. He appeared to be setting the agenda for the 1960s, but in the end he was disappointed with Harold Wilson, the Labour Government and himself.

FURTHER READING

Goodman, G., *The Awkward Warrior: Frank Cousins: his Life and Times* (London: Davis-Poynter, 1979).

KEITH ROBBINS

Craig, Sir **James** [Viscount Craigavon] (*b.* Tyrella, Co. Down, 8 January 1871; *d.* Glencraig, Co. Down, 24 November 1940). Prime Minister of Northern Ireland. During his premiership (1921–40) Craig successfully impressed his personality on the institutions of devolved government in Ulster in the interwar period. In February 1921, shortly before becoming Prime Minister, he declared: 'The rights of the minority must be sacred to the majority . . . it will only be by broad views, tolerant ideas and a real desire for liberty of conscience that we here can make an ideal of the Parliament and executive.' But his political life was dominated by a fear of internal Protestant schism, and unfortunately, in his latter and least impressive years (more particularly in the early 1930s), he found it difficult to maintain this early spirit, and his rhetoric and that of his ministers caused offence within the Northern Irish Catholic and nationalist minority community.

Craig was the son of a Presbyterian whisky millionaire and was educated at Merchiston in Edinburgh. In 1906 he won his parliamentary seat (for Down East, which he held until 1918) in a close contest with an agrarian radical Unionist, James Woods; his speeches on the land question in this period place him firmly in the realistic and reformist wing of Unionism. Amid the ranks of Conservative and Unionist MPs demoralized and decimated by the Liberal landslide, the energetic Craig found it relatively easy to make a name for himself at Westminster, principally as an energetic opponent of Home Rule. Devolution for Northern Ireland after 1921 ended this phase of his career. Although, like many other Unionists, Craig was reluctant to accept such a settlement of the Irish question, he rapidly made a virtue of necessity. His political concerns became increasingly parochial and 'little Ulsterist' in outlook, over-responsive to almost any non-Catholic pressure groups in the province, while remaining more or less indifferent to the London Treasury and to the wider interests of Great Britain and the empire. He justified his attitudes by reference to the violence and disorder which London had left him to deal with in the early 1920s.

As the first Prime Minister for Northern Ireland, Craig was closest to ministers such as R. Dawson Bates and J. M. Andrews who had a markedly suspicious attitude towards

Catholics. He also favoured a rough and ready vulgar patrimonial Keynesianism. Both attitudes infuriated Whitehall officialdom, though London was reassured by the existence of other ministers, notably Craig's Deputy Prime Minister and Minister of Finance, Hugh Pollock, who was more liberal on sectarian questions and more conservative economically. In 1922 S. G. Tallents described Craig in a report for the British cabinet as having 'a great desire to do the right and important thing: not a clever man but one of sound judgement and can realise a big issue.' Craig in this period was prepared to attempt to reach agreements with the nationalist leader Michael Collins, though his efforts were thwarted both by extreme republican provocation and loyalist grass-roots militancy.

After 1925, however – the Irish civil war having contributed to the isolation of northern nationalism – Craig rarely bothered himself with conciliatory gestures. As the South moved towards the adoption in 1937 of what one of its ministers (Sean McEntee) was happy to describe as 'a Catholic constitution for a Catholic state', Craig was equally happy to talk of a Protestant Parliament for a Protestant people. His style of work became increasingly casual; he distributed 'bones' to the 'dogs', as he once described his operation of the spoils system. Yet through all this Craig adhered to one idea – the notion of economic and social parity between Northern Ireland and Great Britain. Paradoxically, the most positive legacy of the Stormont experience in political devolution was the economic and administrative integration of Northern Ireland within the United Kingdom, a development which permitted a significantly improved standard of life for Ulster's citizens. The distinctive legislation of the devolved parliament, on the other hand, tended to exacerbate communal differences.

Craig, in his earlier years, enjoyed a promising career outside Ulster. From 1900 to 1902 he was a brave lieutenant-colonel with the Imperial Yeomanry in South Africa, and by 1920 he had become Parliamentary and Financial Secretary to the Admiralty. It is hard to resist the conclusion that the return to Ulster narrowed his horizons: in this he resembled his great local nationalist rival Joe Devlin, who had,

if anything, an even more promising Westminster career from 1900 to 1918, and who was equally shrivelled by the devolution experiment which made him a mere local tribal leader.

FURTHER READING

Bew, Paul, 'A Protestant parliament and a Protestant state: some reflections on government and minority in Ulster 1921–43', in *Parliament and Community*, ed. Art Cosgrove and J. I. McGuire (Belfast and Salem, Conn.: Appletree Press, 1983).

——, *Conflict and Conciliation in Ireland 1890–1910* (Oxford: Clarendon Press, 1987).

Buckland, Patrick, *The Factory of Grievances: Devolved Government in Northern Ireland 1921–39* (Dublin: Gill and Macmillan, 1979).

——, *James Craig* (Dublin: Gill and Macmillan, 1980).

Jackson, A., *The Ulster Party: Irish Unionists and the British House of Commons* (Oxford: Clarendon Press, 1988).

PAUL A. E. BEW

Cripps, Sir **(Richard) Stafford** (*b.* London, 24 April 1889; *d.* Switzerland, 21 April 1952). Labour Chancellor of the Exchequer. As Chancellor from November 1947 to October 1950, Cripps did more than anyone else to ensure Britain's economic recovery after World War II. At the Treasury he was a key member, with Bevin at the Foreign Office and Attlee at Number Ten, of a triumvirate that was one of the most effective combinations in the history of British government.

Cripps grew up in comfortable circumstances but with a strong tradition of public service on both sides of his family. His father was a successful barrister and Tory MP who migrated to the Labour Party and served, as Lord Parmoor, in the two MacDonald cabinets of 1924 and 1929–31. His mother died when he was four; she was one of the celebrated Potter sisters, of whom the most distinguished was Beatrice (Mrs Sidney) Webb. Cripps was educated at Winchester and University College, London, where he studied chemistry with distinction. But his intention had always been to follow his father to the Bar, which he did immediately after his marriage in 1911 to

Isabel Swithinbank at an unconventionally early age. The marriage was to prove the prop on which much of his career was to rest.

Cripps joined the Red Cross at the outbreak of war in 1914 and served in France until he was recalled in the spring of 1915 to put his scientific training to use as assistant superintendent of a vast explosives factory at Queensferry. His health soon broke down. Two years of serious invalidism left him impaired for the rest of his life and led to the vegetarianism, nature cures and special techniques of exercise for which he came to be well known.

His return to the Bar in 1919 was soon crowned with success, and long before he left it for good in 1939 he had established himself as the leading figure in complex cases, where his powers of logical analysis and ability to state a case clearly were at a premium. Apart from his work, he had only two interests in the 1920s: giving expression of a deep Christian faith, particularly by participation in the affairs of the embryonic World Council of Churches, and the pursuit of quiet country interests at his home in the Cotswolds.

His mind was, however, moving towards politics, and in the summer of 1929 he was persuaded by Herbert Morrison to join the Labour Party. An astonishing transformation of his circumstances then followed. In October 1930 the post of Solicitor-General fell vacant and, there being no suitable candidate already in the Commons, Ramsay MacDonald decided to appoint Cripps. A seat was found for him at East Bristol, which was so safe that he held on to it in the disaster that struck the Labour Party at the general election of 1931. At once he found himself sharing the leadership of the party in the Commons with Lansbury and Attlee, the only other survivors with frontbench experience. But the transformation then went further and deeper. With all the fervour of a convert, Cripps reacted to the events of 1931 by moving rapidly to the left wing of the Labour Party. He was soon the most prominent member of the Socialist League, advocating policies which implied that ordinary constitutional processes might need to be suspended to ensure the establishment of a socialist society in Britain. As the menace of Hitler became more

Sir Stafford Cripps outside the Foreign Office, London, June 1941

apparent, his aim shifted to the establishment of a Popular Front to include the communists.

Cripps was therefore at the centre of most of the disputes that rocked Labour during this period, supported by many of the party's rank and file but bitterly opposed by those leaders, among whom Bevin was pre-eminent, whose aim was electoral and political rehabilitation. The end came in January 1939 when Cripps was expelled from the party. He was not readmitted until 1945.

At the outbreak of war in 1939 Cripps was impatient to be of use. Finding no outlet for his talents in domestic politics, he went on a world tour during which he discussed the problems that the war seemed likely to create with the principal figures in India, China, the Soviet

Union and the USA. In part as a consequence of the views which he expressed on his return, Churchill asked him to go to Moscow as ambassador in June 1940. Months of frustration followed. Cripps found it impossible to make fruitful contact with the Russian leaders and became increasingly clear-eyed about the system over which they presided. But he remained staunch to his view that an exceptional effort should be made to wean Stalin from the close relationship with the Germans that had been forged in 1939. His reward came after Hitler attacked Russia in June 1941. A flurry of Anglo-Russian diplomatic activity was followed, in January 1942, by a triumphal return to the *de facto* leadership of the wave of left-wing enthusiasm which Russian resistance had engendered.

Cripps entered the War Cabinet as Leader of the Commons and Lord Privy Seal in February 1942, but was soon on his way to India. His task was to obtain Indian support in the desperate circumstances created by Japanese military success in return for a promise of self-government after victory had been achieved. The mission was a failure. Cripps had a weak hand to play. Churchill's attitude was at best ambivalent, and Gandhi in particular among the Indian leaders proved obdurate. But although Cripps returned empty handed, his mission had left little room for doubt that India would achieve a large measure of independence once the war was over.

There was little respite from the catalogue of British military failure during most of 1942 and, after India, Cripps was soon engaged in a critique of Churchill's highly personal direction of the war, both military and civil. The matter was effectively resolved in Churchill's favour by Montgomery's victory over Rommel at El Alamein in November 1942. Cripps left the War Cabinet to become Minister of Aircraft Production until the break-up of the coalition in May 1945. But he was increasingly able to put his detachment from both the Labour Party and the central direction of the war to good use in the freedom with which he spoke of his vision of what a postwar government might achieve.

Attlee invited Cripps to become President of the Board of Trade after the Labour Party's victory at the general election of 1945 (see also ATTLEE, CLEMENT); in effect the post was that of Minister for Industry, with the remit of converting industry from war to peace and achieving the levels of production and exports which were needed if any kind of prosperity was to be assured. For Cripps, it was a task that matched his talents. He had always been under compulsion to tackle problems almost as quickly as they had been discerned, but whereas in the 1930s he had been driven by ideology he was now seen increasingly as a minister who concentrated on problems in themselves and was capable of speaking beyond party to the nation. His speeches became more and more a mixture of sermon, arguing moral imperatives, and lecture, expounding the nature of the country's economic problems.

The one major episode which took him away from the Board of Trade was his leadership of the cabinet mission that went to India in the spring of 1946. For all the energy and advocacy that Cripps brought to the task, the mission was a failure, bringing to an end all hope of agreement on a federal structure which might have held the Indian subcontinent together. Partition followed in 1947. Cripps was left with the paradox of having had two failures in India which yet were crowned with the achievement of independence, albeit at a cost which he had feared and striven to avert.

The Labour Government was shaken to its foundations in 1947, firstly by a fuel crisis and then by a run on the pound in the summer, when sterling became fully convertible under the terms of the loan agreement negotiated with the USA in 1945. Cripps emerged as the one man in the government with a grip decisive enough to give a lead to a faltering economy. Attlee was never at his best in economic matters, and Cripps, with some support from other ministers, determined to declare lack of confidence in him. Bevin decided the matter by standing by the Prime Minister. Cripps emerged from the confrontation defeated but promoted to the new post of Minister of Economic Affairs. The infant ministry did not last long. Within two months it was absorbed into the Treasury, Cripps having become Chancellor on the resignation of HUGH DALTON who, on 12 November, had committed the indiscretion of a budgetary leak. For the next three years Cripps exercised the authority of an economic supremo.

In popular recollection these were the years of austerity in which Cripps, who presided over them, gave full rein to his own puritanism and self-denial, inflicting on the country levels of rationing for food, clothing and other necessities that were at wartime levels or worse. But Cripps argued that the country's economic plight was so serious that there was no alternative to the tight control of consumption if the *sine qua non* of a rapid growth of production and a higher level of exports than Britain had known for decades was to be achieved. To these ends there was much admonition by him on the need for managerial efficiency and the use of up-to-date technology. But Cripps was also required to finance and defend the jewels in Labour's crown, the implementation of the Beveridge Report and the setting up of the National Health Service, as well as many lesser features of the welfare state. Nor could there be any going back on the policy of 'fair shares' which had figured so largely in Labour's appeal at the election of 1945.

The Marshall Aid Programme greatly eased problems after mid-1948, and Cripps still had at hand many of the direct controls which were a legacy of the war years. But more significant was his ability to take advantage of the social discipline created by the war, with its expectation that the government, where it could not command, would certainly give a lead. By strength of argument and moral fever Cripps persuaded the trade unions in early 1948 to accept a voluntary wages freeze in return for getting industry to hold dividends, and then kept both sides to the agreement for more than two years.

This was an exemplification of Cripps's approach. There was little by way of major innovation in his policies but they were argued with such persuasiveness and conviction that it seemed at times as though the economy was being driven by the moral fervour of one man. But in pushing so hard for economic recovery Cripps also discarded many of the dogmas of socialist doctrine. His principal weapons were the management of demand through the budget, the control of investment and the encouragement of collaboration between government, industry and the unions in what soon came to be termed 'the mixed economy'. Cripps's one major error was his opposition to the devaluation of the pound in 1949 when it had become all but unavoidable. By then he was a sick man.

Cripps had always been a formidably hard worker. An early riser, he invariably got through half a day's work before most ministers were at their breakfasts. The effect on a weak constitution had often necessitated periods of withdrawal for rest and recuperation. From 1949 onwards the price to be paid for such effort became ever more evident, and by the summer of 1950 Cripps was very ill indeed. He resigned from office on 20 October and died six months later.

Few politicians can begin to match Cripps in the degree to which he brought both intellectual brilliance and a strength of moral conviction to bear on the business of government. But he stood aloof from much of the activity of the political parties and his political judgement was often naïve. If he had died in 1946 he would have been judged an interesting failure. By the time of his resignation in 1950 he had demonstrated his possession of the capacity, command and courage that go to make a great minister. After the Attlee government's false start, Cripps became the main architect of economic recovery, charting the course which was to be broadly followed by succeeding governments for the next quarter of a century.

FURTHER READING

Cairncross, A., *Years of Recovery: British Economic Policy 1945–51* (London: Methuen, 1985).
Cooke, C., *The Life of Richard Stafford Cripps* (London: Hodder and Stoughton, 1957).
Morgan, K. O., *Labour People* (Oxford: Oxford University Press, 1987).

MAURICE SHOCK

Crosland, (Charles) Anthony (Raven) (*b.* St Leonard's-on-Sea, Sussex, 29 August 1918; *d.* Oxford, 19 February 1977). Socialist writer and politician. His reputation was based on *The Future of Socialism* (1956), in which he argued the case for greater social equality. He later rose to hold high office in successive Labour governments.

The son of a senior civil servant, Crosland had a distinguished undergraduate career at Oxford which was interrupted by World War II. Military service served to deepen his socialist commitment, and in 1950 he abandoned a promising academic career as an Oxford economist to become MP for South Gloucestershire. In 1956 he published the work which established his reputation as a writer, *The Future of Socialism*, and his growing influence within Labour ranks was reflected in the series of ministerial offices he held in the first Wilson administration of 1964–70. These included posts at the Department of Education and Science and the Board of Trade. In opposition after 1970, Crosland made his concern about the urgent need for new directions in Labour policy evident in a new collection of published essays, *Socialism Now* (1974). With Harold Wilson back at Downing Street in 1974, he spent the next two years as Secretary of State for the Environment. In spite of his poor showing in the party's leadership contest in 1976, he quickly achieved further promotion. The new Prime Minister, James Callaghan, appointed him Foreign Secretary, a post he was to hold until he was suddenly struck down by an unexpected illness in 1977.

Crosland will be remembered above all as a socialist writer. *The Future of Socialism* – the culmination of the youthful, flamboyant stage of his career – was the most significant product of 'revisionism' within the Labour Party in the 1950s. Crosland set out to examine what was wrong with postwar Britain and what could be done about it. He concluded that the main goal within a more affluent society was the attainment of greater social equality. His claim that the old-style, Morrisonian nationalization had become largely irrelevant to socialist advance inevitably antagonized the Labour left. But the egalitarian and libertarian tone of his writing was unmistakable. His commitment to the breaking down of social-class barriers appealed to a broad band of progressive opinion. And although it was criticized for assuming too readily that Keynesian demand management would ensure uninterrupted economic growth, the power of Crosland's work made it a vital point of reference for the moderate left over the next two decades.

Unlike many left-wing writers, Crosland was also greatly involved with translating ideas into practical reality. He was a conscientious and effective administrator. His years of ministerial office on the whole produced solid achievements: the stimulus given, for example, to the introduction of comprehensive secondary education. Within the Labour Party, Crosland had been a close friend of Hugh Gaitskell, but he gradually became more estranged from his moderate allies, especially over his noncommittal attitude towards British entry into the EEC. By the 1970s he had moved to the centre-left of the party, and was out of sympathy with those who favoured the establishment of a new social democratic grouping in British politics. He remained to the end of his life deeply attached to the working-class constituents of Grimsby, the seat he represented from 1959 onwards. Crosland's distinctive legacy was the idea that socialism was still relevant to the needs of contemporary British society, and should involve greater enjoyment of everyday pleasures. 'Total abstinence and a good filing system', he wrote in 1956, 'are not now the right sign-posts to the socialist Utopia: or at least, if they are, some of us will fall by the wayside.'

FURTHER READING

Crosland, S., *Tony Crosland* (London: Jonathan Cape, 1982).

Lipsey, D. and Leonard, D. (eds.), *The Socialist Agenda: Crosland's Legacy* (London: Jonathan Cape, 1981).

KEVIN JEFFERYS

Crossman, Richard (Howard Stafford) (*b.* London, 15 December 1907; *d.* Cropredy, near Banbury, Oxfordshire, 5 April 1974). Journalist, diarist and senior Labour politician. He held high office in the Labour governments of the 1960s. He is remembered, however, less for his ministerial record than for the publication of his voluminous diaries, which provided a unique insight into the operation of contemporary British government.

The son of a Chancery barrister, Crossman won a scholarship from Winchester to New College, Oxford, where he subsequently taught political and ancient philosophy. He soon became a renowned tutor. In his early writings, he outlined what was to be an abiding political concern: that democracy was fraudulent while it remained that ordinary citizens were deluded by those in authority. But after an unsuccessful first marriage – and a college scandal involving a married woman who became his second wife – Crossman left the academic world to work for the Workers' Educational Association and the *New Statesman*. By this time he was also active in Labour politics. From 1936 to 1940 he was leader of the Labour group on Oxford City Council, and after the war he became Labour MP for Coventry, a seat he was to hold until his death. Promotion from the backbenches, however, remained elusive for several years. This was partly due to the antipathy of the party leader, Attlee, a family friend who resented Crossman's bullying treatment of his parents; it also reflected Crossman's abrasive temperament, which made him many enemies. Although elected to Labour's National Executive Committee in the 1950s, when he emerged as a prominent 'Bevanite', it was not until the early 1960s that Crossman became a frontbench spokesman.

In the leadership contest which followed Hugh Gaitskell's death, Crossman helped to coordinate the successful campaign of Harold Wilson. He received his reward when Wilson became Prime Minister in 1964. As Minister of Housing and Local Government, he demonstrated his administrative capabilities, notably with a Rent Act which remedied some of the inequalities of local taxation. In 1966 he was promoted to become Lord President of the Council and Leader of the House of Commons. The latter position above all provided an opening for Crossman to harness his intellectual abilities to practical problems. His efforts to show that government could be more effectively reconciled with democratic control, however, were to be largely frustrated. The idea of morning sittings of Parliament was soon abandoned; the introduction of specialist select committees met with a mixed response; and reform of the House of Lords was defeated by a crossbench filibuster. In 1968 Crossman was moved on to become head of the newly formed Department of Health and Social Security. Here he proved himself once more a strong minister, but was unsuccessful in attempting to introduce his controversial national superannuation plan, to which he had long attached great importance.

With the defeat of the Labour Government in 1970, Crossman returned to journalism. But his period as editor of the *New Statesman* was fraught with difficulties. Unable to work satisfactorily with the magazine's staff, and with circulation falling, he was removed within two years. This setback ironically paved the way for a triumphant ending to his career. Working from the leisure of his Oxfordshire farm – inherited from his third wife, whom he had married in 1954 – Crossman began to prepare for publication the extensive political diaries he had kept since the 1950s. His original aim was to produce a contemporary version of Bagehot's *English Constitution*. A serious illness (from which he died in 1974) forced him to aim instead at providing a unique contemporary record of the 1964–70 Wilson governments. The appearance of the first volume of his cabinet diaries, however, was delayed by a major legal wrangle, in which the Labour attorney-general sought unsuccessfully to prevent publication. Crossman died while this controversy was unresolved, though he would no doubt have drawn satisfaction from the outcome. In spite of frequent charges of political inconsistency, he had always been hostile to the 'organised hypocrisy of the Establishment'; the excessive secrecy of the British political system, he believed, could be broken down only if the electorate were made aware of exactly how decisions were taken in their name. The diaries were a fitting epitaph.

WRITINGS

The Diaries of a Cabinet Minister, 3 vols. (London: Hamish Hamilton and Jonathan Cape, 1975–7).

FURTHER READING

Dalyell, Tam, *Dick Crossman* (London: Weidenfeld and Nicolson, 1989).

Morgan, J. (ed.), *The Backbench Diaries of Richard Crossman* (London: Hamish Hamilton and Jonathan Cape, 1981).

KEVIN JEFFERYS

Crowe, Sir Eyre (Alexander Barby Wichart) (*b.* Leipzig, Germany, 30 July 1864; *d.* Swanage, Dorset, 28 April 1925). Diplomatist, Permanent Under-Secretary at the Foreign Office. Prime Minister Baldwin's description of Eyre Crowe as 'the ablest servant of the Crown' was a fitting tribute to a man whose whole professional career (1885–1925) was devoted to the Foreign Office. There was nothing conventional about this vivid figure. He was the son of Joseph Crowe, commercial attaché for all of Europe and one of the most eminent British art critics of his day. Crowe's mother and wife were German and he was educated mainly in Germany before going at the age of 18 to Britain to prepare for the Foreign Office examination. Early in his career, he gained a reputation for his intensity, industry and brilliance and was known for his encyclopedic knowledge of British diplomacy and history. He had a special interest in military strategy but read widely in a variety of fields all his life. Crowe was a thorough professional, contemptuous of the snobberies and social preoccupations of the diplomatic world and deeply suspicious of most politicians, publicists and journalists, whose amateur interventions in foreign affairs he deeply deplored.

Crowe's life was the Foreign Office and he served almost his entire career in London. He became associated while still a junior clerk with the 1905–6 Office reforms, a change in the collection, distribution, and keeping of papers that reduced the clerical burden on the Foreign Office establishment and encouraged the participation of its members in the decision-making process. Crowe played an instrumental role in implementing the new system, which still fell short of his hopes for keeping the Foreign Secretary properly informed with the best professional information presented in annual reports from missions abroad as well as by departments at home. Crowe's interest in administrative reform and his concern for those who worked in the department persisted as he made his difficult way up the Foreign Office ladder. He was spoken of as a future Permanent Under-Secretary long before he achieved this lifelong ambition in 1920.

As the knowledgeable senior clerk in charge of the Western Department between 1906 and 1912, Crowe repeatedly, in numerous minutes and memoranda, called attention to the power of the German empire and to the dangers posed to the British position by German restlessness, her military traditions, and her often irresponsible leadership. In January 1907 Crowe submitted to the Foreign Secretary, Sir Edward Grey, his 'Memorandum on the present state of British relations with France and Germany', one of the few memoranda in Foreign Office history subsequently to attract considerable attention within and outside Whitehall. In summarizing the past history of Anglo-German relations, Crowe warned that it was essential to meet German demands by 'the most unbending determination to uphold British rights and interests in every part of the globe'. At the time, Crowe's advice was not always followed; some were offended by his relentless logic and driving energy. In the crisis of July 1914 Crowe insisted that moral obligations to France as well as national interest demanded that Britain take her place alongside France and Russia, but was powerless to do more than advise the Foreign Secretary.

Once Britain entered the war, Crowe threw himself into re-organizing the Foreign Office for its wartime role, irritating those reluctant to abandon traditional ways. He was, ironically enough, the object of a strong press attack in 1915 on the grounds of his German connections, and though defended in parliament, spent most of the war in the Blockade Department, which unexpectedly became the most important part of a Foreign Office much diminished in power and prestige. In 1919 Crowe was head of the Foreign Office section of the British delegation and one of the British plenipotentiaries at the Paris Peace Conference. An active participant in the territorial committees of the conference, he suffered from the lack of order in the proceedings and the absence of communication between the Prime Minister and his expert advisers. There was a major clash with Lloyd George in the autumn of 1919 when, in the absence of Prime Minister and Foreign Secretary, Crowe became the chief British delegate in Paris. Though Crowe was always careful to stay within the bounds of his position, this experience confirmed his suspicion of politicians meddling in foreign affairs.

As Permanent Under-Secretary, Crowe served three Foreign Secretaries, Lord Curzon, Ramsay MacDonald and Austen Chamberlain. Curzon was his most difficult chief; MacDonald and Chamberlain both relied heavily on his unrivalled expertise and experience. Crowe had little confidence in the 'new diplomacy' and even less sympathy with the League of Nations as an alternative to traditional practices. He was a strong anti-Bolshevik and was the British official involved in the Zinoviev letter affair of 1924. Crowe's interests remained centred on Europe. He continued to view the Germans with distrust and favoured the reconstitution of the French *entente*, though critical of the obstructive tactics of Aristide Briand and Raymond Poincaré and strongly opposing the French occupation of the Ruhr. Crowe backed Austen Chamberlain's efforts to improve relations with Paris and was associated with the cabinet deliberations which ultimately resulted in the Locarno agreements (1 December 1925). Crowe's health, always precarious, gave way under the stress of work, and he died, during the early stages of these negotiations, while taking a rare holiday from the Foreign Office.

FURTHER READING

Hinsley, F. H. (ed.), *The Foreign Policy of Sir Edward Grey* (Cambridge: Cambridge University Press, 1977).
Steiner, Zara, *The Foreign Office and Foreign Policy, 1898–1914* (Cambridge: Cambridge University Press, 1969).

ZARA STEINER

Cummings, Michael (*b.* Leeds, 1 June 1919). Cartoonist and caricaturist. The skill of Michael Cummings lies in his mastery of caricature and his shrewdness as a political observer. Although an aggressive cartoonist – his pen is sharp and decisive – his work is always humorous. He is able, despite his strongly held conservative views, to maintain the right to criticize politicians of all parties. His drawings have appeared in the *Daily Express*, the *Sunday Express*, *Punch* and many French publications – among them *Paris Match*. Perhaps the most widely reproduced British political cartoonist, he received the OBE in 1983.

Cummings was educated at The Hall, Hampstead, and Gresham's, Norfolk, but his attendance at the Chelsea School of Art was interrupted after three years by the war. Uncertain that he could make a career as a cartoonist, he trained originally as an art teacher. Ironically for a cartoonist so strongly associated with a conservative viewpoint, Cummings was first published in *Tribune*, whose editor, Michael Foot, persuaded him to try political cartoons. It was his father A. J. Cummings, the political editor of the *News Chronicle*, who encouraged him to seek a job with Lord Beaverbrook. In 1949 he joined the *Daily Express* on a trial basis to provide a serious contrast to the fun of the principal cartoonist Giles. Nine years later he added a further cartoon to his weekly total of three by joining the *Sunday Express*. He has worked for both papers ever since.

Cummings's instantly recognizable style evolved from his early line-and-wash illustrations. His strong black fluent line developed when he realized that a lighter style failed to compete successfully with advertisements. In his time he has been accused of being anti-Liberal, anti-socialist, anti-America, anti-Royal Family – in fact, anti-most things – yet many of his 'victims' ask for the cartoons in which they appear. As one once observed, 'It's a bit like being knighted with the sharp edge of the sword.'

LIZ OTTAWAY

Curzon, George (Nathaniel) [Marquess Curzon of Kedleston] (*b.* Kedleston, Derbyshire, 11 January 1859; *d.* London, 20 March 1925). Imperial statesman and parliamentarian, Viceroy of India and Foreign Secretary. One of the most brilliant but controversial public figures of his day, Curzon attained high office but never fulfilled his ambitions or the expectations of others. He resigned from a long Viceroyalty of India (1898–1905) after a bitter dispute with his Commander-in-Chief and Whitehall, and Lloyd George shackled much of his term as Foreign Secretary (1919–24). The premiership just evaded him in 1923.

Public life came naturally to Curzon, by birth within the aristocratic élite which still dominated Britain in the late nineteenth century (he was heir to the Scarsdale title and his beloved Kedleston Hall); and by education at Eton and Balliol, where he formed friendships and connections essential for a political career. None doubted the intellectual brilliance and amazing capacity for self-discipline and work, to which his academic triumphs bore witness. But the ambition, even arrogance, which sharpened his natural endowments and led him early to scholastic success, an All Souls Fellowship and high public office, ultimately soured his public and private life. His aloofness of bearing was reinforced by a painfully weak spine which needed a constant surgical support, and this belied his talent for conviviality and loyal friendships, as in the company of the confessedly élitist Crabbit Club and 'the Souls'. He made two comparatively late but lastingly happy marriages, the second after his first wife died tragically young.

Curzon's apprenticeship to office was twofold. He entered Parliament as Conservative MP for Southport in 1886, and, having flirted briefly with Tory democracy, settled to nursing his constituency, developing a reputation for elegant and forceful speeches in and outside Parliament, and establishing himself as a reliable assistant and junior colleague in government – as Lord Salisbury's Private Secretary, then Parliamentary Under-Secretary for India (1891–2) and Foreign Under-Secretary (1895–8). Thus he learned the practice of government and acquired knowledge of the two areas which dominated his political vision, India and foreign affairs. He added to this knowledge by extensive travel, particularly from 1887 to 1894. (Since he had only a small income he financed his journeys by writing, both articles and three major tomes, on Russia, Persia and the problems of the Far East.) He visited Canada and the USA; Japan and China; India and Afghanistan; Russia and central Asia via the transcaspian railway; and Persia. He would as cheerfully cook his own food as eat sumptuous official banquets. He endured intense physical exertion and extremes of climate and discomfort, for example in searching for the source of the Oxus, despite his weak back; made astringent political observations yet found time to wonder at the grandeur of the high Himalayas or the delicate beauty of the Taj. Meticulous in preparation, he never forgot his dress clothes in which to meet foreign dignitaries. Once, the fund of gifts packed for his hosts earned him the accusation by Turkish customs officials of being a travelling salesman in cheap jewellery. He became a recognized authority on Asian and Middle Eastern matters. More profoundly, he developed a passionate belief in the divinely ordained responsibility of a benign British imperialism and its civilizing effects on the erratic, effete or untrained oriental mind; and he became haunted by a brooding and darkening Russian presence on the imperial frontier and the need for Britain to deal with this from strength.

In 1898, when Curzon was appointed Viceroy (and created Baron Curzon of Kedleston, as his father still lived), a boyhood dream was fulfilled, and he was released from the shackles of an Under-Secretary's life, becoming freer to exercise real power – but not, in the event, free enough. He was passionately committed to India and bore a punishing workload, not least because he found delegation virtually impossible. He was determined to liberate the administration from the stifling effects of files and red tape; he aspired to a vast range of financial, educational and other reforms; and he was unique in his zeal for the recognition and preservation of India's architectural and archaeological grandeurs. He stamped out crude racialism wherever he found it (as his sovereign had personally commanded), thus earning deep hostility, particularly in military circles. Yet his sense of imperial mission simultaneously led him to misunderstand the burgeoning of modern political aspiration and organization among Western-educated Indians. He was contemptuous of Congressmen and their claims; and stirred up wide, popular opposition by partitioning huge and unwieldy Bengal (1905) – for administrative and political reasons. Educated Bengal Hindus interpreted this as an attack on them and their political and professional aspirations. The royal durbar of 1903 seemed Curzon's most spectacular demonstration of imperial and personal achievement; but tensions soon accumulated which precipitated his resignation. From the outset he had chafed at Whitehall's restraints on the Viceroy, though the breakdown of relations with London came after controversy over control of the Indian army. LORD KITCHENER, appointed Commander-in-Chief in 1902, challenged the existing dual control shared by the Commander-in-Chief and a member of the Viceroy's council. When Curzon lost the battle, in his view abandoned by the India Office, he resigned in great bitterness, which was sharpened because on returning to England he was not honoured as was customary.

During the subsequent decade Curzon mourned his wife and his career, and was isolated by the embittering of old friendships. He still contributed to public life, but not through politics: as Chancellor of Oxford University, President of the Royal Geographical Society, a National Gallery trustee, and a Fellow of the Royal Institute of British Architects, and as a generous restorer and donor of buildings, such as Bodiam Castle, to the nation. He never returned to the Commons, was created Earl in 1911 and from the Lords embarked on a last period of office.

Although a member of the coalition cabinet from 1915, Curzon became a key member only after Asquith's fall. When he eventually achieved the foreign secretaryship in 1919 he suffered disillusion, as he had done in his Indian experience of high office. Despite victory, Britain was entering a new era, and war had eroded old imperial certainties and patterns of influence: Curzon was, further, constrained by Lloyd George, particularly the premier's pro-Greek policy, and could only display his skill and knowledge at the abortive 1923 Lausanne Conference once Bonar Law had replaced Lloyd George. Understandably, when ill-health forced Bonar Law to resign in 1923, Curzon hoped to become Prime Minister, and to the last moment thought he would be. When informed of the king's choice of STANLEY BALDWIN he was bitterly disappointed: yet he gave Baldwin support as Foreign Secretary and as Lord Privy Seal. His greatest final interest and consolation was, however, restoring Kedleston. He was made a KG in 1916 and marquess in 1921; but these honours did not mask the failure of an able and ambitious man to achieve his highest hopes, despite times of apparent triumph, and perhaps the waste of talent and vision which might have been more fully used by his country had it been tempered by greater flexibility and generosity of mind, a talent for cooperation and delegation, and a genuine sense of humour.

FURTHER READING

Dilks, D., *Curzon in India*, i: *Achievement* (London: Hart Davis, 1969); ii: *Frustration* (London: Hart Davis, 1970).

Rose, K., *Curzon: a Most Superior Person* (London: Weidenfeld and Nicolson, 1969).

JUDITH M. BROWN

D

Dalton (Edward) Hugh (Neale) [Lord Dalton of Forest and Frith in the County Palatine of Durham] (*b*. Neath, Glamorgan, 26 August 1887; *d*. London, 12 February 1962). Labour Chancellor of the Exchequer, economist and political writer. He was a leading Labour politician and thinker who had a major role in shaping Labour Party ideas, and national policy, in the second quarter of the twentieth century. He entered Parliament as MP for Peckham in 1924, moving to Bishop Auckland in 1929. He was defeated in 1931, but returned to the House of Commons in 1935 and remained there until his retirement in 1959. He was made a life peer in 1960. Dalton held the posts of Parliamentary Under-Secretary of State for Foreign Affairs (1929–31); Minister of Economic Warfare (with responsibility for the Special Operations Executive) (1940–2); President of the Board of Trade (1942–5); Chancellor of the Exchequer (1945–7); Chancellor of the Duchy of Lancaster (1948–50); Minister of Town and Country Planning (1950–1); and Minister of Local Government and Planning (1951). He was on Labour's front bench from 1925 to 1955, and a long-serving member of the Labour Party National Executive (1926–7, 1928–52). He was also the author or editor of several books, including *Some Aspects of the Inequality of Incomes in Modern Communities* (1920), *Principles of Public Finance* (1922), *Towards the Peace of Nations* (1928), *Unbalanced Budgets* (1934) and *Practical Socialism for Britain* (1935).

Dalton came from an unusual background for a Labour politician. His father, Canon John Neale Dalton, had been tutor to the two young sons of the future Edward VII. Hugh grew up at Windsor surrounded by the atmosphere of the Court, and this undoubtedly affected his attitudes and politics. After attending St George's Choir School at Windsor he went to Summerfields preparatory school, Eton, and King's College, Cambridge, where he read mathematics and economics. At Cambridge he discovered socialism through the currently fashionable Fabian Society, and became part of a circle which included J. M. Keynes and Rupert Brooke. After taking his degree he studied for the Bar and – under the influence of Sidney and Beatrice Webb – began a doctorate (later published) at the London School of Economics on the inequality of incomes. In 1914 he married Ruth Hamilton Fox, a fellow student who shared his Fabian beliefs. In World War I he served in the Army Service Corps in France and later in the Royal Artillery in Italy, where he received an Italian medal for his bravery during the retreat following the battle of Caporetto. After the war he returned to the LSE, where he became a lecturer, and then reader, in the economics department.

Politics, however, was Dalton's first interest, and he fought several contests before eventually gaining a seat as one of an early batch of middle- or upper-class intellectuals in the fast-expanding parliamentary Labour Party. Once elected, he soon made his mark as an expert both in foreign affairs and public finance.

Dalton wrote later that he never had any ambition to be Prime Minister but, from early on, had set his sights on the Foreign Office and the Exchequer. It seems clear that, despite his background as an economist, foreign policy was his greatest passion. In 1929 he became junior minister to Arthur Henderson at the Foreign Office, and for two years helped to guide the second Labour government's doomed attempts to stimulate international disarmament. After losing his seat in 1931 he returned to the LSE, and spent much of the next four years travelling (to Russia and Italy in 1932, to Germany in 1933) and rewriting Labour's domestic programme. His book *Practical Socialism* encapsulated his own thinking about Labour's proposals at the time, and provided a plan of action which, to a remarkable extent, the Attlee government followed after the war.

When Dalton returned to Parliament in 1935, Attlee made him party spokesman on foreign affairs, a portfolio which enabled him to play an important part as an outspoken re-armer and anti-appeaser, leading Labour away from its earlier pacifist inclinations. Dalton deserves much of the credit for making his party available as an ally and potential coalition partner for the Tory rebels against Neville Chamberlain's government in 1940. After the formation of Churchill's administration, Dalton was placed in charge of the blockade against Germany, and also of the clandestine Special Operations Executive, the cloak-and-dagger organization charged with fomenting resistance in occupied territories. Quarrels with Brendan Bracken, the Minister of Information, led to his being moved to the Board of Trade, where he had responsibility for many wartime controls and for aspects of postwar planning. In 1944–5 he successfully steered through his own Distribution of Industries Act, which was the basis for all postwar regional policy.

When Labour won the 1945 election, Attlee first offered Dalton the foreign secretaryship (the post he had asked for) and then, possibly influenced by the King, gave him the Treasury instead (see also ATTLEE, CLEMENT). Here

Dalton – more, perhaps, than any predecessor or successor – sought to relate the direction of financial policy to socialist objectives. He nationalized the Bank of England (which had less effect than he imagined), and his taxation policy was governed by egalitarian principles as well as by a concern to avoid a postwar boom followed by a slump. Dalton's most controversial policy was one on which there was at first a wide measure of agreement. His campaign for lower interest rates, which had the backing of Keynes and other Treasury advisers, at first aroused little comment. Criticism began in the autumn of 1946, and turned to derision after the launching, and collapse, of a $2\frac{1}{2}$ per cent undated stock early in 1947. Shortly afterwards Dalton's policies received a further blow with the fuel shortage, which increased pressure on the currency and hastened the crisis over convertibility in August. Demoralized by this apparent defeat and the need to bring in stringent deflationary measures, Dalton had just introduced a fourth – emergency – budget in November 1947 when an inadvertent leak to a lobby journalist, just before his speech, forced him to resign.

Though Dalton rejoined the cabinet the following year, he never recovered his former standing as one of the dominating members of

Hugh Dalton, as Labour Party candidate for Bishop Auckland, chatting with colliery workers while out canvassing

the government. The Big Five – Attlee, Bevin, Cripps, Dalton and Morrison – who had steered the administration through its dynamic opening phase, became the Big Four (see also CRIPPS, STAFFORD). In his later posts Dalton gradually assumed the role of elder statesman. In the 1951 cabinet crisis he tried unsuccessfully to act as broker between left and right, and lost the support of many in both factions. The following year he was voted off the National Executive, and thereafter he began to disengage, taking a greater interest in younger political protégés (of whom there were many) than in current debates.

Dalton's greatest influence was in the 1930s, when he played a major part in turning the Labour Party from a woolly and sentimental group into an effective political body, and in the 1940s, as an energetic and intellectually powerful minister, who was prepared to outrage financial interests and much of the Whitehall establishment. Though he had loyal friends, his bombastic style made him many enemies, and his reputation suffered as a result. Yet he may be counted as one of the main founders of the postwar Fabian socialist or social democratic tradition in Britain.

WRITINGS

Call Back Yesterday (London: Muller, 1953).
The Fateful Years (London: Muller, 1957).
High Tide and After (London: Muller, 1962).
The Second World War Diary of Hugh Dalton, ed. Ben Pimlott (London: Jonathan Cape, 1986).
The Political Diary of Hugh Dalton, ed. Ben Pimlott (London: Jonathan Cape, 1987).

FURTHER READING

Addison, P., *The Road to 1945* (London: Quartet, 1977).
Durbin, Elizabeth, *New Jerusalems* (London: Routledge, 1985).
Morgan, K. O., *Labour in Power 1945–51* (Oxford: Oxford University Press, 1985).
Pimlott, Ben, *Labour and the Left in the 1930s* (Cambridge: Cambridge University Press, 1977).
——, *Hugh Dalton* (London: Jonathan Cape, 1985).

BEN PIMLOTT

Dash, Jack (*b.* London, 23 April 1907; *d.* London, 8 June 1989).   Trade unionist. Dash sprang to prominence in the 1960s in the disputes in the docks which then seemed endemic. He emerged as the leading figure in the London Docks Liaison Committee and proudly claimed that he had been active in every major dock strike after 1945.

His own direct employment in the industry began only at the end of the war. Dash was born in Southwark. His mother, a professional actress, married 'beneath' herself and was disowned by her family; her husband was a stagehand who had a partiality for drink. Dash was orphaned as a boy and was brought up by other mothers in his street. On leaving school at the age of 14 he drifted into a variety of jobs through the 1920s, including a spell in the army. He was more often than not unemployed and spent some of his spare time reading Tom Paine, A. J. Cronin and Engels. He was impressed by the National Unemployed Workers' Movement and joined the Labour Party, but by 1937 he was a member of the Communist Party. He was then living in Stepney and enjoyed battling against the Fascists. During the war he was in the Auxiliary Fire Service.

The introduction, between 1940 and 1947, of various dock labour schemes was followed by a long period of disruption and militancy. Some 400,000 working days were lost in the peak year of 1949. Small issues erupted into major disputes. The disturbances threatened British exports. The reasons for this volatility are complex and were investigated on two occasions, in 1956 and 1965, by Lord Devlin. To some minds, the short explanation was one man – Jack Dash. He undoubtedly had established a strong personal hold over thousands of dockers who responded to his leadership. Group solidarity was firm. The ascendancy of Dash and his cadre of associates was assisted by the bureaucratic weakness of the Transport and General Workers' Union. It was not only in the docks, however, that Dash became a well-known figure. He toured the country addressing public meetings. His memoirs speak, enigmatically, of a meeting at the University of Stranraer (*sic*) which he addressed. In the 1970s, however, vast and unpredicted changes took place in dockland, which ceased to be the enclosed community that had given Dash its support, and he never again achieved the prominence he had gained in the 1960s.

WRITINGS

Good Morning, Brothers! (London: Lawrence and Wishart, 1969).

FURTHER READING

Jensen, V. H., *Decasualization and Modernization of Dock Work in London* (Ithaca: Cornell University Press, 1971).

Philips, Gordon and Whiteside, Noel, *Casual Labour: the Unemployment Question in the Port Transport Industry 1880–1970* (Oxford: Clarendon Press, 1985).

KEITH ROBBINS

Davidson, Randall (Thomas) [Baron Davidson of Lambeth] (*b.* Edinburgh, 7 April 1849; *d.* London, 25 May 1930). Archbishop of Canterbury. Three Scotsmen became Archbishop of Canterbury during the period of that office's greatest modern public importance. The first was Archibald Tait, Davidson's father-in-law, the last Cosmo Lang, Davidson's successor. Their nationality had something to do with an internationalizing of the authority of Canterbury which corresponded to the spread of both Empire and Anglican Communion. Davidson was archbishop for 25 years (1903–28), longer than anyone since the Reformation, and presided over the emergence of modern Anglicanism and its organs of expression, international and national. Though too young to be at the first Lambeth Conference in 1867, he attended the next five, presiding over two of them and writing a book about the first three. He also presided from 1920 over the new National Assembly of the Church of England (established by the Enabling Act of 1919), which gave the Church a considerable measure of practical independence from Parliament and prepared the way for General Synod.

As Archbishop Tait's chaplain, Davidson was brought early to the centre of ecclesiastical power. On Tait's death in 1882 he was almost immediately appointed Dean of Windsor and Queen Victoria came to put an exceptional degree of trust in his judgement. He soon became a bishop and she would willingly have made him Archbishop of Canterbury, but that promotion actually came a year after her death, at which he was by her side as Bishop of Winchester. With that background and as archbishop through the greater part of two reigns and seven prime ministerships, Davidson came to have an unrivalled experience of the interface of Church and state. The first archbishop to develop warm relations with the Free Churches, he was helped in this by his Presbyterian upbringing and deeply Protestant persuasions. Yet, assisted by Bishop Gore, he took an increasingly accommodating approach to Anglo-Catholics and, indeed, the one great failure of his archepiscopate – the rejection by the House of Commons in 1927–8 of the revised Prayer Book – was the result of his (and the Church's) attempt to go some way in a Catholic liturgical direction (something he personally had no desire for).

Davidson's strength lay in a clear and discriminating judgement, ceaseless work, the ability to make use of excellent assistants and a sure sense of the strengths and weaknesses of his position. Cautious and conservative, he resisted Welsh Disestablishment, the Marriage of Deceased Wife's Sister and other progressive changes, but was able to adapt to such changes once inevitable and at times to meet major crises in a truly primatial way. The two clearest examples are, first, in the constitutional crisis of August 1910, when (despite his sentiments to the contrary) he spoke and voted in the House of Lords for the Parliament Bill; this may well have been crucial for its passing by a narrow majority. Secondly, during the General Strike of 1926, he appealed for the 'simultaneous and concurrent' cancellation of the strike, temporary renewal by the government of the coal subsidy and withdrawal by the mine owners of the new wage scales. This was not government policy and the BBC refused to broadcast the appeal.

Davidson was constantly asked for assistance by those in trouble throughout the empire and beyond, whether over Chinese labour in South

Africa, the execution of Sir Roger Casement or the maintenance of the Ecumenical Patriarchate at Constantinople. In this, when there was no World Council of Churches, he was approaching the role of temporary patriarch of the non-Roman world.

FURTHER READING

Bell, G. K. A., *Randall Davidson*, 2 vols. (London: Oxford University Press, 1935).
Hastings, Adrian, *A History of English Christianity, 1920–1985* (London: Collins, 1986).
Lloyd, Roger, *The Church of England, 1900–1965* (London: SCM, 1966).

ADRIAN HASTINGS

Davies, Clement (Edward) (*b.* Llanfyllin, Montgomeryshire, 19 February 1884; *d.* London, 23 March 1962). Liberal leader. Davies represented Montgomeryshire in Parliament from 1929 until his death. He became Leader of the nine Liberal MPs elected in 1945, following the defeat in the general election of Sir Archibald Sinclair. He saw his task as holding the surviving Liberal Party together rather than revitalizing its message, and his major contribution to new Liberal policy was to advocate from the start British membership of the emerging European Community. He maintained the internationalist tradition of the Liberal Party, becoming President of the Parliamentary Association for World Government in 1951. His spirited defence of Seretse Khama against successive Labour and Conservative Colonial Secretaries showed the passion with which he could take up Liberal causes.

In 1931 Davies had followed the National Liberals led by Sir John Simon who gave unconditional support to the National Government; but in 1942 he returned to the official Liberal ranks led by Sinclair. The parliamentary group he led from 1945 contained the remnants of the Lloyd George and Asquith factions: Lady Megan Lloyd George was his deputy (1949–51), while Sir Rhys Hopkin Morris represented the free trade tradition. Davies rejected Churchill's offer of office in 1951, but made no attempt to win back the National Liberals who by now had been sub-merged in the Conservative Party. During the 1950s the Liberals were assailed by Conservative attacks on 'the wasted vote' (although the main explanation for the drop in Liberal votes was the reduction in the number of Liberal parliamentary candidates). Davies's success was to hand on the Liberal Party reduced but intact to Jo Grimond, the successor whom he virtually appointed in September 1956.

A successful lawyer (QC, 1926) who published on agricultural and commercial law, Davies was also an active member of the Eisteddfod movement. The National Government appointed him to committees and royal commissions on a diversity of subjects: Despatch of Business at Common Law (1934–5), the BBC (1935), Tuberculosis in Wales (chairman, 1936–7), Colonial Empire Marketing (1937) and West Africa (1938–9). After the war he chaired committees on planning Greater London. He was appointed Privy Counsellor in 1947 and, unusually for a party leader, chaired select committees on Delegated Legislation and Members' Expenses in the 1953/4 session of Parliament. His standing as a House of Commons man was shown by his appointment as Chairman of the History of Parliament Trust. He died in March 1962, the month of the famous Liberal victory at Orpington.

C. M. MASON

Dawson [Robinson], (George) Geoffrey (*b.* Skipton-in-Craven, Yorkshire, 25 October 1874; *d.* London, 7 November 1944). Journalist and editor of *The Times*. Dawson – who assumed his surname in 1917 after succeeding to his aunt's entailed estate – though twice editor of *The Times* (1912–19 and 1923–41), became a journalist by chance. He was an ardent imperialist whose memory is sadly tainted with ignominy because he supported Neville Chamberlain's 'appeasement' of Hitler.

Educated at Eton and Magdalen colleges, Dawson gained a Double First, was elected a Fellow of All Souls and joined the Civil Service. In 1901 he was appointed successively Assistant Private Secretary to Joseph Chamberlain and then Alfred Milner. When

Milner returned to England from South Africa, Dawson resigned from the Civil Service to become editor of the Johannesburg *Star*. There, from 1905 to 1910, he promoted the policies and aspirations of the ultra-imperialist followers of Milner known collectively as the 'Kindergarten'. Dawson's experience editing the *Star* gave him an exaggerated notion of the power and political influence wielded by the press.

Northcliffe, who had bought *The Times* and was seeking an editor who shared his ideas, chose Dawson to succeed G. E. Buckle in 1912. At first, relations between editor and proprietor were cordial, but during the Great War, Northcliffe's sudden changes of mood, his irrational animosities, above all, his constant interference in the running of the paper, became insupportable and Dawson resigned. After Northcliffe's death, a new constitution for *The Times* stated that the editor, so long as he retained the confidence of the proprietors, was responsible for the paper's political direction. During his second period at Printing House Square, Dawson developed his fateful rapport with Whitehall and Downing Street. He was always happiest when mingling in high society, gossiping at All Souls' high table, or dining à deux at his club with some politician. Northcliffe had disliked Dawson's 'dining-out' theory of editorship, but this was the prime source of his priceless gift of 'intelligently anticipating events'. Sadly, Dawson abdicated his independence of judgement.

It was widely but falsely assumed that, during the essentially trivial Abdication Crisis in 1936, Dawson colluded with Baldwin. This was not so. Dawson's conduct on this as on other occasions may be censured as too decorous, but his sins were of omission, not commission. A tried and valued intimate counsellor of Baldwin, he loyally supported the government's Indian policy, which culminated in the 1935 Government of India Act. But on domestic and foreign as opposed to imperial affairs, too readily Dawson gave his uncritical support for measures designed to serve party not national interest. It can well be argued that the inevitable consequence of Baldwin's indifference to security was Chamberlain's policy of concession to Hitler's aggression.

Dawson did not have an intimate knowledge of Germany and would not listen to editorial staff who did. He refused to believe that Hitler either wished to dominate Europe or to dismantle the British Empire. German feelings were not to be upset or Hitler's susceptibilities trammeled. He was even prepared to defy the opposition of John Walter, co-proprietor of *The Times*. Dawson remained an 'impenitent supporter' (to use his own words) of Chamberlain's 'appeasement' of Hitler. While British public opinion remained divided, he argued it was not his place to oppose the government and cause unnecessary anxiety – an ingenuous claim for the editor of a newspaper, especially at a time of national crisis. He believed that to resist Germany's demands of Czechoslovakia would be resented and misunderstood by the Empire. Yet it should be remembered that Dawson was far from alone among Britons who recognized the inevitability of war with Germany only after the declaration of hostilities.

Dawson's dealings with Baldwin and Chamberlain in particular invited the suspicion that he sought influence through servility. He would have called it trusting in his own intuitions and loyalties. He wished to remain in step with the circle of 'approved friends' he described as 'thoughtful Englishmen'. Dawson was a member of the squirearchy and deeply conservative by nature; his heart and mind best served and most readily engaged in understanding the gentry and the hereditary English governing class, but his innate snobbery was a fatal professional defect.

FURTHER READING

The History of The Times (London: PHS, 1952), vol. IV, parts I and II.

Koss, S. E., *The Rise and Fall of the Political Press in Britain* (London: Hamish Hamilton, 1984), vol. II.

Wrench, J. E., *Geoffrey Dawson and our Times* (London: Hutchinson, 1955).

A. J. A. MORRIS

Deakin, Arthur (*b.* Sutton Coldfield, Warwickshire, 11 November 1890; *d.* Leicester, 1 May 1955). Trade-union leader. As General Secretary of the Transport and

General Workers' Union from 1946 to 1955, he was the principal industrial buttress of the Attlee Labour governments.

The son of a Warwickshire cobbler (who died when Deakin was ten), he started work as a furnace boy in a steelworks at Merthyr Tydfil at the age of 13, later moving to work in Flintshire. He became a full-time union organizer and in 1932 was brought to London by ERNEST BEVIN. When Bevin joined the National Government in 1940, Deakin became acting general secretary of the union, and was elected to the post in 1945. Deakin was less charismatic than Bevin, but his tight organizational control and ruthless way with opponents allowed him to dominate the union movement and Labour conferences. A combative speaker on the right of the party, he backed Attlee's wage restraint against internal opposition, queried wholesale nationalization, and ran an anti-communist crusade. This led to a ban on communists holding office in the union from 1948, and his splitting of the international trade-union movement by breaking up the World Federation of Trade Unions, of which he was president. The new International Confederation of Free Trade Unions, which he helped to form, excluded communist unions.

Inside the TGWU, Britain's largest union, he refused to deal with shop stewards, insisting on seeing officials, and this led to difficulties with the rank and file, particularly in the docks, where thousands of members were lost to the rival 'blue' union, the National Association of Stevedores and Dockers. Contemptuous of many politicians, stressing 'practical' solutions, he saw the Labour Party as secondary to the unions, but he still played a ferocious part in party arguments, even threatening a union organization to fight the Bevanites. His successors, FRANK COUSINS and JACK JONES, saw him as the symbol of an authoritarian union boss whose policies must be reversed.

MARTIN ADENEY

Denning, Lord [Alfred (Thompson); Baron Denning of Whitchurch] (*b.* Whitchurch, Hampshire, 23 January 1899). Judge and protagonist of individual liberties. Denning has been the best-known and one of the most colourful and distinguished judges of the twentieth century. Called to the Bar by Lincoln's Inn in 1923, he rose rapidly, becoming King's Counsel (1938) and successively a Justice of the High Court (1944), Lord Justice of Appeal (1948) and a Lord of Appeal in Ordinary (1957). But he felt frustrated in the Lords and gladly stepped back into a more active forensic arena in 1962 to become Master of the Rolls. As such, and thereby president of the Civil Division of the Court of Appeal from 1962 to 1982, Denning did his best work and led that court in many noteworthy decisions.

His opinions have a personal style, more colourful and rather more colloquial than is normal; they were frequently couched in short sentences, in which verbs were sometimes optional. He excelled in opening an opinion with an arresting sentence, such as, 'In these three cases the law's delays have been intolerable', or, 'In summertime village cricket is the delight of everyone', or, 'Old Peter Beswick was a coal merchant in Eccles, Lancashire.'

Denning has a profound concern to see justice done, and frequently extended, stretched or even twisted principles of law to enable him to reach what he saw as the right result, a stretching or twisting which in the view of some critics tortured principles beyond breaking point. He once called some of his judicial brethren 'timorous souls'. Thus in one case he boldly advocated extending the scope of liability for negligence to cover economic loss arising from negligent advice; in another he extended the remedy by prerogative writ to cover not only excess of jurisdiction by a tribunal, but error by it in law; in another he extended the remedy by declaration to cover a tribunal which acted contrary to natural justice or made a mistake of law. In commercial law he led his court to invent the use of injunction to prevent debtors making away with their assets to defeat creditors. Some of these advanced decisions have been accepted, even given statutory recognition; some in which he dissented have subsequently been vindicated; but quite a number have been reversed or overruled as unsound, as possibly fair but not warranted by law.

Denning never shrank from controversy, adopted the easy line or was afraid to differ

Lord Denning, Waterloo Station, London, September 1963

from his colleagues, and his approach was always the one which favoured the individual or the claimant. Particularly in later years he frequently fell foul of the House of Lords, as in his repeated attempts to free the Court of Appeal from the shackles imposed by the doctrine that that court is bound by its previous decisions. The House of Lords was also so bound, but in 1966 it relaxed the rule and Denning urged that the Court of Appeal should also free itself from the constraint.

His standing and total integrity caused him to be selected to conduct the inquiry into the conduct of John Profumo, then Minister for War, and the possible security risks involved, and his report (Lord Denning's Report, Cmnd. 2152, 1963) was a best-seller. More importantly, it was a judicious, balanced appraisal of the conduct of the parties and allayed the fears that had been expressed.

Denning was in great demand as a lecturer and speaker and became an idol among law students. Notable sets of his lectures and essays are *Freedom Under the Law* (1949), *The Changing Law* (1953), *The Road to Justice* (1955), *The Discipline of Law* (1979) and *The Due Process of Law* (1980). The academic regard for him can be seen by the creation of the Denning Law Library in the University of Buckingham and the founding of the *Denning Law Journal* to publish articles on matters which relate to the central themes of his vision and attitude to law and society, such as the judicial development of the common law, the essential role played by law in the defence of the individual in the modern state, and the importance of the interplay between law and morality. In his latter years Denning also wrote a number of entertaining, non-technical books about the law, his recollections and reminiscences and interesting and decisive cases.

WRITINGS

The Family Story (London: Butterworths, 1981).
What Next in the Law (London: Butterworths, 1982).
The Closing Chapter (London: Butterworths, 1983).
Landmarks in the Law (London: Butterworths, 1984).
Leaves from my Library: an English Anthology (London: Butterworths, 1986).

FURTHER READING

Blom-Cooper, L. and Drewry, G., *Final Appeal* (London: Oxford University Press, 1972).
Jowell, J. L. and McAuslan, J. P. W. B. (eds.), *Lord Denning: the Judge and the Law* (London: Sweet and Maxwell, 1984).
Pettit, P. H. (ed.), *Denning Law Journal*, vol. I (University of Buckingham, 1986).
Robson, P. and Watchman, P. (eds.), *Justice, Lord Denning and the Constitution* (London: Gower, 1981).
Stevens, R., 'Lord Denning', *Law and Politics*

(London: Weidenfeld and Nicolson, 1979), pp. 488–505.

DAVID M. WALKER

De Valera, Éamon [Edward] (**'Dev'**) (*b*. New York City, 14 October 1882; *d*. Dublin, 29 August 1975). Irish President. De Valera, after service as Commandant in the Irish insurrection of Easter Week 1916, was imprisoned, released and elected to the House of Commons; he was then civil leader of the Irish resistance to the United Kingdom from 1919 to 1922. Opposing the treaty signed by Irish representatives and British Government delegates, he ultimately participated in the republican forces in the Irish Civil War. After a term as leader of the parliamentary opposition to the Irish Free State Government, he was elected to its presidency in 1932, an office altered to Taoiseach Éireann (Prime Minister – lit. 'chieftain' – of Ireland) under the new constitution he sponsored and saw adopted in 1937. Defeated in 1948, he was re-elected in 1951 and (after another three years in opposition) in 1957. He became President of the Republic of Ireland in 1959 and served for two terms, retiring in 1973 (at which point he was the oldest head of state in the world). His austere, nostalgic Irish nationalism dominated Irish politics, as did his intransigent but inactive opposition to the survival of Northern Ireland within the United Kingdom.

The son of an Irish emigrant mother in domestic service and a short-lived Spanish-born father, de Valera was brought up in Bruree, Co. Limerick, by his grandmother and uncle, remaining there despite his wish for reunion with his mother when she married again in the USA. He became a protégé of the local Roman Catholic parish priest, the Very Rev. Eugene Sheehy, previously a vigorous advocate of the Irish Land League to the left of Parnell. Scholarships enabled him to win an education under the Holy Ghost Fathers in Blackrock College, where he showed particular proficiency in theology and mathematics. He taught mathematics in several Irish schools, took up the study of Irish (Gaelicizing his first name) and joined the Gaelic League (Irish language restoration society) in 1908. In 1910

he married the schoolteacher Sinéad (Janet) Flanagan, who had been teaching him Irish. He sought a chair in mathematical physics in University College, Cork, without success, and entered the Irish Volunteers in 1913, later adhering to the minority who opposed John Redmond's commitment of the organization to the British war effort in 1914. Under the influence of the poet Thomas MacDonagh, de Valera held command of a major sector of Dublin in the Volunteers' insurrection of 1916, although he seems to have known little of its planning by the Military Council of the Irish Republican Brotherhood. Having held out for a week, he reluctantly followed the surrender of his superiors; the British military court-martial's death sentence was commuted to life imprisonment, probably because of his American birth. After his release in June 1917 de Valera won a by-election in East Clare and refused to sit at Westminster. Having been re-arrested in May 1918 he was re-elected in November as a Sinn Féin (abstentionist nationalist) candidate. He escaped from Lincoln prison, was elected president of the abstentionists' assembly, Dáil Éireann, after which he travelled in the USA for 18 months, agitating for Irish independence and frustrating Irish-American attempts to embroil his cause in American politics.

On his return de Valera was drawn into negotiations with Prime Minister Lloyd George. The Irish crisis had become a full-scale war of terrorism and counter-terrorism, but de Valera had little connection with military activities. He declined to take part in the formal treaty negotiations, possibly intending to intervene in the event of deadlock; he opposed the resultant agreement, particularly on its requirement of oath-bound allegiance to George V, and narrowly failed to prevent its ratification by Dáil Éireann. De Valera then resigned, campaigned against the treaty and took up arms against the government while playing little part in the fighting. He was arrested and held prisoner for 11 months as Republican resistance was collapsing. In 1926 he resigned the presidency of Sinn Féin, having been defeated on the issue of possible entry to the Free State Dáil, and formed the political party Fianna Fáil (Warriors of Destiny), as whose leader he was elected for Clare in 1927. He complied with entry requirements under the treaty as an 'empty formula'.

The defeat of his former Dáil cabinet officer and present opponent William Cosgrave, President since 1922, brought de Valera into power. He chipped away at the various constitutional provisions of subordination to Westminster, beginning with the Oath: in fact the process of rolling devolution had ably commenced under Cosgrave. In 1936 the abdication of Edward VIII gave de Valera the opportunity of scrapping the link with the British Crown, and he introduced a constitution transforming the 26-county Free State into a Republic in all but name (the name being added in 1949 when his opponents were in power); in other respects the constitution was markedly in keeping with Roman Catholic social teaching (as opposed to the highly secular Free State constitution), although its failure to establish Roman Catholicism as the state church prevented de Valera from obtaining the Papal endorsement for which he had hoped. He was firmly if subtly resisting dangers to his rule from militaristic organizations, a clerical-Fascist 'Blueshirt' movement among his political opponents and a renewal of illegal activities by his former friends in the Irish Republican Army. He had also entered on a bitter 'economic war' with Britain which lasted from 1932 to 1938, when he signed Anglo-Irish agreements with Neville Chamberlain's government by which Britain withdrew from the Irish ports it held under the treaty.

De Valera was a vigorous supporter of the League of Nations, and then and later believed that small powers could manoeuvre among larger rivals to make international bodies somewhat effective peace-keeping institutions. He championed such ideas as Acting President of the League of Nations Assembly (1932) and as its actual President (1938); Irish policy at the United Nations in the late 1950s held to this principle, as did in some degree Irish membership of the EEC after de Valera's retirement from active politics. During World War II he declared Ireland's neutrality, despite British and American pressure and a brief bombing raid from Germany. Covertly he sympathized with the Allies and secretly fell in with some of

their more acceptable requests, but the quasi-republican and extreme chauvinist rhetorical style on which his followers had relied to maintain emotional support for his party meant that many of them simply viewed the conflict in old-fashioned anti-British terms. De Valera intervened with fire-fighting assistance when Belfast was bombed and made his *de jure* constitutional claim to rule of the entire island a pretext for resenting such attacks; he also made the existence of Northern Ireland a basis for his continued refusal to join the Allies at any point, and indeed had he done so he would have made Britain's situation much worse, with inevitable German invasion and Irish civil conflict. At the close of the war Winston Churchill made an unworthy broadcast attack on de Valera, who replied with exceptionally constructive restraint and dignity.

Despite the success of semi-state bodies in electricity deployment, transport direction and fuel reclamation, de Valera's government, an almost unchanged group of former Republican followers from the 1920s traversing virtually the entire spectrum from genius to ineptitude, was moribund when in 1948 he fell before a left–right coalition united in opposition to him. His own success in conceding the trappings of Roman Catholic social teaching while keeping the more meddlesome clerics at arms' length proved impossible for his opponents to imitate, and they fell over an issue of health regulation by government. But neither in 1951 nor in 1957 did de Valera show any signs of rising to the new challenges: culture atrophied, his scheme of Gaelic revival languished under arid state direction, and emigration haemorrhaged. His official hostility to partition prohibited any sign of recognition of Northern Ireland, and its rhetoric, intended to solidify national support behind Fianna Fáil, involuntarily fuelled sporadic outbreaks from the IRA. His retirement to the ceremonial office of the presidencey in 1959 was intended to coincide with the repeal of proportional representation and thus, it was hoped, consolidate his party in power after his departure; but the voters simultaneously elected him and retained PR. He proved an admirable President, making dignified appearances at home and in the USA, and stayed firmly out of the political arena from which his heir, Seán Lemass, cleared out many of the cobwebs of his long rule.

FURTHER READING

Edwards, Owen Dudley, *Éamon de Valera* (Cardiff: University of Wales Press, 1987).
Moynihan, Maurice (ed.), *Speeches and Statements by Éamon de Valera 1917–1973* (Dublin: Gill and Macmillan, 1980).
Ó Néill, Tomás agus Ó Fiannachta Pádraig, *De Valera* (Ath Cliath: Cló Morainn, 1968, 1970; English version by Lord Longford and Thomas P. O'Neill, *Éamon de Valera*, London: Hutchinson, 1970).

OWEN DUDLEY EDWARDS

Devlin [McAliskey], **(Josephine) Bernadette** (*b.* Cookstown, Co. Tyrone, 23 April 1947). Irish nationalist politician. In the late 1960s she was the symbol of the Northern Ireland civil rights movement. Youthful and eloquent, she was typical of the new generation of Queen's University-educated Catholic radicals, which included also Michael Farrell and Eamon McCann, and she easily outwitted local Ulster Unionists in debate. Although she soon lost her early public prominence, she remained a significant figure on the fringes of Irish Republican politics in the 1970s and 1980s.

In April 1969, while a final-year psychology student, Devlin won a by-election in mid-Ulster for Westminster by defeating the Unionist candidate by 4,211 votes in a poll of 92 per cent. Taking her seat on her twenty-second birthday, she thus became the youngest woman ever to be elected to Westminster and the youngest MP for nearly 200 years. Ignoring the usual tradition, she impressively made an hour-long maiden speech attacking the Stormont government led by Terence O'Neill. An extreme but possible solution, she said, would be the abolition of Stormont – an event which was to take place in 1972. In August 1969 her direct involvement in civil violence led to a five-month prison sentence in Armagh jail, which she entered in June 1970. In July 1971 she announced that she was going to have a baby, an event which caused a degree of excitement in the popular media. In January 1972 Devlin punched Reginald Maudling, the Home Sec-

retary, in the House of Commons – on the grounds that he had lied about the events of 'Bloody Sunday' in Derry. She married a schoolteacher, Michael McAliskey, in April 1973, and the following February lost her seat in the general election.

For the next five years Devlin operated on the fringes of militant Republican politics, but returned to the centre of the stage when she was a candidate in the European election of 1979. Standing as a champion of IRA prisoners, she was opposed by the Republican movement itself, but her respectable performance – she was eliminated only on the third count – encouraged the idea that Sinn Fein should adopt a political and electoral strategy. In the 1980s she survived a serious assassination attempt and continued to operate as a free-floating, but hardly sophisticated, critic of what she saw as 'British imperialism in Ireland'. Exceptionally brave and articulate, her personality seemed to lack elements of introspection and caution.

WRITINGS

The Price of my Soul (London: Pan, 1969).

FURTHER READING

Patterson, H., *The Politics of Illusion: Republicanism and Socialism in Modern Ireland* (London: Radius/Century Hutchinson, 1989).

PAUL A. E. BEW

Dimbleby, Richard (Frederick) (*b.* Richmond on Thames, Surrey, 25 May 1913; *d.* London, 22 December 1965). Broadcaster. In 1965 it was inevitable that the televised commentary on the funeral of Sir Winston Churchill should have been given by Richard Dimbleby. This assumption was testimony to the distinctive place he had come to hold in the broadcasting of great national events. His skill in description and his impeccable sense of an occasion came from long experience in the handling of news and information. His father edited the family paper, the *Richmond and Twickenham Times*, and after leaving Mill Hill School in 1931 Dimbleby worked for a variety of papers. Five years later, however, he became one of the BBC's first news reporters. He became one of the best-known war correspondents, initially in France but then in the Middle East, North Africa and elsewhere. He flew with Bomber Command and then covered the final advance into Germany. His description of Belsen was memorable.

After the war he was a familiar voice on the radio as reporter, quiz-master and compere. His face became equally well known with the expansion of television. He seemed just as much at home in this medium and was the obvious person to cover both state occasions and the weekly edition of 'Panorama'. He was, of course, a figurehead, but he seemed to dominate the screen in a manner achieved by no other broadcaster. This was a tribute to his meticulous preparation. His early death, so soon after covering Churchill's funeral, was itself a national shock. The role of the broadcaster has become much more contentious in subsequent decades and the techniques employed in television have changed very considerably. In retrospect, the days of Dimbleby's dominance appear relatively uncomplicated. It would be misleading, however, to believe that he was merely a bulky source of ceremonial reassurance in the decades of imperial dissolution. In his activities as a war correspondent, he had frequently displayed a desire to present the full truth as he saw it, and this zeal had upset his BBC superiors. Even so, although his death from cancer appeared so untimely, it was not altogether incongruous that he should have died in the same year as Churchill. In their different spheres, the two men spoke splendidly and solemnly but with an assurance that was becoming rare and oddly anachronistic.

FURTHER READING

Dimbleby, Jonathan, *Richard Dimbleby* (London: Hodder and Stoughton, 1975).
Miall, Leonard (ed.), *Richard Dimbleby, Broadcaster* (London: BBC, 1966).

KEITH ROBBINS

Douglas-Home, Alexander. See HOME, LORD.

Dowding, Hugh (Caswall Tremenheere) [Baron Dowding of Bentley Priory] (*b.* Moffat, Dumfriesshire, 24 April 1882; *d.* Kent, 15 February 1970). Air Chief Marshal and commander in the Battle of Britain. Dowding commanded RAF Fighter Command during the Battle of Britain in 1940. He was perhaps the only authentic popular hero the RAF high command has produced. Nevertheless, controversy marked even his most famous achievements.

He was educated at Winchester and then, via Sandhurst, joined the Royal Artillery, but his military career changed course when he learned to fly in 1913. He rose to the rank of Brigadier in the Royal Flying Corps in the Great War. In the 1920s Dowding commanded the Inland Area, and served in Iraq and Palestine, interspersed with a spell at the Air Ministry as Director of Training. 1930 saw his appointment as Air Member for Supply and Research, making him responsible for the development of the generation of aircraft with which the RAF was to fight World War II. The 1930s was a period of confusingly rapid technological change in air weaponry, during which Dowding developed the view that a close fighter cordon could provide an effective defence against bomber attack. The all-metal cantilever monoplane fighter, in the shape of the Hurricane and the Spitfire, was the prime source of hope. In 1935 Dowding made the critical decisions that were to concentrate fighter design around the principle of eight-gun armament. Crucially, too, he saw and understood the significance of the first experiments in what came to be known as radar. The following year he was given the chance to put the new material into action when he was appointed Commander in Chief, Fighter Command.

Air policy at the time, however, was geared to the theory of the bomber deterrent, based on the belief that 'the bomber will always get through', in Baldwin's famous phrase. Dowding had to fight hard for recognition of his unfashionable theories until fighter defence was finally given national priority early in 1938. Moreover, he was already 54 years old when he took up his new appointment. He had a right to expect, given his superiority, to attain the position of Chief of the Air Staff: instead, when he failed to secure the highest military post in 1937, he was faced with the prospect of premature retirement as an added burden. On five occasions between 1936 and 1940 he was actually given notice of retirement. By 1940, however, Dowding had welded together the new fighter generation with the radar early-warning system, the whole organized around a sophisticated system of ground control and communications. With a famous letter written on 16 May 1940, just six days after the German attack in Western Europe had begun, he managed to prevent the fuller deployment of Fighter Command in the Battle of France, arguing that any attempt to stem the tide in continental Europe could only weaken Britain when the Germans turned their attention on the Channel. It was a daringly forthright view, given the pressures to continue to help the French, but it saved Fighter Command for the Battle of Britain. Dowding's tactics through the battle were to scramble his fighters and hit the bombers before they could threaten his bases in Kent, realizing that if Air Vice Marshal Park's squadrons were forced to retire north of the Thames, then an invasion was possible along the south coast. Air Vice Marshal Leigh-Mallory, however, believed that the organization of 'big wings' of fighters would destroy more enemy aircraft, even if the delay necessary to mass the big wings allowed the bombers to hit Park's airfields. Dowding's failure to control the ensuing dispute between Park and Leigh-Mallory led to his replacement as Commander in Chief in November 1940.

There can be no doubt that Dowding was a difficult man. His austere, rather humourless approach earned him the nickname 'Stuffy', and his nit-picking attention to detail did not make him an easy colleague. An appointment to the USA to try to increase American aircraft supply to Britain led to another clash, as did his subsequent appointment as Inspector General of the RAF. He was finally allowed to retire in July 1942. In his later years Dowding developed his interest in the occult and in spiritualism, and he enjoyed a long and quiet retirement. His ashes are interred in Westminster Abbey.

FURTHER READING

Collier, B., *Leader of the Few: the Authorised Biography of Air Chief Marshal Lord Dowding of Bentley Priory* (London: Jarrolds, 1957).
——, *The Defence of the United Kingdom* (London: History of the Second World War, 1957).
Wright, R., *Dowding and the Battle of Britain* (London: Macdonald, 1969).

MALCOLM SMITH

Driberg, Tom [Thomas Edward Neil; Lord Bradwell] (*b.* Crowborough, Sussex, 22 May 1905; *d.* London, 12 August 1976). Labour politician and journalist. A member of the Bevanite left in the 1950s, he hovered on the fringes of power for 20 years – being barred from office as a security risk because of his homosexuality.

Driberg's inclinations as a journalist and protégé of Beaverbrook in the 1930s perfectly fitted him for the role of gossip columnist as the original modern 'William Hickey'. Homosexual and high Anglican, he had a view of socialism that was aesthetic rather than economic, being concerned largely with (in Richard Crossman's words) 'getting justice for coloured people and trying to get a Christian social ethic in this country.' In 1942, in defiance of the parliamentary truce, he stood as Independent candidate for New Malden in Essex and was elected. From 1945 to 1950 he took the Labour Whip and was a notable maverick on the extreme left of that party. Disliked by Attlee, Gaitskell and Harold Wilson, he was never a candidate for office while they reigned. He lost his seat in 1955.

Although he was a noted journalist and broadcaster, Driberg's passion for young men and his ambiguous contacts in the world of the secret service made him unemployable in political office. He served as chairman of the party in 1957–8 and was returned to the Commons in 1959 as MP for Barking, but he had to rest content with being on the National Executive Council continuously from 1949 to 1972. The curious guest-list at his Robert Adam house, Bradwell Lodge, was notable for its combination of the high-thinking and the low-living.

As a unilateralist, a Bevanite in the 1950s and a maverick in the 1960s, Driberg enjoyed a place permanently on the fringes of power. Despite his services to his party, his private life barred his way to a seat in the Lords after he left the Commons in 1972. He finally received a peerage in 1976, the year he died, leaving behind him a scurrilous autobiography entitled *Ruling Passions* (1977) which threw a graphic light upon the homosexual underworld of London's public lavatories. His wife's opinion of his activities is unrecorded.

FURTHER READING

Morgan, J. (ed.), *The Backbench Diaries of Richard Crossman* (London: Hamish Hamilton and Jonathan Cape, 1981).

JOHN CHARMLEY

Dyson, Will(iam Henry) (*b.* Ballarat, Australia, 3 September 1880; *d.* London, 21 January 1938). Cartoonist. Dyson was one of the most exceptional Antipodean cartoonists to make his mark in Britain. His radical use of distorted symbolic figures contrasting workers and bosses and his ideological fervour distinguishes his work from that of his contemporaries. The cartoonist David Low once observed that his drawings contained 'a sardonic disrespect for orthodox standards that was an emetic for the complacent'.

Educated at local schools, Dyson was a self-taught artist. By the age of 17 he was contributing to the *Sydney Bulletin* and the *Melbourne Herald*, producing several series of political and theatrical caricatures. In 1909 he left Australia for London and worked as a freelance before joining the socialist *Daily Herald* as chief cartoonist in 1912. Under the editorship of George Lansbury, he enjoyed complete freedom of expression; his cartoons occupied an entire page. It is considered that Dyson was at his most acerbic and did his best work during this period. The death of his wife Ruby in the influenza epidemic of 1919, however, affected him deeply for the rest of his life, and thereafter his work gradually lost its vigour.

Dyson's drawing was inspired by his hatred of greed and militarism, and his own good humour rarely found its way into his work. He was a sound draughtsman with a bold drawing style – penwork over pencil and dark shading – very reminiscent of Daumier.

In 1922 Dyson went back to Australia for five years. While continuing to cartoon, he experimented with new techniques – oil painting, woodcut and dry point etchings. Exhibitions in New York and London of his satirical etchings, depicting artistic and intellectual personalities of the day, were received with much acclaim. In 1931, despite new-found financial security, Dyson rejoined the *Daily Herald* (by then one of the world's biggest circulation papers); he remained there until his death. His last years were marred by persistent ill-health and editorial interference.

FURTHER READING

McMullin, Ross, *Will Dyson: Cartoonist, Etcher and Australia's Finest War Artist* (London: Angus and Robertson, 1984).

LIZ OTTAWAY

E

Ede, (James) Chuter [Baron Chuter-Ede of Epsom] (*b.* Epsom, Surrey, 11 September 1882; *d.* Ewell, Surrey, 11 November 1965). Labour politician, teacher and stalwart of local government. He served as Home Secretary in Attlee's postwar Labour governments, but is best remembered for his part in shaping an important item of wartime social legislation, the 1944 Education Act.

By background and training a Liberal, Ede switched political allegiance to the Labour Party while on active service in World War I. He subsequently became Labour MP for Mitcham and then for South Shields, a constituency he was to represent for 30 years. From 1940 to 1945 he served as a junior minister at the Board (later Ministry) of Education; in this capacity, he played an invaluable role in helping to frame the 1944 Education Act. After the war, Ede went on to serve as a distinguished Home Secretary in Attlee's Labour governments, guiding through Parliament a considerable volume of reforming legislation. He was also Leader of the House of Commons for a brief spell in 1951. He remained influential in Labour politics for several years thereafter, and received a life peerage in 1964 – a recognition of his services both nationally and in local government.

Ede was essentially a liberal nonconformist of the old school. He was brought up to value religious observance, he regarded public service as a duty, and he developed a strong commitment to state education, having begun his career as a schoolteacher. He was, he noted ironically, the only man ever to turn down the offer of promotion from the Board of Education. This self-effacing side to his nature inevitably left Ede overshadowed by the powerful Labour leaders of the period, but he was nevertheless a popular and respected member of the party's frontbench team. He displayed an administrative competence not always shared by his colleagues, and he remained to the end deeply committed to what he termed 'the good old causes of freedom and social justice'.

FURTHER READING

Jefferys, K. (ed.), *Labour and the Wartime Coalition: from the Diary of James Chuter Ede, 1941–1945* (London: Historians' Press, 1988).

KEVIN JEFFERYS

Eden, Sir (Robert) Anthony [Earl of Avon] (*b.* Windlestone, Co. Durham, 12 June 1897; *d.* Alvediston, Wiltshire, 14 January 1977). Statesman. He was Prime Minister from April 1955 until January 1957. His tenure was marked by the Suez Crisis, with which his name is primarily associated in popular memory. But he also deserves to be remembered for the role he had played in shaping British foreign policy for most of the three decades before he became Prime Minister. In particular, he had three terms as Foreign Secretary – from December 1935 until February 1938; from December 1940 until July 1945; and from October 1951 until April 1955.

Eden was acknowledged as the third son of Sir William Eden – though there is circumstantial evidence suggesting that his real father may have been George Wyndham, an unusually literate politician in Arthur Balfour's circle. The Edens had been prominent in County Durham for several centuries, the baronetcy dating back to 1672, and one of his ancestors, Sir Robert Eden, had been the last colonial governor of Maryland. Both Eden's parents were, to say the least, eccentric. The father was noted for his rages, which at times verged on madness and from which his children were not spared. Little better was the strikingly beautiful mother, Sybil, daughter of Sir William Grey, for she was apparently incapable of expressing love for her children and later brought the family to financial disaster by reckless borrowing and crazy generosity to strangers. (R. A.

Butler used to enjoy saying of Eden that his parentage had made him what he was: half mad baronet, half beautiful woman.)

From this unstable home background Eden escaped to preparatory school and Eton (where he was also unhappy). While he was at Eton, World War I broke out and he accordingly proceeded straight from school to the Western Front. He rose to be the youngest brigade major in the army, and he was awarded the Military Cross for rescuing his sergeant. Though he himself emerged physically uninjured from the war, two of his brothers were killed.

After the war, resuming his education, Eden obtained a first class honours degree in oriental languages at Oxford – the beginning of a lifelong interest in the Middle East. After contemplating entering the Diplomatic Service, he opted for a career in politics. In 1922 he contested an unwinnable seat in County Durham for the Conservatives, before being elected to the House of Commons in December 1923 as Member for Warwick and Leamington – a seat he represented until his retirement in 1957.

Once in Parliament, Eden concentrated on international affairs and by 1926 had begun his long association with the Foreign Office. His first role, which lasted until 1929, was to serve as Parliamentary Private Secretary to Foreign Secretary Sir Austen Chamberlain. Loyal to Stanley Baldwin, the embattled leader, during the Conservatives' troubled spell in opposition from 1929 to 1931, he was rewarded by being given his first ministerial post when the National Government was formed in August 1931. The Conservative leader successfully pressed his claims on Prime Minister Ramsay MacDonald, and he duly became Parliamentary Under-Secretary at the Foreign Office.

In the ensuing years he became associated primarily with Geneva, where he often represented his country at meetings of the League of Nations or the World Disarmament Conference. Without ever coming near to resigning, he succeeded in building a public reputation as being more 'progressive' in this sphere than the government as a whole. He was, moreover, widely held to be the most handsome and fashionably attired member of that government. On the whole his chiefs seem to have found his growing popularity useful to them and he accordingly rose steadily on the political ladder while remaining within the Foreign Office. In 1934 he was given the title of Lord Privy Seal. Then in June 1935, when Baldwin succeeded MacDonald as Prime Minister, he was brought into the cabinet as Minister for League of Nations Affairs. Finally, in December of the same year, when his departmental chief, Sir Samuel Hoare, had to be repudiated for his part in shaping an abortive plan with the French for giving Italy a major part of Abyssinia, Eden emerged as the obvious successor as Foreign Secretary. He was only 38 and the youngest man to hold the post since Lord Granville in 1851.

Eden's first term as Foreign Secretary came when the policies of 'appeasement' were in vogue, and, despite his later reputation, his resistance to those policies was far from consistent or vigorous. He acquiesced, for example, in the lifting of the sanctions that had been vainly imposed on Italy for invading Abyssinia; and he made no attempt to rally effective opposition to Germany's remilitarization of the Rhineland. But in May 1937 Neville Chamberlain succeeded Baldwin and began to play a more active role than his predecessor in the making of foreign policy. This seems to have been resented by Eden, and several clashes between the two men resulted. Matters came to a head in February 1938, ostensibly over the issue of recognizing the Italian conquest of Abyssinia, which Eden, after some vacillation, decided to oppose. After a prolonged struggle Eden finally insisted on resigning, though no other cabinet colleague supported him on the relatively narrow issue on which he saw fit to make a stand.

By resigning over Italian policy rather than that pursued towards Germany, Eden for a time found himself in less than complete alliance with the other leading Conservative dissident, WINSTON CHURCHILL, who saw Adolf Hitler as the only real threat. But with the approach of war in 1939 the two men drew closer. All the same, it was the vindicated Churchill, and not Eden, who was given a seat in Chamberlain's War Cabinet. Eden had to be content with the junior role of running the

Sir Anthony Eden and Selwyn Lloyd in Downing Street at the time of the Suez Crisis, August 1956

Dominions Office. And even in May 1940, when Churchill succeeded Chamberlain, there was still no seat for him in the War Cabinet. But he was moved up to the War Office and played a significant role during the Dunkirk Evacuation and the Battle of Britain.

In December 1940 Churchill finally decided to restore Eden to the foreign secretaryship and to bring him into the War Cabinet. According to the former, the latter was like 'a man going home'. Thereafter Eden rapidly emerged as Churchill's second-in-command and would undoubteldy have succeeded to the premiership if a vacancy had arisen during the remainder of the war. In his new capacity Eden was involved in all major decisions and he attended the great majority of wartime international conferences, including those at Teheran, Yalta and Potsdam.

Inevitably, most of the major policy decisions were ultimately made by Churchill. Hence it is not easy to indicate all the areas where Eden's influence was particularly significant. But it is fair to say that he generally proved more sympathetic than his chief towards the Soviet

Union and at times carried the day. In this connection Eden has been depicted by some highly critical historians as more eager than Churchill to promote the supposedly inhumane policy of enforced repatriation of prisoners-of-war to the Soviet Union – where many were summarily executed.

Eden left office in 1945 with the election of Clement Attlee's Labour Government. He was for a time rather dispirited and was also physically and mentally exhausted. For he had served for much of the war as Leader of the House as well as Foreign Secretary. Moreover, his elder son, Simon, had been killed in action in the last days of the war, and his first marriage (to Beatrice Beckett) was on the verge of breakdown – divorce resulting in 1950. In these circumstances he contemplated leaving British politics and becoming Secretary-General of the United Nations. But he eventually resumed his duties at Westminster – suffering much frustration at the unwillingness of the aged Churchill to stand down as Conservative Party leader.

Churchill in fact survived to return to Number Ten in 1951 at the age of 76. Eden was again given the Foreign Office. But on this occasion he was an unwilling and uncooperative partner to the Prime Minister, whom he constantly sought to persuade to retire in his favour. Churchill was to prove a stubborn opponent and held on to power until April 1955. Meanwhile Eden had further and more serious health problems – this time with severe long-term effects. In 1953 he had an apparently routine bile-duct operation but this went wrong. Two further operations – one in the USA – were needed to enable him to return to the Foreign Office, from which he was absent for six months. For the rest of his life he was subject to recurrent bouts of fever and had to take various drugs. It remains a matter of controversy whether his handling of the Suez Crisis would have been different had his health been more normal.

Despite his operations and despite the continuous tension with Churchill, Eden was able during his last term at the Foreign Office to add to his reputation as a world statesman. (The Queen also honoured him in 1954 by making him a Knight of the Garter.) In particular, he is remembered for his work at the Geneva Conference in 1954, which brought a temporary solution to the problem of Indochina, and later in the same year he played a crucial role in reconciling France to the need for West German re-armament under NATO auspices. 1954 also saw Eden reach agreement with Colonel Nasser's Egypt for the withdrawal by 1956 of all British forces from the Suez Canal Zone – especially ironic in the light of later events.

Eden's tenure of Number Ten is generally accounted a stark failure – largely because of the Suez Affair. But it began in impressive fashion when he led the Conservatives to victory with an increased majority in the general election of May 1955. And he followed this by representing his country at the first postwar East–West summit, held at Geneva in July 1955. There he met with American, Soviet and French leaders.

Matters thereafter began to go wrong for Eden. Economic problems re-emerged, requiring an emergency budget in October 1955. Some blamed Eden, whose excessive

concentration on world affairs throughout his career allegedly left him with little practical knowledge of domestic issues in general. He was also to be increasingly contrasted – usually unfavourably – with his distinguished predecessor, and he began to lose the full confidence of some of his colleagues – partly because of his irascibility and his constant interference with detailed departmental matters. To some he seemed too highly-strung to be Prime Minister; to others he was simply capricious or indecisive.

None of this meant that his position was in any way at risk until Nasser nationalized the Suez Canal in July 1956. This at once put him in danger. For if he acquiesced in the coup he was likely to face a major rebellion in the cabinet and in the Conservative Party. And if he sought to reverse it by armed force he was likely to divide the nation, split the Commonwealth, and, above all, come into conflict with the USA. In short, he was probably damned if he did, and damned if he didn't.

After months of fruitless negotiations about the canal's future, during which he completely lost confidence in US Secretary of State John Foster Dulles, Eden decided, with the support of senior colleagues, to try to check or even topple Nasser by means of a secret conspiracy with France and Israel. Under the terms of a secret understanding reached at Sèvres, a suburb of Paris, Israel invaded Egypt on 29 October. Then Great Britain and France, pretending surprise, claimed that the canal was threatened, necessitating the despatch of a task force to take it over and also to separate the combatants. An Anglo-French ultimatum was sent to both Egypt and Israel. Following its rejection by the former, Egyptian airfields were bombed and an armada set sail from Malta.

The reaction at home and abroad to Eden's policy was much harsher than he had expected. A sitting of the House of Commons had to be suspended; most members of the Commonwealth protested; and the USA unequivocally condemned the proposed intervention and mobilized overwhelming support for her view at the United Nations. Clearly the highminded pretext for the Anglo-French invasion of Egypt had been insufficiently plausible.

After some hesitation, Eden's cabinet

decided to disregard UN calls for a ceasefire. Accordingly on 5 November Anglo-French airborne landings took place at Port Said and Port Fuad, and seaborne landings followed on the next day. Meeting little effective resistance, the task force rapidly seized one-third of the canal. But suddenly an order to halt was received. Eden's cabinet, with sterling in desperate need of American support, had after all reluctantly decided to respond to the call for a ceasefire. Eden tried hard to salvage something from the wreck – hoping to bargain withdrawal of the task force against concessions from Egypt. But President Eisenhower insisted on unconditional withdrawal and this was duly completed by 22 December. Great Britain was thus publicly humiliated.

Meanwhile Eden's health problem had intensified. Following a period of rest in Jamaica, he came to the conclusion that he was unfit to continue. He resigned on 9 January 1957. The chances are, however, that he would have been forced to resign in any event. For his Suez enterprise had ended in decisive failure. Moreover, he had been drawn into telling the House of Commons that there had been no foreknowledge of the Israeli attack. This was an outright lie – which was bound to have been exposed sooner or later, with catastrophic implications for his reputation.

Eden spent two decades in retirement, mostly in the Wiltshire countryside, where he died in 1977. One of his principal hobbies there was breeding Hereford cattle. He also completed three volumes of political memoirs, together with a charming account of his early life entitled *Another World*. He became the Earl of Avon in 1961. His closing years were marked above all, however, by great domestic happiness with his second wife, Clarissa Churchill. She ensured a serene end to a turbulent life.

For further illustration, see MACMILLAN, HAROLD.

WRITINGS

Memoirs, 3 vols.: Vol. 1, *Full Circle* (London: Cassell, 1960); Vol. 2, *Facing the Dictators* (London: Cassell, 1962); Vol. 3, *The Reckoning* (London: Cassell, 1965).

Another World 1897–1917 (London: Allen Lane, 1976).

FURTHER READING

Carlton, David, *Anthony Eden: a Biography* (London: Allen Lane, 1981).
——, *Britain and the Suez Crisis* (Oxford: Blackwell, 1988).
Rhodes James, Robert, *Anthony Eden* (London: Weidenfeld and Nicolson, 1986).

DAVID CARLTON

Edinburgh, Duke of. See PHILIP, PRINCE.

Edward VII [Albert Edward] (*b.* London, 9 November 1841; *d.* Sandringham, Norfolk, 6 May 1910). King Edward, who had been Prince of Wales since he was a month old, was nearly 60 when he came to the throne on 22 February 1901. Largely content to leave government policy in home and colonial affairs to his ministers, he considered that he had a more positive role to play as regards the armed forces and foreign policy. He was involved in the achievement of the Anglo-French *entente* in 1904 and the Anglo-Russian Agreement of 1907. His great contribution to the modern monarchy lay in his revival and refurbishing of its public, visible and ceremonial aspects. A pleasure-loving man, his tastes for horse-racing and the music hall were shared by many of his subjects and he was an enormously popular king.

The second child of Queen Victoria and Prince Albert, Prince Albert Edward did not respond to his rigorous and carefully planned education and upbringing to his parents' satisfaction. He grew up to be an affable man, though very conscious of his position, and his social skills were early revealed on his tours of Canada and the USA in 1860, but he had none of the seriousness or the intellectual interests of his father. Queen Victoria blamed him for the distress his affair with an actress caused to Prince Albert in the months before the latter's death in 1861.

During the long period in which he was heir apparent, the Prince of Wales was not given any real share of royal duties and responsibilities.

He devoted himself to social life and pleasure, and his home, Marlborough House, became the centre of fashionable society. He married Princess Alexandra of Denmark in 1863 and they were fond of each other and united in their affection for their five children (the eldest, Prince Albert Victor, died in 1892), but the Prince's sexual liaisons were numerous. His life style involved him in a number of scandals and he was subpoenaed to appear in two court cases, the Mordaunt divorce case in 1870 and the Tranby Croft case in 1891. He was, nevertheless, a popular figure and his recovery from typhoid fever late in 1871 was the occasion for national rejoicing. That he was a shrewd judge of what the nation demanded of its monarchy is shown by his repeated urging of Queen Victoria to abandon the retirement from public appearance that characterized her widowhood and by his enthusiastic support for the successful Jubilee that brought her back into the centre of public celebrations.

King Edward VII and Queen Alexandra on the royal yacht at Cowes, 1909

When, as Edward VII, he entered enthusiastically into his long-awaited inheritance, the King built upon the experience of the Jubilee and, with the aid of Viscount Esher, his confidant and adviser, ensured that state and royal occasions were mounted with great ceremony and panache. He set a stamp upon the public and ceremonial side of the monarchy that has substantially endured, while his delight in showing himself to his subjects on less splendid occasions, on visits to provincial towns or at sporting events, was also to set precedents for his successors.

He did not welcome the decrease in the political power of the Crown that had taken place during Queen Victoria's reign but he largely accepted it. He was, however, very conscious of his dignity and jealous of his prerogatives, and, while he did not consider that, as King, he should make government policy, he did try to ensure that he was consulted. On this he was rebuffed and A. J. Balfour brushed aside his demand to be consulted while policy was in the making.

The King felt, however, that he had the right to greater influence over policy concerning the army and navy, and he intervened on several occasions in disputes concerning their administration and modernization: he threw his influence behind far-reaching reform of the army, crossing swords with two Conservative Ministers for War, St John Brodrick and H. O. Arnold-Forster, in the process, though he achieved more cordial relations with the Liberal Minister, R. B. Haldane; and he gave consistent support to Admiral Sir John Fisher in his long struggle over naval strategy with Admiral Lord Charles Beresford. Despite some blind spots – he detested the thought of khaki replacing red army uniforms – his influence was on the side of greater military and naval efficiency.

More than any monarch since George II, King Edward was at home in Europe and with European royalty, and it is in foreign affairs that the greatest claims have been made for his influence, many contemporaries seeing his hand behind British foreign policy. The King was in a position to influence and felt that he had the right to do so, but it is doubtful that he exercised an independent sway. It is certain, however, that he was an instrument of government policy and that his personal contacts with foreign rulers were useful to his governments. On the whole his views on foreign affairs went with the grain of cabinet and Foreign Office opinion: he favoured close relations with France and an understanding with Russia, combined with a firm but not unconciliatory line with Germany. Influential or merely useful, he fulfilled a unique role.

King Edward VII was a modern constitutional monarch with an acceptance of the control over government of elected politicians that would have horrified the theory, if not the practice, of the older Queen Victoria. Yet the boundaries of royal power were not so clearly drawn as they would be in future reigns. When in the last year of his life, it seemed that he would be called upon to give an undertaking to create sufficient peers to allow the Parliament Bill introduced by Asquith's government to pass through the House of Lords, the King considered inviting the Conservative leader, A. J. Balfour, to form a minority government rather than acquiesce to the Liberal demand. King Edward died before the decision had to be made. But it was not as a political figure that he was so deeply mourned but as a king and a man, at once majestic and popular.

FURTHER READING

Brook-Shepherd, G., *Uncle of Europe* (London: Collins, 1975).

Magnus, P., *King Edward the Seventh* (London: John Murray, 1964).

Middlemas, K., *The Life and Times of Edward VII* (London: Weidenfeld and Nicolson, 1972).

A. W. PURDUE

Edward VIII [Edward Albert Christian George Andrew Patrick David] (*b.* Richmond, Surrey, 23 June 1894; *d.* Paris, 28 May 1972). The reign of Edward VIII lasted only from 20 January to 11 December 1936, when he abdicated in order to be free to marry Mrs Wallis Simpson. He was never crowned. Edward's abdication came as a shock to most of the nation and for a short time it was thought that he had seriously undermined the prestige of the monarchy.

The eldest child of the Duke and Duchess of York, later King George V and Queen Mary, Prince Edward (or David as he was known by

his family) entered the Royal Naval College, Osborne, in 1907. His career in the navy was cut short in 1910 when his father succeeded to the throne. As heir apparent he was created Prince of Wales in the following year.

During World War I Edward's presence at the Western Front earned him the respect of many servicemen. His good looks and personal charm made him an ideal royal representative and after the war, when it was felt that the monarchy had an essential role to play in keeping the empire together, he proved the ideal 'ambassador'. His successful visits in the 1920s to the dominions contributed to making him the most popular member of the royal family both with the press and the public.

From the first, the relationship of Edward with his parents was remote and lacking in demonstrable affection. As he grew older he clashed increasingly with his father over certain royal duties and court procedures, many of which Edward regarded as petty and outdated. Also his liking for parties, night life and a smart circle of friends inevitably conflicted with George's marked preference for a well-ordered and rigorously time-tabled domesticity. What worried George above all was that this most eligible of bachelors and heir to the throne seemed in no hurry to marry and, indeed, clearly preferred the company of married women. His closest companion from 1934 onwards was the sophisticated and elegant Mrs Wallis Simpson. Born in Maryland, USA, in 1896, Wallis Warfield had already experienced one unsuccessful marriage before marrying in 1928 Ernest Simpson, a British shipping broker. This liaison ended in October 1936, when Mrs Simpson successfully sued for divorce.

On George's death on 10 January 1936, Edward emphasized the new style and image of his reign by flying from Sandringham to Hendon to attend his Accession Council at St James's Palace. Although in a sense Edward wanted to appear as 'the People's King', he possessed neither the emotional commitment to be a genuine reformer nor the intellectual stamina to devote much time to affairs of state. Within a few months of becoming king, it became clear that he was paying little attention to state papers, which were often returned by

The Duke and Duchess of Windsor sightseeing at Tregir, near Split on the Dalmatian Coast, 1936

him weeks late and bearing no evidence of having been perused.

In August, Edward, accompanied by Mrs Simpson, went for a cruise along the Dalmatian coast. The American and European press reported their progress enthusiastically and fully but the British media, as a result of a gentleman's agreement, made no mention of Mrs Simpson and the King was represented as a hard-working monarch taking a well deserved rest from the cares of state. The media maintained its silence until early December, and while Edward was given full coverage visiting the Fleet and the depressed areas of South Wales, the public was totally unaware of the drama taking place behind the scenes. In October the Prime Minister, STANLEY BALD-WIN, met Edward to discuss the implications of Mrs Simpson's forthcoming divorce suit. In the following month Edward made it clear to those around him that he was determined to marry Wallis. However, a twice-divorced American commoner as queen was totally unacceptable to the government, the Archbishop of Canterbury

and most of the leading members of the Labour and Liberal opposition parties. Even when a morganatic marriage was proposed, whereby Wallis would not hold the rank of queen and any children born of the union would have no rights to succession, the idea was vetoed by the cabinet and the prime ministers from the dominions who were consulted on the matter.

Edward was faced with three options: renounce Wallis, abdicate, or, if he remained king and married Wallis, face an unprecedented constitutional crisis, for the government would resign and the opposition parties would refuse to take office. Edward chose abdication. The end of the affair came quickly. On 10 December Edward signed the Instrument of Abdication. The following day he broadcast to the nation giving his reasons for quitting the throne and that evening, Edward, now Duke of Windsor, crossed into Europe and into virtual exile.

Stanley Baldwin feared that a 'King's Party', led perhaps by Winston Churchill and Lord Beaverbrook, might emerge in his defence, but Edward made no attempt whatsoever to elicit support in order to remain on the throne. Also, the affair was over too quickly for any popular movement to get under way. Just nine days after it had been made public, Edward was in Europe. Indeed, the Abdication Crisis turned out not to be a crisis. The resilience of the institution proved to be much stronger than the popularity of an individual. When James Maxton proposed an amendment to the Abdication Bill that the monarchy and the hereditary principle should be abolished, it was defeated by 403 votes to five.

Edward married Wallis near Tours on 3 June 1937. No member of the royal family was present. Although Edward retained the title HRH, this right was not extended to the Duchess of Windsor. In October 1937 the Duke and Duchess visited Germany and met Hitler, causing much embarrassment to the royal family and the British Government. In 1940 the Duke escaped from France to Portugal but, fearing that he might be kidnapped by the Germans, the British Government persuaded him to leave Europe. He was appointed Governor of the Bahamas and filled that post from 1941 to 1945. After the war the Duke and

Duchess spent much of the remainder of their lives in France. The Duchess died on 24 April 1986.

WRITINGS

A King's Story (London: Cassell, 1951).

FURTHER READING

Bloch, M. (ed.), *Wallis & Edward: Letters 1931–1937* (London: Weidenfeld and Nicolson, 1986).
Donaldson, F., *Edward VIII* (London: Weidenfeld and Nicolson, 1974).

J. M. GOLBY

Eliot, T(homas) S(tearns) (*b*. St Louis, Missouri, 26 September 1888; *d*. London, 4 January 1965). Poet, playwright, critic and editor. As a poet, he was one of the most potent writers of the first half of the twentieth century; his work is still studied in schools and universities in every continent. His literary criticism, with its emphasis on European tradition, was both challenging and conservative. His criticism of contemporary culture, in such prose works as *The Idea of a Christian Society* (1939) and *Notes Towards the Definition of Culture* (1948), was less influential but equally conservative. In the latter book he insisted that 'culture' and egalitarianism were incompatible.

Eliot was born in Missouri at the intersection of the New England puritan tradition of his family with the racist and agrarian culture of the American South. His businessman father retained the strenuous ethical standards of his distinguished family. Eliot was sent to New England for his education, finally studying at Harvard from 1906 to 1914. Immigration, largely Irish and Jewish, threatened the elite values of the white Anglo-Saxon Protestants. In his poetry, Eliot would find images of purity in the seascapes of New England and its bird life to set against the degeneration of cosmopolitan modern cities which 'spawned' Jews ('Gerontion', 1920) and provided a habitat for the archetypal urbanized Celt, 'apeneck Sweeney'. He arrived in England in 1914 with a travelling fellowship, destined for Oxford. The outbreak of war soon after helped to ensure that he would express his disdain for what Jacksonian democracy had made of America by settling east of the Atlantic. He married an Englishwoman, Vivien Haigh-Wood, in 1915, and became a British citizen in 1927, soon after his confirmation in the Church of England.

Between these dates he moved from the obscurity of avant-garde circles to a position of dominance in English letters. Clerical work in Lloyds Bank supported him from 1917 to 1925, while he established his reputation as reviewer, essayist and editor. His marriage was disastrous and in 1921 he suffered a nervous breakdown which prompted a visit to Lausanne for psychological therapy. Ironically, at this dismal time he finished his sequence *The Waste Land*. It combined erudition with jazzy up to dateness, quasi-biblical prophecy with social satire. After its publication in 1922 it was hailed as a definitive expression of the crisis of European civilization in the aftermath of war. Its impact on young intellectuals was profound, though its quasi-collage technique has never been successfully imitated. It remains his most important work.

In 1925 Eliot joined the publishing firm of Faber. He served it for the rest of his life, building a formidable list of poets. From this time, his own writing became explicitly Christian. Church of England commissions led to his first completed dramatic works – *The Rock* (1934) and *Murder in the Cathedral* (1935). His political position was enigmatic. An anti-semitic aside in a series of lectures given at the University of Virginia in 1933 has been held against him. But he made it under personal strain (he had just left his deeply neurotic wife, who died in a mental hospital 14 years later). He had claimed in 1927 to be 'classicist in literature, royalist in politics and anglo-catholic in religion'. Unlike his old friend Ezra Pound, he had no empathy with Fascism. Some of the younger poets whom he encouraged were explicitly left wing. Herbert Read, an anarchist, was a close friend. In a decade in which many writers professed strong political commitment, Eliot became an eminence above the ceaseless controversy, teased for his sartorial respectability, loved for his kindness.

In World War II he played the role of writer

T. S. Eliot, c.November 1943

as public man to perfection. He served as an air-raid warden and fire fighter. He spoke at Archbishop Temple's Malvern Conference of 1941 on Christianity and social order, though he dissociated himself from the consensus statement which cautiously questioned private ownership of industrial resources. Three of his *Four Quartets* appeared during the war. These are major poems, meditating on time and eternity. But 'East Coker' (1940) and 'The Dry Salvages' (1941) had direct, and even topical, patriotic application. 'Little Gidding' (1942) contained a remarkable evocation of the London blitz as timeless purgatory and suggested that 'History is now and England'. Jibe though he did at left-wing progressivism, Eliot's message connected with the ideal of 'People's War' and with the postwar mood of weary patriotism.

Eliot's influence was at its greatest in the immediate postwar period. In 1948 he was awarded both the Order of Merit and the Nobel Prize for Literature. Next year, his play *The Cocktail Party* was a vast box-office success. Other verse dramas for the West End stage followed. They came to seem tepid and dated

as a vigorous new school of young playwrights emerged in the mid-1950s. But Eliot won personal happiness at last when he married his 30-year-old secretary, Valerie Fletcher, in 1957.

Besides long years of marital misery, then of loneliness, Eliot had often suffered from illness and from 'writer's block'. An inherited puritanical sense of duty seems to have kept him sane. *Old Possum's Book of Practical Cats* (1939), with its delightful light verse, is perhaps more essential to understanding him than one might suppose. Possum-like, he hid much, most of the time. His dogmatic conservative statements arose from and masked underlying scepticism and melancholy. When he gave free rein to his skittish wit, played with words, the effect, as with much major art, was anarchic.

FURTHER READING

Ackroyd, P., *T. S. Eliot* (London: Hamish Hamilton, 1984).
Cairns Craig, R., *Yeats, Eliot, Pound and the Politics of Poetry* (London: Croom Helm, 1982).

ANGUS CALDER

Elizabeth II [Elizabeth Alexandra Mary] (*b.* London, 21 April 1926). Queen of the United Kingdom of Great Britain and Northern Ireland, Queen Elizabeth is also Queen of Canada, Australia, and certain other independent states within the Commonwealth, of which she is head. She succeeded to the throne on the death of her father, King George VI, on 6 February 1952, and was crowned on 2 June 1953. As Princess Elizabeth she had married Prince Philip, Duke of Edinburgh, in 1947; their children are Prince Charles, Prince of Wales; Princess Anne (Mrs Mark Philips), the Princess Royal; Prince Andrew, Duke of York; and Prince Edward. In June 1977 she celebrated the Silver Jubilee of her reign.

Her father, Prince Albert, Duke of York, was second in line to the throne when he married Lady Elizabeth Bowes-Lyon in 1923. It was not until Princess Elizabeth was ten years old that King Edward VIII's abdication brought his younger brother to the throne as a reluctant but dutiful king. This event changed everything for the Princess.

The monarchy under King George VI was, in his words, a 'family firm', and Court and government were anxious to project not just the King but his wife and the Princesses Elizabeth and Margaret Rose (*b.* 1930) to emphasize the domestic felicity and wholesomeness of the new reign. As heir to the throne, Princess Elizabeth was a key figure when, during World War II, the royal family sought to identify with the experiences and hardships of the nation: she spoke on the BBC's *Children's Hour*, joined the Auxiliary Territorial Service and was photographed servicing an army lorry.

The relationship between Princess Elizabeth and her father was close and was to have an abiding influence on her understanding of the responsibilities of the monarchy. Bravely mastering a role for which he had not been prepared, the King was concerned that his daughter should be fully educated in her future duties. At the age of 18 she was made a State Counsellor and was steadily taken further into the King's confidence. Relying heavily upon his united family, the King was reluctant to give his consent to an early marriage between Princess Elizabeth and Prince Philip of Greece, but agreed in 1947 and the royal wedding introduced some colour and romance into a drab postwar Britain.

The married couple hoped that Princess Elizabeth's succession to the throne would be long delayed, that there would be time to concentrate upon a family and for Prince Philip to pursue his naval career. Such time was short, for the King's failing health meant that the Princess had soon to take over many of his duties, and his death came in February 1952 while the Princess and her husband were in Kenya beginning a Commonwealth tour.

A young queen aroused the most romantic feelings of the British people about their monarchy and themselves, and talk of a new Elizabethan age that would bring about a national revival reached a crescendo with the magnificent coronation of 1953. That such a revival was not detected by many in the following years resulted in some disenchantment with the monarchy, especially among intellectuals, which was most evident in the late 1950s; the monarchy, far from giving leadership to natural regeneration, could be seen in an age anxious for modernity and change as redolent of an older Britain, class conscious and traditional. But the monarchy's great strength lies in the expression of the nation's continuity with its past and, if the Queen has sensibly adapted many aspects of style and presentation to suit social change, she has been wise to retain the substance of her inheritance. The Investiture of Prince Charles as Prince of Wales in 1969 and the success of the Jubilee celebrations in 1977 testified to the enduring satisfaction of the majority with the monarchy, a satisfaction that was further demonstrated at the time of the Prince of Wales's marriage to Lady Diana Spencer.

If the question of the presentation of the monarchy and problems of public relations have inevitably concerned the Queen more than they did her predecessors, many of the problems and challenges she has had to meet are similar to those which monarchs have had to deal with in the past. The political duties and influence of the Crown may have diminished but a political role remains. The then lack of formal procedure for electing the leader of the Conservative Party resulted in the Queen having on two occasions to decide, after consultation, which Conservative politician to ask to form a government after the resignation of her Prime Minister; neither the summons to the palace of Harold Macmillan in 1957 nor of Lord Home in 1963 were uncontroversial. The question of the remaining prerogatives of the Crown in respect of the formation of governments and the granting of requests for the dissolution of Parliament is raised every time there is, as in 1974, or seems likely to be, a parliament without an overall majority for any one party. The Queen's constitutional position in Australia led her to dismiss the government of Gough Whitlam, via her Governor-General, in 1975.

The royal finances, a problem for many previous monarchs and a possible cause of dissension with Parliament, were once more a problem in the late 1960s and early 1970s, when inflation required the regular increase of the money provided for the Civil List. A Select Committee of 1971 looked not only at the Civil List but at the whole question of royal expenditure. Even if a complete picture never

Queen Elizabeth II outside
St Paul's Cathedral,
London, after the Service of
the Order of St Michael and
St George, December 1984

emerged, the exercise resulted in an increase in the Civil List and a clearer accounting framework for royal expenditure. A question that had often proved embarrassing to the monarchy was removed from public controversy when the Labour Government provided in 1975 for the royal finances to be regularly updated in line with inflation.

The Commonwealth continues to be a major preoccupation of Queen Elizabeth's at a time when it has ceased to be central to British interests and is not, perhaps, particularly popular with much of the British population.

There has been some criticism of the Queen's Christmas Day broadcasts for concentrating too much on the Commonwealth and not enough on Britain. In 1983 and 1986 there were strong rumours of differences between the Palace and Number Ten and of a clash between the two strong personalities of the Queen and her Prime Minister, Margaret Thatcher, as to the attitude to take to, respectively, the USA's invasion of Grenada and Commonwealth sanctions against South Africa.

One can attempt only an interim assessment

of the reign of Queen Elizabeth II. She has carried out her duties with care and dignity, retains enormous social influence and has the affection and loyalty of the great majority of her subjects. She rules over a very different nation to that of 1952 and she and the institution of monarchy may have played no small part in enabling Britain to adjust to the many changes in its world position and in the nature of its political and social character that have taken place since her accession.

FURTHER READING

Lacey, R., *Majesty: Elizabeth II and the House of Windsor* (London: Hutchinson, 1977).

A. W. PURDUE

Elizabeth, the Queen Mother [née Bowes-Lyon, Lady Elizabeth] (*b.* St Paul's Walden Bury, Hertfordshire, 4 August 1900). Elizabeth became Queen Consort when her husband, as George VI, succeeded to the throne on 11 December 1936 after the abdication of his elder brother, Edward VIII. She did much to support and guide her husband during his 15 years as king and, in so doing, not only helped to restore the prestige of the monarchy after the shock of Edward VIII's abdication, but was also influential in shaping the image of the monarchy to meet the social and political changes that occurred during and after World War II. After the death of George VI in 1952 she retained her popularity, as Queen Mother, both with the public and the media.

The youngest daughter and ninth child of the fourteenth Earl and Countess of Strathmore, Elizabeth married Prince Albert, Duke of York, on 26 April 1923. Whereas royal marriages had hitherto invariably been between other royal houses, Elizabeth was the first commoner for more than 200 years to marry the son of a British king. Despite her lack of royal pedigree, she brought an aura of charm, serenity and domesticity to her position as Duchess of York. She was popular both with other members of the royal family, especially George V and Queen Mary, and with the public. After the birth of her daughters, Elizabeth (*b.* 1926) and Margaret (*b.* 1930), the

Duchess of York, with her sensible appreciation of the importance of public relations, allowed media attention to dwell on the happy and cosy family life of her immediate family, and it was this image of a majestic yet domestic monarchy which was emphasized when the inexperienced Duke of York was unexpectedly thrust into the role of king in December 1936.

At the time there were fears that the institution of the monarchy would be seriously undermined as a result of the abdication of Edward VIII. These fears proved to be exaggerated, but a fundamental reason why the monarchy overcame what could have been a serious loss of prestige was the successful depiction of the new monarch as a father of a close-knit family, as well as king. Elizabeth played an important part in building up this image, and also gave support and guidance to the King, who was hard-working but lacking in confidence. Although younger than George, Elizabeth was more mature, intellectually stronger, and in public appeared more composed than her nervous and diffident husband; especially in the early years of his reign, George leaned heavily upon her for advice and support. While she invariably appeared in a supporting role, there has been no other queen consort who has had such a close contact with the business of the country.

In 1938 the royal couple made a state visit to France. In the following year they toured Canada and then went on to Washington and New York. Elizabeth in particular made a marked impression in the USA, and later in that same year the Americans voted her 'Woman of the Year' for 1939.

During the war years the King and Queen, with the support of the media, made every effort to demonstrate that they were sharing in the hardships experienced by the rest of the population. They remained in London during the blitz and were seen visiting other bombed cities and towns. Again, it was the determined example set by Elizabeth which caught the public imagination and helped maintain morale. When asked whether the Princesses would be sent abroad for the duration of the war, she is reported to have replied, 'The children can't go without me. I can't leave the King, and of course the King won't go.'

Queen Elizabeth with King George VI inspecting air-raid damage, London, September 1940

Throughout the reign, Elizabeth's most important role was in sustaining the confidence of and acting as confidante to the King. After his death in 1952 Elizabeth, unlike Queen Victoria, did not withdraw from her public duties. She took the name Queen Elizabeth, the Queen Mother, to distinguish herself from her eldest daughter, Elizabeth II, who succeeded to the throne, and she maintained a heavy schedule of royal engagements. In March 1953, her mother-in-law, Queen Mary (wife of George V) died, leaving Elizabeth as the family matriarch.

Despite the development of a more intrusive and sensation-seeking press, the Queen Mother has skilfully retained a good relationship with the media and she has remained one of the most popular members of the royal family. However, beneath her public image of sweetness and charm is a strong will and dogged determination to defend the status of the monarchy. Her attitude towards the Duke and Duchess of Windsor, whom she believed had harmed the institution, was one of little compassion and she played no small part in ensuring that they remained virtual exiles from Britain for the remainder of their lives and that the Duchess was denied the title 'Royal Highness'.

Meanwhile, as Queen Mother, she has carried out a wide range of public duties both in this country and overseas. She was Chancellor of the University of London from 1955 to 1980, and is Lord Warden of the Cinque Ports. In 1985 she was president or patron of 312 organizations and in 1986, although in her mid-eighties, she carried out some 130 public engagements.

FURTHER READING

Duff, D., *George and Elizabeth* (London: Collins, 1983).

Mortimer, P., *Queen Elizabeth: a Life of the Queen Mother* (London: Viking, 1986).

J. M. GOLBY

Evans, Harold (Matthew) (*b.* Patricroft, near Eccles, Lancashire, 28 June 1928). Journalist. He became during the 1970s the most admired journalist in Britain as editor of the *Sunday Times* while it was pioneering campaigning and investigative journalism and challenging legal and official restrictions on the right to publish. But his British career ended prematurely in 1982 when he fell out with Rupert Murdoch, who had appointed him editor of *The Times* after acquiring both papers a year earlier.

Evans joined his first newspaper at the age of 16, then served in the RAF and gained a degree at Durham University. He edited the *Northern Echo* from 1961 to 1966, when he conducted a long campaign to clear the name of the wrongly convicted murderer Timothy Evans. He joined the *Sunday Times* in 1966 and was its editor from 1967 until 1981. Among the many campaigns it undertook during his editorship, the most notable was the fight for adequate compensation to children born with deformities after their mothers had taken the morning-sickness drug Thalidomide.

Although he was never openly political, the vigorous anti-Establishment nature of many of the campaigns he masterminded made it inevitable that he should be seen as a radical. He had more friends on the left of the political spectrum than on the right. In his book *Good Times, Bad Times*, he maintains that the main subject of his difference with Murdoch was the politics of *The Times*: the proprietor thought he detected sympathy with the fledgling Social Democratic Party. But another factor was the difficulty he had in forging good working relations with the paper's existing staff after he moved there. Since leaving *The Times* he has worked mainly in the USA, where he lives with his second wife, the magazine editor Tina Brown.

WRITINGS

Good Times, Bad Times (London: Weidenfeld and Nicolson, 1983).

MICHAEL H. LEAPMAN

Ewing, Winifred (Margaret) (*b.* Glasgow, 10 July 1929). Scottish Nationalist politician. She was initially a Westminster MP from November 1967 until the 1970 general election, when she lost her seat. However, in that short period she became a substantial figure in Scottish and British politics. Her victory in a by-election at Hamilton marked the emergence of the Scottish National Party as a serious electoral force. In the 1966 general election Labour had held Hamilton with a very large majority over the Conservatives, and the SNP had not even put up a candidate. It was a remarkable triumph.

Ewing was brought up in Glasgow and studied at Glasgow University. She qualified as a solicitor and was drawn into nationalist politics. In the 1959 general election the SNP fielded but five candidates, and saved only one deposit. In 1966, 23 candidates stood, and 16 kept their deposits. The Hamilton result, therefore, was not an isolated sign of advance, but it was the victory which had been hoped for. Ewing became famous overnight. Frequent television appearances followed and she had columns in the mass-circulation daily newspapers in Scotland. There was heady talk of Scottish independence. An immense burden fell on her since she was expected to articulate the SNP viewpoint on all current issues, but she coped with considerable skill and clarity. However, in 1970 Labour took Hamilton in the general election and the SNP fell back for a few years, but it regained momentum in 1974. Ewing captured Moray and Nairn in that year, but the spotlight was less upon her insofar as she was only one of a clutch of SNP MPs. 1979 the Conservatives regained the seat. Ewing fought Orkney and Shetland unsuccessfully in 1983. It was in Europe, however, that her career blossomed. She became a member of the European Parliament in 1975, and in the first direct elections in 1979 she captured the Highlands and Islands constituency for the

SNP. She retained the seat, with increased majorities, in 1984 and 1989. She has a substantial personal following in the North of Scotland and is well known in the European Parliament, but it is her Hamilton victory which ensures her a lasting place in British political history.

KEITH ROBBINS

F

Faulkner, (Arthur) Brian (Deane) [Baron Faulkner of Downpatrick] (*b.* Helen's Bay, Co. Down, 18 February 1921; *d.* Co. Down, 3 March 1977). Ulster Unionist leader. A scion of a prominent Ulster business family, he enjoyed an intensely varied and agile career. He was in many ways an unlikely moderate. In his early days as a Unionist politician he had identified himself with apparently hardline 'Orange' stances. When the civil rights crisis erupted, he did not use his cabinet position to assist the efforts of the apparently modernizing Prime Minister, Terence O'Neill, though he was always careful by this point to admit the case for reform. Above all, Faulkner was wily and pragmatic; as the last Northern Ireland Premier when the British prorogued Stormont in 1972, he realized that the way back to power was through some kind of alliance with the mainly Catholic and nationalist Social Democratic and Labour Party. After rather fraught negotiations at Sunningdale, he became the leader of the new power-sharing executive in 1974. He performed this role with great skill and tact, a fact which his coalition partners have fully acknowledged.

When he entered Stormont at the age of 28, Faulkner was the youngest MP elected up to that time. He became Minister of Home Affairs in 1959 and was active in defeating the IRA's border campaign. In March 1963 he accepted the Ministry of Commerce within O'Neill's government, and gained a considerable reputation for his energetic pursuit of new investment. However, his relations with the aloof, aristocratic and considerably less competent O'Neill were always tricky, and Faulkner resigned in January 1969 in protest against the setting up of the Cameron Committee to enquire into the causes of violence. Following his own resignation in April 1969, O'Neill managed to secure – by one vote – the succession of his landed cousin James Chichester-Clark, a further indication of the 'Big House' versus business tensions within Unionism at this time.

Faulkner, however, served as Minister of Development within Chichester-Clark's government and carried out the reforms of local government and the establishment of a central housing authority. He now began to appear more as a modernizer and less as a hardliner. But following his election to the premiership, Faulkner, who had broken with tradition and included a Catholic in his cabinet, introduced internment without trial in August 1971. Like other later dramatic initiatives (including the Anglo-Irish Agreement), this move led to an upsurge rather than a decline in violence.

In March 1972, much to Faulkner's surprise, the British Government prorogued Stormont in protest at the 'mini Vietnam' he had allegedly created. Initially, his response was exceptionally bitter; identifying himself with erstwhile hardline opponents such as William Craig, he refused to play any role in advising the British Government, declaring that Northern Ireland could not be treated like a 'coconut colony'. Yet, in another twist, Faulkner eventually took his section of Unionist opinion into the inter-party executive of 1974 with the nationalist SDLP and the ecumenical Alliance Party. In doing so, partly because he was isolated in the Sunningdale negotiations conducted by Edward Heath, Faulkner accepted not only power sharing but the cross-border Council of Ireland. The Council of Ireland had to work on a unanimity rule, and there was then no real danger to the Unionist position, but as a symbol of creeping unification it greatly weakened the appeal of the power-sharing executive to the Unionist population. Faulkner explained in his *Memoirs*: 'If this nonsense was necessary to bring their [SDLP] supporters along I did not see why we should be difficult.' Like so many of Faulkner's political judgements this was sharp enough, but it misunderstood the broader emotions at work in Irish politics. A mass loyalist strike broke down the Faulkner-led executive in May 1974. He briefly formed an unsuccessful breakaway liberal Unionist group (the Unionist Party of Northern Ireland) and then retired from politics in 1976, taking his peerage in 1977.

WRITINGS

Memoirs of a Statesman (London: Weidenfeld and Nicolson, 1978).

FURTHER READING

Bew, Paul and Patterson, Henry, *The British State and the Ulster Crisis: from Wilson to Thatcher* (London: Verso, 1985).
Blakely, P., *Faulkner* (Oxford and London: Mowbrays, 1974).

PAUL A. E. BEW

Fawcett [née Garrett] Dame **Millicent** [Mrs Henry Fawcett; Millicent Garrett Fawcett] (*b.* Aldeburgh, Suffolk, 11 June 1847; *d.* London, 5 August 1929). Pioneer in the causes of women's suffrage and education. Millicent Garrett originally intended to pursue a career as a physician, a profession at that time all but closed to her sex. The frustrations involved in this ambition (over which her celebrated sister, Elizabeth Garrett Anderson, triumphed so singularly) turned her from medicine to politics and the scarcely less frustrating pursuit of reform. She married Henry Fawcett in 1867, the year indeed of the Second Reform Bill, and was thus brought inevitably into contact with the Philosophical Radicals. In that same year she joined the women's suffrage committee, a step which led eventually to her presidency (1897–1918) of the National Union of Women's Suffrage Societies. In 1869 she was a prime mover in the scheme that effected the establishment of Newnham College, Cambridge. Of her several books, *Political Economy for Beginners* (1870) became a best-seller. She worked devotedly for the passage of the Married Women's Property Act (1882).

Fawcett's broader politics certainly lacked a radical edge, and as a suffragist, too, she proved a moderate. In 1887 she joined the Liberal Unionists. She became an enthusiastic opponent of Irish Home Rule and an equally enthusiastic advocate of the British cause in the Boer War. The new generation of militant suffragettes, rallied in 1905 by Emmeline Pankhurst, and the formation of the Women's Social and Political Union did not meet with her approval. She preferred gradualism to the wilder extremities of activism. But she was far from slow, in 1916, to exert her considerable influence upon an embattled wartime government, urging them to stop dragging their feet on the now critical question of women's franchise, a measure of which was finally introduced by Parliament in 1918. Fawcett's role in this albeit only partly satisfactory achievement was historic and of great significance.

WRITINGS

The Women's Victory and After (London: Sidgwick and Jackson, 1920).
What I Remember (London: T. F. Unwin, 1925).

FURTHER READING

Strachey, Ray, *Millicent Garrett Fawcett* (London: John Murray, 1931).

ANDREW MCNEILLIE

Fawkes, Wally. See TROG.

Feather, Vic(tor Grayson Hardie) [Lord Feather of Bradford] (*b.* Bradford, Yorkshire, 10 April 1908; *d.* London, 28 July 1976). Trade-union leader. In his brief but eventful term as General Secretary of the TUC, he played a decisive role in the trade unions' resistance to regulatory legislation, threatened by the Labour Government in 1969 and carried through by the Conservatives in 1971. In his term he aligned the TUC more formally behind the Labour Party than had been the case for years.

An outgoing man with the common touch, sometimes nicknamed 'Vic the Fixer' or 'Uncle Vic', he never allowed anyone to forget his Yorkshire background. After starting work at the age of 14 as a 'flour boy' in a Cooperative grocery, he became a lay official in the shop assistants' union, the National Union of Distributive and Allied Workers, while writing for the local Independent Labour Party newspaper. In 1937 he joined the TUC Organization Department, becoming assistant secretary in 1947 and assistant general secretary in 1960. His matey, informal manner – contrasting with that of his predecessor as general secretary, George Woodcock – served him well when he succeeded to the post in 1969 at the moment when the unions mounted their most major constitutional challenge since 1926.

Feather became acting general secretary in March 1969 (his appointment was confirmed six months later) and led opposition to the Labour Government's 'In Place of Strife' White Paper, which suggested legal restrictions on unions to restrain unofficial strikes. It was replaced by a 'solemn and binding' undertaking with no legal force, which Feather worked hard to fulfil. But in 1970 the incoming Conservative Government led by Edward Heath made the reform of industrial relations a priority, passing the 1971 Industrial Relations Act. Feather ran a brilliant campaign, effectively nullifying the Act by mobilizing TUC unions against the required registration and suspending 32, mainly small, unions which did register. He held the TUC together and led it into talks on the economy with the government which were ultimately abortive. The Act was repealed by the 1974 Labour Government after Feather's retirement in 1973; the lessons learnt from it were reflected in the trade-union legislation carried out 'step by step' by the Thatcher governments from 1979.

FURTHER READING

Silver, Eric, *Victor Feather TUC* (London: Gollancz, 1973).

MARTIN ADENEY

Fisher, Geoffrey (Francis) [Baron Fisher of Lambeth] (*b.* Higham on the Hill, Warwickshire, 5 May 1887; *d.* Sherborne, Dorset, 15 September 1972). Archbishop of Canterbury. Both as a church leader and as a public figure, Fisher touched national and international life at many points during his 16 years as Archbishop of Canterbury (1945–61). The Coronation of Queen Elizabeth II in June 1953 brought him world attention. So also did his epochal visit to Pope John XXIII in 1960. His earlier career, however, gave little hint of these distinctions. His background was that of a public school: first at Marlborough as assistant master, and then, for 18 years, as Headmaster of Repton (1914–32).

Appointment to the bishopric of Chester in 1932 moved him away from this milieu. A further appointment, as Bishop of London in 1939, proved to be a challenging task. The diocese was much divided within itself, and the strong sense of discipline which Fisher was thought to have brought from his headmaster background proved effective. The hazards of war added to his difficulties. His home, Lambeth Palace, was virtually destroyed. It was seen, even so, at the end of his time in London, that Fisher was a spiritual leader of note.

His appointment as 99th Archbishop of Canterbury in 1945 came as a surprise. His predecessor had been William Temple, of whom much had been expected, and whose sudden death in 1944 brought widely felt sorrow. It had been considered that Temple's successor should have been Bell, Bishop of Chichester, a man of wide international contacts – not least with figures in the German anti-Nazi resistance. But Bell had criticized the Allied policy of saturation bombing, and this was held against him, it was supposed, by some in the government of the day. Such was the background to Fisher's archiepiscopate. How he justified his call to this duty is shown by the events which followed.

The major religious initiatives in which Fisher was concerned arose from his long involvement in the cause of Christian unity. During the war, while Bishop of London, he had many contacts with the Roman Catholic Church, especially with Cardinal Hinsley of Westminster and his Sword of the Spirit Movement. At this time Fisher also served as chairman of the British Council of Churches. After the war he became one of the first presidents of the World Council of Churches, presiding at its first assembly in Amsterdam in 1948. Fisher's most notable move in this field was his 'Cambridge Sermon', delivered in Great St Mary's church in that city on 3 November 1946. In this he called upon the Free Churches to move step by step towards greater unity. This evoked a warm response, from the Methodist Church in particular. In later years, however, the movement encountered difficulties which prevented further progress.

Within the Church of England Fisher made his mark as a reformer of some of its structures and forms of government, including the revision of Canon Law. He travelled extensively among the Anglican Communion worldwide, becoming the first Archbishop of Canterbury – and indeed the first church leader – to make use of the opportunities afforded by air travel. Anglican provinces in Africa were visited, and some new ones inaugurated; Canada, Australia and New Zealand saw him on several occasions. His contacts with the Episcopal Church in the USA were especially close, thus offering a valuable preparation for the important Lambeth Conference of 1958 over which Fisher presided.

Fisher also made his mark in the wider world of public affairs. A number of questions arose during his time as Archbishop which led to complex social issues. To all he gave much thought and had important, and often controversial, things to say about them. Chief among these were the Wolfenden Report on the law in relation to homosexuality, the practice of artificial human insemination, AID, and the question of the introduction of Premium Bonds. On homosexuality Fisher made the often-quoted remark that 'in a civilised society all crimes are likely to be sins also; but most sins are not, and ought not to be regarded as crimes.' Nonetheless, in his view, homosexual practice was a sin. AID he condemned as a dangerous development, and Premium Bonds as an extension of gambling into the business of government. On divorce he warned that over-liberalization of its laws would have grave consequences for family life.

These issues, and his views on them, brought Fisher much attention from the media. His relations, especially with the press, were not always happy. In particular, at the time of the possible engagement of Princess Margaret to Group Captain Townsend, it was widely, though inaccurately, reported that Fisher had dissuaded the Princess from taking this step on the grounds of Townsend's involvement in a divorce case. Bitter criticism of the Archbishop's supposed pressures ensued. Similarly, his invitation to President Makarios of Cyprus, then an enemy of Britain, to attend the Lambeth Conference drew hostile reaction.

In contrast, Fisher's contacts with the Royal Family were warm and close. He was, he once said, 'at ease with them'. So were they with him, and the fact that he was so close to them at such junctures as the betrothal, and later the marriage, of Princess Elizabeth to Philip Mountbatten led to an intimate relationship when it fell to him to crown the young Queen in Westminster Abbey in June 1953.

Fisher's visit to Pope John XXIII in 1960 was a notable event. It was the first such occasion since Archbishop Arundel had visited the Roman Pontiff in 1397, and was made entirely on Fisher's own initiative. By the Pope himself, though not wholly by the Vatican, or by all Protestant opinion, the event was well received, and paved the way for later visits by succeeding Archbishops of Canterbury to Rome.

Unexpectedly, and to general surprise, Fisher resigned his archbishopric on 17 January 1961. The recipient of many honours, he was created a life peer in the year of his retirement to Trent in Dorset.

FURTHER READING

Purcell, William, *Fisher of Lambeth* (London: Hodder and Stoughton, 1969).

WILLIAM PURCELL

Fisher, H(erbert) A(lbert) L(aurens) (*b.* London, 21 March 1865; *d.* London, 18 April 1940). Historian and Liberal politician. Fisher became a politician by accident. The new Prime Minister, Lloyd George, decided during his anxious early days of office in December 1916 that educational policy should no longer be left to politicians. He rang the Vice-Chancellor of Sheffield University, whom he had met some years before, called him urgently to London and offered him the presidency of the Board of Education. It was Fisher's only political office and he occupied it – an unusual distinction in the Coalition's slippery cabinet-room – for the whole of Lloyd

George's tenure of power. Since Fisher's father had tutored the Prince of Wales and later held a royal sinecure, this loyalty had its own ironies. Indeed Fisher's own politics had remained Gladstonian – witness his lifelong friendship with Gilbert Murray – and he always claimed to feel closer to Asquith than the new Prime Minister in temperament and outlook. He was MP for Sheffield Hallamshire from 1917 to 1918 and for the Combined English Universities from 1918 to 1926.

In fact he probably formed part of Coalition window-dressing. His one significant initiative – the Education Act of 1918 – proved a great personal triumph and it removed obvious anomalies, in particular the 'half-time' system of education. But Fisher's original ambition to extend the power of government over local authorities and to introduce compulsory 'continuation' schools for juveniles who had left full-time education was allowed quietly to drop. His criticism of the Coalition's Irish policy made similarly little impact. By 1922 he was ill and depressed. He was also (an understandable omission in the printed memorabilia) desperately worried about money. Indeed he seems to have been one of the first twentieth-century politicians to find himself unable realistically to resign for that reason. The collapse of the Coalition in October 1922 brought a crisis, therefore, in Fisher's circumstances and he was reduced to supporting his family largely by writing, until the offer of the wardenship of his old college, New College, Oxford, in 1925 gave him the security he needed. This change in his fortunes allowed him to produce his masterpiece – the three-volume *History of Europe* – ten years later. That phase of his life also ended in accident: he was run over by a lorry in 1940 and died shortly afterwards from his injuries.

WRITINGS

An Unfinished Autobiography (London: Oxford University Press, 1940).

FURTHER READING

Ogg, David, *Herbert Fisher: a Short Biography* (London: Edward Arnold, 1947).

MICHAEL BENTLEY

Fisher, Sir **(Norman Fenwick) Warren** (*b.* Croydon, Surrey, 22 September 1879; *d.* London, 25 September 1948). Leading civil servant. He was Permanent Secretary to the Treasury for 20 years from October 1919. In that year a Treasury minute stated that the Permanent Secretary was ex officio Head of the Civil Service, and, although Fisher himself claimed that the Permanent Secretary's status as such had been well established since the 1870s, both his position and his use of it aroused controversy in Whitehall and Parliament. It was argued by some that Fisher's right to advise the Prime Minister on Civil Service appointments gave both him and the Treasury too much influence. The evidence suggests, however, that Fisher and his department exercised great influence only when ministers allowed them to do so.

The son of a gentleman of independent means, Fisher was educated at the Dragon School, Oxford, and Winchester College, before studying classics at Hertford College, Oxford. He entered the Inland Revenue in 1903, where his administrative ability later attracted the attention of the Chancellor of the Exchequer, Lloyd George. Fisher strengthened his reputation for organizational flair when he was seconded in 1912–13 to the newly established National Health Insurance Commission for England. Subsequently, he became deputy chairman of the Board of Inland Revenue in 1914 and then chairman in 1918.

It was Lloyd George who was responsible for Fisher's appointment, shortly before his fortieth birthday, to the top position in the Civil Service. At the time the Coalition Government of 1919–22 was keen to reduce public expenditure and the size of the Civil Service. Fisher believed that major economies could only be achieved by making changes in policy, and he did not hesitate to proffer advice as to what these changes should be. His chief interest, however, for the greater part of his time as Permanent Secretary, was reform of the Civil Service. He tried, with some success, both to foster team work within Whitehall and to soften the Treasury's image as the 'abominable no-man'. He suspended direct entry into the Treasury, preferring to recruit officials with experience of other departments, in the hope that such men would be better able to form constructive criticism of proposals for public expenditure than young men straight from university. Fisher believed that the Treasury should act as a 'general staff' within Whitehall, forming independent views on policy, including foreign policy. Other departments, especially the Foreign Office, did not always welcome Treasury criticism, however, the more so because of Fisher's habit of talking in an unguarded way about what he regarded as short-comings of people in Whitehall.

Fisher was widely believed to exercise great influence over Neville Chamberlain with regard to 'appeasement' and re-armament in the 1930s. Fisher certainly thought that it was necessary to reach some agreement with Japan and to avoid antagonizing Germany and Italy. He also argued strongly that British defence policy should be designed within limits that would not undermine the British economy, and he therefore advocated reliance on air power, with a low priority for the army. On the other hand, he fell out with Chamberlain over the terms of the Munich settlement and he felt that he had so little influence on defence policy by early 1939 that he went on leave in May, four months before he was due to retire, so as to allow his designated successor, Sir Horace Wilson, to take over. Subsequently, Fisher was involved in Civil Defence work, serving from 1940 to 1942 as special commissioner in the London region to coordinate work in restoring roads and utility services. He was dismissed after publicly criticizing the Minister for Home Security, Herbert Morrison, on a personnel matter.

Fisher was a powerful personality, capable of arousing great affection or great hostility. He married in 1906 and had two sons.

FURTHER READING

Hamilton, H. P., 'Sir Warren Fisher and the public service', *Public Administration*, 29 (1951), pp. 3–38.
O'Halpin, Eunan, *Head of the Civil Service: a Study of Sir Warren Fisher* (London: Routledge, 1989).
Peden, G. C., 'Sir Warren Fisher and British rearmament against Germany', *English Historical Review*, 94 (1979), pp. 29–47.

G. C. PEDEN

Fitt, Gerry [Gerard; Lord Fitt of Bell's Hill in the County of Down] (*b.* Belfast, 9 April 1926). Socialist politician. As MP for West Belfast in the late 1960s, Fitt, more than anyone else, drew the Westminster Parliament's attention to civil rights grievances in Northern Ireland. While remaining almost unshakably in the civil rights and socialist camp, he was appalled by the rise and impact of the IRA. Essentially a reformer and a moderate, he was increasingly disenchanted by the militant fanaticism of many of his republican constituents in West Belfast.

Fitt first worked as a soap boy in a barber's shop and then served with the British merchant navy (1941–53); he was involved in many wartime convoys to Russia. Energetic, witty and profoundly populist in instinct, he established himself as the focal figure of Belfast Catholic working-class politics in the 1960s. In 1966 he was elected as Republican Labour MP for West Belfast, and succeeded in interesting many Labour MPs in the condition of the Catholic minority in Northern Ireland. He was able to build on this when on 5 October 1968, on the occasion of a famous Londonderry civil rights march, he received a head injury from a police baton.

In 1970 Fitt became the first leader of the Social Democratic and Labour Party, an apparently 'modernized' nationalist party. Four years later he acted as deputy chief executive in the power-sharing executive which fell after five months in office. He was always a strong critic of the IRA, and in 1976 he had to defend his Belfast home with a gun against some elements of 'Republican youth'. Still leader of the SDLP, he abstained in the crucial confidence vote in 1979 which brought down the Labour Government, largely because of his disillusionment with Roy Mason, the then Labour Secretary of State. In November 1979, however, declaring himself as socialist rather than nationalist, Fitt resigned as leader of the SDLP. Unfortunately, he had misjudged the mood of his constituents, who replaced him in the general election of June 1983 with the even more militantly nationalistic Gerry Adams. His resignation and the earlier resignation of Paddy Devlin, who held similar views, merely promoted the 'greening' of the SDLP and the movement of that party away from its early roots in the traditions of the Belfast Labour movement.

In the period following his election defeat, Fitt, who took a seat in the House of Lords and thus received the West Belfast soubriquet of 'Fitt the Brit', identified himself more and more with 'socialism' and less and less with mainstream nationalism. Although he voted for the Anglo-Irish Agreement, he became increasingly critical of its effects. In other ways he stepped outside the mainstream Irish nationalist consensus by calling for alteration of the Republic's constitutional claim to the North and urging his erstwhile supporters to vote for the Worker's Party rather than the SDLP, whose leader, John Hume, he increasingly came to regard as a tribal chieftain rather than a political leader. Fitt loved Belfast and bitterly resented the fact that, for reasons of personal safety, he was forced to spend his retirement in London. Genuinely humane, he was one of the few attractive personalities to be thrown up by the Ulster 'Troubles'.

FURTHER READING

Bew, Paul and Patterson, Henry, *The British State and the Ulster Crisis: from Wilson to Thatcher* (London: Verso, 1985).

PAUL A. E. BEW

Fitzgerald, Garret (*b.* Dublin, 9 February 1926). Irish Prime Minister. Garret Fitzgerald, as journalist and academic economist, and subsequently as politician, probably did more than any other person to condition the Republic of Ireland for membership of the EEC, for which it voted by more than 5 to 1 in the 1972 referendum. As Minister for Foreign Affairs in the Cosgrave Coalition from 1973 to 1977 (which included presiding over the EEC Council of Ministers, January–June 1975), he continued his guidance and influence with remarkable success. As Taoiseach (premier) in the 1980s he sought to achieve religious and political reconciliation in Ireland on both sides of the partition divide, notably through the Anglo-Irish Agreement of 1985: in this his political judgement proved tactically shrewd but conceptually naive, although in domestic

politics the converse was true. Fitzgerald's career brilliantly poses the problems of the intellectual in politics, but perhaps his highest achievement was his obvious generosity of spirit and idealism of ethics in an age of politics peculiarly distinguished for cynicism, acquisitiveness and materialism. He had a very good mind, but it could not always keep pace with his heart.

Fitzgerald's first name is an Anglicization but not an English translation of the Gaelic patronymic adopted by the Norman adventurer Fitzgeralds Hibernicized in later medieval times: it symbolizes that middle ground between the vigorous Irish traditions of Anglophilia and Anglophobia. His mother was Protestant, his father Roman Catholic; both were intellectuals and artists. She acted for a time as Bernard Shaw's secretary, he dabbled in Imagism. But for all of his innocence as he became drawn into the developing Anglo-Irish conflict, Desmond Fitzgerald developed into a brilliant director of propaganda and press relations for the rebels in 1919–21; he supported the Anglo-Irish Treaty and was placed by Michael Collins in charge of Foreign Affairs for the Irish Free State, where he sought to obtain steadily greater independence from Britain as Collins had prophesied, and in the process set the example for general devolutionary growth within the Commonwealth. He was still in post when his son Garret was born, and was then Minister for Defence from 1927 to 1932, after which his party fell from power and his talents were unused.

This childhood consciousness of a father thrown from the heights to the wilderness profoundly affected Garret. The boy studied Irish, had a distinguished career in Belvedere College under the Jesuits, and made his mark in University College, Dublin, still a stronghold of his father's party. He took his doctorate in economics, was called to the Bar, became Research and Schedules Manager of the Irish state airline Aer Lingus, published *Semi-state Bodies* (1959) and achieved celebrity as a lucid, engaging and vigorously international economic commentator in the (Protestant) *Irish Times*. He became Lecturer in Political Economy in University College, Dublin, in 1959 and was a successful broadcaster and writer in London for the BBC, the *Financial Times* and *The Economist*. His love of his subject and zest for its deployment in what he saw as a fascinatingly developing economic future for Europe was in the finest traditions of his college, still devoted to its founder Cardinal Newman, and his ideal of knowledge for its own end. Fitzgerald retained his boyish enthusiasm all his life; he enjoyed fun and laughter, but never developed a sense of humour or malice and, unlike his Fine Gael party, had no social pretentiousness. He mastered the complexities of economies other than his own with profound insight and even identification, and whether as evangelist for Ireland's entry into the EEC or guardian angel in its early years therein, he could visualize any problem from the standpoint of government or opposition in any member country, a far cry from the parochialism of his British counterparts, as his Irish admirers well knew.

Political destiny was his whenever he chose to seek it as his father's son and as rising star among Irish economists; Fine Gael valued academic success. But throughout the 1960s Fitzgerald, as economic consultant to a large number of client institutions, and as a major figure in college government, held back: he made his colleagues and his country hunger for his advent. In 1969 he won election to Dáil Éireann and entered an opposition fizzling with excitement; Fine Gael's potential partner in government, Labour, had also revived with the election of its own intellectuals such as Conor Cruise O'Brien. During the subsequent years of the arms importation cabinet scandal, the Lynch government was raked with brilliant fire, from no quarter more than Fitzgerald, of whom it was said he could hold any shadow portfolio at a moment's notice and who was caricatured as the entire Fine Gael front bench. But the hopes that the Fine Gael leader Liam Cosgrave might be edged out in Fitzgerald's interest proved illusory, and Fitzgerald, to his own and Labour's disappointment, found himself at Foreign Affairs after the Lynch government's defeat, instead of heading the government with Foreign Affairs under O'Brien. Both Fitzgerald and O'Brien in cabinet office proved resolute opponents of the IRA and the soft-support patriotic rhetoric filtered in its favour,

but their political opponents made much of it to produce a surprise defeat for Cosgrave in June 1977. Only now, and in opposition, did Fitzgerald inherit the Fine Gael leadership, and when he came into power in 1981 he confronted a condition of economic disaster. His majority was paper-thin, his coalition government fell in 1982, and when it returned to power later that same year he publicly wondered how anyone could wish the responsibility.

His opponent Charles J. Haughey had projected an image of affluence and consumption; Fitzgerald, forced to preach austerity, became an unwelcome prophet. Ironically it was he rather than Haughey who recalled the pursuit of asceticism formerly associated with his father's Nemesis, de Valera. Fitzgerald knew his time would be short. Haughey's Fianna Fáil was easily the single largest party and, like other Puritan regimes, Fitzgerald's would be deemed 'Right but Repulsive'. He did seek a breakthrough in the Northern Ireland crisis, on which his memory of loving Protestant–Catholic parents animated him. Moreover, British premier Margaret Thatcher's public rudeness and intransigence to Irish expressions of concern for Northern Ireland seemed certain to confirm Haughey's return to power. Orchestrating American sympathy and utilizing the attractions to Thatcher of the growing Irish Catholic Tory vote in Britain, Fitzgerald transformed her 'Out, out, out!' into the Anglo-Irish Agreement, but in the excitement of manoeuvring the Tories into acquiescence he and his advisers lost sight of the potential for Ulster Unionist anger. For all of his ecumenism, Fitzgerald had tended to think vaguely of the more pliant Protestantism surviving in the Republic when he should have been contemplating the defiant Northern Ireland Protestant majority. He fell into the de Valera pattern of assuming the problem could be solved in London, and an agreement intended by him to breed reconciliation resulted in destabilization and the loss of more, not fewer, lives as Protestant fear grew. Fitzgerald's government was defeated in February 1987, and he resigned his party leadership as soon as possible thereafter.

OWEN DUDLEY EDWARDS

Foot, Michael (*b.* Plymouth, 23 July 1913). Labour politician and author. He was elected Leader of the Labour Party in November 1980, having been Deputy Leader since 1976, defeating Denis Healey by 139 votes to 129. Labour had lost the general election in May 1979 and Foot knew that he would be around 70 when the next general election came. It was said that he wanted to be Prime Minister, and those MPs who voted for him must have believed such an outcome possible. However, in 1983 Labour won only 209 seats and its share of the votes cast only narrowly exceeded that given to the Liberal–Social Democrat Alliance. Foot announced that he would not stand again for the leadership, but he remained in the House of Commons. It was odd, however, for him to find himself in the position of an 'elder statesman'.

Foot was an hereditary radical. Isaac Foot, his father, was a Plymouth solicitor and Liberal MP for Bodmin on several occasions. He was an ardent bibliophile, teetotaller, Methodist and passionate admirer of Oliver Cromwell. Michael retained the paternal enthusiasm for books and speeches, but later abandoned teetotalism and Methodism. He was sent to Leighton Park, the Quaker school near Reading, and went up to Wadham College, Oxford, in 1931. He mixed in Liberal and socialist circles among people of similar background to his own. It was inconceivable that he would ever fight for King and Country. He became President of the Union. Then came his conversion to socialism. It was not the result of a lengthy study of socialist theory but was triggered off by his experience of conditions in Liverpool, where he briefly worked on coming down from Oxford. He stood unsuccessfully for parliament in 1935 and thereafter threw himself into journalism and politics in London, associating with, among others, Stafford Cripps and Aneurin Bevan. Resignation on a matter of principle from the new journal *Tribune* led him, by way of refuge, into the unlikely arms of Lord Beaverbrook. His work now appeared regularly in the *Daily Express* and the *Evening Standard*. He was one of the authors of *Guilty Men*, an indictment of the 'Old Gang' who had brought Britain to the verge of ruin.

The prospect of a general election always had a magic effect on the Foot family. In 1945 Michael fought in Plymouth for Labour and overturned the large majority of the well-known sitting member, Hore-Belisha. It seemed that there was almost nothing that 'socialism' could not achieve. However, the Labour Government found things a little more difficult and Foot proved unsympathetic to its dilemmas. It seemed to some people at the time that if Foot was not writing an article he must be addressing a public meeting. He became co-editor of *Tribune* in 1948. His activity brought him great popularity in the constituency Labour parties, and his public standing was further enhanced when he regularly appeared on the new BBC television discussion programme *In The News* in the early 1950s. He supported Aneurin Bevan, who had long been his hero.

In 1955, however, he lost his seat at Plymouth Devonport; he lost again, this time heavily, in 1959. A political 'career' was apparently in ruins. Foot threw himself into the Campaign for Nuclear Disarmament after 1958, but was shattered to hear Bevan, of all people, suggest that unilateralists were guilty of 'an emotional spasm'. The two men were later to achieve a personal reconciliation but Foot, who had adored Bevan, still found the episode puzzling. After Bevan's death in 1960, Foot was adopted, in succession, as Labour candidate for Ebbw Vale, and thus returned to the Commons. He embarked on what was to prove a two-volume life of Bevan. Biography, hagiography and contemporary political purpose mingled together in a work of perverse power. Foot was simultaneously engaged in a struggle against Gaitskell. In 1961, following his decision to vote against the defence estimates, Foot and four others found that the party Whip had been withdrawn. It was not to be restored for two years. In the meantime, Gaitskell had died and, under Wilson, Foot initially believed that Labour could regain its proper course.

There was no ministerial post for Foot in the victorious 1964 Labour Government. Wilson's attitude to the Vietnam War proved a severe disappointment. The 'Tribunites' looked to Foot, but he would not bring the government down. After 1966, however, he was less

Michael Foot, Leader of the Labour Party, holding up the party's election manifesto at a press conference, Transport House, London, May 1983; with him is Denis Healey, Deputy Leader

restrained. He voted against the Prices and Incomes Bill, attacked government policy over Rhodesia and deplored the Letter of Intent. He combined with Enoch Powell to defeat Crossman's plans for the reform of the House of Lords. He rejoiced in Wilson's abandonment of Barbara Castle's 'In Place of Strife' proposals for trade-union reform. He vigorously opposed British membership of the Common Market.

Perhaps at this stage, after Labour's 1970 defeat, he took stock of himself. He was 57. He had never held ministerial office. Perhaps he now sensed that his dissent had become so established that people could ignore it. It was time to accept responsibility and perhaps, eventually, achieve some power. In 1970 he became one of the elected members of the Shadow Cabinet and, somewhat unexpectedly, found himself the frontbench spokesman on Fuel and Power. The following year he stood unsuccessfully but respectably against Roy Jenkins for the deputy leadership of the party. In 1972 he topped the poll in the elections for the National Executive and became Shadow Leader of the House. In other aspects of policy

he showed an unusual willingness not to rock the boat; the priority was to get Heath out.

When that was achieved, in February 1974, Foot had a seat in the cabinet as Employment Secretary – a sign that the left would not be ignored. Administration proved less distasteful than might have been supposed. Foot found himself dealing with the intricacies of trade-union legislation in a manner which gave considerable satisfaction to trade-union leaders. He supported an incomes policy, but was wary of any statutory provision. In 1975 he took part in the referendum on the EEC but was disappointed by the outcome. Harold Wilson resigned in March 1976. There was little doubt that Callaghan would be his successor, though Foot survived into the third ballot as his last opponent. This outcome reinforced the view that Foot was now the second man in the government. He was able to obtain his desired post of Leader of the House and Lord President of the Council. Over the next few years he was to display ruthlessness in getting government business through. It surprised some of his colleagues and infuriated the opposition. However, the management of 'devolution' in Scotland and Wales proved to be intractable. Foot's relationship with the Prime Minister became a very close one, but it was achieved at the cost of a certain unreality about the mood in the country. Mrs Thatcher won the general election in May 1979.

As Opposition Leader, Foot stuck to his task manfully, but in 1983 he could not persuade the country at large that he was the stuff of which Prime Ministers were made. Notwithstanding his record in the 1970s, it was difficult to eliminate the impression that he remained fundamentally an awkward rebel incapable of exercising power and responsibility.

FURTHER READING

Hoggart, Simon and Leigh, David, *Michael Foot: a Portrait* (London: Hodder and Stoughton, 1981).

KEITH ROBBINS

Franks, Oliver (Shewell) [Baron Franks of Headington] (*b*. Bristol, 16 February 1905). Civil servant, academic and banker. World War II changed the careers of many university men, and of none was this more conspicuously the case than Oliver Franks. Unexpectedly, he was to become a very distinguished 'public man', occupying a variety of important positions.

In September 1939 he was about to begin his second academic year as Professor of Moral Philosophy in the University of Glasgow. On the outbreak of war he was summoned immediately to London to become a Principal in the Ministry of Supply. In 1945, at the end of the war, he was Permanent Secretary in the Ministry. He could have become a permanent as opposed to a temporary civil servant, a path followed by some of his contemporaries. A number of ex-academics, such as Harold Wilson or Hugh Gaitskell, chose to go into politics. Franks decided to return to Oxford in 1946 and become Provost of his old college, Queen's. However, his experience of the world of affairs placed him in an ideal position to take up further 'temporary' posts of importance, and, as decades passed, his experience gave him an invaluable role as an 'outsider' who was called upon time and again to pronounce upon the activities of 'insiders'.

Franks was the son of a Congregational minister who became Principal of the Congregational Theological College in Bristol. R. S. Franks was a theologian and author of some distinction, and it is scarcely surprising that ratiocinative ability was prized at home. Oliver went from Bristol Grammar School to the Queen's College, Oxford, and after a distinguished academic record was elected a Fellow in 1927. He taught philosophy there for a decade and married the daughter of a well-known Bristol Quaker family. The ethos of serious dissent was not extinguished, whatever the evolution of his own religious views. He was the kind of man Scots would accept for a distinguished Chair of Moral Philosophy, even at the age of 32. It was his capacity for sustained work, coupled with his probing intelligence, that took him to the top of his department in six years of war.

It was expecting too much to suppose that such a youthful Head of House would be allowed to survive untroubled in Oxford for long. In the summer of 1947 Attlee and Bevin persuaded him to go to Paris and chair the complex negotiations which preceded the Marshall Plan. He afterwards went to the USA to explain why a European recovery programme was needed. Bevin, also a Bristol dissenter, though of a rather different background, was clearly impressed by Franks's grasp of issues and his capacity as an expositor, and offered him the Washington Embassy. The four years from 1948 to 1952 which Franks spent in the USA as ambassador were of crucial importance in underpinning the Anglo-American relationship in the postwar world. He played a vital role in establishing NATO and maintaining liaison during the period of the Berlin air-lift and the Korean War. He developed an exceptional rapport and intimacy with the then Secretary of State, Dean Acheson. He did not have the kind of charm sometimes associated with diplomats, but persuaded by calm force of argument.

When Franks came back from Washington, still at a youthful age, he was courted for innumerable prestigious appointments in the years 1952-3. It is supposed that he turned down invitations to be editor of *The Times*, chairman of the BBC, and headmaster of Harrow, to name only a few. Instead, he became a director of Lloyds Bank in 1953 and chairman from 1954 to 1962. In that year he accepted a life peerage (and revealed himself to be a Liberal still) and preferred to accept the headship of another Oxford College, Worcester, rather than become Governor of the Bank of England as Macmillan suggested. The Prime Minister had just defeated him in the contest for the Chancellorship of the University of Oxford. It was unlikely, of course, that such a man would sink into obscurity. Within Oxford itself, the university prevailed upon him in 1964 to chair an enquiry into its own procedures and structure. He remained a director of Lloyds Bank and was frequently pressed to serve on commissions of enquiry both at home and abroad. In 1971–2 he agreed to chair a departmental committee investigating the operation of Section 2 of the Official Secrets Act. He approached that task with his customary thoroughness, though the suggestions put forward did not sufficiently commend themselves to government. He retired as Provost of Worcester in 1976.

It might have been thought that a gentleman in his seventies would not be called again to perform any major public service, though no doubt there would remain many private channels through which his advice could be sought. However, in 1982–3 he accepted the chairmanship of the Committee of Privy Counsellors enquiring into the Falklands War. A great deal of material had to be sifted and appraised swiftly. It is probably true to say that at the time Lord Franks was the only man whose public standing was such that the findings of his investigation would be accepted on all sides. It was a fitting climax to a career which was of such scope and stature as to cause him to be generally considered the most outstanding public servant of his generation.

WRITINGS

The Experiences of a University Teacher in the Civil Service (London: Oxford University Press, 1947).
Britain and the Tide of World Affairs (London: Oxford University Press, 1955).

KEITH ROBBINS

French, Sir **John (Denton Pinkstone)** [Earl of Ypres] (*b*. Ripple, Kent, 28 September 1852; *d*. Deal, Kent, 22 May 1925). General. He was the commander of the British Expeditionary Force (BEF) which was sent to France in August 1914 as a token of Britain's support for her Continental allies, France and Russia.

The son of a naval officer, he was educated at Eastman's Naval Academy, Portsmouth, and entered HMS *Britannia*, the naval training ship, in 1866. However, his own inclinations led him to seek a career in the army. In 1870 he was commissioned into the Suffolk Artillery and four years later he transferred to a cavalry regiment, the 19th Hussars.

His initial promotion was rapid. In 1884 he distinguished himself as the commander of Sir Garnet Wolseley's rearguard during Wolseley's abortive expedition to relieve General Gordon in Khartoum. He was promoted to Brevet Lieutenant-Colonel in 1885 on his return to England and in 1888 was given command of his regiment. He was then only 36 years old and had served in the army for only 14 years. But after duties in India he returned home in 1893 and was placed on half-pay. His career might have been over had it not been for the intervention of the Adjutant General, Sir Redvers Buller, who appointed him as an Assistant Adjutant General at the War Office and gave him the task of writing a new training and tactical manual for the cavalry.

The outbreak of the Boer War in 1899 found French a temporary major-general in command of the 1st Cavalry brigade. He served in South Africa throughout the war, and at Elandslaagte in Natal in 1899 demonstrated his talent as a commander of a force of all arms for the first time. His cavalry subsequently spearheaded the British advance which relieved Kimberley and occupied Pretoria in 1900. He spent the rest of the war slowly hunting down Boer commandos in Cape Colony.

On his return to England he held a series of senior command and staff appointments. He was promoted to Lieutenant-General 1902 and until 1907 he was Commander-in-Chief at Aldershot. He then became a full general and was appointed Inspector-General of the Forces. In 1912 he became the Chief of the Imperial General Staff and thus the pro-

General Sir John French
(left) in France, May 1915

fessional head of the army and the government's senior professional military adviser. It was in that capacity that in March 1914 he initialled a document promising the officers of the 3rd Cavalry brigade stationed at the Curragh in Ireland that they would not be called upon to coerce Ulstermen who were unwilling to accept the Liberal Government's policy of granting Ireland Home Rule. The Liberal Cabinet immediately repudiated the pledge and French resigned.

It would probably have been better for French's reputation if he had remained in retirement. However, in August 1914 he took the BEF to France; until his dismissal in December 1915 he tried, with scant success, to master the twin problems of overcoming the stalemate of trench warfare, which descended upon the Western Front at the end of the first battle of Ypres in November 1914, and cooperating with his French allies. French lacked the formal training of a staff officer and in mid-life he had become mentally lazy. He seemed to prefer to rely upon experience and intuition rather than serious study and staff

work to solve problems. His conduct of the British offensives at Neuve Chapelle (March 1915), Aubers Ridge and Festubert (May 1915) and Loos (September–October 1915) showed that he never mastered the problems of trench warfare. His mercurial temperament led him to quarrel with his subordinates, his superiors and his allies. His relations with the French were never very cordial. In April 1915 he wrote in exasperation, 'Truly I don't want to be allies with the French more than once in a lifetime. You can't trust them.' In May 1915 he secretly encouraged *The Times* and *Daily Mail* to attack Lord Kitchener, the Secretary of State for War, and to blame him for the BEF's failures on the grounds that he had not provided the army with enough high-explosive shells. In reality French was attempting to find a scapegoat for his own failures as a tactical commander at the front and as a staff officer before the war. As CIGS he had not forseen the need for large quantities of high-explosive ammunition. But French was not a chateau general who distanced himself from the reality of the war. His frequent visits to the front meant that he was much beloved by his troops. However, the lengthening casualty lists which his army suffered in 1914–15 preyed heavily on his mind and by the time he was removed from his command in December 1915 he was emotionally exhausted.

On returning to Britain he held the post of Commander-in-Chief Home Forces for two years. He was responsible for training troops who were to be sent abroad and for organizing Britain's defences against German air attacks by Zeppelins and heavier than air bombers. In May 1918 he was appointed Lord Lieutenant of Ireland. Lloyd George's government hoped that his Irish ancestry and his military reputation would enable him to put an end to the violence which had marred Ireland since the Easter Rising of Sinn Fein in April 1916. But these hopes were disappointed. When the government decided to grant the 26 counties of Ireland outside Ulster dominion status in 1921, French resigned his post and retired.

French was a competent cavalry colonel who had the misfortune to be promoted beyond his natural abilities. He was a charismatic leader but he lacked the essential grasp of staff work, logistics and infantry tactics and perhaps also the mental toughness and the political skills needed to be a successful commander in a machine age war.

WRITINGS

1914 (London: Constable, 1919).

FURTHER READING

Cassar, G. H., *The Tragedy of Sir John French* (London: Associated University Presses, 1985).
Edmonds, Sir J. E., *History of the Great War: Military Operations France and Belgium*, 14 vols. (London: Macmillan, 1922–48).
Holmes, R., *The Little Field-Marshal: Sir John French* (London: Jonathan Cape, 1981).

DAVID FRENCH

Fry, (Sara) Margery (*b.* London, 11 March 1874; *d.* London, 21 April 1958). Educationalist and penal reformer. She was born into a Quaker family, the daughter of a distinguished judge, and was educated at Somerville College, Oxford. From 1899 to 1918 she was successively librarian of Somerville, warden of a hostel for women students at Birmingham University, and, during World War I, a worker with the Friends Relief Committee in France. In 1913 she received a considerable legacy which made her financially independent for the rest of her life.

As a young woman Fry had considered politics the only career worth following, but 'Parliament was shut to us, and . . . there was nothing . . . worthwhile to be ambitious about.' However, from 1918 (when she was already 44) she was able to fashion a political career of an unorthodox kind.

In education, she was in 1919 appointed as the only woman among the founder members of the University Grants Committee, and she remained an active member of the committee until 1948. She also helped to advance the cause of women's education by returning to Somerville as Principal for a deliberately limited period (1926–31). Later, she reached a wider audience through her membership of the BBC Brains Trust panel.

In 1918 she was persuaded to accept the secretaryship of the small Penal Reform League. Largely through her efforts, this body was in 1921 merged with the Howard Association to create the Howard League for Penal Reform, the leading English penal reform group until the 1960s. Fry relinquished the secretaryship of the League on moving to Somerville in 1926, but always thereafter remained active in League affairs. She campaigned assiduously for a number of causes, including (in Britain and internationally) the abolition of capital punishment, the improvement of prison conditions and the establishment of a humane juvenile justice system; and (in England) legal aid for defendants in criminal cases and the development of a non-denominationally-based probation service. She also gained practical knowledge of criminal justice from her work (from 1921 onwards) as one of the first women magistrates. She was frequently called upon to sit on Home Office committees, including, most notably, the standing Advisory Council on the Treatment of Offenders (from 1944 until her death).

It is often difficult to trace any particular individual's hand in the penal changes of this period, but this did not worry Fry: 'You march round the walls of Jericho for a number of years, and they do in the end fall down, but how much this is due to your processions and trumpetings . . . you will never know.' One reform, however, was very particularly hers. In the closing years of her life she mounted a strong campaign for state compensation for victims of crimes of violence, which, despite difficulties, was eventually successful. The establishment of the Criminal Injuries Compensation Scheme in 1964 remains her most tangible memorial.

FURTHER READING

Huws Jones, E., *Margery Fry* (London: Oxford University Press, 1966).

Rose, Gordon, *The Struggle for Penal Reform* (London: Stevens, 1961).

ANTHONY BOTTOMS

G

Gaitskell, Hugh (Todd-Naylor) (*b.* London, 9 April 1906; *d.* London, 18 January 1963). Leader of the Labour Party. Gaitskell was elected Leader of the Labour Party in December 1955. He failed to win the general election of 1959 but the prospects for 1964 seemed promising. However, cut off in his prime, he never fought another general election. This tragic circumstance has added to the interest which his career independently excites. It has led to speculation about what would have happened had he dominated British politics through the 1960s and beyond. In a major biography (published ironically in 1979) Philip Williams concluded that Gaitskell 'might have been the great political leader that twentieth-century Britain has badly needed, and sadly failed to find' (p. 787). That so much attention has been lavished upon a man who did not reach 10 Downing Street and whose ministerial experience was both limited in range and brief in time is puzzling. It suggests either that he was indeed a man of exceptional talent and potential, or that his admirers, despairing of the subsequent history of the Labour Party and of Britain in general, have unrealistically supposed that Gaitskell could have led the party and the country in a direction which they find congenial. As a result, they have overstated his capacity and importance.

Gaitskell was the son of an Indian civil servant who spent most of his time in Burma and died in 1915 at the age of 45. His mother was a Scots girl whose father was Consul-General in Shanghai. Hugh went to the Dragon School in Oxford and then followed his brother to Winchester. Intellect was esteemed and Hugh shone, but he was already in modest rebellion from the ethos and atmosphere of an institution which he nevertheless continued to admire in certain respects. At New College, Oxford, he was an 'aesthete' rather than a 'hearty', but an altogether new awakening came with his support for the strikers in the 1926 General Strike. He decided that his future lay 'with the working classes' and, equipped with a First in Philosophy, Politics and Economics, he accepted an adult education job in Nottingham. There, a certain bohemianism on his part was combined with a belief that the newly discovered miners were the nicest sort of people. In 1928, however, he was appointed a lecturer in economics at University College, London, and remained there for 11 years. His political activity continued unabated. He stood unsuccessfully as a Labour candidate in 1935, and when war broke out he was candidate for the working-class constituency of Leeds South. An academic career in economics was still open to him, though his productivity had undoubtedly suffered because of his political involvement. A period he had spent in Vienna had given him an awareness of moods and movements on the European mainland unusual among his contemporaries. He denounced 'appeasement' but found that some of his acquaintances thought imperialism worse than Fascism.

When war did come, Gaitskell, as a German-speaking economist, took up a Civil Service post in the Ministry of Economic Warfare. That post brought him into further contact with Hugh Dalton and, at a time when the lines dividing politicians from civil servants were somewhat blurred, he followed Dalton to the Board of Trade as his personal assistant. Fuel and power dominated his life. In 1945 he could have remained a civil servant or returned to academic life. However, elected for Leeds South, he embarked on the political career to which he had long aspired. He took the first step upwards in May 1946 when he became Parliamentary Secretary at the Ministry of Fuel and Power under Shinwell. Eighteen months later, Gaitskell himself became Minister of Fuel and Power. His understanding of the issues impressed all who came into contact with him, but he was not arrogant. The problems of

Hugh Gaitskell (second from right) at the Labour Party Conference, Margate, 1955

supply with which he grappled were so central to the functioning of the economy that his success or failure would be conspicuous. Gaitskell was undoubtedly a 'success'.

He was brought into the Treasury as a Minister of State after the 1950 election to help in dealing with the problems of sterling in circumstances in which the Chancellor of the Exchequer, Cripps, was ailing. The Korean War, and the re-armament that followed, compounded the problems. It was on his first visit to the USA that Gaitskell learnt that he was to succeed Cripps as Chancellor of the Exchequer; he was 'Number Four' in the government. He had come further and faster than any other Labour MP who had entered the Commons in 1945. Labour's 'old guard' was obviously feeling the strain of many years in office. Gaitskell seemed to be the coming man. On the other hand, while his grasp of economic issues was undoubted, it was possible that he did not have sufficient weight in the party. Tensions centred on the 're-armament budget' of 1951. ANEURIN BEVAN, HAROLD WILSON and John Freeman resigned in protest against the health charges that Gaitskell proposed. Bevan finally based his stand on the notion that the health service should remain entirely free. The issues of principle were important but the struggle was essentially for the future control of the Labour Party. Gaitskell's knowledge of technical issues was greater than that of most Chancellors, but he had no opportunity to prove that he could be a great one. In 1951 the Labour Government came to an end.

It was not until 1955 that the long struggle for the succession to Attlee was settled. The years were marked by squabbles and periodic reconciliations between the 'Bevanites' and other sections of the party on the subject of West German re-armament and other issues. Bevan, Morrison and Gaitskell stood in the ballot in December 1955. Gaitskell had more than twice the votes recorded for Bevan and his vote exceeded the combined poll for Bevan and for Morrison. It was a decisive endorsement, but it did not end the feuding. During the Suez Crisis in 1956 Gaitskell strongly condemned the government's resort to force, though he had not initially been pleased by Nasser's nationalization. Labour seemed to be coming together and a reconciliation with Bevan was achieved. Yet, despite Tory disarray after Eden's resignation, Macmillan was able to win handsomely in 1959. It was a bitter blow, but Gaitskell's hold on the leadership remained secure initially. Inevitably, however, there was an inquest on the outcome. Gaitskell argued that defeat could not be explained by organizational factors. It was time to look more comprehensively at what the party stood for. He elaborated this theme at Blackpool in November 1959. The debate came to focus symbolically on 'Clause Four' of the party's constitution. The rise of the Campaign for Nuclear Disarmament brought further tension and division. Gaitskell resolved to 'fight and fight again' in 1960–1. His courage was unquestioned, but was he wise? Was it leadership or arrogance? In October 1961 he appeared to have achieved a convincing victory for his platform on defence, but recrimination continued. If Gaitskell had fought to have an adverse verdict reversed, why could not others do the same? Then, in 1962, a new problem emerged which also had fissiparous consequences, though not along the same lines. To the dismay of some of his closest admirers, Gaitskell did not share their enthusiasm for British membership of the Common Market. His emotional approach to this question had the incidental benefit that it helped to improve his standing with vociferous opponents of membership on the left. Once again, as Macmillan ran into increasing political difficulty, it began to look as if Labour had a sporting chance of victory. It was not to be Gaitskell's fate to experience it. It could be claimed, however, that his vigorous leadership, despite all the storms, had made that prospect possible.

FURTHER READING

Rodgers, W. T. (ed.), *Hugh Gaitskell* (London: Thames and Hudson, 1964).
Williams, P. M., *Hugh Gaitskell* (London: Jonathan Cape, 1979).
Williams, P. M. (ed.), *The Diary of Hugh Gaitskell 1945–1956* (London: Jonathan Cape, 1983).

KEITH ROBBINS

George V [George Frederick Ernest Albert] (*b.* London, 3 June 1865; *d.* Sandringham, Norfolk, 20 January 1936). King George V came to the throne on 6 May 1910. His reign (1910–36) marked a new stage in the development of constitutional monarchy, in which the decline in royal influence upon government policies was fully accepted, but important political responsibilities remained to the Crown with respect to the granting or withholding of requests for the dissolution of Parliament and the formation of governments. The King handled these responsibilities with tact and sound judgement. By changing the name of the royal family to Windsor in 1917, he symbolically disavowed its German connections and identified it more closely with Britain. His political influence was considerable; it is to be found, however, not in his effect upon government policies, but in the way his evenhandedness between political parties took the monarchy above politics and in the contribution his reputation for integrity and decency made to social and political stability. After a reign in which the monarchy, along with the other institutions of British society and government, was subjected to a severe test, he left it popular and secure.

George was the younger son of the Prince and Princess of Wales, later King Edward VII and Queen Alexandra, and it was only on the death of his brother, Prince Albert Victor, Duke of Clarence, in 1892 that he came into direct line of succession to the throne. He gave up the naval career for which he had been educated and trained, was created Duke of York and in July 1893 married Princess Mary of Teck, who had previously been engaged to his brother. Between 1894 and 1905 the Duchess of York bore her husband one daughter and five sons, the two eldest sons being the future Edward VIII and George VI. An essentially retiring man, George preferred to live quietly with his family at York Cottage, Sandringham, enjoying his shooting and assembling a massive stamp collection. Despite having little zest for the kingship that awaited him, he was determined to do his duty. After he became Prince of Wales in 1901, he was kept informed on government policy by his father, with whom he enjoyed cordial relations.

His accession came at a difficult time, for he found himself in the midst of a constitutional crisis caused by the determination of Asquith's government to introduce a bill curbing the powers of the House of Lords. In November 1910 Asquith demanded that, if the Liberals won the next election, the new king should agree to create sufficient peers to enable the Parliament Bill to pass through the House of Lords (see also ASQUITH, H. H.) Although there was considerable impropriety in this demand, King George complied, but with reluctance and resentment. This resentment hardened when he later discovered that Lord Knollys, one of his two private secretaries, had withheld from him the information that, had he refused, Balfour and the Conservatives might have been prepared to form a minority government.

World War I placed the King and the royal family, with their German ancestry and kinship, in an awkward position. The King considered himself entirely British and, living an austere life and working hard at his morale-boosting duties, he was appalled when, in 1917, Germanophobia led to sneers and criticisms because of his German ancestry. He decided to underline the Britishness of the royal house by changing the name of the dynasty to Windsor, while at the same time junior members of the family also changed their names and took British titles. The name Windsor, redolent of royal tradition, was an inspired choice. In the same year, King George demonstrated that his concern for his throne was greater than the demands of kinship or monarchical solidarity when he argued against allowing the Tsar of Russia and his family to take asylum in Britain.

The political events and circumstances of his reign resulted in this most constitutional of monarchs having to play an active political role on several occasions. In 1923, on the resignation of Bonar Law who was terminally ill, he was required to call upon a leading Conservative to form a government; he chose Stanley Baldwin rather than Lord Curzon, largely on the grounds that it was desirable that a Prime Minister be a member of the House of Commons. In 1931 he persuaded Ramsay MacDonald, who had come to the Palace to tender his and his Labour Government's resignation, to stay on and form a National Government. In both instances he acted after seeking advice from leading politicians and with constitutional propriety.

King George associated the monarchy more closely with the Empire, having fond memories of his imperial tours as Duke of York and Prince of Wales and of his durbar at Delhi in 1911, and thus left a sensitive legacy to his successors. At home his influence was always on the side of consensus, conciliation and cautious adjustment. The most conservative of men, he did not welcome many of the developments of his reign and time. The dissolution of the union with southern Ireland which came with the foundation of the Irish Free State in 1921 was a bitter blow, but he found some comfort from the fact that the Free State remained technically within the Empire. He had little time for the ideology of the Labour Party but did much to ease its transition from opposition to government. After the December election of 1923, he wanted it to be given its chance to form a government and to be seen himself to be even-handed between political parties. If he disapproved of the General Strike of 1926, he had some sympathy with the rank and file of strikers. His personal relations with Labour politicians and trade-union leaders were good and he liked Ramsay MacDonald better than any of his other prime ministers.

It was only at the end of his life, at the time of his Silver Jubilee, that he realized that he enjoyed an enormous popularity he had never courted. He was a plain man who, as Kenneth Rose has put it, '. . . liked a book with a plot, a tune he could hum and a picture that told a story'. In this and in other ways he was close to the majority of his subjects. He disliked many aspects of modernity, including lipstick, cocktails and new fashions in dress, and this led to many clashes with that epitome of postwar modernity, his son, the Prince of Wales; yet he demonstrated a flair for one very modern medium, radio, and his Christmas broadcasts to the nation and the Empire were an overwhelming success. He seemed a suitable father figure who, if stern and a bit irascible, was a cornerstone of decency and rectitude. His contribution to the stability of inter-war Britain should not be undervalued.

King George V (left) with
Victor Emmanuel III of Italy
at the West African Village
at Wembley, May 1924

FURTHER READING

Nicolson, H., *King George V: his Life and Reign* (London: Constable, 1952).
Rose, K., *King George V* (London: Weidenfeld and Nicolson, 1983).

A. W. PURDUE

George VI [Albert Frederick Arthur George] (*b.* Sandringham, Norfolk, 14 December 1895; *d.* Sandringham, 6 February 1952). George VI reigned for 15 years, during which he successfully restored the prestige of the monarchy after the Abdication Crisis. He played an important part in maintaining morale during the traumatic years of World War II and afterwards he assisted in reshaping the relationship of the monarchy with the countries of the Commonwealth.

The second son of the Duke and Duchess of York, later George V and Queen Mary, Albert (or Bertie as he was known by his family) suddenly and unexpectedly found himself king on the abdication of his elder brother, Edward VIII, on 11 December 1936. A quiet, nervous man with a speech impediment, he had lived very much in the shadow of his popular brother. Nevertheless, he had always been a hard-working member of the royal family. He was created Duke of York in 1920, and, in that decade of considerable industrial tension, so many of his public duties involved travelling round the country visiting factories and meeting industrial workers that he was known as 'the foreman' among the family. He also worked closely with the Industrial Welfare Society, and, in an attempt to break down class barriers, he helped set up, and regularly attended, annual camps to which public schoolboys and boys from working-class homes were invited.

After the shock of Edward VIII's abdication and the revelations of his close liaison with a twice-divorced woman, it was felt that the dignity of the Crown needed reasserting, and that in presenting the new king to the people emphasis should be put on his role as a happily married family man which, indeed, he was. In 1923 he had married Lady Elizabeth Bowes-Lyon, an attractive, charming and strong-minded woman who did much to guide his subsequent career. They had two daughters, Elizabeth (*b.* 1926) and Margaret (*b.* 1930). In the years ahead, especially in the war years, it was the depiction of the monarch as father, as well as king, which endeared him so much to so many people.

George VI inherited the throne at a time of grave international tension. He worked hard at his state papers and he expected that his right to be consulted and to encourage should be observed. In 1938 he expressed dissatisfaction at not being fully informed of the events leading up to Anthony Eden's resignation as Foreign Secretary. In the same year, his suggestion to Neville Chamberlain that he write to Hitler, 'as one ex-serviceman to another', showed much naïveté, but there was no doubting his earnestness. He and Elizabeth made two important visits during this period: to France in 1938 and to Canada in May 1939, when the support of the Commonwealth countries in the seemingly unavoidable future war with Germany was being sought. From Canada they moved on to Washington and New York, where they attracted vast crowds and gained the friendship of President Roosevelt and his wife.

George's dedication to duty was best manifested during the war. The decision of the royal family to remain in London during the blitz and be seen visiting bombed towns and factories was important in maintaining morale, as was the decision to reinstitute the Christmas Day broadcasts made popular by his father. He acknowledged the bravery of civilians on the Home Front by creating the George Cross and George Medal, and he awarded the former to the besieged island of Malta which he visited in 1943. He was in Normandy talking to the troops only ten days after the invasion and the

King George VI with Sir John Wilson, the Royal Stamp Curator, 1944

following month he visited the armies in Italy.

After the war, George was confronted with a Labour government pledged to sweeping changes at home and decolonization abroad. Although never fully at ease with Clement Attlee, he performed his duties impartially and positively. In 1945, when first drawing up his cabinet list, Attlee chose Hugh Dalton as Foreign Secretary. The King preferred Ernest Bevin and Attlee agreed, although later he was to deny that his decision had been influenced by the King. It is difficult to assess the extent of a modern monarch's political influence, but, especially in Commonwealth affairs, when acting in concert with his ministers, the King's role was at times an influential albeit not a decisive one. His tour of South Africa in 1947 and his meeting with Nehru in October 1948 both contributed to South Africa and India remaining within the Commonwealth.

Like his father, George was essentially a conservative country gentleman who did not relish change. He was unhappy in 1940 when Chamberlain was forced out of office, and would have preferred as his successor the respectable Lord Halifax to Churchill, a vociferous critic of both Baldwin and Chamberlain and a supporter of Edward during the Abdication Crisis. He was soon under Churchill's spell and by 1945 he felt the British people were ungrateful to vote Churchill out of office.

Throughout his reign George strove hard to ensure that the prestige of the monarchy remained high. He persuaded Attlee that the Order of the Garter should be at the monarch's disposal and not used for political purposes and, like his father, he insisted on maintaining ceremonials and constitutional proprieties. Indeed, in the years of austerity during and after the war, the royal family maintained the mystique of the monarchy, which Bagehot had regarded as so essential, and yet remained popular and acceptable. Compared with their counterparts in the Netherlands and Scandinavia, the royal family retained a far greater degree of glamour and formality and the royal presence could still make occasions memorable. The Festival of Britain only started to capture the public's imagination when the King and Queen agreed to become patrons in March 1950. By this time George was a sick man. Unlike many of his predecessors, he had the good sense to ground his heir in her future duties. Indeed, as his health declined so the spotlight shifted to his daughter Elizabeth. She and her husband, the Duke of Edinburgh, took on an increasing number of public functions and tours, and they were in Kenya on their way to a state visit of Australia and New Zealand when George died suddenly on 6 February 1952.

FURTHER READING

Bradford, S., *George VI* (London: Weidenfeld and Nicolson, 1989).

Middlemas, K., *The Life and Times of George VI* (London: Weidenfeld and Nicolson, 1974).

Wheeler-Bennett, J. W., *King George VI* (London: Macmillan, 1958).

J. M. GOLBY

Gordon Walker, Patrick (Chrestien) [Baron Gordon-Walker of Leyton] (*b.* Worthing, Sussex, 7 April 1907; *d.* London, 2 December 1980). Labour MP and cabinet minister. Gordon Walker was elected MP for Smethwick in October 1945. He made decisive contributions to the Labour Government's imperial and commonwealth policies, both as Under-Secretary of State at the Commonwealth Relations Office (1947–50) and as Secretary of State for Commonwealth Relations in the cabinet (1950–1). In opposition he was one of the party's chief spokesmen on international affairs, becoming Shadow Foreign Secretary in 1963. He was successively Secretary of State for Foreign Affairs (1964–5) and for Education and Science (1967–8).

Raised in the Punjab, where his father was a supreme court judge, Gordon Walker was educated at Wellington College and as a scholar at Christ Church, Oxford. In 1931 he was elected a Student (Fellow) of Christ Church and history tutor. Strongly influenced by his family's public service, his father's Fabianism, and his own experience of studying in Germany, he was active as Labour's parliamentary candidate for Oxford from 1935. His wartime service was spent in British and allied broadcasting; he eventually returned from Radio Luxembourg to become director of the BBC's German service.

He entered parliament after a by-election, and was soon Parliamentary Private Secretary to the Deputy Prime Minister, Herbert Morrison. Upbringing and interest had encouraged his attention to colonial questions; this underpinned his first ministerial appointment, as one of the younger men on the right of the party promoted in autumn 1947. He visited India in February 1948, acquainted himself with the new leaders, and was much used by Attlee at the Commonwealth Prime Ministers' conference in October that year, carrying particular responsibility for press conferences and communiqués.

Gordon Walker played a crucial role in determining India's future relations with the Commonwealth. He helped Attlee persuade the cabinet to accept the importance of a continuing link; then in March–April 1949 he was triumphantly successful as the cabinet's emissary to Asian members in reconciling Indian leaders to the role of the monarch as Head of the Commonwealth. This paved the way for acceptance of republican India as a Commonwealth member at the London Conference (April 1949).

In the new government of 1950–1 Gordon Walker was notably concerned with Africa. He defended the government's decision excluding Seretse Khama from the Bechuanaland Protectorate because of his marriage to a white woman, despite the Bangwatos' wish to see Seretse as chief. He also emerged during two visits in 1951 to South and Central Africa as a staunch proponent of Central African federation. Despite much support from officials for linking Northern and Southern Rhodesia with Nyasaland, other Labour ministers were more reluctant to endorse it in the face of continuing African opposition. The key to Gordon Walker's thinking on both issues was fear of the expanding ambitions and influence of the Union of South Africa under the Nationalists, and the threat this posed to developing multiracial societies in British East and Central Africa. He quietly abstained from voting with his party against the Conservatives' federal legislation in March 1953.

Gordon Walker's Commonwealth commitment continued in opposition; he contributed to Labour's 1957 policy statement *The Smaller Territories*, and attended the first Commonwealth Socialist Conference (May–June 1957). Notwithstanding his support for Gaitskell and Wilson and his work modernizing the party, this commitment cost him dear. After leading opposition to the Commonwealth Immigration Act (1962), he was defeated both at the general election in an overtly racialist campaign and again at Leyton in 1965, before winning that seat in 1966. His career never recovered. As a life peer from 1974 he developed his interest in European affairs, becoming during 1975–6 a member of the European Parliament.

FURTHER READING

Hyam, Ronald, 'The Political Consequences of Seretse Khama: Britain, the Bangwato and South Africa, 1948–1952', *Historical Journal*, 29, 4 (1986), pp. 921–47.
——, 'The Geopolitical Origins of the Central African Federation: Britain, Rhodesia and

South Africa, 1948–1953', *Historical Journal*, 30, 1 (1987), pp. 145–72.
Moore, R. J., *Making the New Commonwealth* (Oxford: Clarendon Press, 1987).

A. N. PORTER

Gormley, Joseph [Lord Gormley] (*b.* Ashton-in-Makerfield, near Wigan, Lancashire, 5 July 1917). Trade-union leader and President of the National Union of Mineworkers. He became a public figure while President of the NUM (1971–82). Almost immediately he was involved in the national strike of 1972 – the first in the mining industry since 1929. This was followed by a further strike in early 1974 which was held to be largely responsible for the fall of the Heath Government. Gormley himself firmly contended that the strike was industrial and not political.

Gormley joined the mining industry at the age of 14. He first became involved in an industrial dispute in 1948, when he displayed the qualities of natural leadership, and was soon elected President of the Colliery Branch Committee. In 1961 he became General Secretary of the Lancashire branch of the NUM. He emerged on the national scene when, in 1968, he stood against Lawrence Daly for the position of General Secretary of the NUM. On that occasion he lost; but in 1971 Sir Sidney Ford, President of the NUM, decided to retire, and this time Gormley defeated Michael McGahey, the Scottish union leader, by a substantial majority.

Gormley's presidency of the NUM coincided with a crucial period in the long history of the mining industry. During the 1960s, faced with strong competition from low-priced oil, mining had been severely contracted. The position of mineworkers in the industrial pay league declined. A reaction set in and led to the strikes of 1972 and 1974, when substantial improvements in miners' earnings were achieved. Although Gormley's reputation was built up largely during the two strikes, his achievements afterwards could be considered more important. The massive increase in oil prices in 1973 and 1979 fundamentally altered the position of coal. Gormley worked positively to rebuild the industry. He supported the introduction of the pit bonus scheme and exercised a moderating influence over subsequent frequently exaggerated pay claims.

After his retirement in 1982 Gormley was made a life peer. He vigorously participated in debates in the House of Lords. Unfortunately, he suffered a stroke in 1983, and in due course returned to his home county of Lancashire.

During his public life Gormley revealed himself as an extrovert with an ebullient sense of humour. He was a vigorous public speaker, using many earthy phrases. He believed in the coal industry and served it well during a momentous phase.

WRITINGS

Battered Cherub: the Autobiography of Joe Gormley (London: Hamish Hamilton, 1982).

DEREK EZRA

Grant, Bernie [Bernard Alexander Montgomery] (*b*. British Guiana [now Guyana], 17 February 1944).   Labour politician. In 1987 he became Labour MP for Tottenham in north London, one of the first Blacks to be elected to Parliament since the 1920s.

A former clerk, telephonist and trade-union official, resident in Britain since 1963, Grant was for a time involved in the Trotskyist movement but became a Labour councillor in the north London borough of Haringey in 1978. In 1985 he was elected Council Leader – apparently the first black head of a local authority anywhere in Europe. He became nationally prominent, and widely vilified, after serious disturbances on the Broadwater Farm housing estate in his borough in October 1985. During these a policeman was murdered, and Grant's comment that local residents believed the police had had 'a bloody good hiding' aroused much condemnation. He and his supporters contend, however, that his articulation of local feelings helped calm racial tensions and draw disaffected black youths into the legitimate political process.

Grant chairs the parliamentary Black Caucus, is active in the Labour Party Black Sections campaign and sits on the executive on the Anti-Apartheid Movement. In the Commons he has specialized in local government affairs,

in race relations and in the politics of Southern Africa and the Caribbean. The oldest and most experienced of Britain's four black MPs, he clearly aspires to a national role as spokesperson for ethnic minority interests. As a member of Labour's Campaign Group, he is equally clearly associated with the left-wing critics of the party leadership. Many observers, however, emphasize his essentially pragmatic political skills and his abilities as a bargainer.

STEPHEN HOWE

Grey, Sir Edward [Viscount Grey of Fallodon] (*b*. London, 25 April 1862; *d*. Fallodon, Northumberland, 7 September 1933).   Liberal Foreign Secretary. His continuous occupation of the office for 11 years (from December 1905 to December 1916) has not been equalled in the twentieth century. Grey bore major responsibility for British policy towards France, Germany and Russia at a time of great tension. He strongly advocated British intervention in August 1914, but sensed the ending of an era: 'The lamps are going out all over Europe; we shall not see them lit again in our lifetime.'

The claims of public life pressed strongly upon Grey from his childhood. His father, a military man, served the Prince of Wales, and his grandfather, Sir George Grey, was a Home Secretary and a Colonial Secretary in several mid-Victorian governments. The family had strong Northumbrian roots. Grey inherited a baronetcy and a modest estate as an undergraduate at Balliol College, Oxford. Neither there, nor previously at school at Winchester, was he academically distinguished, though he already displayed great skill with a rod or racquet.

Grey entered the House of Commons in 1885 as MP for Berwick-upon-Tweed, a constituency he represented until 1916, when he accepted a peerage. Initially, as the youngest member of the Commons, he did not take energetic steps to make his mark. Whiggish by background, he nevertheless supported Home Rule for Ireland and evinced a 'progressive' interest in land reform. His involvement in the countryside was both practical and sentimental: he was an expert fisherman and possessed a formidable knowledge of birds. What attracted Lord Rosebery to appoint him Parliamentary Under-Secretary at the Foreign Office in 1892, however, was Grey's increasing reputation as a man of calm judgement; something which balanced Rosebery's own unstable brilliance. Grey spoke on Foreign Office matters in the Commons under Rosebery's successor until the Liberal Government fell in 1895. In the decade that ensued before Grey was himself to become Foreign Secretary he can scarcely be said to have been grooming himself for this high office. He visited the West Indies, but made no attempt to familiarize himself with the world of European politics and diplomacy at first hand. Rosebery remained his political 'chief', but he increasingly associated with Asquith and R. B. Haldane. Giving general support to the government over the Boer War, he and his Liberal Imperialist friends seemed to be ploughing their own furrow within the divided Liberal Party. He was out of sympathy with its leader, Campbell-Bannerman. Never-

theless, considerations of party balance led Sir Henry to offer Grey the Foreign Office in 1905.

As Foreign Secretary, Grey accepted the Anglo-French *entente* of 1904, signed by his predecessor, as the basis of his diplomacy. He had already developed a suspicion of German ambitions and a dislike of Berlin's diplomatic tactics. His readiness to accept continuity in foreign policy, and his supposed deference to advice from his permanent officials, brought him early criticism from Liberal backbenchers who believed that a Liberal foreign policy required even-handed detachment from European alliances and alignments. Grey supported France in the first Moroccan crisis of 1905–6 and promoted non-binding military conversations with Paris. Nevertheless, he believed that it was neither possible nor desirable to develop the *entente* into a full-scale alliance with specific commitments. He negotiated a convention with Russia in 1907, chiefly regarding the future of Persia. Critics on the

Viscount Grey presiding at the transfer by Stoke Poges Parochial Church Council of Grays Monument Field to the National Trust, May 1925

left did not like an arrangement with an autocratic power; critics on the right suspected that the Russians would not honour the agreement. Liberal backbenchers campaigned that 'Grey must go' in 1911–12 because they disliked the support given to France in the second Moroccan crisis. The Foreign Secretary weathered the storm, but detractors disliked his secrecy and argued that he ought to have shared his opinion on the great foreign issues of the day with the public. Grey remained convinced that naval power was essential, but was prepared to consider possible arrangements with Berlin. Indeed, in general in the years immediately before 1914, there seemed good grounds for believing that Anglo-German relations were improving – in the Balkans, the Near East and Africa. Grey's reaction to the events of the summer of 1914 have been subjected to close scrutiny. Should he have made Britain's position clearer earlier? Did Britain really have 'obligations of honour' to France? Was it a mistake to intervene in the war? At the time, Grey saw no alternative and would have resigned if his cabinet colleagues had failed to support him.

Inevitably, in war the scope for diplomacy is reduced, and, troubled by failing eyesight, Grey was not happy in his last years at the Foreign Office. There was no place for him in the Lloyd George government of December 1916. Brooding over the circumstances and structures that had led to war in 1914, Grey emerged during the conflict as a supporter of the League of Nations idea, and until his death he played an active role in the League of Nations Union. He published his own memoirs, *Twenty Five Years*, in 1925 – something no previous Foreign Secretary had done. Although an 'elder statesman', he remained active in postwar Liberal politics. There was talk of Grey emerging as leader of a Centre Party, but that never materialized.

Grey's public life concerned primarily foreign affairs, but from time to time he spoke and wrote on other aspects of Liberal policy. He supported votes for women. The strength of his career derived not from brilliance of intellect or depth of knowledge, but from that sense of firm and quiet determination, both in speech and demeanour, which he invariably conveyed. His

The Charm of Birds (1927) became a best-seller and testified to his own charm. His courage was displayed amid private tragedies: both his wives predeceased him; two brothers were killed in Africa by wild animals; his family home and his fishing cottage were destroyed by fire; he had no children; and, latterly, he was increasingly blind. He seemed, among it all, to be a model English gentleman who had strayed into politics by accident. It was quite convenient for him that this oversimplification should have existed.

FURTHER READING

Hinsley, F. H. (ed.), *The Foreign Policy of Sir Edward Grey* (Cambridge: Cambridge University Press, 1977).

Karpinski, J. (ed.), *Capital of Happiness: Lord Grey of Fallodon and the Charm of Birds* (London: Michael Joseph, 1984).

Robbins, K. G., *Sir Edward Grey: a Biography of Lord Grey of Fallodon* (London: Cassell, 1971).

KEITH ROBBINS

Grimond, Jo(seph) [Baron Grimond of Firth in the County of Orkney] (*b.* St Andrews, Fife, 29 July 1913). Liberal leader. Grimond led the Liberal Party during a period when its fortunes began to look as though they might one day revive. Yet, though the party was imbued with his personality and his authority was less questioned by members than any other Liberal leader's before or since, it is difficult to point precisely to what he did to produce the results. His personality and ideas were probably the most attractive features of the party to new recruits; his speeches were powerful and well received and he made effective use of the new medium of television. He allowed able men to run the party machine. But he was a philosophical leader rather than a practical strategist: when he told the 1962 Liberal Assembly in the aftermath of the Orpington by-election to 'march towards the sound of gunfire', he left it vague what kind of battle they could expect when they arrived at the front.

Grimond had been brought up among the surviving Liberal grandees in the Asquith tradition; he became engaged to his wife Laura Bonham Carter (Asquith's grand-daughter)

while staying with Sir Archibald Sinclair, the Caithness MP who led the Liberal Party during World War II. When he reached the Commons in 1950 as MP for Orkney and Shetland, Frank Byers had just lost his seat and Clement Davies immediately made Grimond Chief Whip. When Davies decided to retire in September 1956, Byers took some soundings and Davies told the party that Grimond should be his successor; the party did not demur.

By coincidence, Grimond's succession was followed at once by a final purging of the factional squabbles which had hastened the decline of the party; but the purgative agents were death and defection rather than the new leader. As Chief Whip he had borne, with Davies, the brunt of the squabbles between Hopkin Morris, a free trader, and Megan Lloyd George; in November 1956 Morris died, and in the ensuing by-election Megan Lloyd George fought the seat for the Labour Party. That was the end of Simonites, Samuelites and Lloyd Georges in the Liberal Party. When in the 1960s the party's posters carried the message 'Jo Grimond Leads the Liberals', it was not only effective marketing through a brand image, it was true in a sense which had not been applicable since 1916.

In his *Memoirs* (p. 197) Grimond described the Carmarthen by-election as 'an awkward corner to turn' (his candidate insisted on defending the government's Suez adventure), and then remarked: 'From then the fortunes of the Party improved. This was largely due to events outside the Party's control.' The events were partly by-elections, such as at Torrington (1958) and Orpington, fought by the Liberals with a new skill, ferocity and cunning, but more importantly a growing feeling of non-socialist disenchantment with long years of Conservative rule. The party's vote increased to 1.6 million in 1959 and to 3.1 million in 1964, and the number of its MPs reached nine. The increase in vote reflected the increase in the number of Liberal candidates (216 and 366, compared with just over 100 in 1951 and 1955) put up by constituency associations revived by the enthusiasm which Grimond engendered; but the votes per candidate also increased, from over 6,000 in the 1950s to over 7,000 in 1959 and more than 8,000 in 1964. In 1966, when

the general election was about the continuation of a Labour Government, the vote per Liberal candidate fell back to 7,000 (although the vagaries of the electoral system allowed the number of MPs to rise to 12), and in 1970, when Labour was turned out, the number of Liberal MPs was halved and the vote per candidate was back to 6,000.

The rise and fall of Liberal fortunes under Grimond's leadership can be related to his concept of the party as the 'non-socialist radical alternative to Conservatism'. Grimond was very clear about his antipathy to Labour: he regarded socialism as a false doctrine; he had a very Liberal dislike of the bureaucracy that went with Labour governments; and he was appalled by what he saw as the excessive power of trade-union bosses. The radical alternative to Conservatism was set out in a policy campaign which emphasized values of individual liberty, fairness and participation, and policies such as electoral reform, decentralization of power, Home Rule for Scotland and Wales and co-ownership in industry. Grimond himself was particularly interested in the mechanisms of democracy (in marked contrast to the Labour leadership who were fascinated by the machinery of government) and wanted the upper house of Parliament to provide a collegiate representation of the various interests in the nation.

Grimond hoped that this non-socialist radical party would have an opportunity to act as the catalyst for a 'realignment of the Left', which he expected to happen when a significant portion of the Labour Party had had enough of being shackled to socialism and the trade unions. Such an opportunity occurred 20 years later when the Social Democrats broke with Labour, and Grimond's influence prepared David Steel for this eventuality. He failed, however, to prepare his party: when coalition was momentarily on offer in February 1974, only he, Steel and Russell Johnston (the leader of the Scottish Liberal Party) among the MPs were willing to consider it in any circumstances. The members of the party at large were horrified by the suggestion, and their suspicion of coalition was the great handicap of Steel's leadership.

The fundamental problem of the Grimond

strategy was that it left the party without a role in times when Labour was in power and the Conservative Party was the most effective rallying point for those who wanted Labour out of office. Grimond saw this and the need for a policy campaign which would convert voters to preferring Liberal radicalism to Conservatism. But although the party saw itself as radical and opposed to Conservatism as much as to socialism, the voters whom it attracted as its fortunes improved were much more antipathetic to socialism than to Conservatism and readily reverted to Conservatism to get or keep Labour out. The Grimond strategy was entirely dependent on the Labour Party becoming so chaotic that voters would no longer see it as enough of a threat to compel them to vote Conservative.

In 1967 Grimond had had enough of being leader and resigned. He thought he might have been too cautious in pushing forward the Liberal challenge to Labour, and, when in 1977 Steel led the party into the Lib-Lab Pact, Grimond was alone in the parliamentary party in opposing it. Steel believed that the party which preached power-sharing should practice it if the terms were right. Grimond believed that the Labour Party was still tied to bureaucracy, socialism and trade-union bosses and that the Liberal Party should run the risk of forcing a general election which might provoke Labour's final crisis. Grimond lost the argument in the parliamentary party and it was not in him to challenge his young successor in the Liberal Assembly. It is ironic that, had he accepted the leadership which Steel and John Pardoe had urged him to resume after Thorpe's disgrace in 1976, he could have fought in 1977 the one great battle which chance did not bring his way in his years of command. He welcomed the Alliance once the Social Democrats had shaken themselves free of Labour and come back into the political arena prepared to fight, because he thought the Labour Party had come to its final agony; but he played no significant role in its direction.

Grimond's sympathies and interests spread far beyond politics but came together most intensely in the Northern Isles of his constituency, where he continued to live after he left the Commons for the Lords in 1983. In his *Memoirs* (written just before the 1979 election) he summed up his political odyssey 'as starting from the starry-eyed hope that all would be well if only the Liberal Party could return to the forefront of our affairs; passing through a phase when it seemed that the reform of the political system would be enough to put things to rights, ending up with the recognition that we must look at the wider currents in our lives' (p. 291). He was enough of a politician to think that a Liberal Party was necessary; but he did not believe that the party was either indispensable or sufficient for the expression of Liberal values.

WRITINGS

Memoirs (London: Heinemann, 1979).
A Personal Manifesto (Oxford: Martin Robertson, 1983).

C. M. MASON

H

Haig, Sir **Douglas** [Earl Haig] (*b*. Edinburgh, 19 June 1861; *d*. Bemersyde, Berwickshire, 30 January 1938). General. He was the Commander-in-Chief of the British Expeditionary Force (BEF) in France between December 1915 and April 1919. He commanded the largest army the British Empire ever placed in the field and his conduct has remained a matter of intense controversy ever since. Two of the battles which he fought, the Somme in 1916 and the third battle of Ypres, more commonly known as the battle of Passchendaele, in 1917, still seem to epitomize the apparently pointless futility of so much of the trench fighting of World War I.

Haig was educated at Clifton College, and, unusually for a soldier in the late nineteenth century, he attended university, Brasenose College, Oxford. He graduated from Sandhurst in 1885 and was gazetted into the 7th Hussars, where his career followed the normal pattern of a junior cavalry officer. He was an enthusiastic and successful polo player, was appointed adjutant of his regiment in 1888 and promoted to captain in 1891. In 1896 he entered the Staff College at Camberley, where he was an exact contemporary of Sir EDMUND ALLENBY. His two years at the college were one of the major formative experiences of his career. It was while he was there that he developed the ideas about generalship which guided his conduct during World War I.

Haig first saw active service in the Sudan during Kitchener's advance to Omdurman. On returning home he was appointed Brigade Major to the First Cavalry brigade and began an association and friendship with Sir John French which lasted until Haig replaced French as the Commander-in-Chief of the BEF in December 1915. He accompanied French to South Africa as the senior staff officer of the Cavalry Division. After the occupation of Pretoria he received his first independent command, when he became a column commander during the guerrilla phase of the war.

Between the end of the Boer War and the outbreak of World War I Haig held a series of staff appointments and troop commands. When he returned to Britain in 1902 he was given command of the 17th Lancers until 1903, when he was made Inspector-General of Cavalry in India. He was promoted to Major-General and when he returned to Britain in 1906 he spent the next three years serving as Director of Staff Duties at the War Office. Working under the ultimate direction of the Liberal Secretary of State for War, R. B. Haldane, he was responsible for preparing the first British field service regulations and for persuading the dominion governments to adopt regulations and training methods based on those of the British regular army. In 1909 he returned to India as the Chief of Staff of the Indian Army. He continued the reforms begun by Lord Kitchener, which were intended to enable the Indian Army to send troops abroad in the event of a major war.

In the last three years of peace Haig held one of the plum appointments in the British Army, the Aldershot command. This post carried with it command of the First Army Corps when the BEF was mobilized and went to France in August 1914. Haig commanded the First Corps between August and December 1914 during the retreat from Mons and at the first battle of Ypres. As the number of divisions with the BEF grew, Haig's responsibilities also grew. In January 1915 he was promoted to command the First Army and thus had tactical command of Sir John French's offensives at Neuve Chapelle (March 1915), Festubert and Aubers Ridge (May 1915) and Loos (September–October 1915). On the eve of war Haig had private doubts about French's competence as a commander. The latter's reluctance to commit his reserves to Haig's command during Loos so that he could exploit what he thought was a breakthrough led to a professional breach between them which was not healed for several years. Haig actively lobbied for French's removal and succeeded him as Commander-in-Chief in December 1915.

Haig's conduct of operations on the Western Front between 1916 and 1918 was guided by the lessons he had absorbed at the Staff College. They included the notion that the destruction of the enemy's army was the main objective in war. It could be destroyed only in a decisive offensive. The decisive offensive must be divided into four phases, the manoeuvre to bring the enemy to battle, the preparation for battle, the decisive attack and the pursuit of the defeated enemy by the cavalry. Each phase led automatically on to the next. Haig expected the enemy to behave in the same way and therefore victory would go to the side with the higher morale and the general with the stronger will. And finally he believed that once the Commander-in-Chief had set his subordinates their objectives, he must not interfere in the manner in which they carried them out.

These lessons go far to explain his conduct on the Western Front. Haig accepted that a minimum number of troops had to be sent to protect the British Empire in Africa and the Middle East, but throughout the war he was a vehement opponent of diverting forces away from France so that Britain could attack Germany's weaker allies. He always insisted that the war would not be won by defeating the Turks, Austrians or Bulgars. It would be won only when the enemy's main army, the German army, had been defeated in France. His Staff College training also explains his reluctance to remain on the defensive in the expectation that eventually the enemy would wear himself out by attacking the strongly entrenched allied positions in the West. The vacuum in command which developed between Haig's General Head Quarters (GHQ) and his army commanders was partly the result of his training at Camberley, but it was also the product of Haig's own personality. He had considerable difficulty in forming friendships with his contemporaries and colleagues. He was naturally aloof and, perhaps because of the need to overcome childhood asthma, had trained himself to be rigorously self-disciplined. Subordi-

nates often found it difficult to raise awkward issues with him and there was a lack of discussion of alternative tactics and strategy between Haig and his army commanders. Even strong-minded men such as Allenby were afraid of him. He intensified the isolation of GHQ from the front by picking acquiescent staff officers such as Sir Launcelot Kiggell, his chief of staff in 1916–17, to assist him at GHQ. Haig was a deeply religious man and his belief in divine support undoubtedly served him as a psychological prop and confirmed the correctness of his decisions.

In early 1916 Haig wished to mount an offensive from the Ypres salient which would drive the Germans away from the Belgian coast. However, the need to cooperate closely with the French Army took priority and instead he agreed to take part in a joint Anglo-French offensive astride the river Somme. The operation was part of an ambitious allied plan. The French, British, Russian and Italian armies were to mount virtually simultaneous offensives to force the Germans to make peace by the end of 1916. Haig hoped to break through the German line at the first attempt, but he was sadly disappointed. General Rawlinson's Fourth Army lost nearly 60,000 casualties on 1 July 1916. The battle continued until mid-November, by when the BEF had lost approximately 400,000 men and had achieved a maximum advance of about eight miles. When Lloyd George became Prime Minister he was so alarmed at these losses that in February 1917 he resorted to the expedient of placing Haig under the temporary command of the French Commander-in-Chief, General Nivelle, for a second Anglo-French offensive. Haig's part in the operation, the battle of Arras, began well on 9 April, but the French offensive which started on 16 April was a disaster. It resulted in a large part of the French Army going on strike. Lloyd George now had no option other than to allow Haig to revert to his cherished plan to strike north-east from the Ypres salient to clear the Belgian coast. The operation began successfully when Sir Herbert Plumer's Second Army captured Messines ridge on 7 June. But heavy rain, the destruction of the delicate drainage system of the Flanders plain by the artillery, and tenacious German

The statue of Earl Haig in Whitehall, London

defenders meant that when the Ypres offensive proper began on 31 July the assault troops quickly found themselves fighting in a sea of mud. Haig persisted in the offensive until mid-November, encouraged by his chief intelligence officer, Brigadier John Charteris, a notorious optimist who fed him with inflated estimates of German casualties to justify continuing the attack. The one brief success on the Western Front at the end of 1917 was an offensive mounted by the Tank Corps at Cambrai on 20 November. But the Germans counter-attacked swiftly and rapidly regained most of the ground they had lost.

The military and political situation in the winter of 1917 and the spring of 1918 was critical for the Allies. The collapse of Russia enabled the Germans to move large numbers of divisions from the Eastern to the Western Front and to mount a major offensive against Haig's armies on 21 March 1918. Haig's reserves were soon exhausted and the French Commander-in-Chief, General Pétain, wished to protect Paris at all costs. Only the appointment of General Foch as the Allied generalissimo prevented the Germans from cutting off the BEF from the French Army. Fortunately for Haig, in May and June the Germans turned their attention to trying to

break through the French line and he was given time to rest and refit his divisions. On 8 August he began a series of counter-offensives in conjunction with the French and American armies which not only robbed the Germans of most of the gains they had made in the spring, but, more importantly, falsified the German commanders' promise to their troops that they could win the war with one last push. With their weaker allies suing for peace and the morale of their own army crumbling, the Germans signed an Armistice which came into force on 11 November. One possible explanation of why Haig's army did so much better in the summer and autumn of 1918 than it had done in 1916–17 was that the government forced Haig to make significant changes and improvements among the staff at GHQ. Charteris and Kiggell were both sacked early in 1918. Their replacements were men of greater strength of character who were more ready to maintain close liaison with subordinate headquarters and to listen to the ideas of commanders actually in contact with the enemy.

After the Armistice Haig remained in command of the BEF for several months. In 1919 he returned to Britain and took up the post of Commander-in-Chief, Home Forces. He presided over the demobilization of the army until he relinquished his last active command in January 1921. During the war he had become increasingly concerned at the distress many disabled ex-servicemen had suffered and for the rest of his life he devoted much of his time to looking after their welfare. It was largely due to his influence that the various ex-servicemen's organizations were persuaded to unite into one organization, the British Legion.

Haig was very sensitive to anything which he thought was a slur on his own reputation or that of the men who served under him. Although he never wrote his own memoirs, he was ready to assist writers such as John Charteris who were willing to put his case for him. In 1928 he died suddenly at his ancestral home, Bemersyde, which had been purchased for him by public subscription in 1921.

Haig still remains a figure of immense and unresolved controversy. Although John Terraine has tried to rescue his reputation, describing him as an 'educated soldier', he is still widely regarded as the archetypal World War I general, insensitive to the suffering of his troops and responsible for 'creating' an entire lost generation. Both judgements are probably too extreme. Only now are we beginning to glimpse the fact that Haig's style of command was the outcome not only of his own personality, but of a system of training senior commanders suitable to late nineteenth-century colonial warfare but which left them unfitted in too many respects to grapple with the complexities of a war between coalitions of industrialized nations.

FURTHER READING

Blake, R., *The Private Papers of Douglas Haig* (London: Eyre and Spottiswoode, 1952).
Charteris, Brigadier-General J., *Field Marshal Earl Haig* (London: Constable, 1929).
Duff Cooper, A., *Haig*, 2 vols. (London: Faber and Faber, 1935).
Edmonds, Sir J. E., *History of the Great War: Military Operations France and Belgium*, 14 vols. (London: Macmillan, 1922–48).
Groot, G. J. de, *Douglas Haig, 1861–1928* (London: Unwin Hyman, 1988).
Terraine, J., *Douglas Haig: the Educated Soldier* (London: Hutchinson, 1963).
Travers, T., *The Killing Ground: the British Army,*

the Western Front and the Emergence of Modern Warfare 1900–1918 (London: Allen and Unwin, 1987).

DAVID FRENCH

Hailsham, Lord [Hogg, Quintin (McGarel); Baron Hailsham of St Marylebone] (*b.* London, 9 October 1907). Lord Chancellor and eminent jurist. He was MP for Oxford City from 1938 to 1950 and for St Marylebone from 1963 to 1970, and held a number of posts before becoming Lord Chancellor in 1970: Joint Parliamentary Under-Secretary for Air (1945), First Lord of the Admiralty (1956–7), Minister of Education (1957), Deputy Leader of House of Lords (1957–60), Leader of Lords (1960–3), Lord Privy Seal (1959–60), Lord President of the Council (1957–9, 1960–4), Minister for Science and Technology (1959–64), Minister with Special Responsibility for Sport (1962–4) and Minister of Education and Science (1964).

Lord Hailsham has resisted most of the conventional symmetries of political life and the chief impression after a career that stretches back to the 1930s remains one of paradox. He was the author in 1947 of one of the most elegant and persuasive contributions to political polemic produced this century; yet success in the game itself eluded him. He spent a lifetime on the liberal wing of Conservative argument and yet somehow convinced opponents that he flew on the opposite one. He brought to public life an intellectual apparatus of supreme sophistication; but his political reputation came to rest, quite inappropriately, on childish pranks more than sustained achievement. In the absence of the political autobiography that he refused to write, much in Hailsham's party life will retain its mysteries for some years to come, and students must meanwhile enquire between the lines of his wide-ranging publications.

Hailsham's background implied that he would begin adult life with considerable advantages. Eton and Oxford, where he became President of the Union in 1929 and took a first class degree in the following year, plainly helped his progress to the Bar in 1932. Even while these achievements were unfolding, however, the political career of his father, Sir Douglas Hogg, first Viscount Hailsham, also moved into higher gear as he became Baldwin's Attorney-General and later Minister for War in the National Government. That the streams of law and politics would merge in the younger Hogg's life seemed, therefore, a distinct possibility by the early 1930s. In fact the pressures of establishing himself as a barrister, the sheer cost of entering parliament, and difficulties in

Lord Hailsham (as First Lord of the Admiralty) using a hoist on an Admiralty helicopter to inspect the cockpit after opening the National Boat Show at Olympia, London, January 1957

finding a constituency delayed Hogg's appearance in the House of Commons until 1938. It was no ordinary appearance. The Oxford by-election, at which Hogg had defeated the Master of Balliol College, A. D. Lindsay, on a pro-Chamberlain platform just a month after the Munich crisis, won sensational publicity. As Munich then turned from triumph to disaster with Hitler's occupation of Prague in the spring of 1939, so did Hogg's reputation suffer by association. Much of his prolific writing on behalf of the Conservative Party during World War II attempted to justify the 'appeasers' of the 1930s against the allegations produced by their enemies after 1939.

For all Hogg's unease over becoming involved in party bitterness, books such as *The Left Was Never Right* (1945) showed him a tough-minded polemicist. He wanted, nonetheless, to present during the years of opposition after the war a less heated exposition of Tory ideas: a new Tamworth Manifesto that might rally Conservatives rather than merely irritate socialists. This thought lay behind his best and most influential book, *The Case for Conservatism* (1947), which achieved a level of literary craftsmanship unusual, perhaps unique, in postwar political advocacy and still figures in serious discussion of British political traditions. Its image of the Conservative who practices politics not for its own sake but in sympathetic vibration to wider social and spiritual values – 'religion, art, study, family, country, friends, music, fun, duty' – has become a feature of more recent defences of liberal Toryism.

On moving to the House of Lords as second Viscount Hailsham in 1950, moreover, he seemed set to carry out these maxims from an appropriate distance and height. Possibly Churchill fought old fights in keeping Hailsham out of his last government, though he had received minor advancement at the very end of the war. Eden gave him office outside the cabinet; but only with the accession of Macmillan to the Conservative leadership in 1957 did Hailsham's political status grow significantly. Indeed, his relationship with Macmillan through to the stormy leadership crisis in 1963 gave rise to his most important experiences as a politician.

Because Hailsham was a peer, his ministerial and party career followed the contours (and limitations) that a peerage implied in an able man: Leadership of the House of Lords; Lord Privy Seal; Lord President of the Council. But his simultaneous tenure of a new ministry – that of Science and Technology – he took seriously and worked hard to raise levels of consciousness in Britain about the importance of the scientific community. It was nevertheless a weak base from which to become Leader of the Conservative Party, despite his chairmanship of the party organization and a popular success at the party conference in 1957 with his notorious ringing of a bell. Macmillan decided, however, that Hailsham ought to succeed him (perhaps in order that Butler should not do so) when ill-health struck down the Prime Minister in 1963; and, granted the passage of the Peerage Bill at the end of July, Hailsham announced at the famous Blackpool party conference in October his decision to renounce his title. The sequel is familiar. Neither Butler nor Hailsham gained the leadership and, as in 1911 when Bonar Law first emerged, a compromise candidate appeared in Lord Home.

His failure to secure the leadership undoubtedly dealt Hailsham his greatest political blow. Just as Curzon lost interest when rejected in 1923, so Hailsham after 1964 returned to his first love – the law – and little surprise was occasioned by his elevation to the woolsack in 1970 when he re-entered the Second Chamber as Baron Hailsham of St Marylebone, his constituency since 1963. Under both Edward Heath and Margaret Thatcher he made a significant, though as yet inscrutable, contribution to Conservative politics as Lord Chancellor, and his constitutional thought received particular public notice through his support for a new Bill of Rights. He received the Order of Merit in 1988.

WRITINGS

The Door Wherein I Went (London: Collins, 1975).
The Dilemma of Democracy (London: Collins, 1978).

MICHAEL BENTLEY

Hailsham, Viscount. See HOGG, DOUGLAS.

Haldane, J(ohn) B(urdon) S(cott) (*b.* Oxford, 5 November 1892; *d.* Bhubaneswar, India, 1 December 1964). Geneticist, scientific popularizer and political publicist. Haldane was the son of a distinguished Oxford physiologist and nephew of Viscount Haldane. Educated at the Dragon School, Oxford, Eton and New College, Oxford, he obtained Firsts in both mathematical moderations and classics and philosophy, the latter in 1914. During the war he was wounded both in France and Mesopotamia. He was appointed Reader in Biochemistry at Cambridge in 1922 and began to write for a wider audience in such books as *Possible Worlds* (1927). In 1932 he was elected FRS and the following year he took the chair of genetics, later of biometry, at University College, London. His contribution as a scientist came from his wide interests, which took him far beyond conventional departmental boundaries. By the same token, however, he lacked specialist single-mindedness. Haldane had also taken a few paces outside his laboratory and seen the need for political and social reform. He conceived a desire to introduce the 'scientific attitude' into politics. That seemed to mean the Labour Party in the 1920s, though Haldane proved difficult to tie down. He was certainly a progressive spirit, and had a private life to match.

By the later 1930s, however, Haldane had come to believe that Marxism was true. He was much exercised by the Spanish Civil War in which his stepson was killed fighting against Franco's forces. He did his best to extricate himself from his own background and rejoiced in the new insights provided by dialectical materialism. He became chairman of the editorial board of the *Daily Worker* in 1940 and formally joined the Communist Party in 1942. He was relieved of some political embarrassment by Hitler's invasion of the Soviet Union and threw himself (sometimes literally) into diving research on behalf of submariners. In 1945 he devoted a pamphlet to explaining *Why Professional Workers should be Communists*. However, he also had to spend a good deal of time trying to explain why the Russian geneticist Lysenko should be regarded as professional.

By the early 1950s Haldane had ceased to

play an active part in the Communist Party, though he did not formally resign until 1956, and then privately. At the same time, however, he announced that he was leaving Britain in order to dissociate himself from the attack on Egypt. His new destination was India and in 1961 he became an Indian citizen. He dressed in Indian clothes, became an increasingly strict vegetarian and spent a lot of time watching the stars, but also continued research in biometry and genetics. It was in India that he died. His separation from his comfortable childhood world of North Oxford could not have been more complete.

FURTHER READING

Clark, R., *J. B. S.* (London: Hodder and Stoughton, 1968).

KEITH ROBBINS

Haldane, R(ichard) B(urdon) [Viscount Haldane of Cloan] (*b.* Edinburgh, 30 July 1856; *d.* Cloan, Perthshire, 19 August 1928). Liberal imperialist, later Labour politician, Minister for War, Lord Chancellor, philosopher and distinguished jurist. He had no previous ministerial experience when he was appointed Secretary of State for War in December 1905. The reforms he initiated largely determined Britain's military preparedness in 1914. He was twice Lord Chancellor: from June 1912 to May 1915, in Asquith's Liberal administration, and from January to November 1924 as Labour's first holder of that office. While he was endowed with many fine qualities – a capacious intellect, sagacity, patience, moral courage – was an outstanding administrator, magnanimous to foes, and loyal and generous to family and friends, Haldane's handicap as a politician in an age of increasing democracy was a failure to explain his actions clearly to others who were less gifted than himself, a weakness compounded by his desire to pose as a man of mystery. As a consequence he was condemned for being 'too clever by half'.

Haldane grew up in an atmosphere of strict evangelical piety. His undergraduate studies at Edinburgh were troubled by religious doubts, but these were resolved during a brief sojourn at Göttingen University in 1874. Haldane graduated in 1876 with first class honours in philosophy. He read for the Bar at Lincoln's Inn, was called in 1879 and slowly built up a Chancery practice, taking silk in 1890. His success was due not to brilliant forensic skills but to hard work and an unfailing ability to grasp the essence of the most complex issues. As a judge he combined mastery of technical learning with awareness of the social, political and economic implications of his decisions. A gifted equity jurist, he continued his judicial work to the end of his life.

Entering the Commons in 1885 as Liberal MP for East Lothian, he quickly established an unfortunate and generally undeserved reputation as a not very skilful intriguer in the interests of the Liberal imperialists, that faction that cleaved to the reluctant Rosebery as leader and was thoroughly distrusted by the radicals, competitors for the intellectual and parliamentary leadership of the Liberals. With his fellow Liberal imperialists Asquith and Grey, Haldane unsuccessfully conspired to influence Campbell-Bannerman's cabinet-making in the autumn of 1905 (see also ASQUITH, H. H., and GREY, EDWARD). He had sought the woolsack but instead received the War Office.

Haldane was fortunate to be appointed minister when the need for army reform was generally accepted. His less fortunate predecessors bequeathed him an invaluable legacy: ideas, advisers and improved institutions. Haldane's unique contribution to the task was not originality of thought, but conceptual clarity and a readiness to employ others' best ideas. He succeeded in creating both an expeditionary force and an adequate second-line reserve, changes that were effected within strict financial limits. Military and strategic requirements he expected the army to meet by organizational efficiency and ingenuity.

Success was achieved despite formidable parliamentary opposition. Haldane dominated army debates; his speeches induced ennui and confusion among the Tories, while radical opponents were either mollified by financial economies or threatened with conscription should reform fail. In cabinet, Haldane cultivated powerful allies, none more valuable and unexpected than Campbell-Bannerman.

Lord Haldane, the Lord Chancellor, leading the procession at the opening of the Law Courts, October 1913

To avoid criticism Haldane sometimes asserted that his estimates were the necessary minimal response to policy obligations contracted by the Foreign, Colonial or India Offices. After the malign wartime calumnies of unscrupulous political enemies, who accused Haldane of being pro-German, his restoration to favour owed something to his efforts as his own apologist in *Before the War* (1920). He claimed he foresaw and specifically prepared for a Continental engagement as France's ally against Germany, but Haldane's true claim to greatness was the comprehensiveness of his reforms, achieved despite the formidable obstacles he had to surmount as a peace-time Liberal Minister for War.

Education was Haldane's other consuming political interest. He admired and recommended the German model of high culture combined with applied technical knowledge. On organization, his ideas were simple and practical, if unoriginal. He twice served as Chairman of Royal Commissions on university education, was Chancellor of two universities and Lord Rector of another, co-founder of the London School of Economics, for nine years President of Birkbeck College, and an energetic, enthusiastic supporter of the Workers' Educational Association and the British Institute of Adult Education. His interest in education finally determined Haldane's move from the Liberal to the Labour Party. This transition, given his personality and the contemporary political context, was logical and comparatively easy. Though he outdistanced parliamentary Liberalism, Haldane's vague collectivist ideas were illumined by liberal ideals.

He retained a life-long passion for philosophy and frequently claimed that his training in that discipline was of fundamental importance to his judicial and political work. He lectured on philosophy and published a number of books, of which the last, *Human Experience* (1926), offers the most accessible guide to his thinking. Sadly, Haldane's writing on philosophy shares with much of his public oratory a denseness of content and opaqueness of exposition.

Though he never married, there were two important female influences in Haldane's life, his mother and his sister Elizabeth. He was never a popular politician, for his interests were too intellectual and his omniscience too easily suggested self-satisfaction. As a minister he was prodigiously hard working, loyal to colleagues, considerate to subordinates, never reluctant to devolve responsibility. His sweet temper remained unsoured despite the undeserved obloquy he suffered. Deserted by his former Liberal colleagues, defamed by the popular press and certain leading Tories, Haldane was not entirely rejected. As proof of his regard for the man and confidence in his patriotism, George V gave Haldane the Order of Merit. Time has confirmed the appropriateness of that award to a great servant of the state, whose guilelessness survived all the vicissitudes of a political career peculiarly and inextricably linked with the declining fortunes of the Liberal Party.

FURTHER READING

Koss, S. E., *Lord Haldane: Scapegoat for Liberalism* (New York: Columbia University Press, 1969).
'Lord Haldane', in Heuston, R. V. F., *Lives of the Lord Chancellors, 1885–1940* (Oxford: Clarendon Press, 1964).
Sommer, D., *Haldane of Cloan: his Life and Times 1856–1928* (London: Allen and Unwin, 1960).
Spiers, E. M., *Haldane: an Army Reformer* (Edinburgh: Edinburgh University Press, 1980).

A. J. A. MORRIS

Halifax, Earl of. See IRWIN, LORD.

Hankey, Sir Maurice (Pascal Alers) [Lord Hankey] (*b.* Biarritz, France, 1 April 1877; *d.* Redhill, Surrey, 25 January 1963). Leading civil servant. He was Secretary of the Committee of Imperial Defence (1912–38), Secretary of the War Cabinet (1916–19), Secretary of the Imperial War Cabinet (1917–19), Secretary of the Cabinet (1919–38), Clerk of the Privy Council (1923–38), Minister without Portfolio (1939–40), Chancellor of the Duchy of Lancaster (1940–1), and Paymaster-General (1941–2), and was effectively the inventor of the administrative machinery through which modern British cabinet government works.

As the first Secretary of the Cabinet, by definition Hankey was one of the foremost higher civil servants of his day. Yet, born the son of an Australian sheep farmer in Biarritz, and then educated at Rugby, he had been destined for a naval career, graduating with distinction to become a Captain of Marines. He impressed superiors such as 'Jackie' Fisher so much that by 1902 he was transferred to naval intelligence work, and then in 1908 to the post of Assistant Secretary of the Committee of Imperial Defence. In 1912 he became the Secretary of that Committee, a post that he retained until 1938.

It was in December 1916 that Sir Maurice Hankey, as he was by then, was made Secretary of the War Cabinet as part of the administrative changes that accompanied the installation of Lloyd George as Prime Minister. The establishment of the Cabinet Secretariat with Hankey as its official head represented a break with the traditional practice of not recording cabinet proceedings. In the midst of a total war such arrangements were deemed dangerously amateurish and inhibitive of concerted executive action. Thereafter the War Cabinet and the Imperial War Cabinet had the services of the omnipresent Hankey, who, in his various administrative roles, was thought to have attended about 1,240 meetings during World War I and to have recorded probably more than five million words. He was believed to have attended every political and inter-allied conference held during that war, and he was the obvious choice to be the British Secretary to the Paris Peace Conference in 1919 and to be the Secretary of the Cabinet when that body took a peacetime form later that year.

It was only with difficulty that the Cabinet Secretariat survived the fall of Lloyd George and the bureaucratic imperialist ambitions of the Head of the Civil Service, Sir Warren Fisher. Hankey successfully resisted Fisher's plan to bring the Secretariat and himself within the Treasury. Indeed, to the roles of Secretary of the Cabinet and that of Secretary of the Committee of Imperial Defence, Hankey added in 1923 that of Clerk of the Privy Council. He retained all these posts until his retirement from the Civil Service in July 1938, and was subsequently granted a peerage. With the coming of World War II Hankey was Minister without Portfolio in Neville Chamberlain's War Cabinet and then Chancellor of the Duchy of Lancaster and Paymaster-General in Churchill's government, before being dismissed in 1942 following differences with the Prime Minister over military strategy.

Hankey's capacity for dealing with the quarrelsome service chiefs had made his contribution as a central administrator an invaluable one during World War I, and he seems to have possessed very considerable energy, a photographic memory, and the endless tact needed in working with politicians as varied in temperament as Lloyd George and Neville Chamberlain. Only Churchill seems able to have resisted a high estimate of Hankey, whose dynamism modern fashion would ascribe to a spartan diet, forgetting that the indulgent Churchill outlived him.

FURTHER READING

Obituary, *The Times* (28 January 1963).
Roskill, S., *Hankey: Man of Secrets*, 3 vols. (London: Collins, 1970–4).

GEOFFREY K. FRY

Hardie, (James) Keir (*b.* Legbrannock, Lanarkshire, 15 August 1856; *d.* Glasgow, 26 September 1915). Founder and Chairman of the Independent Labour Party and Labour MP. Hardie never held public office. As MP (1892–5 and 1900–15), founder and Chairman (1894–1900, 1913–14) of the Independent Labour Party, and Chairman of the Labour Party (1906–8, 1909–10) he probably did more than any of his contemporaries to establish independent Labour politics in Britain.

Three influences shaped Hardie's social and political consciousness. The first was his illegitimacy, about which he rarely spoke, but which he felt very deeply. He was close to his mother, Mary Keir, but there is still doubt

about his paternity. The hard drinking of his step-father, David Hardie, helped to turn him to the temperance movement. It served, too, to keep a large family in the poverty which also shaped Hardie's social concern. Poverty deprived him of all but minimum schooling and compelled him to work from the age of eight. Thirdly, in 1878 he was converted to Christianity. Although he ceased to be a regular churchgoer after 1884, his socialism always contained religious, puritanical, even quasi-mystical elements which often distanced him from more practically-minded colleagues.

From the age of ten Hardie worked in the mines and soon became actively involved in trade unionism, holding a number of offices. Having made up his education at night school he turned to journalism as a further means of defending the miners' interests. Although initially a Liberal supporter, events in the late 1880s led him to argue for independent working-class action. The failure of the Scottish miners' strike in 1887 fuelled his bitter denunciation of the established pro-Liberal leadership of the TUC in that year. In the aftermath of his defeat in a by-election at Mid-Lanark in 1888, he became Secretary of the newly established Scottish Labour Party. He also began to produce the monthly *Labour Leader*, the best and most influential of all contemporary Labour papers.

In the general election of 1892 Hardie – somewhat fortuitously as his Liberal rival committed suicide – won West Ham in a straight fight against a Conservative. Although his cavalier approach to parliamentary procedure alienated other Labour representatives, Hardie deservedly won the epithet of 'member for the unemployed'. More importantly, his parliamentary position lent weight to what he saw as his primary role – that of prophet for the establishment of a national, independent working-class party. Years of public meetings and written advocacy came to fruition in January 1893 with the formation of the Independent Labour Party. As its only MP and editor of the *Labour Leader*, Hardie was dominant. He was the obvious choice for chairman, a position he retained until 1900. The loss of his parliamentary seat in 1895 gave him more time to publicize the party. It was largely due to his influence that attempts to work more closely with the Social Democratic Federation foundered. Although later in his career Hardie was not averse to working with the SDF, at this stage he believed that its dogmatic Marxism closed the door against cooperation with the Liberals. He also disagreed with the SDF's hostility towards the unions which, in his view, formed the only viable basis for a mass working-class party.

The deterioration in industrial relations in the years immediately before 1900 made the unions more amenable to the idea of political independence. At the founding conference of the Labour Representation Committee in 1900 it was again Hardie who determined the major strategic decisions, and his standing was further enhanced by the capture of a seat at Merthyr in that year. Although he could be flexible and pragmatic in his approach to politics, both his image and rhetoric were those of an extremist. To some extent, therefore, he found himself isolated in a party which had to woo moderate trade unionists and Liberal voters. Only the re-emergence of the unemployment issue in 1904–5 pushed him back into prominence. He was elected first chairman of the parliamentary Labour Party after its electoral successes in 1906 only by a single vote.

Criticism soon began to mount, however. Hardie was not a good organizer, and, distracted by family problems and an overvigorous espousal of the suffragette cause, he was frequently absent from the House. Ill-health provided a convenient excuse for resignation and a world tour in July 1907. Although he again served as chairman in 1909–10 he was increasingly at odds with Ramsay MacDonald's policy of supporting the Liberal Government in return for concessions that would safeguard Labour's electoral position (see also MACDONALD, RAMSAY).

When war broke out in 1914 Hardie opposed British involvement. He had always been a pacifist and an internationalist. He had spoken frequently on foreign affairs since his world tour, and as Chairman of the British section of the Socialist International he had helped commit it in 1910 to the idea of an international strike in the event of war. In 1914,

as during the Boer War, he exhibited considerable courage in opposing mass patriotic sentiment, but there was truth in the observation that the effort destroyed him. Years of public work had already prematurely aged him and in January 1915 he suffered a mild stroke. His mind began to deteriorate and in September he died of pneumonia. He left three children and a wife who had borne with equal fortitude his prolonged absences from the family home and a number of affairs, the most serious of which was with Sylvia Pankhurst.

Hardie was a poor administrator and too much of an individualist to work comfortably with colleagues. He was sometimes erratic, not least in his volatile attitudes towards the Liberals and the SDF. Yet he was consistent in his internationalism, his pacifism, and his advocacy on behalf of women and the unemployed. As the major figure in working-class politics before 1914 he left an enduring influence on subsequent Labour Party policy. His oratory and journalism ensured the success of independent Labour politics and did much to make the British working class politically articulate.

FURTHER READING

Hughes, E., *Keir Hardie* (London: Allen and Unwin, 1956).

McLean, I., *Keir Hardie* (London: Allen Lane, 1975).

Morgan, K. O., *Keir Hardie: Radical and Socialist* (London: Weidenfeld and Nicolson, 1975).

Reid, F., *Keir Hardie* (London: Croom Helm, 1978).

Stewart, W., *Keir Hardie* (London: Cassell, 1921).

KENNETH D. BROWN

Hardinge, Charles [Baron Hardinge of Penshurst] (*b.* London, 20 June 1858; *d.* Penshurst, Kent, 2 August 1944). Permanent Under-Secretary at the Foreign Office, Ambassador to Russia and France, and Viceroy of India. He entered the Diplomatic Service in May 1880 at a time when the Foreign Office and Diplomatic Service were two separate establishments. He was to rise to the top of his profession in both, serving as Permanent Under-Secretary (1906–10, 1916–20) in

London and as Ambassador to Russia (1904–6) and France (1920–22). As Viceroy of India (1910–16) his name was associated with an improvement in relations with the nationalists but also with the unsuccessful Mesopotamian campaign of 1916. His two volumes of memoirs, *Old Diplomacy* (1947) and *My Indian Years, 1910–1916* (1948), provide some insight into Hardinge's character and career.

Coming from a family long associated with the army and service in India, Hardinge was educated at Cheam, Harrow and Trinity College, Cambridge. His rapid ascent up the diplomatic ladder owed much to his capacity for hard work but was undoubtedly assisted by his wife's close connection with the future Queen Alexandra and his own subsequent friendship with Edward VII. 'Capability' Hardinge became ambassador to Russia at the young age of 45, and then again, due in part to Foreign Office manoeuvrings and royal patronage, returned to the Office as Permanent Under-Secretary in 1906, an unusual transfer at the time. Hardinge, though sharing the social snobberies associated with the 'old diplomacy', was an active supporter of the new administrative reforms at the Office (1905–6), which served to strengthen the position of the Permanent Under-Secretary. He enjoyed a close professional relationship with Sir Edward Grey, particularly during the latter's first years in office. Hardinge's expanded advisory role as well as his journeys abroad with the King aroused criticism among Liberal and radical backbenchers, culminating in an unsuccessful attack on the power of the permanent officials in 1912.

Hardinge backed the policy of the *ententes* and was instrumental both in negotiating the Anglo-Russian conventions of 1907 and nurturing the new connection, which he saw as essential for the protection of India. Hardinge was concerned, too, about the hegemonic ambitions of the German government and became a strong proponent of maintaining Britain's naval superiority as the ultimate safeguard against foreign threat. Fully aware of the political objections to turning the *ententes* into alliances, Hardinge rarely pushed Grey beyond the political possibilities posed by a divided Liberal cabinet.

Hardinge's viceroyalty was one of consolidation rather than reform. He was willing to compromise on questions of Indian participation in government but never accepted self-government as practical or desirable. He saw the re-unification of Bengal and the building of the new capital at Delhi (working closely with the architect, Sir Edwin Lutyens) as ways of conciliating opposition groups, while looking to ties with the native princes as a counterbalance to the radicals. Hardinge moved in great viceregal splendour; the royal durbar of 1911 was a magnificent demonstration of British imperial power. Yet despite the implementation of the Morley-Minto reforms, there were continuing signs of discontent; in 1912 Hardinge and his wife were the objects of an unsuccessful bomb attack in Delhi. Even in wartime, relations between the raj and home government remained uneasy, with Hardinge proving more sensitive to Muslim sensibilities than London. When the Indian army moved against the Turks into the Persian Gulf and Mesopotamia, the Viceroy became a strong supporter of the campaign to take Baghdad. A Royal Commission in 1917, looking into the abortive Mesopotamian campaign, condemned both its military and civilian leaders, including Hardinge, who had returned to the Foreign Office for his second tour as Permanent Under-Secretary. His offers to resign were rejected and, as a result of the intervention of the Foreign Secretary, Arthur Balfour, he survived the public censure.

Hardinge's war years at the Foreign Office and at the peace conference, where he was 'organizing ambassador', were not happy ones. He found the Office very much a 'pass on' department dwarfed by the activities of Lloyd George. In spite of Hardinge's efforts to strengthen the position of the professionals and so assure them of an important role in Paris, neither he nor they played a central part in the peace negotiations. Driven to distraction by Lloyd George's tactics, Hardinge, who had lost his wife in 1914 and his elder son from war wounds six months later, came close to nervous breakdown. In July 1920, however, he was offered the highest diplomatic accolade, the Paris embassy, where despite his continuing distrust of Lloyd George and the difficulties of working with Lord Curzon, the Foreign Secretary, he played his part in postponing that rupture with the French which constantly threatened postwar Anglo-French relations. Hardinge retired in December 1921 without again taking an active role in public affairs, though he lived until 1944.

WRITINGS

On Hill and Plain (London: John Murray, 1933).
Old Diplomacy (London: John Murray, 1947).
My Indian Years, 1910–1916 (London: John Murray, 1948).

FURTHER READING

Busch, B. C., *Hardinge of Penshurst: a Study of the Old Diplomacy* (Hamden, Conn.: Archon Books, 1980).

ZARA STEINER

Harmsworth, Alfred. See NORTHCLIFFE, LORD.

Harris, Sir **Arthur (Travers)** [Baron Harris] **('Bomber' Harris)** (*b.* Cheltenham, Gloucestershire, 13 April 1892; *d.* Goring on Thames, Oxfordshire, 5 April 1984). World War II bomber commander. 'Bomber' Harris was one of the most controversial British military figures of the twentieth century. As the Commander-in-Chief of Royal Air Force Bomber Command between 1942 and 1945, he oversaw the major part of the British Strategic Air Offensive against Germany, which produced widespread economic destruction and huge civilian casualties, but which may not have contributed as effectively as it should have done to the defeat of Germany.

Harris went to Rhodesia in 1910, where he worked as a gold digger and a tobacco planter. At the outbreak of the Great War he joined the 1st Rhodesian Regiment and fought in South West Africa. He returned to Britain in 1915 and was commissioned in the Royal Flying Corps, which was absorbed into the Royal Air Force when that new service was formed in 1918. During the postwar years he served with the RAF in India, Iraq and Egypt, earning

himself a reputation as an intemperate champion of air power, and someone clearly destined for high command. Though a rather reserved man, he was a master of the pithy phrase and had a brutally incisive argumentative power. These qualities were acknowledged when he was appointed Deputy Director of Plans at the Air Ministry in 1934. There ensued a series of battles with the War Office and the Admiralty over the priority that ought to be allotted to the re-armament of the RAF. During this period Harris also oversaw the early development of the long-range heavy bombers. He spent 1938 and 1939 in Palestine before returning to command 5 Group (Bomber Command) for the first two years of the war. In 1941 he was sent at the head of an RAF delegation to Washington to try to secure extra aircraft supplies from the USA, then assumed control at Bomber Command.

For the next three years Harris fought tooth and nail to secure the maximum possible apportionment for the Strategic Air Offensive, arguing that success in the air would make a seaborne invasion of the Continent virtually unnecessary. His aim was quite simply to wreck the German economy and to destroy civilian morale by unrelenting attack. Most importantly, he managed to retain the confidence of Winston Churchill in this aim. Harris never got the 4,000 heavy bomber front line he thought necessary, and was frequently ordered to switch his attack to support other areas of the war effort, such as the Battle of the Atlantic or D-Day; he always held that it was these facts that prevented the damage which Bomber Command inflicted from becoming decisive. Other senior airmen, however, gradually came to believe that the tactics of the offensive were wrong; that a selective concentration on target systems such as oil or transport would be more effective than the carpet-bombing of urban areas. After D-Day, in fact, attacks on German oil supplies and on transport proved to be remarkably effective, but Harris still pursued area bombing with the bulk of his force, most famously in the case of the combined Anglo-American attacks on Dresden in February 1945, where the resultant fire-storm may have led to between 80,000 and 100,000 deaths.

After the war, Harris wrote an unrepentant

autobiography in his usual graphic and direct prose. From 1946 to 1953 he was managing director of the South African Marine Corporation. Thereafter, he moved into a very private retirement, outliving virtually all the great commanders of World War II.

WRITINGS

Bomber Offensive (London: Collins, 1947).

FURTHER READING

Frankland, N., *Bomber Offensive: Outlines and Perspectives* (London: Faber and Faber, 1965).
Rumpf, H., *The Bombing of Germany* (London: Frederick Muller, 1963).
Saward, D., *'Bomber Harris': the Authorised Biography of Marshal of the Royal Air Force Sir Arthur Harris* (London: Doubleday, 1984).

MALCOLM SMITH

Hart [née Ridehalgh], Dame **Judith (Constant Mary)** [Baroness Hart of South Lanark] (*b.* Clitheroe, Lancashire, 18 September 1924). Labour politician. Judith Hart, Labour MP for Lanark (1959–83) and Clydesdale (1983–7), and strongly identified with the left wing of her party, held ministerial office from 1967 to 1970 and again from 1974 to 1979, most prominently as Minister for Overseas Development. The cause of third-world aid and development was her especial interest throughout her political life: development agencies and campaigners generally concurred in believing her the most committed and sympathetic politician ever to hold the post.

Born into a middle-class Lancashire family, Judith Ridehalgh attended grammar school and the London School of Economics. In 1946 she married the scientist and anti-nuclear campaigner Dr Anthony Hart; they have two sons. She contested Bournemouth West for Labour in 1951 and Aberdeen South in 1955, entering Parliament for Lanark in 1959. She soon became active in anti-colonial campaigning and development issues, though her first junior ministerial post was at the Scottish Office (1964–6). After a spell as Minister of State at the Commonwealth Office Hart entered the cabinet as Paymaster-General in

1968. The following year she became Minister for Overseas Development – a cause for which the Prime Minister, Harold Wilson, had himself earlier been a prominent advocate.

As the cabinet divided over entry into the European Community, Hart emerged as one of the strongest opponents, in large part because she believed membership would weaken Britain's commitments to the developing countries of the Commonwealth. Here, and in party affairs as a member of the left-wing majority on Labour's National Executive (on which she sat from 1969 to 1983 and which she chaired in 1981–2), she was often at odds with the Labour leadership. This proved also the case in government during the period 1974–9, when she fought hard but unsuccessfully within cabinet against successive cuts in Britain's overseas aid commitments.

Judith Hart retired from Parliament in 1987. She was created a Dame of the British Empire in 1979 (the title carried certain ironies for so strong an opponent of colonialism) and entered the House of Lords in 1988.

WRITINGS

Aid and Liberation (London: Gollancz, 1973).

STEPHEN HOWE

Hattersley, Roy (Sydney George) (*b.* Sheffield, 28 December 1932). Deputy Leader of the Labour Party. Hattersley, Labour's Deputy Leader since 1983 and opposition spokesman on home or economic affairs throughout the 1980s, emerged in the late 1980s as an important architect of the party's changing political thought.

Hattersley came from a Yorkshire family – his local patriotism is evident in much of his writing – which was active in Labour politics. Educated at Sheffield Grammar School and Hull University, he became a journalist and city councillor in Sheffield before entering Parliament, with a safe Birmingham seat, in 1964. He held junior ministerial posts in the 1964–70 Wilson governments, and was opposition spokesman on Defence and on Education from 1970 to 1974. Under James Callaghan's premiership, he served as Secretary of State for Prices and Consumer Protection (1976–9).

In opposition after 1979, Hattersley held successively the front-bench posts for the Environment (1979–80), Home Affairs (1980–3, and again from 1987) and the Treasury (1983–7), though, no economist by training or inclination, he was clearly not at ease in this last role. His advocacy of incomes policies also antagonized some trade-union leaders. The Labour Party was now sharply divided over its future direction, leadership and internal structure. With Denis Healey, Hattersley was the leading voice of the party's right wing (though he repudiated that label) and excoriator of the 'Bennite' left. He was also out of sympathy with the leadership style of Callaghan's successor, Michael Foot. Foot in his turn made clear his preference for his protégé Neil Kinnock to succeed him as leader, spurning Hattersley's own ambitions to lead the party. In the 1983 leadership contest under the new 'electoral college' system, Hattersley was decisively defeated by Neil Kinnock but equally decisively victorious as candidate for the deputy leadership.

A prolific and engaging writer, Hattersley became a regular columnist for several publications, writing on sport, literature and the countryside as freely as on political themes. Puritanical opponents scorned his taste for *belles-lettres* as well as his reputation as a bon viveur. He published a life of Nelson and volumes of childhood reminiscences and non-political essays as well as, in 1987, an important statement of political philosophy, *Choose Freedom*. Drawing on and updating the writings of his mentor, Anthony Crosland, as well as the theory of justice of John Rawls, Hattersley's thinking became a main basis for Labour's late 1980s reappraisal of its objectives. The party's new 'statement of Aims and Values' was essentially a distillation of his book. Although Hattersley is the most prominent inheritor of the 'revisionist' thought of Crosland, and has adapted this to a more individualist ethos, his beliefs still echo many older labour traditions, whether in his emphasis on equality or in his hostility to proposals for a written constitution, a Bill of Rights or proportional representation.

For illustration, see KINNOCK, NEIL.

WRITINGS

A Yorkshire Boyhood (London: Chatto, 1983).
Choose Freedom (London: Michael Joseph, 1987).

STEPHEN HOWE

Haughey, Charles J(ames) ('Charlie') (*b.* Castlebar, Co. Mayo, 16 September 1925). Irish Prime Minister. Haughey was Parliamentary Secretary and subsequently Minister for Justice in the Republic of Ireland from the commencement of the Lemass government in 1959. He was then Minister for Agriculture from 1964. He became Minister for Finance in 1966 when Lemass was succeeded by Jack Lynch, was dismissed in 1970, but was made Minister for Health and Social Welfare in 1977 when Lynch formed his last government. On Lynch's departure in 1979 Haughey became Taoiseach (premier). After falling from power in 1981, he returned from March to December 1982, and again assumed office in 1987; he was re-elected in 1989. Haughey played an important part in modernization of Irish society while somewhat successfully making use of tribalistic sentiments, especially during the years of new violence in Northern Ireland (since 1969). He is perhaps the most astonishing survivor of potentially destructive crises in modern democratic politics, including unsuccessful criminal proceedings against him in 1970 by the government whence he had just been ousted.

Haughey's parents were from Swatragh, Co. Derry, in what became Northern Ireland five years before his birth. His father, John Haughey, unlike the majority of Ulster Catholics at that time, supported Sinn Féin, but followed Michael Collins on the Anglo-Irish Treaty and served in the army of the newly formed Irish Free State during the civil war against intransigent republican former associates. John Haughey left the army in 1928. Charles Haughey grew up in Dublin in financially straitened circumstances. He was educated by the hard-hitting, examination-conscious Christian Brothers, achieving high athletic and scholastic honours, and won a scholarship to University College, Dublin. He qualified as an accountant, was called to the

Bar but did not practice, entered de Valera's party, Fianna Fáil, in 1948 and married in 1951 Maureen, daughter of its most notable evangelist for industrial-commercial expansion, Seán Lemass. Haughey, a highly successful accountant, was unpopular at the polls and only scraped election to Dáil Éireann in 1957 when Eugene Timmons, a more popular fellow-nominee of the party in their multi-seat constituency, was temporarily dropped.

Éamon de Valera's retirement into the presidency gave Haughey his chance: it was a symbolic change from the austere, pedagogical, nostalgic, agrarian 'Dev' to the tough, thrusting, business-minded pragmatist Lemass. Haughey in the Department of Justice did not rest content on the obvious security of his familial standing with Lemass; he undertook drastic and necessary reforms of the Irish legal system which had languished for years in archaic self-obfuscation. He was a phenomenally hard worker, and a skilled, if sometimes McCarthyite, parliamentary debater. He introduced 21 major Bills as minister, and, while he cultivated both a style and a rhetoric asserting the virtues and graces of capitalistic opportunism, he showed beneath them a genuine social concern and humanitarianism. He also exhibited ruthlessness, ill-temper and a readiness to protect associates beyond conventional ethical limits. He won popularity and at this time was widely regarded as a likeable, highly efficient, somewhat raffish rogue with a hard hand and a good heart.

The unexpected resignation of Patrick Smith from Agriculture in protest against Lemass – an unthinkable circumstance during de Valera's long reign – brought Haughey to that department, where he quickly became an abrasive opponent of organized farmers' protest. His rapid self-enrichment by profitable farming and judicious land deals increased hostility to him, as did his misjudgement of the potential of Irish agricultural markets and prices. The controversies prevented his mounting an effective challenge for the succession when ill-health forced Lemass's retirement, but by judicious withdrawal in favour of the compromise choice, Jack Lynch, Haughey earned the prestigious Finance portfolio. He espoused popular, self-serving, but sometimes enlightened measures, such as the emancipation of writers, sculptors, artists and composers from taxation on their creative products. But his dismissal, arrest and trial on the charge of enabling arms to be smuggled into the republic for use in Northern Ireland by insurgent Catholics resulted in legal acquittal and, it was assumed, political oblivion. The real truth of the affair remains unknown. Haughey may have been motivated in his actions, whatever they were, by some identification with the beleaguered Ulster Catholics, and by a desire to link his party with a more aggressive stance on Northern Ireland; and he may have been a scapegoat. One other minister was also dismissed, two resigned, and suspicion of involvement hung over others: Haughey was the only former minister to face a jury. He quietly worked his way back, gaining respect for patient party loyalty, cultivating Fianna Fáil grass roots and back benches, and was elected to shadow cabinet status during his party's time in opposition from 1973 to 1977. His term as Minister for Health and Social Welfare again showed a capacity for inaugurating judicious and necessary reforms, but this time he was conspicuous for his pointed deference to leading Roman Catholic clerical interests as on family planning. He outflanked his opponents, notably his former schoolmate and perennial rival George Colley, when Lynch left office.

Haughey as party leader, in or out of office, faced a succession of ugly revolts. These he survived with characteristic bravado, resourcefulness, intimidation and nerve. Ultimately his party lost several significant dissidents, who formed themselves into the Progressive Democrats in 1985–6. To date it may have taken more electoral support from the leading rival party, Fine Gael, but it prevented his being more than a minority Taoiseach in 1987. But Haughey had never won an overall majority for any of his premierships. This meant that his natural tendency to resort to chauvinistic rhetoric whipped up nationalistic sentiment within his party, which from time to time may have made him dependent on it when he had less reason to cultivate it. It was instinctive with him to question the patriotism of his political opponents and to claim special skills in negotiations with Britain's Margaret Thatcher on

Northern Ireland questions. But his failure to make good his claims meant, for instance, that during the general election of 1981 he was targeted by candidates standing in sympathy with the IRA hunger-strikers in Long Kesh, Northern Ireland; they assisted in his defeat on that occasion, although they faced a far more implacable opponent in Garret Fitzgerald, who replaced him. Haughey's return to power in 1982 coincided with the Falklands War, in which personal volition and political obligations led him to an international stance sharply critical of the UK, whom he embarrassed in the UN Security Council. He was even more embarrassed himself when a murder suspect was discovered to be hiding in the apartment of his Attorney-General. When Haughey sought to palliate his responsibility by describing the situation as 'grotesque, unbelievable, bizarre, unprecedented', his long-term enemy Conor Cruise O'Brien summed his regime up in the acronym 'GUBU', with evident reference to Alfred Jarry's absurdist tyrant Ubu Roi. Proofs of telephone-taps on critical journalists, intimidation of opponents in and out of his party, and a cult of inflexible personality supported by very hard men did nothing to detract from this analogy.

Having fallen from power once more, Haughey used the mid-1980s to consolidate his tribalistic gains by judicious manipulation of reactionary clerical opposition to Fitzgerald's attempts at ecumenical constitutional reforms, and by making the most of British hostility to himself, while the accord between Thatcher and Fitzgerald during the Anglo-Irish Agreement gave way to disillusion as the death-toll continued to mount in Northern Ireland. Ironically, one of Haughey's strongest bases for political appeal is that he is held by friend and foe to be a dirty fighter, and it is widely felt that politics requires such. It seems probable that Haughey's misfortunes in 1970 soured him and radically deepened a cynicism which initially may have been merely superficial. His readiness to court popularity by spendthrift economics at the expense of the morrow finally caught up with him on his return to power, in 1987. Although briefly very popular for coolly resisting what were seen as British bullying tactics to force extradition of

ex-Father Patrick Ryan, an IRA suspect, Haughey still could not hold Irish loyalties; once more he won only a plurality in the snap election of 1989, and regained power with the support of the Progressive Democrats, whose leaders had left Fianna Fáil on his account. The disarray of his opponents may prolong the life of his administration into the 1990s. Should he ever obtain the overall majority for which he thirsts, his probable conduct is still uncertain. It could blunt his abrasiveness and ugly methods by rebuilding his sense of security; it could also give him an opportunity for obtaining greater and more sweeping guarantees of political security together with vindictive measures against opponents. But merely to dismiss him as a political gangster is both intellectually and practically unwise. He is a politician of skills born of survival in the most adverse circumstance; he began as a statesman essentially constructive rather than destructive; and he can still bring to his work the very mixed fruits of his former years. What he probably cannot endure is the moral cost involved in his survival: that is his tragedy, and there is enough stature in him to justify such a word.

FURTHER READING

Dwyer, T. Ryle, *Charlie: the Political Biography of Charles J. Haughey* (Dublin: Gill and Macmillan, 1987).

Joyce, Joe and Murtagh, Peter, *The Boss: Charles J. Haughey in Government* (Dublin: Poolbeg Press, 1983).

MacIntyre, Tom, *Through the Bridewell Gate: a Diary of the Dublin Arms Trial* (London: Faber and Faber, 1971).

Mansergh, Martin (ed.), *The Spirit of the Nation: the Speeches of Charles J. Haughey* (Cork: Mercier Press, 1986).

OWEN DUDLEY EDWARDS

Healey, Denis (Winston) (*b.* Keighley, Yorkshire, 30 August 1917). Labour Secretary of State for Defence and Chancellor of the Exchequer. Out of government he was perhaps the Labour Party's most intellectually imposing postwar foreign affairs spokesman. To his admirers within the party he was also the greatest leader it never had, but to his opponents he was the Labour Chancellor who pioneered Conservative financial policies.

Healey was educated at Bradford Grammar School and at Balliol, where he was loaded with academic honours and was also briefly a student communist. Serving in the Royal Engineers during World War II he attained the rank of Major and was mentioned in despatches. With the war's end he stood unsuccessfully as a Labour parliamentary candidate, and married writer Edna May Edmunds. At the 1945 Labour Conference Healey's speech urging support for international socialist revolution made a deep impression. Thereafter, however, in a series of vigorous pamphlets and policy briefs, he strongly backed the more traditional approach to international affairs of Foreign Secretary Ernest Bevin, and became a scourge of pro-Soviet 'fellow travellers' in Labour's ranks. From February 1946 he ran Labour's International Department, and began to build a formidable intellectual reputation and an equally formidable range of international contacts. The fact that he was on first-name terms with so many European and other politicians was to be a considerable source of both influence and pleasure to him in later years.

Healey entered Parliament in 1952 and the shadow cabinet in 1959, and with Labour's 1964 election victory became Defence Secretary. He remained at this post throughout Harold Wilson's governments (1964–70), his ambition to become Foreign Secretary blocked by Wilson. In 1974, with Labour returned precariously to office, he left his lifelong involvement with international affairs to become Chancellor. Yet in a sense this was no great shift, for the plight of the British economy in these years was such that Healey's role as Chancellor was substantially as a diplomat, negotiating with the International Monetary Fund and other agencies. The cabinet, and the Labour Party, were sharply divided by his advocacy, in 1976, of a £3 billion reduction in public sector borrowing to meet the conditions for an IMF loan. Healey got his way, but the effect of the crisis was to impose on Labour a 'monetarist' strategy, tightly restricting public spending and seeking to limit pay demands. The breakdown of this latter aim in the 'Winter

Denis Healey, Deputy Leader of the Labour Party, preparing his speech for the party conference at Brighton, September 1981

of Discontent' (1978–9) contributed greatly to Labour's election defeat the next spring. Healey, as architect of the government's economic strategy, was widely blamed, especially by Labour left-wingers.

Nonetheless, when JAMES CALLAGHAN resigned as party leader in October 1980, Healey was widely expected to succeed him. Indeed many thought that Callaghan had deliberately timed his departure to maximize Healey's chances – under the electoral college about to be introduced, the left would be stronger than it was among MPs. Instead Michael Foot, the left's candidate, won by 139 votes to Healey's 129. Healey became Deputy Leader, for which post he was challenged by Tony Benn in 1981. This contest, under the new system in which trade-union delegations, constituency parties and Labour MPs all cast votes, was deeply acrimonious; it was also very close run. Healey gained 50.426 per cent of the vote, Benn 49.574 per cent. Healey resigned the post of Deputy Leader in 1983, but continued as Foreign Affairs spokesman until 1987, joking about becoming the Gromyko of British politics. His opposition to unilateral nuclear disarmament, which was for most of this period Labour's official policy, aroused left-wing antagonism once more – and bridging the gap between his personal views and the party's stance demanded all his considerable ingenuity.

A brilliant if sometimes brutal parliamentary debater, Denis Healey was also generally recognized as one of his party's ablest minds. To his supporters, the fact that he never became Labour leader was the party's greatest tragedy of the 1980s, substantially responsible for its successive electoral defeats. To his opponents on Labour's left, he was the most prominent exponent of the traditions and attitudes within the party, especially on international questions, against which they were in revolt. His misfortune, perhaps, was to be so closely identified with support for Britain's nuclear deterrent and with pro-Americanism in foreign policy at a time when these questions were so deeply divisive within Labour, and when a majority of the party's activists held views on them sharply opposed to his. The Labour left's ascendancy, symbolized by Healey's arch-rival TONY BENN, coincided exactly with the years when he might have hoped to win the party leadership. By the time the party moved back towards policy positions which Healey favoured, in the late 1980s, it was under the leadership of a younger generation. He adapted, however, with apparent zest to the role of elder statesman.

For further illustrations, see FOOT, MICHAEL, and KINNOCK, NEIL.

WRITINGS

The Time of my Life (London: Michael Joseph, 1989).

FURTHER READING

Kogan, D. and M., *The Battle for the Labour Party* (London: Fontana, 1982).
Reed, B. and Williams, G., *Denis Healey & the Politics of Power* (London: Sidgwick and Jackson, 1971).

STEPHEN HOWE

Heath, Edward (Richard George) ('Ted') (*b.* Broadstairs, Kent, 9 July 1916). Statesman. He became Prime Minister in 1970, 20 years after first entering Parliament. He has remained in the House of Commons since losing the general election of 1974 and the Conservative Party leadership in 1975, but has not subsequently held ministerial office.

Heath was the only son of a carpenter who was later a master builder. His mother, to whom he was closest, had at one time worked as a lady's maid. He was educated at Chatham School, Ramsgate, and went to Balliol, Oxford, in 1935 to read philosophy, politics and economics. At Balliol he won a music scholarship. The love of music never left him and playing his piano in Downing Street was his way of relaxing after a hard day (in later life he was invited to conduct famous orchestras on special occasions). At university he was active in the Conservative Party and was President of the Union. He was a critic of Chamberlain's 'appeasement' policy, and in the famous Oxford City by-election in 1938 he supported an anti-appeasement candidate against the official Conservative, Quintin Hogg (later Lord Hailsham).

Heath had a good war record. After 1945 he tried a variety of jobs while seeking nomination as a Conservative candidate. He worked briefly as a civil servant, was a sub-editor on the *Church Times*, and then had a spell in banking. He was one of a new breed of young postwar Conservative politicians: he had no family tradition of involvement in politics and did not come from an established profession, business or the land. Above all, he was a professional politician. Without the postwar Maxwell Fyfe reforms of local party nominations, notably forbidding candidates to give large sums to the local party, it is doubtful if he would have been nominated. He was adopted in Bexley and won the seat in 1950. He held the seat (never a safe one) until February 1974, when it was abolished as a result of redistribution; he then became Member for Sidcup.

Heath's maiden speech was, significantly, a call for Britain to respond favourably to attempts to build a united Western Europe. Within eight months of his entry into Parliament he was translated to the whips' office. He was appointed Joint Deputy Chief Whip in 1952, Deputy Chief in 1953 and Chief Whip in 1955, a position he held until 1959. These early years of obscurity in the whips' office deprived him of the opportunity to develop an easy speaking style and probably encouraged an authoritarian manner towards his colleagues. Ironically, the only extensive experience he gained as a backbencher was in 1975, after he had lost the party leadership. Ironically also, for a former Chief Whip, these were the years when he frequently dissented from the party leadership. As Chief Whip he was involved in keeping the party together in the Suez Crisis in 1956, when Macmillan, rather than Butler, emerged to replace the ailing Eden as Prime Minister, and when the Treasury team resigned in 1958. He was extremely close to Macmillan.

In the 1959 Parliament Heath had experience of three departments. Between October 1959 and July 1960 he was Minister of Labour (the National Service part of the departmental title was dropped in November 1959); he then became Lord Privy Seal, and in October 1963 he was appointed President of the Board of Trade by Sir Alec Douglas-Home (see also HOME, LORD). In the leadership battle in 1963, when it was clear that one of the younger generation (Maudling, Macleod or Heath) would not get the leadership, he backed Douglas-Home over R. A. Butler (see also MAUDLING, REGINALD, and MACLEOD, IAIN).

As Lord Privy Seal under Macmillan, Heath was charged with handling negotiations for Britain's entry to the European Community. Macmillan had announced in July 1961 that Britain would apply formally for membership. Heath became Britain's 'Mr Europe', was an enthusiast for entry and was visibly disappointed when de Gaulle vetoed the application in January 1963. He seemed to lose heart and his career marked time for the next few months.

A new opportunity came when Sir Alec appointed him to the Board of Trade. He was looking for a measure which would help him to make his mark and his department had on the file a scheme for the abolition of resale price maintenance. The hand of the department and Heath was forced when the Labour MP John

Stonehouse finished high in the ballot for private members' bills and promised to introduce such a measure. Heath decided to go ahead with his own bill. The measure bitterly divided the party and there was resistance in many constituency parties from small businessmen. Older heads in the party thought it was rash to attempt such controversial legislation in the last year of Parliament. In March 1963, 21 Conservative MPs voted against the measure and 17 abstained. On a later division the majority fell to one. But Heath got his bill through and his skill in negotiations and strength of purpose were not lost on his growing body of admirers.

After Labour narrowly won the 1964 general election, the position of Douglas-Home as party leader was weak; he was no match in the House of Commons for Harold Wilson. The view grew that a younger, more combative man was required to take on the Labour leader. Aware of the weakness of his position, Douglas-Home resigned in 1965 and the party adopted a new system for electing leaders. The choice was confined to Conservative MPs, and the winning candidate had to have an absolute majority and a lead of 15 per cent over the runner-up. At the time Heath enjoyed a high profile: he was chairman of the party's policy review committee and impressed MPs with his vigorous opposition in the Commons to the government's Finance Bill. In the leadership election in July 1965 Heath gained 150 votes to 133 for Reginald Maudling on the first ballot (ENOCH POWELL also stood and gained 15 votes). Maudling immediately stood down, thus precluding the need for a run-off ballot. Heath, aged 49, was the youngest Conservative leader for over a century. In many ways he resembled Wilson, a grammar-school, Oxbridge educated person and a meritocrat, interested in modernizing the British economy.

As opposition leader Heath was determined to chart a new course for the party. He seems to have felt a number of big issues were ripe for tackling. His policy review promised a substantial measure of trade-union reform, tax cuts and constraint on public spending, British membership of the European Community, government disengagement from industry and avoidance of incomes policies. In addition there would be a more selective approach to welfare. Such measures were designed to sharpen up British industry. The full fruits of the review were revealed in a free-market platform for the 1970 election. In the meantime, however, Heath led the party to an expected defeat in the 1966 general election.

Heath was, of all Conservative leaders, perhaps the most consciously interested in policy preparation. He also took the view that shadow spokesmen should concentrate on their departmental briefs. This was one cause of the growing mutual estrangement between himself and Enoch Powell. Powell, the shadow spokesman on defence, would not accept such a limitation, and after his famous speech in Birmingham in April 1968 about immigration he was sacked by Heath. It was a risky decision, for Powell was henceforth a formidable adversary. In fact Heath had no choice: he saw the speech as a challenge to his leadership and sacked Powell with the unanimous support of the shadow cabinet.

In the 1966 Parliament the Conservatives were for a long time the clear favourites to win the next election, but the polls turned in favour of the Labour Government in early 1970. During the 1970 general election campaign the Conservatives lagged in the polls and Heath's chances were widely written off. Senior figures had already begun preparations for getting him to quit. In fact he won a handsome triumph, a victory that was very much his own.

His new government suffered a blow at the outset with the death of Ian Macleod, the Chancellor of the Exchequer, after 31 days in office. A not enthusiastic Anthony Barber was appointed to the Treasury. Heath was very much his own chancellor and was behind the shift to an expansionist economic policy in 1971. The government was hit by the sharp rise in commodity prices in 1971 and then the quadrupling of the Arab oil prices in late 1973. Rising unemployment forced a change in policy in 1971. The government rescued the ailing Rolls-Royce and the Upper Clyde Shipyard because of fears of the loss of jobs which closure would cause, and the Industry Act of 1972 gave the Department of Trade and Industry immense powers to intervene in industry, with funds to match. This switch in policy introduced the term 'U-turn' into British politics. Another difficult issue, with which Heath was closely concerned, was Northern Ireland. There was a clear collapse of law and order in the province, and eventually the government decided to suspend the Stormont Parliament and impose direct rule from Westminster.

A more traumatic experience, however, came over incomes policy. In 1972 the government's attempts to reduce the going rate in public-sector wage settlements had been destroyed by a successful strike by the National Union of Miners. After attempts to negotiate a voluntary wages policy failed, the Heath Government in late 1972 switched to a statutory incomes policy. This was another major 'U-turn' in economic policy. It was the statutory incomes policy which the miners again tried to break in late 1973 by a work to rule and then a strike. The government imposed a three-day working week to save power. Heath felt that the government had no option but to call a general election, and renew a mandate for an incomes policy or to settle with the miners. Although the Conservatives had the most votes, Labour won more seats; Heath's gamble failed. The minority Labour Government called another election in October 1974 and gained a small majority.

The outstanding achievement of Heath's government was entry into the European Community. His support for European unity and integration was a constant theme in his political career. He signed the Treaty of Accession in January 1972 and Britain joined the community in January 1973. He regarded entry as one of the great achievements of the twentieth century.

As Prime Minister Heath left his ministers alone. He later complained that too many decisions were being referred from committees to the full cabinet. He was business-like, not given to speculation about great matters of the world, unlike Churchill and Macmillan. He was also interested in the machinery of government. He established the Central Policy Review staff in 1970, so that the cabinet would be given a collective briefing. He encouraged the formation of giant departments (Environment and DTI), to assist coordination of policy

Edward Heath, Leader of the Conservative Party, addressing a press conference on the eve of the general election, September 1974; with him are Margaret Thatcher and Lord Carrington

before matters came to the cabinet. The creation of 'super-departments' also helped him to keep membership of the cabinet down to 18. The issues in which he particularly involved himself were Britain's entry to the European Community, incomes policy and Northern Ireland.

Heath was not an ideologue. Indeed a frequent criticism was that he was so instrumental that he deviated from his original policies. He wished to reduce inflation and when his policies failed he switched to a statutory incomes policy. He had a great belief in experts. Setting up a committee of wise men would produce the correct 'solution'. He liked working with civil servants and they respected him.

After the Conservatives lost the elections of February and October 1974, Heath's position in the party was weak. He had fought four general elections and lost three of them, though the party's position was virtually beyond rescue in 1966 and the second 1974 election. Many backbenchers felt that the party simply could not win under his leadership. Others felt that having stood on free-market policies in 1970, an interventionist policy platform in February 1974 and then a national unity ticket in October 1974, he was finished. He was eventually persuaded to offer himself for re-election. New rules were drawn up, which provided for an annual election for the leader. To win this time, a candidate needed an overall majority of those eligible to vote (as opposed to those actually voting) and a lead of 15 per cent over the runner-up.

A motley collection rallied to his chief challenger, MARGARET THATCHER. Over the years a number of MPs had become disenchanted with Heath (he lacked tact in dealing with backbenchers and had been niggardly with honours); there was some support for free-market ideas, and a general feeling that it was time for a change. In the first round of the election on 4 February 1975 Thatcher gained 130 to 119 for Heath. He resigned immediately and Thatcher won the second ballot. He had been the first Tory leader to be chosen in a contested election and was the first to be defeated in one.

Heath's later years were busy. He received many honours, enjoyed music and sailing and paid several visits abroad (China and West European capitals still regarded him as a major figure). Thatcher would never have him in a cabinet: he would have opposed many government policies, notably on economics and Europe. There were suggestions that he had been offered the ambassador's post in Washington or translation to the Lords, moves which he regarded as attempts to deny him a platform. The breach widened over the years and in the 1980s he was a vehement critic of the government's policies on the economy, education, social security and poll tax. Conservative critics saw him as a bad loser and he was probably counter-productive to the causes he espoused. Certainly a number of his former supporters, still in the cabinet, found his speeches embarrassing. Unlike other Prime Ministers he did not retire gracefully. Both Balfour and Sir Alec Douglas-Home had continued in government service after they stepped down from leadership, and others had maintained a discreet silence on contemporary politics.

Not so Heath. He was bitter at how Sir KEITH JOSEPH and Margaret Thatcher disowned the work of his government. He thought there was a conscious effort to write him and One-Nation Conservatism out of history. To the end he preached the need for consensus and regarded Thatcherism as an aberration in the Conservative Party's history. In the *Sunday Times* (3 February 1988) he dismissed Thatcherism: 'It's 1860 laissez-faire Liberalism that never was.' Thatcher made a complete breach with so many of his policies – incomes policy, growing public spending, economic growth through reflation, and seeking agreement with trade unions. Apart from Britain's membership of the European Community, his period of government left very few legacies. The Central Policy Review staff was scrapped by Thatcher in 1983, his giant departments were unscrambled, the Industrial Relations Act was largely repealed, and no government has since had a statutory prices and incomes policy. His 'dash' for economic growth was the last attempt by a British government to reflate out of a downturn in the economic cycle.

Many colleagues and observers have commented on Heath's emphasis on the importance of reasoned discussion. He wanted to change public attitudes – to remove the obstacles to faster economic growth, then to cooperate with a prices and incomes policy, and in the 1974 general elections to join a national effort to control inflation. Yet he never managed to communicate his visions – particularly of Europe – to the public. He admitted that he was a poor communicator, though he firmly resisted the gimmicks and image-making which other party leaders accepted.

FURTHER READING

A. Roth, *Heath and the Heathmen* (London: Routledge and Kegan Paul, 1972).

DENNIS KAVANAGH

Heenan, John (Carmel) (*b.* Ilford, Essex, 26 January 1905; *d.* London, 7 November 1975). Archbishop of Westminster. He had Irish parents but English loyalties. From an early age resolved to be a priest, he was educated by the Jesuits at St Ignatius, Stamford Hill, and – most decisively – from 1924 to 1931 at the English College in Rome, where the rector was Arthur Hinsley. When in 1935 Hinsley became Archbishop of Westminster, Heenan was soon helping draft his speeches. He later wrote the cardinal's biography.

In 1936, at the height of Stalinism, Heenan visited Russia disguised as a lecturer in psychiatry to be better informed of communism, which he regarded as the principal threat to Christianity and the West. His account of the visit is fascinating and shows him at his ablest – observant, pragmatic and fearless.

During the war he became well known as a broadcaster. By the late 1940s he was already grasping, what he retained for 25 years, the effective leadership of English Catholicism. In 1951 he was appointed Bishop of Leeds, in 1957 Archbishop of Liverpool, in 1963 Archbishop of Westminster and in 1965 a Cardinal. In the days of Pope John and the second Vatican Council he appeared warmly different from his reserved, highly conservative predecessor at Westminster, Cardinal Godfrey. The early influence of Hinsley made him naturally ecumenical – up to a point. He developed an excellent relationship with Archbishop Michael Ramsey and the Chief Rabbi. As a television debater he could be masterly. He had a conservative view of the priestly role and, outside the defence of Catholic schools and the fight against communism, thought political interests inappropriate in a priest. He trusted the laity, but as leader of the Catholic church in what may well be judged the age of its greatest social weight in modern British history, his own contribution to public life may seem surprisingly small.

Heenan was profoundly distressed by the intellectual and spiritual upheaval following the Vatican Council, the deeper implications of which he failed to understand. He distrusted the influence of liberal theologians. The last years of his life were ones of ill-health, alienation from current trends and loss of the ability to communicate a sense of direction which had earlier been so strong.

WRITINGS

Not the Whole Truth (London: Hodder and Stoughton, 1971).
A Crown of Thorns (London: Hodder and Stoughton, 1974).

ADRIAN HASTINGS

Henderson, Arthur (*b*. Glasgow, 20 September 1863; *d*. London, 20 October 1935). Foreign Secretary and Secretary of the Labour Party. Along with Hardie, MacDonald and Snowden, he was one of the key figures in the establishment of the Labour Party and its development into a party of government. Although consistently on the right of the party, Henderson stayed with it in the crisis of 1931. A cabinet minister in Asquith's and Lloyd George's coalition governments of 1915–17, he was to be Home Secretary in the first Labour government and Foreign Secretary in the second. A moderate and a loyalist, Henderson represented the link between the trade unions and the Labour Party. He was unfortunate in losing his seat not only in 1918 but also in 1922, 1923 and 1931.

Henderson may well have been the illegitimate son of a domestic servant, Agnes Henderson. When he was nine, the family moved to Newcastle-upon-Tyne, where his mother married Robert Heath, a policeman, in 1874. He was apprenticed as an iron moulder after leaving school at the age of 12 and worked mostly in his trade at the Stephenson locomotive and foundry works. He joined the Iron Founders' Union, and was soon branch secretary. In 1892 Henderson became his union's district delegate for the Northumberland, Durham and Lancashire area. He came into prominence when the hitherto most costly dispute in the union's history took place in his area from March to September 1894. The dispute was settled by means of the creation of a board of conciliation. Henderson, then and thereafter, was a strong advocate of joint committees of employers and employed settling disputes. Hence he was a leading trade unionist, involved both in the National Industrial Council set up in 1911 and the National Industrial Conference of 1919.

Henderson also owed his early advancement in his union to his views fitting in well with its predominantly Liberal leadership. He was a Liberal Party member, and in 1894 was elected to Newcastle City Council as a Labour man, clearly backed by the Liberals. In 1895 the Liberal executive selected him to fight the two-member Newcastle parliamentary constituency with John Morley, but the Liberal membership preferred their previous candidate, a wealthy businessman. Henderson stayed loyal, and soon became full-time Liberal agent to Sir Joseph Pease, MP for Barnard Castle. Henderson was elected onto Darlington Council in 1898, in effect as a 'Lib-Lab', and was mayor in 1903.

Henderson's union affiliated to the Labour Representation Committee in 1900, and when it agreed to finance a parliamentary candidate Henderson successfully stood in the election for that role. With Pease's decline in health, the LRC arranged for Henderson's selection as candidate for Barnard Castle. In spite of the Liberals running a candidate, when a by-election occurred in 1903 Henderson beat the candidate by 47 votes and held it until 1918.

Henderson was a leading Christian figure in the Labour Party, making many major speeches before Christian-organized meetings throughout his career. Having been converted to evangelical Christianity at the age of 16, he found the Christian fellowship he needed with the Wesleyan Methodists and became a well-known lay-preacher. He was also an active speaker in the 1890s for the North of England Temperance League and was prominent later in other temperance organizations. He married Eleanor Watson, a fellow Wesleyan, in 1889. They had three sons (one was killed in World War I; the others became Labour politicians) and a daughter.

In Parliament, before World War I, Henderson was very much a trade-union rather than a socialist Labour MP, pressing labour issues but otherwise having priorities close to those of the Liberals. As chairman of the Parliamentary Labour Party between 1908 and 1910 he received criticism for putting too much emphasis on such issues as the Licensing Bill rather than on unemployment. In 1911 he supported MacDonald to be leader of the Parliamentary Party and in 1912 took over as Secretary, a post he held until 1934.

Henderson supported Britain's war effort, being the most prominent Labour figure on the Parliamentary Recruiting Committee. He succeeded MacDonald as chairman of the Parliamentary Party in August 1914, was made a Privy Councillor in January 1915 and entered Asquith's Coalition Government in May as President of the Board of Education. He acted as the government's main labour adviser, helping Lloyd George push dilution of labour into munitions factories and shipyards, often in the face of serious rank-and-file trade-union opposition. In August 1916 he regularized this role by resigning his education position and becoming Paymaster General and Labour Adviser. With Lloyd George's accession to the premiership, Henderson became one of the small War Cabinet and a key figure in the government.

His position in politics was transformed when, in the summer of 1917, he went on an official mission to Russia to try to maintain the Provisional Government's support for the war effort. Henderson enthusiastically supported it and deplored the activities of the Bolsheviks, but he returned advocating British Labour's participation in a socialist conference in Stockholm which would include representatives from all belligerent countries. Lloyd George forced Henderson's resignation over this issue. For years afterwards Henderson was smeared by his political opponents as a 'hobnobber with Bolsheviks', a charge which helped lose him the East Ham seat in the 1918 general election and troubled him in his successful by-election contest in Widnes in August 1919.

Out of office, Henderson devoted himself to organizing the party. He was a key figure in revising the Labour Party constitution, reorganizing the party in the constituencies and revising policies for the postwar world. This continued work he had been involved in as first chairman of the War Emergency Workers' National Committee in 1914–15.

Though Henderson and MacDonald personally disliked each other, Henderson loyally supported MacDonald until 1931 (see also MACDONALD, RAMSAY). In the Parliamentary Party he was chief whip from 1921 to 1924 and again from 1925 to 1927 (a post he had also held before the war), and ruled it with a very firm hand. In the first Labour government (1924) he was Home Secretary. In the second (1929–31), after an attempt by MacDonald to give him lesser office, he became Foreign Secretary and was one of the successes of that government. After MacDonald's defection in 1931, Henderson was elected leader of the Labour Party. He lost his seat in the 1931 election and resigned the leadership the following year. He was re-elected to Parliament in September 1933, representing Clay Cross until his death.

Henderson was a strong supporter of the League of Nations. He was president of the Geneva Disarmament Conference which commenced in 1932, and in 1934 he was awarded the Nobel Peace Prize. He wrote *Labour's Way to Peace* (1935) and several pamphlets and articles on this theme in his last years.

FURTHER READING

Hamilton, M. A., *Arthur Henderson* (London: Heinemann, 1938).

Leventhal, F. M., *Arthur Henderson* (Manchester: Manchester University Press, 1989).

McKibbin, R., *The Evolution of the Labour Party 1910–1924* (Oxford: Oxford University Press, 1974).

Morgan, K. O., *Labour People* (Oxford: Oxford University Press, 1987).

Winter, J. M., *Socialism and the Challenge of War* (London: Routledge and Kegan Paul, 1974).

CHRIS WRIGLEY

Henderson, Sir **Nevile (Meyrick)** (*b.* Horsham, Sussex, 10 June 1882; *d.* London, 30 December 1942). Ambassador to Germany. As British Ambassador in Nazi Germany from April 1937 until the outbreak of World War II, and believing he had been selected by Providence to preserve the peace, he worked tirelessly to improve the atmosphere in Anglo-German relations and to implement the 'appeasement' policies of Neville Chamberlain. He viewed with sympathy Hitler's restoration of German confidence and prosperity and accepted as just the claims upon which the latter rested his demands for territorial change. Believing in the limited nature of Hitler's ambitions, Henderson sought to justify the dictator's actions and to moderate expressions of British opposition to his expansionist policies during both the Austrian and Czechoslovakian crises. He remained convinced that through a policy of concessions it would be possible to strengthen the influence of Hermann Goering, with whom he had excellent relations, and the 'moderates' as against the 'extremists', von Ribbentrop, Himmler and Goebbels, who were urging Hitler to war. Anxious, above all, to avoid offending Hitler, Henderson was a leading actor in formulating and implementing the policies that culminated in Munich. The Ambassador continued to seek an accommodation with Berlin even when the Foreign Office turned to a policy of deterrence in the winter and spring of 1939. With the German occupation of Prague, Henderson was recalled to London, and returned to Berlin five weeks later. While recognizing the increasing hopelessness of the situation, he still sought ways of settling the Danzig crisis without provoking a German attack on Poland. Henderson delivered the British ultimatum on 3 September and had his last interview with von Ribbentrop. His mission had ended in failure.

Henderson came from a prosperous Glasgow merchant family trading in the Far East. His father, who died when Henderson was four, had inherited an estate in England, Sedgwick Park, where the future ambassador was born and brought up. Due to his mother's influence, he joined the Diplomatic Service rather than the army after Eton and four years language study on the Continent. Except for two very brief periods, this quintessential Englishman in appearance and temperament, who loved the countryside, hunting and fishing, spent his whole working life abroad, with assignments in all parts of the world. A key turning point was Henderson's first embassy in Belgrade, where he developed an exceedingly close relationship with the Yugoslavian dictator, King Alexander, whom he much admired. Henderson never married and, having no home base, his 'Englishness', but also his deep conservatism and distrust of change, was exaggerated by exile.

Henderson was appointed Ambassador to Germany in January 1937 by Anthony Eden at the urging of Robert Vansittart. He was to follow a more independent path than was customary for modern British ambassadors, querying instructions and, contrary to what the Foreign Office had intended, conveying in personal conversations with the Nazi leaders at critical moments an impression of limited concern. In September 1938 he rejected Lord Halifax's demand that Hitler be warned of the consequences of a military solution to the Sudeten crisis and succeeded in having his instructions rescinded. Henderson had Chamberlain's ear and support, though his inclination to stress the positive aspects of Nazism and to argue the German case evoked criticism at the Foreign Office. After Munich, Henderson's judgements were increasingly questioned and his overoptimistic view of German intentions discounted. When war broke out and the Ambassador returned to London, he faced bitter public opprobrium. Already terminally ill, he wrote a defence of his actions and the policies of the Chamberlain government in *Failure of a Mission* (1940) as well as two autobiographical books, *Hippy: In memoriam: the Story of a Dog* (1943) and *Water under the Bridges* (1944), before his death.

WRITINGS

Failure of a Mission: Berlin, 1937–9 (London: Hodder and Stoughton, 1940).

Hippy, in Memoriam: the Story of a Dog (London: Hodder and Stoughton, 1943).

Water under the Bridges (London: Hodder and Stoughton, 1945).

FURTHER READING

Gilbert, F., 'Two British Ambassadors: Perth and Henderson', in *The Diplomats, 1919–1939*, ed. G. A. Craig and F. Gilbert (Princeton, NJ: Princeton University Press, 1953).

ZARA STEINER

Heseltine, Michael (Ray Dibdin) (*b.* Swansea, Glamorgan, 21 March 1933). Conservative Minister of the Environment and Minister for Defence. Michael Heseltine is the man who, arguably, came nearer than anyone to bringing down Margaret Thatcher – nearer than Argentina's General Galtieri did, certainly nearer than any of her Labour opponents in the House of Commons. Other ministers have departed from the Thatcher cabinet, almost always unwillingly, often sullenly, and sometimes in humiliation. On the spectacular day in January 1986 when Michael Heseltine walked out of her cabinet, it seemed for a brief moment of history that he might have brought down the whole Thatcherite temple on top of him.

As a Tory, Heseltine is not one of nature's Thatcherites. Around Liverpool there are still people, people who would never vote Conservative, who talk of him warmly as their favourite politician because when he descended on Merseyside, like a blonde *deus ex machina* in the wake of the Toxteth riots, he conveyed a real awareness of the despair that comes from joblessness and of the challenge to government to provide hope.

It was the message that her 'wet' ministers had been trying to get across to Mrs Thatcher. But it is hard to attach the word wet to Heseltine. This was the man who, as Defence Secretary (1983–6), took a big stick to the fellow-travellers and 'woolly' liberals of CND. As Environment Secretary (1979–83), while he took his message of hope to Merseyside, he was also taking a big stick to 'loony lefty', or free-spending, councillors in local authorities around the country.

His vigorous anti-socialism led him, on one of the most memorable parliamentary occasions of modern times, to snatch the Mace in the Commons and advance towards the Labour benches with the idea of who knows what breach of privilege before being thwarted by his colleague Jim Prior. This episode did him no harm at all among the voting classes. Indeed the central fact about Heseltine is not his administrative ability as a minister, nor the profundity of his insight, nor his loyalty to this or that 'ism' of political theory. His great gift is a larger-than-life quality and a talent – one he shares to a degree with Enoch Powell, or even, if you like, with Churchill – to strike resounding chords in the hearts of an astonishingly wide range of people.

He may be suspect among monetarist gurus; and the stuffier kind of Conservative may wince at his bumptiousness (why doesn't the fellow get a proper short-back-and-sides haircut?). But he has notoriously been the darling of the Conservative conference (maybe reflecting the fact that it is at the conference, in contrast to Westminster, that the women of the party come into their own). The annual Heseltine conference speech became one of the great events in the political calendar, making the trip to Brighton or Blackpool worthwhile. The great mane of hair would seem to explode into a golden cascade as he worked up the audience. His success, not to mention his photogenic appeal, could make colleagues, conscious of their bald patches, sick with envy, but they knew better than to show it.

Heseltine is no intellectual. He did not shine academically at school or at Oxford. Oxford, incidentally, was by way of being a consolation prize; he actually wanted to do a B.Comm. at Bristol but they turned him down.

His lack of rapport with books derives from a mild kind of dyslexia. As a minister, faced with the challenge of a daily mass of paper to digest, he turned this slight handicap into an advantage by making his civil servants digest it for him: he insisted on information being turned into graphs and diagrams or lists of basic facts, or he would elicit the facts by questioning the officials orally. It provided a livelier picture of a given situation than other ministers might get.

Heseltine comes from what he has described

as 'the commercial middle classes of South Wales' (and his political hero is Lloyd George). After Oxford, and without a B.Comm., he started training as an accountant but never finished because he found he had a sound grasp of commercial technique without a qualification. With £1,000 given him by his grandparents he teamed up with an Oxford friend to invest in a rooming house, moved on into other property investment, then into a publishing enterprise.

But his little financial empire disintegrated. Heseltine's way of dealing with the crisis says a lot about him, his toughness, his ambition and his sense of honour. He could have got out by putting his companies into liquidation, with limited liability. Instead he announced that, since he had got the companies into trouble, he would get them out of it. He went to his bank manager, whose judgement may have been influenced by the fact that he was due to retire the next day, and handed over his shares, his house deeds, the keys to his car, his gold watch. With the cooperation of the bank he began the long haul – ten years – to get his finances sorted out. It was an achievement that showed immense business skill as well as guts and determination. And after that he was a rich man.

When Mrs Thatcher came to power, it was inevitable that Heseltine should join her cabinet – his standing with the conference made him a major party figure. The department he would have liked would have been Industry – he felt he knew something about the subject. But she significantly kept him away from the industrial-economic mainstream of strategy, and sent him to the Environment. Heseltine left several lasting monuments to his time there: among them the sale of council houses; a strengthening of the 'Green' factor in planning decisions; and a new managerial system for the Environment Department itself. The Merseyside initiative earned him credit among the Wets – credit that he lost by acquiescing in the monetarist rigours of the government's general policy.

But it was partly because Mrs Thatcher regarded him as 'not one of us', and wanted him even farther from the economic mainstream, that she promoted him sideways

in 1983 to be Defence Secretary. If he was still ambitious to get the Department of Industry, a knife was turned in the wound when Leon Brittan secured that job in 1985. Rivalry between the two was one factor in the way the Westland crisis developed.

Westland ought not to be what is mainly remembered from Heseltine's Defence years. He achieved a massive departmental reorganization there too, over the heads of the generals and admirals, with more lasting effect than the reorganization of a helicopter company. As a supplier to the Defence Department, Westland was a major Heseltine interest. But it was also an ailing company, and as such came under Brittan, who eventually favoured its sale to the American manufacturer Sikorsky. Heseltine, a sincere and passionate European, favoured a pan-European link-up. The details were less important politically than the fact that it developed into a nasty intra-cabinet lobbying battle. The Prime Minister sought to cool it – but on terms which Heseltine saw as being neutrality very much on the anti-Heseltine side. He characteristically declined to be gagged by Downing Street.

The nastiness culminated in the selective leaking, intended to weaken his case, of a confidential document. The responsibility for this was confused: it was Brittan who paid the price of the impropriety, by resigning. There is no doubt that by the general rule that ministers have to take responsibility for their officials' actions, the Prime Minister carried some responsibility for the leak too. But before Brittan was sacked, Heseltine had walked out. It was unpremeditated. It left the Prime Minister looking very vulnerable, if only for a few weeks. It hurt Heseltine too, but not irreparably. He is a hard man for the electorate to hate.

WRITINGS

Where There's a Will (London: Hutchinson, 1987).

FURTHER READING

Critchley, Julian, *Heseltine* (London: André Deutsch, 1987).

JULIAN CRITCHLEY

Hetherington, (Hector) Alastair (*b.* Llanishen, Glamorgan, 31 October

1919). Journalist. He was editor of *The Guardian* for nearly 20 years, from 1956 to 1975. During that time he transformed the former *Manchester Guardian* into a truly national newspaper by overseeing first its move to two-centre publication and then the transfer of its main office to London.

Hetherington joined the *Manchester Guardian* from the *Glasgow Herald* in 1950. Under his stewardship, the paper successfully broadened its appeal to gain a significant younger readership, partly by expanding coverage of the arts and increasing the space allotted to features. As the only quality newspaper that consistently supported the left, *The Guardian* became the natural mouthpiece for the radical movements of the 1960s, and its circulation grew steadily to more than 300,000 a day. Hetherington steered it away from its traditional support for the Liberals and tended to back Harold Wilson's Labour Party.

He quit the paper to begin a new and less successful career in broadcasting as controller of BBC Scotland. In 1975 the talk of devolution for Scotland and Wales was at its height: his mandate was to carve a degree of autonomy for Scottish broadcasting within the BBC system. But he was unable to cope with the corporation's centralized bureaucracy and lasted only three years in the job. He became professor of media studies at Stirling University and in 1985 was appointed a member of the Peacock Committee on the future of broadcasting. He exerted a strong influence on the committee's report. With its recommendations for funding the BBC by subscription, more programmes made by independent producers and looser regulatory controls on commercial television, it provided the basis for the far-reaching White Paper on broadcasting in 1988 and the legislation that followed it.

WRITINGS

Guardian Years (London: Chatto and Windus, 1981).

MICHAEL H. LEAPMAN

Hicks, William Joynson-. See JOYNSON-HICKS, WILLIAM.

Hoare, Sir **Samuel (John Gurney)** [Viscount Templewood] (*b.* London, 24 February 1880; *d.* London, 7 May 1959). Conservative politician. His political career spanned most of the first half of the twentieth century and included some of the highest ministerial offices. As Secretary of State for Air in the 1920s he successfully defended the infant RAF from take-over bids by the older services. As Secretary of State for India in the 1930s he presided over the enactment of what would have been, had it been fully implemented, the greatest measure of Indian constitutional reform prior to the granting of independence. His short term at the Foreign Office in 1935 was overshadowed by the international crisis provoked by the Italian invasion of Abyssinia and ended with his resignation after the failure of a diplomatic initiative (the Hoare–Laval Pact) which still continues to arouse controversy. Restored to office after a brief period in the political wilderness, Hoare became a member of the inner group of four in the Chamberlain cabinet most closely associated with the policy of 'appeasement'. Discarded from the War Cabinet by Churchill in 1940, he emerged as a highly effective ambassador to Spain, his last official appointment.

There was a strong element of social reform in Hoare's family background. His great-grandfather was brother-in-law of both Elizabeth Fry and Fowell Buxton and, with them, founded what later became the Howard League for Penal Reform. Hoare's father forsook the family banking firm in London for the life of a Norfolk squire, combining it with loyal service as a Norfolk Conservative MP from 1885 to 1906. His reward was a baronetcy, to which his son succeeded in 1915. Hoare was the elder son in a family of six children. After a distinguished academic career at Harrow he went to New College, Oxford, where he not only gained firsts in both classics and history but also blues for rackets and tennis. Despite his spare frame and, at times, uncertain health, Hoare excelled at tennis and, more unusually, at ice-skating; he was also one of the best shots in England, the scourge of all game birds.

Hoare's political career was launched almost immediately he left Oxford. Adopted as one of two Conservative candidates for Ipswich early in 1905, he combined nursing a constituency with gaining useful administrative experience as Assistant Private Secretary to the Colonial Secretary, Alfred Lyttelton. After a not unexpected defeat in the 1906 election he was the successful candidate for Brixton in the 1907 LCC elections, at which the Conservatives (as Municipal Reformers) wrested control of the country's largest local authority from the Liberals. A year later he was nominated for the Chelsea constituency and won it comfortably from its Liberal incumbent in January 1910 (holding it securely for the next 34 years). A few months earlier he had acquired a priceless asset for a rising politician when politics were still dominated by an élite based upon social position: he married a daughter of the sixth Earl Beauchamp.

Hoare was an active backbencher in the Conservative opposition to a weakened Liberal government. On at least two occasions he stood out from the ruck. In the so-called Holmes Circular affair the permanent secretary at the Board of Education, Sir Robert Morant, wrote critically of the educational and social abilities of local-authority schools inspectors as compared with the overwhelmingly university-educated HM inspectorate. The document was leaked and Hoare, a recent member of the LCC education committee, led the attack on this apparent evidence of government class bias. After numerous debates and parliamentary questions Morant was forced to resign and his minister was moved to another post. Hoare's other notable backbench campaign was less successful. A devout Anglo-Catholic

Sir Samuel Hoare returning from Geneva, September 1935

(despite Quaker forbears), he and others bitterly opposed the disestablishment and disendowment of the Church in Wales. Although they secured some amendments, they were unable to prevent the passage of the legislation.

On the outbreak of war in August 1914 Hoare joined up immediately, but a serious illness forced the postponement of active service. When he eventually departed for overseas, in March 1916, it was to head the British intelligence mission attached to the Russian general staff at Petrograd. He left Russia just before the February Revolution but continued his secret service work in a similar post in Italy where, among other things, he procured a British subsidy for a pro-war editor named Benito Mussolini.

It was not until January 1919 that Hoare was able to resume his parliamentary career, after an overwhelming victory in Chelsea as a coalition supporter in the 1918 election. One of his special fields as a backbencher was foreign affairs, especially relations with the new Soviet Russia (he was for a time League of Nations Deputy High Commissioner for Russian Refugees). Another was Ireland, where he generally supported government policy and worked closely with Lord Beaverbrook. This was one of his most important, if surprising, political friendships and Beaverbrook remained a staunch ally, advocate and occasional financial supporter for the rest of Hoare's career.

As the coalition proceeded, Hoare became increasingly dissatisfied with Lloyd George as Prime Minister and the Conservative Party's role within it. When he heard, in late September 1922, that leading Conservative ministers were planning an early coalition election with their Liberal colleagues, Hoare set about organizing a backbench revolt. He, as much as anyone, was responsible for the historic anticoalition vote at the Carlton Club meeting on 19 October, which led to Lloyd George's resignation and the subsequent Conservative electoral victory.

Hoare could confidently expect senior office in the new Conservative administration formed by Bonar Law. But his appointment as Secretary of State for Air, outside the cabinet, was an ambiguous one. Many, including the Prime Minister, assumed that it would be only a

matter of time before the newly created RAF ceased to exist as a separate service (and with it the Air Ministry), as the older services resumed control of the air arm. But they reckoned without Hoare, promoted to the cabinet by Baldwin in 1923, and his formidable Chief of Air Staff, Trenchard. Over a period of seven years, apart (for Hoare) from the brief Labour Government of 1924, these two, joining political with technical expertise, put the autonomous role of the RAF beyond challenge. Hoare was also responsible for the development of civil aviation. Here he did much, by personal example, at a time when flying was very much a minority activity. With his wife he made the inaugural flight on the new Indian route, a round trip of 12,000 miles.

Hoare was by now a close political colleague of Neville Chamberlain, and shared the latter's concern over Baldwin's leadership of the party during the years of opposition, 1929–31. It was they, not Baldwin (holidaying in France), who played the decisive part in the formation of the National Government in August 1931. Hoare became Secretary of State for India, and his four years in that office were the most impressive of his ministerial career. His was the primary responsibility for devising a policy for the future government of the vast Indian subcontinent, of ensuring its political acceptability, above all by his own party (in which Churchill was his most virulent critic), and of piloting through the lengthy and complex legislation involved. The fact that the Government of India Act of 1935 was never fully implemented was no fault of Hoare (who had moved on to other things) and does not detract from his achievement.

In the cabinet changes which accompanied Baldwin's succession to MacDonald as Prime Minister in June 1935, Hoare was appointed Foreign Secretary. The most difficult of the many problems with which he had to deal was the containment of the newly resurgent Germany. This was seen to require a close alliance with France and, to a lesser extent, with Mussolini's Italy. But in 1934 Italy deliberately provoked a quarrel with Abyssinia, long the object of its imperialist ambitions, and in October 1935 invaded the country. The resultant crisis dominated Hoare's tenure.

Military measures against Italy were opposed both by France (fearful they would divert attention from the German menace) and the British Chiefs of Staff, whose advice the cabinet accepted. There was much talk of collective action by the League of Nations, to which Hoare contributed in a much-publicized speech in Geneva in September 1935. But to be effective these needed the full commitment of Britain and France, which neither was prepared to give while other countries were unwilling to share the dangers involved. In the end, Hoare, with cabinet approval, sought to save some of Abyssinia from Italian depredations by the agreement he made in Paris with the French premier, Laval. The cabinet, after first backing this Hoare–Laval Pact, within a few days reversed its position in face of an extraordinary display of public outrage at the apparent rewarding of an aggressor. Hoare, who at this vital time was incapacitated by a skating accident in Switzerland, was repudiated. He resigned with dignity to save the government's face and a few months later the Italians completed the total subjugation of Abyssinia which it had been the object of the Hoare–Laval plan to avoid.

Hoare had only six months to wait for a return to high office, a tacit recognition of the shabby way he had been treated. After less than a year as First Lord of the Admiralty he moved to the Home Office when Chamberlain succeeded Baldwin as Prime Minister. Here his chief interest lay in penal reform. He introduced a radical new Criminal Justice Bill which, among other things, included the abolition of corporal punishment. In the teeth of much backbench opposition Hoare had seen it through most of its stages when the outbreak of war compelled its abandonment. Many of its provisions were later incorporated in the 1948 Act.

Hoare was more than just a departmental minister, however important. He was Chamberlain's loyal supporter in seeking 'appeasement' of the dictators and formed, with Chamberlain, Halifax and Simon, the cabinet's inner group. But Hoare was not an unquestioning appeaser. In the early summer of 1939, much against Chamberlain's inclinations, he pressed strongly for a defensive alliance with the Soviet Union. When war came he became Lord Privy Seal in the War Cabinet, with major coordinating functions. In April 1940 he once again became Secretary of State for Air. But the Norwegian campaign was already doomed and with it the fate of the Chamberlain Government. When Chamberlain resigned in favour of Churchill, Hoare knew that his ministerial career was over. Alone among the four principal appeasers, he was denied office in the new administration: Churchill had neither forgiven him for appeasement nor for worsting him in the India Bill debates. But useful employment was not at an end. Hoare would have dearly loved to have gone to India as viceroy but this Churchill would not countenance. Instead he went as ambassador to Spain, where for over four years he successfully implemented the British Government's policy of dissuading Franco from entering the war on the side of his fellow-dictators. Hoare returned to England in 1944 as Viscount Templewood, after the Palladian-style house he had built in Norfolk.

Hoare's retirement was largely spent writing his memoirs, pursuing the cause of penal reform – he became a passionate advocate of the abolition of capital punishment – and attending the Lords. On his death 15 years later the usual tributes were paid, but the Hoare–Laval Pact and appeasement were still seen as fatally tarnishing his reputation. He had never been a popular figure. A somewhat prim personality was combined with an intense and often all-too obvious ambition. Nevertheless, it could be argued that his ministerial career overall was one of the most outstanding of the inter-war period.

WRITINGS

Ambassador on Special Mission (London: Collins, 1946).
Nine Troubled Years (London: Collins, 1954).
Empire of the Air (London: Collins, 1957).

FURTHER READING

Cross, J. A., *Sir Samuel Hoare* (London: Jonathan Cape, 1977).

J. A. CROSS

Hogg, Douglas (McGarel) [Viscount Hailsham] (*b.* London, 28 February 1872; *d.* Carter's Corner Place, Sussex, 10 August 1950). Conservative Lord Chancellor. He was a distinguished barrister and Conservative politician, rising through the law officerships to be twice Lord Chancellor and to hold several other cabinet posts under Baldwin and MacDonald.

He was the eldest son of Quintin Hogg, a successful sugar grower and a major educational philanthropist who had effectively founded the Regent Street Polytechnic. As a young man, Douglas Hogg gained experience in his father's commercial concerns, including work in the West Indies, which was to give him useful commercial insight when he entered politics. He served and was wounded in the Boer War. On returning from South Africa he was called to the Bar and began a new legal career when already over the age of 30. A clear, lucid mind and great powers of persuasion proved to be a secure basis of success in this second career, a practice based on commercial and common-law knowledge. He was one of the leading juniors in the profession when he took silk in 1917 and became a bencher of Lincoln's Inn in 1920. By that time he would no doubt have entered parliament had not the 'Coupon' Election of 1918 required him to stand down as Conservative candidate for St Marylebone to make way for a Lloyd George Liberal. When his opportunity came with the end of the Lloyd George coalition in 1922, he seized it: he was elected for St Marylebone and remained its MP until 1928.

Hogg had the unusual distinction of joining the government of Bonar Law before getting into parliament at all, when Law made him Attorney-General in 1922. As a frontbencher in a government which had few effective speakers in the Commons he rapidly rose in his colleagues' estimation; he was especially important in getting Conservative MPs to vote for the Irish Free State Bill, about which many had severe doubts. Experience in the Commons certainly sharpened his political skills; Baldwin retained him as Attorney-General and encouraged him to speak on a wider range of issues when the party was in opposition in 1924. He made a formidable speech in the

Douglas Hogg, first Viscount Hailsham

attack on MacDonald over the Campbell Case, an attack which helped to bring down the government. In November he again became Attorney-General but with a seat in cabinet, and was offered the lord chancellorship when it fell vacant in 1928. This presented a difficult choice: some, perhaps he himself, saw him as a future Prime Minister, and the events of 1923 indicated that a peer could not succeed Baldwin. Equally, as the law stood until 1963, a peerage would inhibit not only his own career but his son's, already a significant consideration. All the same he accepted, perhaps drawn more by the actual promise of the highest post in his twin professions than by future uncertainties.

From this point Hogg was an essential member of the Conservative front bench as long as he was active in politics. He led the party in the Lords during the stormy party crisis of 1930–1 and was included in the National Government as Secretary of State for War in 1931; the independent line that he had taken in the party crisis possibly ensured his exclusion from the original National Cabinet, but he returned when the cabinet was restored to normal size in November. Four years at the War Office provided few opportunities to shine at a time of disarmament, low expenditure and widespread pacifism, and when re-armament began in 1934 the army had the lowest priority. He continued to play a full part in cabinet, however; he may have suggested the formula of 'agreeing to differ' which saved the unity of the government in 1931, and he was an active member of the delegation to the Ottawa Economic Conference in 1932. Nonetheless he was happier when Sankey's retirement enabled him to return to the woolsack in 1935. As Lord Chancellor he again demonstrated his legal skills in a number of appeal cases, and presided over the last ever trial of a peer by his peers, when Lord de Clifford was charged with manslaughter in 1935.

Declining health necessitated Hogg's move to the Lord Presidency in March 1938 and out of the government altogether in the following October. By that time, however, he had seen his son establish himself both at the Bar and in the Commons, a career in which he too would come near the highest office and be twice Lord Chancellor. Throughout his life Hogg remained active in outside organizations, notably as President of the Marylebone Cricket Club – an interest happily shared with Baldwin – and continued his father's active work in the Polytechnic.

JOHN RAMSDEN

Hogg, Quintin. See HAILSHAM, LORD.

Home, Lord [Douglas-Home, Alexander (Frederick); Sir Alec; Lord Home of the Hirsel] (b. London, 2 July 1903). Conservative Prime Minister. His political career bridged the prewar and modern Conservative parties. He served under Neville Chamberlain (1937–40) and Winston Churchill (1951–5), became Prime Minister for one year (1963–4), subsequently served under Edward Heath (1970–4), and continued to play an active role in the House of Lords after Margaret Thatcher became Prime Minister in 1979. Like Anthony Eden, he spent the bulk of his political life engaged in foreign and Commonwealth matters. Like Eden, too, he was at his best in the number two position rather than at the helm.

Home's is the least written-about career of any twentieth-century Prime Minister. His premiership has attracted no scholarly study, and his political career before 1963 has failed to excite much interest or comment from historians or biographers. It might be easy, therefore, to dismiss him as a lightweight, but such a conclusion is seriously misleading.

He was born into an upper-class Borders family and enjoyed the traditional aristocratic education of Eton and Christ Church, Oxford. Shunning the life of estate management and farming, which his father had favoured, he turned to politics, standing unsuccessfully as a Conservative in the 1929 general election at Coatbridge and Airdrie in Lanarkshire. There had been no long-term plan to become a politician, let alone a Conservative, but he was genuinely moved by the high unemployment in the areas around his home in Lanarkshire, and saw himself, on balance, having a potentially more useful role in politics than in any other career.

His wish was fulfilled in the 1931 general election, when he successfully stood for the South Lanark constituency, which he held, albeit with a reduced majority, in 1935. His first six years in parliament passed relatively quietly, his initial step up the ladder coming with his appointments as Parliamentary Private Secretary to ministers at the Scottish Office and the Ministry of Labour. His big opportunity came in 1937 when Neville Chamberlain asked him to become his Parliamentary Private Secretary just as he was leaving the Treasury to become Prime Minister in succession to Stanley Baldwin. The deteriorating international position in Europe naturally claimed the bulk of Chamberlain's time. Home did not attend Chamberlain on his visit to see Hitler at Berchtesgaden, but he did go with him to their final meeting, in Munich. There he witnessed Hitler sign the declaration drafted by Chamberlain which stated that, in future, disputes between Britain and Germany would be settled by peaceful means. He became close to Chamberlain personally: the Chamberlains came up to stay with the Homes at the Hirsel, their home on the Borders, shortly after the return from Munich. That Home shared the same broad drift of Chamberlain's policy is beyond doubt but, although he provided support, he did not influence the Prime Minister in his chosen policy.

The fall of Chamberlain in May 1940, and his replacement by Churchill, removed Home from the centre of politics, and a two-year recuperation from a serious spinal operation then rendered him a temporary invalid. The five years in the wilderness were not wasted: during this time Home formulated his moderate Conservative philosophy, which was to be the guiding force of his subsequent ministerial career.

Home's association with Chamberlain and 'appeasement' did not appear to damage his political career, and, in May 1945, Churchill invited him to serve in the Caretaker Government as Parliamentary Under-Secretary at the Foreign Office. The experience was short-lived; in the July general election the Conservatives were defeated, as was Home himself. For another five years he returned to political obscurity, a period ended by his recapture of his Lanarkshire seat in the 1950 general election.

Shortly after his return to Westminster, Home's political aspirations appeared to have met yet another handicap when, during the life of the eighteen-month parliament, his father died, and he succeeded him as the 14th Earl of Home. Becoming a peer did not exclude him from political office, but it was not the custom then for members of the House of Lords to reach the highest offices. When the Conservatives won the October 1951 general election, with Churchill again at the helm, the Secretary of State for Scotland, James Stuart, asked for Home to be appointed to the new post of Minister of State for Scotland. It was to be Home's first sustained experience of ministerial office, and was one he filled with some distinction. His special task was to promote the Conservative cause in Scotland and head off the Scottish nationalism which had been enjoying one of its periodic bouts of resurgence. Home, based in Scotland, worked hard, visiting far-flung areas and talking to wide sections of the community. Although only infrequently in London, and then in the House of Lords, his work began to receive attention. His star was clearly in the ascendant.

In April 1955, Churchill retired, and Eden, his successor, invited Home to become Secretary of State for Commonwealth Relations, with a seat in cabinet. Although now in a position of some influence, Home remained a relatively passive figure in cabinet throughout his period at the Commonwealth Office (1955–60). The job was essentially a public relations exercise (as that at the Scottish Office had been), working with the Commonwealth. His persuasion skills were at a premium in his two most challenging tasks: holding the Commonwealth together during and after the Suez Crisis of 1956, in which he excelled, and trying to make work, albeit unsuccessfully, the ill-fated Central African Federation of Southern and Northern Rhodesia and Nyasaland.

Home's safe and effective handling of Commonwealth affairs, and the regard in which he was held as Leader of the House of Lords from 1957, suggested to Macmillan that he would make a suitable Foreign Secretary when, in 1960, he had to find a successor to Selwyn Lloyd, who had held the post since Macmillan himself ceased to be Foreign Secretary in December 1955. Lloyd had always allowed himself to be dominated by Macmillan at the Foreign Office: it is possible that, in Home, Macmillan thought he might find a similarly accommodating lieutenant. If this thought was in his mind, he found he had backed the wrong man, and Home proved himself a more independent-minded politician than in his previous offices.

This period at the Foreign Office (1960–3) proved in every way the making of Home. The scale of the promotion in 1960 was, of course, immense, from relatively junior cabinet minister to one of the highest positions in the government. The appointment was also remarkable because Home was in the House of Lords, and it was felt, particularly on the left and in certain sections of the media, that the Foreign Secretary should be in the lower house: Macmillan calmly rode out the storm, and, in doing so, paved the way for Lord Carrington's appoint-

Sir Alec Douglas-Home greeting Ian Smith, Prime Minister of Southern Rhodesia, on the steps of 10 Downing Street, September 1964

ment as Mrs Thatcher's first Foreign Secretary (1979–82).

Home's two main objectives were to preserve the military strength of Western Europe in the face of what he regarded as a serious Soviet intention to expand westwards. This meant warm support for the American contribution to NATO. Secondly, he came increasingly to favour closer European integration, but primarily for political rather than economic reasons. In both these areas Home had to contend with the major interest of Macmillan in his department's work. Indeed, Macmillan's interest in foreign affairs from 1960 to 1963, with his close relationship with President Kennedy (1961–3), the Polaris deal at Nassau and his enthusiasm for British entry into the Common Market, was arguably greater even than it had been from 1957 to 1960.

In October 1963, to the surprise of many, not least himself, Home found himself propelled into the premiership. Historians have still to analyse fully the frenzied events of the leadership crisis of that month, but it seems likely that the worst Home can be accused of is not duplicity but only excessive secrecy. To have remained in the Lords was unthinkable, so, utilizing the recently passed legislation on renunciation of peerages, he was found a seat (Kinross and West Perthshire) and translated into the Commons as Sir Alec Douglas-Home. His was to be the briefest period at Number Ten in the postwar period, and it has been judged harshly by pundits and commentators. He is criticized for being insufficiently dynamic or forward-looking to have led the Conservative Party at that point in its history.

Such criticisms are largely unfair. Home did much to rally the party in the 12 months before the general election, which came in October 1964. The party's standing in the polls was considerably higher then than it had been 12 months earlier, and it came within a handful of seats of winning. Home took over in the least propitious circumstances, with a demoralized and tired party, a sceptical media, and a strong challenge from the Liberal and Labour parties, the latter under a dynamic new leader, Harold Wilson. Home's prospects were dented by the refusal of two prominent former ministers, IAIN MACLEOD and ENOCH POWELL, to serve under him. Home himself thought their abstention proved decisive in the electoral defeat. The major item of domestic legislation in the 1963–4 session, the Resale Price Maintenance Bill, caused deep divisions within the Conservative Party, which further damaged electoral prospects. Any leader taking over in October 1963 would have encountered severe problems.

In the end, his innate conservatism probably counted against him. He determined not to make any major policy or personnel changes (bar bringing back Selwyn Lloyd). With hindsight, one can argue that a dramatic, fresh approach would have appealed more to the media and the electorate, and would have been more in tune with the spirit of the age. Home certainly was little match for Wilson, then at the height of his powers, who gained immense credence with his rallying cries of modernization and technological revolution.

After the election defeat, Home became Leader of the Opposition, a position for which he had no great personal liking. He announced that the position of the Conservatives was to support the government when it acted in the public interest and to offer implacable opposition when it did not. Such a statement from a leader might have been appropriate in foreign affairs, but was not for domestic politics, and it did little to endear him to the young Turks in the party eager for full-blooded combat. Murmurings of rebellion came increasingly into the open as discontent manifested not only with his lack of fire, but also with his limited grasp of domestic politics, and especially economics. Before standing down, Home, on his own initiative, introduced a new system for choosing the party leader, in which, replacing the former method of informal consultations among senior Conservatives, Conservative MPs voted in a two-ballot election.

EDWARD HEATH, the successful candidate in the 1965 leadership election, invited Home to remain in the shadow cabinet with responsibility for foreign affairs. It was typical of Home that he assented. A man less motivated by service might have declined. In choosing to remain in politics, for what was to be another nine years, Home added to his reputation. He became an elder statesman in the party whose counsel was frequently sought and who was always listened to with respect. When Labour lost the close election in June 1970, it was little more than a formality that Heath appointed Home again to the Foreign Office.

In his second and final period as Foreign Secretary (1970–4), Home found himself with a freer hand. Heath, unlike Macmillan, lacked a background and a burning interest – with one exception – in foreign affairs. The exception was, of course, European integration, and here Heath placed responsibility for detailed negotiation over entry into the EEC in the hands of Geoffrey Rippon. Instead, Home had two preoccupations. The first was Rhodesia, where he made a brave, but ultimately fruitless, attempt to unfreeze the impasse which had existed since Ian Smith had unilaterally declared independence in 1965 following the break-up of the Central African Federation. As a former Commonwealth Secretary, Home brought not just determination but also a deep understanding to the negotiations, and it was a great sadness to him personally that his initiative failed. The second theatre was the Middle East, where Home had the twin problems of presiding peacefully over Britain's withdrawal from the Gulf, initiated by the Labour Government, and asserting Britain's interest in Arab–Israeli relations. In the latter, Home made a brave attempt to urge Israel that its long-term interest lay in abandoning its newly conquered territories and retiring behind the 1967 frontiers, with the UN providing a policing and peace-keeping role. Home brought vision and statesmanship to this last ministerial post, and it can be considered his most successful period of office.

Following the election defeat in February 1974, Home, now aged 70, decided to retire from political life, and returned to the House of Lords with a life peerage as Lord Home of the Hirsel.

Home's was not the most spectacular or innovative of political careers. He was neither an original thinker, nor an especially astute party politician. His skills in managing the House of Lords often deserted him in the lower chamber. Where he excelled was as a man of firm conviction and principle at a time when integrity in British politics was being brought increasingly into question. Motivated by a deep Christian conviction and a belief in a middle-of-the-road Conservatism in the tradition of Churchill and Macmillan, he will be remembered as a popular and trusted politician and a more than averagely successful Foreign Secretary.

WRITINGS

The Way the Wind Blows (London: Collins, 1976).

FURTHER READING

Young, K., *Sir Alec Douglas-Home* (London: Dent, 1970).

ANTHONY SELDON

Hope, Victor. See LINLITHGOW, LORD.

Hore-Belisha, (Isaac) Leslie [Baron Hore-Belisha of Devonport] (*b.* London, 7 September 1893; *d.* Reims, France, 17 February 1957). Liberal and later National Liberal MP, Secretary of State for War (1937–40). He was generally regarded as the most successful reforming War Minister since R. B. Haldane (1906–12).

Jacob Isaac Belisha, a businessman of Sephardic Jewish origins, died when his son Leslie was an infant, and when his mother married Sir Adair Hore, Leslie became Hore-Belisha. He was educated at Clifton, the Sorbonne, Heidelberg and St John's College, Oxford, and after World War I, in which he was commissioned in the Army Service Corps, he was the first postwar president of the Oxford Union. In 1923 he was elected Liberal MP for Devonport (a seat which he retained until 1945), and was also called to the Bar. He was a prolific journalist, writing regularly for the *Daily Express, Sunday Express* and *Evening Standard*, and acquiring a taste for personal publicity which later irritated some of the more conventional generals. In 1931 he helped organize the Liberal National Party to support Ramsay MacDonald, trebling his own majority in the election. The following year Neville Chamberlain made him his Financial Secretary at the Treasury and he was henceforth a Chamberlain protégé. Between 1934 and 1937 he was a successful Minister of Transport: among other reforms he reduced road accidents (installing the 'Belisha beacons' which perpetuate his name), introduced driving tests and revised the highway code.

When Chamberlain became Prime Minister, he sent Hore-Belisha to the War Office with the express purpose of shaking up the conservative army hierarchy and the notoriously obstructive bureaucracy. This he did very impressively in the remaining months of peace, beginning with a variety of measures designed to make the army more popular; in his own apt phrase, 'the Army should be a part of the nation not apart from the nation'. He improved recruiting figures by removing many of the petty restrictions on the soldier's liberty, increased pay and family allowances, and offered better opportunities for promotion from the ranks to a commission. He continued his predecessor's programme in the modernizing of barracks, and brought in Sir Isadore Salmon, Managing Director of Joe Lyons, as Honorary Catering Adviser to the Army. More significantly and controversially, he regularly consulted Capt. B. H. Liddell Hart, defence correspondent of *The Times*, on every aspect of military reform (see LIDDELL HART, B. H.). An early, and wholly beneficial, result of this collaboration was the drastic overhaul of the officer career structure. The retiring age for senior officers was lowered, as was also the period of command and staff appointments; the half-pay system was abolished; and time-promotion was introduced so that the rank of major would normally be attained after 17 years' service. On 5 August 1938 more than 2,000 officers – the largest number in the army's history – were promoted in a single list taking up 20 pages of the *London Gazette*.

Hore-Belisha's flamboyant personality and unconventional methods made him popular in the press and with the general public (as 'the soldier's friend'), but he also had an unhappy knack of making enemies. For example, in the summer of 1938 he mishandled the 'Sandys affair' when Duncan Sandys, a young Conservative MP, made public confidential information about the inadequacy of anti-aircraft defences. Hore-Belisha further alienated Lord Gort, the Chief of the Imperial General Staff, whom he had promoted in December 1937 after boldly purging the Army Council of its more reactionary members; and he also antagonized Winston Churchill, Sandys' father-in-law, who had previously supported him. In

December 1938 Hore-Belisha survived a junior ministers' revolt because on this occasion the Prime Minister supported him, but it was an ominous sign that his trusted Parliamentary Under-Secretary, Lord Strathcona, was among the malcontents.

Meanwhile Hore-Belisha had radically altered his views on the priority of roles for the army. As a supporter of Chamberlain he had given the highest priority for the home defence role against air attack at the expense of preparing the small field force for Continental war, believing (as did Liddell Hart) that the French army and the Maginot Line could be relied upon to protect Britain's interest in Western Europe. But Hore-Belisha became disenchanted with Chamberlain's policy at Munich, and by the end of the year he was fighting in cabinet for a change of priorities (and hence of larger funds) for the army. In February 1939 he succeeded in getting the Continental commitment accepted by cabinet and at last the army began to receive modern equipment. In April he displayed great political courage in persuading Chamberlain that conscription must be introduced, and he also succeeded at last in July in establishing a Ministry of Supply.

The advent of war entailed that Hore-Belisha had to rely increasingly on his senior military advisers and this was soon to bring about his downfall. On 3 September 1939 Lord Gort joyfully escaped from the War Office to become Commander-in-Chief of the army in France, but his successor, General Sir Edmund Ironside, proved to be equally antagonistic towards his political superior. In the opening weeks of the 'Phoney War', Gort and his Chief of Staff, Major-General Pownall, felt that they were not receiving proper support from the War Office. Hore-Belisha's well-meant attempt to put this right by visiting the forces in France in mid-November in fact proved disastrous. His inept criticisms of the field works on his return to London was seized upon by his enemies (Gort, Pownall and Ironside chief among them) and magnified into 'the Pill Box affair'.

As a Liberal National in a predominantly Conservative administration, Hore-Belisha was critically dependent on the Prime Minister's support. On 14 December Chamberlain re-affirmed his confidence in Hore-Belisha and even offered to remove Gort and Ironside if he so wished. But Hore-Belisha showed a fatal insensitivity to his predicament and soon afterwards the Prime Minister decided to move him to another ministry. The Ministry of Information was a possibility, but the Foreign Office gave Chamberlain the curious advice that Hore-Belisha's Jewish origins made him unacceptable. The Prime Minister then offered the astonished Hore-Belisha the Board of Trade but since no satisfactory explanation for the move was given he understandably resigned. This proved to be the virtual end of a promising political career. He was briefly Minister of National Insurance in Churchill's caretaker government in 1945 but never again held office. He became a Conservative in 1945 but no seat was found for him, and in 1954 he accepted a peerage. In 1944 he had married Cynthia Elliot; there were no children.

Though he had irritating faults, such as unpunctuality and impatience, Hore-Belisha possessed personal charm and considerable ability, not least as a brilliant debater. His practical reforms constitute a watershed in army history, particularly in improving the terms of service for all ranks and for bringing the army and nation together. He was on the threshold of a distinguished political career but for his encounter with the inflexible and vindictive generals and the unfortunate circumstances of his resignation.

FURTHER READING

Bond, Brian (ed.), *Chief of Staff: the Diaries of Lt. Gen Sir Henry Pownall*, vol. I (London: Leo Cooper, 1972).

Bond, Brian, 'Leslie Hore-Belisha at the War Office', in *Politicians and Defence*, ed. I. F. W. Beckett and J. Gooch (Manchester: Manchester University Press, 1981).

Liddell Hart, B. H., *Memoirs*, vol. II (London: Cassell, 1965).

Minney, R. J., *The Private Papers of Hore-Belisha* (London: Collins, 1960).

Trythall, A. J., 'The Downfall of Leslie Hore-Belisha', *Journal of Contemporary History*, 16 (1981), pp. 391–411.

B. J. BOND

Horne, Robert (Stevenson) [Viscount Horne of Slamannan] (*b*. Slamannan, Stirlingshire, 28 February 1871; *d*. Farnham, Surrey, 3 September 1940). Conservative Chancellor of the Exchequer. He rose to become Chancellor under Lloyd George in 1921, after only the briefest of political apprenticeships, but went into an equally rapid eclipse when Lloyd George fell in 1922, and, like Lloyd George, never held office again. He had in fact three quite separate careers, first as a successful Scottish lawyer, second and most briefly at the summit of politics, and finally among the leaders of British industry between the wars.

Horne was the son of a Scottish Presbyterian minister and developed from the first outstanding abilities and a gregarious nature that was to remain his reputation for life. He achieved a first class degree in mental philosophy at the University of Glasgow, where he was also president of the students' union and winner of several university prizes. He seemed determined on an academic career, lecturing and examining for the universities of Wales and Aberdeen over the next five years. He then began to shift his career towards the law, which had formed part of his undergraduate studies, and was called to the Bar by the Scottish Faculty of Advocates in 1896. Over the next two decades he developed a successful but hardly spectacular career at the Scottish Bar, mainly in Glasgow, though seemingly without committing himself to a legal career for life. Over the same period he made valuable contacts in Scottish industry and in political circles: he was the unsuccessful Unionist candidate for Stirlingshire, the constituency of his birth, in both the elections of 1910.

His opportunity came, though, with World War I, which provided him, as a talented man just too old to fight, with an opportunity for entry and rapid promotion through national administration and London society. A short period at the National Service Department led

Sir Robert Horne, Chairman of the Great Western Railway, unveiling the name crest on the new 'Lloyd's' engine at Paddington, February 1936

on to bigger executive responsibilities. He was in many ways typical of the men of talent from outside the political mainstream recruited by wartime government under Lloyd George's auspices. After a term as Assistant Inspector-General of Transportation (with the honorary rank of Lieutenant Colonel of the Royal Engineers) devoted to gearing up the logistical support for the army in France, he moved to support Sir Eric Geddes at the Admiralty. There he was first director of the Department of Materials, and later of the Department of Labour, before joining the Board of Admiralty as Third Civil Lord in 1918. He was in effect a problem-solver for Geddes – himself one of Lloyd George's own trouble-shooters – and achieved thereby a considerable reputation as a man who could get things done in very different fields.

It was therefore natural that the merging of his earlier Scottish connections with his newly acquired metropolitan reputation should ensure Horne a safe seat and a political career. He was elected MP for the new Glasgow Hillhead constituency in 1918 and represented it until his transition to the Lords in 1937. The four years of Lloyd George's postwar government produced for Horne four years in cabinet in three successive posts, as well as a privy councillorship and a knighthood. He was at once appointed Minister of Labour on being elected to Parliament, a post for which his Admiralty experience was highly relevant; this was also a key job in what was expected to be – and was – a time of high postwar Labour militancy. He proved to be both a strong and a flexibly pragmatic minister, helping Lloyd George to ride out the storm of militancy without making major long-term concessions. From here he went on to be President of the Board of Trade in 1920, another trouble-shooting appointment at a time when the country's international trade was beginning to fall away and unemployment was beginning to rise. He finally moved to the senior economic post in cabinet as Chancellor of the Exchequer in April 1921, occupying that post while the government was trying to cut back its expenditure to appease critics on the right. Horne was essentially a pragmatic administrator who could be trusted to perform well in any

post, though he was also an active participant in cabinet debate. His several moves of post while in government – particularly in a time of continuing economic crisis – did not allow for the accumulation of lasting personal achievements, and, while he was both popular and admired by ministerial colleagues, he did little to build up a party following in the Commons or outside.

Lloyd George's steady promotion of Horne owed much to his and Austen Chamberlain's estimation of Horne's abilities, as well as to the latter's congenial nature and pragmatic politics at a time when the coalition was under attack by Tory diehards. It is not therefore surprising that Horne stood by Chamberlain when Lloyd George fell in October 1922, and refused to join Bonar Law's new Conservative cabinet. The decision meant the end of his governmental career: when Baldwin later tried to heal the party breach with the coalitionists by bringing in Chamberlain, Birkenhead and others, he had too few posts on offer to satisfy all aspirants for office. Horne rejoined the front bench in opposition in 1924, but when the party returned to office in November he was offered only the Ministry of Labour and without the certainty even of a cabinet seat. When he refused he was offered nothing else. A man without a real party base was a natural casualty of the process whereby the split of 1922 was healed.

Horne remained, though, an active back-bencher, a regular participant in debate, and an experienced and encouraging adviser to such young men of talent as Harold Macmillan as they sought to make their names as economic radicals. He enjoyed the role of a senior back-bencher, often on deputations to ministers, as for example over defence policy in 1935–6. He was at times an important go-between, most importantly between Beaverbrook and Baldwin in the party crisis of 1930–1, though he came out strongly on Baldwin's side when forced to choose.

A man of his experience, however, could not be satisfied with the life or the income of a backbencher when eclipsed from office in his prime. He was much in demand in industry and became an active director of such companies as P. & O., the Suez Canal Company, Lloyd's Bank, and Commercial Union; he was chairman of the Great Western Railway and of the Burmah and Zinc Corporations. Such wide connections in important industrial concerns naturally enhanced his influence still further as a speaker on industrial matters in Parliament.

His last years were enlivened by a continuing active involvement in the politics of the Lords, and also by a lively life in industry and society, where his company as an entertaining companion and a lively raconteur was much in demand.

JOHN RAMSDEN

Howe, Sir (Richard Edward) Geoffrey (*b.* Port Talbot, Glamorgan, 20 December 1926). Chancellor of the Exchequer and Foreign Secretary. In the first decade of Conservative government after 1979, Sir Geoffrey Howe occupied two of the most important offices of state. His capacity to work with a Prime Minister who in no way distanced herself from the concerns of the Treasury and the Foreign Office was crucial. Howe shares with Thatcher an extraordinary ability to master detail and to manage without sleep. There are strong similarities in their backgrounds – law as a springboard for politics, and the grocery trade. In temperament, however, they appear to be very different; a fiery Anglo-Saxon works with a phlegmatic Welshman.

South Wales during the year of the General Strike might appear to be an unlikely birthplace for a major Conservative politician. Conventional wisdom would suppose that such an environment could nurture only socialist convictions. The central clue to Howe's career is to be found in the constant challenge which he presents to such assumptions. His father was a solicitor in Port Talbot who later became a county coroner. His mother was the daughter of a Scotsman who eventually built up a chain of grocery shops in South Wales. It was Welsh chapel culture mixed with the cosmopolitan commerce of Cardiff and politics that were vaguely Liberal. In his childhood Howe saw poverty and unemployment at first hand, though his own family was never less than comfortable. His ambitious parents sent him to Winchester in 1940. He won an award to Trinity Hall, Cambridge, at the end of the war

but first he did his national service in the Royal Signals; he went up to Cambridge in 1948. There he took part in university Conservative politics but did not become President of the Cambridge Union. After his law degree he went into chambers in the Middle Temple and was called to the Bar in 1952. He threw himself into the affairs of the new Bow Group and started to write pamphlets. The reduction in the role of the state began to emerge as one theme in his writings.

Newly married and beginning to make his way as a barrister, Howe stood for Aberavon in the 1955 general election and again in 1959. He performed respectably but realized that even a local boy could never win. Elected for Bebington in Cheshire in 1964, he lost two years later and began a rather long search for a new seat. At this time he took on a good deal of legal work – including the Aberfan enquiry – and became a QC. In 1970 he was elected for Reigate and was immediately made Solicitor-General in the Heath government and received a knighthood. In this capacity he had an unusually central political role. His major initial impact lay in the drafting of the government's Industrial Relations Bill. Agreements between employers and unions were to be enforceable at law and there was to be a National Industrial Relations Court to try cases arising out of the legislation. It did not take long for difficulties of enforcement to manifest themselves. Howe remained convinced that this basic approach was correct but the government could not sustain the initiative. He also played a major part in drafting the European Communities Bill. In 1972 he was given the role of Consumer Affairs Minister with a seat in the cabinet. He set in motion the Office of Fair Trading and appeared firmly to endorse the legal controls on wages and prices on which the government embarked. Howe seemed to be in the van of the increasingly despairing efforts of the Heath government to maintain its authority. When it was defeated, he did not rush to distance himself from the policies which he had been lately advocating.

In February 1975 he put his name forward in the second ballot for the leadership of the Conservative Party, but the main contest was between MARGARET THATCHER and WILLIAM

Sir Geoffrey Howe (left) and Douglas Hurd arriving at Downing Street for a cabinet meeting, April 1986

WHITELAW. Howe gained 19 votes and was made Shadow Chancellor by Mrs Thatcher. He had an uncomfortable time confronting Denis Healey, whose comment that to be attacked by Geoffrey Howe was like being savaged by a dead sheep caught the public imagination. Nevertheless, Sir Geoffrey stuck to his task and moved quietly in the direction of greater economic liberalism. When the Conservatives won the 1979 general election the Treasury team was determined to make a fresh start, though there remained a general expectation that it would not be long before there was once again talk of a prices and incomes policy. However, the first budget set the tone of much of what was to follow. Reductions in both the standard and higher rates of taxation were accompanied by increases in VAT and prescription charges. The public sector borrowing requirement was to be reduced, an objective which found further expression in the 1980 budget which elaborated a medium-term financial strategy. Keynesian orthodoxy was further challenged in the 1981 budget in circumstances of acute public controversy about high unemployment and the control of inflation. By 1983 substantial progress in the reduction of inflation could be recorded, though bitter argument continued about the means which had been brought to bear and the cost of success. There was nothing exciting about Howe as a speaker, but, under the eye of the Prime Minister, there was no doubt that he was a major figure in the policy changes of these years.

Foreign Secretaries traditionally have rather more space in which to operate than ministers with major domestic responsibilities. Sir Geoffrey has conducted British foreign policy since 1983 with the same dogged determination that he displayed as Chancellor. Immediately he had to deal with the invasion of Grenada by the USA and the ban on union membership at GCHQ in Cheltenham. In Europe he had to play himself in amid another protracted budgetary wrangle. His patience and persistence were both displayed in the negotiations with Beijing which eventually produced the accord on the future of Hong Kong in December 1984. Howe has played a full part in complex East–West negotiations and in the problems of the Near East and Southern Africa. Inevitably, however, it has been the Prime Minister who has had the greatest impact on these issues. In the summer of 1989, against his wishes, he was moved from the Foreign Office and became Deputy Prime Minister, a position of uncertain political weight.

Howe has been at the centre of British politics for a decade. His role has been that of a subordinate whose gifts have nonetheless been vital in the consolidation of Conservative government. That may, or may not, be all that can be said about his career.

FURTHER READING

Hillman, J. and Clarke, P., *Geoffrey Howe: a Quiet Revolutionary* (London: Weidenfeld and Nicolson, 1988).

KEITH ROBBINS

Huddleston, (Ernest Urban) Trevor (*b.* Bedford, 15 June 1913). Bishop. A strong opponent of the apartheid policies of the South African government, Huddleston has always identified himself with the cause of black Africans. It was a relationship which began in the period when he was priest in charge of the Sophiatown and Orlando Mission of the Anglican Community of the Resurrection. He had been sent there by the community's mother house in Mirfield, Yorkshire (which he had entered in 1943 after being ordained to the Anglican priesthood in 1937), to further educational and social work. Huddleston came to feel deeply what he came to see as the injustices under which the people lived, and the police state brutalities of the regime as it affected native peoples. Among them, both as a pastor and as a defender of their rights (he was Provincial of the Order in Johannesburg from 1949 to 1955), he became much admired. Many have testified to his influence, including Desmond Tutu, first black Archbishop of Cape Town, whom Huddleston helped in his early days.

With his book *Naught for Your Comfort*, published in 1956, Huddleston drew international attention to the South African scene. A plea for the rights of black Africans there, it was a denunciation of those who denied them, and spoke prophetically of the ills which would arise from any continued denial of essential freedoms. The book's title, drawn from a poem of G. K. Chesterton's, echoes this theme:

I bring you naught for your comfort
Yea, naught for your desire,
Save that the sky grows darker yet
    And the sea rises higher.

Huddleston was Bishop of Masasi, Tanzania, from 1960 to 1968. After his return to Britain, as Bishop Suffragan of Stepney (1968–78), and subsequently, as Bishop of Mauritius and Archbishop of the Indian Ocean, he has continued to be a prominent opponent of apartheid, and is active in promoting the cause of social justice for all in South Africa and elsewhere.

WILLIAM PURCELL

Hume, (George) Basil (*b.* Newcastle upon Tyne, 2 March 1923). Archbishop of Westminster. Christened George, he took the name of Basil on becoming a monk. He was Abbot of the Benedictine monastery of Ampleforth, Yorkshire, from 1963 until 1976, when he was appointed ninth Archbishop of Westminster. It seemed a surprising choice. Every previous archbishop had been a diocesan priest; none since Manning had attended an English university; the last four had been trained at the English College, Rome; every one appointed in the twentieth century had been moderately working class. In contrast Hume's father, Sir William, was a distinguished physician and a Protestant, his mother French. He was educated at a public school, read history at Oxford and studied theology in Fribourg, Switzerland. Added to which, in 1976 his brother-in-law, Sir John Hunt, was Secretary of the Cabinet. Socially and educationally Hume was a member of the establishment in a way many Anglican bishops have been but Catholic ones have not.

Other characteristics remain more important. Hume is manifestly a monk, a man of prayer who has written about little except the spiritual life. Not much of an academic or originator of ideas, Hume's strength has lain rather in a frequent willingness to admit he does not know the answers. His fondness for squash and support for Newcastle United add the human touch. Beneath the gentle smile and slightly diffident manner lies, nevertheless, a clear and effective mind.

Hume has been the willing heir to the ecumenical breakthrough of the second Vatican Council. On the evening of his episcopal ordination in Westminster Cathedral, the monks of Ampleforth, joined by other Benedictines, Catholic and Anglican, sang Latin Vespers in Westminster Abbey, the first such service there since the sixteenth-century dissolution. An extraordinarily evocative ceremony, it seemed almost the beginning of a new era in English religion, and subsequently Hume's personal rapport with Archbishop Runcie has been very close indeed.

With his French mother (and he always spoke to her in French), Hume has been a natural European. His election in 1979 (and re-election in 1983) as President of the Council of European Bishops' Conferences reflects this and greatly extended his influence internationally and in Rome. In the public and political field he intervened effectively over arms sales to El Salvador in 1978 and over Ethiopia's famine in 1984, but he has never appeared a politically contentious bishop. He is reluctant to take sides and his heart is clearly elsewhere.

As an ecclesiastical leader he has been criticized for indecisiveness (as he was, it seems, when abbot). He is anxious to act from consensus rather than by the imposition of authority and he wants to provide space for others rather than to impose his own plans. However, he quickly and effectively reformed the administration of his diocese, dividing it between five area bishops, and he has carried over an abbot's care for his monks to one for his diocesan clergy. But his primary ecclesiastical role seems that of principal advocate for the mind of the second Vatican Council, and especially its central constitution *Lumen Gentium* in an age when, under John Paul II, the dominant tendency is to belittle the council and reassert a monarchical model. How long his influence can prevail is unpredictable but, at least to date, its effect has been to transform England from being one of the more conservative into one of the more liberal areas of world Catholicism.

WRITINGS

Searching for God (London: Hodder and Stoughton, 1977).
To Be a Pilgrim (London: Hodder and Stoughton, 1984).

FURTHER READING

Castle, Tony (ed.), *Basil Hume: a Portrait* (London: Collins, 1986).
Hastings, Adrian, *A History of English Christianity, 1920–1985* (London: Collins, 1986).

ADRIAN HASTINGS

Hume, John (*b.* Derry, 18 January 1937). Leader of the Social Democratic and Labour Party and Northern Ireland MEP. He was a founder member of the Catholic SDLP in 1970 and soon emerged as the party's key thinker; indeed he became the principal political strategist for constitutional nationalism in Ireland as a whole.

An ex-teacher (a graduate of St Patrick's College, Maynooth), Hume first came to prominence in the civil rights movement in Derry in 1968. In the Stormont general election the following year he was returned as MP for Foyle. He was heavily involved in the establishment of the power-sharing executive and was head of the Commerce Department. After the collapse of the executive, provoked by the Ulster Workers' Council strike of 1974, Hume devoted himself to internationalizing the 'Ulster question.' In 1979 he became leader of the SDLP and was elected to the European Parliament with an impressive 24.6 per cent of the vote. A fluent French speaker, he transcended the normal parochialism of Irish politics and had a major influence on élite opinion within both Europe and the USA.

Hume argued that Britain ought to lance the 'Protestant boil' (in his words) in order that moderate and accommodating tendencies would emerge within Unionism. Conveniently, he attributed Unionist obduracy not to the violent tactics or the unappealing sectarian face of Irish nationalism; rather it was owing to a lack of nerve on the part of the British state. Thus, the collapse of the power-sharing experiment was a result not of the Council of Ireland (and which SDLP leaders at the time claimed was an agency of Irish unification), but of the pusillanimity of the Labour Government in London in failing to resist 'the extremes of Unionism'. Undoubtedly Hume's greatest achievement was the signing in November 1985 of the Anglo-Irish Agreement, which was widely recognized as embodying his analysis. The agreement apparently gave the Dublin Government significant influence within Northern Ireland and was vigorously supported at first by the British Prime Minister, Margaret Thatcher. Hume, in accordance with his analysis, predicted Unionist accommodation with nationalism by the end of 1986. In this, at least, he proved to be over-optimistic.

Hume was, undoubtedly, the most skilful Ulster politician thrown up by the Troubles – a fact that should not be obscured by his penchant for ponderous 'history lessons' and inappropriate clichés. His thinking, though, lacked an economic dimension; the material benefits of the Union explained Unionist acquiescence in the Anglo-Irish Agreement, but the agreement did not lead to any wider reassessment of the Unionists' place within Ireland, nor indeed the much advertised isolation in urban areas of Sinn Fein.

Unlike his predecessor as leader of the SDLP, the MP for West Belfast Gerry Fitt, Hume came from an area where Catholic nationalists were in a majority. He often seemed to have correspondingly less grasp of the strength of communal feeling on the opposing side. As his admiring biographer Barry White makes clear, Hume sees himself in the Parnell mould. In 1984, addressing the SDLP conference, he attractively quoted Parnell on the need to 'leave no stone unturned . . . to conciliate the reasonable or unreasonable prejudices' of Irish Unionism. Simultaneously, he warned against the New Ireland Forum Report – which he inspired – becoming a 'nationalist revival mission'. His critics would allege that by his talks with Sinn Fein in 1987–8, and his rhetoric of 'lancing the Protestant boil', Hume has failed to live up to these high principles.

WRITINGS

'The Irish Question: a British problem', *Foreign Affairs*, 58 (1979–80).

FURTHER READING

Bew, Paul and Patterson, Henry, 'The New Stalemate: Unionism and the Anglo-Irish Agreement', in *Beyond the Rhetoric: Politics, the Economy and Social Policy in Northern Ireland*, ed. Paul Teague (London: Lawrence and Wishart, 1987), pp. 41–57.
White, Barry, *John Hume: Statesman of the Troubles* (Belfast: Blackstaff Press, 1984).

PAUL A. E. BEW

Hurd, Douglas (Richard) (*b*. Marlborough, Wiltshire, 8 March 1930). Conservative Home Secretary, Foreign Secretary and writer. He was appointed Home Secretary in 1985, having entered the cabinet in the previous year as Northern Ireland Secretary. An ability to write novels was no obstacle in the nineteenth century to becoming Prime Minister, and an aptitude for producing thrillers has not impeded Hurd's political progress. He has, however, other substantial attributes. His father was a Conservative MP, subsequently ennobled, who wrote for *The Times* for many years as its agricultural correspondent. Douglas was a King's Scholar and Newcastle Scholar at Eton and a major scholar at Trinity, Cambridge. He became President of the Cambridge Union in 1952 and then entered the Diplomatic Service. He served in Beijing (1954–6) and at the United Nations (1956–60), then spent three years as Private Secretary to the Permanent Under-Secretary at the Foreign Office and three years in the Rome Embassy. At this point, however, with a successful diplomatic career virtually guaranteed, he decided to change to politics.

In 1966 Hurd joined the Conservative Research Department and two years later headed its foreign affairs section. He then joined Edward Heath's private office as Private Secretary to the Leader of the Opposition some weeks after Heath had dismissed Enoch Powell from the shadow cabinet. It was the first of the many crises which Hurd, as his political aide, was to go through with Heath. He remained in this position after 1970 when Heath became Prime Minister. The account of his experiences – *An End to Promises* (1979) – remains of considerable value. It gives an insight not only into Heath's character and way of working but also into Hurd's own beliefs about the significance of the 'Heath experiment'. He did not disguise either the shortcomings of Heath's personality or the failures of the government, but argued that it had brought the country up against reality.

In 1974 Hurd himself entered the Commons as MP for Mid-Oxon, a seat, under a new name, which he has represented continuously since. It was not a very auspicious time to begin a parliamentary career. The Conservatives were in opposition and Heath, whom Hurd had served so loyally and intimately, was about to be overthrown. Nevertheless, his diplomatic background made him immediately useful and he became opposition spokesman on European Affairs from 1976 and Minister of State at the Foreign and Commonwealth Office in the first Thatcher government. Unlike some others who had been Heath associates or protégés, Hurd was able to make a successful transition under the new leadership. He was moved to the Home Office as Minister of State in 1983, a step which indicated that he was to be tested as an all-round minister rather than simply thought of as the Foreign Office specialist he was by background. That was followed by the appointment to Northern Ireland in 1984, suc-ceeding Jim Prior. It was a post for which he seemed well suited and in which he made a promising beginning, despite the intractable difficulties of the task. He had scarcely settled in, however, when he was brought back to the Home Office as Secretary of State. It is only in this office that he has had a period of sustained major responsibility, and he has impressed by his clear powers of exposition and judgement. Hurd's career began relatively late but it has flourished. In October 1989, as a result of the cabinet shuffle following Nigel Lawson's resignation, he became Foreign Secretary – the first former official in the Foreign Office ever to have become its political head. His interpretation of Conservatism, given his capacity to blend emphases often thought antagonistic, may be of major significance in the 1990s.

For illustration, see HOWE, GEOFFREY.

WRITINGS

An End to Promises (London: Collins, 1979).

KEITH ROBBINS

I

Illingworth, Leslie (*b.* Barry, Glamorgan, 2 September 1902; *d.* Sussex, 20 December 1979). Cartoonist. Illingworth has been described by the American cartoonist and historian Draper Hill as 'simply the finest draughtsman of our times to have devoted his energies to editorial caricature'. He was not a political animal in the way that Vicky was – he had no such allegiances. He was a perfectionist who was able, through his elegant balanced compositions, to transcend the use of labels and symbols so beloved by his predecessors.

Illingworth's professional career began while he was still a student at Cardiff Art School. In 1920 he gained a scholarship to the Royal College of Art, where he studied drawing, etching and architecture. Six months later he was offered and accepted a full-time job on the *Western Mail*, a post he held until 1926. In 1927 he made his first contribution (a joke cartoon) to *Punch*, and in due course he graduated to sharing the so-called big cuts (the leading political cartoons on prescribed topics) with Bernard Partridge and Ernest Shepard. It was during this time that he developed his unique and distinctive style of scraperboard work – a technique which involves the scratching of a black-coated board.

In 1939, in order to reach a wider audience and achieve greater editorial freedom, Illingworth joined the *Daily Mail* as chief political cartoonist. Coincident with this new era his style evolved further – penwork was replaced by brush, solid blacks, crayon and hand-lettered captions. Over the next 30 years he produced three or four cartoons a week for the *Daily Mail* while continuing to be responsible for a good proportion of *Punch* cartoons. He felt increasingly restricted by that magazine's policies until 1953, when, encouraged by Malcolm Muggeridge (who had just taken over the editorship), his satires became more trenchant.

Illingworth retired in 1969. He later re-emerged as guest cartoonist on *The Sun* and drew for the *News of the World* for three years.

FURTHER READING

Hill, Draper, *Illingworth on Target* (Boston: Wiggin Gallery, Boston Public Library, 1970).

LIZ OTTAWAY

Irwin, Lord [Wood, Edward (Frederick Lindley); Earl of Halifax] (*b.* Powderham Castle, Devon, 16 April 1881; *d.* Garrowby, Yorkshire, 23 December 1959). Viceroy of India. An outstanding representative of Britain abroad, his most creative tenure of office was as Viceroy (1926–31); although subsequently Foreign Secretary (1938–41) and Ambassador to the USA (1941–6), he was in both posts subordinate to the Prime Minister of the day.

The youngest child of 2nd Viscount Halifax, the early deaths of his brothers left him heir to great Yorkshire estates, which he inherited in 1934. He was temperamentally a countryman and scholar, and deeply rooted in his Christian faith. After Eton and Christ Church, Oxford, he became a Fellow of All Souls, served in the Great War, and was Ripon's Conservative MP from 1910 to 1925, when he was created Lord Irwin, prior to his Indian appointment. Although unambitious politically, and more reflective than effective in government, he rose to cabinet rank in the 1920s via colonial affairs and education before being called to the Viceroyalty (on the king's suggestion) – a challenge which elicited the best from him.

Irwin's Indian years were stormy because of the increasing tempo of nationalist political agitation orchestrated by Congress and Gandhi. The Statutory Commission, appointed in 1927 to report on India's constitution, was totally British, and consequently unanimously criticized by political India as indicative of British reluctance to grant real reform. Opposition to its work under Sir John

Simon was strident and populist, wherever it travelled. Irwin shared with Birkenhead, Secretary of State for India, responsibility for this miscalculation. Thereafter he was sensitive and imaginative in handling Indians and their sentiments. Although adamantine against violence and civil disobedience, he was radical in pursuing conciliation as the true foundation for peace in India and for a British presence. In 1929 he persuaded the new Labour government to announce a round table conference of British and Indian representatives in London to consider India's future constitution, combined with a statement ('the Irwin Declaration') that India's constitutional goal was dominion status. Even this, and Irwin's patient discussions with Indian leaders, could not deflect Congress from its demand for independence and a civil disobedience campaign (1930–1), which began with Gandhi's famous Salt March. Profoundly aware of Mahatma Gandhi's uniqueness in Indian eyes, and convinced that he was that enigmatic blend of the saintly and the political, Irwin handled Gandhi's arrest most delicately; and then in 1931 laid aside self-importance or any false dignity of office to hold prolonged conversations with Gandhi which enabled the Mahatma to persuade Congressmen to abandon opposition temporarily and send him as Congress representative to the forthcoming London conference. Acute observers were convinced that like had met like: two men of deep faith met in warmth and trust and drove a hard bargain (though Conservatives at home were hostile to his declaration and the spectacle of his meetings with an ex-prisoner). Sadly their initiative floundered at the end of 1931 under another Viceroy and growing political pressure for a tough stance on both sides. (Irwin was appointed GCSI and GCIE in 1926 and KG in 1931.)

Irwin would have preferred after India to devote himself to Yorkshire, the Middleton foxhounds and Oxford University, of which he became Chancellor in 1933. But he was persuaded back into government, not least to help prepare the new Government of India Bill, which was to be the fruition of the discussions he had initiated in 1929. He was drawn into foreign affairs, and has been criticized for naïvely meeting Hitler in late 1937 and failing to discern the true nature of the Nazi leadership. He became Foreign Secretary when Eden resigned early in 1938, and thereby accepted that, unlike Eden, he would follow his Prime Minister rather than initiate in foreign policy. (He weakened his position thereby; but he also later escaped public odium.) Acutely conscious of British military weakness and the practical problems of defending Czechoslovakia, he did not oppose Chamberlain's policy of 'appeasement': symptomatic of his subordination was his absence from Chamberlain's crucial meetings with Hitler. Nor did he use his full influence on Chamberlain to achieve a more national government determined to re-arm. But rapidly he recognized how inadequate conciliation was in these European circumstances, and threw his weight behind re-armament and British support for Europe's remaining 'small nations'. Further, he welcomed Churchill as leader of a national government in 1940, particularly as there had briefly been a prospect of his own summons to that role, for which he felt quite unfitted.

Within months his new chief urged him to go as envoy to Washington: this was not his milieu or *métier*, and there was suspicion that Churchill was getting rid of him, but his sense of duty overcame personal inclination. Although he became increasingly effective as an envoy, and then after Pearl Harbour in coordinating the war effort of the British and American governments, he was overshadowed by Churchill and weakened by the Prime Minister's intimacy with Roosevelt, which excluded him; and, indeed, he wished to come home. Ever the patriot, he stayed, and participated in the beginnings of the United Nations and in negotiations for an American postwar loan to Britain. Just as he had misread Nazi Germany in 1937, now he underestimated events in Russia. But his political career was ending. An earldom in 1944 and the OM in 1946 were fitting honours for great labours for Britain, at home and abroad.

His last years were more private and tranquil, though saddened by one son's wartime death. He resumed his ties with Eton and his beloved All Souls, his work for Oxford, his estates, his hunt and his local church, and entered new pastures by becoming Chancellor of Sheffield University, chairman of the BBC's advisory council, and author of memoirs redolent of himself but which revealed little new of the turbulent events in which he had been a central figure. He died at home in Garrowby just after his golden wedding – one devoted to wife and children, to his country, and his God. Halifax was a man of simplicity and humility, despite high birth and office and a commanding presence (even though one arm was atrophied and handless from birth); for him inner peace was more important than political achievement.

WRITINGS

Fullness of Days (London: Collins, 1957).

FURTHER READING

Birkenhead, Lord, *Halifax* (London: Hamish Hamilton, 1965).
Brown, Judith M., *Gandhi and Civil Disobedience: the Mahatma in Indian Politics* (Cambridge: Cambridge University Press, 1977), chaps. 1–4.
Gopal, S., *The Viceroyalty of Lord Irwin 1926–1931* (Oxford: Clarendon Press, 1957).

JUDITH M. BROWN

Isaacs, Rufus. See READING, LORD.

Ismay, Hastings (Lionel) [Baron Ismay of Wormington] (**'Pug'**) (*b.* Naini Tal, India, 21 June 1887; *d.* Wormington, Worcestershire, 17 December 1965). General, member of the secretariat of the Committee of Imperial Defence (Secretary, 1938–40) and Chief Staff Officer to the Prime Minister (1940–5). Completely trusted by Churchill, he was an invaluable bridge between the civil and military sections of the government and, later, between the British and American authorities as the counterpart of Roosevelt's emissary and go-between, Harry Hopkins. Ismay's value as a top liaison officer and an 'oiler of wheels' has been widely attested, notably by Churchill and Eisenhower, but his precise contribution to specific decisions remains elusive. He shunned the limelight, did not keep a diary and played

down his personal achievements in his *Memoirs* (1960). His career still awaits a thorough assessment.

After education at Charterhouse and Sandhurst, Ismay was commissioned into an Indian Army cavalry regiment in 1905. He served throughout World War I in Africa and thereafter made his mark as a staff officer, notably in his first term with the Committee of Imperial Defence secretariat (1925–30). After a further period in India as Military Secretary to the Viceroy, Lord Willingdon (1931–3), Ismay returned to the CID as Deputy Secretary and succeeded his mentor, Lord Hankey, as Secretary in 1938. Appointed a non-executive member of the Chiefs of Staff Committee just before Churchill's advent to the premiership, and retained by him, Ismay ensured that the War Cabinet secretariat would develop into a first-class machine.

Ismay accompanied Churchill to nearly all the wartime allied conferences and his responsibilities were greatly increased, after the USA entered the war, as the chief liaison officer between the Chiefs of Staff and the American Joint Chiefs of Staff. Ismay's main role seems to have been to mollify Marshall and Eisenhower, when Churchill's ebullience and Alanbrooke's abrasiveness had irritated or confused them, by explaining Britain's willingness to cooperate fully with her ally. Thus after the Casablanca Conference (January 1943) Ismay convinced Eisenhower that the British had complete confidence in him as supreme commander in the Mediterranean, and also that the invasion of Sicily was the next logical step after victory in North Africa. Ismay from the outset (June 1941) had taken a more favourable view of Russia's ability to survive the German invasion than most of his colleagues, and in October 1943 he convinced Stalin that the Allied invasion of North-West Europe could not take place before the early summer of 1944.

Ismay's main personal responsibility was to supervise and promote deception measures. He enjoyed a brilliant success with Operation Mincemeat, which distracted German attention from the Allied preparations to invade Sicily. As early as the Teheran Conference he gained Russian cooperation for the wide range of deception measures ('the Bodyguard of

Lies') which completely misled the Germans as to the intended landing beaches for Operation Overlord.

By 1944 relations between the Chiefs of Staff and Churchill were becoming strained, with Ismay uncomfortably in the middle. The crisis came at the Quebec Conference in September 1944 when, to prevent a mass resignation by the Chiefs of Staff, Ismay formally offered his own, only to have it rejected by the Prime Minister. The end of the war brought only a brief respite.

In 1947 Ismay performed the most distasteful assignment of his career as Chief of Staff to Lord Mountbatten, the last Viceroy of India. He hated the role of 'undertaker to the Raj', but was convinced that partition was unavoidable. After a brief period as Secretary of State for Commonwealth Relations (1951–2), Ismay accomplished his last great public service as the first Secretary-General of NATO (1952–7) in Paris, where his tact, geniality and vast experi-

ence turned what might have been a cumbersome bureaucracy riddled with intrigue and mutual suspicions into something approaching a model of international cooperation.

In retirement Ismay, who was happily married with three daughters, took up the country life he had always hankered after on his estate in Worcestershire.

FURTHER READING

Bryant, Sir Arthur, *The Turn of the Tide* (London: Collins, 1957).

——, *Triumph in the West* (London: Collins, 1959).

Colville, J. R., *The Churchillians* (London: Weidenfeld and Nicolson, 1981).

Wheeler-Bennett, Sir John (ed.), *Action this Day: Working with Churchill* (London: Macmillan, 1968).

Wingate, Sir Ronald, *Lord Ismay: a Biography* (London: Hutchinson, 1970).

B. J. BOND

J

Jellicoe, Sir **John (Rushworth)** [Earl Jellicoe] (*b.* Southampton, Hampshire, 5 December 1859; *d.* London, 20 November 1935). Admiral of the Fleet. Jellicoe came from a Hampshire family which had close links with seafaring over several generations. His father commanded one of the Royal Mail Steam Packet Company's vessels and went on to become commodore of its fleet and a director of the firm. Young John was educated at private schools in Hampshire and Sussex before joining the training ship *Britannia* in 1872. The teenage cadet distinguished himself both in his examinations and at games. At the conclusion of this period, two years later, he joined HMS *Newcastle*, a sailing frigate with auxiliary steam-power, and proceeded to see the world. Service in other vessels followed, interspersed with gunnery courses at Greenwich and Portsmouth. Jellicoe was promoted Commander in 1892 and Captain five years later. In the latter year he departed for East Asia, where he served on the China Station. He was injured when taking part in the international expedition against the Boxers in 1900; a bullet entered his lung and remained there undisturbed until the end of his life.

On his return to England in 1901 it was apparent that Jellicoe was a marked man professionally. He went to the Admiralty, where his task was to inspect ships being built in private yards and suggest improvements in the light of his practical experience. On Clydeside he also inspected a daughter of the owner of the Clan line of steamers with considerable approval: they were married in 1902. The marriage to Gwendoline Cayzer gave Jellicoe a social position and a wealthy and energetic wife. A further period of service at sea followed in the Atlantic and the Mediterranean before he was appointed Director of Naval Ordnance in 1905. Two years later, Jellicoe was promoted Rear-Admiral and became Second-in-Command of the Atlantic Fleet. He was

knighted in the same year. In 1908 he returned to the Admiralty as Controller. In this capacity he was at the heart of the discussions and decisions about gunnery in the new *Dreadnought* era. The calibre of the British guns appeared to be greater than those of their German potential opponents but there were doubts about the quality of the British shells. Sir John had a reputation as a hard and efficient worker, though doubts on the gunnery question had not been resolved when he again left the Admiralty in 1910 to take command of the Atlantic Fleet. At the end of 1911 he became Second-in-Command of the Home Fleet, leapfrogging more senior admirals in the process. The First Lord of the Admiralty, Winston Churchill, had been persuaded that Jellicoe was to be the Nelson of the war that might well lie ahead. When Sir John returned to the Admiralty as Second Sea Lord in December 1912, however, his relationship with the First Lord was somewhat stormy, particularly on matters of naval discipline. Jellicoe was also far from confident that British ships were in fact as superior as his political master supposed.

A few days before the outbreak of war in 1914, Jellicoe was appointed Commander-in-Chief. This step did not come as a surprise. He appeared to be about the right age, nearly 55, and to have acquired the necessary mixture of experience, except perhaps in the matter of tactics and strategy. He was not a demonstrative or flamboyant figure but he inspired trust. His responsibility was awesome. It was widely believed that the Royal Navy would play a decisive role in the war. Jellicoe was uncomfortably aware that he might lose it in an afternoon. By the spring of 1916 no major full confrontation between the British and German fleets had occurred. There was some criticism that Jellicoe was unenterprising. Impatient spirits wanted to see action against the German High Seas Fleet. On 31 May, at the Battle of Jutland, they had their wish, though it did not produce a clear-cut conclusion; neither side dealt the other a crippling blow. Arguably, the balance of advantage lay with the Royal Navy, but the British public looked for a more decisive victory than had in fact happened. Jellicoe was the obvious scapegoat and he was indeed deeply depressed by the outcome. In sections of the press he was adversely compared with the more glamorous and accessible figure of DAVID BEATTY. Perhaps he had indeed erred on the side of caution, though the detailed decisions of the day continue to be debated down to the present. After Jutland Jellicoe worked hard to 'learn the lessons' of the engagement, but by the end of the year Beatty succeeded him as commander of the Grand Fleet.

In December 1916 Sir John became First Sea Lord, where his major responsibility was to deal with the U-boat menace. To some minds, the organization of convoys was an obvious solution. Jellicoe took his time to be persuaded, but he was not as unimaginative as he has sometimes been presented, not least by the Prime Minister of the time, Lloyd George. By this stage in the war, however, the combination of burdens he had assumed adversely affected Jellicoe's health and nerves. He was out of his depth in the political manoeuvrings which undermined his position. Lloyd George thought him too pessimistic. In turn, he expressed a predictable contempt for politicians. However, in December 1917 he was unceremoniously dismissed. A peerage followed by way of compensation. Jellicoe began to prepare accounts of his wartime experiences. After the war he undertook an extensive Empire tour to advise the various dominion governments on their naval forces, though he still personally hankered after the idea of a unitary imperial navy. He became Governor-General of New Zealand from 1920 to 1924, and accepted an earldom on laying down that office. In the last decade of his life he interested himself in scouting and shooting but was inevitably drawn into controversy about Jutland, however much he tried to avoid it. The decisions he took in the evening of 31 May 1916 overshadowed everything he had previously done and was to do subsequently. He had not turned out to be the Nelson of World War I, but neither had he lost that war in an afternoon.

FURTHER READING

Bacon, Sir R. H., *The Life of John Rushworth, Earl Jellicoe* (London: Cassell, 1936).
Patterson, A. Temple, *Jellicoe* (London: Macmillan, 1969).

KEITH ROBBINS

Jenkins, (David) Clive (*b*. Port Talbot, Glamorgan, 2 May 1926). Trade-union leader. Jenkins was among the most articulate and controversial British trade-union leaders of the 1970s and 1980s, a pioneer in white-collar trade unionism, and an important influence on the left wing of the Labour Party. Educated at local state schools and in evening classes at Swansea Technical College, he started work at the age of 13 and soon became active in the Association of Scientific Workers. With the influential support of Harry Knight, left-wing leader of the rival Association of Supervisory Staffs, Executives and Technicians, he rose rapidly: an ASSET national officer at 28, General Secretary at 34. (His elder brother Tom also gained high trade-union office, being General Secretary of the Transport Salaried Staffs Association from 1977 to 1982.)

When ASW and ASSET amalgamated in 1968 to form the Association of Scientific, Technical and Managerial Staffs, Jenkins was first joint leader, then from 1970 General Secretary. This was a strategic post in the 1970s: the areas where Jenkins's union recruited were among Britain's fastest-growing spheres of employment, and even more of union membership. In 1968 ASTMS had 70,000 members; by 1977, more than 430,000. White-collar workers to whom union organization had previously often been anathema were now amenable to recruitment; an expansion in which Jenkins's own persuasive appeals to what he christened the 'rebellious salariat' contributed much.

The union's role, and that of Jenkins himself, was somewhat paradoxical. Members were on average considerably more affluent than those of most unions and more likely to be Conservative voters; but ASTMS was not only affiliated to the Labour Party, it took a consistently left-wing stance there and within the TUC. Jenkins was a crucial advocate of the left's campaign for constitutional reform within Labour in the late 1970s, helping introduce a new method of electing the party leader and mandatory reselection for Labour MPs. He was also a strong supporter of unilateral nuclear disarmament. In 1988, having steered his union into merger with Ken Gill's Technical, Administrative and Supervisory Staffs, he retired to Tasmania with his second wife.

The author or co-author of numerous books on trade unionism and the future of employment, and an enthusiast for workers' education and labour market planning, Jenkins gained a deserved reputation as one of the few real intellectuals among British union bosses. But this, when combined with his personal flamboyance, taste for political intrigue and apparent delight in irritating the more traditional brethren, won him more admirers than friends within the movement.

WRITINGS

Jenkins, C. and Sherman, B., *The Collapse of Work* (London: Eyre Methuen, 1979).
——, *The Rebellious Salariat: White Collar Unionism* (London: Routledge and Kegan Paul, 1979).

STEPHEN HOWE

Jenkins, Roy (Harris) [Lord Jenkins of Hillhead] (*b.* Pontypool, Monmouthshire, 11 November 1920). Labour Home Secretary and Chancellor of the Exchequer, President of the EEC Commission, and first leader of the Social Democratic Party. Jenkins ranks with R. A. Butler among the best prime ministers Britain never had. He was the most distinguished Home Secretary (1965–7 and 1974–6) and one of the best Chancellors of the Exchequer (1967–70) of the postwar period. In 1976 he withdrew from domestic politics to become the first British President of the EEC Commission (1977–80); but he made a bold re-entry in 1981 to help found the Social Democratic Party, of which he was the first leader (1981–3). Neither in 1983 nor in 1987, however, did the SDP–Liberal Alliance

achieve the electoral breakthrough which would have brought him back to power.

From a mining background in South Wales, Jenkins became one of the grandest figures in British politics. But his impeccable roots are misunderstood by those who accuse him of betraying them. He was born into the party purple. His father, Arthur Jenkins – a gentle, moderate, widely read and civilized man from whom his son derived liberal values and a European outlook – was MP for Pontypool and wartime Parliamentary Private Secretary to Clement Attlee. Jenkins was brought up in a confident Labour tradition of civic responsibility and steady social improvement; his was never the Labour Party of class war and strident protest.

From Abersychan County School he won a place at Balliol College, Oxford, where his contemporaries included Edward Heath, Denis Healey and Anthony Crosland, who became a close friend, but he twice failed to become President of the Union. From Oxford he progressed naturally, after war service decoding signals at Bletchley, into Parliament – first for the condemned seat of Southwark Central, which he won at a by-election in 1948, then for Birmingham, Stechford, which he represented from 1950 to 1976.

From the outset of his career he saw Labour as the successor to the Edwardian Liberal Party – a non-doctrinaire party of moderate progress, capable of appealing to the whole of the non-Conservative part of the nation. This was a view he expressed explicitly in a characteristic personal manifesto, *Pursuit of Progress* (1953), and implicitly in several elegant historical biographies, most notably *Asquith* (1964), with whom he closely identifies. During the bitter internecine battles of 1951–63, Jenkins was a prominent supporter of Hugh Gaitskell; he differed from Gaitskell only in having become an ardent champion of Britain's entry into the EEC.

When Labour came to power in 1964 Jenkins made an immediate mark as Minister of Aviation, and was quickly promoted to Home Secretary – an office whose reactionary ethos he set out to transform. As a backbencher he had already piloted through Parliament an Act liberalizing the law on censorship of printed material. He now abolished theatre censorship as well and gave crucial government time to Bills legalizing homosexuality and abortion. These measures both symbolized and embodied the relaxation of social restraints on personal morality characteristic of the 1960s. While the press hailed the 'permissive society', Jenkins preferred to speak of the 'civilized society'.

Following devaluation in 1967, Jenkins replaced James Callaghan as Chancellor of the Exchequer at an exceptionally difficult time. Though he found time to introduce a number of structural reforms, his principal effort had to be devoted to holding down consumption and boosting exports in order to get the balance of payments back in surplus. After 'two years' hard slog' the figures finally came right in August 1969. Scrupulously, however, Jenkins disappointed Labour hopes of a generous pre-election budget. In consequence he was widely – though the poll evidence suggests unfairly – blamed for the loss of the 1970 general election.

In July 1970 Jenkins was elected deputy leader in succession to George Brown, but was soon isolated as the party swung leftwards, repudiating in particular the Wilson government's commitment to seek entry to the EEC. In October 1971 Jenkins led 69 Labour MPs in voting against the party whip in support of the Conservative Government's negotiated terms; but in April 1972 he was driven to resign. Many felt that he should have stayed and fought. It was an unhappy period in which Jenkins' sense of direction faltered. When Labour returned to office in 1974 Jenkins went back to the Home Office; but his second period there was overshadowed by Irish terrorism, while politically he was preoccupied with winning the EEC referendum. When, on Wilson's retirement, he won only 56 votes in the contest for the succession, he chose instead to accept the presidency of the EEC Commission.

Coming fresh to Brussels, Jenkins found some difficulty learning to operate the complex multinational bureaucracy. On the other hand he had considerable success in giving the commission a higher political profile; in particular he established the president's right to attend world economic summits. But the major achievement of his term was the creation in 1978 of the European Monetary System – which, to his chagrin, successive British governments have refused to join.

In 1981 Jenkins returned dramatically to British politics. With Labour, following its loss of office in 1979, swinging ever further to the left and the Conservatives, under Margaret Thatcher, moving sharply to the right, there was unsatisfied public demand for a credible third party that might fill the gap. Jenkins joined with three other disillusioned Labour ministers and a score of MPs to form the SDP. In electoral alliance with the Liberals the new party won a string of by-elections: Jenkins himself returned to the Commons in March 1982 for Glasgow, Hillhead. But then the Falklands War transformed the political landscape. Despite 26 per cent of the vote in 1983 the Alliance won only 23 seats; Jenkins surrendered the leadership to DAVID OWEN, whose relationship with the Liberals was much less positive. After a second disappointment in 1987 the SDP split. Jenkins helped lead the larger faction into a new merged party, the Social and Liberal Democrats; but the standard which he had raised in 1981 was now severely tattered. Elected Chancellor of Oxford University in 1987, he accepted a peerage, resumed his historical writing with studies of *Truman* (1986) and *Baldwin* (1987), and settled urbanely into the role of elder statesman.

Jenkins' reputation will rest principally upon three achievements, the ultimate importance of two of which it is still too early to assess. Britain's belated membership of the EEC represents an historic shift to which Jenkins, second only to Edward Heath and at great personal cost, contributed decisively. The 'civilized society', however, has provoked a backlash which has called in question many of the libertarian gains then made. Similarly the attempt to reshape the mould of British politics, after coming tantalizingly close to success in 1981, seems at the end of the 1980s to have foundered. Yet unquestionably, whatever the eventual outcome of these developments, Roy Jenkins has been one of the most creative, lucid and widely admired politicians of the postwar years.

Roy Jenkins returning to the House of Commons after his by-election win at Hillhead, Glasgow, March 1982; with him is Shirley Williams

WRITINGS

Pursuit of Progress (London: Heinemann, 1953).
Asquith (London: Collins, 1964).
What Matters Now (London: Fontana, 1972).
Partnership of Principle (London: Secker and Warburg, 1985).

FURTHER READING

Campbell, John, *Roy Jenkins: a Biography* (London: Weidenfeld and Nicolson, 1983).

JOHN CAMPBELL

Jones, Jack [James Larkin] (*b.* Liverpool, 29 March 1913). Trade-union leader. As the General Secretary of the Transport and General Workers Union (1969–78), he was arguably the most powerful and effective trade-union leader in Britain in the second half of the twentieth century. Sometimes attacked as 'the Emperor Jones' and 'the most powerful man in Britain', he dominated the TUC and was the architect of the Social Contract which sustained the Labour governments of the 1970s.

Brought up in Liverpool, he was first an engineering worker and then, after a period of unemployment, a docker. He took part in hunger marches and the Spanish Civil War, in which he was wounded, before becoming a full-time official of the TGWU. In Coventry during World War II he multiplied union membership and backed the emerging shop-stewards movement – a trend opposed by the national leadership under ARTHUR DEAKIN. He became general secretary in 1969, with the aim of 'giving the union back to the members', and moved it towards the left. With membership reaching two million, he dominated Labour Party conferences. He campaigned successfully against industrial-relations legislation and for a huge increase in old-age pensions, until that time an issue frequently championed by the Conservatives. Jones was to campaign for pensioners throughout the rest of his life.

When the Labour Party returned to power in 1974, it largely followed the Jones blueprint – a liaison committee between government, party and TUC, and a conciliation and arbitration service, based on his wartime experiences, removing the government from most disputes. The Social Contract restricted wages in return for what were, effectively, guaranteed minimum increases and social legislation that included improved family allowances and better health and safety at work.

Jones worked for the end of union proscription on communists and, as Chairman of the TUC International Committee, for closer relations with Eastern-bloc unions. Exceptionally thorough, and personally austere (his politics closely supported by his wife Evelyn), he managed both to allow more democracy into the union and to retain tight control until his last conference (he retired in 1978) – something his successors failed to manage.

WRITINGS

Union Man (London: Collins, 1986).

MARTIN ADENEY

Jones, Thomas ('T. J.') (*b.* Rhymney, Monmouthshire, 27 September 1870; *d.* London, 15 October 1955). Deputy Secretary of the Cabinet, political diarist, and academic. The eldest of nine children of a local storekeeper, Jones grew up in a strong cultural and religious context of Welsh literacy and nonconformity. He left grammar school at the age of 13 and earned a living as a time-keeper in the Rhymney Ironworks, hoping initially to become a Methodist Minister. Able though he was as a preacher, however, he lost the taste for evangelical religion during his time at University College at Aberystwyth; instead, he went to Glasgow University in 1895 and emerged with first class honours in economic science. Deeply influenced by the teachers he had come across, most of all by Sir Henry Jones (moral philosophy) and William Smart (political economy), he built an array of interests on these Welsh and Scottish foundations, principally in social problems of poverty and working conditions.

Local involvement through the Glasgow Fabian Society, and in slum rehabilitation, aroused his political conscience. He joined the Independent Labour Party in 1895 and by the early 1900s had acquired a wider reputation as a socialist of practical orientation, in the Fabian tradition, concerned with research into problems of housing, health or trade unionism as a means to promote state action, guided by the wisdom of an informed élite. Much of his life's work was to consist of subtle brokerage between intellectuals, politicians and other 'great contemporaries'; but, unlike most of the ILP and the Fabians, his inner vision was un-English and returned habitually to Wales. For this reason, Lloyd George found him congenial. Their first meeting, when Lloyd George was Chancellor of the Exchequer, led to the offer of appointment as Secretary of the Welsh National Health Insurance Commission in 1912.

By then Jones's experience had been broadened as the result of a tour as Barrington Lecturer in Political Economy, speaking all across Ireland in the summers of 1904 and 1905, and by his appointment as Professor of Economics at the Queen's University of Belfast in 1909. The contacts made here were to be immensely valuable when, as Lloyd George's private negotiator, he dealt secretly with the leaders of Sinn Fein in 1920–1. Meanwhile friendships had grown in circles of progressive opinion and among wealthy philanthropists such as the Liberal supporter and coal-owner David Davies.

Thus Jones was far from being 'the little Welsh socialist' that some Civil Service mandarins dubbed him when, in December 1916, Lloyd George, now Prime Minister, offered him a post as Assistant Secretary in the newly formed Cabinet Office after Asquith's downfall. His was a network of acquaintance which made it easy, for example, serving Ramsay MacDonald in 1929, to assemble the most celebrated economists of the day to form the Economic Advisory Council; equally his own qualifications as political analyst justified his position on the cabinet's Reconstruction Committee in 1917.

Jones remained as Deputy Secretary of the Cabinet under Sir Maurice Hankey until his retirement, aged 60, in 1930. Here, in a way unusual in Whitehall and with no subsequent parallels, he served four Prime Ministers as administrator, adviser, fount of ideas, part-time speech-writer and, occasionally, conscience. A lifelong negotiator, he never lost the radical impulse, and he saw himself as 'a believer in ordered progress . . . a sort of Burke with a leaven of Shelley'.

With Lloyd George he was on terms of closest intellectual understanding, and probably Jones's greatest service to national politics lay in his role as go-between with the Irish, in the north as well as the south, interpreting each side to the other, a work crowned with the Treaty in 1921. Friendly as he became with Baldwin, there was a gulf of political philosophy; perhaps sadly it was the relationship with MacDonald that was least easy. He played a significant part, beyond that of cabinet bureaucrat, in a range of issues, such as post-war planning; policy towards Russia; the various European conferences of the early 1920s (at one of which Welsh briefly became the language of diplomacy); the great strikes of 1919, 1921 and 1926 and the government's emergency preparations to meet them; unemployment; the rationalization of industry; and the future of India. His observations of episodes such as Black Friday in 1921 or the Zinoviev letter are those of an insider habituated to the wheelings and dealings of politicians climbing and descending the greasy pole.

There was time in all this for other concerns, such as the Gregynog Press, which produced fine editions for 20 years, for voluminous correspondence, much of which appeared in *Diary with Letters 1931–50* (1954), and above all for the diary, which records in their original vigour what ministers actually said and did in the cabinets and committees Jones served for 14 years. Sparkling accounts of Lloyd George's table talk or Baldwin's weekends at Chequers, of Churchill's indiscreet comments and the characteristic flavours of Robert Horne, A. J. Balfour and Jimmy Thomas fill the 17 small volumes privately printed in Switzerland. He was prevented by the dictates of official secrecy from publishing even extracts in his own lifetime and the work – of incalculable value to British historians – was finally issued in 1969–70 as *Whitehall Diary*.

Jones retired in 1930 and became first secretary of the Pilgrim Trust which, by appealing to the millionaire American Edward Harkness, he had helped to create. For more than a decade he combined a variety of charitable and public services before returning to Aberystwyth

in 1944 as College President and immersing himself in the politics of Welsh academe. His last achievement was the foundation of Coleg Harlech, a 'college of the second chance' for adult education. Apart from the many lectures and essays on government, public administration, education or Welsh affairs, a huge range of material survives in the National Library of Wales, witness to his remarkable range and intellectual fertility.

WRITINGS

Diary with Letters, 1931–50 (London: Oxford University Press, 1954).
Thomas Jones: Whitehall Diary, 3 vols., ed. Keith Middlemas (London: Oxford University Press, 1969–70).

KEITH MIDDLEMAS

Joseph, Sir **Keith (Sinjohn)** [Baron Joseph of Portsoken in the City of London] (*b.* London, 17 January 1918). Senior Conservative minister. Lord Joseph – still thought of by most people as 'Sir Keith' – has left more monuments than it is given to most politicians to leave behind them. Several of them he is thoroughly ashamed of (and there was never a politician more enthusiastic about apologizing for past sins: the popular image of Sir Keith was always of an anguished face and hands wrung in agonized contrition). As a big-spending Housing Minister from 1962 to 1964 he pulled down acres of little terraced houses and put up tower blocks that were memorials to all that was worst – but best intentioned – in the days of government-provided housing. He is ashamed, too, of his record, as a big-spending Social Services Minister (1970–4), in reorganizing the Health Service in a way that pleased nobody. His much bigger monument is an intellectual and spiritual one: in a sense Keith Joseph invented Thatcherism.

There is much at the DHSS that he remains proud of: he switched resources to what he called 'the afflictions', such as rheumatism and senility, which a health service can alleviate if it cannot cure. He focused attention on the 'cycle of deprivation', a phrase he invented and which passed into the vocabulary of social workers trying to break through the seeming inevitability of problem parents producing problem children, and so on, indefinitely. It was to do something about poverty, he always claims, that he entered politics in the first place. For some Conservative tastes, he was always a bit 'pi': 'The only boring Jew I've ever known', was what Harold Macmillan called him.

For a few brief, extraordinary weeks in 1974 it seemed that Joseph might be the man to whom the Tory Party, at one of its lowest ebbs, would turn as leader. It was only when he stepped down from the leadership battle that Margaret Thatcher entered it. He had ceased to be a serious contender when he created a storm with a speech which the media seized on as a suggestion of compulsory birth control for the lower social classes. He was deeply hurt that, given his record on behalf of the poor, he could be so misrepresented. But he could see, as the whole party could now see, that there were parts of the rough old world of politics that Keith Joseph was unable to cope with.

Most politicians, thwarted from the top job,

Sir Keith Joseph, June 1983

are bitter. Characteristically, however, he threw himself wholeheartedly behind the new leader. His joy was that of a schoolmaster watching his favourite pupil rocketing to heights to which he could never aspire himself.

The contrast between the rigorous Thatcherite Keith Joseph and the free-spending Keith Joseph of the 1960s and early 1970s is one of the intriguing paradoxes of modern politics. Joseph himself, never missing a chance for self-effacement, makes much of his own inconsistency, and of his 'conversion' to true Conservatism. He puts a precise date to his conversion: April 1974.

In fact his politics were more consistent than he likes to suggest. He was always a rigorous believer in free-enterprise economics as the key to prosperity. There was no inconsistency between that and the ambition to spread prosperity where it is needed; or with holding 'liberal' views, which he has always held, on matters such as capital punishment and race relations. In that sense, Joseph was, and remains, much more of an old-fashioned, pre-Thatcherite Tory than he is prepared to admit.

But after his conversion of 1974 he was convinced that little can be done for the underdog until society repents its old sins of trying to solve social problems by throwing taxpayers' money at them. State planning cannot create the wealth needed for a dignified society: only entrepreneurs can do that.

In the period 1974–9 Joseph threw himself into the process of getting this point across – to politicians, to industrialists, to academics, to the media, to young people. His base of operations was the Centre for Policy Studies, which won over hearts and minds to the new Conservatism in quarters, in the business world and elsewhere, where the traditional Tory Party had been regarded with despair or cynicism.

Unlikely revolutionary that he is, Joseph thus contributed massively to the revolutionary change effected by Margaret Thatcher in the character of the Conservative Party. It is a party which does not take kindly to revolutionaries, and it would have known how to destroy, or laugh out of court, anyone else doing what he did; Joseph's reputation for total honesty and sincerity helped him to survive, to lay an intellectual foundation for the policies to be followed when Mrs Thatcher formed her government in 1979.

In that government, Joseph's role was to provide her with moral and intellectual encouragement when she was under pressure to make a 'U-turn': he gave her, so to speak, the convictions of her courage. As Industry Secretary (1979–81), although frequently portrayed as indecisive – for he saw every side of every question – he was in fact tougher, more Thatcherite, than the Prime Minister in dealing with a major steel strike and in trying to cut losses at British Leyland.

His passionate belief in the right of all sections of society to a dignity in their life remained, even when he was being arraigned as the cruellest of the cruel Thatcherites. One story from the early 1980s sums up both the passion and the unworldliness with which he manifested it. He came back, angry, from a visit to an old people's home in his constituency. There was ample funding for the home, he complained – but it was used so unimaginatively: a treat for the old folk meant what? – Fish and chips! Why shouldn't they be getting boeuf bourguignon?

The same passion inspired his last ministerial job, at Education (1981–6), where his battle cry was to do something for the 'bottom forty per cent'. Deep down, perhaps, he could not see why every child should not have the benefits he had given his own children (forbidden to watch television) when he introduced them to good literature and good music. The fruits of this idealism had to be for the long term: the short term was dominated by bitter disputes with the teachers' unions that lasted almost all his years at Education.

JULIAN CRITCHLEY

Joynson-Hicks [Hicks], **William** [Viscount Brentford] (**'Jix'**) (*b.* London, 23 June 1865; *d.* London, 8 June 1932). Conservative Home Secretary. He was a leading Conservative politician of the 1920s, and Home Secretary in Baldwin's second government, from 1924 to 1929. As a staunch conservative as well as an evangelical, he was somewhat out of sympathy with the spirit of the 'Roaring Twenties', and

his popular nickname 'Jix' came to symbolize outdated and unfashionable social attitudes.

Hicks began his career, however, with a mind very much open to the future, even as a man ahead of the times. Born into a prominent City family, he embarked on a solicitor's career in 1882 and rapidly acquired a reputation: he was co-author in 1894 of one of the first books on the law relating to motor vehicles, and as a young politician he showed a similarly prescient awareness of air power. The opening for a career in public life came when in 1895 he married the only daughter of a prosperous Manchester silk manufacturer, Richard Joynson. In 1896 Hicks added 'Joynson' to his name and over the next decade his position as Joynson's heir led to an active involvement in politics, charitable work and evangelical religion in Manchester. He was defeated as Unionist candidate for North Manchester in 1900, and by Winston Churchill for North West Manchester in 1906. Revenge came when he defeated Churchill in the 1908 by-election occasioned by Churchill's promotion to the cabinet, but he was again defeated at the general election of January 1910, and at Sunderland in December. He finally secured a safe seat, and moved the centre of gravity of his political life back to London, when elected for Brentford in March 1911. Redistribution required his move to the Twickenham constituency in 1918, which he represented until his own elevation to the Lords in 1929.

Joynson-Hicks's return to the Commons in 1911 coincided with the Unionist onslaught on Asquith's government, and his special knowledge of such technical matters as motor cars, air transport and telephones was particularly appreciated on Unionist benches that were deficient in such skills. He scored a personal success in 1912 when he drew attention to the poor state of provision for military aviation, and it is apparent that his efforts contributed significantly to the preparations that underpinned the work of the Royal Flying Corps when war came in 1914.

During the Great War, too much a critic by nature to be in office, Joynson-Hicks remained a vigilant critic of all governments, and he concentrated his attentions on the progress of war in the air. With Lloyd George's postwar coalition he was if anything even more critical, resenting the way in which his party kept in office old foes such as Lloyd George and Churchill. He was prominent in the party's 'diehard' faction on many occasions, above all in mobilizing support for General Dyer after the Amritsar massacre. He naturally voted against coalition at the Carlton Club meeting of 19 October 1922 and was offered junior office by Bonar Law at the Board of Trade, in a government itself singularly lacking in experienced men.

Once in office, though, Joynson-Hicks proved to possess abilities that his colleagues had not expected in a man whose career had been almost entirely negative. After less than five months he was appointed Postmaster General, in March 1923, and when Baldwin succeeded Bonar Law, in May 1923, he became Financial Secretary to the Treasury with a cabinet seat, an unusual arrangement made because Baldwin remained Chancellor when he became Prime Minister. Joynson-Hicks had to do much of the detailed work involved in steering the Finance Bill through the Commons, and so far impressed as to retain a cabinet seat when Neville Chamberlain took over the Exchequer in August, when he moved to Chamberlain's post as Minister of Health. He therefore held four posts in the year between the 1922 and 1923 elections, a period in which he could make no departmental impact, but could and did confirm his own claim to higher office later.

His appointment to the Home Office when Baldwin returned to power in November 1924 was welcomed in the party as that of a man whose diehard politics would guarantee a firm hand when both strikes and espionage were feared, but also a man whose philanthropic work and religious convictions exhibited a more human face. The outcome was a disappointment. His reforming intentions were undoubtedly based on a generous spirit, but his abilities and experience seem to have been inadequate for the weight of the task. For example, over factory reform, where he was buffeted both by progressive young MPs such as Harold Macmillan who wanted a radical reform, and by the employers' associations who wanted no change at all, the outcome was endless procrastination and eventually no real reform at all.

He was more active in the field of public order. He supervised from the Home Office the preparations that enabled Baldwin's government to defeat the General Strike of 1926, both through official channels and by working with the unofficial Organization for the Maintenance of Supplies. With the strikes over, he was a strong supporter of those in the cabinet who wanted retaliatory legislation against the trade unions, and more generally of the government's move to the right in 1927–8. He was responsible for – and rather mismanaged – the Arcos Raid, which provided the pretext for breaking off relations with the Soviet Union. This was typical too of his support for an actively interventionist role for the Metropolitan Police; he encouraged them in raids on nightclubs and in prosecutions for public immorality, a veritable campaign to clean up London which alienated progressive opinion and led to one or two spectacular rebuffs in the courts.

While Home Secretary Joynson-Hicks continued to be active in the politics of Anglicanism, especially over the proposed modernization of the Prayer Book in 1927; he led the cross-party campaign to defeat the Church's plans and was successful both in 1927 and when modified proposals came forward in 1928. His last years at the Home Office did produce achievements too, notably the Shops Act of 1928, which greatly benefited a generation of shop assistants, and the Summer Time Act. But 'Jix' seemed increasingly out of harmony with the times and it seemed an almost perfect paradox that an incautious remark of his should have forced the government into one of its most far-reaching reforms, the extension of the right to vote to women between the ages of 21 and 30.

Joynson-Hicks was 64 when the 1929 general election came, and chose not to seek re-election, being raised to the peerage as Viscount Brentford. High office and its associated strains seem to have impaired both his health and his optimism (never perhaps his greatest quality), and he died shortly after retirement.

FURTHER READING

Blythe, Ronald, 'The salutary tale of Jix', in *The Age of Illusion* (London: Hamish Hamilton, 1963).

Taylor, H. A., *'Jix': Viscount Brentford* (London: Stanley Paul, 1933).

JOHN RAMSDEN

K

Kaldor, Nicholas [Baron Kaldor of Newnham in the City of Cambridge] (*b.* Budapest, 12 May 1908; *d.* Cambridge, 30 September 1986). Economist and economic adviser to successive Labour governments and several developing countries. He was made a life peer in 1974 for political services to the Labour Party. During the Labour Government of 1964–70 he served as Special Adviser on the social and economic aspects of taxation policy to James Callaghan, Chancellor of the Exchequer (1964–7); as Special Consultant to Roy Jenkins, Chancellor (1968), and as Special Adviser to Richard Crossman, Minister for Health and Social Security (1969). Before that, he had been active in Labour Party circles since World War II, and was a close friend of Hugh Gaitskell, leader of the party from 1955 to 1963. In the Labour Government of 1974–9, Kaldor was again made Special Adviser to the Chancellor of the Exchequer, Denis Healey, but resigned in 1976 in protest over the conduct of economic policy. He retreated to the Lords and used his platform to great effect, particularly as a trenchant critic of the economic policies pursued by the Conservative Government from 1979. His collected speeches *The Economic Consequences of Mrs. Thatcher* (1983) are reminiscent of the style of Keynes in their mixture of incisiveness, wit and righteous indignation.

Kaldor was one of the most original and distinguished economists of his generation, who made lasting contributions to economic theory and to applied economic analysis. He was born in Hungary into a middle-class Jewish family. His father was a successful lawyer and legal adviser to the German Legation in Budapest. From 1914 to 1925 he was educated at the famous Minta school in Budapest, and then went as a student to Berlin to study economics, but spent most of his time as an accredited journalist. He did not like the university, and in 1927 went to London to enrol

at the London School of Economics. There he blossomed and became the favourite pupil of the influential Lionel Robbins, graduating with first class honours in 1930. He stayed on at the LSE as a research student and in 1932 was appointed to the staff, becoming a lecturer in 1938 and a reader in 1945. In the 1930s he made major theoretical contributions to both micro and macro economics in such fields as the theory of the firm, welfare economics, trade cycle theory, and Keynesian economics. He was one of the first converts at the LSE to the Keynesian revolution and played a major proselytizing role, never deviating from the faith.

During the war the LSE was evacuated to Cambridge, and Kaldor came into direct physical contact with the Cambridge school of Piero Sraffa, Joan Robinson, Richard Kahn and Keynes himself. The exigencies of war turned his mind to applied economic issues relating to the war economy and to planning for the peace. He made major contributions to the two Beveridge Reports, on Social Insurance (1942) and Full Employment (1944). He also participated in the process of international reconstruction after the war as Director of Research at the Economic Commission for Europe in Geneva (1947–9) and as a member of various Commissions and Expert Committees, including the US Strategic Bombing Survey (1945), the Berlin Currency and Trade Committee (1948), and the UN Group of Experts on National and International Measures for Full Employment (1949).

In 1949 Kaldor returned to England as a Fellow of King's College, Cambridge; he was lecturer in the Department of Economics, where he stayed to his retirement in 1975, having been made a reader in 1952 and a professor in 1966. From 1951 to 1954 he served as a member of the UK Royal Commission on the Taxation of Profits and Income, and produced a minority report which laid the foundations for tax reform during the Labour

Government ten years later. His book *An Expenditure Tax* (1955) became a minor classic. His tax expertise led him as an official adviser to India (1956), Sri Lanka (1958), Mexico (1960), Ghana (1961), British Guiana (Guyana) (1961), Turkey (1962), Iran (1966) and Venezuela (1976). During the 1950s he was also one of the foremost architects of the post-Keynesian school of economics which pioneered new ways of thinking about equilibrium growth and the functional distribution of income along non-neoclassical lines. In the 1960s, while an adviser to the Labour Government, he turned his attention away from growth theory to the applied economics of growth, and strongly opposed Britain's entry to the EEC on the proposed terms. In the 1970s he led worldwide the intellectual assault on the doctrine of monetarism.

During his long and distinguished career as an academic economist and public servant, many honours came his way, including honorary doctorates of the universities of Dijon (1962) and Frankfurt (1982); he was Fellow of the British Academy (1963), President, Section F of the British Association for the Advancement of Science (1970), President of the Royal Economic Society (1974–6), and Honorary Member of the American Economic Association (1975) and the Hungarian Academy of Sciences (1978).

Kaldor never wrote a grand treatise in the tradition of Ricardo, Mill or Marshall, but his eight volumes of *Collected Essays* (1980) are a testament to his originality and endeavour, and provide a lasting memorial to one of the most innovative and controversial economists of the century.

WRITINGS

'Recollections of an Economist', *Banca Nazionale del Lavoro Quarterly Review* (March 1988).

FURTHER READING

Passinetti, L., 'Nicholas Kaldor', *International Encyclopedia of the Social Sciences*, 18 (New York: Free Press 1979).

Thirlwall, A. P., 'Symposium on Kaldor's Growth Laws', *Journal of Post-Keynesian Economics* (spring 1983).

——, *Nicholas Kaldor* (Brighton: Wheatsheaf Press, 1987).

Wood, A., 'Nicholas Kaldor', *The New Palgrave Dictionary of Economics* (London: Macmillan 1987).

A. P. THIRLWALL

Kent, Bruce (*b.* London, 22 June 1929). Campaigner for nuclear disarmament. He was General Secretary of CND from 1980 to 1985 and was appointed its chairman in 1987.

Kent was educated at Lower Canada College, Montreal, Stonyhurst College, and Brasenose College, Oxford. His education, after he had returned to Britain, gave some indication of the important posts within the Church for which he was clearly destined. After reading law at Oxford he was ordained to the Catholic priesthood in 1958. He held only a brief curacy in Kensington from 1958 to 1963 before entering the service of the Cardinal Archbishop of Westminster as Secretary at Archbishop's House. This was followed by the important posting as Catholic Chaplain to the University of London (1966–74) and his creation as Monsignor. During this time, however, and subsequently while working as parish priest in Somers Town (1977–80), he became progressively involved with peace issues; from 1974 to 1977 he was Chaplain to Pax Christi, a Catholic body devoted to this question.

Kent had come to see peace as all important for the world's future, and therefore held that the proliferation of nuclear weaponry was a major threat to the human condition. This conviction led him increasingly into active membership of the peace movement, nationally and internationally. As General Secretary of CND he became well known as a powerful advocate for disarmament in all forms. Eventually deciding to devote himself entirely to this work, and after a short while attached to a parish in Islington, he resigned his ministry, to the surprise of many, in 1987. The same year he received an Honorary LLD from Manchester University and in 1988 he married Valerie Flessati. Kent has written widely on disarmament issues and on the matter of Christians and peace.

WILLIAM PURCELL

Kerr, Philip. See LOTHIAN, LORD.

Keynes, J(ohn) M(aynard) [Baron Keynes of Tilton] (*b.* Cambridge, 5 June 1883; *d.* Tilton, Leicestershire, 21 April 1946). Publicist, economic policy adviser to the government and academic economist. He was the most influential economist of the twentieth century, and his importance in British political life was threefold. First, he was a publicist who presented the classic critique of the Versailles peace settlement. Secondly, he emerged as a spokesman for radical changes in British economic policy between the wars, and during World War II exercised an official responsibility for restructuring international financial relations. Thirdly, through his book *The General Theory of Employment, Interest and Money* (1936), he challenged the theoretical assumption that the economy was in principle self-righting, and thereby established 'Keynesianism' as a doctrine of demand management by the state, aimed at maintaining full employment.

Keynes came from an academic family in Cambridge. His father was Registrary of the university; his mother was the first woman mayor of the city. He was sent to Eton as a scholar and went on to King's College, Cambridge, to read mathematics. He was Twelfth Wrangler in the mathematics tripos in 1905 – a good but not brilliant result. As an undergraduate he was president of both the Liberal Club and the Union Society, with a well-formed aptitude for political debate, especially on the side of free trade. He was also a member of the select society known as the 'Apostles', which was the core around which the Bloomsbury group was to coalesce. Keynes's close friendship with such figures as the writer Lytton Strachey and the painter Duncan Grant was reinforced by their homosexuality.

After two years as a civil servant in the India Office, Keynes returned to Cambridge in 1908 to teach economics, with a stipend provided by Professor Alfred Marshall. It was as Marshall's protégé that Keynes became an economist, though his strictly academic research was still in the field of probability, on which his dissertation won him a fellowship at King's in 1909. With such connections, Keynes became editor of the *Economic Journal* in 1911 as a young don; he was to discharge this duty for more than 30 years until, as a peer and a director of the Bank of England, he stepped down in 1945 – an important thread of professional continuity in an otherwise extraordinarily diverse career. Already in 1913 he was combining his academic expertise with his administrative experience in sitting as a member of the Royal Commission on Indian Finance and Currency. During World War I he entered the Treasury and was soon entrusted with wide responsibility for the external finance of the war.

Keynes's attitude to the war was the product of conflicting claims upon him. He was not a pacifist but, like many of his Bloomsbury friends, he asserted a conscientious objection to conscription – a gesture of which he was spared the consequences by his privileged position in the Treasury. Moreover, the replacement of Asquith as Liberal Prime Minister by Lloyd George, at the head of a Conservative-dominated coalition, made the atmosphere in the government increasingly uncongenial to Keynes. He went to the Versailles peace conference as the official representative of the Treasury, but one who nourished an unofficial sensitivity over his own liberal credentials. It is not altogether surprising that he resigned in June 1919, dismayed by the heavy scale of reparations demanded from Germany, and determined to expose the treaty's shortcomings. Within a few months *The Economic Consequences of the Peace* (1919) was ready to be launched upon a tide of already expectant public opinion, which it caught with an unanticipated plenitude of success. Keynes fused high moral passion with hard economic analysis, and revealed, moreover, his striking distinction as a writer. The nub of his case was that reparations implied a transfer of wealth from poverty-stricken Germany in the form of real resources, which Germany could generate only by establishing an unlooked-for economic domination over the rest of Europe.

The fulsome reception accorded to the book, which made its author a household name in educated circles on both sides of the Atlantic, gave Keynes a platform of which he made full use thereafter. Though keeping his fellowship at King's, he did not revert to full-time academic teaching and research after the war, but instead divided his time between Cambridge and his house in Bloomsbury, where the cultural and business life of London, as well as politics, were open to him. He became a rich man through speculation, worth half a million pounds at the peak in 1936. He married the ballerina Lydia Lopokova in 1925 and they appear to have had a happy if childless marriage, sustained by a common interest in the arts, of which Keynes was a great patron. (He was later to play a vital role in enlisting government support through the formation of the Arts Council.)

Called on periodically by government for expert advice over economic policy, Keynes found his view overruled in 1925 on the undesirability of an imminent return to the Gold Standard at the traditional parity of $4.86. When the Chancellor of the Exchequer, Winston Churchill, announced Britain's return to Gold, Keynes used the press to make his criticisms public. He argued that, with an inappropriately high parity for sterling, the monetary mechanism would not in fact work smoothly to deflate domestic prices but rather would provoke unemployment. At this stage, however, Keynes did not doubt the (Marshallian) postulate that a market-clearing equilibrium would be established in the long run. But his most famous aphorism – 'In the long run we are all dead' – was intended to alert policy-makers to the more immediate consequences of their actions, which they would ignore at their peril.

In the 1920s Keynes was actively involved in Liberal Party politics. From 1923 he was chairman of the weekly paper the *Nation* (later amalgamated with the *New Statesman*) which, under the editorship of the Cambridge economist Hubert Henderson, pressed for a more radical policy stance. This brought Keynes and Henderson into close cooperation with Lloyd George, despite their old Asquithian affiliations, and the activities of the Liberal Summer Schools cemented this alliance. When the party entered the 1929 general election with a pledge to cut the high level of unemployment to 'normal' proportions, Keynes and Henderson produced their famous pamphlet *Can Lloyd George Do It?* in support. Public works, it suggested,

notably a loan-financed scheme of road-building, could stimulate a cumulative process of economic recovery. Keynes was thus identified as a prominent partisan opponent of Baldwin's Conservative Government and of the 'Treasury view' which it espoused. There were certainly other arguments against public works on the grounds of feasibility, but in 1929 the crucial objection was the Treasury view: that public expenditure necessarily diverted resources from more productive uses by private enterprise.

What was Keynes's case for a radical policy? His was essentially a plea for a bold state-led initiative, in the confidence that, with spare capacity available, such a programme would succeed in mobilizing idle resources. Unavailing in the electoral arena in 1929, Keynes was given a chance to influence inside opinion under the Labour Government of 1929–31 through his concurrent membership of the (Macmillan) Committee on Finance and Industry and the newly instituted Economic Advisory Council (especially its committee of economists, of which Keynes was chairman). Keynes was able, moreover, to found his policy advice on a more coherent theoretical basis with the completion of his *A Treatise on Money* (1930), a rigorous academic work in two volumes. The novelty of the *Treatise* was to repudiate the identity of investment and saving. Instead it talked of enterprise and thrift as different processes controlled by different people – albeit in theory brought into equilibrium by the adjusting mechanism of interest rate. With cheap money, enterprise could be relied upon to do the trick. But Keynes urged other policies like public works in Britain at this time because, he contended, cheap money was not on offer so long as bank rate had to be kept up in order to protect the high parity of sterling fixed under the Gold Standard.

Thus, given these rigidities in the real world, Keynes was ready to outline the case for a number of unorthodox policy expedients – incomes policy, devaluation, tariffs and bounties, as well as public works – and other leading economists, notably Professor A. C. Pigou and Sir Josiah Stamp, were likewise ready to countenance some of these 'second-best' options.

Vol. 6 No. 11. **PICTURE POST** March 16, 1940

UNOFFICIAL ECONOMIC ADVISER TO GREAT BRITAIN : *John Maynard Keynes in His Study in Bloomsbury*
It was he who foresaw the evil results of Versailles while that treaty was still under construction—and resigned an important job to make them known. To-day, at the age of 56, he has produced a plan for financing the war and avoiding its most disastrous economic consequences.

Mr. KEYNES
HAS A PLAN

To carry on a war successfully we must spend over £2,000 millions a year. How are we to pay? How are
we to avoid inflation ? In this article Kingsley Martin, Editor of "The New Statesman and Nation," writes
of the man who has given an answer to those questions, describes the answer which he gives.

WHEN "The Economic Consequences of the Peace," by John Maynard Keynes, was published in 1919 it caused a prodigious sensation. Here was an important member of the British delegation at Versailles, who had resigned his post in order to tell the truth about the Treaty. The sensation was due at least as much to the book's literary quality as to its expert substance. Those who knew nothing of economics could appreciate, if only from quotations in the press, Mr. Keynes's brilliant picture of M. Clemenceau, Mr. Lloyd George and President Wilson at Versailles. It successfully put over the point that the American President had kept his Puritanical conscience clear by insisting on verbal consistency with the Fourteen Points, while allowing cunning men to find ways of getting round them. It convinced us all that, whatever the other merits or evils of the Treaty, its real vice was its failure to treat Europe as an economic whole and to reconstruct it for the benefit of the common people. It was a treaty of strategy and national greediness—with the League of Nations thrown in to make it look pretty.

PICTURE POST

J. M. Keynes as portrayed in
'Picture Post', 16 March
1940

They were agreed, too, that in theory the current level of wages was too high, even if they saw little prospect of successfully bringing it down. Keynes therefore joined forces with others who were prepared to consider appropriate action: he supported Sir Oswald Mosley's proposals within the Labour Government; he pushed the committee of economists towards a programme of public works and tariffs; he incurred Liberal wrath by publicly questioning free trade; he drafted an addendum to the Macmillan Report, signed by five other members including Ernest Bevin, along congruent lines. By the time the report was published in the summer of 1931, however, the mounting economic crisis at home and abroad vitiated such proposals, and events rapidly overwhelmed the Labour Cabinet. Only when the position seemed untenable did Keynes himself opt for devaluation, though he was relieved when the new National Government found itself forced off Gold in September 1931.

After 1931 Keynes severed many of his direct political connections and, with an unaccustomed single-mindedness, devoted his energies to economic theory. Within a surprisingly short time he had stepped outside the analytical framework of the *Treatise* and was arguing out his new theory of effective demand. He was crucially stimulated at this point by the 'Circus' of younger economists at Cambridge, especially the ideas of R. F. Kahn and J. E. Meade, suggesting a fresh approach to the problem of saving and investment. Instead of investment depending upon prior saving – the orthodox assumption – savings were seen as being generated by an initial act of investment through a process which multiplied income, output and employment. Thus saving and investment were brought into equality by the equilibrating mechanism of changes in income or output. It followed that equilibrium might be reached while output was still below full capacity or full employment. It followed, too, that changes in output were now assigned the equilibrating task which was fulfilled under orthodox theory (including *A Treatise on Money*) by changes in interest rate. What role, then, did interest play? Keynes proceeded to explain interest in terms of 'liquidity preference' – the premium which wealth-holders exacted for tying up their resources in ways which sacrificed the liquid advantages of holding cash.

The General Theory of Employment, Interest and Money thus gave a wholly new account of how the economy worked – or failed to work. No longer did Keynes point to particular rigidities in the real world as the crucial reason why prices were prevented from making efficacious adjustments which would clear the market. He argued now that reductions in wages or interest rates, even if forthcoming, might simply be incapable of restoring full employment, which was a function of effective demand (that is, of prospective consumption plus investment). In a homely saying, one man's expenditure was another man's income. Keynes claimed that his theory would 'revolutionise the way the world thinks about economic problems'; but he acknowledged that it would necessarily be infused with political considerations in the process. *The General Theory* itself was largely silent on policy. Keynes, moreover, was fairly tentative and cautious in his subsequent practical recommendations, well aware that bottlenecks in production constrained the full use of resources, and reluctant to advance a practicable target for 'full employment' above a level of 95 per cent.

It was only with World War II that Keynes's ideas gained widespread acceptance. In 1940 he was invited back into the Treasury, where he served as an adviser for the rest of his life. A macro-economic approach – designed to contain inflation by restraining demand for finite resources rather than simply to raise revenue – became the basis of the 1941 budget. Conversely, the feasibility of maintaining full employment after the war was proclaimed in the Coalition Government's White Paper of 1944. But Keynes's own attention was increasingly consumed by planning for the postwar international economy, seeking new means of discharging the functions of the historic Gold Standard. Keynes played a large part at the Bretton Woods conference (1944) which helped to set up the International Monetary Fund and the World Bank. In contrast to his advocacy of tariffs in the conditions of the 1930s, he now reverted to fundamentally liberal trade policies. His abilities as a negotiator were put to a supreme test at the end of the war when American support for Britain under the lend-lease agreement was abruptly terminated. Keynes was largely responsible for securing a large dollar loan from the USA and Canada to tide Britain over the transition to peace. It was an arrangement which he recognized as at once imperfect and necessitous – a case which he made out with telling effect in the House of Lords in December 1945. There can be little doubt that these wearisome transatlantic negotiations taxed Keynes's strength – he had suffered a major heart attack in 1937 – and he died suddenly at Easter 1946, just before the Order of Merit could be conferred.

FURTHER READING

Clarke, Peter, *The Keynesian Revolution in the Making, 1924–36* (Oxford: Oxford University Press, 1988).

Harrod, R. F., *The Life of John Maynard Keynes* (London: Macmillan, 1951).

Hession, Charles H., *John Maynard Keynes* (London: Collier Macmillan, 1984).

Moggridge, D. E., *Keynes*, 2nd edn (London: Macmillan, 1980).

Skidelsky, Robert, *John Maynard Keynes: Hopes Betrayed, 1883–1920* (London: Macmillan, 1983).

P. F. CLARKE

Kinnock, Neil (Gordon) (*b.* Tredegar, Monmouthshire, 28 March 1942). Leader of the Labour Party. Kinnock became Labour Party leader in October 1983. He took the party to defeat in the general election of 1987. He is both a conventional and an unconventional leader. His family background, unlike that of most Labour leaders, is 'working class' (his father was a miner and his mother a district nurse) and, as a Welshman of mixed Welsh and Scottish descent, he is the first leader since Ramsay MacDonald not to be English. Fortuitously, perhaps, these aspects of Kinnock's personal story mirror the Labour Party's retreat to strength outside England and, within England, to areas of 'traditional' industry. Kinnock does not speak to his party members as a middle-class radical burdened by social guilt and possessed of a romantic notion of what the 'working class' is. He is a truly representative Labour man, but, by that same token, vulnerable to the accusation that he might betray his roots in the search for power.

Despite his 'representativeness', however, Kinnock was not himself a miner. Growing up in postwar Britain, he had opportunities which his parents lacked. He lived in a bungalow with a bath, central heating, a fridge and a smokeless fuel grate. He passed his 11-plus and attended Lewis School, Pengam, a school with a well-established reputation for sending clever boys into a wider world than that of the valleys and therefore often considered pretentious. Certainly, that was what Kinnock called it, and he did not particularly want to escape from South Wales. To study history and industrial relations at University College, Cardiff, seemed the logical next step. His academic record was undistinguished, though he revelled in the world of student unions. He married Glenys Parry in 1967 in a chapel in Anglesey – a gesture to tradition rather than belief.

Kinnock took a job with the Workers' Educational Association, but his mind was already on a political career. In 1969 he was adopted as the candidate for Bedwellty and the following year he entered the House of Commons. His majority was and has remained impregnable. His reputation was that of a 'left-winger': he moved in *Tribune* circles and was soon a popular speaker. He campaigned vigorously against membership of the EEC and was a supporter of CND. When Wilson resigned in

Neil Kinnock handing Roy Hattersley a copy of the Labour Party manifesto at the start of the general election campaign, May 1987; on his left are Denis Healey and Gerald Kaufman

1976, Kinnock unsuccessfully worked on behalf of Michael Foot for the party leadership. He had already made his dissent from the government's acceptance of the IMF cuts abundantly plain. The mantle of Aneurin Bevan, mediated through Bevan's acolyte, Michael Foot, seemed to be descending upon this new fluent son of Wales, but it became apparent that his Welshness did not extend to any great sentimentality about Wales itself. Devolution seemed to him a dead end and he engaged in strident controversy with Plaid Cymru. He did not believe that the misfortunes of 'working people' in Wales stemmed from their being British. Kinnock appeared to be vindicated in his opposition to a measure on which the Labour Government had expended a vast amount of time when the electors of Wales decisively rejected devolution in March 1979. However, his 'success' in this matter served only to compound the difficulties of a Labour government which was already floundering.

Labour's election defeat in 1979 was naturally a disappointment to Kinnock, though he did not at first suppose that it would be a prelude to a long spell of opposition. Callaghan offered him the position of Labour's spokesman on education. It was the first time that he had accepted a kind of responsibility. His popularity among rank and file members of the party continued to grow. There was a good deal of talk about traditions of collective and democratic decision-making which had been flouted. However, in the fratricidal conflicts which threatened to engulf the Labour Party, left found it increasingly difficult to talk to left. Kinnock was of the left, but not the hard left, and he could actually smile as well as clench his fist. When Callaghan stood down, Kinnock could hardly fail to support Michael Foot's candidature for the party leadership. He accepted Healey as deputy leader. He was no admirer of Anthony Wedgwood Benn, even when transmogrified into Tony Benn, and for a time that opposition appeared to cause him to forfeit some of his general popularity in the Labour Party at large. The struggles of individuals within the party made interesting reading, but they contributed to Labour's defeat in 1983 under Foot. Foot, in turn, now encouraged the notion that Kinnock should succeed him, and departed precipitately with this end in view. In the leadership election, Kinnock defeated Hattersley handsomely. His task was both to seek to heal the splits within his own party and to provide effective opposition to a Prime Minister who had grown steadily more confident and dominant.

The 1987 election demonstrated that Labour still had a long way to go. A third defeat in a row prompted fresh debate on specific policy issues, on relations between the Labour Party and the trade unions, and on the party's organization and image. Kinnock held his position, but not without difficulty. His rhetorical powers came near, on occasion, to Michael Foot's propensity for vacuous long-windedness, and his capacity for a sharp phrase was not invariably matched by a grasp of detail. There were times when his lack of any ministerial experience became evident. Even so, with the 'Alliance' disintegrating, it was not altogether beyond the bounds of possibility that Kinnock might eventually succeed. When he first entered parliament he talked frequently about his commitment to 'the emancipation' of 'his' class: paradoxically, Labour might only achieve that objective if Kinnock in turn persuaded the party to emancipate itself from the prejudices of class.

FURTHER READING

Harris, Robert, *The Making of Neil Kinnock* (London: Faber and Faber, 1984).

KEITH ROBBINS

Kipling, (Joseph) Rudyard (*b.* Bombay, 30 December 1865; *d.* London, 18 January 1936). Author and poet. Kipling began his professional life as a journalist and reporter in 1882 with the *Civil and Military Gazette* in Lahore, and from 1887 to 1889 worked on the Allahabad *Pioneer*. By 1890, when he settled in London, he was already well known for his verse and short stories. He rapidly became and remained until his death the most celebrated British literary exponent of imperial and patriotic themes. His literary eminence, recognized by the Nobel Prize for literature in 1907, gave him access to the highest social and political circles. He persistently used his contacts and wide popularity to rally Britons to the defence of their country and to performance of their duty as an imperial race.

Both his parents were from strongly Methodist families; from 1865 his father taught at government art schools in Bombay and Lahore. Although he was educated in England from 1871 to 1882, it was on Indian subjects that Kipling first revealed his skill with words, talent for observation, humour and forceful imagery. These were variously combined both to convey something of India itself and to popularize the role of the British there, especially as soldiers, administrators and engineers. Books such as *Plain Tales from the Hills* (1888), *Barrack-room Ballads* (1890), *The Jungle Books* (1894-5) and *Kim* (1901) provided many of the ingredients from which adults and children of all classes fashioned their mental pictures of empire.

Kipling married an American in 1892, and until 1896 lived in Vermont, where his two daughters were born. He was criticized for his vulgarity and rudeness; many found his writing offensive for its violence, obsessive detail and contrived dialogue. His intolerance and bigotry often represented the worst in imperial assertiveness. However, poems such as 'The English Flag' (1890), 'Recessional' (1897) and 'The White Man's Burden' (1898) illustrate his parallel concerns with the grandeur of empire and its capacity to improve the conditions of its subjects, his pessimism about the fragility of law and civilization, and his insistence on the perennial obligations of rulers despite popular ingratitude.

By 1900 Kipling had begun to lose confidence in Britain's ability to live up to these quasi-religious ideals. For him, as for others, the South African War (1899-1902) was a turning-point. It exaggerated his tendency to hero-worship commanding acquaintances such as Field-Marshal Lord Roberts, Cecil Rhodes and Lord Milner; his hatred of politicians and his loathing of 'liberalism', intellectuals and administrative incompetence reached vitriolic heights. Both as writer and political activist, he adopted the obsessions of the extreme right – external defence and the threat posed by Germany, naval expansion, compulsory military service, and Ulster's Unionism.

From his home in Sussex he simultaneously evolved in books such as *Puck of Pook's Hill* (1906) and *A History of England* (1911) an idealized vision of the country and its past, which this frenetic militarism was intended to protect.

World War I confirmed his gloomiest predictions, and his 17-year-old son's death at Loos in 1915 enhanced his bitterness at the national failure to take his warnings of two decades to heart. Combined with persistent illness, events after 1918 only depressed him further: Lloyd George's Irish settlement and later concessions to nationalism in India he felt were treasonable, and he condemned even his cousin Stanley Baldwin as a socialist. Some compensating comfort he drew from working for the Imperial War Graves Commission and the Rhodes Trustees. The influence and esteem generated by his earlier writing also persisted, bringing him the freedom of the City of London, the Royal Society of Literature's gold medal, and finally burial in Westminster Abbey.

FURTHER READING

Birkenhead, Lord, *Rudyard Kipling* (London: Weidenfeld and Nicolson, 1978).

Carrington, C. E., *Rudyard Kipling: his Life and Work* (London: Macmillan, 1955).

Sandison, Alan, *The Wheel of Empire: a Study of the Imperial Idea in Some Late Nineteenth and Early Twentieth-Century Fiction* (London: Macmillan, 1967).

A. N. PORTER

Kitchener, Lord [Horatio Herbert; Earl Kitchener of Khartoum and of Broome] (*b.* Co. Kerry, 24 June 1850; *d.* at sea, 5 June 1916). General and statesman. After long military service in different parts of the British Empire, Kitchener was the man the government needed in August 1914 to become Secretary of State for War.

He was educated in Switzerland, where he learnt to speak fluent French, and at the Royal Military Academy, Woolwich. His active service career began, unusually for a British officer, in the Franco-Prussian War in 1870. On the eve of being gazetted as a lieutenant in the Royal Engineers he travelled to France and for a short time served with the French Army of the Loire. The inability of the French to resist the Prussians had a powerful influence on the development of his own strategic policy in 1914–16.

After a period of home service he was seconded to the Palestine Exploration Fund in 1874. This enabled him to learn Arabic and marked the beginning of his connection with Britain's empire in the Middle East, where he was to build the real foundations of his career. In 1878 Britain acquired Cyprus under the terms of the Treaty of Berlin and Kitchener was sent to the island to map it. In 1882, after the British conquest of Egypt, he was seconded to the Egyptian Army as the second in command of the cavalry. Two years later the Mahdist rising in the Sudan began to assume formidable proportions and General Gordon was besieged in Khartoum. Although the expedition under Sir Garnet Wolseley failed to relieve Gordon, Kitchener emerged from the campaign with a reputation for energy and ability, and thereafter he rose rapidly. Kitchener was an intensely ambitious man. Although he pretended to despise the press, he quickly realized that he could use it to further his own career. He took posts which kept him in the limelight and he was ready to use his personal friendship with the wives and cousins of important politicians to improve his own prospects.

Gordon's death touched him very deeply. Between 1886 and 1888 he was the Governor-General of the Eastern Sudan before being appointed Adjutant-General of the Egyptian Army in 1888 and Sirdar (Commander-in-Chief) in 1889. Until 1895 he devoted himself to rebuilding that force so that with it he could reconquer the Sudan and avenge Gordon. He was successful. In 1896, despite the very severe financial constraints which the British administration in Egypt imposed upon him, he began the reconquest. By 1898 his troops had arrived at Khartoum and on 2 September they routed the Dervish army led by the Mahdi's successor, Khalifa Abdullah, at the battle of Omdurman. Kitchener then demonstrated that he could be a diplomat as well as a soldier. A small French expedition under Captain

Field Marshal Earl Kitchener, Secretary of State for War

Marchand had marched from the Congo to Fashoda on the White Nile. Kitchener went to meet him and, with a judicious blend of tact, courtesy and a show of overwhelming force, convinced Marchand that it would be impossible for him to claim the region for France.

Kitchener was raised to the peerage in 1899 and appointed Governor-General of the Sudan. But his period in office was a brief one. In October 1899 war broke out between the British and the Boer republics of the Transvaal and the Orange Free State. After a series of military defeats, Lord Roberts was appointed to command the British Army in South Africa and he took Kitchener with him as his Chief of Staff. When Roberts returned home after the fall of Pretoria in 1900, Kitchener succeeded him and fought a protracted guerrilla war which led to the final surrender of the Boers in

May 1902. On his return to London he was made a Viscount.

Between 1902 and 1909 Kitchener served as Commander-in-Chief of the Indian Army. He was responsible for ending the system by which control of the army in India was divided between the Commander-in-Chief and the Military Member of the Viceroy's Council. The Viceroy, Lord Curzon, was intensely suspicious of any measure which threatened to increase the authority of the military at the expense of the supremacy of the civil power (see also CURZON, GEORGE). Although Kitchener had his way, he did so only at the cost of a bitter row with Curzon which culminated in the latter's resignation. Kitchener also introduced administrative reforms which ensured that in 1914 India was able to send several expeditionary forces abroad. However, financial stringency meant that they were not properly equipped to fight European enemies.

In September 1911, after being promoted to the rank of Field-Marshal, Kitchener was appointed British Agent and Consul-General in Egypt, a post which made him the effective head of the Egyptian Government. He only enjoyed the post for a short time because on the outbreak of World War I in August 1914 the Liberal Prime Minister, H. H. Asquith, made him the Secretary of State for War. His most significant contribution to the British war effort was his decision to raise a volunteer army numbered in millions to supplement Britain's small prewar professional army and her Territorial Force. Unlike most of his contemporaries he did not believe that the war would be over in a matter of months. His experiences in the Sudan and South Africa had taught him that victory would go to the side with the biggest battalions. He believed that by the beginning of 1917 the armies of Britain's allies, France and Russia, would have fought the armies of her enemies, Germany, Austria-Hungary and, after November 1914, Turkey, to a standstill. But Kitchener's 'New Armies' would be unblooded. They would be able to intervene in the Continental land war and deliver the knock-out blow against the Central Powers; Britain would then be able to impose her own peace terms on her enemies and her allies.

Until the autumn of 1915 Kitchener's control over British strategy was virtually unchallenged. But the collapse of Britain's ally Serbia, his vacillation over the evacuation of the allied army from the Gallipoli Peninsula and the growing disquiet of many of his cabinet colleagues at his obsessive secretiveness combined to erode his power. When Sir William Robertson became the Chief of the Imperial General Staff in December 1915 he effectively supplanted Kitchener as the government's chief military adviser. But Kitchener's standing with the public remained so high that Asquith did not dare to sack him. His removal from office in June 1916 was effected only when the cruiser HMS *Hampshire*, which was carrying him to Russia, struck a German mine and he was drowned.

Kitchener had long been recognized as an outstanding imperial soldier and pro-consul. But his reputation as a strategist in World War I suffered from the fact that his premature death meant that he wrote no memoirs to defend his name. He was the ideal whipping-boy for surviving generals and politicians anxious to find a scapegoat for their own mistakes. Only at the end of the twentieth century have historians begun to recognize the full scope of his achievements as a strategist in 1914–15.

FURTHER READING

Cassar, G. H., *Kitchener: Architect of Victory* (London: William Kimber, 1977).

French, D., 'The evolution of attrition, 1914–1916', *English Historical Review*, 103, 40 (April 1988), pp. 385–405.

Neilson, K., 'Kitchener: a reputation refurbished?', *Canadian Journal of History*, 15, 2 (1980), pp. 207–27.

Royle, T., *The Kitchener Enigma* (London: Michael Joseph, 1985).

DAVID FRENCH

L

Laidler, Graham. See PONT.

Lancaster, Sir Osbert (*b.* London, 4 August 1908; *d.* London, 27 July 1986). Cartoonist, writer and illustrator. Best known as the inventor of the one-column feature or pocket cartoon style of drawing, Lancaster was also a prolific writer, caricaturist and critic, a distinguished designer for both opera and ballet, and an architectural historian.

Educated at Charterhouse School, Lancaster gave up his law studies at Lincoln College, Oxford, to attend the Byam Shaw School (1925–6), the Ruskin School of Drawing (1929–30) and the Slade School of Art (1931–2), where he studied stage design under Victor Polunin. His importance as an illustrator dates from the 1930s, when he established a reputation, while working for the *Architectural Review*, for writing and illustrating humorous books and articles on architecture and design. His bestsellers – *Progress at Pelvis Bay* (1936), *Pillar to Post: a Pocket Lamp of Architecture* (1938) and *Homes, Sweet Homes* (1939) – categorize architectural pretensions in a tongue-in-cheek way.

In 1939 Lancaster joined the *Daily Express* and continued there with only one break – he served with the News Section of the Foreign Office and at the British Embassy in Athens from 1944 to 1946 – until his death. Initially, his drawings appeared on the William Hickey page as column-breakers; they later moved to the front page as the paper contracted due to wartime paper shortages. Although the small one-off daily cartoon remains a permanent feature of the British press, only Lancaster's work ever retained the title 'pocket cartoon'. His magnificent creation was the miniature upper-class world of Lady Maudie Littlehampton (a character who has proved as enduring as David Low's Colonel Blimp) through which, by using a permanent cast of regular characters, he reflected his comments on news in the real world.

Lancaster's artistic talent lay in his ability to combine a sophisticated style with the humour of a child's vision. Alongside his cartooning, he continued his architectural writing as well as designing costumes and sets for the Royal Ballet and Glyndebourne Opera. He was knighted in 1975.

WRITINGS

All Done From Memory (London: John Murray, 1963).
With an Eye to the Future (London: John Murray, 1967).

FURTHER READING

Lucie-Smith, Edward, *The Essential Osbert Lancaster* (London: Barrie and Jenkins, 1988).

LIZ OTTAWAY

Lang, Cosmo (Gordon) [Baron Lang of Lambeth] (*b.* Fyvie, Aberdeenshire, 31 October 1864; *d.* Kew, Surrey, 5 December 1945). Archbishop of Canterbury. Lang was a central figure in the life of the Church of England in the first half of the century. He was Bishop of Stepney from 1901 to 1908, when, at the youthful age of 44, he was appointed Archbishop of York. He moved to Canterbury in 1928 and remained Archbishop until his resignation in March 1942 at the age of 77.

When Sir William Orpen painted Lang's portrait he reputedly commented that he saw in front of him seven archbishops. Which of them was he to paint? On the surface, Lang was emphatically a man of the English Establishment. He appeared to move securely among the society of his time and to be the perfect courtier. He was on good terms with successive monarchs. Edward VII wisely reminded him of the need to prevent the clergy from growing moustaches. It fell to Lang to crown George VI in 1937, just as his had been, in Baldwin's words, 'the voice of Christian England' in his broadcast after Edward VIII's abdication, in which he regretted that the King had been led astray by a social group whose standards and ways of life were alien to the best instincts and traditions of his people. His critics found him unctuous and smug: they suspected that Lang was fundamentally a great actor.

Part of the grounds for this suspicion lay in the fact that Lang was not even an Englishman. His father and grandfathers were Scottish Presbyterian ministers and Lang had graduated from Glasgow University. At this point he had made one trip to London – the excitement of a visit to the House of Commons brought on a severe nose-bleed. He contemplated a political career and had already thought of a suitable title for his future peerage. It was not Lambeth.

In 1882 he went up to Balliol College, Oxford, and loved it. He became President of the Union and took a First in history, although he had been disappointed about a Second in Greats. In 1888 he became a Prize Fellow of All Souls at the second attempt. Three years earlier he had himself commented that his character was Janus-like and double-faced. On the one hand he was metaphysical and dreamy, while on the other he had an almost insufferable amount of common sense and a capacity for business. A legal career seemed ideal, but he was rescued from it by the thought of the priesthood. A dream in which John Henry Newman urged Lang to join him in a third-class railway carriage and forsake the comforts of first-class travel had its obvious implications, but they were resisted. He was already attracted by ritual, though his mother in Glasgow was not. Separation from Presbyterianism and Scotland was now inevitable. A short period at Cuddesdon College was followed by a spell at Leeds Parish Church, where the curates wore top-hats and long frock-coats. Lang then spent three years as Dean of Divinity at Magdalen College, Oxford, and in 1895 became vicar of Portsea where, in a manner of speaking, Queen Victoria was a neighbour. Visits to Osborne introduced him to various members of the royal family and helped his promotion.

The major legacy left by Lang is in the sphere of ceremonial and ritual in worship. Of course, he was not alone in seeking to 'catholicize' the Church of England, but at York he was able to establish certain practices as normal and acceptable. Wherever he went, there was dignity and colour, but evangelicals worried about his sincerity. Christian Socialists thought that the Archbishop, whether in his York or Canterbury phase, was not sufficiently sympathetic to their blueprints for social and economic reform. Ecclesiastical 'middle England' felt left out by an archbishop who liked top people and knew something about slums but had never been in much contact with 'ordinary parish life'. He was the only celibate Archbishop of Canterbury in this century.

Lang's mind was good. As a Glaswegian boy he had wrestled long with neo-Hegelianism, but he was never able to address the intellectual problems of his age in a manner that attracted the attention of his contemporaries. The descent of Europe towards another war was beyond the understanding of an archbishop in his seventies. Dogged by success, he never sufficiently came to terms with greatness. He is, however, the most puzzling of archbishops and the only one whose heart, in a certain sense, remained in the Scottish Highlands.

FURTHER READING

Lockhart, J. G., *Cosmo Gordon Lang* (London: Hodder and Stoughton, 1949).

KEITH ROBBINS

Lansbury, George (*b.* near Lowestoft, Suffolk, 22 February 1859; *d.* London, 7 May 1940). Labour politician, editor of the *Daily Herald*, and Christian pacifist. He spent his life in Labour politics but came into particular prominence as MP for Bow and Bromley, when he was the only cabinet member of the second Labour Government to survive the 1931 general election. This accident made him leader of the 46 members of the opposition in Parliament, a burden he carried effectively despite limited resources until 1935. Since the Great War he had achieved an extraordinary position in the affections of the Labour Party, to the extent, as Ronald Blythe points out in an evocative essay, of being immobilized by respect, a figure one criticized only at the risk of stirring thoughts of sacrilege and patricide. Nevertheless, his political destruction was brought about by one devastating speech from Ernest Bevin at the 1935 Party Conference. The issue was an executive committee resolution calling for the government to take appropriate measures to stop the invasion of Ethiopia by the Italians. Lansbury, whose pacifism led him into increasingly desperate resorts as war in Europe approached, spoke against it. Bevin is reported to have replied to critics of his savage rejoinder that 'Lansbury has been going about dressed in saint's clothes for years waiting for martyrdom. I set fire to the faggots.'

Lansbury and Bevin, however, had much in common: a fierce loyalty to the working class to which they belonged (Lansbury's father had been a hard-drinking navvy), an exceptional capacity to make ordinary people feel themselves part of the process by which decisions affecting their lives were made, and a talent for sustaining militant activity by pushing legal and organizational constraints to the limit. Both men at times seemed to menace the extensive middle ground of British politics with a revolutionary threat neither of them in fact believed in. Reactions to the pacifism of Lansbury's later years have got in the way of an appreciation of the militant Christian socialism which was his real contribution to the Labour movement.

Lansbury was drawn into the movement by issues and contestable causes rather than theories, though, in a handful of books and a steady output of articles and pamphlets, he worked round a core of general insights into the contradictions and consequences of capitalism, the nature of class conflict and the position of women. These were only sharpened by his selective response to Marx and his early association with H. M. Hyndman. They survive obstinately in contemporary political debate.

In 1885 Lansbury returned from a catastrophic year in Queensland with his wife, three small children and a younger brother, and immediately started agitation against the misleading propaganda that had tempted him and many others into emigration. The outcome was the establishment of the Emigration Information Department in 1886. His performance brought him to the attention of the Liberal MP for Whitechapel, for whom he acted as agent in the election of that year. But he had already, as Honorary Secretary of the Liberal Association in Bow, embarked on a career as a catholic and somewhat unreliable organization man. In 1892 he left the Liberals for good, joined the Social Democratic Federation and subsequently the Independent Labour Party and the Labour Party, taking up membership of the Fabian Society for a period along the way. In 1889, the year of the London dock strike, he joined Will Thorne's Gas Workers' Union, of which he was a trustee for many years and which he represented at the Labour Party Conference from 1921.

The chairman of his representative committee for the emigration agitation was a Clerkenwell curate, and the conference which was its climax was chaired by the suffragan Bishop of London. Lansbury's highly charged relationship with the Church of England went back to his youth, when the Reverend J. Fenwick Kitto, Vicar of Whitechapel, had caught his imagination with his attractive services, and had confirmed him in a robust interpretation of the Christian message. Lansbury poured the routine anathemas of the left on the heads of profiteers and capitalists, but his capitalists were victims as well as villains, and his most passionate hostility was for those who repudiated the spirit behind the simple injunctions of Christ, which offered, as it seemed to him, the only hope of escape from a system that inflicts avoidable pain on so many of its members. His targets were often the clergy and men of affairs who took their churchmanship very seriously, though the social message they drew from it was very different from his. Among them there were also important figures on the right of the Labour movement itself, those he identified as 'preachers', Methodists such as Arthur Henderson and the miners' leader Frank Hodges. Their social concern, with its anxious commitment to established institutions and its ideology of 'cooperation' between classes and interests, was effectively focused after the Great War by the inter-denominational crusading of the Industrial Christian Fellowship. Lansbury regularly found himself confronting its supporters across the institutional barricades. As editor of the *Daily Herald* he had supported the Clydeside strikers in 1916. Sir Lynden Macassey was Lloyd George's trouble-shooter on the Clyde, and conscientiously supported the mission of the postwar ICF for a disciplined and organic social order, as did the industrialist Alfred Mond, the Minister of Health directly confronted by Lansbury's later rebellion in Poplar. Ship builders and owners with the same 'Christian' vision of industrial relations patronized Havelock Wilson, the accommodating leader of the seamen's union. Lansbury made the tactical error of contesting Middlesbrough against Wilson in 1906.

For Lansbury, the trouble with the organized Christianity of the day was that it shirked the obligation to take sides and fight. The fight, however, did not call for the mobilization of class violence, though it certainly called for direct action. He was encouraged by an apparent concession from Lenin, whom he met in 1920 and greatly liked, that a peaceful revolutionary process might be a possibility in Britain, for Lansbury believed that the institutions for creating a democratic society already existed.

His assault on the Poor Law began with his election to the Poplar Board of Guardians in 1892, and was strengthened by the influence of his energetic group of socialists on the borough council. He pressed a spoonful of workhouse porridge on an embarrassed chief officer, documented peculation, used his exchange with the Prince of Wales at the hearings of the Royal Commission on the Aged Poor in 1894 to blackmail royalist officials, charmed funds from the American soap millionaire Joseph Fels to provide work for the indigent at Laindon Farm Colony and Hollesley Bay, and drove the Prime Minister Arthur Balfour into a corner in 1905 by leading a large deputation of desperate women from the East End into his room in the House of Commons. Asked in that year to serve on the Royal Commission on the Poor Laws, Lansbury made a major contribution to the famous minority report of 1909, generally taken to be the work of Beatrice Webb, which led eventually to their abolition.

Returned at the second election of 1910 for the Bow and Bromley Division, and in the same year becoming an LCC member for Woolwich,

he assailed the 'ninepence for fourpence' principle of the Asquith government's Insurance Acts as a fraud by which the poor would have to pay for their own relief. But always, as he put it, in hot water with his party, he demonstrated his independent conception of the class struggle, in a period when the conventional evidence for it was becoming particularly obvious, by an uncalculating absorption in the cause of the militant suffragettes. Well aware of the economic reasons for the subjection of women, he saw it as an expression of the degraded moral sensibility of a social system based on competition and greed. All dominance was class dominance, including the economic dependence of empire, and even the well-intentioned paternalism of the Cadburys and Rowntrees. Over the treatment of suffragettes Asquith found himself insulted to his face on the floor of the House, and Lansbury was expelled, before resigning from the House in disagreement with his party over the franchise for women. He had his first brief experience of prison in Pentonville, having finally, as he conceded, overstepped the line between legal and illegal public speech, and went on unrepentant hunger strike.

Resignation kept him out of the House until 1922, a period that covered all but the last two years of his editorship of the *Daily Herald*. This was also the period in which his pragmatic local militancy matured, for in 1919 he became Mayor of Poplar, and Labour took control of the borough. Unlike party bureaucrats such as Herbert Morrison, Lansbury could not suppose that the mere making of law and its administration would bring about great changes. His advice to the political activist was to join the movement and master the dull committee business, because, in a phrase from *Your Part in Poverty* (1916), 'in these meetings men and women get to understand one another's point of view, and are also able to think out and organise their plans of campaign.' The Poplar campaign was highly cohesive and, for Morrison, irritatingly effective.

The general problem was the familiar contradiction of capitalism: profusion, located in the boroughs of Kensington and Westminster, and poverty, in the boroughs of East London, with their very low rateable value and their

George Lansbury speaking at a rally called to demonstrate against the Unemployment Assistance Regulations, Trafalgar Square, London, August 1936

huge numbers of unemployed. Many men had by mid-1921 run through their claim on insurance benefits and had to be relieved from the borough rates. The council's solution was to refuse to pay the 'precepts', fees due to the LCC for centralized services. Duly summoned, the councillors processed to the High Court from Bow, complete with mace and insignia of office, and a banner announcing 'Poplar Borough Council marching to the High Court and possibly to PRISON'. The possibility was realized, in Brixton for the men and Holloway for the women, on a charge of contempt. While they effectively harrassed the prison authorities, the virus of 'Poplarism'

began to spread, and the LCC and the government caved in. Mond rushed through legislation to transfer the burden of outdoor relief to the Metropolitan Common Poor Fund.

The victory of 'Poplarism' generated anomalous pressures on the system of relief in the 1920s and early 1930s: the East End boroughs became a 'haven for paupers' (Gilbert, p. 217). But it also represented a development of the idea of redistribution through state action which was to be more fully realized in the 1945 government of Lansbury's protégé in the opposition group of the 1930s, Clement Attlee.

The *Daily Herald* in its legendary years

under Lansbury was a means for the unfettered expression of anti-official perspectives of all kinds, and writers such as G. K. Chesterton and Hilaire Belloc, who were in no sense socialists, wrote brilliantly for it. For Lansbury himself it was the vehicle for causes, among them a variety of strikes; Home Rule for Ireland; objective reporting of events in revolutionary Russia; independence for India; and the electoral contests between John Scurr of Poplar and C. F. G. Masterman, Lloyd George's chief assistant on the Insurance Bills of 1911, and prototype of the Oxbridge young men who paddled worthily in East End social work before retreating into anodyne parliamentary careers.

Lansbury was only briefly in the cabinet, as First Commissioner of Public Works in the Labour Government of 1929. His 'liberation' of the decorous metropolitan parks reflected the personal qualities for which he was widely loved. But his greatest contribution to the spirit of democratic freedom was the survival of the *Herald* in the face of wartime officialdom and Fleet Street economics. His contribution to the Labour movement itself was the grass-roots militancy derived from his religious faith.

WRITINGS

My Life (London: Constable, 1928).

FURTHER READING

Blythe, R., *The Age of Illusion: England in the Twenties and Thirties, 1919–1940* (London: Hamish Hamilton, 1963), chap. 14.

Cole, M., 'Lansbury', in *Dictionary of Labour Biography*, ed. Joyce M. Bellamy and John Saville, vol. 2 (London: Macmillan, 1974), pp. 214–21.

Gilbert, B. B., *British Social Policy: 1914–1939* (London: Batsford, 1970).

Postgate, R., *The Life of George Lansbury* (London: Longmans, 1951).

Studdert-Kennedy, G., *Dog-Collar Democracy: the Industrial Christian Fellowship, 1919–1929* (London: Macmillan, 1982).

GERALD STUDDERT-KENNEDY

Laski, Harold (Joseph) (*b.* Manchester, 30 June 1893; *d.* London, 24 March 1950).

Political theorist and Professor of Political Science at the London School of Economics. His academic work combined with left-wing politics gave him considerable influence, especially in the 1930s (described by one historian as the 'Age of Laski'), and even more notoriety. He was the archetypal scholar-politician and 'red professor'.

The son of a prosperous Manchester businessman, prominent in that city's Jewry and Liberal politics, Laski was a child of precocious brilliance. This manifested itself in his schooldays at Manchester Grammar School, then as a scholar at New College, Oxford. It was a precocity which also estranged him from his family, for he met and married (in 1911, as an 18-year-old schoolboy about to go to Oxford) the older Frida, eugenecist and Gentile. His father was unforgiving, and insisted that the marriage remain secret and that the couple remain separate while Harold was at Oxford (with Frida in Glasgow). This unhappy arrangement lasted until Harold took his finals, in which he obtained a first in modern history, in 1914; but the breach with his family lasted for many years longer.

Rejected for military service on medical grounds (his health was always poor) when he tried to enlist on the outbreak of war, Laski went to North America to teach. After a spell at McGill University in Montreal, he moved in 1916 to Harvard, where he remained until his return to England in 1920. His relationship with the USA continued to be close and affectionate, reflected in his remarkable 20-year correspondence with Mr Justice Holmes of the Supreme Court (a correspondence published after their deaths).

Back in England, in a teaching post at the London School of Economics, Laski rapidly established his academic reputation and his role as the intellectual in politics. His academic work (he had already published two books) had hitherto been concerned with advancing a theory of political pluralism against the monistic claims of state sovereignty, but when he produced his massive *magnum opus*, *A Grammar of Politics* (1925), it was rightly regarded as the textbook of Fabian political science. However, subsequent events (the collapse of the 1929–31 Labour Government, and the rise of Fascism) soon gave Laski's writings a new urgency and focus. In a series of books through the 1930s (starting with his *Democracy in Crisis*, 1933) he warned of the contradiction between capitalism and democracy and of the perils in store if the contradiction remained unresolved. His writings were characteristic of much of the left of the period in their popular Marxism, their blind eye to Stalinism and their sweeping ideological rhetoric. This gave them great influence at the time (Laski was also one of the triumvirate which presided over the Left Book Club) but has diminished their subsequent interest and reputation.

Laski's prominence in the politics of the left during the 1930s (for example, in the Socialist League, and Unity Campaign) commended him to Labour's constituency activists, who elected him to the party's National Executive Committee in 1937 and kept him there for over a decade, as chairman of the party in the crucial year of 1944–5. It was during this period, of war and its immediate aftermath, that Laski became a controversial public figure. He took it upon himself to instruct the Labour leadership on its duty (to end the coalition, not to participate in the Potsdam talks and, in the case of Attlee, to resign as party leader). All this meant that Laski was rarely out of the headlines during the 1945 election campaign, with Churchill depicting him as the devilish power behind the Labour throne. His notoriety was further augmented when, following newspaper reports that he had condoned revolution at an election meeting, he brought an action for libel (which he subsequently lost). His assorted interventions eventually provoked the memorable rejoinder from Attlee that 'a period of silence on your part would be welcome.'

Laski was a prodigious scholar, prolific writer, fine teacher and generous human being. He was also a romancer who liked to think, and liked others to think, that he consorted with the mighty rather more than he did, and more than Britain's cold climate for political intellectuals allowed. His academic and political reputation has declined since his early death in 1950, but he was, in his own difficult time, a republican apostle of liberty (even when this became 'Marxism plus habeas-corpus', as his position

was once dubbed) who kept the faith and never stopped calling others to it.

FURTHER READING

Deane, H. A., *The Political Ideas of Harold J. Laski* (New York: Columbia University Press, 1955).
Eastwood, G., *Harold Laski* (Oxford: Mowbrays, 1977).
Martin, K., *Harold Laski: a Biographical Memoir* (London: Cape, 1953).
Zylstra, B., *From Pluralism to Collectivism: the Development of Harold Laski's Political Thought* (Netherlands: Van Gorcum, 1968).

ANTHONY WRIGHT

Law, (Andrew) Bonar (*b.* New Brunswick, Canada, 16 September 1858; *d.* London, 30 October 1923). Conservative Prime Minister. He was a most unexpected success, a man of the humblest origin who rose to lead the Conservative Party at the time of its battle to defend the House of Lords and the Irish Union, and who returned from retirement to take back the leadership of his party and the prime ministership in 1922. Despite his national prominence he remained a solitary and remote figure; as one of his chief rivals said, after Law was buried in Westminster Abbey, the 'unknown Prime Minister' was buried near the Unknown Warrior.

Law was the son of a Presbyterian minister of Ulster stock and a Scottish mother, born and brought up in a remote manse in rural New Brunswick. After the early death of his mother he was taken to Scotland by an aunt, and suddenly found himself in more affluent surroundings in Glasgow. Nonetheless, there is no doubt that the influence of his earliest years remained with him, as did the memory of his dour and uncommunicative father: in later life Law took no delight in food and drink, or in society, and he himself became melancholy and withdrawn as his father had been. In Glasgow he proved himself a talented child at school, but without any particular distinction. When 16 he entered his mother's family business and rose rapidly; he was soon a junior partner in Jacks and Co., ironmasters, and went on to be also a director of the Clydesdale Bank. Having married in 1891, he lived in Helensburgh and

Bonar Law: caricature by Bert Thomas

travelled the 20 miles each day to Glasgow, practising Conservative politics like the rest of his family and rising to be chairman of the Glasgow Iron Trade Association. In the 1890s he seemed to have a position typical of hundreds and to be marked out by no special quality. The one sign of clear difference lay in his attitude to political debate. He had joined as a young man the Glasgow Parliamentary Debating Association and remained an active member for many years, impressive by the thoroughness with which he researched his case and the dryly effective way in which he presented it. He was also noted for the breadth of his political and economic knowledge, essential tools for the successful debater, and indeed spent much leisure time reading blue books for usable information. This no doubt brought him to wider prominence and paved

the way for his adoption as candidate for the Glasgow Blackfriars constituency, a Liberal seat which he was not expected to win.

Glasgow responded to the Boer War in an outburst of patriotic fervour, and a convinced imperialist such as Bonar Law who was also a well-known local figure was well placed to take advantage of the fact. He won Blackfriars from the Liberals in the election of 1900. In Parliament he did not shine among the new intake of MPs, hardly even getting mention beside Winston Churchill, who made his maiden speech on the same day. Time provided better opportunities, though, and a specially admired speech on the budget in April 1902 secured him office as Parliamentary Secretary to the Board of Trade four months later. It was the only office he held before becoming Leader of the Opposition in 1911. His early speeches, often, to the consternation of his departmental officials, delivered without notes, drew on his Glasgow experience, and he gradually acquired a sure sense of the House, though often in an unconventional way: if his audience had grasped the point he was making, he did not trouble to finish what he was saying, and the speeches that are recorded in Hansard often bore only a passing resemblance to what had been said. With the onset of the split in the Conservative Party between tariff reformers and free traders in 1903, Law lined up unhesitatingly with Joseph Chamberlain, and his knowledge of both imperial and industrial issues rapidly made him one of the ablest exponents of tariff reform in the House. The split no doubt also contributed to a personal setback, for when his party was defeated at the election of 1906, Law lost his Glasgow seat to a Labour candidate. His importance to the party was signalled, though, by his almost immediate return for the safe seat of Dulwich at a by-election, at a time when many distinguished casualties were seeking constituencies.

In the parliament of 1906, the much-depleted Conservative ranks were in need of all the debating talent they could find, especially after Joseph Chamberlain's incapacitation. Law rose quickly to the front rank of speakers, and was included in meetings of ex-ministers now being first referred to as a 'shadow cabinet', although he had not held cabinet office as such. He was especially effective when the mood of politics darkened with the battles over the People's Budget and the House of Lords in 1910–11, since he was prepared to be direct to the point of rudeness when he felt that the occasion justified – a very attractive feature to a party that felt impotent in the face of revolutionary changes being carried by the Liberals. He thus acquired the reputation of a strong man, in marked comparison with the then leader, Balfour; that reputation was no doubt further enhanced by his involvement in various of the pressure groups that sought to push Balfour further towards a simple commitment to tariffs and harry free traders out of the party.

Law's opportunity to emerge more publicly as a front-ranking Conservative came with the party's search for a standard-bearer to carry the battle into the crucially marginal area of Lancashire; after others with wider experience had turned down the honour, Law agreed to give up his safe seat and fight a marginal in Manchester instead. He did not win the seat, but he won a national reputation in the party by trying and was anyway returned to parliament within three months at a by-election in Bootle. By this stage, Balfour's leadership was drawing to a messy close and a scarcely concealed battle for the succession was going on, a battle that came into the open when Balfour resigned in November 1911. Despite his lack of hard experience, Law was 'meekly ambitious' and let it be known that he was available to succeed Balfour, though probably more as a marker for the future than from hope of being chosen. He was aided, though, by the deadlock between Walter Long and AUSTEN CHAMBERLAIN, both supported by more MPs than Law, but neither with a clear majority or much chance of re-uniting the party. By simply refusing to withdraw from the contest, Law found himself chosen as Lord Home was to be in 1963, as the least unpopular contender in a party desperate for unity. Lloyd George, more perceptive than most Conservatives about the abilities of such a self-made man, noted that 'the fools have stumbled on the right man by accident.'

As Opposition Leader for the last three years before the Great war, Law gave his party its head. He had neither the authority nor the inclination to take a moderate or a responsible course, and sought instead to unite the party in a common hatred of Asquith's government. His former uncomplicated commitment to tariffs was an early casualty of that strategy, for once again unity proved to be impossible without a compromise which would push the issue off the immediate agenda, so as to clear the decks of politics for constitutional issues.

In the battles over Home Rule, Law's background and Glasgow Unionist connections both ensured a natural affinity to the cause of Ulster. In this he went to the very edge of treason, committing his party to back Ulster's resistance, even by force if necessary, and almost certainly knowing of and approving the steps that were being taken to arm Ulster's Protestants. It may be argued that he had a far clearer insight into Ulster's sense of history and its determination to resist Home Rule than had the Liberal Government, but it remains unclear how far the official Unionist encouragement of Ulster actually contributed to resistance, or how far Law himself saw it merely as a tactic with which to recover power. In purely tactical terms it was certainly successful, for by 1914 the government was being forced to make concessions to avert the real threat of civil war, concessions, however, that Law could not now accept since he had raised his party's hopes so high. The party's morale soared, by-elections went well and the Unionists expected to return to office in 1914–15, especially (as Law somewhat melodramatically told Asquith) if there were to be a bloodbath in Ireland.

All of this changed with the outbreak of war in 1914, and with it came a steady transition of Law from irresponsible party leader to national figure of government. When Asquith first widened the base of his government in 1915, Law went only to the junior post of Colonial Secretary, so low was his personal reputation among Unionists as well as Liberals. The fall of Asquith in December 1916 marked Law's transition to the centre of politics, for it was achieved with Lloyd George by a combination on which the central focus of Britain's war effort rested until the armistice of 1918. Lloyd George provided the flair and drive in the management of both policy and politics, but

Law was the essential second in command, a workhorse Chancellor of the Exchequer, but also a sound critic of the Prime Minister's ideas and a vital communicator with Parliament. The alliance of reactionary and Liberal progressive probably owed much to common origins outside the mainstream of British public life and to a common disregard for the concerns of society and respectability; both placed more emphasis on getting things done. In all of this Law continued to rely heavily on his sense of what his party would stand, and from this position steered it past the shoals of coalition, feared revolution, franchise reform and the other pitfalls of the war years. It was a major contribution to Conservative strength in the next generation. Despite that, Law's alliance with Lloyd George remained largely negative – a device to defeat Germany, a device to take the country through the perils of postwar politics, a means to speak to the disaffected working classes; there seems never to have been much warmth in the friendship, nor the admiration for Lloyd George that many Conservatives increasingly felt. It was perhaps that detachment that made Law so valuable to the coalition, above all when the uniting forces of a German war and the fear of revolution faded away in 1921. By then, though, Law himself was exhausted by the strains of office, devastated by family losses from the war, and probably already suffering from the illness that was to kill him within two years.

Once out of office in March 1921 his importance to the government became clear. His successor Austen Chamberlain could neither stem nor ride the tide of Tory anti-coalitionism, and Law himself was courted by the anti-coalitionists who now saw him as an alternative leader of a new government. Ambition conflicted with loyalty to recent colleagues and it was only at the last moment that he decided to attend the Carlton Club meeting of 19 October 1922, to speak against coalition and hence to make himself the legitimator and leader of the Conservative revolt against Lloyd George. The initiative made him Prime Minister, but in a state of health that ensured only a short tenure of office. He set himself the task of returning politics to a normal peacetime condition, just as his own premiership marked the return of party government, and in doing so brought on a whole new generation who were to be the Conservative leaders of the next 20 years. Age and illness, though, had made him more negative and gloomier than ever, and, while a policy of 'tranquillity' and promises of a moratorium on legislation had proved a good election cry in 1922, it was a poor basis for government in a time of economic and diplomatic difficulty. It may well be that Law's final illness and retirement in May 1923 came at the right time for his reputation, but he retired much loved by his party and was succeeded by Baldwin, who set himself to carry forward some of Law's traits, in particular his honest and unaffected style.

Through all, Law remained an enigma. He hardly ever entertained and rarely went into society; he spent many hours playing bridge with friends, generally political friends from his own party, another testament to the extent to which from 1900 the House of Commons was the entire focus of his life.

FURTHER READING

Blake, Robert, *The Unknown Prime Minister: the Life and Times of Andrew Bonar Law* (London: Eyre and Spottiswoode, 1955).

Ramsden, John, *The Age of Balfour and Baldwin* (London: Longman, 1978).

Taylor, H. A., *The Strange Case of Andrew Bonar Law* (London: Stanley Paul, 1932).

JOHN RAMSDEN

Lawrence, T(homas) E(dward) [later Shaw, T. E.] **('Lawrence of Arabia')** (*b.* Tremadoc, Caernarfonshire, 16 August 1888; *d.* Bovington, Dorset, 19 May 1935). Writer, diplomat and soldier. Lawrence is best known for his role as a British liaison officer with the Arab forces during their revolt against the Turks (1916–18). From 1915 onwards, however, he played a significant part in the formation of British policy towards the Arab provinces of the Turkish Empire. This role culminated in his appointment in 1921 to the Colonial Office, where he worked during several crucial months as adviser to Winston Churchill on Arab affairs. He was an ardent supporter of the concept of Arab self-determination, and once wrote that his object had been 'to save England, and France too, from the follies of the imperialists, who would have us, in 1920, repeat the exploits of Clive or Rhodes. The world has passed by that point.'

Lawrence's father, Thomas Chapman, came from a well-connected Anglo-Irish family with estates in County Westmeath. His marriage was unsuccessful, and in 1885 he eloped with his daughters' governess. The couple was never free to marry, but adopted the name Lawrence and maintained the appearance of a middle-class family with private means. They settled in Oxford, where their five sons attended school and university.

During his childhood T. E. Lawrence developed a strong interest in archaeology, and, after gaining first-class honours in history, he went in 1911 to join the British Museum's excavations at Carchemish in northern Syria. He was to work in the Middle East for nearly four years, during which time his views would be greatly influenced by the sufferings of the native population at the hands of a corrupt Turkish administration. By the outbreak of war he was convinced that the Arabs should be given the opportunity to govern themselves.

In January 1915 he joined the British Military Intelligence Department in Cairo. His personal knowledge of Syria led him to take a special interest in the evolution of policy towards this region and in the correspondence which took place during 1915 between Sir Henry McMahon, British High Commissioner in Egypt, and Sherif Hussein of Mecca. The British drafts of this were framed by Gilbert Clayton, the head of Lawrence's department. Knowledge of the correspondence, and of the proposed postwar settlement of Syria contained in the secret Sykes–Picot Agreement between Britain and France, played an important part in Lawrence's motivation while he was working as a British adviser to the Arab forces between October 1916 and October 1918. In particular, he understood the need for the revolt to spread northwards into Syria from its starting point in the Hejaz.

At the Paris Peace Conference, Lawrence attempted without success to secure Arab self-government in Syria and Mesopotamia. Instead, the mandate for Syria was given to France, while Britain took over Mesopotamia and Palestine. Within two years, however, attempts to impose British colonial rule in Mesopotamia led to a costly rebellion. Winston Churchill was appointed to the Colonial Office with the task of finding a new policy that would reduce expenditure, and in January 1921 he took Lawrence as his adviser on Arab affairs. Their combined efforts led to solutions which provided for a large measure of self-government in Mesopotamia and Trans-Jordan.

In August 1922, having resigned from the Colonial Office, Lawrence enlisted in the ranks of the RAF. He devoted much of his energy over the years that followed to his book *Seven Pillars of Wisdom* and to other literary work. Despite the humble position he had chosen, he retained many contacts with figures in public life; his friends in Parliament included Nancy Astor, Winston Churchill and the Labour MP Ernest Thurtle. Although he took no further interest in the Middle East, he occasionally used his influence to improve the conditions of his fellow servicemen. For example, he strongly advocated the abolition of the death penalty for cowardice. Shortly after retiring from the RAF, after more than 12 years' service, he received fatal injuries in a motor-cycle accident.

WRITINGS

Seven Pillars of Wisdom (London: Jonathan Cape, 1935).
The Letters of T. E. Lawrence, ed. D. Garnett (London: Jonathan Cape, 1938).
T. E. Lawrence to his Biographers Robert Graves and Liddell Hart (London: Faber and Faber, 1938).
The Letters of T. E. Lawrence, ed. M. Brown (London: Dent, 1988).

FURTHER READING

Wilson, J. M., *Lawrence of Arabia: the Authorised Biography* (London: Heinemann, 1989).

J. M. WILSON

Lawson, Nigel (*b*. London, 11 March 1932). Conservative Chancellor of the Exchequer. To the student of economics, Nigel Lawson's monument – it sounds a remarkably boring monument for a fairly colourful character – will probably be the Medium Term Financial Strategy. The MTFS, for which Lawson was to a large extent responsible as Financial Secretary to the Treasury, gave a measure of stability to the Thatcher administration's economic policy after the stormy early months of the crudest monetarism, which meant appallingly high interest rates and a wave of fatalities among British businesses. It was announced in the 1980 budget and set a target of steadily declining growth of money supply over the next few years.

When Mrs Thatcher strengthened her position in the general election of 1983, Lawson succeeded Geoffrey Howe as her Chancellor. The worst of the economic blizzard was over, and it fell to Lawson to play a more agreeable role than had been available to Howe.

Lawson is one of the most accomplished performers of the art of monetarism. He is a bright boy – as he was at school. His home background, financially comfortable, was Jewish; his grandfather had come from Latvia and the religion had lapsed. At Westminster he won a scholarship to Oxford, where he took a First in philosophy, politics and economics. He then did rather well in the Foreign Office exam, but when it came to the interview, according to his own account, it was decided that he wasn't a Foreign Office type of person.

Diplomacy's loss was journalism's gain. He was recruited by the *Financial Times*, which at that time had a reputation for collecting the cream of the cream of aspiring journalists. Where he really made his name as a writer, however, was on the newly founded *Sunday Telegraph*, which he joined as City Editor. He was not yet 30, a fact which, according to folklore, was glossed over, lest canny *Telegraph* readers might be alarmed at the idea of planning their financial affairs on the advice of a mere lad.

Lawson was now very much at home in the

Nigel Lawson and his wife in St James's Park, London, March 1989, being pursued by an anti-smoking demonstrator

world of the City – and with putting words together. It was the latter facility – along with a degree of self-confidence which some found distasteful – that took him into politics: he was appointed speech-writer to Sir Alec Douglas-Home when he was Prime Minister in 1963–4. The then director of the Conservative Research Department, Sir Michael Fraser, has put on record how the 31-year-old would march up and down, 'looking like Napoleon in his youth, telling me how everything ought to be done . . . whether he thought I was being stupid, whether everyone else was being stupid.'

Lawson entered the Commons in 1974, which was a year when the heavens seemed to be falling in on the Tory Party and most of the blame was being heaped on Ted Heath, whose government had been brought down by the miners. Lawson was by no means an out-and-out anti-Heath man – he admired Heath's Europeanism, for instance – but he certainly believed in the need for market forces, in a way that the Heathites did not. On the other hand, as a young MP he was not in the forefront of the campaign to get Mrs Thatcher into power. But when the latter became Prime Minister Lawson proved an invaluable part of her team from the outset. He understood the economics of what she was trying to do, which was more than could be said of most of his colleagues, and he proved to be adept at political infighting. He likes to win. Like Mrs Thatcher, he does not care very much whether people like what he is doing.

But after he had been Chancellor for a couple of years, it emerged that the Tory Party liked what he was doing very much indeed. He was cutting personal income tax (while at the same time achieving an important reform of company taxation, which was more controversial) and he was starting to pay off the National Debt. He had improved public expenditure procedures. The economy was visibly growing, and the unemployment figures were even beginning to come down. It seemed, after the long, hard slog of the early Thatcher years, that he had squared the economic circle (even if part of the balancing of the books had been achieved by selling off the nationalized industries). But by 1989 some of the magic had dulled. The price of tax cuts appeared to be rising inflation and rising interest rates.

Nigel Lawson is his own man. This has enabled him often to stand firm against a less economically literate Prime Minister. He let it be known that if she wished to get rid of him, he would be quite happy to move into the City, where he expected probably to be happier, and certainly to be far richer. Even so, after many months during which it appeared that there was tension between him and Mrs Thatcher, notably on the question of British participation in the Exchange Rate Mechanism of the European Monetary System, it came as a surprise when he resigned in October 1989.

JULIAN CRITCHLEY

Lever, William (Hesketh) [Viscount Leverhulme of the Western Isles] (*b.* Bolton, Lancashire, 19 September 1851; *d.* London, 7 May 1925). Multinational soap manufacturer, salesman, and nonconformist paternalist. He was senior member of Lever Brothers from 1885 until 1890 and then chairman of Lever Brothers Ltd until his death. His great achievement was to convert his inheritance as a modest Victorian shopkeeper into a multinational business which, four years after his death, merged with its Dutch rivals to form Unilever.

The elder son of James Lever, a retail grocer and Congregationalist, and his wife Eliza (née Hesketh), daughter of a Manchester cotton mill manager, William Lever was raised as a nonconformist but educated at the Church Institute, Bolton. At the age of 16 he joined his father in business. He proved to be a born salesman, studying working-class housewives' tastes and circumstances and noting emerging American marketing techniques. At 21 he was taken by his father into partnership at a salary of £800 a year.

The turning point in Lever's career came in 1884 when, on the verge of retiring to the Orkney Islands, he hit upon the distinctive brand name of 'Sunlight' for his laundry soaps. One soap, made from vegetable oil rather than tallow, lathered more easily and sold so well that Lever decided to manufacture it. With withdrawals from the family firm and loans from relatives he raised £27,000 to pay for the soap works of Winser & Co. of Warrington. To a distinctive brand name and a distinctive soap he added distinctive packaging by substituting scented tablets in cartons for the old paper-wrapped bars. Demand for the soap soared. Lever used all his creative powers to advertise it to the large working-class market. Slogans, doggerel verse, even a painting by a Royal Academician (which deeply offended the artist W. P. Frith) were pressed into service to advertise Sunlight soap in newspapers and magazines, on hoardings and railway stations. When competitors, such as Pears or Joseph Watson's, threatened, Lever introduced a variety of ingenious 'prize schemes'. New soaps, too, kept imitative competitors at bay. Lifebuoy carbolic soap came in 1894; Monkey Brand, an abrasive soap, in 1899; Lux soap flakes soon after.

Lever Brothers Ltd went public in 1894 with a capital of £1.5 million. By 1906 the business was the leading soap firm in the country and an early British multinational. It had 3,000 UK employees, who produced more than 60,000 tons of soap per annum, and seven overseas factories (two in the USA and one each in Canada, Australia, Belgium, Germany and Switzerland). Total capital employed was £4.7 million, of which Lever himself held all the ordinary shares (£1.8 million). His success rested on a strategy of increasing his market share by aggressive marketing techniques and buying out rivals. However, his attempt in 1906 to form a soap manufacturers' cartel, through a holding company controlling all the firms in the industry, was defeated by Lord Northcliffe.. The *Daily Mail* and the *Daily Mirror* raised the spectre of monopolistic trusts and inflated soap prices. Lever Brothers' shares fell by over 20 per cent and the cartel was abandoned. Lever sued the Northcliffe press for libel and was awarded £91,000 in compensation.

Lever's ambitions grew with success. Motivated by a mixture of commercial calculation and benevolence he moved his works from Warrington to the Wirral side of the Mersey in 1888 and built a spacious model company town which he named Port Sunlight. By 1909 many of his 3,600 employees lived in the 720 houses then erected. The halls, schools, institutes, library, church (non-denominational), swimming pool and art collection he donated made the community one of the inspirations of the Garden City movement. Lever influenced the life of the village almost as much as the work of the factory. His co-partnership scheme of 1909, when he distributed to over a thousand long-serving employees £500,000 of non-marketable shares (which by 1912 yielded dividends totalling £40,000), further strengthened employee loyalty.

A dread of monopolistic competitors fuelled Lever's megalomaniacal tendencies. To guarantee supplies of vegetable oils he bought plantations in the Solomon Islands (1902) and the Belgian Congo (1911). To secure the supply of palm oil from West Africa he bought merchant firms in Nigeria (1910) and a fleet of six steamers (1916). As his commercial empire grew so his autocratic traits became more evident. He visited his Congo plantations with much pomp in 1912–13 and 1924–5. He purchased the Outer Hebrides in 1917–19 and attempted to revitalize the depressed island economies of Harris and Lewis with modern farming methods, canning factories and, on the mainland, a chain of 360 retail fish shops, the MacFisheries. To his bewilderment, the Hebrideans rejected his schemes of philanthropic rationalization with vigour and violence.

Lever's control of his firm lasted longer than his powers of commercial judgement. Planning greater conquests in the postwar speculative boom, in 1920 he bought for £8 million control of the Niger Co., his chief rival in West Africa. Within months, prices collapsed and it was discovered that the Niger Co. had a bank overdraft of £2 million. The banks insisted on placing a professional accountant, Francis D'Arcy Cooper, in charge of the subsidiary. Thereafter, Cooper discreetly but increasingly controlled Lever Brothers.

In public life Lever sat as MP (Liberal) for the Wirral from 1906 to 1909, but his essentially autocratic personality found the Commons uncomfortable. He was High Sheriff of Lancashire in 1917–18 and Mayor of Bolton in 1918. In the last 30 years of his life he gave many speeches and wrote numerous pamphlets about the relations of labour and capital.

Lever's philanthropic activities centred on Bolton and the Wirral, particularly Port Sunlight, and were funnelled often through his masonic activities. He built and endowed four Congregational churches, one with his invalid brother James Darcy Lever (*d.* 1910).

Lever married in 1874 Elizabeth Ellen, daughter of Crompton Hulme, a Bolton linen draper. She died in 1913 and in her memory he built the magnificent Lady Lever Art Gallery at Port Sunlight. One of their children, William Hulme Lever (1888–1949), reached adulthood. From 1888 Lever lived at Thornton Manor on the Wirral and had a London house near Hampstead Heath. He was created a baronet in 1911, a baron in 1917 and a viscount in 1922. At his death he left £1.6 million and a business with employed capital of £64.5 million and more than 20,000 employees worldwide.

FURTHER READING

Jeremy, David J., 'The Devices of a Paternalist: William Hesketh Lever and Port Sunlight, 1889–1914', unpublished paper for a conference on entrepreneurship at the Ecole des Hautes Etudes Commerciales, University of Montreal, 1986.

Lever, William Hulme, *Viscount Leverhulme* (London: George Allen and Unwin, 1927).

Nicolson, Nigel, *Lord of the Isles: Lord Leverhulme in the Hebrides* (London: Weidenfeld and Nicolson, 1960).

Reader, W. J., 'William Hesketh Lever', in *Dictionary of Business Biography*, ed. David J. Jeremy and Christine Shaw, 6 vols. (London: Butterworths, 1984–6).

Wilson, Charles, *The History of Unilever: a Study in Economic Growth and Social Change*, 2 vols. (London: Cassell, 1954).

DAVID J. JEREMY

Liddell Hart, Sir B(asil) H(enry) [Liddell Hart, Capt. B. H.] (*b.* Paris, 31 October 1895; *d.* Medmenham, Buckinghamshire, 29 January 1970). Defence correspondent, military historian and philosopher of war. He was an outstanding military journalist, critic and historian in the era of the two world wars. He went up to Corpus Christi College, Cambridge, in 1913 to read history, but volunteered for the army on the outbreak of war, served on the Western Front in 1915–16 and never returned to complete his degree course. His experience at Ypres and on the Somme, where, respectively, he was wounded and gassed, made him a lifelong critic of war and generalship, though never a pacifist. He began to write on infantry tactics while still serving, and soon after being obliged to resign on health grounds he became successively military correspondent for the *Daily Telegraph* (1925–35) and defence correspondent of *The Times* (1935–9). In these years, despite his comparative youth, he probably reached the peak of his military and political influence. He rapidly expanded his tactical ideas (the 'expanding torrent' of attack based on the German offensive of 1918) to the strategic sphere ('the strategy of indirect approach' culled from a wide reading of history), to grand strategy and national policy (the 'British Way in Warfare' based on naval power and economic blockade, and 'limited liability' with regard to an army commitment in Europe). Above all, with his mentor and friend Major-General J. F. C. Fuller, Liddell Hart became internationally famous as the proponent of mechanization, armoured warfare and what was later to be termed blitzkrieg. His books and articles were widely read in progressive circles in the British Army, where he fostered a remarkable number of influential contacts, and also in Germany, though it is doubtful if he was quite so influential there as he was to claim after 1945. He emphasized the importance of air support to tanks, as well as the need for mechanical infantry, arguing that such forces would restore mobility and decisiveness to warfare. His early political contacts included John Buchan, Sir Samuel Hoare and Lord Thomson, and in the 1930s he was consulted by successive war ministers. Neville Chamberlain specifically urged Hore-Belisha to read Liddell Hart's book *Europe in Arms* (1937), and in 1937–8 he reached the peak of his influence as Hore-Belisha's close – though unofficial – adviser (see also HORE-BELISHA, LESLIE).

This partnership between 'H-B' and 'L-H' proved to be a mixed blessing for the latter. With re-armament at last gathering momentum and war threatening it was a hectic and exciting time for the young journalist, who used his modest army rank of captain to cock a snook at those senior officers whom he considered to be reactionary. He advised Hore-Belisha on virtually every aspect of military reform, including reduction of the establishment in India, changing the Cardwell system (named after Edward Cardwell, Secretary of State for War, 1868–74), anti-aircraft defences and mechanization. Above all, he exercised a key influence on senior appointments, including a 'purge' of the Army Council and wholesale changes in the commands. Most of his choices proved successful, but even some of the officers promoted (such as Lord Gort, the new Chief of the Imperial General Staff) resented his influence, while he was understandably detested by those whose careers he brought to a sudden end. He was also blamed for some of Hore-Belisha's shortcomings for which he had no responsibility, and came to believe that he had made a bad mistake in sacrificing his independence as a commentator.

Worse still, in the late 1930s his personal and professional lives were simultaneously in crisis. His first marriage (by which he had one son) broke up (he was to re-marry in 1942). He was at odds with the editorial line of *The Times*, which supported 'appeasement' further than he was prepared to go, while his fervent opposition to sending an army to the continent, arguing that the defensive was now superior, seemed to clash with his earlier support of armoured warfare. In the summer of 1939 he suffered a collapse, whether physical, nervous, or both remains unclear, and a few months later lost his post on *The Times* for advocating a negotiated peace with Hitler.

Thus in the years 1939–45 Liddell Hart's reputation suffered a severe decline. With considerable moral courage, he continued to oppose Churchill's policy of total war, particularly conscription, strategic bombing and 'unconditional surrender'. Not surprisingly he was *persona non grata* with Churchill's circle and also lost many of his military contacts. His call for a negotiated peace had seemed almost treasonable in the early war years, but with the turn of the tide by 1943 his opposition to the destruction of Germany began to acquire respectability as a future Soviet threat arose.

After the war Liddell Hart was remarkably successful in rebuilding his reputation as a prescient and influential military theorist. He championed some of the German generals, such as Manstein, accused of war crimes, and convinced the public that their early victories had owed much to his influence. He was among the first to see that atomic weapons would at best deter all-out conflict between nations possessing them but would not prevent conventional warfare. He wrote persuasively about the kind of conventional defences needed by the West to deter a Soviet attack, stressing that once any atomic (and later nuclear) weapons were used escalation to total destruction was inevitable. Altogether, Liddell Hart's philosophy of restraint, mutual tolerance and avoidance of show-downs (such as the Cuba missile crisis threatened to be) seemed much more appropriate in the nuclear age than it had done in the dark days of Hitler's ascendancy.

Liddell Hart secured a prominent place among the early international pundits of the nuclear era, and in 1960 his book *Deterrence or Defence* was praised by the then Senator J. F. Kennedy. But he felt increasingly ill at ease in a new age of ballistic missiles, war gaming and 'think tanks', and devoted his last years mainly to his *Memoirs* (2 volumes, 1965) and his *History of the Second World War* (published posthumously in 1970).

Always helpful to aspiring writers and historians, in his later years he became something of a guru, consulted by statesmen and scholars of many nations. He was awarded an Hon. D.Litt. by Oxford University in 1964 and received a knighthood in 1966. He was certainly influential for more than 40 years in that his enormous output of books and articles was widely read: he was at least equally important as a 'gadfly', stinging and sharpening the wits of soldiers and politicians in positions of authority even if they did not always agree with him. He was also a self-publicist with an insatiable craving for fame who was apt to overestimate his influence on individuals and events. Nevertheless, one can confidently predict that his name will always figure prominently in any account of military history and theory in the mid-twentieth century.

FURTHER READING

Bond, Brian, *Liddell Hart: a Study of his Military Thought* (London: Cassell, 1977).

——, *British Military Policy between the Two World Wars* (Oxford: Oxford University Press, 1980).

Howard, Michael (ed.), *The Theory and Practice of War* (London: Cassell, 1965).

Howard, Michael, *The Causes of Wars* (London: Temple Smith, 1983).

Lewin, Ronald, 'Sir Basil Liddell Hart: the captain who taught generals', *International Affairs* (January 1971).

Luvaas, Jay, *The Education of an Army* (London: Cassell, 1965).

Mearsheimer, John J., *Liddell Hart and the Weight of History* (London: Brassey's, 1989).

B. J. BOND

Lindemann, F(rederick) A(lexander) [Viscount Cherwell] ('The Prof') (*b.* Baden-Baden, Germany, 5 April 1886; *d.* Oxford, 3 July 1957). Scientist, government adviser and minister. Lindemann was the son of wealthy parents – an Alsatian father and an American mother – but was brought up in Britain. In 1902 he left for further education in Germany for most of the next dozen years, and in Darmstadt and Berlin he came to specialize in low temperature physics. He returned to Britain on the outbreak of the war and found an outlet for his scientific skills at the Royal Aircraft Factory at Farnborough. Lindemann distinguished himself by his study of 'spin' in aircraft and how it could be prevented. In 1919 he was elected Dr Lee's Professor of Experimental Philosophy (Physics) at Oxford. He had responsibility for the Clarendon Laboratory and energetically set about reviving its reputation, but was often involved in clashes with the university authorities as a result of his single-minded concentration on what he regarded as important.

Lindemann's wealth and continental background made him an unusual Oxford figure, as did the fact that he played tennis at Wimbledon while a professor. He early made political contacts on the right and particularly liked dukes. Churchill became a friend in the early 1920s. However, it was not until the 1930s, after Hitler came to power, that Lindemann came close to the centre of government. In June 1935 he joined an Air Ministry committee to consider scientific aspects of air defence under the chairmanship of Sir Henry Tizard. His advent upset other members of the committee. The arguments in part concerned the priority to be given to radar, or at least to its invulnerability to jamming, but also involved the status of the committee itself. Lindemann's links with Churchill were contentious, and it did not help that this 'adviser' was actively though unsuccessfully seeking election to parliament as MP for Oxford University.

Lindemann served under Churchill at the Admiralty in 1939 as head of his statistical section, and acted in the same capacity when he became Prime Minister. In fact, Churchill used him in a wide variety of roles, and greatly admired his short and lucid memoranda on many topics. Lindemann's major concern, however, was with bombs of all types and counter-measures against them. He had an arrogant confidence in his own judgement and it was fortunate that he often turned out to be right. He was made a peer in 1941 and became Paymaster-General in the following year. He frequently attended meetings of the War Cabinet. Churchill regarded him as his right-hand man. It was inevitable, therefore, after 1945, that he should return to Oxford, though he continued to play a prominent part in the House of Lords on economic as well as scientific questions. In 1951 he joined the Churchill cabinet again as Paymaster-General but resigned two years later. He resigned from his chair in 1956.

'The Prof', as he was known, operated effectively at the interface between science and government, though he was not popular either among his fellow-scientists or even Conservative politicians. He was contemptuous of 'proper channels' and knew little at first hand about the people of the country to whose survival he so substantially contributed. It was the accident of his close relationship with Churchill, and the recovery of Churchill's own career, that gave Lindemann an opportunity to exercise an influence in policy-making which could not have happened in any other way.

FURTHER READING

Harrod, R., *The Prof* (London: Macmillan, 1959).
Birkenhead, Earl of, *The Prof in Two Worlds* (London: Collins, 1961).

KEITH ROBBINS

Linlithgow, Lord [Hope, Victor (Alexander John); Marquess of Linlithgow] (**'Hopie'**) (*b.* Hopetoun House, West Lothian, 24 September 1887; *d.* Hopetoun, 5 January 1952). Viceroy of India. Before becoming Viceroy in 1936 he was Civil Lord of the Admiralty (1922–4), deputy chairman of the Conservative Party (1924–6) and the Navy League's president (1924–31); he had chaired the MRC, the governing body of Imperial College, a committee on agricultural produce, the royal commission on Indian agriculture (1926–8) and the joint select committee on Indian constitutional reform (1933–4). After leaving India in 1943 he became Chairman of the Midland Bank, a commissioner of the Church of Scotland, Chancellor of Edinburgh University and Chairman of the Trustees of the National Gallery of Scotland, but assumed no political role. He received many honours: KT (1928), GCIE (1929), GCSI (1936), and KG (1943); in 1935 he became a Privy Councillor.

Public life came early and naturally to Linlithgow. His father died at the age of 48 but had already been the first Governor-General of Australia, among other posts. His son succeeded to the title just before his majority, after education at Eton. He served in the Great War, but was invalided home. He declined the Governorship of Madras in 1924, for family and financial reasons. However, his committee work on India's agriculture and politics later made him a clear candidate for the Viceroyalty – a difficult post demanding political expertise, a dignified presence and aristocratic connections. Of the last two there was no doubt in Linlithgow's case. But his political vision and expertise can rightly be criticized.

Linlithgow was Viceroy in particularly difficult circumstances. He had to inaugurate the 1935 constitution, which made British India's provinces virtually self-governing, and ease Indian politicians away from opposition into constitutional politics, particularly Congress-men under Gandhi and Jawaharlal Nehru. He also had to lure the princes nearer to an all-India Federation, which the raj envisaged as the buttress of a continuing imperial presence. From 1939 his task including mobilizing India's resources for the war effort. In peace Linlithgow was not unsuccessful. Elections in 1936–7 demonstrated Congress popularity in much of British India, and Linlithgow eventually contrived a formula whereby Congressmen took provincial office yet the Governors' reserve powers remained intact. The new constitution worked well and provided valuable political experience for the rulers of free India after 1947. The Viceroy failed to persuade the princes of the virtues of federation; and so the continental provisions of the 1935 Act remained dormant. His lack of pressure on the princes has been criticized, but their reluctance probably stemmed more from their dislike of Congress and their knowledge that Indian divisions (particularly on communal lines) had lessened their need for radical political changes.

When war broke out negotiations for federation were suspended. Congress withdrew from provincial government, choosing instead non-cooperation, culminating in civil disobedience and the Quit India campaign of 1942; Linlithgow's government vigorously suppressed this, incarcerating leading Congressmen until 1945, laying waste the Congress organization. Consequently Jinnah and the Muslim League gained time and space to build a separate Muslim political identity and militancy, which ended in their claim to nationality and the partition of the subcontinent. Linlithgow was not the man for this juncture. Caught between India's own disunited politicians (still sensitive and uncertain of British commitment to self-government) and his London masters, particularly Churchill, he lacked the skill to achieve conciliation and collaboration. His sense of imperial obligation was heightened by the war, compounding his profound distrust of Congress and its leaders, and his misreading of its significance in India's developing political life. (An English academic noted in 1942 how he was clearly weighed down by his wartime responsibility, and openly critical of Indians as lacking politi-

Lord Linlithgow, as Viceroy of India, arriving to take the salute at the march past of the annual proclamation parade, Calcutta, January 1939

cal instinct and competence, and moral courage.) He still envisaged a British presence in India for many decades and was determined not to weaken fundamentally the British position as the price of wartime collaboration. Further, he lacked the warmth and either the capacity or the wish to make imaginative personal contact with Indian politicians which might have led to cooperation. Linlithgow's declaration of war for India without consultation, his failure to take any solid initiative to attract Congress collaboration early in the war, and his alliance with Churchill, which helped to wreck the Cripps Mission (1942), were symptomatic of this personal and political stance. All his office yielded was an expansion of his council to include more Indians. However, under him India provided much financial and material support for the Allies and more than two million recruits, and became the base for the offensive back into South-East Asia. The price for India and Linlithgow was high. The imperial machine was terminally enfeebled. Administrative inefficiency, as much as the loss of Burmese rice, caused

catastrophic famine in Bengal in 1943. Linlithgow went home tired and saddened.

Aloof and cautious in public, Linlithgow was privately a happy family man. He married in 1911 (his wife died in 1965) and had five children. He enjoyed serious literature and light music; loved paintings, including his own inherited collection; was a keen sportsman; and, not least, was a sincere Christian and elder of the Church of Scotland. His were skills and qualities more appropriate for a careful landowner than an imperial politician in turbulent times.

FURTHER READING

Brown, Judith M., *Gandhi: Prisoner of Hope* (New Haven, Conn.: Yale University Press, 1989).

Glendevon, J., *The Viceroy at Bay: Lord Linlithgow in India 1936–1943* (London: Collins, 1971).

India: the Transfer of Power 1942–7 (London: HMSO, 1970–1), vols. 1–3 [includes material from the Linlithgow Collection in the India Office Library].

Moore, R. J., *Churchill, Cripps and India, 1939–1945* (Oxford: Clarendon Press, 1979).

JUDITH M. BROWN

Livingstone, Ken(neth Robert) (*b.* London, 17 June 1945). Labour politician. During the 1980s, as Leader of the Greater London Council, he became the most publicized and controversial local politician of his time – and perhaps of any time.

A working-class south Londoner who trained as a teacher and worked as a laboratory technician, Livingstone sat on Lambeth Borough Council from 1971 to 1978 and on Camden Council from 1978 to 1982. Both were left-wing, Labour-controlled authorities where his skills as a political infighter were honed. He also became a Greater London Councillor in 1973, and in 1981 Labour's sweeping victory in the GLC elections was immediately followed by Livingstone's replacing Andrew McIntosh as Labour Group leader. Thus he also assumed leadership of the council, in what many saw as a carefully staged left-wing coup. A rising tide of controversy immediately began to engulf him. This was partly on account of the innovative measures the council itself undertook between 1981 and 1986. It stemmed partly also from the long and, in public-relations terms, highly successful campaign the GLC fought against its abolition by the Conservative Government. But it probably owed most to Livingstone's own radical statements on many sensitive issues, notably his opposition to the British military presence in Northern Ireland. These made him for a time the pet-hate figure of some newspapers, but he seemed to relish the attention and eventually his relaxed and often humorous style disarmed much of the hostility. Admirers soon saw him as the leading British exponent of the 'Rainbow Coalition' mode of radical politics espoused by black American leader Jesse Jackson.

Livingstone's efforts to enter Parliament, representing London's Brent East constituency, were thwarted by a long dispute between his supporters and those of the sitting Labour MP Reginald Freeson, but finally bore fruit in the 1987 general election. Once he was in Parliament his public profile diminished somewhat – he often complained that back-bench MPs wielded far less real power than local council leaders – and he was out of sympathy with his party's new direction under Neil Kinnock. But as an articulate spokesman

for left-wing views on Labour's National Executive, to which he was also elected in 1987, he could still catch the headlines. Although he lost his position on the NEC in 1989, few doubted that, still relatively young, he could still make his mark on Labour politics in some way.

WRITINGS

Livingstone's Labour: a Programme for the Nineties (London: Unwin Hyman, 1989).

FURTHER READING

Carvel, J., *Citizen Ken* (London: Chatto and Windus, 1984).

STEPHEN HOWE

Lloyd, (John) Selwyn (Brooke) [Baron Selwyn-Lloyd of the Wirral] (*b.* West Kirby, Cheshire, 28 July 1904; *d.* Preston Crowmarsh, Oxfordshire, 17 May 1978). Senior Conservative politician. Lloyd was Foreign Secretary during the Suez Crisis of 1956 and the Chancellor of the Exchequer dismissed by Harold Macmillan in the 'Night of the Long Knives' in July 1962. In a frontbench career spanning 25 years he served under four Conservative Prime Ministers and was a respected Speaker of the House of Commons in the 1970s. Like Bottom the Weaver, a part he once acted at school, Lloyd 'undertook' many parts.

Lloyd was born into the Edwardian professional class. His family, of Welsh extraction, had settled in the Wirral, where his father was prominent in the local Methodist church. The values of his nonconformist upbringing remained with him throughout his life. He won scholarships to Fettes and Magdalene College, Cambridge, where he became President of the Union in 1927. Initially a Lloyd George Liberal, he was adopted as parliamentary candidate for Macclesfield at the age of 22. At Criccieth he became a political associate of Megan Lloyd George. After his defeat in the 1929 general election he concentrated on his legal career on the Northern Circuit (he had been admitted to Gray's Inn in 1926 and was called to the Bar in 1930). His legal experiences gave him a concern for the under-dog and he was a consistent opponent of the death penalty. He served on the Hoylake District Council, becoming chairman at the age of 32, and his career in local government proved a pragmatic apprenticeship. Nationally Lloyd broke with the Liberals over the 1931 financial crisis. Convinced of the necessity for a protective tariff, he voted thereafter for the Conservatives.

On the outbreak of war Lloyd went to the Staff College, Camberley; he rose to the rank of Brigadier and became Deputy Chief of Staff, Second Army. One of General Dempsey's right-hand men, he was a close observer of Field Marshal Montgomery during the invasion of Normandy, in which he had important staff responsibilities. He entered the House of Commons as Conservative MP for the Wirral in July 1945. At a time of Labour landslide this proved to be five years ahead of many of his contemporaries, and he was the first of his generation to achieve one of the 'great' offices of state. In six years of opposition he worked closely with Anthony Eden and R. A. Butler, both of whom sought his services when the Conservatives were returned to power in October 1951. His most significant contribution in opposition was as the dissenting voice in the Beveridge Broadcasting Committee, his minority report on the BBC's monopoly making him in many eyes 'the father of commercial television'.

As Minister of State Lloyd worked for three years on disarmament questions at the United Nations. Subsequently he served as Minister of Supply and Minister of Defence. He developed useful working relationships with Churchill and Eden and owing to the intermittent illnesses of both men achieved unexpected autonomy. He attended more than 100 cabinet meetings before entering the cabinet. His rapid promotion to the Foreign Office in December 1955 was seen by some observers as a sign that Eden wished to conduct his own foreign policy after the independent initiatives of HAROLD MACMILLAN, with whom Eden had an uneasy relationship, an impression not dispelled by the subsequent Suez Crisis. Following President Nasser's nationalization of the Suez Canal in July 1956, Lloyd never wavered from his belief that a negotiated settlement was both possible and preferable to the course of action Eden actually followed, which he described laconically as 'The Plan for which I did not care'. Had his negotiation of the Six Principles with his Egyptian counterpart, Dr Fawzi, been reached ten days earlier at the United Nations, some colleagues felt the situation might have been saved. After his reluctant presence at secret talks with the French and Israelis at Sèvres in October 1956, Lloyd was tied by collective cabinet responsibility to the military invasion of Egypt in November. However, he continued to ask awkward military and political questions, based on his experience in Second Army and as Minister of State. After the withdrawal of British troops from Egypt he offered his resignation on 28 November, but this was refused.

Lloyd was retained as Foreign Secretary by Harold Macmillan in January 1957 and the next three years saw the resolution of the Cyprus question and the Formosa Straits dispute. As Sancho Panza to Macmillan's mercurial Quixote, Lloyd also played an important steadying role when accompanying the Prime Minister to international summits in Bermuda, Moscow and Paris. His position in the upper echelons of the cabinet was seemingly assured and Macmillan was at home with his dependable presence, though there was an edge to their complex political relationship that Lloyd's antennae did not always detect.

In 1960 Macmillan transferred Lloyd to the Treasury. His years as Chancellor of the Exchequer were marked by several important initiatives. He set up the National Economic Development Council, a tripartite organization for government, employers and trade unions; he made the first steps towards an incomes policy and encouraged the concept of long-term expenditure planning; and he provided government funding for the National Theatre. Lloyd's chancellorship was to founder on the cumulative political difficulties that arose in the spring of 1962. The pay pause was particularly unpopular with nurses and teachers, who had a large measure of public support, and contributed to a series of by-election reverses for the government. On 13 July 1962 Macmillan moved with uncharacteristic haste and dismissed seven cabinet ministers, including the

Chancellor. Privately Lloyd decided that 'a bitter resentment against Macmillan would destroy my peace of mind', and he found in forgiveness the best form of revenge. As a backbencher he loyally undertook in the severe winter of 1962–3 an inquiry into the Conservative Party organization. When Macmillan resigned as Prime Minister in October 1963, Lloyd played a key part in influencing the succession in favour of Lord Home, and it was no surprise when he was recalled to the cabinet as Lord Privy Seal and Leader of the House of Commons. His success in this latter role, in one of the happiest years of his life, paved the way for the speakership to which he was elected in January 1971. In this office he was respected for his inherent fairness and his concern for the backbencher.

Lloyd was underestimated by his contemporaries. Lacking the fashionable quality of 'charisma', he achieved his ends by more solid nonconformist virtues. At times he appeared the political staff officer, yet at others he proved innovative and independent. Shy in public, he was wittily gregarious in private, especially with trusted friends, compartmentalized from the diverse strands of his career, though after the failure of his marriage he remained a loner who guarded his emotional privacy. Nevertheless, he was a man to be taken seriously in everything he did, who was concerned to play a constructive part in his country's welfare, and who left a significant legacy in unexpected areas of public life.

For illustration, see EDEN, ANTHONY.

WRITINGS

Mr Speaker, Sir (London: Jonathan Cape, 1976).
Suez 1956: a Personal View (London: Jonathan Cape, 1978).

FURTHER READING

Thorpe, D. R., *Selwyn Lloyd* (London: Jonathan Cape, 1989).

D. R. THORPE

Lloyd George, David [Earl Lloyd-George of Dwyfor] (*b.* Manchester, 17 January 1863; *d.* Llanystumdwy, Caernarfonshire, 26 March 1945). Liberal politician and Coalition Prime Minister. Lloyd George was Prime Minister from December 1916 to October 1922, but was a substantial, though enigmatic, figure at the centre of British politics for far longer. He was in fact continuously in office from December 1905 until his resignation in 1922 – an unusual record, which no doubt encouraged the view that he was indispensable. The prospect of his return to office was a topic of endless political speculation, but he never did make a political come-back, though not for want of trying. His ministerial achievement, therefore, was concentrated in the first quarter of the century.

J. M. Keynes, who knew that Lloyd George was not educated at Eton and King's College, Cambridge, and was not even English, seems to have supposed, in a celebrated phrase, that this 'goat-footed bard' was 'rooted in nothing'. He was a 'half-human' visitor to the twentieth century from the enchanted woods of Celtic antiquity and was medium and vampire rolled into one. Since this description was penned, historians have exerted themselves energetically to provide Lloyd George with roots. Welsh historians, personally lacking any vampire tendencies themselves, have been at pains to point out to fen-dwellers that Llanystumdwy was a real community. After the death of his father when he was a baby, Lloyd George was brought up by his mother and his uncle, the local shoemaker and lay pastor of a Campbellite Baptist chapel in nearby Criccieth. The household was modestly prosperous by local standards. Lloyd George early inhabited two linguistic worlds – Welsh and English – and also contrived to be a moderately rebellious nonconformist who nevertheless attended the village 'National' or Anglican school maintained by a Church that was still established. His circumstances inevitably gave the schoolboy a capacity to see that 'facts' have no automatic social location. Different traditions 'see' the same phenomena in different lights. What nothing can explain is why one particular boy should have had the 'supreme idea' of 'getting on'. He told the girl he was to marry that, if it obstructed his path, he was prepared to thrust even love itself under the wheels of his juggernaut. 'Getting on' led him swiftly to abandon the project of following in his father's footsteps and becoming a schoolteacher. He took law exams and in the mid-1880s established himself as a solicitor in Porthmadog and other nearby towns. He also threw himself into other 'causes' – against drink and against the tithe – and seemed a model nonconformist radical, though one who expressed private satisfaction at the practice British guns had obtained in the bombardment of Alexandria in 1882. Active on the new Caernarfonshire County Council, his local fame was such that he gained the Liberal nomination for the Caernarfon Boroughs constituency and entered the House of Commons at a by-election in 1890. He sat for this constituency – though initially it was by no means 'safe' – until 1945, when he took a peerage.

It is easy to argue that this youthful figure at Westminster was 'the great outsider'. Clearly, he had neither wealth nor social connection, but he was not unique in these respects even in the House of Commons of the 1890s. He neither cultivated a self-conscious 'cloth-cap' image nor fawned before his social superiors. He had an inner arrogance which rendered such strategies superfluous. Nevertheless, there were strains in trying to maintain a parliamentary life in London and a home life in North Wales. He had to support his growing family by journalism and by serving the legal needs of expatriate Welshmen in London. Gradually, through the 1890s, in an age when oratorical ability still mattered, he was becoming known as a forceful speaker.

It seemed as if Welsh concerns were closest to his heart, and during this period Lloyd George has sometimes been described as a Welsh nationalist. Certainly, he associated with other Welsh Liberals who tried to act as a 'Welsh Party' and to achieve distinct legislation for Wales relating to drink, land laws and the established Church. He talked, from time to time, of Home Rule for Wales. It seems fairly certain, however, that he was never separatist in either sentiment or intention. Even from a very early stage, 'Wales' evoked very ambivalent emotions, whether conceived in terms of climate or culture. He retained a certain nostalgia for 'chapel culture' all his life, particularly when people began to sing, so long as it

was not necessary to be too fussy about meanings. On the other hand, there was a stultifying narrowness which caused him to express his desire to escape from the 'stunted' principality. It was his wife who retained a home there; he preferred to live in Sussex or Surrey. He loved Wales, but the prospect of 'Wales alone' was intolerable.

It was his opposition to the South African War of October 1899 that gave Lloyd George a 'British' reputation for the first time. It is well known that he opposed the war and was involved in stormy meetings in Birmingham, Glasgow and even Bangor in his own constituency when he made 'anti-war' speeches. The problem is to interpret his motives. It seems hardly sufficient to suppose that he was 'pro-Boer' because of his fellow-feeling, as a Welshman, for a small people. He was not a Calvinist. He was not a pacifist, if that word is taken to mean opposition to fighting in any circumstances. He was not an anti-imperialist, if that be taken to mean opposition to empire as such. British rule in South Africa was desirable, but what was unnecessary was to fight, in the clumsy way that had been engineered, in order to consolidate that rule. Old-age pensions, to name only one measure, were going to be lost because of the antics on the veldt. Lloyd George's stance made him appear 'left-wing', which was no bad thing at this juncture, but it has been pointed out that the notorious meeting at Birmingham, if only it had been prepared to listen, would have heard a speech praising Lord Rosebery, the enemy of Campbell-Bannerman and the Gladstonians. In other words, even at this point, it is not easy to characterize Lloyd George as either 'left' or 'right'. Similarly, with the other contemporary issue which brought him fresh prominence, his opposition to Balfour's Education Act of 1902, he seemed to be the voice of nonconformity galvanizing Wales against the financial support being given to 'voluntary' schools. In private, however, it looks as if he believed that the act was quite reasonable. After the immediate hue and cry was over, Lloyd George slipped away. He had no wish to be typecast as a Welsh nonconformist.

When Campbell-Bannerman formed his cabinet in December 1905, prior to the general election in the following month, Lloyd George became President of the Board of Trade and, at the age of 43, the youngest member of the cabinet. He was understandably elated. He had a department of 750 people and responsibilities in the area of labour relations and the supervision of railways and harbours, among other matters. Like most of his cabinet colleagues, he did not have much first-hand knowledge of trade; nevertheless, his legal training served him in good stead in piloting through measures relating to patents, company law and shipping. It did not seem to matter that he had not been to Balliol. Although slightly puzzled that this should be so, his civil servants were impressed by his dexterity and energy. He could obviously read, though he seemed disinclined to write if it could be avoided. He was a 'success' and the government was coming to need success. When Asquith became Prime Minister in 1908, Lloyd George was the obvious man to succeed him as Chancellor (see also ASQUITH, H. H.).

At the Treasury, Lloyd George was at the height of his powers. It was still suspected that he did not fully understand all the financial detail with which he had to appear to cope, but he grasped the opportunity to thrust 'welfare' to the fore, though he would probably have been somewhat surprised to find himself later described as the pioneer of the welfare state. Poverty did distress him, but so did the prospect of Labour advance, though to relate the precise proposals of the 1909 budget to either anxiety in simple fashion is unsatisfactory. Old-age pensions could come now that the skirmishing in South Africa was over. The taxation increases proposed were modest by some later standards but were deemed excessive by Conservatives. Taxation of motor cars and petrol was interesting but not thought likely to yield much revenue in the longer term. The Conservative majority in the House of Lords might throw out the budget on the pretext that it was not an orthodox money bill. Some have believed that the Chancellor goaded the opposition with a provocative budget in order to bring on a major constitutional crisis. That seems unlikely. Nevertheless, he was not afraid to take up the challenge. He attacked dukes with a relish that caused consternation in

Buckingham Palace, not to mention some quarters in his own party. Nevertheless, at the end of November 1909 the Lords rejected the budget. Under the cry of the Peers versus the People, Lloyd George took a leading part in both the January and December election campaigns of 1910. The Liberals lost their overall majority in the Commons, but could still govern reasonably effectively. The Parliament Act of 1911 removed the power of the Lords to veto legislation and replaced it by the right to delay.

At this stage, the Chancellor appeared to be the radical darling. The National Insurance Act of 1911 consolidated his legislative reputation. Yet at the very time when the division between government and opposition appeared most sharp, Lloyd George was dabbling in private with the idea of a coalition to put through necessary measures on an 'agreed' basis. Party squabbles could drag the country down at a time when there were difficult issues across the Irish Sea and continental war might be a possibility. That the Chancellor felt mature enough to offer a wide view beyond his Treasury brief was instanced by his Mansion House speech in 1911 which warned the powers of Europe that Britain could not be ignored. By 1914, however, as the summer crisis unfolded, there were many Liberals who hoped that Lloyd George was the man to keep Britain out of the war. Lloyd George did not go out of his way to clarify his stance at too early a stage, but it seems unlikely that he seriously contemplated such a role. In any event, the violation of Belgian neutrality clinched matters. Belgians and Serbs really were little people.

Lloyd George remained at the Exchequer, but early made it clear that he had views on the general conduct of the war. He had a temperamental impatience with the way things seemed to be going, but he was not disloyal. When the first Coalition Government was formed in May 1915 he stepped down from the lofty heights of the Treasury to take over the new Ministry of Munitions. The task was deceptively simple – to find out what was really needed and then to supply those needs. He seemed intuitively to grasp what running a war required and his achievement was considerable. When Kitchener was drowned in June

David Lloyd George at the British Zionist Federation dinner at the Savoy Hotel, London, April 1931

1916, Lloyd George succeeded him. Six months later he was installed in Downing Street. This outcome has been analysed frequently and different conclusions have been reached. On the whole, the concatenation of circumstances which brought about this result has not been seen as the climax to a deliberate plot to depose Asquith, though some have not been persuaded.

As Prime Minister, Lloyd George brought determination and vigour to the war. He was prepared to innovate and short-circuit. He still believed that victory was obtainable, but drastic changes were necessary. Lloyd George's record has been generally praised. He was the man who won the war, but it was far from clear that he could be the man who would win the peace. His coalition government had been a government of individuals. It was doubtful if the Liberal Party could reunite under his

leadership. The Prime Minister was determined to carry on, but the election of 1918 saw the Conservatives as the largest single party. They accepted his leadership – but for how long? Opinion differs on the strategy Lloyd George was following to ensure his own political survival. Were the Liberals to reunite? Were 'his' Liberals to fuse with the Conservatives? Was an emerging Labour Party an enemy or a potential ally? These uncertainties also make it difficult to characterize the government as a whole as it struggled with industrial issues and the Irish question. The Prime Minister appeared as inventive as ever, but in October 1922 the majority of Conservative MPs decided that they had had enough. The Lloyd George era was over.

Nevertheless, in the Commons and the country, he remained a figure of stature. The Liberals were reunited, after a fashion, and

Lloyd George became leader after Asquith's retirement at the end of 1926. His supreme effort was made in the general election of 1929 but the outcome was disappointing. The Liberals could only help keep a Labour government in office, something some of their number found distasteful. Lloyd George had made great play with a programme which claimed that the Liberals could conquer unemployment, and over the previous few years he had drawn upon the advice of economists such as Sir Walter Layton and Keynes in proposing measures which would supposedly achieve this object. There was consolation, however, in the acclaim accorded to the *War Memoirs*, which he did not in fact write, though he embellished them at suitable intervals. He still liked to be thought in the big political league, and Herr Hitler found time to receive him at Berchtesgaden in 1936. Lloyd George was rather impressed. He and his wife celebrated the golden anniversary of what had been a not altogether straightforward marriage in Cannes in 1938. In 1940 he denounced Neville Chamberlain for his handling of the Norwegian campaign, but his old friend Winston Churchill could not persuade him to resume the struggle in this new war. Indeed, he thought the Germans would soon be in Surrey. Should they be opposed? The exposure to unpleasantness in South-Eastern England led him in 1944 to move back to Llanystumdwy. There, lately equipped with an earldom, the magnificently ambiguous journey came to an end.

In the 1930s, Lloyd George spent a lot of time farming on an estate in Surrey to which he gave a Welsh name. A new strain of raspberry was produced and named after him. Perhaps he derived a certain mischievous pleasure from the fact that he delivered a raspberry to his contemporaries.

For further illustration, see ASQUITH, H. H.

FURTHER READING

Campbell, J., *Lloyd George: the Goat in the Wilderness* (London: Jonathan Cape, 1977).
George, W. R. P., *The Making of Lloyd George* (London: Faber and Faber, 1976).
Gilbert, B. B., *David Lloyd George: a Political Life: the Architect of Change 1863–1912* (London: Batsford, 1987).
Grigg, J., *The Young Lloyd George* (London: Eyre Methuen, 1973); *The People's Champion 1902–11* (London: Eyre Methuen, 1978); *From Peace to War 1912–1916* (London: Methuen, 1985).
Morgan, K. O., *Lloyd George* (London: Weidenfeld and Nicolson, 1974).
Pugh, Martin, *Lloyd George* (London: Longman, 1988).

KEITH ROBBINS

Lothian, Lord [Kerr, Philip (Henry); Marquess of Lothian] (*b*. London, 18 April 1882; *d*. Washington, DC, 12 December 1940). Publicist and diplomat. Lothian deserves to be better known as Philip Kerr, under which name he achieved considerable success as an administrator in South Africa, an imperialist journalist at home and an important member of Lloyd George's 'garden suburb' after 1916. But fame follows notoriety; and it was after the death of his cousin in 1930, which brought him the title of eleventh Marquess of Lothian, that Kerr became implicated in the so-called Cliveden Set and entered the histories of 'appeasement' by remarking, at the time of the Nazi regime's remilitarization of the Rhineland in March 1936, that Hitler was only going into his own back garden.

Following his first-class degree in modern history at Oxford, Lothian became the youngest of Lord Milner's 'Kindergarten' in South Africa, where he served as Private Secretary to the Lieutenant Governor of the Transvaal, Sir Arthur Lawley, and worked closely with a lifelong friend, R. H. (later Lord) Brand. He came home in 1909 and helped found an influential imperialist periodical, the *Round Table*, which threw him into contact with a number of gifted journalists and academics – some of whom joined him in either the Lloyd George secretariat or the loose connection with Lloyd George's style of Liberalism that was to characterize Lothian's politics for the rest of his life. He was Private Secretary to Lloyd George from 1916 to 1921. In mid-career, the academic element of Lothian's personality overrode the political: he resigned from the secretariat in 1921 and spent the next decade in journalism, serious writing and travel. Journalism made him director of United Newspapers for a year or so. With Lionel Curtis he wrote a book called *The Prevention of War* (1923), announcing an abiding interest which Kerr's involvement in the Versailles conference had further stimulated; it also reflected his passion for American experience, on which the book predominantly drew. Travel tended, naturally, towards America and, as secretary to the Rhodes Trustees after 1925, Lothian discovered a number of opportunities to visit the USA.

The collapse of Ramsay MacDonald's second Labour government in 1931 allowed the new National Government to include among its Liberal contingent a sympathetic voice in the House of Lords. Lothian took the Duchy of Lancaster until after the general election of October, when he became junior minister to Sir Samuel Hoare at the India Office. But the collective withdrawal of Liberal ministers when the Ottawa agreements of 1932 contravened their commitment to free trade meant that Lothian played no significant part in developing policy. Instead he spent increasing time with the Astors. Waldorf Astor he had known through the garden suburb, but it was Astor's wife, Nancy, who became an especially close friend, not least through an interest in the Christian Science that dominated the Astor household and that had supplanted Lothian's original Catholicism (which he had abandoned at Oxford). Versailles still weighed heavily with him: it was said that he himself had drafted the preamble to the treaty. And through the tortuous unwinding of foreign policy in the 1930s Lothian shared a widespread horror of going to war with Germany to defend an increasingly indefensible settlement. These sympathies made him a central member of Claud Cockburn's infamous Cliveden Set, which in fact approximated more to a Victorian salon than a Nazi cell. America continued to command Lothian's preoccupations as a way forward through the tangle of European concerns and made him critical of Neville Chamberlain's refusal to involve the USA in his thinking. Just before the outbreak of World War II a vacancy occurred at the Washington Embassy and Lothian seemed an obvious choice for what appeared a post of great future importance. His diplomatic career proved as

brief, however, as his ministerial one. He died just over a year later.

FURTHER READING

Butler, J. R. M., *Lord Lothian, Philip Kerr 1882–1940* (London: Macmillan, 1960).
Sykes, C., *Nancy: a life of Nancy Astor* (London: Collins, 1972).
Turner, John, *Lloyd George's Secretariat* (Cambridge: Cambridge University Press, 1980).

MICHAEL BENTLEY

Low, Sir David (*b*. Dunedin, New Zealand, 7 April 1891; *d*. London, 19 September 1963). Cartoonist and caricaturist. Low was the most celebrated cartoonist of his age. After precocious success in Australia, he worked in Fleet Street from 1919 until his death. During his heyday on the *Evening Standard* (1927–49) he set standards of technique and content by which other cartoonists came to be judged. An uncomfortable period on the *Daily Herald* (1950–3) was followed by a final move to the *Manchester Guardian* (now *The Guardian*). He was most famous for his sustained ridicule of the Fascist dictators, who banned his work and blacklisted him, and for his hostility to the policy of 'appeasement'. In domestic politics his sympathies were left of centre. He devised cartoon symbols such as Colonel Blimp and the TUC carthorse that became more famous than their creator, and his portrait caricatures, many first published in the *New Statesman*, became collectors' items. He wrote perceptively on his art, and he was an accomplished broadcaster.

Low's first drawing was published in a children's comic when he was 11. He was a full-time cartoonist in New Zealand in his teens and moved to Australia to join the famous weekly *Bulletin*, 'the Bushman's bible', in 1911. His wartime cartoons of the combative Australian Prime Minister, Billy Hughes, led to an offer of employment with the Liberal Cadbury press in Fleet Street. He leapt at it and quickly made a mark with lively cartoons of Lloyd George for the evening *Star*. In 1927 Lord Beaverbrook tempted him to the *Evening Standard* with a high salary and – more important – a guarantee not to interfere with the content of his cartoons (though not in fact a guarantee to publish them). The relationship worked happily. Low's cartoons gained force by often contradicting editorial policy, while Beaverbrook enjoyed the rumpus (and Low's impish cartoon image of him).

Low left the *Evening Standard* in 1949 mainly for a change of scene, but he soon fretted at the *Daily Herald*'s touchiness about occasional criticism of the Labour Party. The *Guardian* proved a haven and greeted him with delight and a certain deference. He had long been syndicated worldwide and was indeed a celebrity.

The fluency of Low's brushwork concealed immense pains. He was not a 'natural' artist but developed his skill by laborious practice. His cartoons were carefully drawn in pencil, then brushed in. He worked in a studio, never at the office. His achievement was to re-introduce wit, verve and caricature into the bland, post-Victorian conventions of British cartooning, still dominated on his arrival by what Max Beerbohm called 'comic ideas, seriously illustrated'. Low purveyed serious ideas, comically illustrated: 'It is easier to impress an Englishman by exciting his sense of humour than his sense of horror.' Gillray and Rowlandson were his models.

Low's geniality reflected a basic optimism. 'Here lies a nuisance who was dedicated to sanity', he once suggested for his epitaph. He thought the world's problems were due to stupidity more than wickedness. Blimp and the carthorse were both symbols of stupidity ('Baldwin may have no brains', explains Blimp, 'but he's a true Englishman'). He mistrusted emotion in politics, preferring a rational, pragmatic reformism. This was insufficiently rigorous to be called socialism but kept him in line with the broad aims of the Attlee government, for example. Above all he was an individualist, disliking the 'totalitarianism of the left' as much as Fascism. The individualist streak in American society appealed to him, and he was an effective exponent of Britain's wartime and postwar condition to the USA and to Australasia, in print and on radio.

Low married a New Zealand girl, proposing by cable from London, and had two daughters. He accepted a knighthood in 1962.

WRITINGS

Low's Autobiography (London: Michael Joseph, 1956).
Ye Madde Designer (London: Studio, 1935).

FURTHER READING

Mellini, P., 'Colonel Blimp's England', *History Today*, 34 (October 1984).
Seymour-Ure, C. and Schoff, J., *David Low* (London: Secker and Warburg, 1985).

COLIN K. SEYMOUR-URE

M

MacDonald, (James) Ramsay (*b.* Lossiemouth, Morayshire, 12 October 1866; *d.* at sea, 9 November 1937). Labour and National Prime Minister. Few careers in modern British political history have been more stormy, more controversial or, in the final stages, more tragic than MacDonald's. He was the illegitimate son of a farm labourer and a servant girl, born in poverty in a remote fishing village on the coast of North-East Scotland. He had to fight his way to prominence and, in his early years at any rate, did so with remarkable *élan*. He was a parliamentary candidate in his twenties and an MP at the age of 39. At 44, he was chairman of the Parliamentary Labour Party. Thirteen years later he was the first Labour Prime Minister in British history. His second government, however, collapsed in acrimony and humiliation during the sterling crisis of August 1931; and he is remembered as much for his reluctant decision to form a National Government with the Conservatives and Liberals as for his earlier role as one of the chief architects of Labour's rise to major-party status. His last six years were a sad diminuendo of failing powers, ebbing authority and gathering derision.

Partly because of these shifts of fortune, his career is extraordinarily hard to assess. At every stage he was surrounded by intense controversy. Before World War I he was one of the most persuasive exponents of a gradualist, evolutionary socialism stressing the need for slow, organic change. Under his chairmanship the Parliamentary Labour Party acted, to all intents and purposes, as a junior partner in a broad-based coalition headed by the minority Liberal Government of the day. This led to bitter conflicts with the socialist purists of the Independent Labour Party, which MacDonald had joined soon after its foundation and which provided him with his base in Labour politics. The war years brought more violent altercation of an uglier kind. MacDonald was a leading member – perhaps the leading member – of the Union of Democratic Control, which held that Britain was as much to blame for the war as Germany and which campaigned for a compromise peace. As such, he was the victim of press attacks of extraordinary savagery, Horatio Bottomley's notorious paper, *John Bull*, even publishing a facsimile of his birth certificate in order to make the fact of his illegitimacy public. The controversy surrounding his actions in 1931 had louder echoes and more enduring effects. For a while, he was the darling of what would now be called the Establishment. 'Every duchess in London will be wanting to kiss me!' was his own (often-misinterpreted) ironic comment. But its adulation soon wore off. Meanwhile, most of his old followers in the Labour Party had turned on him with a mixture of bitterness and contempt which left deep wounds and which scars his reputation even today.

Yet in his prime, ordinary members of the Labour Party idolized him as no leader has been idolized since. Egon Wertheimer, the German socialist writer, described him in the 1920s as the 'focus for the mute hopes of a whole class'; and the phrase was not hyperbole. In part, this was the product of the commanding presence and mellifluous voice which made him a great platform orator in the histrionic style of the period and helped to earn him the soubriquet of 'the Gladstone of Labour'. His private personality, on the other hand, was not an unmixed asset for a political leader. Magnetism jostled with reserve, warmth with shyness. Attacks on his aloofness and complaints about his brusqueries in personal relationships were legion. Even one of his closest and most admiring supporters described the 'chill' of going into his room and 'being looked at, if looked at at all, as though not there'. Yet he was an unusually considerate employer, took great pains to help old friends or colleagues in trouble and won something close to devotion from a small circle.

Apparent aloofness was, in part, the product of real loneliness. MacDonald's wife died in 1911, leaving him to bring up a family of five small children. He was hit hard by her death – years later one of his children recalled his 'tear-stained agony of grief' on its anniversary – and, in some respects, never recovered from it. He was a handsome man of middle height, with flowing locks, a noble brow and, when he chose to exercise it, considerable charm. He was attractive to women, needed their company and relaxed more easily in it than in men's. But although he formed close friendships with a few women, he never remarried; and for the last 25 years of his life he was emotionally alone. After 1931 he was accused of having succumbed to the 'aristocratic embrace'. He

was, it was said, a snob and social climber who had betrayed his party to win the approval of the class enemy – more at home in society drawing rooms than with the dispossessed whose aspirations he was supposed to represent. But these judgements reveal more about the Labour Party's need to find a scapegoat than about the intricacies of MacDonald's character. In his last few years, it is true, a friendship with the flamboyant Conservative hostess Lady Londonderry brought some light into an otherwise bleak private life, but there is no evidence that it influenced his political attitudes or values.

Perhaps because his powers declined so dramatically and so publicly after 1931, it became conventional after his death to dismiss

Ramsay MacDonald taking part in a tug-of-war match at Easton Lodge, June 1923

him as a sentimental dreamer, with no grasp of the practicalities of office. Winston Churchill's savage nickname, 'the boneless wonder', was endlessly repeated. The truth was more complicated. MacDonald's political creed can fairly be described as utopian and his platform style strikes a modern ear as sentimental. But he won his spurs in politics as an organizer, as a master of committee detail, and these traits survived almost until the end. As Prime Minister and (in his first government) as Foreign Secretary he displayed impressive mastery of the details of complex international negotiations. He lacked Winston Churchill's insatiable administrative appetite and could not emulate Lloyd George's driving will. But that is only to say that he was not in the very front rank of twentieth-century British political leaders. Had it not been for 1931, he would almost certainly have gone down as a perfectly competent Prime Minister of the second rank. His greatest failure lay in his inability to stop the dramatic rise in unemployment which haunted his second government. But, although it later became commonplace to argue that he should have adopted the teachings of J. M. Keynes, it is not so clear from the vantage point of the 1980s that they would have been any more successful than the Treasury orthodoxy of the day. Perhaps the real charge against him is not so much that he found no solution as that he did not appear to be looking for one with sufficient energy. That, however, is a criticism of his public relations rather than of his administrative capacity.

MacDonald was educated – first as pupil, then as pupil-teacher – at the Drainie village school, four miles across the fields from the Lossiemouth cottage where his mother and grand-mother brought him up. At the age of 19 he left home to seek his fortune in the south, first in Bristol and then in London. He became a socialist, joining the Bristol branch of H. M. Hyndman's Social Democratic Federation and then the breakaway Socialist Union. In London he suffered a spell of unemployment, found work addressing envelopes for the National Cyclists Union and then became an invoice clerk in the City. He took evening courses in science at the Birkbeck Institute, but his hopes of a scientific career were wrecked when a nervous breakdown prevented him from sitting a scholarship examination.

His political career really began in 1888, with his appointment as private secretary to Thomas Lough, a future Radical MP. He joined the recently founded Fabian Society and became secretary of a more obscure socialist sect called the Fellowship of the New Life, which believed in moral regeneration and communal living. Shortly after the 1892 general election, by now a freelance journalist, he was adopted as prospective parliamentary candidate by the Dover Labour Electoral Association. In 1894 he switched to Southampton – a two-member constituency where it looked as if the local Liberal Association might adopt a Labour candidate to run in harness with the sitting Liberal MP. The Liberals, however, turned him down. He joined the 18-month-old Independent Labour Party and stood unsuccessfully as ILP candidate for Southampton in the 1895 general election.

The following year he married Margaret Gladstone, a distant relative of Lord Kelvin and daughter of Dr John Gladstone, professor of chemistry at the Royal Institution. Her private income of around £460 a year gave MacDonald a degree of economic security unique in his generation of Labour leaders and made it possible for him to devote himself, almost full-time, to politics. He rose rapidly in the ILP and, together with KEIR HARDIE, played a crucial part in the manoeuvres which led to the establishment of the Labour Representation Committee – the fore-runner Labour Party – in 1900. He was chosen, without opposition, as its secretary and was largely responsible for the secret electoral pact with the Liberal chief whip, Herbert Gladstone, which made it possible for the new party to win nearly 30 seats in the 1906 general election. In 1900 he stood as ILP candidate for Leicester, again unsuccessfully. Thanks to his pact with Gladstone, the next election brought him better luck. Leicester was another two-member constituency, and after complex negotiations the Labour Party and the Liberals agreed that each should run only one candidate. In 1906 MacDonald was elected.

The next big milestone in his career was his election as chairman of the Parliamentary Labour Party in 1911. In the next three-and-a-half years he steered his occasionally restive, but mostly acquiescent, followers into an increasingly close relationship with the Liberals. August 1914, however, brought a sharp, almost seismic, break in this pattern. Despite his approval of the government's domestic policies, MacDonald had consistently opposed its foreign and defence policies as provocative and dangerous. When war came in the end, it seemed to him to prove his earlier warnings well-founded. The German invasion of Belgium, he believed, was only the proximate cause of the tragedy. The real cause was 'the policy of the balance of power through alliance'; of that the British Government was as guilty as the German. When the Parliamentary Labour Party decided to vote for war credits, he resigned from the chairmanship. As war fever rose, he and the handful of dissident Radicals and socialists who took a similar line had to plough an increasingly lonely furrow. By a curious irony of political mutation, however, his wartime isolation – his position as the voice of principle, scourge of authority and outcast from respectability – gave him a hold on the imagination of the Labour movement which was to be of incalculable benefit in the turbulent politics of the postwar period. His commitment to evolutionary methods still put him on the right of the party. But in style, image and personal association, the war turned him into a man of the left. It was an ideal combination for a party torn, then as always, between a left-wing heart and a right-wing head.

These benefits were slow in coming. In the 1918 general election MacDonald was defeated by a crushing majority. In 1921 he stood in a by-election for Woolwich – held by Labour since 1903 – only to lose again. Outside Parliament, however, the tide of party opinion gradually turned in his favour as the Coalition Government alienated working-class voters and Labour's drab and cautious parliamentary leaders failed to satisfy a rank and file hungry for battle against it. In 1922 he returned to Parliament as member for Aberavon. The largely left-wing ILP caucus decided to run him for the leadership against the sitting tenant, J. R. Clynes, and he was duly elected with a majority of five votes.

His strategy as party leader must be seen against the background of the complex, three-party politics of the time. The Liberals were on a downward escalator, Labour on an upward one. But although Labour had come ahead of the Liberals in the 1922 election, no one could be sure it would stay ahead. MacDonald's main objective was to ensure that it did – to make it the chief anti-Conservative party in the state and, in doing so, to create a new, Conservative-versus-Labour two-party system in place of the familiar Conservative-versus-Liberal system of prewar days. He succeeded triumphantly. The 1923 election produced a hung Parliament, with Labour as the second largest party; early in 1924 MacDonald kissed hands as Prime Minister of a minority government. It held office for nine months, achieving little in home affairs but settling the reparations crisis which had led to the French occupation of the Ruhr – a success for which MacDonald, who doubled as Foreign Secretary, could claim much of the credit. The government fell in humiliating circumstances, following a botched decision not to proceed with the prosecution of the communist paper the *Workers' Weekly* for sedition; in the subsequent general election the Conservatives won a decisive victory. But the real victims of the 1924 election were the Liberals, who returned with only 40 seats and saw their vote fall by more than a million. Although the Labour Party also lost seats, their vote actually rose, making their claim to have supplanted the Liberals that much more believable.

In the 1924 Parliament MacDonald's leadership came under heavy fire from the leftward-moving ILP. The most serious threat to his strategy, however, came when Lloyd George succeeded Asquith as Liberal leader and launched a brilliant campaign for a programme of national development and loan-financed public works to mop up unemployment. In the end, both threats were beaten off. In the 1929 election Labour still fell short of a majority, but became, for the first time, the largest party in the House of Commons; once again, MacDonald became Prime Minister of a minority government. Had he died that summer, he would probably have gone down as one of the greatest leaders in the history of the British Labour movement.

As things were, he and his colleagues were soon overwhelmed by the onset of the world depression and the remorseless increase in unemployment which it brought in its train. They struggled on until the sterling crisis of August 1931, which brought the government down. The Treasury and the Bank of England believed that the only way to prevent a collapse of the currency was to cut public expenditure, including expenditure on unemployment benefit. This was anathema to the Labour movement, and particularly to the TUC; partly because of this, it was opposed by a powerful group of cabinet ministers, including Arthur Henderson, the Foreign Secretary. Mac-Donald and Philip Snowden, the Chancellor of the Exchequer, accepted the Bank's solution, but although a narrow majority of the cabinet agreed with them, it became clear that the government could not carry on. To the astonishment of most of his colleagues and against his own original inclinations, Mac-Donald then bowed to King George V's insistent urgings and agreed to form an emergency National Government. A few weeks later he led his new colleagues into a general election, in which the Labour Party was crushed. To all intents and purposes, he was now the political prisoner of the Conservative Party – a position which became steadily more humiliating as his physical and mental capacities deteriorated. He resigned from the prime ministership in the early summer of 1935, but remained in the cabinet for another two years, as an increasingly isolated and uninfluential Lord President of the Council. When he died suddenly on a voyage to South America, a few months after leaving office, he was a broken man, execrated by his old followers and unloved by his new ones. Yet it is at least arguable that he had done more than any other single person to turn the loose-knit and fissiparous 'Labour alliance' of the turn of the century into a major party of state. Few of the Labour ministers who held office in the governments of Clement Attlee or Harold Wilson acknowledged any debt to him. They owed it just the same.

WRITINGS

Ramsay MacDonald's Political Writings, ed. Bernard Barker (London: Allen Lane, 1972).

FURTHER READING

Elton, Godfrey, *The Life of James Ramsay MacDonald* (London: Collins, 1939).
Hamilton, M. A., *Remembering My Good Friends* (London: Jonathan Cape, 1944).
Marquand, David, *Ramsay MacDonald* (London: Jonathan Cape, 1977).
Weir, L. MacNeill, *The Tragedy of Ramsay MacDonald* (London: Secker and Warburg, 1938).

DAVID MARQUAND

MacGregor, Sir Ian (Kinloch) (*b.* Kinlochleven, Argyll, 21 September 1912). Industrialist. His main contribution to British political life did not come until he was past retirement age. Then, in a move that demonstrated the desperation of British governments about the management of nationalized industries, he was brought back from the USA to run first the British Steel Corporation (1980–3) and then the National Coal Board (1983–6). At the latter he precipitated the epoch-making 1984 Miners' Strike, which polarized politics and the country. Ultimately successful in his aims, he gave his name to a style of confrontational management and challenge to the unions which became a trademark of the Thatcher years.

Born and brought up in Scotland, MacGregor trained as a metallurgist. During World War II he was sent to the USA as part of a government purchasing mission as an expert in tank armour. He remained after the war and became chairman of the American metal company AMAX, which grew rapidly under his direction from 1967 to 1977, expanding into mining of all kinds. Criticized – ironically, in view of later events – for overexpansionism, it was not until he left AMAX that the British Government employed him to reorganize and retrench its loss-making industries. It was seen as a comment both on the competence of British managers and on the government's desperation to contain their huge losses.

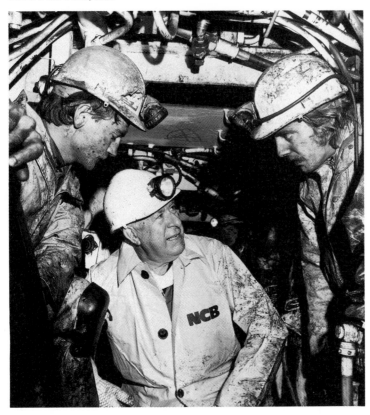

Sir Ian MacGregor while Chairman of the National Coal Board

In 1975 MacGregor had joined the board of the troubled British Leyland motor company, and strongly backed moves to sack its best-known union convenor. But in 1980 a political storm broke when he was appointed chairman of BSC for a 'transfer fee' payment to his then company, the bankers Lazard Frères of New York, which eventually reached over one and a half million pounds. This was still less than the two million pounds a day the corporation was losing. Helped by cuts set in train by his predecessors, he reduced losses in his first full year from £668 million to £338 million. More crucially, he re-established the corporation's morale, particularly among managers, refusing to cut below what he termed an 'Alamein line'. Although it was never in the black under Mac-Gregor, BSC owed much of its subsequent return to profit and its eventual privatization to him.

MacGregor's appointment to the NCB in 1983 was a clear signal that the government, though still wary of the industrial power of the National Union of Mineworkers after their strike victories, wanted to end the 'most-favoured industry' treatment of coal and to cut back subsidies. To the left-wing leadership of the NUM it appeared a 'declaration of war' and an opportunity to mobilize for industrial action which might change government policy – and not just in the mining industry. Although he was initially cautious, MacGregor's patience was exhausted by an overtime ban imposed by the union soon after his arrival. He accelerated pit closures, giving the NUM leadership under ARTHUR SCARGILL the opportunity to call out all its members without the required ballot, on the pretext of supporting other areas which had taken precipitate action. The resulting strike – the longest major dispute in twentieth-century Britain – led to picketing that was more violent than any seen since World War II.

While he was outwardly tough, MacGregor's erratic public performance (talking, for example, of 'a small fire on the other side of town') and his unexplained shifts of attitude alarmed government ministers, and after three months they cast aside the fiction of non-involvement to wage a major propaganda campaign. Mac-Gregor saw the strike in cataclysmic terms. He later told a newspaper, 'it is not generally known how close to the abyss we came. We could so easily have gone down the tube. We were that close to disaster.' He resented having to keep in touch with the government and was elusive and evasive in discussions, criticizing what he called 'interference from the front office', and was summoned to Downing Street to explain his strategy. He lost credibility when he sacked key executives, provoked a threatened strike by deputies – the industry's junior managers – and appeared at one negotiation meeting with his face obscured by a plastic bag in an unfortunate joke.

A long series of talks made no progress and MacGregor took what was an unfamiliarly tough line in the British context, attempting to break the union, successfully promoting the formation of a breakaway union, and encouraging a strike-breaking return to work. After the strike he made no concessions, abrogating local understandings with the unions and asserting management's right to manage. The government, grateful for victory but alarmed at his erratic conduct, recommended a knighthood but denied his wish for a further top job, perhaps as supremo of the National Health Service. After 1986 MacGregor was left to pursue his business interests in Scotland and elsewhere.

MacGregor's success against the NUM, until then seen as the trade unions' untouchable 'brigade of guards' after their strike victories in the 1970s, effectively removed the fear of the elected government being defeated by industrial action. It encouraged a series of further confrontations with the unions in a variety of industries, notably the heavily unionized printing industry in Fleet Street.

WRITINGS

The Enemies Within (London: Collins, 1986).

FURTHER READING

Adeney, Martin and Lloyd, John, *The Miners Strike: Loss Without Limit* (London: Routledge, 1986).

MARTIN ADENEY

Mackay, James (Peter Hymers) [Baron Mackay of Clashfern, of Eddrachillis in the District of Sutherland] (*b*. Edinburgh, 2 July 1927). Lord Chancellor. He graduated in mathematics at Edinburgh and lectured on that subject at St Andrews before going to Cambridge, where he became a senior wrangler. He then studied law at Edinburgh and was called to the Scottish Bar in 1955. Mackay rose rapidly by professional skill and ability and latterly frequently represented the British Government at the European Court. He was successively vice-dean (1973–6) and dean (1976–9) of the Faculty of Advocates and also served as a part-time Sheriff Principal and a part-time member of the Scottish Law Commission.

In 1979, though he had not previously exhibited any political leaning, Mackay accepted the office of Lord Advocate with a life peerage. In 1984 he was made a judge of the Court of Session, but a year later was promoted to be a Lord of Appeal in Ordinary and in 1987 was made Lord Chancellor; his was the first appointment to that office from the Scottish Bar since 1707, though he was by no means the first Scot to have held it.

Mackay is a frank, friendly, totally unassuming man with profound religious convictions (he was brought up in the Free Presbyterian Church) and a very undogmatic attitude to government. In 1989 he threw the whole legal world into a ferment with the publication of a series of radical proposals for drastic reorganization of the legal profession: for solicitors to be allowed to plead in the higher courts and to become Queen's Counsel and judges, for partnerships among barristers, for banks and building societies to be allowed to undertake conveyancing for clients, for 'no win, no fee' litigation, and other changes. All these provoked bitter attacks, and were condemned by senior judges as evil and sinister.

DAVID M. WALKER

Maclay, Joseph (Paton) [Baron Maclay] (*b.* Glasgow, 6 September 1857; *d.* Kilmacolm, Renfrewshire, 24 April 1951). Shipowner and head of the Ministry of Shipping as Shipping Controller. He was the son of Ebenezer Maclay and Janet Paton. At the age of 28, with T. W. Mcintyre, he established a trampship firm. This company expanded rapidly to become one of the largest shipping concerns on the Clyde. By the beginning of World War I it operated more than 50 ships.

During the war the efficient use of mercantile shipping became vital for two reasons: firstly to supply the military with men and material and secondly to keep Britain fed and producing. Up until 1916 control and direction of shipping was *ad hoc* and limited, but with the formation of Lloyd George's government in that year control was centralized. One of the new ministries established to direct the war economy was the Ministry of Shipping. Sir Joseph Maclay, created a baronet in 1914, was appointed to head this new ministry as Shipping Controller and became a member of the Privy Council.

His role was initially a dual one: he was to allocate the shipping resources available and to oversee the construction of new vessels. In 1917 the level of U-boat attacks was reaching a peak and taking an ever-growing toll of ships. This increased the workload beyond the capabilities of a single controller, so the task of overseeing construction was hived off to a new Controller-General of Merchant Shipping. Maclay's role was now to concentrate on making the most of the remaining fleet and to decide on the types of vessel to be built. He proved a very able and popular Controller. Winston Churchill, in *The World Crisis*, described Maclay as able, knowledgeable and charming. These qualities enabled him to gain the confidence of colleagues and to execute his duties well.

After the war Maclay did not remain very active in the public service. However, he did become a member of the Business Committee on Finance in 1921 and was made a peer in 1922. He was also concerned, as a shipowner in the inter-war period, with safeguarding the British shipbuilding industry. He argued that the managers had not improved the operating efficiency of their ships for 30 years. He saw virtue in using the type of standard ship used in the war to reduce production costs. Others at the time, such as James Lithgow, were putting the emphasis on cutting the labour costs of the builders rather than improving the product.

Maclay married Martha Strang in 1889; they had five sons and two daughters. He held the local positions of JP and Deputy-Lieutenant of Renfrewshire, and was awarded an honorary LL D of Glasgow University.

FURTHER READING

Campbell, R. H., *Scotland Since 1707: Rise of an Industrial Society*, 2nd edn. (Edinburgh: John Donald, 1985).
Churchill, Winston S., *The World Crisis, 1916–18*, pt. 2 (London: Butterworths, 1927).
Obituary, *The Times* (25 April 1951).

ANTHONY GANDY

Maclean, Donald (Duart) (*b.* London, 25 May 1913; *d.* Moscow, 6 March 1983). Diplomat and Soviet spy. Even as a boy at Gresham's School, Norfolk, where he became a close friend of James Klugman, already a Marxist and later to serve on the political committee of the British Communist Party, Maclean was troubled by two misgivings: first, whether God existed; and second, why he felt so contemptuous of his father's belief in the dwindling Liberal Party. (Sir Donald Maclean, lawyer and Liberal MP, was a staunch Presbyterian and had been knighted in 1917 under Lloyd George.) The two quarrelled in August 1931 over Ramsay MacDonald's decision to stay as Prime Minister. Sir Donald was a member of that crisis Coalition Government then set up. His sudden death in June 1932 at once released the son from past obligations. At Trinity Hall, Cambridge, he consorted with Marxist undergraduates such as GUY BURGESS, Maurice Cornforth and David Haden-Guest and his school-friend Klugman. He did not, however, neglect his work, taking a double first in modern languages, and coming in the first half-dozen names at the top of the Foreign Office examination list. Asked, during the oral interview, whether he had renounced his radical views, Maclean admitted: 'Not completely.' The examiners thanked him for his honesty. Not long afterwards he was recruited as a probationary Soviet agent.

Maclean joined the Diplomatic Service in 1935 and during his first posting, to the British Embassy in Paris, he became engaged to an American girl, Melinda Marling, marrying her in June 1940, while the German armies were approaching the French capital. Unlike his fellow 'Cambridge spies' Burgess, ANTHONY BLUNT AND KIM PHILBY, Maclean remained a 'sleeper' until Hitler's attack on the Soviet Union in 1941. His war years were spent at the Foreign Office in London, where he had ample opportunity of passing material to the Russians, increasingly so during his four years as First Secretary at the British Embassy in Washington (1944–8). There he was appointed joint secretary of the new Combined Policy Committee on nuclear development, with a special pass to admit him to the Atomic Energy Centre at night. Twice a month he would drive to his mother-in-law's home near New York, stopping off to hand over consignments of information to the Soviet consulate. Posted to Cairo as Head of Chancery in 1948, his unpredictable and often drunken behaviour caused him to be sent back to London on sick leave after only 18 months. Ironically, his next assignment was the American desk at the Foreign Office. This gave him further opportunities of passing on material to his Soviet controller. By 1951, however, British security and the CIA, already warned by Soviet defectors that a 'mole' was active at the Foreign Office, had narrowed the field from four possible suspects to Donald Maclean. Forewarned by his fellow-spies Philby and Blunt, and helped by Burgess, who at the last moment decided to accompany him, he escaped to Moscow on his 38th birthday, 25 May 1951. Maclean at first enjoyed his life as an honoured citizen of the USSR and his work for the Soviet Foreign Ministry and the Institute of World Economic and International Relations. His wife and children followed him there, but she left him for a brief marriage with Philby. She and the children eventually returned to America, and Maclean finished his days, lonely and sad, his family dispersed.

FURTHER READING

Boyle, Andrew, *The Climate of Treason* (London: Hutchinson, 1979).

Cecil, Robert, *Donald Maclean* (London: Bodley Head, 1988).

Connolly, Cyril, *The Missing Diplomats* (London: Chatto and Windus, 1953).

Hoare, Geoffrey, *The Missing Macleans* (London: Cassell, 1955).

Muggeridge, Malcolm, *Chronicles of Wasted Time*, 2 vols. (London: Collins, 1972).

Rees, Goronwy, *A Chapter of Accidents* (London: Chatto and Windus, 1972).

ANDREW BOYLE

MacLeod, George (Fielden) [Lord MacLeod of Fuinary] (*b.* Glasgow, 17 June 1895). Minister of the Church of Scotland. From a privileged background, MacLeod chose to become minister of the distressed Glasgow parish of Govan (1930–8) before founding the Iona Community in 1938. He inspired many in and beyond the Church of Scotland to take up radical political causes, particularly that of peace. He was created a life peer in 1967.

MacLeod's grandfather, Norman MacLeod, was Queen Victoria's favourite Scottish churchman, and his father, Sir John, was a Glasgow Unionist MP from 1915 to 1922. Although the second son, MacLeod inherited his father's baronetcy through a nephew in 1944. His education at Winchester, Oriel College, Oxford, Edinburgh and Union Theological College, New York, was interrupted by war service as a captain with the Argyll and Sutherland Highlanders. After working as minister at the fashionable St Cuthbert's Church in Edinburgh (1926–30), he served during the depression years at Govan Old Parish Church, where he pioneered ventures such as clubs for the unemployed and a parish mission. A broadcast preacher from 1929, he responded to the communist challenge by blending incarnational orthodoxy, a social gospel, an aesthetic sacramentarianism and a quest for community with veneration for the Celtic Church of St Columba.

These trends of thought culminated in the foundation of the community and the rebuilding of Columba's abbey on Iona, off the west coast of Scotland. The community, which MacLeod led until 1967, trained young ministers through work in the company of craftsmen for mission in urban Scotland. Increasingly, lay people were drawn in, particularly through summer courses. Politics were freely discussed. Although MacLeod had become 'an uncomfortable socialist', he insisted on no particular party allegiance and was to sit as an Independent in the Lords.

MacLeod's mission was peace. He called for pacifism in the 1930s, during the war and afterwards. Opposition to the atomic bomb was a theme of his address as Moderator of the General Assembly of the Church of Scotland in 1957. His autocratic and impatient ways pushed the Iona Community into a unilateralist declaration in 1966. Subsequently he discerned international finance behind the reluctance to disarm. MacLeod persuaded many, especially in Scotland, of the incompatibility of Christianity and warfare.

FURTHER READING

Ferguson, R., *Chasing the Wild Goose* (London: Fount, 1988).

D. W. BEBBINGTON

Macleod, Iain (Norman) (*b.* Skipton, Yorkshire, 11 November 1913; *d.* London, 20 July 1970). Conservative minister. Few Conservative politicians played a more pivotal role than Iain Macleod during a period of sustained political turbulence between the disaster of the Suez campaign in 1956 and the controversy surrounding Macmillan's successor as Conservative leader in 1963. He earned his reputation as a Tory Radical – 'too clever by half', as Lord Salisbury later complained – as Macmillan's Minister of Labour (1955–9) and, more especially, during his short spell as Colonial Secretary (1959–61), when he showed a disposition to accelerate the pace of decolonization in Africa. He attained a long-standing ambition when he became Chancellor of the Exchequer in Edward Heath's government in 1970 – only to die of a heart attack within weeks of his appointment.

His parents were Scots (both had originated from the Isle of Lewis) but Macleod's father had since developed a medical practice in Skipton. Neither his home background nor his school (Fettes College) placed Macleod on an obvious inside track for reception into the Conservative Party. He showed no interest in politics in any case. His years at Cambridge were spent mostly in London, where he played bridge at a level that provided an income and suggested one possible career; he nevertheless managed a second class degree in history. It was World War II which initiated a switch in direction. Following a trouble-free landing on D-Day, Macleod sustained a wound that, together with a disease that had already affected his spine, restricted his movements and brought him home in the autumn of 1944. He meditated his future and decided to fight a constituency when the war ended. He lost the Outer Hebrides in 1945 by a crushing margin and only with his adoption by Enfield did his parliamentary career begin at the 1950 election.

Macleod's sympathies lay with the liberal wing of the Tory party and expressed themselves through his role in the Conservative Research Department, dominated by one liberal teacher, R. A. Butler, and through his concern with social reform, suggested by another hero, Neville Chamberlain, whose biography Macleod later wrote. His attack on Aneurin Bevan, which first brought Macleod to Churchill's attention in 1952, perhaps had its roots more in the party game than in any developed sense of social policy, but the promotion to which it led gave Macleod the ministry that Chamberlain had held in the 1920s – that of Health. As if in ironic and cruel answer, Macleod's wife, Eve, contracted meningitis and polio just two months later and turned their marriage into a battle against physical disability that continued to Macleod's premature death.

Cabinet rank came at the end of 1955 in Anthony Eden's first reshuffle of appointments. The Ministry of Labour, which Macleod ran until after the general election in 1959, promised to provoke serious problems because of its vulnerability in a climate of mounting unemployment, its embarrassments at the hands of powerful trade-union leaders, and its fielding of questions about national service which had become highly unpopular among the young. This last problem Macleod tackled head on, and announced in 1957 the phasing out of conscription. Challenges from the TUC proved more intractable and came to a head in the London bus strike of May–June 1958. The defeat of Frank Cousins made Macleod a major public figure, just as his dexterity in the House of Commons – he was widely regarded as the sharpest and most attractive speaker on the Tory benches – helped him turn even unfavourable issues such as unemployment to his advantage in debate. Doubtless Macleod's successes at Labour helped nerve Macmillan to offer him the Colonial Office when the Conservatives had been returned again in 1959 (see also MACMILLAN, HAROLD).

In one sense the move consolidated Macleod's status; in another it threatened to undermine his career. For, quite as much as economic protection or the future of India had disturbed Conservative politics in the 1930s, so in the 1960s the realities of decolonization seized the emotions of both left and right inside the Tory party. That figures so disparate as Sir Ian Gilmour and Sir Roy Welensky came to compare Macleod to Joseph Chamberlain says something for the panache with which he addressed his task. Possibly the opportunity for radical achievement owed as much to the context of policy in 1959–60 as to Macleod's own thinking; but, once pledged to releasing Jomo Kenyatta in Kenya and Hastings Banda in Nyasaland, or to the strengthening of the hand of Julius Nyerere in Tanganyika, Macleod followed his thinking with a dour determination that made him enemies at home as well as in white-dominated Central Africa. It was Macleod's enthusiasm for change in Northern Rhodesia, however, which gave rise to doubts even in Macmillan, who had heretofore supported Macleod's drive to pull Britain out of Africa, and precipitated a clash with Duncan Sandys, the Commonwealth Minister. It was controversy over the future of Rhodesia that led to Lord Salisbury's accusations of lack of scruple and a surfeit of cleverness.

Macmillan's appetite for crusades had steadily weakened. In October 1961 he switched Macleod to the Duchy of Lancaster (sweetened by the Leadership of the House). Unbeknown to himself, and implausibly in a man of 48, Macleod's contribution to British politics had come to an end. His tenure of seniority in the House, and the chairmanship of the party organization that he also assumed, suffered from deep rifts in the party which characterized the years 1961–3. He did not stand for the leadership when Macmillan was forced into resignation by illness in October 1963; he supported Butler and, when Lord Home emerged as front runner, refused to serve under him. Some journalism followed – he edited *The Spectator* until 1965 – and he played a significant part as Shadow Chancellor through the Wilson governments. But continued over-strain caught up with him within weeks of attaining a long-standing ambition when he became the occupant of 11 Downing Street in Edward Heath's new government. He died there in July 1970.

FURTHER READING

Fisher, Nigel, *Iain Macleod* (London: Deutsch, 1973).

MICHAEL BENTLEY

Macmillan, (Maurice) Harold [Earl of Stockton] (*b*. London, 10 February 1894; *d*. Birch Grove, Sussex, 29 December 1986). Conservative Prime Minister. Macmillan was Prime Minister from January 1957 to October 1963. The choice had been made by the Crown in the wake of Eden's resignation on grounds of health (the Conservative Party at that time did not have a clear mechanism for electing a leader). Butler had recently been Acting Prime Minister while Eden had been recuperating. Macmillan read *Pride and Prejudice* and calmly awaited the outcome of the soundings. There is little doubt that the Crown's choice reflected the broad view of both cabinet and the Conservative Party. Initially, there were those who supposed that Macmillan would be a stop-gap: he was older than his predecessor and he would probably be defeated at the next general election. The Suez debacle of a few months earlier was still in the public mind and the Conservative Party was in an unhappy condition. These forecasts proved mistaken. Macmillan's record of six years and nine months as Prime Minister was, in 1963, the longest continuous term since that of another first-class scholar from Balliol College, Oxford – Asquith.

Like Churchill, Macmillan was the product of an Anglo-American marriage. His father was a director of the publishing house founded by Harold's grandfather, who had left poverty on the Isle of Arran to make his way in England. His mother came from Indiana and aspired to see her third son rise to great influence within her adopted country. At Birch Grove, her home in Sussex, her grandchildren were told not to kick doors because the house would belong, in due course, to the Prime Minister. It must be doubtful, however, whether his school contemporaries would have shared that vision. Harold was clever and bookish, but he was also delicate. He nearly died from pneumonia and had to leave Eton early. Private tutors helped him to an Exhibition to Balliol in 1912 and to a First in Classical Moderations in June 1914. Macmillan was attracted to wittiness and holiness among his companions and teachers, preferably in combination. In 1914 he found himself initially in the King's Royal Rifle Corps, but in the following year he joined a special battalion of the Grenadier Guards. He was wounded on three occasions and his life was in jeopardy; he spent most of the latter part of the war in hospital in pain, reading and reflecting on life and conduct. His religious convictions deepened, but did not lead him to Rome. He admired discipline and courage and met 'ordinary' men for the first time. Macmillan could not face a return to Oxford – so many of his friends were dead. He wanted something quite new, and his mother's influence resulted in his appointment as ADC to the then Governor-General of Canada, the Duke of Devonshire. Thirteen months after his arrival in Ottawa, he was back in London marrying Devonshire's youthful third daughter at St Margaret's, Westminster. The reinforcements brought in by the Macmillans to counter the aristocratic swells included Henry James and Thomas Hardy. Harold went into publishing, but had already developed a taste for both politics and aristocratic society.

He found it difficult to decide what party he should support. His family tradition was Liberal, merging into Liberal-Unionism with a dash of Christian socialism. At Oxford Macmillan had declared no firm allegiance. He could have been a Liberal, but despite his admiration for Lloyd George he guessed that the Liberal Party was disintegrating, and thought that he could only be a Conservative. In December 1923 he fought Stockton-on-Tees and was narrowly defeated by a Liberal. It was his first experience both of campaigning and of life in the industrial north. He stood again in 1924 and won, with Labour coming in second place. Together with other young members, Macmillan was active putting forward what they regarded as progressive policies. The year after the General Strike they published *Industry and the State* and earned themselves the nickname 'The YMCA'. A promising career seemed to be developing, but in 1929 Macmillan lost his parliamentary seat. He also realized in the same year that his wife had developed an intense attraction for Robert Boothby, his associate and co-author, and this relationship, though concealed before the public, was to last until her death in 1966. In the early months of 1931 he seems to have had a nervous breakdown and his war wound was again troublesome. He went to Germany for treatment but recovered sufficiently to regain his Stockton seat in 1931.

During the 1930s he operated politically at two levels. He sought to develop an economic philosophy between unadulterated private enterprise on the one hand and socialism on the other. The family firm published the writings of Keynes, and Macmillan was influenced by them. In 1933 his *Reconstruction: a Plea for a National Policy* argued that planning was required on a national basis – though a visit to the Soviet Union in the previous year had left him unimpressed by communism. A manifesto, *The Next Five Years*, was similarly designed to appeal to moderate opinion. Its author was prepared to countenance public control of transport, gas and electricity. In May 1938 he published *The Middle Way*, and the thrust of such a book is self-evident. There was a need for a mixed economy. State planning should and could be combined with private enterprise.

These serious works were the reflection of his deep concern for his North-Eastern constituency, but in the short term they did Macmillan little good except to confirm his reputation as an intellectual rebel. At this time his discontent was not confined to domestic matters. In June 1936 he voted against the government on a vote of censure in protest against the failure to stop Italian aggression against Ethiopia and resigned the party whip. He sat as an Independent Conservative until May 1937, when Chamberlain took office. However, after Eden resigned in February 1938, Macmillan continued to express sharp criticisms of the government's foreign policy (see also EDEN, ANTHONY). The effigy of Neville Chamberlain was burnt on the Birch Grove bonfire on 5 November 1938. There was, not surprisingly, no call to join the government.

However, when Churchill became Prime Minister, Macmillan accepted the parliamentary secretaryship to the Ministry of Supply and served in this capacity modestly for 20 months. For most of 1942 he was Under-Secretary of State for the Colonies, but at the end of the year he accepted appointment as Minister of State in North Africa with cabinet rank. It was a curious post, requiring much tact and judgement. His fluent French was useful, as was his ability to get on well with Americans. He gave up his post in May 1945, having become thoroughly familiar with the personalities and problems of the Mediterranean as a whole. His understanding with Eisenhower was much greater than his intimacy with de Gaulle. He was already conscious of American power; perhaps it was the British role to be the Greeks in the new Roman Empire. After VE day he visited Klagenfurt in Austria and sanctioned the repatriation of Cossacks to the Soviet Union and anti-communist Yugoslavs to Yugoslavia. Much later, this decision was to cause him difficulty.

Macmillan had not visited his constituency since 1942, and it is not surprising that he was defeated at Stockton in the 1945 general election. He came back into parliament in November 1945 as MP for Bromley and retained this seat for the remainder of his years in the Commons. His position at this time was not easy. He spoke cleverly and frequently, but it

seemed to many that he could not fundamentally object to Labour's programme since parts of it at least were close to what he had himself advocated in the 1930s. He dabbled with the idea of European integration, but did not take his involvement too far. He was a prominent Tory, but by no means dominant among his contemporaries. When Churchill formed a new government in 1951, Macmillan was given the task of building the 300,000 houses to which the party had committed itself in the late election. He gathered an excellent team around him and in October 1954 he was able to announce that the target had been achieved. Churchill promoted him to the Ministry of Defence, but he found the task somewhat dispiriting. The three individual service ministries still had much power and Churchill himself was looking over Macmillan's shoulder. Eden made him Foreign Secretary in 1955, but in this post, too, he was to find that the Prime Minister took a very close interest. Within six months, SELWYN LLOYD had been installed in the Foreign Office and Macmillan had moved to the Treasury. Here, at last, was an opportunity, over time, to show his colours, but the chief legacy of his first and only budget was the introduction of Premium Bonds. As the Suez Crisis developed over the summer, Macmillan was not a waverer and initially gave the Prime Minister strong support. In the end, however, he was as keen to come out as he had originally been to go in. It opened him to the accusation that he was 'First in, first out'.

His tenure of all these offices was so short that his power of sustained leadership was still largely an unknown quantity when he became Prime Minister. He seemed to revel in an 'Edwardian' image which some advisers initially thought a great mistake. They were to discover, over the next six years, that Macmillan was a shrewd and sharp operator, whatever the image he conveyed. His immediate task was twofold. He had to restore the morale both of the Conservative Party and of the country at large, and he had to repair the ruptured relationship with the USA. Some maintained that these two objectives were in contradiction but Macmillan achieved success in both respects. However, despite his air of unflappability, Macmillan's hold on his party was more pre-

Harold Macmillan (left) as Foreign Secretary with his Prime Minister Sir Anthony Eden at the Geneva conference, July 1955

carious than it sometimes seemed. In January 1958 he had to face the resignation of his entire Treasury team, who opposed the planned level of government expenditure. He successfully dismissed the affair as 'a little local difficulty', though it has been seen subsequently by critics of Macmillan as a symbolic turning point which was to lead to years of inflation ahead. Macmillan dismissed such fears and continued to adhere to his preferences of the 1930s in this and other economic issues. He was also prepared to ride out the storm occasioned by Lord Salisbury's resignation in protest against the release of Archbishop Makarios of Cyprus from prison. He visited the Soviet Union in February 1959, and its limited utility seems mysteriously to have encouraged the notion that he was 'Supermac'. In August he welcomed his wartime associate President Eisenhower to Britain and, together, they gave what was supposed not to be a party political broadcast. In October the Conservatives won their third victory in a row and Macmillan had a majority of 100 seats.

The years that followed, which augured so well, saw a steady decline in his skill and success. His appointment of IAIN MACLEOD as Colonial Secretary signalled an acceleration of decolonization, particularly in Africa, and he gave a celebrated speech to both Houses of the South African Parliament in February 1960 in which he spoke of a 'wind of change' blowing through the continent. Macmillan set much store by East–West summits. By 1961 he had at length come round to the view that Britain should seek to join the Common Market. Some play was made with his alleged 'Europeanism' in the 1940s. It is true that he had shown more interest than Eden, but that is to say very little. In the event, the protracted negotiations were to come to nothing. Eighteen months after Macmillan's announcement of British intentions in the Commons, he was confronted by de Gaulle's veto in January 1963. Among other matters, de Gaulle was annoyed by the fact that Macmillan had persuaded President Kennedy to substitute Polaris for Skybolt and thus preserve a British independent deterrent. The strategy of the government had collapsed and Macmillan's fortunes never recovered. There was a Liberal by-election victory at Orpington in 1962 which precipitated a drastic cabinet purge in July. His handling of the Vassall case (in which a minor civil servant was convicted of spying for the Soviet Union) seemed clumsy. In the following summer he survived with some difficulty the Profumo Scandal arising out of the relationship between his Minister for War and Miss Christine Keeler. He seemed determined to struggle on, fortified by the belief that his 'special relationship' with President Kennedy had made possible the signature of the Test Ban Treaty. However, in October, illness led him to announce his resignation.

Macmillan's career presents many paradoxes. He was one of the rare Prime Ministers to have enhanced his reputation by his conduct after ceasing to be Prime Minister. That was only partly because he lived to a very great age. He became Prime Minister with only a slim record of achievement behind him, and his reputation, where it existed, was as a rather conscientious bore. His religion meant a great deal to him but it remained entirely private. He admired wit, but neither his pre-1939 treatises nor his laborious six volumes of post-retirement memoirs contained much in the way of verbal sparkle. He was often thought to be a survivor from a previous age, but it was not clear what age it was. In his last 20 years, however, he matured and ripened in a marvellous way. The University of Oxford was singularly fortunate in its Chancellor. The ideas he advanced in speeches of tantalizing charm still harped back to the 'middle way' at a time when the consensus which he had sought to embody in his government was already disintegrating. It was significant that when, after all, he did accept an earldom, in 1984, his title gave continuing life to the Stockton years when his political ideas had first crystallized.

WRITINGS

Winds of Change (London: Macmillan, 1966).
The Blast of War (London: Macmillan, 1967).
Tides of Fortune (London: Macmillan, 1969).
Riding the Storm (London: Macmillan, 1971).
Pointing the Way (London: Macmillan, 1972).
At the End of the Day (London: Macmillan, 1972).

FURTHER READING

Fisher, Nigel, *Harold Macmillan: a Biography* (London: Weidenfeld and Nicolson, 1982).
Horne, Alistair, *Macmillan*, vol. 1: *1894–1956*

(London: Macmillan, 1988); vol. 2: *1957–1986* (London: Macmillan, 1989).
Sampson, Anthony, *Macmillan: a Study in Ambiguity* (London: Allen Lane, 1967).

KEITH ROBBINS

Major, John (*b*. London, 29 March 1943). Conservative Foreign Secretary and Chancellor of the Exchequer. It is not given to many men to be appointed to two of the highest offices in government within the space of three months. The cabinet reshuffle of July 1989, which removed Sir Geoffrey Howe from the Foreign and Commonwealth Office, resulted in Major's promotion. He had scarcely accustomed himself to his new role when Lawson's resignation as Chancellor in October 1989 led to his appointment to the Treasury. It would seem likely that Major's talents are better employed as Chancellor.

He was brought up in South London and educated at Rutlish Grammar School. He took various jobs after leaving school as accountant, builders' labourer and community worker in Nigeria. He then joined the Standard Chartered Bank in 1965 and gained his AIB. His family background was not political, but he joined the Conservative Party as a teenager and served on Lambeth Borough Council for three years from 1968, with a particular interest in housing. He unsuccessfully contested St Pancras North in both 1974 general elections before being elected for Huntingdonshire in 1979 (Huntingdon since 1983). Major quickly gained junior posts in the Home Office, as a Whip and in the DHSS. He early gained a reputation for clear expression and grasp of detail. His promotion as Chief Secretary at the Treasury in 1987 seemed to follow logically. He adjusted the competing claims of his colleagues calmly. However, his promotion to the Foreign Office in 1989 occasioned some surprise because of his youth and of his inexperience in foreign affairs. He had little opportunity to display his talents in this office before his return to the Treasury. Major had become overnight the leading parliamentary Conservative of his generation, but he had yet to make his mark in the country at large.

KEITH ROBBINS

Marples (Alfred) Ernest [Baron Marples] (*b.* Manchester, 9 December 1907; *d.* Monte Carlo, 6 July 1978). Businessman and minister. The two great interests of Marples's life were construction and communications. He was the son of a foreman engineer and trained as an accountant after leaving school. He moved to London on qualifying and in the late 1920s went into property development; he established Marples, Ridgway and Partners, which was to become a major contracting business. He served in the Royal Artillery during World War II, leaving with the rank of captain. In 1945 Marples entered the Commons as MP for Wallasey. His expertise on housing matters was of great value to a depleted Conservative Party not overendowed with builders. It was almost axiomatic that he should go to the Ministry of Housing and Local Government in 1951 as Parliamentary Secretary under Harold Macmillan, where he played a notable part in reaching the target for house-building which the government had accepted. In 1954 he moved to Pensions and National Insurance as Parliamentary Secretary, but he had no office in the Eden government and devoted himself largely to his continuing business interests.

Macmillan appointed Marples Postmaster-General in 1957. The new minister was frequently in the public eye, partly because he had an exceptionally developed sense of publicity but also because he could readily be identified with new technology. Under his stewardship, subscriber trunk dialling was introduced, and it came as no surprise that the electronic random number indicating equipment used to pick out lucky Premium Bond winners was christened 'Ernie'. In 1959 he became Minister of Transport and entered the cabinet. Marples exuded a confidence that the problems caused by the inexorable growth of road transport could be solved. On the one hand there had to be a major programme of 'motorway' building, and on the other strenuous efforts to deal with traffic in towns by such varied means as parking meters, yellow lines and flyovers. He was aided to some extent by the recommendations of Sir Colin Buchanan, and he brought in Beeching from ICI to investigate the railway network. The closure programme which Beeching advocated, and which Marples largely accepted, caused great controversy. The railway lobby urged that 'Marples Must Go', but he did not. In opposition after 1964, he initially shadowed on technology questions, but his political career had reached its peak. There was no place for him in the Heath government after 1970 and in 1974 he took a life peerage. He spent an increasing amount of time in France, where he owned a vineyard.

In his old age Marples became well known as a fitness fanatic; his enthusiasm for cycling was widely advertised. He did not solve the problems he encountered but he did carve for himself a distinct political niche in his efforts to do so. Public school and university men in the Conservative Party were no doubt capable of dealing with more abstruse issues of policy. Marples concentrated on being a practical man dealing with practical problems. And he made sure that everybody knew what he was trying to do.

KEITH ROBBINS

Marquis, Frederick (James) [Earl of Woolton] (*b.* Salford, Lancashire, 24 August 1883; *d.* Sussex, 14 December 1964). Businessman and Conservative organizer. A successful retailer with his roots in Lancashire, he rose to national fame as Food Minister in World War II and went on to preside as Party Chairman over the Conservative recovery from defeat in 1945.

Marquis seemed destined for a career in university or in charitable work. He took a B.Sc. from Manchester in 1906, going on to be a research fellow in economics, and an MA in 1910. Over that period he was also a part-time teacher and warden of a social settlement in Liverpool's dockland. Despite later fame as a businessman and politician, these early experiences left him with a valuable grasp of ordinary peoples' attitudes and a capacity to communicate. When turned down for military service on health grounds in 1914 he volunteered instead for Whitehall, where his Liverpool work was already known. He held posts in supply organizations before taking effective charge of the government's coordination of the leather trade as Controller of Civilian Boots. This led to an invitation to re-organize the Boot Manufacturers' Federation when the war ended and to an introduction to Rex Cohen of the Liverpool store Lewis's. Marquis was the first Gentile to join Lewis's board, but proceeded to become joint managing director and then company chairman. As a businessman prominent in retailing he was heavily involved in advising government in the 1930s on trade and industrial matters, and was knighted in 1935.

As government prepared for another war, Marquis was drawn back into the Whitehall machine, serving on groups that considered home defence, fire brigades and air-raid precautions; in April 1939 he was commissioned to devise a crash programme for the clothing of a mass army after conscription was introduced, a job that he later cited as his biggest achievement. When war broke out in September he became Director General at the new Ministry of Supply; he preferred to remain in such a backroom post, but his elevation to the Lords indicated that Chamberlain saw him as a potential minister. He was duly appointed Minister of Food in April 1940, where the task was not to improvise an organization from scratch but to provide direction, political leadership and public communication for a team central to the war effort on the home front. He became a regular and most effective broadcaster with a flair for putting over his case to the radio audience, and he rapidly gained the nickname 'Uncle Fred'. The same flair came with other publicity campaigns of the Ministry, as with such ideas as 'Woolton Pie' for eking out unappetizing foods, but all was based on a firm administrative grasp. The Woolton touch could be seen in the slogan over the ministry's door – 'We not only cope. We care.' It was the face of intrusive wartime control he sought to show.

He was less effective as Minister of Reconstruction from 1943, though he did important work in reconciling differing ministerial views, as over the Employment White Paper of 1944. When Labour left office after the end of the European war in 1945, Woolton stayed on in Churchill's caretaker team, still as an independent; he joined the Conservatives only after the shattering defeat of 1945, and became Party Chairman a year later. At Central Office he used the gifts that had worked so well at the Ministry of Food – an inspirational avuncularity, a sure managerial sense, and a willingness to aim for very large results. It was mainly his achievement that membership reached its all-time high in the early 1950s; the general level of organization also peaked, one of the foundation stones of the party's recovery of power in 1951. He remained Party Chairman until 1955 and no successor has matched his rapport with the rank and file. He was also a cabinet minister in various coordinating and non-departmental posts from 1951 to 1955; this was less of a success, partly perhaps through failing powers, partly though the general failure of Churchill's experiment with 'overlord' ministers. He remained, though, a very powerful advocate for his party in the Lords with a shrewd sense of public appeal: his entreaty for the country to have more 'red meat' in 1951 was an effective blow in the demand for a quicker end to rationing, not least coming from the man who had done so much to accustom the public to rationing in the first place. It was on both counts a particular triumph for him when meat rationing was in due course ended by a government of which he was still a member.

WRITINGS

Memoirs (London: Cassell, 1959).

JOHN RAMSDEN

Marsh, Richard (William) [Lord Marsh of Mannington] (*b*. Swindon, Wiltshire, 14 March 1928). Labour minister and businessman. As Minister of Power and of Transport in the 1966 Labour Government of Harold Wilson, and later chairman of the British Railways Board, Marsh had a career in many ways emblematic of the meritocratic and corporatist currents in postwar British society. From a working-class background, he rose via public-sector trade unionism and a scholarship to Ruskin College, Oxford, entering Parliament in 1959 and becoming the youngest cabinet member in 1966. Marsh several times adopted minority or unpopular positions within cabinet.

In the devaluation crisis of July 1966 he was among those members urging deep cuts in public spending – a position historian Clive Ponting described as 'masochistic', and in May 1967 he was one of the strongest opponents in cabinet of Britain's entering the European Community.

Placed in charge of Labour's steel nationalization programme, Marsh argued the case on pragmatic rather than ideological grounds, as a means of rationalizing an inefficient and underinvested industry, but experienced considerable difficulty in finding suitable personnel for the new public board. Wilson moved him to the Transport post in 1968. Here he inherited a dock nationalization plan from his predecessor, Barbara Castle. This he abandoned, but progress in devising an alternative was slow. Marsh's personal relations with many cabinet colleagues had apparently by now become strained, and Wilson no longer felt confidence in him. In August 1969 he was dismissed from his cabinet post in a reshuffle. Although given the frontbench Housing portfolio when Labour returned to opposition in 1970, he found Edward Heath's offer of the chairmanship of British Rail more attractive. After resigning his Commons seat in 1971 he served on a wide range of public bodies and on the boards of numerous private companies. As well as running the railways from 1971 to 1975, he became chairman of the Newspaper Publishers' Association in 1976 and of the broadcasting company TV-AM in 1983. He was knighted in 1976 and created a life peer in 1981.

WRITINGS

Off the Rails (London: Weidenfeld and Nicolson, 1978).

FURTHER READING

Ponting, C., *Breach of Promise: Labour in Power 1964–1970* (London: Hamish Hamilton, 1989).

STEPHEN HOWE

Martin, (Basil) Kingsley (*b.* Hereford, 28 July 1897; *d.* Cairo, 16 February 1969).

Academic, journalist, Labour activist and editor of the *New Statesman and Nation*. His editorship of the *New Statesman and Nation* between January 1931 and 1960 established the paper as a widely read and internationally respected forum of radical opinion. Ironically, for such an ardent critic of colonialism and so inveterate a traveller, he embodied a uniquely English tradition of intellectual dissent, too often dismissed by Labour Party leaders as unnecessarily querulous. Biographer, political theorist and former don, Martin served his journalistic apprenticeship on the *Manchester Guardian* from 1927 to 1930; in those same years he co-founded and jointly edited the *Political Quarterly*. He was a relentless campaigner, a persuasive if idiosyncratic polemicist, and a dominant personality in the weekly press for almost three decades; he proved a valuable patron of liberal pressure groups such as the Union of Democratic Control, the National Council for Civil Liberties and the Campaign for Nuclear Disarmament.

Martin's political philosophy and personal values were moulded by his upbringing in a family whose staunch nonconformity embraced all aspects of the secular as well as the religious life. His father's pacifism, socialism and tolerance deeply influenced an already complex personality. Registering as a conscientious objector while still at Mill Hill School, Martin subsequently served in France during 1917 and 1918 as an orderly in the Friends' Ambulance Unit. The experience reinforced an already deep strain of pacifism, abandoned only with great reluctance in the late 1930s. In 1919 Martin went up to Cambridge, where a First in history secured a byefellowship back at Magdalene after a year's scholarship at Princeton. His appointment as an assistant lecturer at the London School of Economics, scholarly publications and involvement in the *Political Quarterly* all suggested a potentially distinguished academic career. In fact, it lasted only until 1927.

Martin's close friend and colleague Harold Laski proved a lasting influence as well as a useful introduction into the higher echelons of the Labour Party, albeit at the expense of useful contacts in the trade-union movement such as Ernest Bevin, scourge of so-called Hampstead intellectuals. Clashes with the LSE's Director, William (later Lord) Beveridge, led Martin to commence a three-year appointment as a leader-writer on the *Manchester Guardian*. A frustrated dissenter and idealistic crusader, he soon encountered difficulties in reconciling a wholehearted adherence to democratic socialism with the constraints C. P. Scott placed upon his more fiery editorials.

Martin's relentless lobbying to secure a fresh post back in London paid off when the sickly Fabian weekly, the *New Statesman*, merged with its Liberal counterpart, the *Nation*, in late 1930. Having masterminded the union of their respective papers, Arnold Bennett and John Maynard (later Lord) Keynes gambled on a relatively fresh face to launch their new venture as the flagship of British radicalism. Circulation in January 1931 stood at 14,000; in 30 years it increased sixfold. Martin set out to make the 'Staggers and Naggers' a commercial success *and* an attractive but rarely compromising organ of unashamedly socialist thinking (in the front half at least, as a succession of literary editors enjoyed an enviable degree of discretion). As chairman, Keynes applauded evidence of commercial enterprise while sensibly bowing to editorial integrity in matters of potential conflict.

By intuition as much as logic, Martin and his colleagues articulated the ideas and ideals of liberal middle-class opinion in mid-twentieth-century Britain. By the 1940s the *New Statesman and Nation* was extending its influence to anti-imperialists in Africa and Asia, most especially in India. Its editor was always infuriatingly inconsistent; well-intentioned yet often astonishingly naïve; unusually prone to being influenced by the last person spoken to; and on occasions, such as the 1938 Czechoslovakian crisis, culpably wrong. All these failings notwithstanding, Kingsley Martin gave his beloved weekly a persistent 'standard of compulsive readability', which his colleague Richard Crossman judged his greatest attribute.

FURTHER READING

Hyams, E., *The New Statesman: the History of the First Fifty Years, 1913–1963* (London: Longmans, 1963).

Rolph, C. H., *Kingsley: the Life, Letters & Diaries of Kingsley Martin* (London: Victor Gollancz, 1973).

ADRIAN SMITH

Mary [Victoria Mary Augusta Louise Olga Pauline Claudine Agnes] (*b.* London, 26 May 1867; *d.* London, 24 March 1953). Princess Victoria Mary, the daughter of the Duke and Duchess of Teck, married Prince George, Duke of York, on 6 July 1883 and was, successively, Duchess of York, Duchess of Cornwall and Princess of Wales before becoming Queen Consort on George's accession to the throne in 1910. She bore her husband one daughter and five sons: Princess Mary, later Countess of Harewood and Princess Royal; Prince Edward, in turn Prince of Wales, King Edward VIII and Duke of Windsor; Prince Albert, later Duke of York and then King George VI; Prince Henry, later Duke of Gloucester; Prince George, later Duke of Kent; and Prince John, who died at the age of 13. She devoted herself to the promotion of King George's comfort and the protection of the dignity of his position; she was a guardian not just of the King but of the institution of monarchy. After her husband's death she largely retired from public duties but led an active private life and continued to exert considerable influence at court; along with Queen Elizabeth, George VI's consort, she did much to ensure the virtual exile of the Duke of Windsor and to see that the style of monarchy of George VI was substantially that of his father.

Princess May, as she was known, was born into a junior and somewhat impoverished branch of the royal family. Her father, Prince (later Duke) Francis of Teck, was a grandson of the King of Würtemburg, but his royal status was qualified by the fact that he was the child of a morganatic marriage. Her mother, the very stout and good-natured Princess Mary of Cambridge, was a grand-daughter of George III. Queen Victoria allowed the Duke and Duchess the use of Kensington Palace, where Princess May was born, and later also White Lodge, Richmond Park, but the couple's extravagant life style was unequal to their income and the family was forced to escape their creditors by living abroad between 1883 and 1885. This background of precarious royal status and equally precarious financial position does much to explain Queen Mary's awe of her husband, her obsession with royal genealogy, her frugality and her legendary acquisitiveness. Royal, but not royal enough, her marriage prospects seemed unfavourable, and that she became engaged to the eldest son of the Prince of Wales, the Duke of Clarence, and, after his death, engaged and then married to his younger brother, Prince George, owed much to the match-making of Queen Victoria, who was unconcerned by the morganatic strain in the Tecks' royal blood.

The first years of married life were not without problems: Princess May, now Duchess of York, was not made over-welcome by Princess Alexandra and her daughters, and, since she was essentially a city person, it is unlikely that she took easily to the country life favoured by Prince George, for so much of the time, both while he was Duke of York and later as Prince of Wales. The marriage was, however, a success and the couple became close. The future Queen was at once a willing subordinate to her husband and a dominant mother to her growing family. She was certainly a better wife than a mother, for she appears to have disliked babies and, although she became fond of her children (born between the years 1894 and 1905) as they grew older, she never allowed maternal warmth to come between them and the strict quarter-deck regime imposed on them by her husband, who was their king as well as their father. That this attitude played a part in the creation of the future strained relations between her eldest son and his father cannot be doubted.

Queen Mary made a dignified and imposing Queen Consort. Her style of dress became increasingly anachronistic, for she obeyed her husband's tastes and dictates, and her long skirts, tocques and parasols gave her an endur-

Queen Mary on a visit to Silverwood Colliery, Yorkshire, July 1912

ing Victorian appearance. An interest in charities and philanthropy has become obligatory for royal females, and Queen Mary, who had early acquired a dutiful interest in this sphere, was indefatigable in opening and inspecting institutions which relieved the unfortunate. World War I gave her many opportunities to extend her welfare work. The war also revealed a talent for public relations, as shown by her gift of a cigarette box to every soldier at the front at Christmas 1914. But, above all, she saw her duty as being wife, supporter and protector of the King, to which end she ensured that his daily life and that of the court followed the precisely timed routine and austere ceremony that he preferred. It was not a role without influence for, if she carried out the King's wishes, she often also interpreted them.

There was a contrast between the Queen Mary who subordinated herself to the service of her husband and king, and the regal and dominant figure that her children, her courtiers and the public knew. In some respects she was a matriarch who, after the death of George V, continued to have a profound influence on the style and ethos of the House of Windsor. The institution of the monarchy which she so revered was associated for her with the dutiful service that was George V's conception of it. If she briefly transferred her loyalty to her son as Edward VIII, that loyalty was strained by the combination of wilfulness, spontaneity and dereliction of mundane duties which Edward brought to kingship, and could not withstand his desire to marry the twice-divorced Mrs Wallis Simpson. Her eldest son, she considered, had failed in his duty towards the institution she so revered. Although she claimed in a letter to him after the Abdication that 'My feelings for you as a mother remain the same', the Duke of Windsor, writing at the time of her death, characterized her as 'hard and cruel'. With the aid of his consort, Elizabeth, Queen Mary moulded her second son, George VI, into an acceptable successor to his father. She lived to pay homage, at the age of 85, to her grand-daughter Queen Elizabeth II, and, zealous to the end in her defence of George V's memory and legacy, helped bring about the 1952 declaration that Windsor would remain the family name.

FURTHER READING

Duff, David, *Queen Mary* (London: Collins, 1985).

Pearson, J., *The Ultimate Family: the Making of the Royal House of Windsor* (London: Michael Joseph, 1986).

Pope-Hennessy, J., *Queen Mary, 1867–1953* (London: Allen and Unwin, 1959).

A. W. PURDUE

Maudling, Reginald (*b*. London, 7 March 1917; *d*. London, 14 February 1979). Conservative Chancellor of the Exchequer and Home Secretary. Reginald Maudling, it has to be said, looks – at this remove of time – to be a profoundly sad figure. It may seem a tragic thing to say of a politician who filled several of the great offices of state with great ability, intellectual distinction and manifest humanity, and who was moreover himself a man of great charm. His political downfall came because he did not choose his business contacts carefully enough. The 'might-have-been' technique of political history is fruitless, but the simple, sorry, mundane fact about the Maudling story is that he might have gone on to greater things if the British did not expect their politicians to be able to accumulate enough money to give them independent means. His chosen path to financial independence led to problems.

Maudling was an easy-going personality, which gave him an air of indolence. In fact, behind the easy-going exterior was one of the best minds in politics in modern times. There have been few Chancellors of the Exchequer more at home among the nitty-gritty of Treasury facts and figures on which economic and fiscal policy must be built.

His Conservative politics he learned from one of the purest sources, at the knee of 'Rab' Butler. Maudling was one of the bright young men – others were Iain Macleod and Enoch Powell – taken by Butler into the Conservative Research Department after the war to rebuild a Tory Party demoralized by the Labour landslide of 1945 and determined to avoid the unpopularity earned by the party in the 1930s. So, for good or ill, Maudling was in at the start of what came to be called the 'postwar consensus', based largely on the contemporary inter-

Reginald Maudling, Home Secretary, arriving at Aldergrove Airport, Belfast, June 1970; James Chichester-Clark, Prime Minister of Northern Ireland, is on the left

pretation of Keynesian economics and characterized by what was later seen as an all but superstitious over-emphasis on the prevention of unemployment at almost any cost. Intellectual flaws there may have been in the doctrines of the postwar consensus, but at least Maudling could claim to be one of the most intelligent practitioners of it.

His obvious ability earned him early preferment in the Churchill government of the 1950s, and by the time that Harold Macmillan came to power Maudling was recognized as being in the alpha class of politician. As President of the Board of Trade (1959–61) he was picked by Macmillan to put together what was considered the most realistic compromise available when the original Common Market 'Six' went ahead to form a European Community without Britain. The compromise was EFTA, the European Free Trade Association: a poor thing, but more useful than it would have been without Maudling's skill.

In 1961 Maudling was appointed Colonial Secretary to continue the process launched with the Macmillan 'wind of change' speech. He disarmed African suspicions about British intentions, and was held to have achieved a particularly notable success in his formula for independence in Kenya. Maudling's part in dismantling the old empire did not, however, help his reputation on the right of his party.

But now Macmillan's charmed political life was at a low ebb. In 1962, in a bid to give his administration a more forward-looking face, he carried out the 'Night of the Long Knives', when a third of his cabinet were dismissed, including the Chancellor, Selwyn Lloyd, who was seen as taking too stuffy a view about the importance of controlling public expenditure. Maudling, at the age of 45, stepped into the Chancellor's shoes, with policies which the later monetarists were to condemn as having fuelled the fires of inflation. It was a charge against which Maudling was adept at defending himself. He never accepted the monetarist argument.

When Macmillan resigned in 1963 Maudling was a front runner for the succession, which in fact went to Lord Home. When Home lost the next general election, and the Tories looked for another leader in 1965, Maudling was favourite. This was the first time the leadership was determined by a ballot of MPs, and in the event the voting was Maudling 133, Edward Heath 150. It seemed that the Tory Party wanted something more robust than the supposedly bland Maudling.

The Tories were now out of office, and Maudling had substantial responsibilities as Deputy Leader of the Opposition but only the salary of an MP to provide his political income. An ex-Chancellor of the Exchequer need not be short of invitations to earn fees by giving his name to commercial enterprises, and it was now that he failed in his financial affairs to show the shrewdness that was a characteristic in his politics. He accepted two invitations which led to deep trouble. One was to become president of the Real Estate Fund of America, whose affairs led to long litigation. The other was to link himself with the business empire of the architect John Poulson. Maudling did not draw a salary, but had arranged for Poulson to make a large contribution to a non-commercial repertory theatre which was an enthusiasm of Mrs Maudling, a former actress.

However, before these chickens came home to roost, the Tories returned to power. In 1970 Maudling became Home Secretary, with responsibility on a host of quasi-moral issues, the more pressing because this was the era of the so-called Permissive Society. Maudling made his own liberal outlook clear when he said it was more meaningful to talk of the Compassionate Society. But a more specific Home Office responsibility was the Metropolitan Police – who became liable to be called in to investigate Poulson. Maudling resigned in 1972. There was actually also an attempt to expel him from the Commons.

Thus in the wilderness, he was in no position, when Heath's government later collapsed in confusion, to take part in the great debate that ensued inside the Tory Party, the debate on monetarism – between the 'Wets' and the 'Dries' – on which he was so well qualified to provide much-needed intellectual rigour to the Wet cause.

When Mrs Thatcher emerged as Heath's successor, she rather surprisingly invited the Wet as well as discredited Maudling to join her shadow cabinet, proving that she was more generous and more catholic in her taste of colleagues than she received credit for among critics. But he did not last long. His job was Shadow Foreign Secretary, and his relaxed style outraged the fire-eaters in Mrs Thatcher's entourage anxious to build up her reputation as an iron maiden.

In fact his life had not long to last. He died a couple of years later, at the age of 61.

WRITINGS

Memoirs of Reginald Maudling (London: Sidgwick and Jackson, 1978).

JULIAN CRITCHLEY

Maxwell, (Ian) Robert [Hoch, Jan] (*b.* Slatinske Doly, Czechoslovakia [now USSR], 10 June 1923). Businessman and newspaper proprietor. Fearing persecution by the Nazis, Maxwell left Czechoslovakia in 1939 and travelled to Palestine; he joined the Czech Legion which, after fighting briefly in France, arrived in Britain in 1940. He served with distinction in the British Army, winning the Military Cross in Belgium, and from 1945 to 1947 worked as the British Military Government's press control officer in Berlin. On his return to London, excited by the possibilities of publishing, Maxwell took advantage of Britain's status as an occupying power and established a joint company with Ferdinand Springer, Germany's largest scientific publishers, to sell Springer's publications worldwide. At the same time, with his ability to speak nine languages, he entered the international barter trade and forged uniquely close and profitable relations with the governments of communist Europe and Soviet Russia.

Supported by Springer's reputation, Maxwell cultivated contacts in London with government, political, business and publishing personalities. In 1951 he took over the ailing book wholesaler Simpkin Marshall. Three years later Simpkins crashed, earning Maxwell criticism from the Official Receiver and permanent suspicion from some publishers.

Undaunted, he committed his enormous energy to developing the fledgling Pergamon Press, and in 1968 he announced Pergamon's sale for $25 million to an American. The sensation was eclipsed by the news, just weeks later, that the deal was cancelled. Pergamon's accounts were subject investigation by the Take Over Panel, the Department of Trade and Industry and the Fraud Squad. The DTI inspectors' first report, published in July 1971, stated that Maxwell 'is not in our opinion a person who can be relied on to exercise proper stewardship of a publicly quoted company.'

Maxwell's future business career seemed doomed. His political opportunities (he was Labour MP for North Buckinghamshire from 1964 to 1970) were also bedevilled by an unflattering reputation in the House of Commons and poor relations with a section of his constituency, which prompted in 1974 an official Labour Party enquiry.

Yet after a blitz of legal initiatives, business coups and the exertion of his remorseless personality, Maxwell regained control of Pergamon. In an unexpected coup in July 1980 he bought 30 per cent of the ailing British Printing Corporation. By 1981, with Maxwell in total control, BPC's losses were drastically cut. Using BPC's forecast profits as collateral for bewildering but often profitable take-over bids and acquisitions, Maxwell relaunched himself at the centre of British business life. His first major prize was Mirror Group Newspapers in 1984, so overcoming past frustrated attempts to own a national newspaper; then followed a succession of other print works and minor newspapers around the world.

Throughout the 1980s, heavily promoted by his own newspapers, Maxwell cultivated the image of a globe-trotting power-broker involved in a myriad of disparate activities – journalistic, political, financial and charitable – simultaneously boasting that his strategy would produce a £3 to £5 billion printing and publishing mega-corporation by 1990. In 1989 he publicly abandoned his target and strategy. Having bought Macmillan Publishers of New York, Maxwell offered for sale all his print works and announced that 80 per cent of Maxwell Communications Corporation was now concentrated in the USA, committed only

Robert Maxwell at a news conference at the launch of his biography 'Maxwell' by Joe Haines, February 1988

to publishing. Despite his wealth, which is unquantifiable because of his use of secret Liechtenstein trusts, Maxwell says that he remains a socialist and is committed to finance various charities, especially those devoted to Jewish causes.

FURTHER READING

Bower, T., *Maxwell the Outsider* (London: Aurum, 1988).

Haines, J., *Maxwell* (London: Macdonald, 1988).

TOM BOWER

Melchett, Lord. See MOND, ALFRED.

Milner, Alfred [Viscount Milner of St James's and of Cape Town] (*b.* Giessen, Hesse-Darmstadt, 23 March 1854; *d.* Sturry Court, near Canterbury, Kent, 13 May 1925). Civil servant. Milner was one of the most distinguished civil and public servants of the early twentieth century. As High Commissioner for

South Africa and Governor variously of the Cape Colony, the Transvaal and the Orange River Colony from 1897 to 1905, he bore much of the responsibility for Britain's policy both in the years which preceded the war of 1899–1902 and in the difficult postwar period of reconstruction. A highly respected elder statesman and influential spokesman on imperial themes, he again held major office in the War Cabinet (1916–18) and as Secretary of State for the Colonies (1918–21).

Milner's early upbringing was divided between London and Germany. After three years at school in Tübingen and an outstanding career at King's College, London, he won a scholarship to Balliol College, Oxford, in 1872. There again his record was brilliant: a string of university scholarships, presidency of the Union and a Double First in classics were followed by a Fellowship at New College in 1876. From 1879 to 1885 he tried his hand first at law and then at journalism, on the *Pall Mall Gazette* under John Morley and W. T. Stead. Under the influences of Benjamin Jowett's Balliol, Oxford friends such as Arnold Toynbee, and Stead, Milner's political views matured in directions antithetical to those of traditional Gladstonian Liberals. He stressed the responsibility of the whole community, and the efficacy of an efficient interventionist state, for promoting the social and economic welfare of the people; he also took very seriously Britain's world role as an imperial power, and vigorously opposed the separation of Ireland from Great Britain espoused by the Liberal Party after 1885.

As private secretary to G. J. Goschen, Milner was drawn into public life when in 1886 Goschen became Chancellor of the Exchequer. His growing interest in financial policy was given full rein, first in appointment to the Egyptian finance ministry (1889–92) and then as chairman of the Board of Inland Revenue in London. His book *England in Egypt* (1892), a major statement of Britain's imperial achievement and responsibility, was both popular and influential.

Milner's appointment at Joseph Chamberlain's request to a most difficult post at Cape Town was a tribute to his ability and to his acceptability to both Liberal and Conservative politicians; it nevertheless overlooked his limited capacity for painstaking negotiation and compromise. Britain faced many problems: there was the challenge presented by the independent-minded Transvaal, courting international support to weaken British influence in a region economically and strategically vital to Britain's imperial network; the Transvaal's new mineral wealth had created seriously strained relations with Britain's colonies, Natal and the Cape; and inside the Transvaal, tensions were acute between the Afrikaners and the new immigrants (Uitlanders) who dominated Johannesburg and the mining industry. Milner came to the conclusion that the Transvaal's leaders were fundamentally unreasonable and that only an outspoken policy – uncompromising to the point of being prepared to face war – would secure Britain's interests. During 1899 his acceptance of the necessity for war, his apparent harshness towards the Dutch throughout South Africa, and his public support for the Uitlanders eroded public confidence in him. This contributed much both to the serious division of British opinion about South African policy and to the revival of general reservations about imperial expansion which the war itself (1899–1902) only accentuated.

Milner's hopes for a quick victory and a clean slate on which to reconstruct a thoroughly British South Africa proved illusory. The war was prolonged and very destructive, while Afrikaners' bitterness and nationalist sentiment greatly increased. Economic recovery was slow and British immigration limited; political divisions among the British in South Africa opened the way for Dutch political recovery. Although Milner, with young Oxford-trained recruits such as Lionel Curtis and Geoffrey Dawson (his 'Kindergarten'), helped rebuild the material foundations for a South African political union, its completion, which was in Milner's opinion seriously flawed, was left to his successors in 1910.

Despite the public tributes and his elevation to the peerage (1901, 1902), Milner returned to Britain in July 1905 conscious of limited achievement and sensitive both to criticism and to the changed climate of metropolitan opinion. Like other staunch imperialists, he commonly blamed democratic politics and weak leadership for his failure to do more and for growing signs of imperial weakness. Such convictions fired his vigorous opposition to major Liberal policies, such as the People's Budget of 1909 and reform of the House of Lords, and his activity for imperial causes, such as tariff reform. As ever he was convinced that empire, especially its political and economic consolidation, and domestic social reform were inseparable. Books such as *The Nation and the Empire* (1913) and his support for the Round Table movement were designed to counteract the empire's centrifugal tendencies.

The Liberal Government's distrust of Milner did not prevent it harnessing his administrative experience after 1914 to help solve problems of wartime supply. In 1916 he became still more involved in the war effort, first as one of Lloyd George's small War Cabinet, concerned with questions which ranged from shipping, to negotiations with Russia and France, and postwar reconstruction. In 1918 he was appointed Secretary of State for War and at the end of hostilities took the Colonial Office. Colonial questions were of some significance to the peace-making at Versailles. However, Milner's most important achievement was his negotiation with Egypt's nationalist leaders of what became the basis for the Anglo-Egyptian settlement of 1922. His reconciliation of Britain's regional strategic interests with her withdrawal from political control was not immediately accepted in London, a rebuff which contributed to his resignation in February 1921. It was nevertheless of major assistance to Britain in meeting the fundamental postwar challenge of reducing imperial claims and ambitions to match the finance and manpower available in an economy seriously weakened by the war. It also revealed in Milner himself an unusual flexibility of approach.

FURTHER READING

Gollin, A. M., *Proconsul in Politics: a Study of Lord Milner in Opposition and in Power* (New York: Macmillan, 1964).
Headlam, Cecil (ed.), *The Milner Papers: South Africa 1897–1905*, 2 vols. (London: Cassell, 1931–3).
Marlowe, John, *Milner: Apostle of Empire* (London: Hamish Hamilton, 1976).
Porter, A. N., *The Origins of the South African War* (Manchester: Manchester University Press, 1980).

A. N. PORTER

Monckton, Sir Walter (Turner) [Viscount Monckton of Brenchley] (*b.* Plaxtol, Kent, 17 January 1891; *d.* Folkington, Sussex, 9 January 1965). Conservative politician and lawyer. He was the eldest child of a paper manufacturer, F. W. Monckton, but on completion of his education at Harrow and Balliol chose not to pursue a business career. While President of the Oxford Union in 1913, he made the acquaintance of the Prince of Wales, then at Magdalen. When war came he was refused entry into the armed forces; he could hardly see out of one eye, although this had not prevented him from hunting and playing cricket for Harrow. He managed to secure a commission in the Queen's Own West Kent Regiment and served in France, winning the MC. In 1919 he was called to the Bar by the Inner Temple and soon built a flourishing practice in common law; he took silk in 1930. Monckton was Recorder of Hythe (1930–7), Chancellor of the Diocese of Southwell (1930–6) and Attorney-General, first to the Prince of Wales (1932–6), and then to the Duchy of Cornwall (1936–51). He also acted as the constitutional adviser to the Nizam of Hyderabad and to the Nawab of Bhopal from 1933, at a time when the Indian princes were considering whether they should join in the proposed scheme for a federal India which became the Government of India Act, 1935. Monckton counseled that Hyderabad's future was best assured by accession to the federation on favourable terms.

Monckton was recalled from Hyderabad to advise the Prince of Wales, now King Edward VIII, during the events which led up to his abdication in December 1936. Despite the fact that he was the King's closest adviser and confidant, Monckton also retained the complete confidence of the Prime Minister, Stanley Baldwin, with whom he met frequently in efforts to resolve the crisis. These were unsuccessful, but Monckton's part was recognized by the conferment of a KCVO in the New Year's Honours list. He continued to act as go-between for the royal brothers on financial and other matters until after the outbreak of World War II, and persuaded the Duke of Windsor to leave Lisbon and take up appointment as Governor of the Bahamas in 1940.

At the outbreak of war Monckton was appointed chairman of the Aliens Advisory Committee, which heard appeals from those detained under section 18B of the Defence of the Realm regulations; anxious to play a more active part, he applied to join the RAF Volunteer Reserve. Instead Chamberlain appointed him Director-General of the Press and Censorship Bureau, and in April 1940 he was made Deputy Director-General of the Ministry of Information. Promoted Director-General in December 1940, he was sent on a mission to the Soviet Union the following October, from which he proceeded to Cairo as a member of the Middle East War Council and Director-General of Propaganda and Information Services. He acted as Minister of State from February to May 1942, but a quarrel with Churchill in April put him out of favour. Although he continued in government service until the end of the war, he was given no further prominent position. However, he was appointed Solicitor-General in the caretaker government from May to June 1945, an office which he had refused ten years earlier. He led the UK delegation on the Reparations Commission, but on Labour's accession to office resumed his successful practice at the Bar.

Monckton spent much of 1946 in India, vainly trying to secure the future of Hyderabad as the subcontinent moved towards independence, and in 1947 had the invidious task of trying to persuade the Nizam that its future would be best secured by some form of alliance with India. Rejection of his advice led to the Indian occupation of Hyderabad in September 1948.

In February 1951, at Churchill's wish, Monckton successfully contested the Bristol West by-election, and after the general election in October he became Minister of Labour and National Service in Churchill's government.

His 'riding orders' were to keep on good terms with the unions, and he quickly built up a good relationship with their leaders based on trust and a mutual respect for each other's point of view. Hindsight perhaps indicates that he was on occasion too conciliatory, but, if so, it was with the full backing of the Prime Minister and most of his colleagues.

When Eden became Prime Minister in April 1955, Monckton was appointed Minister of Defence and found himself engaged first in cooperating with and later resisting Treasury pressure for cuts in defence, particularly in the numbers of service personnel. He was unhappy at the drift of policy during the early stages of the Suez crisis and voiced his doubts at the Egypt Committee on 23 August and in cabinet on the 28th. His loyalty to Eden inhibited him from resigning, although, when it became clear on 18 October that the Israelis might become involved in the operations against Nasser, he insisted on moving to a cabinet post without portfolio. While he was among those who opposed the landings on 4 November, he acquiesced in the decision to intervene and did not resign when the landings went ahead.

Monckton had hoped to become Lord Chief Justice, but the current incumbent of the post was equally determined that he should not – probably because of his chequered marital career – and instead he turned to banking, acting as chairman of the Midland Bank from 1957 to 1964. He also chaired the Iraq Petroleum Company from 1958 until his death.

In 1959 Macmillan asked Monckton to chair an advisory commission preparatory to the review of the constitution and working of the Federation of Rhodesia and Nyasaland, which was due to take place in 1960. This was a difficult assignment since Monckton and his colleagues were precluded from considering anything which might lead to the break-up of the federation, and yet became convinced that it could hope to survive as a workable multiracial state only if the possibility of secession was admitted. Their report, which suggested greater devolution of powers, parity in the number of seats for Blacks and Whites, a wider franchise and safeguards against racial discrimination, in addition to the controversial recommendation that secession be permitted after a further period, was well received when published in October 1960, but the anger it aroused in the federal government and the subsequent controversy were not helpful to those who strove in vain to hold the federation together. The attempt was abandoned in 1963.

During the course of the commission's visits to Africa, Monckton had to return frequently to England to attend to the affairs of the bank. This undoubtedly contributed to the increasing difficulty he had with his health. Despite a kidney operation in February 1963 and the onset of arterio sclerosis, he was installed as Chancellor of Sussex University in June 1963 and presided over the launching of Midland and International Banks Ltd in December. He resigned as chairman in June 1964 and died six months later.

FURTHER READING

Birkenhead, Lord, *Walter Monckton* (London: Weidenfeld and Nicolson, 1969).

Lamb, Richard, *The Failure of the Eden Government* (London: Sidgwick and Jackson, 1987).

Seldon, Anthony, *Churchill's Indian Summer* (London: Hodder and Stoughton, 1981).

JOHN BARNES

Mond, Sir **Alfred (Moritz)** [Lord Melchett of Landford] (*b.* Farnworth, Cheshire, 23 October 1868; *d.* Melchett Court, Hampshire, 27 December 1930). Industrialist, 'rationalizer' of industry, creator of ICI, and Minister of Health. He was an important figure in both industry and politics in the first third of the century.

Mond was the second son of the successful chemical manufacturer Ludwig Mond and his wife Frederike. He was educated at Cheltenham College and St Johns College, Cambridge, where he read natural sciences, but after taking a relaxed attitude to study failed his final examinations. However, after talking to his father's partner Sir John Brunner, he decided to pursue a career in politics, and to prepare the ground he studied law at Edinburgh. In 1894 he was called to the Bar at the Inner Temple and for about a year practised on the North Wales and Cheshire circuit.

In 1894 Mond married Violet Goetzes,

daughter of a London coffee merchant. They had three daughters and one son, Henry, who subsequently played an important role in his father's company and in politics. The following year Mond joined the board of his father's firm Brunner, Mond, but his main energies went elsewhere. His major business activity was in another family firm, Mond Nickel Co., of which he was made chairman in 1902.

His second and growing interest was in his political career. In 1900 he failed to win Salford for the Liberals, not being helped by his opposition to the Boer War, but in 1906 he ran a much more successful campaign to take Chester from the Conservatives. He held this seat until 1910, when he won Swansea, a town with a major Brunner, Mond plant. He lost this to Labour in 1923, but a year later won the Carmarthen constituency, which he held until 1928.

In the years before World War I Mond was an advocate of free trade and made speeches on other aspects of industrial and financial policy. He criticized Conservative policies and supported calls for the reform of the House of Lords. In 1913 he was made a baronet and a member of the Privy Council. During the war his political importance grew. He had supported the replacement of Asquith by Lloyd George. After Asquith's resignation in 1916, he was rewarded by being made the First Commissioner of Works. He was well-suited to the immense task of building the facilities needed for war. He had royal parks planted with vegetables and even employed his own capital and buildings to provide hospital facilities.

Mond received abuse earlier in the war because of his German background and was involved in two lawsuits to clear his name, winning £5000 damages in one of them. Those that knew him considered he had reacted against his father's German ways and some rejection at school by becoming the very epitome of Englishness.

After the war Mond was made responsible for constructing the cemeteries for the War Graves Commission and helped establish the Imperial War Museum. In Lloyd George's coalition government he was made Minister of Health (1921–2) and was employed by Lloyd

Lord Melchett and his son
out pheasant shooting at
Woodfalls, Melchett Park,
Hampshire

George to bring his business acumen to bear on the housing programme. But his political influence declined after the collapse of the coalition in 1922. Being on the right of the Liberal Party (many of his most notable speeches had been on the theme of defending capitalism against socialism), he became increasingly alienated by Lloyd George's move leftwards. In 1926 Mond left his old party to join the Conservatives. Having been unopposed by the Conservatives in Carmarthen he did not feel obliged to stand down. Neither party found his new position comfortable. He was therefore elevated to the Lords in 1928.

Following the European war and the postwar growth of commercial nationalism Mond turned away from free trade. He now supported protection of the Empire market, which he saw as providing many varied and complementary aspects: unlimited raw materials, the industrial might of Britain and large areas of untapped demand. This he saw as a firm for Britain to assault the world's other markets. He established the Empire Economic Union campaign. Before he left the Commons the emphasis of his activity had returned to commercial fields. He became famous for his efforts to 'rationalize' British industry, especially the chemical sector. He believed mergers would promote greater efficiency, outweighing the drawbacks of monopoly business. As the MP for Swansea, for example, he became involved in bringing together the Welsh anthracite industry. He aided the formation of Amalgamated Anthracite Collieries, which, after mergers in 1923 and 1928, controlled 85 per cent of South Wales production. Mond was made Chairman of this company. He was also instrumental in the merger of Mond Nickel with its competitor International Nickel Co. of New Jersey, and in the formation of the Finance Corporation of Great Britain and America.

However, the largest merger in which he was involved was the formation of ICI. Having rejoined the board of Brunner, Mond, which he had left in 1916, he replaced Roscoe Brunner as chairman in 1925. Discussions concerning consolidation within the industry rapidly ensued. Initially Mond was pursuing a grand alliance of British firms and the large German company of IG Farbenindustrie. This company had expertise in two technologies in which Mond, with his strong imperial views, was particularly interested. The first was the process of turning coal into oil; the second was the manufacture of synthetic ammonia, which was vital in peacetime for agriculture and in war for the manufacture of explosives.

The crucial negotiation took place on the *Aquitania* between Mond and Harry McGowan of Nobel Industries. It led to a new British company, consisting of Brunner, Mond, Nobels, British Dyestuffs Corporation and United Alkali Co., which had in total 125 subsidiaries and 70,000 workers. Talks with IG foundered and McGowan achieved his aim of making ICI's international link with Du Pont rather than with the Germans. Following the crash of 1929 the new company was plunged into financial crisis. The major problem it faced was the massive but unprofitable investment made in ICI's Billingham synthetic ammonia plant.

In 1928 Mond made a notable contribution to the difficult labour problems of the post-General Strike period by instituting, with Ben Turner of the TUC, the Mond–Turner conference. This brought together labour leaders and employers and was seen as a success in reducing mutual suspicions, though it produced no specific agreements. He was himself proud of the progressive and successful employee relations in his own companies.

Mond's other concern at the time of his death was the Zionist cause. He met Chaim Weizmann in 1922 and visited Palestine. He became president of the Economic Board and the English Zionist Federation, and joint chairman of the Jewish Agency, from which he later resigned in protest at government policy.

For further illustration, see ASQUITH, H. H.

FURTHER READING

Bolitho, H., *Alfred Mond, First Lord Melchett* (London: Secker, 1933).

Emden, P. H., *Jews of Britain* (London: Sampson Low, 1945).

Morris, P., 'Mond, Alfred Moritz', *Dictionary of Business Biography*, ed. David J. Jeremy and Christine Shaw, 6 vols. (London: Butterworths, 1984–6).

Reader, William J., *Imperial Chemical Industries: a History* (Oxford: Oxford University Press, 1975).

ANTHONY GANDY

Montagu, Edwin (Samuel) (*b.* London, 6 February 1879; *d.* London, 15 November 1924). Liberal statesman. He was the second son of Lord Swaythling, a wealthy merchant banker. He received his education at Clifton College, the City of London School and Trinity College, Cambridge. Soon after graduation he secured the Liberal nomination for West Cambridgeshire and was elected to Parliament in 1906.

Asquith, at once appreciating Montagu's ability, chose him as his private secretary, and then ensured that he rapidly ascended the ministerial ladder. Junior posts at the India Office and the Treasury were followed by entry into the cabinet in February 1915 as Chancellor of the Duchy of Lancaster. From July to December 1916 Montagu served as Minister of Munitions. With the collapse of Asquith's Coalition Government, he retired to the back benches, only to return to office in July 1917 when Lloyd George offered him the Indian secretaryship. He retained this position until he was dismissed in March 1922 for releasing a sensitive telegram from the Indian Viceroy without cabinet authorization. In the 1922 general election Montagu suffered a humiliating defeat. He died, embittered, two years later, still only 45 years of age.

In all the posts which he held, Montagu showed administrative and financial flair. But his main claim to fame now rests on his work as a reforming Indian Secretary. His 1919 Government of India Act was an important step to fulfilling the objective he had announced in his 'Declaration' two years earlier: 'the progressive realisation of responsible Government in India as an integral part of the British Empire'.

Montagu was a man of acute sensitivity and volatile moods, and this made him vulnerable to personal attack; moreover, as a member of a prominent Jewish banking family, he had to endure repeated anti-Semitic gibes. Another source of personal distress was his inability in December 1916 to prevent the breach between

Asquith and Lloyd George, for both of whom he felt genuine affection and respect. Disappointment thus clouded his short life and brilliant career.

FURTHER READING

Waley, S. D., *Edwin Montagu: a Memoir and an Account of his Visits to India* (London: Asia Publishing House, 1964).

G. R. SEARLE

Montefiore, Hugh (William) (*b*. London, 12 May 1920). Bishop. Born into a distinguished Jewish family, Montefiore was educated at Rugby and St John's College, Oxford. He served in the Royal Artillery from 1940 to 1945 and was ordained in 1950. After a curacy in Newcastle he moved to Westcott House, Cambridge, as chaplain and tutor (1951–3) and as Vice-Principal (1953–4). He was Fellow and Dean of Gonville and Caius College from 1954 to 1963 and Vicar of Great St Mary's from 1963 to 1970, leaving in 1970 to become Bishop Suffragan of Kingston-upon-Thames. He was translated to the bishopric of Birmingham in 1978. He retired in 1987.

As a liberal theologian, Montefiore has taken part in the religious debates of the day, as in his contribution in 1962 to the exploratory volume of new Christian thinking, *Soundings*. At the same time he has produced other considerable academic works, such as his *Commentary on the Epistle to the Hebrews* (1964). He has also been a popular, and popularizing, writer on Christian themes and issues, as in *God, Sex and War* (1963), *Can Man Survive?* (1970), *Man and Nature* (1976), *Yes to Women Priests* (1978) and others. His activities in the public sphere made a particular mark during his chairmanship of the Church of England Board of Social Responsibility, which was working to promote the thought and action of the Church in matters affecting man's life in society; Montefiore's many writings reflect these varied interests. While chairman of the Independent Committee on Transport in 1973 he startled public opinion by his criticism of the motor car as a wasteful and polluting use of energy.

WILLIAM PURCELL

Montgomery, Bernard (Law) [Viscount Montgomery of Alamein] (*b*. London, 17 November 1887; *d*. Isington, Hampshire, 23 March 1976). General. Few soldiers in modern times have aroused so much controversy as Montgomery. His achievements in command of the 8th Army in the Western Desert and the Mediterranean between August 1942 and December 1943, and as commander of the Allied 21st Army Group in North-West Europe after June 1944, were totally overshadowed by his extraordinary personality and assiduous creation of historical myths of self-justification. The wartime legend has also obscured his role as NATO's Deputy Supreme Commander from March 1951 to September 1958.

Montgomery was the fourth of eight children of the Rev. Henry Montgomery, who was himself the son of a former Lieutenant-Governor of the Punjab. Brought up in Tasmania, of which his father became Bishop in 1889, Montgomery had a harsh and largely loveless upbringing dominated by his mother, which appears to have left him with a lifelong inner insecurity and a conscious need to prove himself. In short, he was something of a maladjusted youth and, indeed, he was almost dismissed from the Royal Military College, Sandhurst, after setting fire to a fellow cadet's shirt-tails, an escapade that led to the severe burning of the victim. His mother's intervention alone saved his career at this early stage. Montgomery had expressed an early interest in the army during his education at St Paul's School, which he attended after the family returned from Tasmania in 1901, and he proceeded to Sandhurst in 1907.

Montgomery was commissioned into the Royal Warwickshire Regiment in September 1908, serving with the 1st Battalion in India until almost the outbreak of the Great War. After being severely wounded at Meteren near Ypres in October 1914 and winning the DSO for his gallantry in the same action, he was posted as Brigade-Major to what became the 104th Infantry Brigade in 35th Division while recuperating. He accompanied the division back to France in 1916 and rose to be GSO 2 to 33rd Division, GSO 2 to IX Corps and, by 1918, a temporary Lieutenant Colonel as GSO

1 to 47th Division. After a short spell commanding the 17th Battalion, Royal Fusiliers, Montgomery went to the Staff College as a student. There followed a series of staff appointments: Brigade-Major to the Cork Infantry Brigade in 1920 during the Anglo-Irish war, Brigade-Major to the 8th Infantry Brigade in 1922, then GSO 2 to the 49th West Riding Territorial Division.

During this period of military retrenchment and slow promotion in the peacetime army Montgomery made his reputation as a trainer of troops. Regimental service in 1925 was followed by a period as a Staff College instructor and, in 1929, a temporary appointment to the War Office to revise the Infantry Training Manual. A permanent battalion command was forthcoming only in 1931. Montgomery took his unit to Palestine and India before being appointed GSO 1 at the Staff College, Quetta, in 1934 and to the command of the 9th Infantry Brigade in England in 1937. He had married a widow, Betty Carver, in 1927 but, tragically, she died while Montgomery was with his new brigade command from complications following an insect bite on an English beach, leaving Montgomery with the two young sons from her previous marriage. Her death resulted in an emotional gap in Montgomery's life which was not essentially filled until his friendship with a young Swiss boy in the twilight of his own years.

Montgomery's character had already made him some enemies within the army, and a number of appointments he might have expected did not come his way until he was promoted to Major-General commanding the 8th Division in Palestine in October 1938. With customary zeal he threw himself into combating the Arab revolt which had erupted in Palestine two years earlier, but in April 1939 he was recalled to England to command 3rd Division, an appointment he owed largely to the influence of ALAN BROOKE. The division was thoroughly exercised according to Montgomery's theories both that summer and during the 'Phoney War' period from September 1939 to May 1940. During the retirement on Dunkirk, Montgomery took over II Corps when Brooke was brought home to start rebuilding the army, but he then reverted to commanding 3rd Division in Sussex. In

September 1940 he was elevated to Lieutenant-General commanding V Corps, and was side-posted to command XII Corps in Kent in April 1941. Montgomery continued to impress in his management of exercises and he was again elevated to become GOC, South-Eastern Command, in November 1941, an appointment which involved him in the later stages of planning for the Dieppe raid. It was Montgomery who chose the 2nd Canadian Division as the main raiding force, but he had left England before the catastrophe that befell the Canadians at Dieppe.

Brooke had proved to be something of a patron in the past and it was again Brooke who urged Montgomery's appointment to the 8th Army in August 1942 when Prime Minister Winston Churchill demanded changes in the Middle East Command. However, Churchill favoured Lieutenant-General Gott, and on 6 August Montgomery was designated to command British forces participating in the planned 'Torch' landings in North Africa. Then, on the following day, Gott was killed when his aircraft was attacked by German fighters, and Montgomery was appointed after all. His predecessor, General Sir Claude Auchinleck, had already halted the advance of Rommel's 'Afrika Korps' at the first battle of Alamein in July 1942, and had made extensive preparations to defend the current 8th Army line in the vicinity of Alamein and Alam Halfa before launching a counter-attack sometime in September. Arguably, the 8th Army's morale was at a low ebb despite these successes, and Montgomery's appointment certainly had a major impact in terms of his imposition of personality on the army. A slight, uncharismatic figure, he nonetheless seized the imagination of his troops by such means as wearing unconventional headgear and an ability to express objectives in simple terms. Sadly, part of the personality cult involved the conscious and unnecessary denigration of his predecessor Auchinleck, whom Montgomery falsely claimed had intended to retreat to the Nile Delta if the Germans attacked again. Similarly, while strengthening the defensive positions Auchinleck had already laid out, Montgomery chose to claim all credit to himself when Rommel attacked along the expected axes and was

Viscount Montgomery, in the caravan he used as a study, sitting under a portrait of General Rommel, May 1946

beaten back in the action known as the battle of Alam Halfa from 31 August to 6 September 1942.

Another emerging trait of Montgomery's was to claim that all his battles were fought to a precise plan which never required amendment. In fact, one of his strengths was the ability to refashion plans that had gone astray, and it was again entirely unnecessary to claim, as he did consistently, that the second battle of Alamein (23 October to 4 November 1942) went exactly as he had intended. In reality it was a close-run battle despite the considerable numerical and materiel superiority which, in contrast to his predecessors, Montgomery enjoyed over his opponent. It was the chaotic state of the 8th Army – and not rain as Montgomery claimed – that prevented effective pursuit of Rommel. In any case, as the subsequent plodding advance across North Africa indicated, Montgomery preferred conducting methodical set-piece attacks. Consequently, he failed to capitalize on

the wealth of intelligence derived from 'Ultra' which provided full information on German intentions and the pitiful state of their forces. Nevertheless, Montgomery's methods suited the limited capabilities of his army. Alamein was also a most necessary victory in the context of national morale and Montgomery reaped the reward, being knighted and promoted to General in November 1942.

Pursuit of Rommel brought the 8th Army to Tunisia, where Allied forces had already landed in the German rear. It would no longer be a 'private' war in the Mediterranean, and Montgomery resented the intrusion of American commanders, for whose capability he had little regard. He was able to impose his will on the planning for the Allied assault on Sicily in June 1943, but he was enraged by his army being subsequently confined to a subsidiary role in southern Italy after the Allied invasion in September 1943. Consequently, he showed little enthusiasm for the advance up the spine of

Italy. His clashes with the Americans had hardly endeared him to his allies and his appointment to command 21st Army Group for the invasion of North-West Europe, confirmed in December 1943, was not a foregone conclusion. However, his contribution to invasion planning, not least an insistence on widening the frontage of the initial landing, was considerable.

Montgomery's conduct of the land battle in Normandy was again controversial and his attempted breakout plan using British armour east of Caen on 18–20 July ('Goodwood') was disastrous. He was all but dismissed in July through a failure to accommodate a visit to Normandy planned by Churchill and he greatly resented Eisenhower's assumption of the direction of the land operations in August. Thereafter, he consistently advocated the so-called narrow front strategy of throwing Allied resources into a direct drive on Berlin, whereas Eisenhower favoured the far more attainable objective of a 'broad-front' advance across Western Europe. Eventually, Eisenhower forbade any advance on Berlin in March 1945 and took the US 9th Army out of the 21st Army Group. In the meantime, Montgomery, who was promoted to Field Marshal in September 1944, had insisted against all professional advice on proceeding with the gamble of using Allied parachute forces to seize bridges over the Rhine ('Market Garden') between 17 and 25 September. In particular, British airborne forces suffered heavily at Arnhem. However, Montgomery retrieved some of his reputation by commanding all Allied forces north of the salient created by the German Ardennes offensive in December 1944, and the set-piece crossing of the Rhine by his forces in February 1945 was also successful.

Left to clear German forces from Denmark and the Netherlands, Montgomery received the surrender of all German forces there and in northern Germany at Luneburg Heath on 4 May 1945. He became Military Governor of the British occupied areas of Germany and Commander-in-Chief of the British zone before succeeding Alan Brooke as Chief of the Imperial General Staff in June 1946, six months after his elevation to the peerage as a Viscount. In October 1948 Montgomery virtu-ally self-selected himself as first Chairman of the Commander-in-Chiefs Committee of the newly formed Western Union. However, when this became the basis of NATO, Eisenhower became Allied Supreme Commander and Montgomery his deputy in March 1951. Montgomery had enjoyed an uneasy relationship with Labour politicians as CIGS and it was no better when General Ridgway replaced Eisenhower as Supreme Commander in June 1952. Montgomery clung on however. He retired in September 1958, having had a central role in the early development of NATO strategic policy.

In retirement, his vanity and egotism having increased with the years, Montgomery became involved in refighting wartime controversies through the publication of his memoirs and as a presenter of television programmes based upon them. In this way his career and achievements remained a matter of public debate to the very end of his life and beyond.

WRITINGS

Memoirs (London: Collins, 1958).

FURTHER READING

Barnett, Corelli, *The Desert Generals*, 2nd edn (London: Allen and Unwin, 1983).

Chalfont, Alun, *Montgomery of Alamein* (London: Weidenfeld and Nicolson, 1976).

Hamilton, Nigel, *Monty*, 3 vols. (London: Hamish Hamilton, 1981, 1983, 1986).

I. F. W. BECKETT

Morris, William. See NUFFIELD, LORD.

Morrison, Herbert (Stanley) [Baron Morrison of Lambeth] (*b.* London, 3 January 1888; *d.* Sidcup, Kent, 6 March 1965). Labour politician. Morrison was a figure of the first rank in twentieth-century British history. His active involvement in the Labour Party spanned half a century. He led the London Labour Party to victory in the London County Council elections of 1934 and 1937, laying the basis for 30 years of Labour rule, and more than any other London politician he gave a visible identity to the inchoate government of the capital. For over 25 years he occupied a central place in the leadership of the national party, shaping its domestic policies more than any other individual. As a parliamentarian he was widely regarded as the best Leader of the House of Commons in 40 years, ahead even of Baldwin. Above all, however, Morrison was a man of government, both local and national. The one ministerial success of the 1929 Labour Government, he made a major contribution to the domestic front during World War II as Home Secretary and Minister for Home Security. In the postwar Labour Government he was the chief coordinating minister and the source of much of the dynamism of the government. As the architect of its nationalization programme, he put his stamp on the economy for 30 years. No Labour politician then or since has matched his all-round abilities and achievements.

Morrison was born in Brixton, the youngest of seven children of Henry Morrison, a police constable with a tendency to drink, and Priscilla Lyon, the daughter of an East End carpet fitter. An inadequately treated eye infection deprived Morrison of the sight of his right eye, though he was to overcome this handicap with great fortitude. After leaving school at the age of 14 he moved through a variety of 'blind alley' jobs, from errand boy to shop assistant, until in 1912 he became the circulation manager for the Labour newspaper the *Daily Citizen*. Although his disability disqualified him from military service, Morrison insisted on registering as a conscientious objector on pacifist grounds. In April 1915 he found his vocation when he became part-time secretary of the London Labour Party; thereafter he lived on and for politics. In the previous decade Morrison had become actively involved in socialist politics, moving, as did many, back and forth between the Independent Labour Party and the Social Democratic Federation, though finally settling in the ILP; as secretary of the South West London Federation of branches he played a significant role in the decision to form the London Labour Party. A diet of socialist literature and street-corner speaking was accompanied by an ascetic life style and a concern with the machinery of local govern-ment and the minutiae of building a party organization.

Between the wars Morrison became by far the most important figure in London politics. Largely through his work the London Labour Party was built into a highly efficient mass-membership organization which enjoyed particular success in the mobilization of women. The necessity for, and even the beauty of, organization became Morrison's constant theme in the stream of articles, circulars and pamphlets which he produced. He did not, however, see organization as an end in itself, but as the only means by which power could be gained and a programme of social improvement carried out. The implementation of such a programme, he believed, required representatives with expertise who knew how to run council committees and deal with the business of local government. To that end he sought to recruit able middle-class figures and to train Labour candidates, both for the LCC and the boroughs. Morrison himself, whether on the Hackney Borough Council or on the LCC, combined mastery of the detail of the work of local government with great effectiveness in debate. As leader of the LCC after 1934 he enjoyed unquestioned success. Under him the Labour majority pursued progressive policies designed to improve the education, health, housing and environment of London. Throughout, Morrison insisted on the efficient conduct of public administration, which he believed required a clearly defined collaborative but formal relationship with the officers, and on the complete avoidance of any suggestion of patronage or lax administration. His views here led him into sharp conflict with the advocates of Poplarism in the 1920s and with some of the borough parties in the 1930s. In many ways Morrison was typical of the Labour local government leaders who emerged between the wars as the party won control of a number of major cities. The much greater prominence which he enjoyed was a consequence of the symbolic importance of Labour control of the capital, especially after the debacle of 1931, and of Morrison's use of advertising experts who projected him as the personification of Labour's policies.

Morrison's success in London politics made

Herbert Morrison asking
Barbara Castle to dance,
1945

him a national figure. He had first attracted
national attention in 1919, when he spoke for
the London Labour mayors who visited Lloyd
George at Gairloch to press for action on
unemployment. Throughout the 1920s he was
seen as a young rising star of the party. He was
elected as MP for South Hackney in 1923 and
again in 1929, when Ramsay MacDonald
appointed him Minister of Transport. Morrison's most significant achievement was to
block the Bill designed to make London
Transport into a private monopoly and to
introduce his own measure to create an auto-

nomous London Passenger Transport Board.
His desire to see this latter Bill onto the statute
book, his admiration for MacDonald and his
own approach to politics led him to hesitate
over the course to adopt in August 1931. That
hesitation, which was widely suspected though
not known, undoubtedly affected attitudes to
him subsequently. This was apparent in 1934
when he was thwarted in his desire to succeed
Henderson as party secretary, and in 1935
when he unsuccessfully challenged Attlee for
the party leadership (see also ATTLEE,
CLEMENT). On both occasions he was handi-

capped by a certain provincial resentment of London, always a strong force in the party, and by a fear that he was likely to prove too dominant a leader. Despite being frustrated in these ambitions, Morrison played a central role in the national party during the 1930s, though from his power base on the National Executive Committee, even after being re-elected for Hackney South in 1935. Together with Hugh Dalton, Morrison took the lead in reshaping the party's domestic policies after 1931. In particular, in his book *Socialisation and Transport* (1933), he outlined a coherent model of the form and practice to be adopted by the public corporation. After considerable debate the Morrisonian model was accepted as the basis on which the party's nationalization programme would be carried out.

In the late 1930s, when Labour's chance of national office seemed still remote, a number of suggestions were made that Morrison should replace Attlee. Although nothing came of them, they served to give an additional edge to Attlee's resentment. It was Morrison who in 1940 insisted that Labour divide the House at the end of the debate on the Norwegian campaign, so precipitating the fall of Chamberlain and the formation of the Coalition. Morrison resumed office as Minister of Supply before becoming Home Secretary and Minister of Home Security in October (later with a seat in the War Cabinet). During the blitz Morrison displayed to the full his administrative genius in coordinating the varied aspects of civil defence and his instinctive understanding of popular sensibilities. In the House his performances grew increasingly assured and authoritative. During the later stages of the war he made a series of detailed speeches setting out a comprehensive programme for reconstruction which was to provide the basis for the manifesto *Let Us Face the Future*, on which Labour fought the 1945 election. Morrison himself chose to contest the seat of East Lewisham to symbolize the party's intention to win middle-class support. In the immediate aftermath of victory he made a further unsuccessful bid for the leadership when he urged Attlee to observe the procedures laid down after 1931 and to delay accepting the King's commission to form a government until the

parliamentary party had had the opportunity to elect a leader. With the support of Bevin, Attlee ignored this suggestion.

In the new government Morrison became Deputy Prime Minister, holding the non-departmental offices of Lord President of the Council and Leader of the House of Commons. For the next five years he occupied the central role in the government, coordinating domestic policy, shaping the legislative programme and managing both the House of Commons and the Parliamentary Labour Party. His understanding of the parliamentary process was never better demonstrated than during the first session of the new Parliament, when he steered 70 bills through the Commons. The strain of overwork finally exacted its price in 1947, when Morrison suffered a thrombosis which required several months of recuperation. His illness coincided with the growing concern over a lack of coordination in economic affairs, and culminated in the transfer of his functions in this area to Sir Stafford Cripps. The problems which were apparent in the area of economic planning owed far more to institutional conflicts and to personal rivalries among the leading ministers than to Morrison's supposed lack of feel for economic policy.

After his recovery in mid-1947 Morrison became the exponent of a policy of 'consolidation', arguing that electoral considerations and administrative realities required not the pursuit of further measures of nationalization, but a period of stability during which to consolidate both the performance and the public image of the newly nationalized industries. 'If we go on always stretching out our hands for more and not making good the gains we have claimed, only disaster can follow', he warned the party conference in 1948. As he feared, the response of the voters in 1950 to Labour's so-called shopping list of industries for further nationalization was a negative one. Although those to the left of the party continued to demand further advance, their arguments were rhetorical rather than substantive; in practice they accepted Morrison's strategy, though admitting that was to prove far more difficult. While Morrison was winning the domestic arguments, he was less successful in establishing his authority as Foreign Secretary – having succeeded Ernest Bevin in March 1951. His period at the Foreign Office was politically an unhappy one, however his policies are evaluated. The demands of political management and the organization of the successful Festival of Britain inevitably distracted his attention from the central demands of the post. It was with some relief that after the election defeat in 1951 Morrison once more concentrated on domestic affairs.

During the 1951 to 1955 parliament Morrison remained one of Labour's most effective spokesmen. However, his position within the party was waning. The loss of his seat on the NEC at the ill-tempered Morecambe conference in 1952 revealed a loss of support among the constituency parties, while his understandable hesitations over challenging the dying Greenwood for the post of party treasurer, the office which he had failed to gain in 1943, led the major trade-union leaders to look for another champion in the internal battles provoked by the Bevanites. By the time that Attlee finally retired in 1955, Morrison's chance of succeeding him had gone. As his friends warned, in the leadership election he was 'rolled in the mud', polling just 40 votes. In 1959 he accepted a life peerage and in 1960 the office of president of the British Board of Film Censors. He made his last significant contribution to political life in leading the fight against the London Government Bill abolishing the LCC.

In contrast to most politicians, Morrison also made a contribution to the study of British government. While a visiting Fellow of Nuffield College, Oxford, he wrote, with the advice of Norman Chester, *Government and Parliament: a Survey from the Inside* (1954), an attempt to produce a new Erskine May. Essentially the book provided a descriptive account of how the system of government worked in theory; Morrison was too discreet to reveal how government had worked in practice, despite the urgings of Chester. What the book did reveal was the extent to which Morrison had formed an emotional attachment to the House of Commons in particular and to an idealized version of the British system of government in general. His *Autobiography* (1960) struck a similar note,

in that it too was extremely reticent about the inner life of both government and the Labour Party.

Morrison was an unusual figure in the higher ranks of the Labour Party, representing neither the trade-union movement, with the leaders of which he enjoyed an uneasy relationship, nor the middle-class intelligentsia. A perceptive contemporary portrait in 1949 saw him as epitomizing the same suburban classlessness as H. G. Wells; his socialist version of technocratic progressivism offered a vision of a well-ordered meritocratic society with which the lower-middle class of minor civil servants, municipal employees, teachers and technicians could identify. Both in the policies which he advocated and in the ideology which he espoused, Morrison was, as Hugh Gaitskell saw, the closest the Labour Party has come to producing an equivalent to the leaders of the Scandinavian social democratic parties.

For further illustration, see ATTLEE, CLEMENT.

FURTHER READING

Donoughue, B. and Jones, G., *Herbert Morrison: Portrait of a Politician* (London: Weidenfeld and Nicolson, 1973).

Morgan, K. O., *Labour People* (Oxford: Oxford University Press, 1987).

J. S. ROWETT

Mosley, Sir **Oswald (Ernald)** (*b.* London, 16 November 1896; *d.* Orsay, France, 3 December 1980). Fascist leader. For most of his life, Mosley was a 'coming man' whose moment never came. He was most prominent in the public eye as leader of the British Union of Fascists, launched in October 1932. However, while it was in this role that his beliefs and activities were most contentious, his forceful personality exerted an influence in many areas of British public life over a much longer period.

Mosley came from a landed Staffordshire family. His father, the fifth baronet, separated from his mother when he was five. His mother adulated him and he was prepared to do extraordinary things, including crashing an aeroplane, to impress her. At Winchester he showed great distinction as a boxer and fencer.

In his own words, he began to be less half-witted when he was 16, the age at which he left school. He was rusticated from Sandhurst in June 1914 as a result of a fight – the culmination of a distinctly boisterous six months at the college. Such manly qualities were no obstacle when it came to war. Mosley wanted to be a flyer: the élite of a *corps d'élite*. He served with the Royal Flying Corps as an observer after his flying accident and did not return to France as a pilot, but joined the 16th Lancers. By the end of 1916, however, he had been invalided out of the army with a permanent limp. The leg injury sustained in the flying accident had become worse. Mosley worked subsequently in the Ministry of Munitions and the Foreign Office and, by his own account, read voraciously and omnivorously. However, this latter activity did not prevent an active London social life at the houses of various scintillating hostesses. He became Conservative MP for Harrow in 1918 (the youngest member) and advanced the notion of 'socialistic imperialism'. In May 1920 he married a daughter of Lord Curzon, then Foreign Secretary. She brought her own fortune to supplement Mosley's by no means meagre resources. They glittered in the social life of the capital.

However, Mosley saw himself as a serious and independent-minded politician. He and his generation, so he believed, had a new perspective on the crumbling world to which, socially, he belonged. He denounced British policy and actions in Ireland. He crossed the floor of the House and sold his polo ponies. He developed a great enthusiasm for the League of Nations under the guidance of Lord Robert Cecil. Children arrived, though their development was left largely to 'professionals'. In 1922 Mosley stood for Harrow as an Independent and defeated the Conservative candidate. He told the electorate that he could not have his freedom of action restricted. The war had destroyed old party issues and the old parties.

Sir Oswald Mosley at the head of a Fascist march through London, October 1937

He was again victorious as an Independent in 1923, but the following year Ramsay Mac-Donald gave him a hearty welcome into the Labour Party. Mosley seemed to some the most brilliant man in the House of Commons and he had certainly dismissed the Tory record as drivel. In 1924 he nearly defeated Neville Chamberlain in his Birmingham Ladywood fief, and set off for India, reading Keynes *en route*.

Stimulated by John Strachey, among others, Mosley turned his mind to economics and came to see 'finance' as the enemy. In his writing he advocated *Revolution by Reason* and put forward the 'Birmingham Proposals' of 1925. In 1926 he went fishing with Franklin Roosevelt and paid for the publication of a strike bulletin in Birmingham. By the end of the year he won a by-election at Smethwick with a large majority. Perhaps, as some of his friends hoped, he would be Prime Minister for a very long time. He had the 'divine spark'. MPs found him arrogant. He found them mediocre. In consequence, Mosley decided to address mass meetings in the Midlands, engage in philandering, and play clever games with the artistic élite. This formed the prelude, when Labour returned to power in 1929, to his role as assistant to J. H. Thomas, who was supposed to be solving the unemployment problem. The following year, despairing of Thomas, Mosley produced a memorandum advocating, among other things, an extensive public works programme. The cabinet did not accept it and he resigned. He found less support elsewhere in the Labour Party than he had hoped for, and in March 1931 he founded the New Party which lasted less than a year. Mosley lost his seat in the 1931 general election.

Following a visit to Italy in 1932 Mosley formed the BUF, and his oratory struck a chord in the conditions of the time. He campaigned against 'decadence' in *The Greater Britain*. After June 1934, when violence occurred at a great meeting in Olympia, middle-class support (and Lord Rothermere) fell away. Anti-Semitism became more pronounced and there were street battles in the East End. In 1936, his first wife having died, Mosley married Diana Mitford (Mrs Diana Guinness) in Goebbels's house in Berlin. Hitler gave them, as a present,

a photograph in a silver frame of himself and a German eagle. Mosley campaigned vigorously in favour of peace but was not a pacifist. It was a Jewish conspiracy which wanted war. He claimed still to be a British patriot after 1939, though he believed a disastrous mistake had been made. Most people in 1940 wanted him locked up, though he denied that he would have been a British Quisling. He was in prison from May 1940 to November 1943, and was then under house arrest until May 1945.

After the war Mosley wrote various books in self-justification and from 1948 to 1966 led the Union Movement. His revived theme was European unity. He stood unsuccessfully for parliament, but even when he did so in ethnically mixed communities he failed to make a major impact. For most of the postwar period he lived out of Britain and was substantially ostracized. Only in the last decade of his life was there a modest rehabilitation which focused on the positive features of his economic ideas in the early 1930s. He energetically lived a hero's life but never found the outlet for his talents which he so impatiently sought.

WRITINGS

My Life (London: Nelson, 1968).

WRITINGS

Mosley, Nicholas, *Rules of the Game: Sir Oswald and Lady Mosley 1896–1933* (London: Secker and Warburg, 1982).
——, *Beyond the Pale: Sir Oswald Mosley 1933–1980* (London: Secker and Warburg, 1983).
Skidelsky, Robert, *Oswald Mosley*, rev. edn (London: Macmillan, 1981).

KEITH ROBBINS

Mountbatten, Louis (Francis Albert Victor Nicholas) [Earl Mountbatten of Burma] **('Dickie')** (*b*. Windsor, 25 June 1900; *d*. Mullaghmore, Co. Sligo, Ireland, 27 August 1979). Admiral, Viceroy of India and Chief of the Defence Staff. Prince and professional sailor, Mountbatten played a significant and often heroic role in the events of the quarter-century following the outbreak of World War II when British power surged and subsided in world affairs. As Supreme Allied Commander South-East Asia, 1943–6, he coordinated the liberation of South-East Asia from the Japanese; as Viceroy of India in 1947 he was instrumental in Britain's disengagement from the subcontinent. He later became deeply involved in the postwar re-appraisal of national defence. He was assassinated by the Irish Republican Army in a bomb explosion which destroyed his boat and killed others on board during a family outing.

The younger son and youngest of the four children of Prince Louis Alexander of Battenberg (later Marquess of Milford Haven) and Princess Victoria (daughter of Louis IV of Hesse-Darmstadt), Mountbatten was a great-grandson of Queen Victoria. His sisters married King Gustav VI of Sweden and Prince Andrew of Greece. He accompanied his cousin, the Prince of Wales (later Edward VIII), on tours of Australasia (1920) and India and the Far East (1921–2). Although he had grown apart from Edward by the time of the Abdication (December 1936) and readily transferred his allegiance to George VI, he provided thereafter one of the few links between the former king and his successors. His nephew, Prince Philip of Greece, married Princess (later Queen) Elizabeth in 1947 and Mountbatten remained their friend and adviser, becoming 'honorary grandfather' to their eldest son, Charles. An avid genealogist and campaigner on behalf of Europe's remaining monarchies – he was dubbed 'the shop steward of royalty' by Harold Wilson – he was gratified when his family name was formally linked to that of Windsor in the designation of Queen Elizabeth's descendants.

On the outbreak of World War I his father was forced from office as First Sea Lord on a wave of anti-German feeling in the country. This incident led to the anglicization of Battenberg to Mountbatten and reinforced the young Louis's determination to pursue a naval career and avenge his father. He had entered naval college at Osborne in 1913, moved to Dartmouth in November 1914 and in July 1916 was appointed midshipman on HMS *Lion*, Admiral Beatty's flagship. Marriage in 1922 to Edwina Ashley (1901–60), grand-daughter of Sir Ernest Cassel, brought him a dynamic wife,

a bitter-sweet marriage, two daughters and a considerable fortune which allowed him to indulge his tastes for polo and fast cars. Beneath the playboy image, however, he developed his naval expertise particularly in the fields of equipment and signals.

As Captain of HMS *Kelly* (1939–42) Mountbatten displayed courage and panache; the destroyer was damaged by a mine in 1939, torpedoed in May 1940 and sunk in the Battle of Crete in May 1941. Mountbatten was mentioned in despatches twice and awarded the DSO. The ship's exploits inspired Noel Coward's film *In Which We Serve*. He next commanded the aircraft-carrier *Illustrious*, but in April 1942 Churchill picked him to be Chief of Combined Operations. It was a period of mixed fortunes, from the success of the St Nazaire raid to the Dieppe debacle, but in these preparations for what became the Second Front Mountbatten displayed a fascination for technology, enthusiasm for experimentation and, above all, organizational zeal and diplomatic flair. On the strength of these qualities Churchill decided to transfer him to one of the bleakest theatres of the war. In August 1943, when only 43 years of age and still at the substantive rank of Captain RN, Mountbatten leap-frogged his seniors to the position of Supreme Allied Commander South-East Asia and acting Admiral.

The Japanese had driven Europeans and Americans from South-East Asia and the Pacific in 1941–2. In 1943 the British and Indian forces drawn up for counter-attack in Burma were dispirited, ill-equipped and ravaged by malaria. Only Orde Wingate's 'Chindits' provided a gleam of hope. Morale was not helped by inter-service and Anglo-American feuding. British commanders resented a Supremo for South-East Asia Command (SEAC) who threatened to usurp their authority, while his American deputy, General Stilwell, was an abrasive Anglophobe who discounted SEAC's Burma campaign as a bid to 'Save England's Asiatic Colonies'. A major contribution to the Allied cause was Mountbatten's skilled handling of the delicate relations between British, American and Chinese commands. He was also tireless in revolutionizing the health, efficiency and determination of the troops. Here he worked harmoniously with General Slim, whose 14th Army repulsed the Japanese at Arakan and Imphal-Kohima (February–June 1944) and entered Rangoon in May 1945. The planned seaborne invasion of Malaya was overtaken by the atomic bomb and Japan's surrender on 15 August. Mountbatten received the formal Japanese surrender in Singapore on 12 September.

During the next nine months SEAC's task was the re-occupation of a huge and disparate region embracing Siam, much of French Indo-China and the whole of the Netherlands East Indies in addition to British territories. The presence of Japanese troops and the plight of Allied prisoners-of-war, the resistance of local nationalists and the social upheavals caused by war and food shortages, all stretched SEAC's resources but did not sap the energy of its Supreme Commander. Romanov scion he may have been, but Mountbatten was not wedded to the restoration of Europe's *ancien régime* overseas. He recognized the necessity for local collaboration and had a keen eye for the up-and-coming leaders of postwar Asia. His accommodation of Aung San in Burma and his sympathy for Indonesia's Sukarno delighted progressives but appalled some 'old hands' as naïve and dangerous. Mountbatten has been portrayed as the impetuous seaman, sensing the direction of the wind, trimming his sails accordingly and racing before it without heed to the shoals beneath the surface. SEAC was wound up by the end of May 1946. Created Viscount and promoted to Rear-Admiral, Mountbatten looked forward to resuming his naval career. Soon, however, Attlee offered him a different assignment.

By the end of 1946 India was racked by communal conflict and government was on the verge of breakdown. Viceroy Wavell, who had never enjoyed the full confidence of the British Cabinet in his attempts to end the deadlock between Congress and Muslim League, was advocating a staged military withdrawal from the subcontinent. Attlee, however, was committed to a political settlement and decided to 'change the batting': he approached Mountbatten in mid-December and somewhat peremptorily dismissed Wavell in the New Year. With his royal aura and liberal ideas, his

military triumphs and political skills, his interest in Asia as well as his proven patriotism, Mountbatten seemed an inspired choice as the last Viceroy of India.

He went to India in March 1947 with full freedom of manoeuvre and the mandate to complete the transfer of power by June 1948. Working towards an Indian union acceptable to both Congress and League, Mountbatten plunged into a hectic round of talks with Indian leaders. Viceroy and Vicereine established cordial relations with Congress principals, particularly Nehru, though they failed to make the same impact upon Jinnah of the League. By May, a draft allowing the provinces considerable autonomy and correspondingly reducing the powers of central government was despatched for cabinet approval. Assuming that the scheme carried the endorsement of the major Indian politicians, Mountbatten was shaken by Nehru's outright rejection of a plan which, the latter argued, would lead to the 'balkanization' of the subcontinent. The Viceroy rapidly regained his poise, however, and flew to London with a different scheme, this time for partition. First cabinet and then, on 2–3 June after his return to Delhi, Congress and League were persuaded to accept this. While none (not even the League) welcomed partition, all acquiesced in it, believing it to be the least damaging of the options by then available.

Agreement secured, Mountbatten advanced the date for its implementation to 15 August 1947. In the final weeks of the British Raj he supervised the division of assets, notably the armed forces, while Sir Cyril (later Lord) Radcliffe drew the boundaries of the new states through Bengal and the Punjab. The transfer of power has been hailed as an act of statesmanship that saved South Asia for the Commonwealth and enhanced Britain's global authority. On the other hand, it has been presented as a shabby scuttle thinly disguised by the glamour of Mountbatten: an empire was lost and a subcontinent was unnaturally divided against itself. In their haste to quit, it has been said, the British ditched loyal princes, abandoned minorities such as the Sikhs and condemned hundreds of thousands of Hindus and Muslims to death in communal massacres.

Lord and Lady Mountbatten
on their arrival at the Durbar
Hall

In defence of Mountbatten it must be said that he was the servant of a government firmly committed to Indian independence, that the possibility of partition had been envisaged as long ago as the Cripps Mission (1942), and that the speed of the operation may actually have saved lives which would have been lost if the British had lingered over their departure.

Mountbatten had hoped to stay on as Governor-General of both India and Pakistan, thereby easing the tensions between the newly independent states and perhaps paving the way to subcontinental unity. As it happened, while Nehru gladly accepted his continuing presence in India, Jinnah insisted on himself becoming Pakistan's first Governor-General. Until they left in June 1948 the Mountbattens were crucial in the improvement of Anglo-Indian relations following the struggle for independence.

Mountbatten now returned to the sea as Commander of the First Squadron, Mediterranean. He was promoted Vice Admiral in June 1949 and in June 1950 moved to the Admiralty as Fourth Sea Lord, responsible for supplies and transport. In 1952 he was appointed Commander in Chief, Mediterranean, and early the following year was promoted Admiral and also became NATO's Allied Commander in Chief in the Mediterranean. In 1955 he fulfilled his ambition of becoming First Sea Lord, a position he occupied (together with that of Chief of Naval Staff) until 1959. While he supported the general military build-up in response to Nasser's nationalization of the Suez Canal (July 1956), he had grave misgivings about a full-scale invasion of Egypt and on 2 November vainly urged Eden to turn back. As Chief of the Defence Staff between 1959 and 1965 he presided over the defence re-organization and review of global strategy conducted by the second Macmillan government (1959–63), although he was disappointed in achieving only the partial integration of the services. When Labour formed a government in 1964, he added his considerable authority to the arguments against unilateral disarmament. During his active retirement he wrote a report on prison security (1966) and was president of the United World Colleges.

A royal and a man of action, Mountbatten was also a democrat who prided himself on being above party politics. Both Churchill and Attlee singled him out, and he got on well with Macmillan and Wilson. He declined invitations to be Minister of Defence in a Labour government (1949) and a Conservative one (1962). When, after he had left office, he speculated with others in high places on ways to re-invigorate British morale – a curious episode that has been called 'the coup d'état that never was' (1968) – he insisted that a government of National Unity could be attained only through constitutional methods and that it would be best led by the Prime Minister of the day, Harold Wilson. Honours were showered upon him, notably KG (1946), OM (1965) and FRS (1966). His drive was matched by showmanship, his ability to get the best out of others by a distorted view of his own historical significance, witness the television series *The Life and Times of Lord Mountbatten* (1969). That said, however, Mountbatten was pivotal in the salvation of British interests and the adjustment of Britain's position in Asia between 1943 and 1948.

FURTHER READING

Campbell-Johnson, Alan, *Mission with Mountbatten* (London: Robert Hale, 1951).

Dennis, Peter, *Troubled Days of Peace: Mountbatten and South East Asia Command, 1945–46* (Manchester: Manchester University Press, 1987).

Mansergh, Nicholas (ed.), *Constitutional Relations between Britain and India: the Transfer of Power 1942–47*, vols. ix–xii (London: HMSO, 1980–3).

Moore, R. J., *Escape from Empire* (Oxford: Oxford University Press, 1983).

Ziegler, Philip, *Mountbatten: the Official Biography* (London: Collins, 1985).

A. J. STOCKWELL

Murdoch, (Keith) Rupert (*b.* Melbourne, Australia, 11 March 1931). Newspaper proprietor. At the age of 21, not long down from Oxford, he inherited a daily and Sunday paper in Adelaide, South Australia, from his father, the distinguished press executive Sir Keith Murdoch. From that slender base, Rupert Murdoch built News Corporation, the second largest media empire in the world.

Having made his mark in Australia, his entry into British press ownership came at the end of 1968, when he was invited to act as a 'white knight' in staving off an unwelcome bid for the mass-market Sunday paper *News of the World*. Within months Murdoch had taken full control. In 1969 he bought *The Sun*, a failing middle-market paper, and turned it into a racy tabloid concentrating on sex and near-naked pin-ups. By the mid-1970s it had overtaken the *Daily Mirror* to become Britain's largest-selling daily paper.

In 1981 Murdoch acquired two of the most influential papers in the country. Under Thomson Newspapers, *The Times* and the *Sunday Times* had been beset with industrial relations difficulties – but it was still a surprise when the Department of Trade and Industry allowed the sale to go through without a reference to the Monopolies and Mergers Commission. Some saw it as a reward for his support of the Thatcher administration.

The politics of Murdoch's papers have been inconsistent: in Australia and Britain he has at various times supported both main parties. Left-wing in his youth – he belonged to the Labour Club at Oxford – he advocated in 1970

Rupert Murdoch being interviewed by reporters about his plans to buy Times Newspapers, Grays Inn Road, London, December 1981

the re-election of Harold Wilson's Labour Government, which the old *Sun* had always supported. But the Conservatives won and by the next election, in 1973, he had switched his support to them. His British papers have since remained in the Conservative camp and have been especially strident in support of Margaret Thatcher, who rewarded Larry Lamb, *The Sun*'s first editor, with a knighthood. (Murdoch himself shows no interest in honours and in an early interview claimed he had once rejected a knighthood, presumably offered by the Australian Government.) *Sun* editorials are pithy expressions of chauvinism, populism and prejudice. *The Times* and *Sunday Times*, before he acquired them, occupied a centre-right political position: under his ownership they are firmly Thatcherite.

Murdoch supports administrations that provide a favourable climate for people like him to do business. He has wide interests in the USA, including newspapers, television and the film industry, and has become a US citizen. He owns Sky Television, beamed by satellite to homes in Britain. He has long been a demon figure to the left, particularly when, at the end of 1985, he dismissed members of the print unions and produced his four London papers at a new plant in Wapping, East London, using workers from another union. This was a key factor in the national press proprietors' even-

tual defeat of restrictive labour practices, enabling them to move away from Fleet Street to new plants with the most modern labour-saving machinery.

Newspaper magnates are seldom popular heroes and Murdoch has never shown signs of wanting to be one. His mass-market papers are criticized for lowering ethical standards and for intruding into the private lives of celebrities and others – yet they remain immensely popular and profitable.

FURTHER READING

Leapman, Michael, *Barefaced Cheek: the Apotheosis of Rupert Murdoch* (London: Hodder and Stoughton, 1983; rev. edn, Coronet, 1984).

Munster, George, *Rupert Murdoch: a Paper Prince* (London: Viking, 1985).

MICHAEL LEAPMAN

Murray, (George) Gilbert (Aimé) (*b.* Sydney, Australia, 2 January 1866; *d.* Oxford, 20 May 1957). Internationalist and classicist. A distinguished classical scholar who also enjoyed some fame as a translator of Greek drama, he was of political significance mainly as a campaigner for the cause of liberal internationalism over a period of 40 years. In particular, he served the League of Nations Union

(LNU) as chairman of its executive committee from its foundation in 1918 until 1938 (with a break from late 1919 to 1923 when he was vice-chairman) and thereafter until its demise as joint president. He then served its successor body, the United Nations Association, as joint president from its inception in 1945 until his death, except for the period from 1947 to 1949 when he was sole president.

He was born in Australia of Irish descent, the second son of Sir Terence Murray, a stock-farmer and local politician (president of the legislative council of New South Wales), who ran into debt, took to drink, and died young in 1873. Brought to England in 1877 by his mother, he was educated at Merchant Taylors' school and St John's College, Oxford, where he proved so outstanding a classicist that he was elected a Fellow of New College immediately upon graduating in 1888, and a year later became Professor of Greek at Glasgow University at the controversially precocious age of 23. He held this chair for only ten years, however. Like Lady Mary Howard, the wealthy daughter of the Earl of Carlisle, whom he married at Castle Howard in December 1889, Murray was a hypochondriac as well as a work-aholic, and interpreted as serious illness the exhaustion produced by adding Oxford-style tutorials to Scottish-style lecturing and his own textual study of Euripides. He was financially secure enough to resign in 1899 and move his family to Surrey, where he wrote plays and published translations. In this period the ten-sions within his personality became particularly apparent: he has commonly been regarded as an ultra-rational Victorian Liberal, being as he was a convinced home ruler, free-trader, pro-Boer, atheist, teetotaller, vegetarian, non-smoker, and dutiful paterfamilias; but recent biographies have stressed that he also had the temperament of a creative writer rather than technical scholar, enjoyed the company of beautiful actresses (such as Mrs Patrick Campbell) and playwrights (such as Shaw), and dabbled in psychical research.

By 1905 Murray felt sufficiently recovered to be able to return to academic life, and was re-admitted to a tutorial fellowship at New College, Oxford. Once again his stay was a short one: in 1908 he migrated to Christ Church as a

Gilbert Murray

consequence of securing the Regius Professorship of Greek at Oxford – an appointment which reflected the success of his book *The Rise of the Greek Epic* (1907) as well as the fact that, as a dedicated Liberal, he was politically congenial to the Prime Minister (Asquith), in whose gift it was. He was to hold the chair until 1936, consolidating his reputation as a learned and imaginative teacher rather than a technical scholar of the highest calibre.

Murray did not achieve political prominence until the outbreak of World War I. A neutralist until he heard Sir Edward Grey's Commons speech of 3 August 1914, he was transmuted into a champion of the Foreign Secretary against his radical critics. He published two contributions to the 'Oxford Pamphlets 1914' series, and a longer work, *The Foreign Policy of Sir Edward Grey* (1915), which combatively rebutted the arguments of two of his friends who had joined the Union of Democratic Control, Bertrand Russell and H. N. Brailsford. He undertook propaganda work for the government, and visited the USA and Scandinavia, but became depressed by the conduct of the war following the departure of Grey and Asquith from office in December 1916. In January 1917 he was persuaded by his old friend H. A. L. Fisher to join the Board of Education as a temporary and part-time civil servant, and spent the rest of the war as Principal Assistant Secretary to its Universities Branch. Despite these official connections, however, Murray retained the respect of anti-war opinion because he helped conscientious objectors, accepted a vice-presidency in the League of Nations Society (which had been set up in May 1915), and publicly supported Lord Lansdowne's letter to the *Daily Telegraph* (29 November 1917) advocating a negotiated peace with Germany.

As an internationalist with official connections, Murray was well qualified for the unifying role he was called upon to play in a polarized League of Nations movement. Once Woodrow Wilson's commitment to a League had turned it from a dangerously utopian and 'pacifist' idea into an official war aim, many in Whitehall decided that, if a League was inevitable, it should be used to institutionalize the existing mechanisms of allied cooperation against Germany. Having failed to convert the idealistic League of Nations Society to this approach, David Davies and Charles McCurdy (two pro-Lloyd George Liberal MPs) formed with Murray's help in June 1918 a separate League of Free Nations Association to advocate the immediate creation of a League without enemy participation. Almost immediately, however, merger talks were held with the League of Nations Society; and, when the resulting LNU was officially created two days before the armistice, Murray was the obvious choice to be its chairman.

On Lord Robert Cecil's return from the Paris peace conference, Murray surrendered the chair, resuming it only when Cecil returned to ministerial office in 1923 (see also CECIL, LORD ROBERT). He served as Cecil's loyal second in command, often acting as a moderating or soothing influence. Indeed Murray's integrity and tact were of inestimable value to

the LNU as it struggled to be both a quasi-official body (with a royal charter and the party leaders as its honorary presidents) and a protest movement against government policy. His diplomatic qualities were recognized in his appointment as delegate to four League of Nations Assemblies (in 1921 and 1922 for South Africa, in 1923 and 1924 for Britain); and he came close to becoming British Ambassador in Washington in 1929. He was also active in the League's Committee for Intellectual Cooperation, a forerunner of UNESCO.

Though Murray had few illusions about the League's prospects, particularly after 1936, or about those of the United Nations, he refused to give up the struggle. By the 1950s, however, the path for a Liberal and internationalist was no longer a straightforward one: Murray found himself voting Conservative, for want of a viable Liberal Party, and supporting the Suez invasion, for world-order reasons. He twice (in 1912 and 1917) declined a knighthood, but accepted the Order of Merit in 1941 – an honour that George V had been prevented only by Lloyd George's objections from bestowing 20 years previously. He died at Yatscombe, his home on Boar's Hill, a venerated and stoical figure who had outlived his wife, three of his five children and most of his friends.

FURTHER READING

Birn, Donald S., *The League of Nations Union, 1918–1945* (Oxford: Oxford University Press, 1981).

West, Francis, *Gilbert Murray: a Life* (London: Croom Helm, 1984).

Wilson, Duncan, *Gilbert Murray OM, 1866–1957* (Oxford: Oxford University Press, 1987).

MARTIN CEADEL

Murray, Len [Lionel; Baron Murray of Epping Forest] (*b.* Hadley, Shropshire, 2 August 1922). Trade-union leader. He was General Secretary of the TUC from 1973 to 1984 and played a major part in concluding the Social Contract with the Labour Government of 1974–9 which restrained wages to help reduce 30 per cent inflation in exchange for social measures and what were, effectively, guaranteed minimum increases for the lower paid. But he saw the corporatist tide ebb with the number of union members and its influence reducing sharply after the Conservative's victory in 1979.

The archetypal TUC bureaucrat, Murray joined the Economic Department straight from Oxford, and played an important role as its head from 1954 to 1969, the period in which it became accepted that the TUC had a legitimate place in discussions of government economic strategy. This role was formalized by the creation of the National Economic Development Council, a tripartite body with government, employers and unions, in 1963. Murray, working closely with George Woodcock, prepared the TUC's annual Economic Review – its prescription for the economy. But he remained a shadowy figure before becoming general secretary in 1973. He had a difficult start, as powerful union general secretaries such as JACK JONES were unwilling to allow him as major a role as that of his predecessors. But the return in 1974 of the Labour Government with an elaborate formal and informal liaison machinery with the unions gave him the powerful central part. He argued through the Social Contract, and, with Jones, pressed for further measures, including the statutory obligation for trade-union elected representatives to sit on company boards, a measure which divided union activists.

But it was a step too far for the corporatist approach, and, when Murray and others failed to convince the Callaghan Government that they could not deliver another year of tight income restraint, the government collapsed under the pressures of the so-called winter of discontent, which saw widespread industrial disruption. Faced by an incoming Conservative administration determined to exclude the unions from discussions, Murray at first waited for a change of heart, but then, in the vacuum of leadership following the retirement of Jones and others, launched what was called 'new realism' after the re-election of the Conservatives in 1983. Insisting that 'we have to argue our case where it counts', he carried the 1983 congress for a programme of limited dialogue with the government, resisting moves to withdraw from tripartite bodies such as the NEDC. But his strategy was exploded by the government when it banned unions from GCHQ, its radio monitoring 'spy' centre, in spite of a rapid offer by the TUC of a pledge of no disruption. Murray took it personally, both as a reflection on the patriotism of union members and as a sign of a government decision to spurn even a moderate approach.

Later that year, with increasing ill-health and the pressures of the miners' strike, which divided the unions and in which efforts by the TUC to get some control were spurned by the NUM, Murray resigned. After heart surgery he became an active Labour Party spokesman in the Lords and spent much of his time in Christian community work.

MARTIN ADENEY

N

Namier, Sir **Lewis (Bernstein)** [Bernstein, Ludwik] (*b.* Wola Okrzejska, Poland, 27 June 1888; *d.* London, 19 August 1960). Historian. Namier made his academic name as the leading historian of eighteenth-century England in his generation. His *The Structure of Politics at the Accession of George III* (1929) set a standard and established a methodology which dominated the historiography of the period for many decades. It is only recently that the 'Namierite' interpretation has lost its supremacy among scholars – who nonetheless continue to acknowledge the weight of his work. The 'Namier School' constituted a formidable force and brought Namier himself invitations to deliver the most prestigious lectures in his profession and honorary degrees from the most distinguished universities. From Oxford he received both a D.Litt. and, in the last year of his life, a DCL: recognition that he was not only a great historian but also a significant public man.

Namier felt the weight of the past from early childhood; the circumstances of his upbringing made it almost inescapable. He was born into a polonized Jewish family living in Austrian Poland near the Russian frontier. One could not fail to be aware of the complex local mixture of languages, races and religions. Family relationships were difficult. Namier moved westwards for his higher education, to Lausanne, the London School of Economics and Balliol College, Oxford. He graduated with a First in 1911 and two years later he became a British subject, changing his surname for the second time – he had come to England as Ludwik Bernstein and in 1910 he had become Lewis Bernstein Naymier. He began to collect eighteenth-century material, though ostensibly active on his father's behalf in business in the USA. In 1914 he joined the army but was then discharged because his knowledge of East-Central Europe was more useful both to the Foreign Office and to the propagandists of Wellington House. At the end of the war he was working in the Political Intelligence Department of the Foreign Office. For some years subsequently his personal life was in turmoil as he divided his time between research, article writing and business commissions. Estranged from his father, he never went home again. It is from this unlikely background that *The Structure of Politics* and *England in the Age of the American Revolution* (1930) emerged and in 1931 brought Namier to the Chair of Modern History at Manchester University, which he held for 22 years.

A. J. P. Taylor, his junior colleague at Manchester, maintains that Namier conspicuously failed to distinguish in the university between such things as 'faculties' and 'senates', a distinction of some significance. If so, it was because his mind was not only on eighteenth-century England but once more on contemporary Europe. The plight of German-Jewish scholars and students drove him to start reading and writing in the field of what would now be described as contemporary history. He submitted official recollections of documents to fierce scrutiny and his analyses were subsequently published. At the same time, he agonized on Jewish identity and the allegiance he increasingly gave to Jesus Christ. Eighteenth-century England seemed rather remote from his immediate personal and political concerns, but he still clung to it, perhaps somewhat romantically, as an example of a society which, supposedly, could resolve its conflicts and offer decent stability by keeping both rhetoric and ideology under control. It is not surprising that he turned his attention during and after the war to the relationship between revolution, nationalism and freedom in modern European history. He retained his Manchester Chair but also presided over the major *History of Parliament* on which he set such store. The project was far from complete when Namier died.

All his life, Namier struggled with difficulty to resolve inner conflicts and understand external ones. The very diversity of the influences that had played upon him gave him a breadth of knowledge and a depth of experience which explain why Sir Lewis, as he became in 1952, was a great, but not a complete, historian and a great, but flawed, human being.

FURTHER READING

Colley, Linda, *Lewis Namier* (London: Weidenfeld and Nicolson, 1988).
Namier, Julia, *Lewis Namier: a Biography* (London: Macmillan, 1971).

KEITH ROBBINS

Neil, Andrew (Ferguson) (*b*. Paisley, Renfrewshire, 21 May 1949). Editor of the *Sunday Times*. He was appointed to the post in 1983, when he was only 34. He had formerly worked for *The Economist* and the Conservative Research Department. The appointment was surprising and controversial not simply because of his age, but because a number of senior journalists on the paper were thought to have strong claims. Rupert Murdoch, the proprietor of the *Sunday Times*, had chosen to bring in an outsider partly because he thought the paper had become too complacent: Neil, with his abrasive approach to personal relations, helped to cure that. He had come to the proprietor's attention because of their common support of broadcasting deregulation and their belief in the future of satellite television. When Murdoch launched his Sky satellite service in 1989 he appointed Neil to run it, while retaining him as editor of the *Sunday Times*.

Given the editor's political background, it was not surprising that under Neil the paper gave firmer support to the Conservatives than it had under his predecessors. On economic matters its policy could be described as Thatcherite, but Neil's essential libertarianism prevented him from seeing eye-to-eye with the Thatcher government on a number of issues, especially those involving freedom of publication. The paper published extracts from Peter Wright's MI5 memoirs, *Spycatcher*, against the government's wishes, but won the ensuing court case.

His instinctive opposition to cartels and restrictive practices meant that Neil was one of the most outspoken supporters of the move of the Murdoch papers to Wapping at the beginning of 1986, breaking the print unions' stranglehold over Fleet Street production processes. Pro-union demonstrations continued outside the Wapping plant for a year, during which Neil ranked second only to Murdoch himself in the demonology of the left.

FURTHER READING

Melvern, Linda, *The End of the Street* (London: Methuen, 1986).

MICHAEL H. LEAPMAN

Norman, Montagu (Collet) [Baron Norman of St Clere] (*b*. London, 6 September 1871; *d*. London, 4 February 1950). Banker. He was Governor of the Bank of England from 1920 to 1944. His length of service in this office was highly unusual, but Norman himself was highly unusual. His position at the hub of financial affairs for so long gave him a status of which he was very conscious, and he remains the one governor in the twentieth century whose name is known beyond banking and financial circles. The role he sought to play was one of the reasons why Labour after 1945 wished to 'control' the Bank by nationalizing it.

Norman was born into banking. He was the grandson of a director of the Bank of England and his father was a partner in Martins Bank. His mother was the daughter of a former Governor of the Bank of England. After Eton and King's College, Cambridge, Norman spent time on the Continent before entering Martins Bank in 1892. Two years later he joined his maternal grandfather's merchant banking firm of Brown, Shipley & Co. He was despatched to New York and might have settled there had it not been for patriotic sentiments stirred by the outbreak of the South African War in October 1899. He saw service there for two years and collected a DSO, though he complained about the exaggerated system of rewards. He then resumed banking and threw himself into reconstructing his London house, Thorpe Lodge. Disagreement with his business partners precipitated a nervous breakdown in the years immediately before 1914. However, the war enabled him to end his connection with Brown, Shipley, and from 1915 Norman worked at the Bank of England as a kind of 'devil'. By the end of the war he had become Deputy Governor. He had displayed both a capacity for hard work and a brilliant neurotic personality. Neither of these things stood in the way of his elevation to Governor. His term was thereafter regularly renewed, and in 1931 extended without time limit. He might have left in 1939 but his experience was deemed essential in another world war. Medical advice, following a somewhat mysterious fall, forced Norman to stand down in 1944. He lingered long enough thereafter to witness the end of the old-style Bank of England which he had so long dominated.

Norman had two broad objectives throughout his long career. On the one hand, he sought both for himself personally and the Bank as an institution a central advisory role to government in financial and monetary matters. He established that being Governor was a full-time occupation, and the duties of other staff became more severely professional. He never hesitated to express his views on currency questions and was an early advocate of a return to the gold standard. His efforts in 1931 to avert the abandonment of that standard proved of no avail, though, despite his disappointment, he clung to office. On the other hand, he remained anxious to stress that the Bank should not become a direct instrument of government. He thought that a central bank should continue to be independent and participate internationally to the best of its own judgement. To this end, Norman built up a strong network of banking contacts in Europe and North America.

Norman's skill lay in pursuing both objectives simultaneously, though they were sometimes in conflict. He was an enigmatic character who contrived to convey a sense of mystery above and beyond the techniques of banking which he had mastered over many years.

FURTHER READING

Boyle, Andrew, *Montagu Norman: a Biography* (London: Cassell, 1967).
Norman, Sir Henry, *Lord Norman* (London: Macmillan, 1957).

KEITH ROBBINS

Northcliffe, Lord [Harmsworth, Alfred (Charles William)] (*b.* near Dublin, 15 July 1865; *d.* London, 14 August 1922). Newspaper proprietor and politician. He pioneered the 'popular' press in the early twentieth century and sought to use his papers to advance his own political views and, to an extent, a political career.

Alfred Harmsworth, named after his father, was the eldest son of an unsuccessful barrister and the daughter of a prosperous Dublin land agent. He was a good-looking boy who, despite a lifelong mother fixation, grew up into a handsome young man attractive to women. In 1888 he married Molly Milner (*d.* 1963). There were no children of the marriage, but Harmsworth had at least four illegitimate offspring. His wife had her own affairs, but continued to act as hostess at the family's houses, of which Harmsworth's favourite was Elmwood, near Broadstairs in Kent. In 1905 he took his title from a nearby stretch of coast – Northcliffe.

The initial 'N' was chosen deliberately, for Northcliffe liked to be known as 'the Napoleon of Fleet Street'. Partly because of such posing, superior contemporaries inclined to dismiss him as superficial, even commonplace. Others, not seeking depth, were impressed by his breadth of interest in the world. Certainly, Northcliffe's formal education had been limited; but on leaving school at the age of 16 he was sure that he wanted to be a journalist.

He began as a freelance, contributing to various papers, including *Titbits*. In June 1888 he launched his own similar weekly, entitled *Answers to Correspondents*. This contained a mass of miscellaneous information, appealingly presented. It was followed by *Comic Cuts*, *Chips*, *Home Sweet Home* and other popular titles. Within five years total sales of all Harmsworth publications were approaching one and a half million copies weekly. Alfred contributed the journalistic flair; his younger brother Harold

(1868–1940), the future Lord Rothermere, the financial acumen. Both eventually became millionaires.

'The Chief', as Northcliffe became known to his staff, ceased to write regularly once his press empire had expanded, but his oversight remained close. He possessed an instinctive sense of what would interest the new urban lower-middle-class public – clerks, teachers, shop assistants and the like. By the 1890s about half of them had been educated in the new board schools created under the 1870 Education Act; the remainder had attended religious denominational schools. The famous Act thus assisted Northcliffe's success, but it was not a precondition for it.

After successfully reviving the *Evening News*, bought in 1894, the Harmsworth brothers made their breakthrough into mass morning journalism. On 4 May 1896 appeared the first number of the *Daily Mail*. Although the *Mail* owed a little to the strident example of Pulitzer journalism in the USA, Northcliffe always claimed that his papers were seeking not crude sensation but 'brightness'. This meant giving space to the trivial alongside the important. Helped by new technology, which cut costs and speeded production, the *Daily Mail* was able to appear as 'a Penny Newspaper for one Half-penny'. Yet it did not so much take readers from existing penny papers as recruit hundreds of thousands of new daily readers. The number of daily newspaper readers in Britain has been estimated to have doubled between 1896 and 1906, thanks especially to Northcliffe, and to have doubled again by 1914.

The *Mail* flattered its readers by labelling itself as 'the Busy Man's Daily Journal'. It was written, Northcliffe explained, not for comfortable £1000 a year men, but for those who vaguely hoped to attain such an income one day. Circulation of the *Daily Mail* – the world's first truly national newspaper in its range of outlets – approached a million during the Boer War, averaged 750,000 daily during the Edwardian years, and finally passed the million during World War I. The *Daily Mirror* had reached the million mark in 1912, being the first newspaper in the world to do so. The Harmsworths had launched it in 1903 as a paper for ladies. It had been saved in the

following year by transformation into an illustrated paper, the Fleet Street pioneer in the use of half-tone photographs. Northcliffe's Associated Newspapers Limited, incorporated in 1905, was the first public company to give the general public the chance to invest in newspapers.

In the same year Northcliffe moved up-market by taking over *The Observer*, a Sunday paper. He sold this in 1911 to concentrate upon *The Times*, of which he had secured control in 1908. Traditionalists were alarmed. But Northcliffe saved *The Times* from extinction by gradually modernizing it without destroying its traditional character.

Many politicians were jealous of Northcliffe because of the influence which they attributed to his publications. His personal political ambitions fluctuated, becoming strongest during World War I. He believed that, if given office, he could make a better contribution to achieving victory than most existing ministers. His papers gave loud support to the campaign for the removal of Asquith from the premiership in 1916. Lloyd George, who was not intimidated but sometimes exasperated by Northcliffe, made good use of his drive, firstly by appointing him in 1917 as head of the British war mission in Washington, and then in 1918 as Director of Propaganda in Enemy Countries.

In his last months Northcliffe became mentally unbalanced. Collections of his private papers are held in London at the British Library and the archives of *The Times*, and in Oxford at the Bodleian Library.

FURTHER READING

Clarke, T., *My Northcliffe Diary* (London: Gollancz, 1931).

Ferris, P., *The House of Northcliffe* (London: Weidenfeld and Nicolson, 1971).

The History of The Times, vols. iii–iv (London: The Times, 1947, 1952).

Linton, D. and Boston, R. (eds.), *The Newspaper Press in Britain: an Annotated Bibliography* (London: Mansell, 1987).

McEwen, J. M., 'Northcliffe and Lloyd George at War, 1914–1918', *Historical Journal*, 24 (1981), pp. 651–72.

Pound, R. and Harmsworth, G., *Northcliffe* (London: Cassell, 1959).

Taylor, A. J. P., 'The Chief', *Essays in English History* (London: Hamish Hamilton, 1976).

DONALD READ

Nuffield, Lord [Morris, William (Richard); Viscount Nuffield] (*b.* Worcester, 10 October 1877; *d.* Nuffield Place, Oxfordshire, 22 August 1963). Industrialist and philanthropist. Nuffield was the founder of Morris Motors and controlled some of Britain's most famous motor car marques. He is, however, often confused with his Victorian namesake William Morris, who contributed notably to the arts and philosophy. Like Henry Ford in America, he was largely responsible for mobilizing Britain's upper and middle classes by providing low-cost, reliable motor cars. In the first two decades of the twentieth century he revolutionized the British motor industry by targeting the mass market with a low-price, high-output policy and assembly instead of centralized manufacturing production. An entrepreneur rather than an engineer or manager, he owed much of his success to improving an existing product, sensing market direction and then exploiting the trend. Although he was regarded as a major force in the industry until his death, his positive influence upon his firm waned from the 1930s as his energies were drawn toward charitable, social and political activities.

Morris was the eldest of seven children of a rural Oxfordshire farmer. A self-taught man, he had little regard for formally educated managers and apprenticed labourers, preferring those who had worked through the ranks of the company. Fiercely independent, he left his position in a bicycle firm at the age of 16 to establish a cycle assembly and repair business in Oxford. After several years of uneven success Morris joined several others in forming the Oxford Automobile and Cycle Agency, which eventually failed. Undaunted, but more cautiously and without partners, he set up in 1907 the Morris Garages to repair and sell only

Lord Nuffield explaining various parts of the new Morris Eight engine to dealers at Grosvenor House, London, August 1934

motor cars. The prosperous business gave him valuable mechanical knowledge and convinced him that an enormous demand existed for popularly priced cars. Using retained profits, a practice he held sacrosanct, and £4,000 worth of preference shares sold to the Earl of Macclesfield, Morris built his first model, the two-door Morris Oxford, in March 1913. Unlike his rivals, who manufactured their own parts, he purchased his components from specialist concerns. This allowed him to lower the real price of his cars by avoiding high capital investment and reaping the benefits of his suppliers' economies of scale. The formula worked so well that Morris built a new factory in Cowley to produce the larger Cowley model in 1915.

In the decade following World War I Morris became the predominant British motor manufacturer through price leadership and acquisition. He lowered prices by utilizing more efficient production methods developed for munitions manufacture and demanding large quantities of inexpensive components. However, when Morris's requirements overwhelmed certain suppliers, he preserved his production system through vertical integration. He purchased the engine manufacturer Hotchkiss, the bodybuilder Pressed Steel, and the carburettor producer SU. Simultaneously he expanded his market appeal by offering the indigenous Morris Commercial Car and MG and the acquired Wolseley marques (Riley was taken over in 1936). While horizontal expansion allowed Morris to cover the entire range of tastes, eventually all the models used standardized parts produced by the new subsidiaries.

Although Morris's success peaked in 1929, when he held 51 per cent of the market, by 1933 his share had fallen to 29 per cent. The decline resulted from a shift in demand to smaller cars and revitalized competition, but, more importantly, his empire suffered from severe management problems as Morris became more detached from the business. He frequently took long holidays and avoided board meetings, but insisted that only he make major decisions. Yet he seemed more interested in trivia, leaving the company to drift without a streamlined organization and long-term strategy. Additionally, Morris's ambi-

guous directives and challenging temperament alienated many of his top managers. His chief lieutenants during the early years, F. G. Woollard, A. A. Rowse and E. H. Blake, left in frustration. L. P. Lord, who as managing director from 1933 until 1936 created the corporate, model and market strategy that invigorated the company, moved to rival Austin, vowing revenge.

It was during Lord's tenure that Morris began to concede some authority over corporate affairs to his board. This resulted, in part, from Morris Motors becoming a public company in 1926 and the sale to it, a decade later, of the remainder of the empire which Morris still owned outright. Already a wealthy man, he donated time and considerable sums of money to relief societies, medical charities and, ironically, educational institutions. Elevated to the peerage in 1934, he also dabbled in politics by using his industrial status to advocate his staunch nationalistic and right-wing views. Nuffield gained notoriety by actively participating in industrial lobby groups, contributing money to Mosley's New Party, opposing the repeal of the McKenna Duties and championing re-armament. After World War II he was an outspoken critic of steel rationing and nationalization. His outside interests, coupled with changes in the company's structure, left him with little direct power over its operations. But he believed that he still had a right to rule. His input, however, usually consisted of second-guessing and criticizing his managers. Nuffield remained chairman until the Nuffield Organization merged with Austin to form the British Motor Corporation in 1952. He retired without ceremony after serving barely a year as president of BMC.

Historians and biographers still debate William Morris's life. Some claim he was an eccentric dictator whose nostalgic outlook and vanity prevented him from adapting to change. They argue that he always viewed his complex firm in terms of the early Morris Garages and interfered long after his authority had been eroded. Others maintain that he was a benevolent genius by citing his paternalistic labour policies and patriotic export orientation. They also point to his seemingly instinctive ability to create a demand for a product that he efficiently produced. More probably, his supporters describe his early life and his detractors characterize his later years. Clearly, however complicated, Nuffield was an entrepreneur. He relied on his ambition and skill to make the motor car a common feature of British life, while increasing his own wealth and status. He was married without children, but many claim that his company was his offspring.

WRITINGS

'Policies that Have Built the Morris Business', *Journal of Industrial Economics*, I (1954).

FURTHER READING

Andrews, P. W. S. and Brunner, E., *The Life of Lord Nuffield: a Study in Enterprise and Benevolence* (Oxford: Oxford University Press, 1959).

Church, R. and Miller, M., 'The Big Three: Competition, Management and Marketing in the British Motor Industry, 1922–1939', *Essays in British Business History*, ed. B. Supple (Oxford: Clarendon Press, 1977), pp. 163–86.

Overy, R. J., *William Morris, Viscount Nuffield* (London: Europa, 1976).

Turner, G., *The Leyland Papers* (London: Eyre and Spottiswoode, 1971).

TIMOTHY R. WHISLER

O

O'Neill, Capt. **Terence (Marne)** [Lord O'Neill of the Maine] (*b.* London, 10 September 1914). Prime Minister of Northern Ireland. The first Unionist Prime Minister perceived to have liberal tendencies, O'Neill flattered only to deceive. In an admittedly difficult conflict in which extremists on both sides tried to undermine him, he failed to set in process the modernization and hence, possibly, the preservation of Ulster's devolved system of government, of which, ironically, he was intensely proud. As a result the O'Neill era (1963–9) is often seen as one of missed opportunity in Northern Irish affairs.

O'Neill was educated at Eton. He was Minister of Finance at Stormont from 1956 to 1963, and was appointed Prime Minister largely, his critics alleged, because of his aristocratic connections rather than for the possession of any particular political skill. In his early years in office he was concerned primarily to strengthen his position by winning back Protestant support which the Unionist party had lost to the Northern Ireland Labour Party in the period after 1958. 'Stealing Labour's thunder' (to use O'Neill's own term) – rather than allaying Catholic resentments – was the main preoccupation. While capable of the occasional conciliatory grand gesture – such as a famous visit to a Catholic school – O'Neill espoused a rhetoric of planning and modernization by which nationalist grievances would be dissolved by a shared participation in the benefits of economic growth. He saw no role for structural reform.

O'Neill's lack of responsiveness to Catholic grievances was bitterly criticized by liberal Unionist groupings, such as the leadership of the Northern Ireland Labour Party and the *Belfast Telegraph*, but in the short term O'Neillism was quite effective politically. His manifesto for the 1965 election crystallized the ideology of modernization – 'Forward Ulster to Target 1970'. The result showed an average swing to the Unionist Party of 7 per cent and was a major defeat for Labour. Ironically, O'Neill had played a key role in marginalizing a party which gave radicals from the Catholic community an outlet for their energies; many of these same figures were to re-emerge in the civil rights movement.

Serious Unionist opposition to O'Neill in 1966 was caused, therefore, not by his pro-Catholic reformism – which was, in fact, non-existent – but by his tone: O'Neillism came increasingly and controversially to define sectarianism as a matter of culture and tradition, while politics was redefined in terms of technical and administrative capacity. Harold Wilson was convinced by the ensuing loyalist furore 'that O'Neill had carried through a remarkable programme of easement', and thus the Labour Government postponed the implementation of civil rights reforms in the 1964–8 period. The emergence of the civil rights movement presented O'Neill with an excruciating dilemma. On the one hand, placating the reformers was likely to mean consolidation of the Unionist internal opposition. On the other, failing to do so would probably lead – in his eyes at least – to British intervention and a complete dissolution of local autonomy. O'Neill chose the path of minimal reform ('the five point programme of November 1968') but, caught between the pressures generated by loyalist and nationalist militants, he resigned from office in April 1969, even though it is clear that he still retained substantial Protestant support even at the end.

O'Neill's legacy is an ambiguous one; even the reputation of his pathbreaking talks with the Irish Premier Sean Lemass suffered from later claims by Lemass's widow (bitterly repudiated by O'Neill) that they had been about 'Irish unity'. His famous statement on resignation continues to haunt his reputation: 'It is frightfully hard to explain to Protestants that if you give Roman Catholics a good job and a good house, they will live like Protestants . . . [and] they will refuse to have eighteen children on national assistance . . . in spite of the authoritative nature of their church.'

WRITINGS

The Autobiography of Terence O'Neill (London: Allen and Unwin, 1972).

FURTHER READING

Bew, Paul and Patterson, Henry, *The British State and the Ulster Crisis: from Wilson to Thatcher* (London: Verso, 1985).

Farrell, Michael, *Northern Ireland: the Orange State* (London: Pluto, 1985).

PAUL A. E. BEW

Orwell, George [Blair, Eric Arthur] (*b*. Motihari, Bengal, India, 25 June 1903; *d*. London, 21 January 1950). Writer. Though his obsessions with poverty and with international politics typified the concerns of his generation of writers in the troubled 1930s, he then seemed an outsider, a deviant. But after his death at the height of the cold war he became a hero and touchstone, paradoxically both for right wingers and the New Left. For the former, his last and most important works of fiction – *Animal Farm* and *1984* – were the definitive exposure of communist totalitarianism. But those who rethought their Marxism after the Soviet invasion of Hungary in 1956 found inspiration in Orwell's democratic socialism, his warm interest in popular culture, and his intellectual honesty.

Orwell was born in India, where his father worked for the government's Opium Department. His upbringing was suburban and, in his own phrase, 'lower-upper-middle-class'. Though he later claimed that his experiences of brutal discipline and snobbery at a highly regarded preparatory school, St Cyprian's, had been traumatic, he worked hard enough there to win a scholarship to Eton. He found the Etonian atmosphere 'tolerant and civilised', but his academic record was so poor that he went on, not to Oxford, but to the Imperial Indian Police.

His service in Burma from 1922 to 1927 coincided with an upsurge of nationalist resentment. He developed a revulsion against imperialism, resigned, and resolved to earn his living by writing. During almost a decade of obscure struggle, he experimented with life as a tramp, washed dishes in a Paris hotel, taught in a private school and worked in a Hampstead bookshop. Blair became Orwell in 1933 when Victor Gollancz, who published *Down and Out in Paris and London*, chose this out of four possible pseudonyms. Three novels, not very successful, followed. Anxious to earn enough to marry Eileen O'Shaughnessy, Orwell accepted Gollancz's idea that he should write a book about the unemployed in the North of England. He spent two months there early in 1936. His stay in cheap lodgings over a tripe shop and his descents into coalmines provided unforgettable images. His contact with ordinary northerners confirmed the socialist ideas which he had already begun to pick up from Hampstead friends. *The Road to Wigan Pier* fell into two parts. The first detailed bad living conditions so powerfully that it stirred the consciences of many middle-class readers, the second sniped fiercely at the intellectual left and its prescriptions. Through Gollancz's Left Book Club it became a controversial best seller.

By the end of 1936 Orwell was in Spain, with letters of introduction from the Independent Labour Party which took him straight into the POUM, the smallest of the political militias fighting for the republic against Franco. He was a brave and popular soldier for four months before he was shot in the neck. He had been delighted on arrival by the egalitarian revolutionary atmosphere in Barcelona. Hence his dismay was all the greater when he returned as an invalid to witness battles between the anarchists and government-backed communists out to destroy them. The POUM itself was illegal. Communist and fellow-travelling journalists denounced it as 'Trotskyite' and 'pro-Fascist'. Loathing of Stalinism and concern over the corruption of political language became recurrent themes in Orwell's writing.

When *Homage to Catalonia* appeared in 1938 from the so-called Trotskyite house of Secker and Warburg, it was savaged by most left-wing reviewers, and sold only a few hundred copies. Orwell confirmed his heterodox position –

George Orwell at work

independent socialist revolutionary – by briefly joining the quasi-Marxist ILP. At this stage, like the ILP, he opposed British involvement in the foreseeable European war. But when war came, his patriotism asserted itself. He tried to enlist, but he had recently suffered severely from tuberculosis and he had to make do with the Home Guard, which he hailed as a potentially revolutionary 'People's Army'. His pamphlet *The Lion and the Unicorn* (1941) combined a glowing essay on English national character with a call for the socialist transformation of Britain, as a necessity if the war was to be won.

Orwell was now well known as a literary essayist. His insistence that literature was inseparable from politics, and his serious interest in 'popular culture' – seaside postcards, boys' stories, thrillers – were to prove especially influential. From 1941 to 1943 he worked for the BBC, creating propaganda programmes aimed to whip up Indian support for the allies (in fact, very few Indians listened). He then became Literary Editor of *Tribune*, at that time the mouthpiece for Aneurin Bevan and George Strauss, Labour MPs who were opposed to the Coalition Government, and critical of Britain's Soviet ally, but who were vehemently 'pro war'. He flourished in this congenial environment. His conversational, controversial 'As I Please' column had a wide audience in the Labour movement.

Meanwhile, he wrote *Animal Farm*, an incisive Swiftian fable on the history of Soviet communism. Gollancz turned it down, and so, following a hint from the Ministry of Information, did Jonathan Cape. T. S. Eliot, for Faber, declared, 'we have no conviction that this is the right point of view from which to criticise the political situation at the present time.' Secker and Warburg came to the rescue, the book appeared just as the war ended, and it sold very well indeed.

The sudden death of his wife in 1945 left Orwell to bring up alone their recently adopted son. In 1947, he took him to live in a farmhouse on the Isle of Jura. Here he wrote *1984*, which would make 'Orwellian' a universally understood adjective, with its nightmare vision of a totalitarian Britain. From its publication in 1949, it was first an instant, then an enduring, best seller. But Orwell's tuberculosis was now terminal. He married Sonia Brownell on his deathbed in University College Hospital, London.

Orwell was distressed in his last years by the use to which right-wing cold warriors put his writings. He was never anti-socialist, nor even anti-revolutionary. The final scene of *Animal Farm* emphasizes that the ruling pigs, now feasting with the farmers, have *betrayed* the revolution. His underlying temperament may have been 'anarchist Tory', but throughout his maturity as a writer he argued a left-wing case, attempting to speak for lower-middle- and working-class English people whose values he saw as essentially, to use one of his key words, 'decent'.

FURTHER READING

Crick, B., *George Orwell: a Life* (London: Secker and Warburg, 1980).

ANGUS CALDER

Owen, Dr **David (Anthony Llewellyn)** (*b.* Plympton, Devon, 2 July 1938). Labour Foreign Secretary and leader of the Social Democratic Party. He had a brilliant career as a Labour MP, rising to become Foreign Secretary in 1977 at the age of 38 – an achievement matched in the twentieth century only by Anthony Eden. He took a leading part in setting up the Social Democratic Party; the Limehouse Declaration of January 1981, the SDP's foundation document, was written in his house (and typed for the press by his American wife Deborah, a leading literary agent). He served as leader of the SDP from 1983 to 1987, when he resigned to form his own political grouping (also known as the SDP).

Rather against superficial appearances, Owen's family roots were Welsh, with some affinities for Lloyd George Liberalism. His father was a doctor, his mother a dentist, in Plymouth; and Owen was sent away to public school (Bradfield) before going to Cambridge to read medical sciences at Sidney Sussex College. He completed his medical training at St Thomas's Hospital, London, where he was a houseman when – somewhat inconsequentially – he was adopted as Labour candidate for Torrington, which he fought unsuccessfully in 1964. Selected for the marginal Sutton division of Plymouth (where his father had practised), he gained the seat in 1966 and held it until 1974 when, after redistribution, he scraped home in the Devonport division instead. Perilously unsafe as a Labour MP, Owen was to become more secure in his local position as a Social Democrat – significantly, he was to be the only member of the 'Gang of Four' whose parliamentary career was continuous.

Owen was a late starter but a fast learner in politics. He quickly made a mark in the parliamentary Labour Party, associating with young revisionist MPs who were close to Anthony Crosland and Roy Jenkins, but never simply one of them. His openly expressed dissatisfaction with Harold Wilson as Prime Minister in 1968 paradoxically led to his first ministerial appointment, as Under-Secretary for the Royal Navy. He continued to specialize in defence as opposition spokesman until his resignation from the front bench in 1972. Owen emerged at this stage as one of the organizers of the vote by 69 Labour MPs, in defiance of the party whips, to join the Common Market – in some ways a foretaste of later developments and an episode which set him with Jenkins rather than Crosland.

Owen broadened his ministerial experience in Wilson's second government, initially at the Department of Health and Social Security under Barbara Castle, with whom he worked surprisingly effectively in limiting consultants' private practice in National Health Service hospitals. He moved as Minister of State to the Foreign Office in 1976; Crosland's unexpected death in office the following year prompted Callaghan's unexpected choice of Owen to succeed him. It was an opportunity which Owen seized with both hands, with the dashing mien of a tough and energetic minister, constantly in the public eye. He was particularly active in working towards a settlement of the Rhodesian problem, by involving the USA in negotiations which paved the way for eventual agreement with the Zimbabwe nationalists under the subsequent Conservative Government. Over Iran, Owen's support for the Shah attracted left-wing criticism at the time but his fears about the course of a putative Islamic revolution were to some extent borne out by later events.

Labour's swing to the left after losing the 1979 general election saw Owen's emergence as a spokesman for the beleaguered social democratic wing, and, with Shirley Williams and William Rodgers, he formed a 'Gang of Three' staking out their position. In a move which Owen subsequently regretted, the Limehouse Declaration signalled full cooperation with Jenkins, who had been acting independently outside the Labour Party, as a fourth founder of the new SDP (see also

David Steel (far left) talking to David Owen (front, left) in the House of Commons before the State Opening of Parliament, April 1981

JENKINS, ROY); and it is clear that Owen disliked the growing moves towards an accommodation with the Liberals. The Falklands War in 1982 saw Owen taking a decisive line. He had a good record behind him as Foreign Secretary in pre-empting Argentinian threats, and could thus reproach the Thatcher Government for negligence; but what made – and left – an impression was his firm support for the government in mounting a military expedition. When Owen stood for the leadership of the SDP shortly afterwards, he ran Jenkins a fairly close second. His popular impact, indeed, was greater than that of his leader, and in the House of Commons, too, Owen developed an effective probing style of his own.

The 1983 general election saw an impressively high vote for the SDP–Liberal Alliance, but it was hardly a major parliamentary breakthrough for the SDP, which won only six seats. It was not surprising that Owen was unanimously elected to the leadership on

Jenkins's resignation at this point. He succeeded in making the SDP presence felt at Westminster; if it was, as critics alleged, a one-man band, it was still a virtuoso performance, against all numerical odds. But the Alliance entered a more traumatic phase. Owen resisted moves towards closer affiliation, especially the joint selection of candidates, which, in many parts of the country, was the trend within the Alliance. Owen's vision was of a multi-party future under proportional representation, with the SDP maintaining a distinctive image, notably upon issues like defence, where he took a hard line in favour of Britain's independent nuclear deterrent. The arguments for closer union within the Alliance were often more practical and pragmatic, with a greater readiness to seek compromise. Owen's talk of a 'social market' also suggested to some that his economic views were disconcertingly close to Thatcherism. In an embarrassing internal disagreement over defence policy in 1987, the polarized reactions of Owen and the Liberal rank and file confirmed their mutual antipathy.

Owen's relations with DAVID STEEL as Liberal leader were civil but not close. In the 1987 general election the double leadership of the Alliance was widely seen as a disadvantage, especially when Steel seemed to incline towards the left, Owen towards the right. In its aftermath, Steel's prompt initiative for merger was met by Owen's dismissive rejection. Repudiated by the bulk of SDP members voting in a national ballot, Owen resigned the leadership in August 1987. There was no reconciliation; and in 1988 Owen rallied his own followers in a tightly organized movement of uncertain size, claiming to perpetuate the independent identity of the old SDP. Widespread predictions that this grouping would simply fade away awaited a protracted fulfilment, while the sapping effect of the split upon the merged party proved that Owen still could not be ignored.

FURTHER READING

Harris, Kenneth, *David Owen* (London: Weidenfeld and Nicolson, 1987).

P. F. CLARKE

P

Paisley, Rev. **Ian (Richard Kyle)** (*b*. Armagh, 6 April 1926). Leader of the Democratic Unionist Party and Northern Ireland MEP. Paisley has been a substantial figure in Ulster and British politics for a quarter of a century. The son of a Baptist preacher, he was ordained in Belfast on 1 August 1946. In 1963 he decisively emerged in politics as a street demagogue and opponent of the alleged 'sellout' policies of Terence O'Neill. O'Neill reciprocated by describing Paisleyism as 'Nazism', and spoke of the need to 'lance' this 'boil of simmering nastiness'. Paisley soon won the 'martyrdom' of a short spell in jail in 1968. In fact, he was a man driven by a few simple imperatives – saving the last stronghold of evangelical faith, Protestant Ulster, from the clutches of Rome, Dublin and, later, the IRA – rather than an elaborated political ideology. A man of great energy, wit, and rather less intellect – as his pursuit of various paper qualifications and distinctions revealed – he reacted often with little deliberation to the circumstances that arose around him. In April 1969 Paisley challenged O'Neill in his Bannside seat and was only narrowly defeated, by 1,414 votes; in April 1970, however, Paisley won the seat at Stormont, and on 18 June 1970 he was elected to Westminster for the North Antrim seat.

In his early years, Paisley – who was then under the influence of a maverick Belfast QC, Desmond Boal – had supported integration. In October 1973 he argued that Britain might hold a referendum in Ulster to test support for this proposal. He opposed the devolved power-sharing executive (involving moderate unionists and nationalists) formed in December 1973, though he had little real role in its fall. He was, in fact, in Canada when the loyalist workers' strike, which brought the executive down, began. Later, as Boal's influence waned, Paisley came to be influenced more by the support base of his party, the Democratic Unionist Party. Many of those who joined this party were small-town and rural evangelicals consumed by the desire to protect Ulster against the materialist and secular tide which had triumphed in the rest of the UK.

A form of majority-rule devolution became Paisley's principal political objective, despite the fact that it was never likely to be accepted by the British Government. In May 1977, in alliance with loyalist paramilitaries, Paisley attempted to break the direct-rule system, again by applying the mass-strike weapon. This time key sections of the Unionist population refused their support and Paisley was humiliated. Despite, however, a pledge to resign if the strike failed, Paisley stayed in politics and gained increasingly massive majorities in the European elections of 1981 and 1985. But his party, the DUP, peaked in 1981 and then began to lose support to the more 'respectable' Official Unionist Party, and his personal church, the Free Presbyterian (established in 1951), remained at about 14,000 members.

The Anglo-Irish Agreement of November 1985 cast a shadow over Paisley's later years. Visibly aged, and rumoured to have health problems, he failed to provide a vigorous and dynamic focus for Unionist resistance. Indeed, he agreed a pact with James Molyneaux, the leader of the Official Unionist Party, which effectively deprived the DUP of much of its independence, hence creating a context which led to the resignation from political life of some of Paisley's most ardent young lieutenants. To the surprise of those commentators who had stressed the importance of evangelical Protestantism to the Unionist tradition in crisis, Paisley's famed electoral support actually began to wane; in the general election of 1987, after a career marked by a steadily increasing electoral popularity, his vote fell from 33,937 to 28,383. Having routinized his charisma through involvement in the electoral process, Paisley could not find his fire when it mattered most.

Paisley's redeeming features – his pleasant family life, the 'good living' practised by many of his religious followers, and the fact that his bark was worse than his bite – were invisible to those who lived outside Ulster. At his peak, he never took more than 230,000 of a total pro-Union vote of 590,000, but he was widely seen to be the spokesman of Ulster Unionism, and almost every time he opened his mouth his booming rhetoric alienated UK and international opinion.

FURTHER READING

Bruce, Steve, *God Save Ulster* (Oxford: Clarendon Press, 1987).

Moloney, E. and Pollock, A., *Paisley* (Dublin: Poolbeg Press, 1986).

Nelson, S., *Ulster's Uncertain Defenders: Loyalists and the Northern Irish Conflict* (Belfast: Appletree Press, 1984).

Smyth, Clifford, *Ian Paisley: Voice of Protestant Ulster* (Edinburgh: Scottish Academy Press, 1987).

PAUL A. E. BEW

Pankhurst [née Goulden], **Emmeline** (*b.* Manchester, 4 July 1858; *d.* London, 14 June 1929). Leader of the militant campaign for the enfranchisement of women. She founded the Women's Social and Political Union (WSPU) and became, with her daughters Christabel and Sylvia, the best-known campaigner for women's enfranchisement. Her reputation rests upon the use of militant tactics between 1905 and 1914 and on the dedication which her own self-sacrifice inspired in others.

The daughter of Robert Goulden, a self-made cotton manufacturer, she grew up in the radical atmosphere of late-Victorian Manchester. At an early age she was encouraged to read newspapers, and attended a women's suffrage meeting when she was 14. In 1879 she married Dr Richard Pankhurst, a lawyer of radical-socialist views, who was 24 years her senior. They had five children.

In 1885 the couple moved to London, where Emmeline enjoyed the gracious life style of Russell Square and opened a fancy-goods shop in an unsuccessful attempt to improve the family's precarious finances. After returning to Manchester in 1893 they joined the Independent Labour Party. Emmeline was elected to the Chorlton Board of Guardians in 1894 and the Manchester School Board in 1900. Following Richard's death in 1898 she gained employment as a Registrar of Births and Deaths. She now fell increasingly under the influence of her wilful eldest daughter, Christabel. Not until 1903, when Christabel became attracted to women's suffrage, did this cause begin to dominate her life. Offended by the hostility to women displayed in the ILP, they decided to set up their own organization (the WSPU), though Emmeline retained socialist connections through her friendship with Keir Hardie.

Initially the WSPU found it difficult to make an impact; it was only a peripheral element in the women's suffrage movement in Lancashire. In 1905 Emmeline gladly returned to London, where she began to tap the funds and frustration of well-to-do women. The WSPU attempted to put pressure on the incoming Liberal Government by intervening in by-elections and by 'militant' methods; these included heckling, invasions of the House of Commons, window-breaking, arson, and attacks on golf courses, art galleries and politicians' houses. The campaign culminated after 1908 in hunger-strikes in prison, during which the 'suffragettes' suffered forcible feeding. Her oratorical powers and fine physical presence made Emmeline a superb figurehead for the organization. The WSPU attracted immense publicity and by 1908 could draw 250,000 people to Hyde Park rallies. However, the government made no concessions to militancy, and from 1909 the WSPU went into decline. It lost funds and suffered three serious splits; it alienated sympathetic politicians; and the suffrage was overshadowed by other controversies. Emmeline became permanently estranged from her daughters Sylvia and Adela; and from 1912, when Christabel left for Paris, she bore the brunt of a debilitating cycle of imprisonment, hunger-strikes, forcible feeding, release and re-arrest.

From this dilemma Emmeline was rescued by the outbreak of war in August 1914. Swiftly abandoning women's suffrage, she devoted herself to the war effort and grew closer to the establishment through her cooperation with Lloyd George as Minister for Munitions. During 1916–17, when the suffrage question was being settled, she was away on visits to the USA and Russia. After Christabel's failure to win election to Parliament in 1918 she was left with no purpose in life, and little means of supporting herself. She therefore undertook another American lecture tour, and in 1921 became a lecturer for the National Council for Combating Venereal Disease in Canada. After returning, exhausted, to Britain in 1926 she agreed to contest Whitechapel as a Conservative, but died before the election. Though Emmeline remains a heroine to many feminists, her role in the women's movement has been much diminished by modern scholarship.

FURTHER READING

Pankhurst, E. Sylvia, *The Suffragette Movement* (London: Longman, 1931).
——, *The Life of Emmeline Pankhurst* (London: Laurie, 1935).
Rosen, A., *Rise Up Women* (London: Routledge, 1974).

MARTIN PUGH

Paynter, (Thomas) Will(iam) (*b.* Whitchurch, Cardiff, 6 December 1903; *d.* Edgware, Middlesex, 12 December 1984). Leading Communist Party member and Secretary of the National Union of Mineworkers. As Secretary of the NUM (1959–68), Paynter was confronted by the relative decline of coal in the face of oil and had to deal with the problems arising from many pit closures. He gained a reputation as a solid, moderate trade-union leader. As he wrote in his autobiography, *My Generation* (1972), he put his trade-union loyalties first and his political loyalties second. As a communist, however, he was kept off the General Council of the TUC, except for the year 1960–1.

Paynter came from a poor but respectable South Wales family. After leaving school at the age of 13 he was employed on a farm before working in coal mines from his fourteenth birthday. He educated himself in the Cymmer workmen's library, reading socialist classics.

He joined the Communist Party in June 1929, and in September he was elected a checkweigher. The following year, following a clash with the police when he was supporting Arthur Horner and the militant Mardy Lodge, Paynter was sentenced to four months' hard labour. In 1931 the Cymmer Colliery Company secured a court injunction for his removal as a checkweigher.

From the ranks of the unemployed Paynter played a prominent role in the hunger marches from South Wales in 1931, 1932 and 1936. He went to Moscow to study at the Lenin School in December 1932, and in 1933 he was a Comintern courier to the communist underground in Nazi Germany. In March 1937 he was sent by the CP to Spain as a political commissar to the British Battalion of the International Brigade, receiving the support of the South Wales Miners' Federation. Paynter had been elected to its executive in 1936. He was elected in 1939 a miners' agent for Rhymney and, from 20 November 1951 until 1959, when he was elected to succeed his fellow Welshman and communist, Horner, as secretary of the NUM, he was President of the South Wales Miners.

On his retirement Paynter left the CP and accepted an appointment on the Commission on Industrial Relations, resigning when the Heath Government brought forward its industrial relations legislation. He published in 1970 *British Trade Unions and the Problem of Change*. He rejoined the CP in 1977, and was campaigning in support of the miners in the 1984 strike at the time of his death. He left a widow and seven sons.

FURTHER READING

Ashworth, W., *The History of the British Coal Industry*, vol. 5: *1946–1982* (Oxford: Clarendon Press, 1986).
Francis, H. and Smith, D., *The Fed: a History of the South Wales Miners in the Twentieth Century* (London: Lawrence and Wishart, 1980).
Francis, H., *Miners Against Fascism: Wales and the Spanish Civil War* (London: Lawrence and Wishart, 1984).

CHRIS WRIGLEY

Philby, Kim [Harold Adrian Russell] (*b.* Ambala, Punjab, India, 1 January 1912; *d.*

Moscow, 11 May 1988). Journalist, intelligence officer and Soviet spy. Nicknamed after the boy hero of Kipling's *The Jungle Book*, Philby seldom saw his maverick and often difficult father, whom he both admired and feared. Harry St John Philby, Arabist, explorer and advisor to King Ibn Saud, was briefly imprisoned in 1941 under Section 18b of the Defence Regulations. Philby's mother, Dora Johnson, had also been reared in an Indian Civil Service family; she bore three other children, all girls. The family lived in Hampstead, London, St John Philby staying in Saudi Arabia. Like his father, Philby was educated at Westminster School, where he developed the pronounced stutter he would never lose; but he did well academically, winning a first-class scholarship to Trinity College, Cambridge, in 1929. Regarding Ramsay MacDonald as a traitor to the working class, he joined the Socialist Society there and met GUY BURGESS, DONALD MACLEAN and ANTHONY BLUNT, who subsequently became his fellow Soviet 'moles'.

By 1933 Philby had acquired 'the firm conviction that my life must be devoted to communism.' In 1933 and 1934 he went to Vienna, where Alice ('Litzi') Kohlmann, a fervent Marxist, enrolled him in an underground communist cell. It was there, too, that he was recruited by a Soviet controller. He returned to England, having married Litzi (in danger of her life) to give her British nationality. He lay low, feigning Fascist sympathies, until the outbreak of the Spanish Civil War, when he went to the front on the Franco side as correspondent for *The Times*, even being awarded a decoration by the Caudillo himself. Leaving *The Times* after the fall of France, in 1944 he managed, through Burgess, to enter Section D ('D for Destruction'), part of British Secret Intelligence, soon to be disbanded. He worked next as instructor in the Special Operations Executive, eventually joining Milo's Section Five, an important wartime post in Secret Intelligence; he rose to run the Iberian desk and Section Five itself. By an irony, he was later chosen as chief of counter-espionage against the Soviet Union, thus being responsible for unnumbered deaths in Turkey and elsewhere.

From 1949 to 1951 Philby worked in Washington as MI6 liaison officer with the CIA and FBI. Ruthless, though equally charming, he acted throughout as the classic double agent, passing on information to Moscow. By 1951, however, partly because of revelations by Soviet defectors, partly through Russian mistakes in disclosing code names, Donald Maclean, now at the Foreign Office in London, came under direct suspicion as a Soviet spy. Philby warned Burgess of Maclean's imminent danger of arrest on Friday, 25th May 1951, giving time for Maclean to escape. To the consternation of their Soviet controllers, Burgess on the spur of the moment decided to accompany him. Philby was recalled to London and had to resign from MI6 after interrogation. There were still differences between members of MI5 and MI6 about Philby's involvement and his role, especially when Harold Macmillan in 1955, as Foreign Secretary, prematurely exonerated him in the Commons. The next 12 years he spent in the Middle East, combining work for the British secret service with journalism for *The Observer* and *The Economist* and still spying for both sides. In 1963, with exposure inevitable following information from fresh defectors, he escaped to Moscow, where he lived as an honoured Soviet citizen with, eventually, his fourth wife, a Russian. He was given the honorary rank of Major-General in the KGB and awarded Lenin's Order of the Red Banner.

WRITINGS

My Secret Life (London: MacGibbon and Kee, 1968).

FURTHER READING

Boyle, Andrew, *The Climate of Treason* (London: Hutchinson, 1979).

Cookridge, E. H., *The Third Man* (New York: Putnam, 1968).

Knightley, Phillip, *Philby: Life and Views of the KGB Master Spy* (London: André Deutsch, 1988).

Page, Bruce, Leitch, David and Knightley, Phillip, *The Philby Conspiracy* (London: André Deutsch, 1968).

Philby, Eleanor, *The Spy I Loved* (London: Pan Books, 1968).

Trevor-Roper, Hugh, *The Philby Affair* (London: William Kimber, 1968).

ANDREW BOYLE

Philip, Prince [Duke of Edinburgh] (*b.* Corfu, 10 June 1921). Prince Philip married Princess Elizabeth (later Queen Elizabeth II) on 20 November 1947. He was made HRH the Duke of Edinburgh before his marriage and became a prince of the United Kingdom in 1957. Since 1960 his adopted surname, Mountbatten, has been hyphenated with Windsor as the patronymic of the royal family. He has been an energetic, outspoken and sometimes controversial consort to the Queen. Among the interests he has pursued and the causes he has supported are national scientific and technological development, greater opportunities for achievement by young people (the Duke of Edinburgh's Award Scheme) and the protection and conservation of wild life (the World Wild Life Fund, later the World-Wide Fund for Nature).

His father, Prince Andrew of Greece, was a brother of King Constantine I of Greece, and his mother, Princess Alice, was a daughter of Admiral Prince Louis of Battenburg, who changed his name to Mountbatten and became Marquess of Milford Haven in 1917. With his father exiled from Greece, and his parents estranged, Prince Philip was largely brought up by his British relatives. He was educated at Cheam and Gordonstoun and at the Royal Naval College, Dartmouth, which he entered in 1939 as a special entry cadet. During World War II he served in the Royal Navy, first in the Mediterranean, where he took part in the battle of Matapan, and then in the Pacific, being present at the Japanese surrender in Tokyo Bay.

Prince Philip first met Princess Elizabeth at Dartmouth in 1939, when she accompanied the King and Queen on a visit to the Royal Naval College. An incipient romance was furthered by a series of visits the Prince made to the royal family at Windsor and by the correspondence which he maintained with the Princess during the war. The match was assiduously promoted by his uncle, Lord Louis Mountbatten (Earl Mountbatten of Burma, 1947), and by the Greek royal family, and from early in the war there were rumours in informed circles that an eventual marriage was a possibility. There were advantages and disadvantages to the Prince's suit: he was royal

and from a family closely connected with the British royal line, anglicized, and a serving naval officer; but he belonged to the rather shaky Greek dynasty, was not a British subject, and had a number of rather embarrassing pro-Nazi German relatives. That betrothal and marriage had to wait until 1947 is explained partly by George VI's reluctance to see his daughter marry young and partly by the political situation in Greece, which made it inapposite for Prince Philip to renounce his Greek and take British nationality. In 1947 a series of steps were taken: in March HRH Prince Philip

Prince Philip addressing a conference on utilization of wasteland and dockland, July 1980

of Greece and Denmark took British nationality and changed his name from Schleswig-Holstein-Sonderburg-Glucksburg to the anglicized form of his mother's name, Mountbatten; on 10 July the engagement of Princess Elizabeth to Lieutenant Philip Mountbatten RN was announced; and on 20 November HRH the Duke of Edinburgh married the heir to the throne.

In the first years of his marriage Prince Philip was able to continue his career as a naval officer and, with the rank of Lieutenant-Commander, to command his own ship, HMS *Magpie*, but the failing health of King George VI required that in 1951 the Prince take indefinite leave from the navy to support his wife in her royal duties. With George's death, on 6 February 1952, he found himself in the full-time job of husband to the Queen.

It is in many respects an unsatisfactory position for an energetic man with a forceful personality. The husband of a queen has no role or position set by constitutional law, and Queen and Parliament have not seen fit to make Prince Philip a king or even a prince consort. Until 1957 he was a prince only by courtesy, having given up his Greek title and not yet been made a prince of the United Kingdom; until 1967 he was given a chair rather than a throne alongside the Queen at the State Opening of Parliament. For some time it appeared that he would not be able to pass on his adopted family name of Mountbatten to his children and descendants, for in April 1952 the Queen, advised by Winston Churchill, declared that she and her children would be 'styled and known as the House and Family of Windsor'. In 1960 this decision was modified, and a further statement by the Queen declared that Mountbatten-Windsor would be the family name, though the name of the House remained Windsor.

In his interpretation of the role required of his position, Prince Philip has, wisely, disavowed that of political adviser to the Queen favoured by his predecessor Prince Albert. In addition to the essentially passive duty of supporting the Queen in her engagements, he has fulfilled a demanding programme of state and other public engagements on his own; he has been an independent voice promoting the causes with which he sympathizes, criticizing institutions, professions or the nation as a whole when he finds it necessary. Some historians have discerned a muted clash of wills in the early years of the Queen's reign between Prince Philip, bent on refashioning the court and the royal life style, and more traditional influences, including that of Queen Elizabeth, the Queen Mother, concerned to retain a fundamental continuity with the traditions established by the House of Windsor. It was Prince Philip who raised the question of the royal family's financial position, which had been eroded by years of inflation, with his comment on an American television programme in 1969 that the palace was 'in the red'. His remark led to a Select Committee the following year.

Apart from his enthusiasm for outdoor sporting pursuits, Prince Philip shares few of the dispositions of the British aristocracy; essentially a modernizer, he is interested in technical problems and has often appeared irritated by the conservatism and lack of drive and efficiency of his adopted country. His determination not to be merely a bland adjunct to the Queen but to speak his mind and promote his own causes has, at times, made him a controversial figure, for professional bodies and august institutions do not always welcome advice from a well-informed princely amateur. His relations with the press have not been harmonious, and an early dislike, inspired by Lord Beaverbrook's vendetta with the Mountbattens, has been exacerbated by the increasing intrusion of reporters and photographers into the royal family's life. A bluffness of manner can lead to gaffes, but Prince Philip was entrusted in January 1989 with the most delicate of missions in being selected as Britain's principal representative at the funeral of Emperor Hirohito of Japan. Like the Queen, he is an enthusiast for the Commonwealth and is the royal family's greatest traveller, fulfilling more engagements abroad than any other member. His Duke of Edinburgh's Award Scheme, founded in 1956, has proved an enduring success, while his association with the World-Wide Fund for Nature is in tune with the growing British concern for ecology.

FURTHER READING

Judd, D., *Prince Philip: a Biography* (London: Michael Joseph, 1980).
Pearson, J., *The Ultimate Family: the Making of the Royal House of Windsor* (London: Michael Joseph, 1985).

A. W. PURDUE

Pont [Laidler, Graham] (*b*. Newcastle upon Tyne, 1908; *d*. London, 23 November 1940). Cartoonist. It is impossible to make any assessment of what English middle-class life was like in the 1930s without reference to the penetrating and subtle work of the comic artist Graham Laidler. Discovered by E. V. Knox (the art editor of *Punch*), he was one of the few artists whose services were exclusively retained by the magazine.

Laidler drew incessantly as a child. He was educated at Glenalmond before spending five years at the Architectural Association (qualifying ARIBA). It was not until 1932 that his work first appeared in *Punch*. The name 'Pont', a family nickname, is derived from *Pontifex Maximus*, meaning bridge builder. He chose to use the name for his comic work in order to differentiate it from his architectural work.

From 4 April 1934 until his death Pont contributed 104 drawings to *Punch* on the subject of the British character. He was an instant success. Obviously the result of meticulous preparation, it is notable that his work never lost its freshness. The backgrounds in his drawings, with detail spreading right to the edge, demanded to be noticed. The major appeal of his work lay in the fact that contemporary readers of *Punch* were able to recognize each scene. He once said, 'I do not try to draw funny people. I try very hard to draw people exactly as they are.' He was funny because he had no stock characters. He drew and used real people in the way that Mark Boxer did – exaggerating the situation for comic effect without showing any obvious viciousness towards the 'victims'. His work has remained consistently popular with modern readers who take pleasure in a common nostalgia.

Several well-received collections of Pont's work – *The British Character – Studied and Revealed* (1938), *The British at Home* (1939) and *The British Carry On* (1940) – were published during his lifetime. A further volume, *Most of Us are Absurd*, appeared posthumously in 1946. Pont died from poliomyelitis at the age of 32.

FURTHER READING

Hollowood, A. Bernard, *Pont: an Account of the*

Life and Work of Graham Laidler (1908–1940) (London: Collins, 1969).

LIZ OTTAWAY

Powell, (John) Enoch (*b*. Birmingham, 16 June 1912). Conservative politician and classical scholar. Powell had only a modest ministerial career – as Minister of Health from 1960 to 1964 – but his speeches and actions have excited much attention. He has been a prophet in the wilderness, though the wilderness has had no intrinsic attraction for him. He would have preferred to have been his country's saviour, and there were indeed moments, in the late 1960s and early 1970s, when he was conspicuously waiting in the wings – for a call that never came. He has remained into old age a formidable speaker, articulating varied opinions pungently and pugnaciously in a manner which has produced a grudging admiration even from those who have dissented sharply from those opinions.

Powell was the son of two elementary-school teachers. The fact that he was reading Harmsworth's Encyclopaedia with enthusiasm at the age of four suggested that he had an unusual brain. At King Edward VI School, Birmingham, and Trinity College, Cambridge, that brain applied itself with unwavering intensity to the study of Greek. At the age of 22 he was a Fellow of Trinity. Three years later he was in Sydney, Australia, as Professor of Greek. When war broke out he enlisted as a private in the Royal Warwickshire Regiment, but intelligence work suited both his punctilious application to detail and his formidable forensic capacity. He served in Cairo and, latterly, in India, rising to the rank of Brigadier. India had cast something of a spell over him and he had little notion that the end of the raj was near. He supposed that the Indian Army, whose future he was planning, would continue to have a substantial quota of British officers.

In 1945 he decided to plunge into politics. He could only be a Tory, though the scale of the Labour victory in 1945 was discouraging. Powell worked in the Conservative Research Department alongside REGINALD MAUDLING and IAIN MACLEOD. Their task was to provide briefs for Conservative policy under the pre-

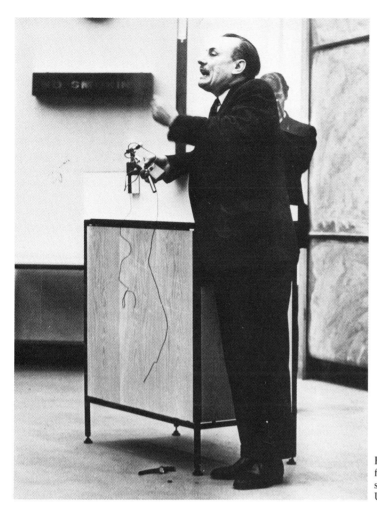

Enoch Powell making a
forceful point during a
speech at Reading
University, October 1968

siding aegis of R. A. BUTLER. There had to be a
positive 'New Conservatism' which would
entail embracing the welfare state. Only with a
new charter could the party regain its electoral
appeal. Powell did not appear rigidly hostile to
these tendencies, though he was shocked by the
party's readiness to 'abandon' India in 1947. In
1950 he narrowly won Wolverhampton South-
West, a constituency which he represented
until he withdrew in the February 1974
election.

In the Commons his knowledge and powers
of exposition were speedily recognized on both
sides, but Powell was somewhat lonely in his
intellectual eminence and inclined to follow an
individual path. He opposed British participa-

tion in the United Nations force in Korea and
voted against his party line in opposing British
membership of the European Coal and Steel
Community. He did not take a junior post
under Churchill. He remained, however, a
'coming man', although his opposition to withdrawal from the Suez Canal Zone caused irritation. Eden made him Parliamentary
Secretary to the Ministry of Housing and Local
Government in 1955, and he settled down to
the partial derestricting of rents. He kept his
head down during the Suez Crisis of 1956. In
1957 Macmillan put Powell into his Treasury
team as Financial Secretary. Here was a
stepping-stone which might lead to the
chancellorship. However, a year later Powell

345

joined the Chancellor, PETER THORNEYCROFT, in resigning; the spending departments wanted more than the Treasury ministers deemed prudent. Only when Thorneycroft came back into the government in 1960 did Powell accept another appointment, this time as Minister of Health, initially not in the cabinet. That elevation came in 1962 when Macmillan sacked some colleagues. As Minister of Health, Powell gained a high reputation as an effective administrator and communicator. He had his first experience of the problems involved in trying to run even a rudimentary 'incomes policy'.

EDWARD HEATH, Maudling, Macleod and Powell had emerged as the leading quartet of the Tory 'next generation'. The others might seem to be slightly more experienced, but some commentators believed that Powell had a more striking personality than any of them. His patriotism was a special feature. He was already agonizing over Britain's post-imperial identity in a way that some of his colleagues found puzzling – though he did not consider the government's (unsuccessful) application to join the European Economic Community an occasion for resignation. He had made a striking speech in 1959 in which he called upon Parliament to accept responsibility for the misdemeanours which had taken place in the Hola Camp in Kenya. He was against capital punishment. He was neither 'right' nor 'left'. His independent voice was further confirmed in 1963 when, his support for Butler in the succession to Macmillan having failed, he declined to serve under Lord Home. He liked Home, but that was not relevant. However, he did serve under Home in opposition.

Powell contested the leadership when Sir Alec stood down but obtained merely 15 votes. He served as shadow Minister of Defence under Heath but took a different view from his leader not only on the merits of Britain staying 'East of Suez' but also on floating the pound sterling and on immigration policy. Speeches he made on this last topic, in which he predicted in colourful language the social consequences of continued immigration, led to his dismissal from the shadow cabinet in April 1968. It was clear, nevertheless, that his views on this topic had considerable public resonance. He had apparently jeopardized his career by his language but he had gained a popular following. His supporters also liked his opposition to membership of the EEC and perhaps his support for Ulster Unionists as well. In addition, Powell criticized the industrial and economic policy of the government. His attacks on Heath developed over a wide front. Powell placed his concern for the survival of the British nation, as he conceived it, above even party loyalty. He stood down at Wolverhampton and his behaviour was widely believed by his erstwhile party colleagues to have substantially assisted a Labour victory. It would be difficult for Tories to forgive him.

Powell transferred his battle for national identity to the border constituency of South Down in Northern Ireland, which he won as an Ulster Unionist in the October 1974 election and retained until his defeat in 1987. He sought to defend Ulster against what he considered to be the malign attempts of successive governments, prompted by sinister Foreign Office and American influences, to drive Northern Ireland into the Republic. His central concern with Ulster prevented a complete accommodation with Mrs Thatcher after her assumption of the party leadership in 1975, although in other respects he found certain of her policies and emphases much more congenial than those of Heath. He remained, as perhaps he had essentially always been, a very individual voice in British politics.

FURTHER READING

Cosgrave, P., *The Lives of Enoch Powell* (London: Bodley Head, 1989).

Lewis, Roy, *Enoch Powell* (London: Cassell, 1979).

Roth, Andrew, *Enoch Powell* (London: Macdonald, 1970).

Schoen, Douglas, *Enoch Powell and the Powellites* (London: Macmillan, 1977).

KEITH ROBBINS

Prior, James (Michael Leathes) [Baron Prior of Brampton] (**'Jim'**) (*b.* Norwich, Norfolk, 11 October 1927). Conservative MP and businessman. Prior was Minister of Agriculture, Food and Fisheries (1970–2) and Lord President of the Council and Leader of the House of Commons (1972–4) in the Heath government. Under Mrs Thatcher, he was Employment Secretary (1979–81) and Northern Ireland Secretary (1981–4). On leaving the government, he became director of a number of important companies and banks and, most notably, chairman of the General Electric Company, but he also managed to write a political autobiography. He received a life peerage in 1987.

The son of an East Anglian country lawyer, Prior went to Charterhouse and after the war served in India and Germany with the Royal Norfolk Regiment. At Pembroke College, Cambridge, he decided upon a political career, but he went initially into work as a land agent, having graduated with a First in estate management in 1950. In 1959 he won Lowestoft from Labour and paid his first visit to the House of Commons, where he knew no one. He became a Parliamentary Private Secretary at the Board of Trade and then at the Ministry of Power (1963–4) but his path to future promotion came some months after the Conservatives were defeated in 1964. He was made a Vice-Chairman of the party in 1965 and then was called upon to be Heath's Parliamentary Private Secretary in opposition, although in personality the two men were not alike. It was this experience which led to Prior's promotion straight into the cabinet in 1970 and to a more central post two years later.

When it became clear that Heath could not retain the party leadership, Prior put himself forward, with only very modest support. Throughout the years of opposition he was the Conservative spokesman on Employment, and in 1979 Mrs Thatcher made him Employment Secretary. However, his approach to trade-union legislation did not commend itself to the Prime Minister. From 1981 to 1984 he served as Northern Ireland Secretary and threw himself energetically into the province's economic and political problems. At the same time, however, his unease at the main thrust of government policy overall in these years was evident. His mind increasingly turned to business and he left the Commons in 1987.

WRITINGS

A Balance of Power (London: Hamish Hamilton, 1986).

KEITH ROBBINS

Profumo, John (Dennis) (*b.* London, 30 January 1915). Conservative politician and Minister of War. Profumo belongs to that select and unfortunate group of politicians whose chief claim on posterity consists of having resigned office after a sex scandal; his name will forever be linked with that of the call-girl Christine Keeler.

When first elected to the Commons in 1940, Profumo was, at the age of 25, the youngest member of the House. In an act of considerable political bravery, he voted against Neville Chamberlain in the famous vote of 8 May which led to Churchill's rise to power. For the rest of the war he served with his regiment, rising to the rank of brigadier. His neglected constituency, Kettering, was among those which responded to the 1945 election by dismissing its Conservative member. For the next five years Profumo worked in Conservative Central Office.

He was elected for Stratford-upon-Avon in 1950 and received preferment in November 1952 as Parliamentary Secretary for Civil Aviation at the Ministry of Transport. The long period of Conservative rule gave him the chance to rise up through the ranks (serving in junior posts at the Colonial and Foreign Offices) until in 1960 he became Secretary of State for War. A saturninely handsome man, married to the glamorous actress Valerie Hobson, he seemed well set into a successful political career when, in early 1963, came the first intimations of the scandal with which his name will always be associated. Allegations in the press that he had had a sexual relationship with a young woman of ill-repute, Christine Keeler, led him successively to sue foreign newspapers and deny the allegations in the Commons.

Under pressure from the Opposition and press speculation, Profumo admitted in June that he had lied to the Commons and resigned his seat. His career and reputation blasted, and the position of the Macmillan Government shaken, he showed great dignity in the manner of his departure from political life. Despite all offers from the press, he has remained silent about the whole affair and has devoted himself to charitable work in the East End of London. He was appointed CBE in 1975.

FURTHER READING

Hyde, H. Montgomery, *A Tangled Web* (London: Constable, 1986).
Lord Denning's Report (London: HMSO, Cmnd. 2152, 1963).
Young, Wayland, *The Profumo Affair* (Harmondsworth: Penguin, 1964).

JOHN CHARMLEY

R

Radcliffe, Cyril (John) [Viscount Radcliffe] (*b.* Llanychan, Denbighshire, 30 March 1899; *d.* Hampton Lucy, Warwickshire, 1 April 1977). Judge and chairman of enquiries. Radcliffe was a Law Lord more widely known for service on public commissions and enquiries than for his judicial work. He was a Fellow of All Souls from 1922 to 1937, was called to the Bar in 1924, and rose very rapidly, becoming the outstanding man at the Chancery Bar in the 1930s; he took silk in 1935. During World War II he worked in the Ministry of Information, from 1941 as director-general, and ably complemented the minister, Brendan Bracken.

In 1949 Radcliffe was appointed direct from the Bar to the House of Lords to be a Lord of Appeal, a jump extremely rare save in the case of some ex-law officers. He sat there for only 15 years, excelling in property, company and revenue cases. He accepted that judges made law by re-interpreting principles in the light of new combinations of facts, but did not do so openly. He had a concern for civil liberties but was also troubled by the erosion of authority, the tendency of some to deny the validity of any rule of law which did not accord with their views, which could lead, he held, to the country becoming ungovernable.

Over some 30 years Radcliffe was chairman of a series of vitally important commissions and committees, notably the two boundary commissions established to implement Indian independence by delimiting the boundaries between India and Pakistan (1947); the Royal Commission on the Taxation of Profits and Income (1951–5); the Constitutional Commission for Cyprus (1956); the Committee of Enquiry into the Monetary System (1957–9); the Committee on Security Procedures and Practices in the Public Service (1961); the Tribunal of Enquiry into the Vassall Case (1962); the Committee of Privy Councillors investigating the *Daily Express* and D-notices (1967); and the Committee on Ministerial Memoirs (1975–6). He enjoyed the new challenges of these investigations. Legal and judicial work, even at the highest level, seemed to have lost its interest for him, though he sat regularly as Law Lord when not engaged on one of the enquiries.

Before he retired from judicial office, but increasingly thereafter, Radcliffe devoted his energies to public services, and was chairman of the trustees of the British Museum (1963–8), chairman of the governors of the School of Oriental and African Studies (1960–75), a member of the BBC Advisory Committee, and chancellor of the University of Warwick (1966–77). He had a most powerful intellect and was very well versed in literature, history and the fine arts.

Despite his extensive knowledge of government – he has been said to have had one of the strongest analytical minds ever encountered in the Lords – he was not active in the legislative work of the House, but was a lucid and persuasive speaker and delivered many notable lectures, in particular the 1951 Reith lectures on 'The Problem of Power' and the 1960 Rosenthal lectures on 'The Law and its Compass'.

FURTHER READING

Blom-Cooper, L. and Drewry, G., *Final Appeal* (London: Oxford University Press, 1972).
Stevens, R., 'Lord Radcliffe', *Law and Politics* (London: Weidenfeld and Nicolson, 1979), pp. 445–59.
Thompson, E. P., 'A Report on Lord Radcliffe', *New Society* (1970), p. 737.

DAVID M. WALKER

Ramsey, (Arthur) Michael [Baron Ramsey of Canterbury] (*b.* Cambridge, 14 November 1904; *d.* Oxford, 23 April 1988). Archbishop of Canterbury and theologian. Ramsey was

Archbishop from 1961 to 1974. It did not seem immediately obvious that he was the man to cope with the 'permissive' impulses of his time. He seemed about the last man to whom one could apply the adjective 'swinging'. He could appear remote and aloof, though not censorious. His marriage was childless and he was thought to be out of touch with current preoccupations. However, he had two positive advantages that marked him out from his immediate predecessors in the job: he had never been a headmaster and he would not wear gaiters and an apron – his ample form was much more appropriately housed in a purple cassock. In the event, he surprised many by the skill with which he wrestled with theological and social ideas that at first sight were uncongenial to him. The fact that he looked like an old man, though he was not, perhaps explains this surprise. In his measured response he neither sought refuge in untrammeled trendiness nor in intransigent conservatism. The voice was clearly personal and his opinions had not been processed into life by an ecclesiastical machine.

Ramsey's father was a Cambridge don who hovered between town Congregationalism and college Anglicanism; Frank, his brilliant brother, died prematurely and had no religious belief. Michael Ramsey seemed so much the quintessence of a liberal Anglo-Catholic that his mixed ecclesiastical pedigree and family knowledge that belief was difficult were often overlooked. It was also often forgotten that, despite a deep shyness and lack of small talk, he had been a successful President of the Cambridge Union as an undergraduate. There had then been talk of a political career, though, since he was undoubtedly a Liberal, it might not have been a very flourishing one. Instead, after ordination, his life seemed likely to be spent in universities. At the age of 36 he was Professor of Divinity at Durham, and he stayed there for a decade before moving to Cambridge (and to his father's old college) in the same capacity. He was there for only two years before going back to Durham as bishop. He then served as Archbishop of York for five years before his translation to Canterbury.

Although Ramsey retained his scholarly interests and outlook, the pressures of the office ruled out sustained writing, though he had the intellectual equipment to produce a response to John Robinson's *Honest to God* (1963), a book which shaped the outlook of many. He had to preside over the diocese of Canterbury in some fashion. He contributed to the ongoing work of Christian reconciliation, both at home and abroad. His sympathies were wide, and he disliked 'party' within his own church and denominational smugness outside it. He had hoped to bring about Anglican–Methodist reunion but the scheme narrowly failed in 1972. This disappointment clouded his last two years at Canterbury.

Inescapably, however, an archbishop remains a national figure. His liberalism remained intact, particularly in matters of race. He abhorred apartheid and was worried about restrictions on immigration into the United Kingdom. He thought the British Government should have used force against Ian Smith following his unilateral declaration of independence in Rhodesia in 1965. The Prime Minister did not agree. Ramsey did not campaign stridently or believe that the Christian gospel could be reduced to a social programme, but neither did he believe that it had nothing to say to society at large. It was the impression conveyed to a sceptical generation by his own manifest spirituality which left its mark. He was a man of words by training and conviction, but more could sometimes be achieved by being a simple Canterbury Pilgrim.

KEITH ROBBINS

Rank, J(oseph) Arthur [Baron Rank of Sutton Scotney] (*b.* Hull, Yorkshire, 22 December 1888; *d.* Sutton Scotney, Hampshire, 29 March 1972). Flour manufacturer, film magnate and Methodist leader. He was the single most influential figure in the promotion and shaping of the modern British film industry, enabling it to rival that of Hollywood.

His father, Joseph Rank (1854–1943), a stern but passionate Wesleyan Methodist, independently built up an immensely successful business in Hull by substituting steamdriven roller-milling for the windmill. Joseph Rank Ltd, registered with a capital of £700,000 in 1899, had purpose-built dockside mills in

Hull and London by 1904, when headquarters were moved to the metropolis. While this suggested a privileged upbringing for Arthur Rank, it was subject to the strict but certainly not joyless discipline of the Wesleyans. His five years at The Leys School, Cambridge, a Wesleyan public school, were undistinguished. From school he followed his two brothers, James Voase (1881–1952) and Rowland (1884–1939), into the family firm. He trained in the London office, then on the London Corn Exchange, next with an independent miller, then in Rank's Premier Mills in the Royal Victoria Dock, London, and finally as production manager at the firm's Clarence Mills, Hull, four and a half years in all. During World War I he joined an ambulance unit raised by Sir Arthur du Cros, rising to captain in the Royal Field Artillery. In 1917 he married Laura Ellen, eldest daughter of Sir Horace Marshall (later 1st Baron Marshall of Chipstead), a wholesale newspaper distributor and Wesleyan friend of Rank's father.

Between the wars, demand for flour remained buoyant and the Rank business continued to expand, though one acquisition managed by Arthur Rank was not a success. In 1933 the private firm of Joseph Rank Ltd was converted into a public company, Ranks Ltd. With a capital of £7.295 million, it reputedly produced nearly a third of all the flour sold in the UK. Under the ageing Joseph Rank as chairman, James and Arthur Rank and a brother-in-law became managing directors. Following the acquisition of Associated London Flour Mills Ltd in 1932, Arthur developed the animal feeds side under the Blue Cross trade mark. Paradoxically it was Christian conviction which nudged this reticent suburban-dwelling city businessman into that most extrovert and epidermic of industries, films.

Characteristically, Rank had moved slowly from indifference to faith. After the war he started teaching in the Wesleyan Church Sunday School at Reigate and soon recognized the limitations of old-fashioned visual aids in the age of Hollywood films. Passionately concerned to share his Christian faith with the unchurched masses (to this end he bought the *Methodist Times* in 1925), he started showing films in the Reigate Methodist Church. He presented projectors to this and later to other Methodist churches around the country. Poorly produced religious films spurred him to join the Religious Film Society in 1933, to commission a 20-minute film on the life of Christ and then, in October 1934, to form a film production company, British National Films, with Lady Yule. The adventuresome widow of a Calcutta jute magnate, she had two things in common with Rank: both were teetotallers and millionaires. For the British film industry, the latter was exceedingly important.

While Lady Yule's interest proved casual, Rank's was enduring. From financing filmmaking he moved into distributorship and studio ownership and later into film exhibition. With Charles Moss Woolf (previously of Gaumont-British Picture Corporation, the major British distributor), he formed General Film Distributors, which thrived by acquiring films from the new independent production companies and renting them to the rapidly expanding circuits of cinemas. Two months later, in August 1935, he joined Charles Boot, of the large Sheffield contracting firm Henry Boot & Son, in promoting Pinewood Studios. The following year a more powerful group of financiers, including Lord Luke, Lord Portal of Lavenham, Paul Lindenburg of Japhets Bank, Arthur Rank and his Methodist associate Leslie W. Farrow, an accountant, formed the General Cinema Finance Corporation. This (with Manorfield Investments) became the major holding company owning most of J. Arthur Rank's film industry interests. Among businesses acquired were Denham Studios (1938), Elstree Studios (1939) and the largest integrated film producer, distributor and exhibitor, Gaumont British Picture Corporation (1941). After the death of Oscar Deutsch in 1941 Rank gained control of the Odeon Theatre chain (and with it the financial and managerial skills of John (later Sir John) Davis, who became his right-hand man). Since most potential rivals had died or retired during the early part of the war, Rank emerged as the dominant capitalist in the British film industry.

Such power as he gained was neither actively sought nor heavily wielded. Rachael Low judges that 'Rank's progress in the industry in the thirties was not so much a deliberate attempt to take it by storm as a step by step response to changing events, drawing him further and further along the road to power.' He was concerned to make profits but not at the expense of quality. He saw his role as mobilizing finance for creative film-makers; beyond that, as contributing to the war effort, competing with Hollywood and, in his religious films or Sunday film sermonettes, exerting direct Christian influence. The wide latitude he gave his film-makers produced some flops but it also resulted in such classics as *Henry V*, *Hamlet*, *The Way to the Stars* and *In Which We Serve*. Against charges of monopoly power must be set his relationship with his film-makers, the exoneration of the Palache Committee (1943–4) and the substantial losses made in 1947 when the Labour Government suddenly replaced a high duty on imported films with a more liberal quota arrangement. For Rank, who had just patriotically embarked on a programme of 47 films costing more than £9 million in a government-instigated bid to stem or reverse the flow of dollars to Hollywood, this was a stunning blow. It led to layoffs and losses of £6 million for the Rank empire by 1951. Rank's soft-spoken manner, liberal policies and private generosities earned him the affection and regard of his film-makers and stars, who respectfully nicknamed him 'Uncle Arthur'.

On the death of his eldest brother in 1952 Rank, now in his mid-sixties, became chairman of the flour company, Ranks Ltd. In 1953 he surrendered his film interests to a new company, the Rank Organization, and set up a charitable trust to distribute most of the income. He then devoted his energies to the family firm. Over the next two decades he made numerous acquisitions and merged Ranks with Hovis McDougall (1962), transforming the flour company into a diversified giant with bakery, agricultural merchanting, flour milling and grocery divisions. He retired in 1969.

In the Methodist Church he served as denominational treasurer and on numerous national committees; many of his generous and usually anonymous benefactions went in this direction. Sunday School work, shooting on his Hampshire estate and bridge were among his private delights. In 1957 he was created a baron.

FURTHER READING

Davis, Sir John, 'Joseph Arthur Rank', in *Dictionary of National Biography 1971–1980*, ed. Lord Blake and C. S. Nicholls (Oxford: Oxford University Press, 1986).

Low, Rachael, *The History of the British Film: Film Making in 1930s Britain* (London: George Allen and Unwin, 1985).

Manville, Roger and Rank, Joseph, 'Joseph Arthur Rank', in *Dictionary of Business Biography*, ed. David J. Jeremy and Christine Shaw, 6 vols (London: Butterworths, 1984–6).

Obituary, *The Times* (30 March 1972).

Rhode, Eric, *A History of the Cinema from its Origins to 1970* (London: Allen Lane, 1976).

Wood, Alan, *Mr Rank: a Study of J. Arthur Rank and British Films* (London: Hodder and Stoughton, 1952).

DAVID J. JEREMY

Rathbone, Eleanor (Florence) (*b.* London, 12 May 1872; *d.* London, 2 January 1946). Feminist, social reformer and Independent MP. She was a major influence on British feminism and an Independent MP for 16 years. Prominent in the constitutional movement for women's suffrage, she propagated the idea of a 'New Feminism' in her capacity as President of the National Union of Societies for Equal Citizenship (NUSEC) after 1919. As a humanitarian reformer, her greatest achievement was family allowances, for which she campaigned for 28 years.

The daughter of William Rathbone, a Liverpool shipowner and Liberal MP, she grew up steeped in a tradition of public service. A serious, intellectual young woman, and a habitual smoker, she read philosophy at Somerville College, Oxford (1893–6). Never interested in the male sex, she shared most of her life with another suffrage campaigner, Elizabeth Macadam. Rathbone embarked on a career of philanthropy and social research in Liverpool, producing reports on casual labour and the problems of widows under the Poor Law. In 1909 she became the first woman to be elected to Liverpool City Council. At the same time she campaigned for women's suffrage, favouring a strictly non-militant and non-party strategy. It is a sign of her far-sightedness that in 1913 she established the first Women's Citizens Association in order to educate women in the use of the parliamentary vote.

Rathbone's work for the dependents of servicemen in Liverpool during the war stimulated her interest in the idea of a system of allowances for children paid directly to mothers. She argued that since the wages earned by men bore no relationship to the needs of their families, poverty was unlikely to be overcome by industrial means; family allowances were a highly effective and economic way of raising living standards. Moreover, the idea was feminist in that it implied recognition of motherhood as an important occupation worthy of support by governments. However, Rathbone faced opposition from traditionalists, who believed the system would undermine parental responsibility, and from the Labour movement, where trade unionists claimed it would weaken their ability to bargain with employers.

During her ten-year presidency of NUSEC Rathbone endeavoured to extend the reach of the women's movement to women not involved in the suffrage campaign. This involved a merger between NUSEC and the Women's Citizens Association, and the creation of the Townswomen's Guilds in 1929. She was also instrumental in persuading NUSEC to adopt the 'New Feminism' in which reforms like family allowances occupied a central place. She believed that with the achievement of many 'equal rights' reforms, culminating in equal suffrage in 1928, the movement needed a fresh direction; it was time to stop 'measuring everything that women want, or that is offered them, by men's standards.'

In 1929 Rathbone stood successfully as Independent candidate for the Combined English Universities. As a backbencher she proved to be persistent and formidable in harrying ministers. She took up the issue of child marriage and women's franchise in India, and was active in the League of Nations Union. During the 1920s she moved away from disarmament, and favoured strengthening the League's powers to deter aggressive states. Increasingly concerned by the threat from Fascism, she made several visits with other women MPs to Romania, Czechoslovakia, Yugoslavia and Spain in 1937. During World War II her campaign for family allowances gained momentum from the fears about the declining birth rate and from the Beveridge Report. As a result the Coalition Government introduced a Bill for family allowances in 1945, although Rathbone had to threaten to oppose it until ministers agreed to make the payments to mothers rather than to fathers. Shortly after this triumph she died suddenly from a heart attack.

FURTHER READING

Stocks, M., *Eleanor Rathbone* (London: Gollancz, 1949).
Strachey, R. (ed.), *Our Freedom and its Results* (London: Hogarth Press, 1936).

MARTIN PUGH

Reading, Lord [Isaacs, Rufus (Daniel); Marquess of Reading] (*b*. London, 10 October 1860; *d*. London, 30 December 1935). Advocate, Liberal Party stalwart, Lord Chief Justice and Viceroy of India. Although his dazzling career was not exactly a fable of 'rags to riches', it did nevertheless represent a remarkable rise from obscurity to international prominence. Born the son of a modestly successful Jewish fruit merchant, he became one of the most celebrated, and highly paid, barristers of his age; he went on to become a Liberal MP and cabinet minister, Lord Chief Justice, special wartime Ambassador to the USA, Viceroy of India and Foreign Secretary. It was a triumph which led to comparisons (mostly inaccurate) with Disraeli, and which helped to create a special bond with another, and even more spectacularly gifted, outsider, David Lloyd George.

There was nothing in Reading's early life to suggest his later success. He left school at the age of 14, became a ship's boy, spent a dreary time in the family fruit business, and worked as a jobber on the Stock Exchange, but was 'hammered', or expelled, when he was unable to cover his debts. At the age of 25, and almost by accident, he entered a firm of solicitors, and promptly decided to become a barrister. Reading's legal career was meteoric. He cast off his feckless youth and transformed himself into the sober, shrewd, and dedicated barrister. Supported by a loyal and ambitious wife, he became a Queen's Counsel in 1897 and was soon immersed in cases such as the 1901 Kynoch affair, involving Joseph Chamberlain, and the Taff Vale dispute. In 1904 he won a by-election victory at Reading and entered the House of Commons as a moderate, rather passionless, Liberal. The great Liberal landslide of 1906, allied to his glittering legal reputation, was soon to deliver into his hands, in sequence, the offices of Solicitor-General, Attorney-General and finally, in 1913, Lord Chief Justice, when he assumed the title Baron Reading of Erleigh.

But before this last promotion, he faced ruin and disgrace. His close friendship with Lloyd George led to his involving the Chancellor of the Exchequer in the highly charged Marconi Scandal of 1912–13. Accused essentially of insider dealing, both ministers misled the House of Commons over their modest investments in the American Marconi Company and were saved only by the anti-Unionist majority in the Commons and by Asquith's unflinching support.

Reading did not enjoy his work as Lord Chief Justice. Luckily for him the outbreak of the Great War provided an escape. Lloyd George, never a Chancellor with a thorough understanding of finance, called upon his advice at the Treasury and later sent him to the USA to negotiate a massive loan to help pay for the war. In 1918, with Lloyd George now premier, he was appointed Ambassador to the USA, where his urbane diplomacy smoothed Anglo-American relations. After a brief involvement in the postwar peacemaking, Reading returned reluctantly to the lord chief justiceship in 1919.

Two years later, Lloyd George again rescued him from the legal doldrums by appointing him, after some machination, Viceroy of India. Reading's viceregal career was an indisputable triumph. The first Viceroy to negotiate face to face with Gandhi – whom

he later had arrested – he proceeded to disrupt the fragile post-1916 Hindu–Muslim accord. But he also strove to implement the 1919 Montagu–Chelmsford reforms, and to assert justice and impartial administration under the fading power of the raj.

Created a marquess on his return to Britain, and without office, he became involved in the world of commerce, accepting a place on the board of ICI and those of several other companies. Now a respected, if not particularly powerful, elder statesman, Reading put some effort into reviving the ailing Liberal Party – but without much success.

In 1931, at the age of 70, fate again offered him stimulating work when he became a stop-gap Foreign Secretary in the first National Government. Although he was soon relieved of office, his final years were full of activity: among other things, he was involved in the round table negotiations over India's constitutional progress and remained a potential healer of the Liberal Party's wounds. His final office was that of Warden of the Cinque Ports.

Reading's career was an odd mixture of the conventional and the unorthodox. He had great personal charm, if little charisma. He was essentially an administrator and a conciliator, rather than an innovative politician. He was also an opportunist, though not dishonourably so. Lord Beaverbrook recalled, 'In conversation he had little to say, but when he spoke it was with authority. He did most of his talking and much of his public speaking with his hands on the lapels of his coat.' It will serve as an epitaph.

FURTHER READING

Hyde, H. Montgomery, *Lord Reading* (London: Heinemann, 1967).

Jackson, Stanley, *Rufus Isaacs* (London: Cassell, 1936).

Judd, Denis, *Lord Reading* (London: Weidenfeld and Nicolson, 1982).

Reading, Second Marquess of, *Rufus Isaacs: First Marquess of Reading*, 2 vols. (London: Hutchinson, 1942, 1945).

Walker-Smith, Derek, *Lord Reading and his Cases* (London: Chapman and Hall, 1934).

DENIS JUDD

Rees, Merlyn (*b.* Cilfynydd, Glamorgan, 18 December 1920). Labour politician. He is one of Labour's longest-serving postwar MPs, and acted as Secretary of State for Northern Ireland during the deeply troubled years of 1974–6 and as Home Secretary from 1976 to 1979.

Rees served in the RAF during World War II and taught economics and history at Harrow Weald Grammar School – where he had himself been educated – from 1949 to 1960, meanwhile three times unsuccessfully contesting the local Harrow East constituency for Labour. He entered Parliament at a by-election in June 1963, winning South Leeds, which he has held throughout his Commons career. He occupied various junior ministerial posts in the governments of Harold Wilson (1964–70), and on Labour's return to power in 1974 was placed in charge of Northern Ireland, where direct rule from London had been introduced in 1972.

Rees immediately faced a crisis. The United Ulster Unionist Council had won 11 of the province's 12 Westminster seats, and treated the result as a mandate to destroy the Sunningdale power-sharing agreement implemented two months earlier. On 13 May their supporters launched a general strike which brought down the new authority. The only power Rees possessed which might have thwarted the strike, the army, could not in his view be used. In July 1974 he tried to break the deadlock with a Constitutional Convention, simultaneously phasing out internment without trial and approving an unofficial ceasefire with the IRA which began in February 1975. Yet the ceasefire gradually eroded, the Convention talks collapsed, and ending internment did not seem to diminish terrorism. All the initiatives of 1974–6 had failed; but Rees's task was very likely an impossible one in any case. At the Home Office, to which he was moved in 1976, life was less stormy, though he aroused the hostility of civil libertarians by several of his decisions, notably over the Official Secrets Act trial of two journalists and a former soldier in 1978. After Labour's 1979 election defeat he shadowed his former post for a year and then was Labour energy spokesman and industry and employment coordinator until 1983, when

he returned to the back benches. Identified with the moderate right wing of the Labour Party, Rees was hardly a charismatic figure or an inspiring orator. But his conscientiousness and essential decency were recognized by political opponents as well as friends.

WRITINGS

Northern Ireland: a Personal Perspective (London: Methuen, 1985).

STEPHEN HOWE

Rees-Mogg, William [Baron Rees-Mogg of Hinton Blewitt in the County of Avon] (*b.* Temple Cloud, Somerset, 14 July 1928). Editor of *The Times*. He held the post from 1967 to 1981, in effect throughout Lord Thomson's proprietorship. During that time the paper gave broad support to the moderate Conservatism represented by Edward Heath. On stepping down from the editorship when Rupert Murdoch bought *The Times*, he won appointment to a number of public bodies and became a firm advocate of the Thatcher government's monetarist economic policy.

Rees-Mogg was educated at Charterhouse and Oxford. He had thoughts about a career in politics, and stood as a Conservative candidate in a safe Labour seat, but decided to concentrate on journalism, working for the *Financial Times* and the *Sunday Times* before joining *The Times*. He was one of the last national newspaper editors to see his role as setting a mood in which good work could be done, rather than being involved personally in all editorial processes. Under him, the circulation of *The Times* initially rose above 440,000 but then declined to below 300,000. However, it remained influential, especially among Conservatives. Rees-Mogg supported the management in closing the paper from November 1978 to November 1979 to persuade the print unions to agree to less extravagant production methods. The failure of the tactic led to the paper's sale and Rees-Mogg's resignation.

His first major appointment after *The Times* was as vice-chairman of the BBC, where he angered programme-makers by seeking to assert the governors' right to suppress programmes they thought unsuitable. From 1982 to 1989 he was chairman of the Arts Council, where a reduction in government subsidies meant that he had to perform the unpopular task of trimming back grants to struggling theatre and music companies. In 1988 he was appointed the first chairman of the Broadcasting Standards Council, aimed at driving excessive sex and violence from television screens; he was also created a life peer. He writes an idiosyncratic weekly article in *The Independent*.

MICHAEL H. LEAPMAN

Reith, Sir **John (Charles Walsham)** [Baron Reith of Stonehaven] (*b.* Stonehaven, Kincardine, 20 July 1889; *d.* Edinburgh, 16 June 1971). Architect of the BBC and public servant. The name of Reith remains firmly linked with the early years of broadcasting in Britain. In December 1922 he was appointed the general manager of the British Broadcasting Company and began his 'great work', and on its establishment in January 1927 he became the first director-general of the BBC. He left in June 1938, having been urged by the Prime Minister to accept the chairmanship of Imperial Airways: his hope that he might become a governor of the BBC was disappointed. At the time of his departure there was a strong feeling in many quarters that he had been in complete charge for long enough.

Reith was the son of a Scottish father and an English mother. Whether in life, on the battlefield, or in the battlefield of life, he wrestled to apply the standards and principles he had learnt in the Glaswegian manse of his father, a leading but not wealthy United Free Church minister. The young Reith was awkward and self-absorbed both at Glasgow Academy and at Gresham's School, Holt. He was early blessed with the conviction that he was to do something considerable in the world. An engineering apprenticeship with the North British Locomotive Company in Glasgow was the perhaps unpromising starting point. By 1914 Reith had reached London and was working on the Royal Albert Dock Extension. Then came the war. He served as a regimental soldier from August 1914 until October 1915 but was then severely wounded. His great powers of organization and

improvisation were displayed as Transport Officer but so also were his obstinacy and arrogance. He then went to the USA between March 1916 and August 1917 in charge of a rifle factory, and ended the war in Sussex working on a scheme to construct a submarine barrage in the Channel.

Intermittently throughout this challenging period, Reith's mind returned to the possibility of becoming a cabinet minister. Believing that a 'Gladstone–Cromwell' combination was much needed in British politics, he was convinced that he could fit the bill. However, it was not easy to relate this prescription to the actual structure of politics at the time, and from March 1920 until the autumn of 1922 Reith successfully managed a factory in Coatbridge. He was then determined to try his luck in London, and after a few months working as a political secretary to a group of London Unionist MPs he applied for and obtained the job with the new broadcasting company. He knew little about broadcasting – nobody knew about it – but his strong physical presence, dominating personality and engineering background carried the day. In the early years he battled both to establish the independence of broadcasting in relation to government, the press and the wireless industry on the one hand, and on the other to set up a fully national coverage with a strong central direction over the regions. He worked unremittingly to create a service which was educative and elevating and not merely entertaining. Early on, however, it became evident that the power of the new medium raised fundamental issues concerning access and control. The role of the BBC during the 1926 General Strike was an important case in point. Reith found himself being jostled between opposing sets of politicians as he sought to maintain a certain detachment and impartiality. Labour felt that Reith had been too obsequious before Baldwin, but Churchill was furious at his refusal simply to broadcast government propaganda. Battles of a different but related character continued after 1927 between Reith and some of the governors of the corporation under its new charter. The new director-general had himself played a major part in establishing the 'public service' concept, funded by licence fee, which became charac-

Sir John Reith speaking at the National Conference for Wireless Group Leaders at the London School of Economics, January 1932

teristic of the British system, as compared, for example, with the commercial plurality in the USA. There were pressures from Parliament, the press and certain querulous governors which Reith deemed it his duty to resist. The rapid expansion of the BBC owed much to Reith's drive and determination, but within and beyond the new Broadcasting House there was criticism of his autocratic style. From time to time in the mid-1930s, particularly when he had bouts of ill-health, Reith wanted some new mountain to climb, though his actual departure proved extremely wounding, as was perhaps inevitable. He seems not to have supposed that his successor would have found his presence on the board in any way inhibiting. He also thought that the restructuring of Imperial Airways was a challenge of insufficient magnitude.

Reith believed after 1939 that the war offered him the chance to put his talents at the disposal of the nation. Chamberlain somewhat reluctantly made him Minister of Information in January 1940, again a post which disap-

pointed but which might lead to greater things. Under Churchill, however, his prospects were not good. The two men simply did not get on. Reith was Minister of Transport from May to October 1940 and of Works from October 1940 until February 1942, when he was dismissed. He was bitter at this outcome, felt himself unjustly treated and loathed Churchill's 'rotten gang'. For the remainder of the war Reith worked modestly but effectively in the Admiralty. He never held political office again, but for 15 years after the war found imperial roles which suited his imperious disposition, particularly as chairman of the Colonial Development corporation from 1950 to 1959. In the 1960s Scottish honours came his way – Lord Rector of Glasgow University, Lord High Commissioner to the General Assembly of the Church of Scotland – and these posts restored to some degree a sense of well-being to a life which finally fruited where it had begun. Even so, despite his pioneering work at the BBC, Reith had thrust the goal of greatness upon himself and could not disabuse himself of the notion that lesser men had succeeded.

WRITINGS

Into the Wind (London: Hodder and Stoughton, 1949).
Wearing Spurs (London: Hutchinson, 1966).

FURTHER READING

Boyle, A., *Only the Wind Will Listen* (London: Hutchinson, 1972).
Stuart, C. (ed.), *The Reith Diaries* (London: Collins, 1975).

KEITH ROBBINS

Robbins, Lionel (Charles) [Baron Robbins of Clare Market] (*b*. Sipson, Middlesex, 22 November 1898; *d*. London, 15 May 1984). Economist and public servant. He had a long and distinguished academic career, notably as Professor of Economics at the London School of Economics from 1929 to 1961. Robbins played an important part in introducing professional economic advice into the machinery of government. He was latterly an eminent public man, one of the great and the good, and his name became synonymous with the expansion of British higher education in the 1960s.

Robbins did not undergo a conventional academic education. The son of a farmer, he left the Southall County High School to serve in the Royal Field Artillery as a subaltern (1916–19). On demobilization he threw himself into the guild socialist movement; soon disillusioned, his politics moved steadily towards the right. Only in 1920 did he enter the LSE as a student, gaining first class honours in 1923. The two teachers with whom he established the closest rapport were the neoclassical economist Edwin Cannan and the rising Labour politician Hugh Dalton. It was Dalton who was instrumental in smoothing Robbins's path to an academic career, initially bringing him back from Oxford to the LSE as a lecturer in 1925 and repeating the manoeuvre by securing Robbins's return from his fellowship at New College, Oxford, to the LSE chair in 1929 – a striking appointment.

The young Robbins, moreover, was invited through Keynes to serve as one of the five members of the committee of economists of the newly instituted Economic Advisory Council in 1930. The composition of its report left Robbins in an isolated position, especially in his steadfast refusal to countenance tariffs as a possible expedient. He emerged as a courageous defender of the free market, even when faced with an unprecedented slump, and from 1931 was reinforced in his doctrinaire approach by his colleague F. A. von Hayek. Together they made LSE into a counterweight against Cambridge economics. Robbins's own analysis is lucidly explained in his book *The Great Depression* (1934), which argued that too much investment had been the root of a problem which the market alone – given time – could solve; state intervention merely impeded this process. Robbins lived to make a handsome retraction of his disparagement of reflationary policies, while reaffirming the validity of his defence of free trade – both upheld at the time in the face of Keynes's opposition.

The reconciliation between him and Keynes dated from World War II, when Robbins served as Director of the Economic Section of the War Cabinet (1941–5). It was a post for which his subtle diplomatic gifts, as well as his robust intellectual grasp, well suited him; and he succeeded in gaining the ear of important ministers and civil servants, especially through the Lord President's Committee. Robbins was not, however, to be tempted permanently from the LSE, to which he gave his first loyalties, and he returned after the war, the effective head of a formidable department. His own scholarly work showed a mastery of the history of economic thought, with *The Theory of Economic Policy in English Classical Political Economy* (1952), perhaps his finest book. He lavished his time also upon the administration of the arts, with notable service to the National Gallery, the Tate Gallery and the Royal Opera House; he became one of the first life peers, in 1959; and he finally gave up his academic chair to become chairman of the *Financial Times* (1961–70). His appointment as chairman of the Committee on Higher Education (1961–4) converted him into a well-briefed advocate of expansion. The principle which the Robbins Report enunciated – that places should be made available for all suitably qualified school-leavers – became the basis on which new universities and polytechnics were founded in the 1960s. Little wonder that it rained honorary degrees in Robbins's retirement.

WRITINGS

The Autobiography of an Economist (London: Macmillan, 1971).

P. F. CLARKE

Robens, Alfred [Lord Robens of Woldingham] (*b.* Manchester, 18 December 1910). Labour minister and businessman. He was briefly Minister of Power in the second Attlee Government and a member of Labour's leading circle in opposition throughout the 1950s, but he left politics in 1960 to head the National Coal Board. Robens had entered Parliament in Labour's 1945 landslide election victory, after ten years as an official of the shopworkers' union and three as a Manchester city councillor. In October 1947 he became Hugh Gaitskell's Parliamentary Secretary at the Ministry of Fuel and Power, thus beginning a long and close political association with Labour's future leader. He also became, with George Brown, Barbara Castle, Anthony Crosland and others, one of the group of able young Labour politicians to whom Hugh Dalton acted as mentor. Identified firmly with the right wing of his party, Robens thus had three overlapping sources of support: the trade-union bloc of Labour MPs, the followers of Dalton and Gaitskell's associates. He developed into one of the sharpest critics of Labour's 'Bevanite' left, and on Aneurin Bevan's resignation in April 1951 he took over as Minister of Power.

As the question of Attlee's retirement became urgent, some talked of Robens as a likely future leader of the Labour Party. Dalton frequently pressed his claims, as his diaries record. Yet he was by general judgement not a success as Shadow Foreign Secretary in 1955–6, his performance during the Suez Crisis being especially harshly judged by the press and his colleagues. He stood down voluntarily,

to be replaced ironically by Bevan. In 1960, apparently despairing of ever again holding office after Labour's third successive election defeat, he decided to abandon his political career, and assumed the chairmanship of the National Coal Board. While he also gathered a wide range of directorships elsewhere, he served for a decade at the NCB, where he fostered close links with the miners' union and became the leading exponent of a consensual management style and of a major trade-union role in decision-making for the public sector. This approach was sharply to be repudiated by NCB chairmen after 1979. Robens was created a life peer in 1961.

WRITINGS

Ten Year Stint (London: Cassell, 1972).

FURTHER READING

Pimlott, B. (ed.), *The Political Diary of Hugh Dalton 1918–40, 1945–6* (London: Jonathan Cape, 1987).
Williams, P. M., *Hugh Gaitskell* (London: Jonathan Cape, 1979).

STEPHEN HOWE

Robertson, Sir William (Robert) ('Wully') (*b.* Welbourn, Lincolnshire, 29 January 1860; *d.* London, 12 February 1933). General, and military opponent to Lloyd George. The only British soldier ever to have risen from the lowest army rank to the highest, he was Chief of the Imperial General Staff (CIGS) from December 1915 to February 1918, at a time when British civil–military relations were under particular strain. Before taking office as the professional head of the army, Robertson had been Haig's Chief of Staff in the British Expeditionary Force (BEF) in France. While CIGS he strongly supported Haig and came into conflict with Lloyd George, who criticized the strategy of attrition adopted on the Western Front. Although Lloyd George was not able to remove Haig, his manoeuvrings forced Robertson to resign and the outcome of this conflict was a partial confirmation of the British constitutional principle of civil supremacy over the military arm of government.

Robertson came from a modest family – his father was a village shopkeeper – with no army tradition. He served in the ranks for ten years before in 1887 he gained a commission in the 3rd Dragoon Guards. Apart from some regimental soldiering as a junior officer in India, and a spell in high command at the end of his career, most of Robertson's service was spent in staff appointments. His first major job was as Commandant of the Staff College from 1910 to 1913. In 1913 – by now Sir William – Robertson was appointed Director of Military Training in the War Office, responsible not only for training and military education, but also for home defence. During the Curragh Incident in the spring of 1914 Robertson was given the unwanted task of managing any large-scale operations which might be conducted in Ulster against the Unionists. The impact of the crisis certainly demonstrated the extent to which 'politics' could intrude upon the army. In his memoirs, *From Private to Field Marshal*, Robertson claimed that he counselled colleagues against resigning and urged them to ignore the fuss and 'get on with their work', since 'in the long run any intention there might be of employing troops against Ulstermen would be abandoned.' Yet Robertson himself took steps to ensure that result by raising a large number of practical obstacles to the deployment of troops in Ireland. He also wrote an uncritical letter of support to one of the leaders of the 'mutiny', John Gough. Robertson's opposition to the use of troops to suppress Unionist resistance to government policy was subtle and bureaucratic, and was clearly more effective (and personally less damaging) than the wilder conduct of his fellow War Office Director, Sir HENRY WILSON.

In August 1914 Robertson went to France on the staff of the BEF. He and Sir Douglas Haig became concerned that the commander of the BEF, Sir John French, was not up to the job and they made no secret of their worry, especially to the War Minister (Kitchener) and to King George V, with whom Robertson had enjoyed a warm friendship since well before the war. French was replaced by Haig at the end of 1915, and at the same time Robertson was brought home to become CIGS. Kitchener, Haig and Robertson enjoyed great public esteem which placed them in a very strong position *vis-à-vis* any politicians who tried to alter, or even influence, military policy (see also HAIG, DOUGLAS, and KITCHENER, LORD). To a very great extent the contest between soldiers and politicians emerged as a dispute over strategy. The 'Westerners', including Haig and Robertson, believed that the war could only be won by devoting the country's full resources to direct assaults on the German forces in France and Flanders, while the 'Easterners', including Lloyd George, were horrified by the 'mincing machine' of static trench warfare and hoped to find some alternative route to victory.

Relations between the government and the leading soldiers deteriorated after Lloyd George became Prime Minister in December 1916. He had a low opinion of Robertson's abilities, describing him as having only 'the brains of a superior clerk'. Anxious to improve allied cooperation, during 1917 Lloyd George worked towards the establishment of an inter-allied council, to which, moreover, he could appoint his own men and which he could perhaps use as a means of bypassing Robertson and Haig. Robertson equally appreciated this point and objected (in vain) to the establishment of the Supreme War Council (SWC) in November 1917. The politicians' intention, he asserted in his memoirs, 'was not so much to provide effective unity of military command, as to acquire for themselves a greater control over the military chiefs.' How right he was. When Lloyd George supported the expansion of the SWC's functions with the creation of an 'Executive War Board', on which the British representative would not be Robertson but Sir Henry Wilson, the CIGS refused to work under the new arrangement and he resigned. He was replaced by Wilson.

Robertson served out his active career in a number of comparatively unimportant posts at home and as Commander of the British Army of the Rhine after the Armistice. While serving in Germany Robertson nursed hopes, initially encouraged by the Secretary for War, Winston Churchill, of taking over the Irish Command. But here he was disappointed. Lloyd George refused to appoint him to a job which above all others in the British army of the time required political finesse. As in February 1918, Lloyd

George was again able to override War Office opinion and secure an important military command for his own candidate, in this case Sir Nevil Macready.

In many ways Sir William Robertson was an archetypal soldier. Among his virtues were loyalty, steadfastness and a reluctance to express himself hastily. These, of course, were completely antithetical to Lloyd George. Like Haig (and the King), Robertson had apparently complete faith in the rightness of the British case and the correctness of the military tactics adopted on the Western Front. His mistake was to regard these truths as self-evident. Notoriously gruff and quiet, he relied too much on the right of the accused to remain silent, with the result that Lloyd George and his associates pronounced him guilty unheard. Robertson, too, represented an old-fashioned style of military command, where politicians left the business of war entirely in the hands of soldiers. In the changed circumstances of mass mobilization and 'total' war, he failed to appreciate the growing need for popular leaders, such as Lloyd George, to take a major share in the running of warfare.

WRITINGS

From Private to Field Marshal (London: Constable, 1921).

Soldiers and Statesmen, 1914–1918 (London: Cassell, 1926).

FURTHER READING

Beckett, Ian F. W. (ed.), *The Army and the Curragh Incident, 1914* (London: Army Records Society/Bodley Head, 1986).

Bonham-Carter, Victor, *Soldier True: the Life and Times of Sir William Robertson, 1860–1933* (London: Muller, 1963).

Woodward, David R., *Lloyd George and the Generals* (Newark, NJ: University of Delaware Press/London: Associated University Presses, 1983).

KEITH JEFFERY

Rowntree, (Benjamin) Seebohm (*b.* York, 7 July 1871; *d.* High Wycombe, Buckinghamshire, 7 October 1954). Manufacturer, philanthropist and social investigator. He developed the practice of 'scientific management' and took a lifelong interest in social problems, helping to pioneer methods of social investigation and publishing influential surveys of social conditions. Despite service on various official bodies, he retained a low public profile, and his contribution to the evolution of social policy and practice was exercised primarily by example and advice.

The third child of Joseph Rowntree and Emma Antoinette Seebohm, Rowntree entered the family cocoa-manufacturing firm in York in 1889 after being educated at Bootham School, York, and Owens College, Manchester. He was made a director in 1897, when the firm became a limited liability company, and was chairman from 1923 to 1941.

Rowntree's long business career established one of his two main areas of achievement: industrial management. Sensitive to the family Quaker tradition, cherished by his father, of obligation towards the workforce, he was the first labour director of the firm. He was personally accessible to employees, and presided over the introduction of various welfare measures: an eight-hour day – without reduction in wages – in 1896; a works doctor in 1904, followed soon afterwards by a dental service; a retirement pension in 1906, extended in 1917 to widows' benefit; works councils and a 44-hour, five-day week in 1919; a supplementary insurance scheme in 1921; a psychological department in 1922; and a profit-sharing scheme in 1923. Special attention was also given to the needs of women employees and to educational and recreational facilities.

Rowntree encouraged the adoption of these practices in munitions factories while director of the Welfare Department of the Ministry of Munitions between 1915 and 1918. He was a member of the Reconstruction Committee in 1917 and was involved in the founding of the Industrial Welfare Society in 1918 and of the National Institute of Industrial Psychology in 1921, serving on its executive committee until 1949 and as chairman from 1940 to 1947. He helped to establish the Oxford Conferences of Employers, Managers and Foremen in 1920 and the Management Research Groups in 1927. In 1936 he became a trustee of the Nuffield Fund for Special Areas. Rowntree

361

developed his ideas on management in various publications, notably *The Human Needs of Labour* (1918, rev. edn 1937) and *The Human Factor in Business* (1921). His contribution to management was recognized when he became an Honorary Fellow of the British Institute of Management in 1952. He was also president of the Outward Bound Trust and the War on Want Committee and chairman of the Nuffield Committee on Old Age.

Rowntree argued that good management contributed to business efficiency and success. His ideas were influential in Britain and the USA, and his position as the doyen of 'scientific management' is secure – although his practices were neither entirely new nor unique, and, despite their emphasis on benevolence and participation, retained elements of discipline and paternalism.

Rowntree's other main concern and source of reputation was his interest in and investigation of wider social questions: poverty, unemployment, old age, housing. His *Poverty: a Study of Town Life* (1901), based on York, became a classic text. A second survey of York was conducted in 1936 (published as *Poverty and Progress* in 1941); and in 1951 he wrote, with G. R. Lavers, *Poverty and the Welfare State*, a third study of York, and *English Life and Leisure*. Rowntree also investigated rural conditions. He published *Land and Labour: Lessons from Belgium* (1911) and, with May Kendall, *How the Labourer Lives: a Study of the Rural Labour Problem* (1911). In the 1930s the findings of various agricultural inquiries, with Viscount Astor, appeared.

Rowntree's investigative methods represented an advance on earlier techniques, and in the 1901 survey the direct questioning, the distinction between primary and secondary poverty and concept of a life-cycle of poverty broke new ground and made for greater precision. But the survey was also partly impressionistic and arbitrary; and *English Life and Leisure*, if interesting, was highly subjective.

Rowntree's work did, however, help to shape attitudes and social policies. It exposed the limitations of voluntarism in dealing with poverty and strengthened the case for state intervention; and, in that sense, the surveys of 1901 and 1941 contributed to the social legislation of the periods after 1906 and 1945. Yet Rowntree was also much concerned with personal and moral issues, such as gambling and drink, and, distrustful of socialism, he remained a Liberal throughout his life.

Rowntree was predeceased in 1944 by his wife, Lydia, whom he married in 1897; there were four sons and a daughter. He was personally reserved and unostentatious: he became a CH in 1931, but was indifferent to honours. His advice was often sought by official bodies and he served on several; but his style was better suited to an environment which he himself could control than to public or political life.

FURTHER READING

Briggs, A., *A Study of the Work of Seebohm Rowntree, 1871–1954* (London: Longmans, 1961).

Fitzgerald, R., *British Labour Management and Industrial Welfare 1846–1939* (London: Croom Helm, 1988).

Williams, K., *From Pauperism to Poverty* (London: Routledge and Kegan Paul, 1981).

GEOFFREY B. A. M. FINLAYSON

Runcie, Robert (Alexander Kennedy) (*b.* Crosby, Lancashire, 21 October 1921). Archbishop of Canterbury. He has been a critical commentator on government policy during the Thatcher years and was the inspirer of Terry Waite's roving missions.

Runcie became Archbishop in March 1980. He was educated at Merchant Taylor's School, Crosby; Brasenose College, Oxford; and Westcott House Theological College, Cambridge. His university education was interrupted by war service (1942–6), during which he won the Military Cross and gained a breadth of experience generally denied to earlier generations of church leaders. In common with many other Anglicans of his generation, he was also influenced by such leading churchmen as William Temple. The net result was a set of moderate socially critical attitudes that were shared by many recruited, from the 1960s onwards, into the Anglican episcopate.

Runcie entered the priesthood in 1951 but, apart from a curacy in Gosforth (1950–2), he was not directly involved in parochial ministry. From 1952 to 1956 he was at Westcott House, first as Chaplain and subsequently as Vice Principal. In 1956 he became Dean of Trinity Hall, Cambridge, and, in 1960, Principal of Cuddesdon Theological College. From the latter he moved, in 1970, to become Bishop of St Albans prior to his final translation to Canterbury.

As teacher and bishop Runcie developed a particular interest in relationships between the Anglican and Orthodox Churches. Such ecumenical and international concerns have especially characterized his period as Archbishop. Thus, in 1982, he welcomed Pope John Paul II to Canterbury in celebrations without any post-Reformation precedent. In 1989 this was followed up by an official visit to the Vatican and a controversial indication that Anglicans might accept a redefined Papacy at the head of a reunited Church. Also, as part of a general attempt to provide himself with a more effective staff and so more fully to realize the potentialities of his office, he appointed Terry Waite (a Church Army Officer) as special counsellor for Anglican affairs. The latter, as the Archbishop's roving ambassador, became particularly famous for attempts to secure the release of Western hostages held in the Middle East. Successful missions in Iran and Libya were preludes to Waite's own capture (1987) in Lebanon. Despite this outcome the Archbishop's emissary demonstrated a previously unacknowledged capacity for international action at points where conventional diplomacy had failed.

Similar international concerns were evident in a service held in St Paul's Cathedral (1982) to celebrate the conclusion of the Falklands War. The Church's refusal to make the service simply a celebration of national victory earned Runcie the displeasure of parts of the governing Conservative Party. The priority given by the Church to Anglo-Argentinian reconciliation clashed with some traditional nationalist responses.

Conflict with Mrs Thatcher's government has in fact been a recurring feature of Runcie's primacy. Given that many Anglican activists wish to maintain the Church of England's traditional alliance with the Conservative Party,

this conflict has involved friction within the Church itself. The erosion of the post-1945 political consensus, the general preference of modern episcopal leaders for that consensus and the absence of an obviously strong party political opposition frequently impelled the Church's official spokesmen to assume the role of governmental critic. Clashes occurred over the miners' strike (1984–5), housing, local government reform, tax and social security policy, immigration, overseas aid and Southern Africa. The report *Faith in the City*, personally commissioned by the Archbishop and critical of the impact of free market policies upon 'the inner city', was a particular source of conflict. Further official opprobrium was attracted in 1989 by the Archbishop's well publicized comments upon 'pharisaical' attitudes towards the poor and unsuccessful in contemporary British society.

Controversy has also surrounded the Archbishop's handling of ecclesiastical affairs. He has sought to innovate on the basis of consensus and to develop a more collegiate form of episcopal leadership. This has led spokesmen for the Church's Evangelical and Catholic wings to complain of an undue inclination towards theological liberalism. Particularly on the matter of allowing the ordination of women, radicals have complained of unnecessary indecision. Such disputes underline the difficulty of leading a theologically heterogeneous Church in an era of rapid change.

FURTHER READING

Duggan, M., *Runcie: the Making of an Archbishop* (London: Hodder and Stoughton, 1985).
Medhurst, K. N. and Moyser, G. H., *The Church and Politics in a Secular Age* (Oxford: Clarendon Press, 1988).

K. N. MEDHURST

Russell, Bertrand (Arthur William) [Earl Russell] (*b*. Tintern, Monmouthshire, 18 May 1872; *d*. Penrhyndeudraeth, Merionethshire, 2 February 1970). Philosopher, social reformer and peace campaigner. His historical importance derives principally from his stature as philosopher. However, given his pedigree and connections (he was grandson of the mid-

Victorian Whig premier Lord John Russell, and godson 'in a secular sense' of J. S. Mill), it is not surprising that he exploited his scholarly renown to promote a diversity of radical causes through more than 70 years of public life. He was aided by remarkable gifts as a stylish communicator and popularizer of ideas – qualities exemplified by his impish best-seller of 1945, *A History of Western Philosophy*, and his inaugural series of BBC Reith Lectures (1948–9) on *Authority and the Individual*. Throughout his career he managed to stir controversy on every side: Trotsky abused him as a 'moth-eaten old aristocrat', while conservatives stereotyped Russell even more simply as a leftist crank. Despite all his notoriety as a scourge of the establishment, he went to the grave laden with honours. Among them were Fellowship of the Royal Society (1908), the Order of Merit (1949) and the Nobel Prize for Literature (1950).

Having been schooled at home by private tutors, Russell entered Trinity College, Cambridge, in 1890. Five years later he was made lecturer. Over the following two decades or so of outstanding intellectual fertility he won a major international reputation for philosophical work, especially on mathematical and symbolic logic and on epistemology in the analytic tradition. Contacts with G. E. Moore and A. N. Whitehead, and latterly with Ludwig Wittgenstein, helped stimulate a corpus of truly seminal writings. These included a book on Leibniz (1900), the *Principia Mathematica* (with Whitehead, 3 volumes, 1910–13) and *The Analysis of Mind* (1921). However, political interests were also increasingly apparent. Russell's very first book had been a survey of *German Social Democracy* (1896), and in 1907 he had stood unsuccessfully at a parliamentary by-election with some Liberal support as a champion of female suffrage. Such public concerns were intensified by the Great War. The reckless vigour of his campaigning (especially with the No-Conscription Fellowship) against the futility of the conflict led him to be first fined, then dismissed from Trinity and denied a passport, and eventually condemned to six months in Brixton gaol for insulting the USA as Britain's ally. Similar anxieties over issues of war and peace would become the principal preoccupation of his later years.

Meanwhile, Russell had outlined his prescriptions (loosely, guild-socialist) for the postwar order in *The Principles of Social Reconstruction* (1916). In 1922–3 he made token attempts to implement these by standing as Labour parliamentary candidate at Chelsea. Thereafter he exercised his influence, and earned most of his living, through his prolific pen. His 'progressive' ideas on how to nurture the young, for example, led him to publish *On Education* (1926) and *Education and the Social Order* (1932), and also to attempt running Beacon Hill School with Dora, the second of his four wives. Critics condemned his libertarian and anti-Christian views on sex as well as education. There was much cheap comment that his increasingly tangled marital and extra-marital adventures made him a dubious guide to topics such as *Marriage and Morals* and *The Conquest of Happiness*, on which he published widely read books in 1929–30. If, in the late twentieth century, Russell's early support for such features of our more 'permissive' society as sex education in schools, pre-marital intercourse, and public backing for contraception seem scarcely controversial, that change of mood itself owes something to advocates such

Bertrand Russell, 1953

as he. On a more directly political front, his *Practice and Theory of Bolshevism* (1920) made plain his refusal to follow the Marxist-Soviet road to socialism; and works of the following decade, such as *Freedom and Organization* (1934) and *Power* (1938), reflected growing fears about Fascist authoritarianism too.

Russell, a sponsor of the Peace Pledge Union, was initially inclined to appease Hitler and indeed to have Britain unconditionally disarmed. By 1939, however, he conceded that civilized values would suffer even more gravely if they were not forcibly defended against Nazi tyranny. Thus he endowed the second war with a validity refused to the first. After the defeat of Germany and Japan he actually advocated that the USA should risk further conflict by quickly using its otherwise transitory monopoly of nuclear weapons in order to compel Soviet subservience as well. Once the USSR had its own atomic bomb, Russell accepted that the terms of the problem were altered and that a more conciliatory approach was prudent. As he reiterated in his typically unsolicited and haughty messages to world leaders, reciprocal nuclear warfare had now to be tackled (preferably by some form of 'world government') as an imminent peril to all civilization. Henceforth Russell argued not only against the spread of atomic weapons but also for a balanced programme of nuclear disarmament and a ban on testing by the two superpowers. Thus he deplored the development of a British arsenal, and in 1958 became the first president of the Campaign for Nuclear Disarmament – something to be sought, if necessary, on a unilateralist basis. Two years later he resigned to form the Committee of 100, which pursued the same ends through the dramatic and media-orientated tactic of civil disobedience. Press and television pictures of the ancient philosopher leading 'sit-down' protests were soon embedded in the folk memory. In 1961, after his arrest for inciting participation in such a demonstration outside Parliament, worldwide publicity was given to the cause of a man condemned to spend a week of his ninetieth year once again behind bars at Brixton.

After 1963 he channelled his remaining energies into the new Bertrand Russell Peace Foundation. He had now concluded that the greatest danger of war stemmed from the policies pursued (with British backing) by successive US governments. Russell's foundation was soon sponsoring the Stockholm Tribunal of intellectuals who declared the Americans guilty of war crimes in Vietnam. This rather bizarre episode did occasion some palpable hits against the USA, but the impact was lessened by the silliness of Russell's converse romanticization of the Vietcong. During much of the 1960s it was hard to disentangle his own views from those of Ralph Schoenman, the secretary and spokesman whom the philosopher only belatedly repudiated. However, none could doubt that by the end of his life Russell had proved himself to be, over many years and on an international scale, perhaps the most distinguished intellectual within the ranks of those determined to heighten public awareness of the horrors attaching to the threat of global thermonuclear warfare.

WRITINGS

The Autobiography of Bertrand Russell, 3 vols. (London: Allen and Unwin, 1967–9).

FURTHER READING

Clark, R., *The Life of Bertrand Russell* (London: Weidenfeld and Nicolson, 1975).
Ryan, A., *Bertrand Russell: a Political Life* (London: Allen Lane, 1988).

MICHAEL BIDDISS

S

Samuel, Herbert (Louis) [Viscount Samuel of Mount Carmel and Toxteth] (*b.* Liverpool, 6 November 1870; *d.* London, 5 February 1963). Liberal minister, party chairman and diplomat. After holding minor office from 1905, he served as Postmaster General (1910–14, 1915–16), President of the Local Government Board (1914–15), and Home Secretary (until December 1916). From 1920 to 1925 he was British High Commissioner in Palestine. Subsequently, he became Chairman of the Liberal Party and Home Secretary in the National Government between 1931 and 1932. His political career ended in the House of Lords. He was an intellectual, fairminded man of considerable administrative skill and humanity, but he lacked personal dynamism.

A member of a politically conscious Jewish banking family, Samuel set his sights on a parliamentary career as a result of his experiences during the London dock strike of 1889. He was a political activist during his years at Balliol (1889–93) and contested his first parliamentary election in 1895. Of independent means, he worked for various radical and Liberal organizations. He was a member of the Rainbow Circle, dined frequently with Beatrice and Sidney Webb, and was one of the young radicals responsible for developing the 'New Liberalism'. He was defeated in the 1900 general election but two years later won the Cleveland by-election. As Under-Secretary of State at the Home Office from 1905 to 1909 Samuel helped establish the probation system and made his own contribution to the Liberals' welfare programme in the form of the Children Act of 1908. In 1909 he entered the cabinet as Chancellor of the Duchy of Lancaster, and further confirmed his administrative skills as Postmaster General from 1910 to 1914. After a short spell as President of the Local Government Board he returned briefly to the Post Office, before becoming Home Secretary in the Asquith Coalition Government. He refused to continue in this office, however, when Lloyd George replaced Asquith as Prime Minister in 1916. In the general election of 1918 Samuel was beaten by a Coalition Conservative. He then spent some time as Special Commissioner to Belgium before going to Palestine as High Commissioner in 1920.

It was the strategic importance of Palestine that had first roused Samuel's interest in 1914. Although he had renounced Judaism during his university days he remained attached to the Jewish community and gave the Zionist movement great help. His Palestinian administration was marked not only by its modernity and integrity, but also by his skilful handling of the region's numerous religious and political factions.

Perhaps for this reason he was asked in 1925 to head a royal commission on the British coal industry. Although he had intended to retire to pursue his intellectual interests – he was the author of numerous philosophical works and later became President of the British Institute for Philosophic Studies – Samuel did not feel able to refuse. The commission failed to prevent a general strike in 1926 but Samuel himself was instrumental in paving the way for its speedy conclusion. This further proof of his conciliatory powers, combined with his long absence from domestic politics, made him the obvious choice as party chairman when the warring factions of the Liberal Party tried to come together in 1926. He did much to rejuvenate the Liberals' organization and programme but could neither disarm distrust of Lloyd George, nor turn the party's electoral fortunes. He was himself elected as member for Darwen in 1929 and subsequently became Home Secretary in the National Government. As a Liberal, however, he could not agree with the protectionist policies on which Baldwin subsequently embarked. In 1932 Samuel resigned. He lost his seat in 1935, and accepted a viscountcy in 1937. This was the effective end of his political career, although he lived on until 1963, outlasting his wife by four years and leaving four children.

WRITINGS

Memoirs (London: Cresset Press, 1945).

FURTHER READING

Bowle, J., *Viscount Samuel: a Biography* (London: Gollancz, 1957).

KENNETH D. BROWN

Scarfe, Gerald (*b*. London, 1 June 1936). Cartoonist and caricaturist. Gerald Scarfe's work is instantly recognizable. From the mid-1960s he has built a reputation as a key satirist and cartoonist who deals incisively with world events and leading political figures by making grotesque drawings and caricatures of them. He has worked for *Punch*, *Private Eye*, the *Daily Mail*, the *Sunday Times* and as cover artist for *Time*. The author and art critic John Berger once described him as 'a natural satirical draughtsman' in the tradition of Gillray and George Grosz. He has had major one-man exhibitions of sculptures and lithographs all over the world and his extraordinary versatility has taken him into the fields of animation, theatre design and television film direction.

Bed-ridden as a child with chronic asthma, Scarfe used drawing as a means of coping with his fears. His first published drawing appeared in *The Eagle*, where it won first prize. (A certain David Hockney of Bradford was a runner-up.) Virtually self-taught, his first cartoon drawings were initially, by editorial decree, conventional 'funnies'; his violent political work gained prominence only later when he joined *Private Eye*. Discovering that he could make social comment through his drawings was the breakthrough and his career gathered momentum. In 1967 he joined the *Sunday Times*.

Scarfe's method of caricature is to start with the eyeball and to build up the drawing from that – stretching the face to see how far it will go before becoming unrecognizable. He aims to distil the essence of the person, above all to establish a symbol that represents that person.

Not wishing to be type-cast, Scarfe has always striven to develop his style and technique. Some recent activities – the writing and directing of the animated sequences in the film *Pink Floyd The Wall* (1982) and the designs for *Orpheus in the Underworld* for the English National Opera (1985) – have won him much acclaim, serving to remind us that he has always been more than a political cartoonist.

WRITINGS

Scarfe by Scarfe: an Autobiography in Pictures (London: Hamish Hamilton, 1986).

LIZ OTTAWAY

Scargill, Arthur (*b*. Barnsley, Yorkshire, 11 January 1938). Trade-union leader. As President of the National Union of Mineworkers from 1982, he led the longest major strike of the twentieth century in Britain, in 1984. In the 1970s and 1980s he was the most prominent industrial spokesman for the policy of using industrial action for political ends and refusing compromise – what he called 'collaboration' – between unions and a Conservative government.

A product and a force in the radicalization of the moderate Yorkshire coalfield in the 1960s, encouraged by the influx of communist miners from Scotland, Scargill had followed his father down the pit at the age of 16 and into the communist party at 17. He joined the Labour Party in 1966.

He made his name as a leader of flying pickets at the Saltley coke depot in Birmingham in the 1972 strike, when hundreds of local engineering workers marched to join miners and shut the gates. Scargill described it as the moment when 'everything I have always believed in and idolised crystallised'. He saw it as the blueprint for effecting political change.

Scargill became president of the union's Yorkshire area in 1973, and was critical of the national wage settlements, particularly under the Social Contract with the Labour Party. By the time he became president of the union in 1982 his support for picketing in other disputes, as at the Grunwick film-processing plant or in support of the health workers, and his stand against further legal restraints on the unions had made him a national figure. After two unsuccessful ballots on strike action, acceleration of pit closures by Sir IAN MAC-GREGOR allowed him to manoeuvre the union into a strike without a ballot. It lasted eleven months, polarizing the country and the Labour Party and splitting the union. Scargill's intransigence and refusal to condemn his members' violence prolonged it, infuriating Labour's leadership, and led to defeat. But Scargill remained uncompromising, and was re-elected in 1988.

FURTHER READING

Adeney, Martin and Lloyd, John, *The Miners' Strike: Loss Without Limit* (London: Routledge, 1986).
Crick, Michael, *Scargill and the Miners* (Harmondsworth: Penguin, 1985).

MARTIN ADENEY

Scarman, Leslie (George) [Lord Scarman of Quatt] (*b.* London, 29 July 1911). Judge, law reformer and social critic. Although a distinguished judge, he made his major impact by his vigorous promotion of law reform and his examination and analysis of the causes of social troubles and disturbances.

Scarman was called to the Bar in 1936 and, after war service, took silk in 1957. He was made a judge of the High Court in 1961 but really came to public notice when selected in 1965 to be the first chairman of the Law Commission, set up under the Law Commissions Act of that year as a standing body to plan and undertake the systematic reform of English law (there is a separate Scottish Law Commission). As such he set on foot bold and far-reaching plans for the examination and statutory reshaping of many important areas of law. Several of the commission's proposals have resulted in amending legislation. He was also vice-chairman of the Statute Law Committee and accordingly involved in changes which greatly improved the published form of the statute law, notably by the production of the constantly updated loose-leaf Statutes in Force.

Scarman left the Law Commission on pro-motion to the Court of Appeal in 1973, then in 1977 was further advanced to the House of Lords as a Lord of Appeal in Ordinary (1977–86). In these capacities he was less distinguished, being overshadowed by some giants, but yet delivered some noteworthy judgements, such as on a hospital patient's 'right to know' about the risks inherent in treatment (the doctrine of 'informed consent').

He again came to public notice when invited to investigate the events in Red Lion Square, London, in 1974, and the causes of the riots and disturbances in Brixton and Notting Hill in 1981. His reports on these incidents and his recommendations prompted serious rethinking in government on the social problems resulting from the decay of the inner cities.

Scarman has a strong concern for civil and human rights and favoured the enactment in United Kingdom law of a Bill of Rights founded on the European Convention on Human Rights of 1950. He also did valuable work for legal education, being President of the Senate of the Inns of Court and the Bar (1976–9) and in the government of London University.

FURTHER READING

Benyon, J., *Scarman and After: Essays Reflecting on Lord Scarman's Report, the Riots and their Aftermath* (London: Pergamon, 1984).

DAVID M. WALKER

Scott, C(harles) P(restwich) (*b.* Bath, 26 October 1846; *d.* Manchester, 1 January 1932). Newspaper editor and confidant of politicians. He saw the *Manchester Guardian* as the voice of provincial probity in politics, and its columns under his editorship were respected by Liberal MPs.

Scott, the fourth son of Russell Scott, a prosperous Unitarian coal merchant, was educated at Hove House, Brighton, Clapham Grammar School and Christ Church, Oxford, where in 1869 he took a First in classics and philosophy. His career was decided for him when his cousin, J. E. Taylor, proprietor of the *Manchester Guardian*, offered him a post. Within less than a year Scott had become editor. He grew a bushy beard to hide his youthful appearance, and he exercised a strict discipline. None the less, during his first years as editor the paper lacked sharpness in both opinion and layout. Its politics remained old-fashioned Whig until the Irish political crisis of 1886. The *Manchester Guardian* then followed Gladstone in his conversion to support for Home Rule. W. T. Arnold, the chief leader-writer and a staunch Home Ruler, was one of the best of a long succession of able recruits whom Scott attracted to Manchester from Oxford University. These included C. E. Montague, who became Scott's son-in-law; L. T. Hobhouse, who became the first non-family director of the paper; and J. L. Hammond, who eventually became Scott's biographer.

During the final Victorian years Scott steered the *Manchester Guardian* leftwards in support of the 'New Liberalism'. This sought social justice through social reform which stopped short of socialism. The paper revealed its new sympathies with great effect during the dock strike of 1889. Scott became Liberal MP for Leigh in 1895. He was not a ready debater, however, and after ten years he gave up his seat in order to concentrate upon journalism.

Scott's leader-writing fluctuated in quantity, but rarely in quality. He wrote little during his years in parliament, but much during World War I and after. He was a fierce exponent of correctness and clarity in written English. At the *Manchester Guardian* centenary dinner in 1921, Lord Robert Cecil praised him for 'making righteousness readable'. In a centenary leader, Scott himself cautioned: 'Comment is free, but facts are sacred.'

In 1907, following the death of J. E. Taylor two years earlier, the Scott family finally became sole owners of the *Manchester Guardian*, although only after paying an extortionate price. The paper remained moderately profitable during most of Scott's editorship, but he was always to rate influence above sales and income. The main readership continued to be concentrated in the greater Manchester area (and Scott was a familiar local figure as he cycled daily to and from the Cross Street offices), but by the Edwardian period the *Manchester Guardian* was reaching readers in many other parts of the country. Sales peaked at almost 70,000 daily in 1919. Scott's *Manchester Guardian* thus never became a mass circulation paper. Instead, it set a standard for daily quality journalism. That standard was sustained through not only high-principled political writing, but also informed attention to the arts.

The success of the *Manchester Guardian* under Scott won him national and international respect. Even so, his subordinates remained well aware of his shortcomings alongside his virtues. His total commitment to the paper caused him to be overdemanding, and yet reluctant to delegate; he could be insensitive in handling people, even though sensitive in handling principles; and he could be tight-fisted in financial management to the point of false economy.

Scott's position gave him considerable influence within the Liberal leadership, notably with Lloyd George. The two men first came into close accord during the Boer War, when both Lloyd George and the *Manchester Guardian* courageously stood out on the unpopular anti-war side. Scott retained his public faith in Lloyd George through many vicissitudes in peace and war, but he was always ready with frank criticism in private. Lloyd George, in the words of his secretary and mistress, treated Scott as 'his touchstone not only for what was Liberal and was not, but for right and wrong'.

In 1874 Scott married Rachel Cook (*d.* 1905), the pretty and intelligent daughter of a professor of ecclesiastical history at St Andrews University. They had three sons and one daughter, each of whom became variously associated with the *Manchester Guardian*. Collections of Scott's papers are held in Manchester at the John Rylands University Library and the offices of *The Guardian*, and in London at the British Library.

FURTHER READING

Ayerst, D., *Guardian: Biography of a Newspaper* (London: Collins, 1971).

Clarke, P. F., *Lancashire and the New Liberalism* (Cambridge: Cambridge University Press, 1971).

Hammond, J. L., *C. P. Scott of the Manchester Guardian* (London: Bell, 1934).

Linton, D. and Boston, R. (eds.), *The Newspaper Press in Britain: an Annotated Bibliography* (London: Mansell, 1987).

Taylor, A. J. P., 'Manchester', *Essays in English History* (London: Hamish Hamilton, 1976).

[Wadsworth, A. P. (ed.),] *C. P. Scott 1846–1932: the Making of the Manchester Guardian* (London: Muller, 1946).

Wilson, T. (ed.), *The Political Diaries of C. P. Scott 1911–1928* (London: Collins, 1970).

DONALD READ

Shaw, (George) Bernard (*b.* Dublin, 26 July 1856; *d.* Ayot St Lawrence, Hertfordshire, 2 November 1950). Anglo-Irish writer and radical political activist. Bernard Shaw, playwright, Fabian, enthusiast and eccentric, was born into a family of 'downstarts', members of the Irish Protestant Ascendancy, with good connections and an inherited social status, but very little money to give that position practical expression. Shaw left school at the age of 15 and worked in Dublin as a clerk until 1876. He then moved to London, where for nearly ten years, supported partially by a small inheritance, he built up a modest reputation as a journalist. During these years he also educated himself. He gained from his home – especially his mother – a broad knowledge of music and art, but much of his prodigious learning (which was not always worn very lightly) was acquired in the Reading Room of the British Museum, where, for example, he read *Das Kapital* in French before it had been translated into English.

In the mid-1880s Shaw enthusiastically took up politics. In 1884–5 he began to work specifically in the three areas where he achieved his most important political impact: in the Fabian Society, as a political writer and as a dramatist. In 1884, attracted by the ideals of social democracy, Shaw joined the Fabian Society, just nine months after its foundation. He subsequently persuaded his friends Sidney Webb and Sydney Olivier to join and they, together with Graham Wallas, remained among the society's most powerful members for some 20 years and more. Shaw put his literary gifts and his talents as a public speaker at the service of the society. He acted as literary editor of the early Fabian Tracts. He himself wrote three of the first six published, although each of these was criticized and revised by the society as a whole. The final article of Tract Number 2, *A Manifesto* (1884), 'That we would rather face a Civil War than such another century of suffering as the present one has been', demonstrates that not all early Fabian thought was irrevocably gradualist. Indeed, at the beginning there was a considerable overlap in membership between the Fabians and more revolutionary organizations, such as the Social Democratic Federation (SDF) and the Socialist League. Nevertheless, within a few years the Fabians had decisively broken with the Marxists of the SDF, rejected revolutionism and firmly adopted an evolutionary path. Shaw, who had originally been attracted to the revolutionary approach, estimating that working socialism could actually be established within a fortnight, had by 1889 (in one of the *Fabian Essays in Socialism*) rejected it as 'impracticable'. He later maintained that the same volume presented socialism for the first time as 'a completely constitutional political movement, which the most respectable and least revolutionary citizen can join as irreproachably as he might join the nearest Conservative Club.'

Shaw also participated directly in London city politics. In keeping with the early Fabian tactic of 'permeation', for a short time in the late 1880s he served on the executive of the South St Pancras Liberal and Radical Association. In 1893 he was one of the two Fabian representatives at the inaugural conference of the Independent Labour Party. Between 1897 and 1903, having been elected unopposed, he served as a local councillor in the borough of St Pancras. Here his practical socialism led him to champion such necessary but unglamorous causes as the provision of public lavatories for women. In 1904 he stood unsuccessfully on the Progressive Party ticket for election to the London County Council. He regarded himself, rightly, as an 'eminently unelectable person'. In the years just before World War I Shaw began to reduce his involvement in politics. He resigned from the Fabian Society executive in 1911, ostensibly to make way for younger men. His growing literary success and the demands this placed on his time must, however, have been a contributory factor.

Bernard Shaw

While he abandoned electoral politics, Shaw continued to lecture to the Fabians and to write on political topics. His pamphlet *Commonsense about the War* (1914) was not very well received. Although he generally supported the war, he was quite critical of Sir Edward Grey and British policy. Predictably, the tone of his remarks did not easily accord with the jingoistic hysteria of the time. 'No doubt the heroic remedy . . .', he wrote, 'is that both armies should shoot their officers and go home to gather in their harvests in the villages and make revolutions in the towns.' Shaw's most important political writings after 1914 were instructive works. In 1928 there was the 200,000-word *The Intelligent Woman's Guide to Socialism, Capitalism, Sovietism and Fascism*, which had a very wide sale: in 1937 it was issued in two volumes as the first 'Pelican' paperbacks. He published his last significant political work, *Everybody's Political What's What*, in 1944. Throughout nearly 60 years Shaw's major writings were supplemented by a host of lesser publications – lectures, articles, letters to the press – and pronouncements on an extraordinarily wide range of topics: eugenics,

vegetarianism, the excellence of the Soviet system (after a visit in 1931), Hitler's admirable methods of government (though he deplored his anti-Semitism), and the promotion of a 40-letter British phonetic alphabet, which he intended to be the first charge in his estate.

St John Ervine, one of Shaw's biographers, describes him in the 1920s as being 'beyond question the most famous living dramatist in the world'. In 1925 Shaw received the Nobel Prize for Literature. Like all of his other work his plays were suffused with political meaning. His own description of his very first drama, *Widowers' Houses* (1892, but begun seven years earlier), aptly sums up his improving intention: 'an original didactic realistic play'. In its preface Shaw announced that the plot, which dealt with the evils of slum landlordism, was 'deliberately intended to induce people to vote on the Progressive side at the next County Council election in London.' Although less explicitly 'political', subsequent plays (and their prefaces) dealt with equally contentious topics: *Mrs Warren's Profession* (1893) considered prostitution as well as slum life; *John Bull's Other Island* (1904) tackled contemporary Irish issues such as land reform and Home Rule; *Major Barbara* (1905) examined the arms trade. Despite his professed socialism, Shaw was unashamedly elitist and his later work contains a powerful anti-democratic element. *Man and Superman* (1903) suggested that only by the selective breeding of supermen could humanity escape the inevitable catastrophe produced by 'Proletarian Democracy'. *Back to Methuselah* (1921) picked up this evolutionary theme and left mankind's future in the hands of wise 300-year-old 'Ancients'. In *The Apple Cart* (1929) liberal democracy is denounced and enlightened despotism proposed.

In the end, however, Shaw's plays have survived, not as didactic political tracts, but as stimulating and enjoyable theatrical entertainments. Shaw's utterly sincere social moralizing is continually undermined by his irrepressible facetiousness. Ironically, the very qualities which made him so popular and such a joy to read – wit, a love of paradox, unpredictability, irony itself – largely (and in his lifetime increasingly) disqualified him from consideration as a serious thinker by the British political classes.

Thus he remains above all a brilliant dramatist and, literally, a figure of fun, but not a political heavyweight.

WRITINGS

Sixteen Self Sketches (London: Constable, 1949).

FURTHER READING

Holroyd, Michael (ed.), *The Genius of Shaw* (London: Hodder and Stoughton, 1979).
——, *Bernard Shaw*, vol. 1: *1856–1898: The Search for Love* (London: Chatto and Windus, 1988); vol. 2: *1898–1918: The Pursuit of Power* (London: Chatto and Windus, 1989).
Laurence, Dan H., *Bernard Shaw: Collected Letters*, 4 vols. (London: Max Reinhardt, 1965–88).
O'Donovan, John, *G. B. Shaw* (Dublin: Gill and Macmillan, 1983).

KEITH JEFFERY

Shinwell, Emanuel [Baron Shinwell of Easington] (**'Manny'**) (*b.* London, 18 October 1884; *d.* London, 8 May 1986). Labour politician. Shinwell played a prominent and often highly controversial part in Labour politics for more than half a century, serving in the governments of 1924, 1929 and 1945 and as chairman of the Parliamentary Labour Party for three years during the Wilson governments of 1964 to 1970.

The eldest of 13 children of a Jewish tailor and shopkeeper, Shinwell left school at the age of 11 to be apprenticed as a tailor's cutter. Within a year he had abandoned the trade, and for the next decade he drifted through a range of the 'blind alley' jobs for adolescent boys so characteristic of the Edwardian economy, until in 1909 he joined the Scottish Cooperative Wholesale Society. He had already by this time revealed that autodidact tendency so common among the pioneers of the Labour Party by amassing a somewhat haphazard collection of more than 250 books, which included the usual range of the classics of English literature and semi-scientific works such as Haeckel's *Riddle of the Universe*. He had also acquired that lifelong fascination with the forms of the English language which was so evident in his speeches. Indeed, it was the clear-cut language

of Robert Blatchford's writings that attracted Shinwell to socialism and membership of the Independent Labour Party in 1903. Within six years he had become an active propagandist in the West of Scotland, a member of the Glasgow Trades Council and an organizer for the National Union of Seamen. It was his work in the shipping industry that led to his being placed in a reserved occupation during World War I. Although not initially opposed to the war, by 1917 he was supporting the campaign within the Labour movement for a negotiated peace.

It was the events in Glasgow in the immediate aftermath of the war which first brought Shinwell to national prominence. A movement for the introduction of a 40-hour week led to a series of strikes and demonstrations, culminating in a huge meeting in George Square on Bloody Friday, 31 January 1919, which was dispersed with great violence by the police. Immediately afterwards the government, influenced by fears of revolution, despatched 10,000 troops to the city as a precautionary measure. As one of the strike leaders, Shinwell was tried, found guilty of incitement to riot and sentenced to five months in prison. Ironically, since throughout he had counselled moderation, he was portrayed as a revolutionary. On his release he resumed a central role on the Glasgow Trades Council and the city council. In the 1922 general election he was returned for the Linlithgow seat, which he had contested in 1918.

Once in Parliament, in contrast to a number of the other new Clydeside members, Shinwell showed himself to be an effective debater, not simply a street-corner evangelist, and a firm supporter of Ramsay MacDonald, whom he proposed as leader at the first meeting of the PLP. In the 1924 government Shinwell became Parliamentary Secretary to the Department of Mines, a post which he occupied for a period in the second Labour Government after 18 months as Financial Secretary to the War Office. On each occasion he sought to bring forward minor bills which would appeal to party opinion. In the crisis of August 1931 Shinwell was one of the few members of the government asked directly by MacDonald to join the new National Government, though he rejected the request out of hand. After losing his seat in the subsequent election he was given a full-time job as a party propagandist at a salary of £250 a year by the party secretary, Arthur Henderson. He continued in this position until 1935 when, after a bitter campaign, he was returned for Seaham, unseating MacDonald himself.

On his return to the Commons, Shinwell once more demonstrated his capacity as a parliamentary debater, but he played little part in the leadership of the party. Throughout his career he relied upon his powers of oratory and his quick wits to deal with issues and problems as they arose. He had little sympathy, therefore, with the detailed policy-making exercise being conducted by Dalton and Morrison, and held firm to his previously expressed view that the party should simply concentrate on criticizing whatever the government was doing without worrying about alternative policies of its own. That attitude was again evident after Shinwell's election to the National Executive Committee in 1941, when consideration turned to Labour's policies for reconstruction. Having turned down a junior position in the Coalition Government in 1940, Shinwell spent the war on the back benches, acting as a self-styled 'constructive critic' of the government. His criticisms of Labour ministers for not pressing strongly enough for socialist policies, together with his own open manoeuvrings for position within the party, gave him a reputation for disloyalty and aroused resentment across the PLP.

In 1945, however, Attlee made what seemed the logical choice in view of Shinwell's past ministerial experience, and appointed him as Minister for Fuel and Power with responsibility for the nationalization of the mining industry. The structure devised, although created 'virtually from scratch', owed little to any original ideas from Shinwell. His Parliamentary Secretary, Hugh Gaitskell, quickly came to the conclusion that as an administrator Shinwell was a failure, lacking any conception of 'either organisation, or planning or following up', doing everything by fits and starts and on impulse, and avoiding for as long as possible any unpleasant decisions. That damning judgement came to be almost universally

shared in the fuel crisis of 1947, when after ignoring repeated warnings from other ministers Shinwell was forced to announce to an unprepared and shocked House of Commons an immediate emergency programme of fuel rationing. Shinwell's performance in the House seemed to his colleagues to be the height of cynical irresponsibility, as he sought not merely to pass the buck but 'to pick it up and hurl it'. In the aftermath of the crisis the pressure to move him was irresistible, and in the autumn he took over the War Office, losing his seat in the cabinet. As in 1929–30, he found himself at home with his military staff and quickly became a strong advocate of the modernization of the armed forces and of NATO. In 1950 he returned to the cabinet as Minister of Defence, and adopted the most hawkish posture of all on the scale of the re-armament programme.

In 1950 Shinwell lost his seat on the NEC and failed to regain it subsequently. Disliked by both the left and the right, he found his position within the party weakened, and in 1955 he retired from the shadow cabinet. Thereafter he spoke out increasingly against any dilution of the commitment to public ownership and against British possession of nuclear weapons, though later he once more became an equally strong supporter of retention. Between 1964 and 1967 he served as Chairman of the PLP. However, the growth of resentment at what some saw as his authoritarian handling of party meetings, clashes with the Leader of the House, Richard Crossman, and the Chief Whip, John Silkin, over the management of the PLP, and his own bitter hostility to the application to join the EEC led to his resignation.

In 1970 he accepted a life peerage and quickly became an active and outspoken member of the House of Lords, playing an especially active role in the all-party Defence Study Group. In March 1982 he resigned the Labour Whip in protest against what he saw as an unchecked drift to the left, though he remained a member of the party.

During his last decade Shinwell became, partly by design, something of a national 'character', for example, pipeman of the century, widely regarded on all sides as an elder statesman. He published several volumes of entertaining but unreliable memoirs which offer his version of the history of the Labour Party and his place within it. Throughout his political life Shinwell found great support from his family; each of his three wives predeceased him. His political gifts, oratory, quick wittedness and vivid personality were typical of those of the first generation of Labour Party leaders. Like them, he was more at home on the platform than in office. The resentment and suspicion which he aroused among colleagues from all sections of the party inevitably limited his effectiveness as a major politician. In many ways his most significant political achievement was his own career.

WRITINGS

Conflict without Malice (London: Odhams, 1955).
Lead with the Left (London: Cassell, 1981).

FURTHER READING

Williams, P., *Hugh Gaitskell* (London: Jonathan Cape, 1979).

J. S. ROWETT

Simon, Sir **John (Allsebrook)** [Viscount Simon of Stackpole Elidor] (*b.* Manchester, 28 February 1873; *d.* London, 11 January 1954). Liberal statesman and lawyer. He combined a distinguished career in the law with a long political career in which he held almost all the major offices of state apart from the premiership. The leading barrister of his age, said to have earned up to £50,000 per annum in the years immediately after World War I, Simon's list of political offices included the Home Office (twice), the Treasury, the Foreign Office and the woolsack, and is unique in twentieth-century history.

Unlike the majority of his political contemporaries, Simon was not born into a life of luxury and ease. His father was a Congregational minister, his first home a terraced house in Manchester. It was his academic distinction that enabled him to rise above his modest origins. A scholarship to Fettes College in Edinburgh was followed by one to Wadham College, Oxford, where his contemporaries included F. E. Smith and C. B. Fry. After securing a First in Greats and becoming President of the Union, Simon was elected a Fellow of All Souls in 1897. It was a connection which he maintained to the end of his life and which became especially important to him in his final years.

Called to the Bar in 1899, Simon entered parliament as member for Walthamstow in the landslide Liberal general election victory of 1906. It was a mark of his abilities that he rapidly emerged from the ruck of new Liberal MPs as a man of exceptional talent, becoming Solicitor-General in 1910 at the remarkably early age of 37. Promoted to Attorney-General with a seat in the cabinet in 1913, Simon played an important role in the Irish and constitutional problems which beset the Liberal Government in the period before the outbreak of European war. Simon, however, never regarded the law as an end in itself, but rather as the vehicle by which a man of humble means could establish his position in the world of politics. When, therefore, on the formation of Asquith's coalition in May 1915, he was offered the Lord Chancellorship, he turned it down in favour of the Home Office: 'rather the sack than the woolsack'. Had he agreed, Simon would have been the youngest Lord Chancellor in modern times.

Simon had accepted British involvement in the war with reluctance. His resignation was withdrawn only after pressure from Prime Minister Asquith. During 1915, however, his position within the government became increasingly difficult and he finally resigned in January 1916 over the introduction of conscription. This event brought to an end Simon's meteoric rise. It was to be more than a decade and a half before he again held government office. Not himself a pacifist, Simon served with distinction in the Royal Flying Corps, but at the end of hostilities was a victim of the nationalistic tide which destroyed independent Liberalism in the 'Coupon' Election of 1918, losing his seat in parliament.

In the 1920s Simon's career was blighted by the internal problems of the Liberal Party. He returned to Westminster as Member for Spen Valley in the general election of 1922, but failed to emerge as Asquith's successor in the party leadership, as had at one time seemed possible.

His relations with Lloyd George were never again good, despite the apparent reconciliation of the warring Liberal factions. Simon had first established his Liberal credentials on the radical wing, but in the 1920s his views became increasingly conservative. It was he who made the famous pronouncement on the illegality of the General Strike of 1926, which some believed played a part in the ending of that event. By the end of the decade he had even begun to question the central Liberal doctrine of free trade. While out of office the government made use of his talents at the head of the Statutory Commission on India (1927–30) and the enquiry into the R101 airship disaster (1930–1). His report for the former was a model of lucid exposition, but was largely pre-empted when the Viceroy, Lord Irwin, issued his declaration on dominion status in October 1929.

Simon's final breach with Liberalism came over Lloyd George's unwillingness to put the minority Labour Government of 1929–31 out of office. In 1931 Simon and his followers broke away to form the Liberal National Group, and he received his reward when appointed Foreign Secretary that November in Ramsay MacDonald's National Government. It was an unenviable period in which to hold this office, and Simon's handling of the Manchurian crisis (1931–3) and the World Disarmament Conference (1932–4) and his response to the rise of Nazism in Germany were severely criticized by contemporaries and also later historians. It was said that he was indecisive and could not make up his mind on any major issue. In truth the diplomatic problems of the early 1930s were not susceptible to easy solutions and this most cerebral of politicians was only too aware of the difficulties which each policy option opened up.

Transferred to the Home Office in 1935, Simon played a significant role in the Abdication Crisis of the following year and, upon the accession of Neville Chamberlain to the premiership in 1937, succeeded the latter as Chancellor of the Exchequer. He continued Chamberlain's policy of financial restraint, regarding a sound economy as the fourth arm of the nation's defence. As a loyal supporter of the Prime Minister and a leading advocate of 'appeasement', his removal from the higher direction of the war effort was inevitable on the formation of Churchill's government in May 1940, but he served with great distinction as Lord Chancellor – the post he had rejected a quarter of a century earlier – until the end of the war. Simon remained active in politics to the end of his life, even entertaining hopes of returning to the woolsack in Churchill's post-war government in 1951. By this stage he recognized that the Liberal Nationals had no independent future and took comfort in the belief that the modern Conservative Party had been liberalized.

By nature a shy man, particularly after the early death of his first wife in 1902, Simon craved popularity and affection, but did not have the personal qualities which alone could win them. His intellectual capacity was beyond dispute, but he lacked the common touch and that impression of fallibility which would have made his public image more human. He was, as Asquith said, 'the Impeccable'.

For illustration, see Asquith, H. H.

WRITINGS

Retrospect: the Memoirs of the Rt. Hon. Viscount Simon (London: Hutchinson, 1952).

FURTHER READING

Dutton, D. J., *Sir John Simon* (Bolton: Ross Anderson, forthcoming).
Heuston, R. F. V., *Lives of the Lord Chancellors 1940–1970* (Oxford: Clarendon, 1987).

DAVID DUTTON

Sinclair, Sir Archibald (Henry Macdonald) [Viscount Thurso] (*b.* London, 22 October 1890; *d.* Twickenham, Surrey, 15 June 1970). Liberal parliamentary leader, Secretary of State for Scotland (1931–2) and Air Minister (1940–5). His most notable achievements came during his leadership of the parliamentary Liberal Party after 1935, when his forthright opposition to the National Government enhanced his reputation and that of his party.

Educated at Eton and Sandhurst, Sinclair

joined the 2nd Life Guards in 1910, and two years later inherited the baronetcy of Ulbster and the family estate in Caithness. He served with distinction in the Great War, most notably as second-in-command to his close friend Winston Churchill during the latter's sabbatical from Westminster.

Sinclair entered parliament as MP for Caithness and Sutherland in 1922. As the size of the parliamentary Liberal Party steadily decreased, his influence within it increased. When the Liberals divided over free trade, Sinclair sided with Herbert Samuel, in opposition to the protectionist Sir John Simon. The Samuelites joined the National Government in 1931, but, alarmed by the slide towards protectionism, they resigned after the Ottawa conference.

Samuel's defeat in the 1935 election catapulted Sinclair to the party leadership. Over the next four years he steered his depleted ranks on a steady, independent course, attacking the National Government on 'appeasement', re-armament and domestic policy, while rejecting any proposed centrist political alliances. His period as Air Minister, though often turbulent and controversial, enhanced his reputation nationally. Nevertheless, in 1945, his constituents surprisingly rejected him. Later, illness prevented him from duplicating in the Lords the active role he had enjoyed in the Commons.

Sinclair confessed that he valued love and honour above all else. Both probably limited his political advancement. His family was at least as important as politics, and Liberalism meant more to him than power. His perceived mission was to keep the Liberal flag flying in anticipation of his country's return to sanity; that the party survived was largely due to his courage and integrity. Some of his private papers are held in the collection of Thurso Papers at Churchill College, Cambridge.

FURTHER READING

Cook, C., *A Short History of the Liberal Party* (London: Macmillan, 1984).
Wilson, T., *The Downfall of the Liberal Party* (London: Fontana, 1966).

GERARD J. DE GROOT

Smith, F(rederick) E(dwin) [Earl of Birkenhead] (*b.* Birkenhead, Cheshire, 12 July 1872; *d.* London, 30 September 1930). Conservative lawyer-politician, Attorney-General, Lord Chancellor and Secretary of State for India. He was one of the most brilliant political personalities of the years before and after World War I. Beaverbrook called him simply 'the cleverest man in the kingdom'. He remains to this day a legendary figure whose mere initials still evoke a whole anthology of well-loved anecdotes and epigrams.

From a modest provincial background he won a scholarship to Wadham College, Oxford, where he gained a dazzling reputation at the Union. After returning to Merseyside he made an equally sensational success at the Liverpool Bar before exploding into the House of Commons in 1906 with the most impudent maiden speech ever delivered there, rallying the depleted Unionist benches after the Liberal landslide.

Unashamedly ambitious, endowed with a cutting tongue and an inexhaustible appetite for life and pleasure, Smith quickly assumed by sheer force of personality and intellectual ability a leading role in the Tories' opposition, first to Lloyd George's 1909 budget and then to the curbing of the power of the House of Lords in the constitutional crisis of 1910–11. In 1912–14, reflecting the virulent Orange traditions of his Liverpool constituents, he went to the very brink of treason in supporting, with Sir Edward Carson, Ulster's resistance to Irish Home Rule. Yet all the time he maintained the closest cross-party friendships with leading Liberals, most notably with his fellow-adventurer Winston Churchill, with whom in 1910 he founded the celebrated 'Other Club'.

But for the Great War he was well placed to succeed Bonar Law as Tory leader; but the war diverted him into the legal offices. After a brief spell as press censor and a somewhat inglorious interlude at the front, he succeeded Carson as Attorney-General, initially under Asquith, then under Lloyd George. In 1916 he achieved a new notoriety with the controversial prosecution for treason of Sir Roger Casement. At the end of the war Lloyd George outraged the legal establishment by appointing him (aged only 46) the youngest Lord Chancellor since Judge Jeffreys. Taking the title Lord Birkenhead, Smith proceeded to astonish his detractors by proving one of the greatest Lord Chancellors of the century, displaying a wisdom, erudition and statesmanship hitherto unsuspected. His major legislative monument was the Law of Property Act, 1922: reform was long overdue but it took the energy of a young Lord Chancellor to bring it to the Statute Book. At the same time he was an unusually political Lord Chancellor, pulling his full weight in cabinet. In 1921 he played a critical role in helping to negotiate the treaty with Sinn Fein which recognized the independence of Southern Ireland. By this courageous affront to his Unionist past, however, he both sacrificed his own remaining credit with the Tory right and helped seal the fate of the coalition.

Birkenhead was now one of Lloyd George's closest colleagues, and shared in the increasing odium with which his government was regarded. When in 1922 the Tory Party voted to end the coalition, Birkenhead found himself in the political wilderness. He was now a somewhat soured figure, drinking too much and acidly contemptuous of those who had supplanted him. In 1924, however, Baldwin reunited the Tory Party by bringing back the former coalitionists and Birkenhead became Secretary of State for India. His attitude to India was generally reactionary; in dealings with his two Viceroys, Reading and Irwin, he adopted a stance of cynical scepticism towards hopes of constitutional advance. In 1926, on the other hand, he played a constructive role in trying to avert the General Strike: his intellect was still powerful when he chose to apply it. In 1928 he left politics to try to earn in the City the money to keep his family in the extravagant style to which he had become accustomed. But he died only two years later, burned out at the age of 58.

FURTHER READING

Campbell, John, *F. E. Smith, First Earl of Birkenhead* (London: Jonathan Cape, 1983).
Heuston, R. F. V., *The Lives of the Lord Chancellors, 1885–1940* (Oxford: Oxford University Press, 1964).

JOHN CAMPBELL

Smuts, Jan (Christian) (*b.* near Riebeeck West, Cape Colony, 24 May 1870; *d.* Doornkloof, Irene, Transvaal, 11 September 1950). Statesman, soldier and Prime Minister of South Africa. Smuts was a South African of Afrikaner descent. He fought against the British in the South African War (1899–1902) but went on to become a British Field Marshal and the most influential Commonwealth leader before Nehru. A member of Lloyd George's War Cabinet during World War I (1917–18) and a close confidant of Winston Churchill during World War II, he achieved a position in British political life unequalled by any other Commonwealth figure. The only statesman of world stature yet to emerge from South Africa, he played a key role in the foundation of the League of Nations in 1919 and wrote the preamble to the Charter of the United Nations Organization in 1945.

Smuts grew up on a farm and began school only at the age of 12, on the death of his elder brother. After Stellenbosch and a Double First in law at Cambridge, he started work as a lawyer in Cape Town but soon moved to the Transvaal, where he became State-Attorney in 1898. He played an important part in the events leading to war between Britain and the Transvaal republic in October 1899 and in the peace negotiations which brought the war to an end at Vereeniging in May 1902. Together with Louis Botha, Smuts led the postwar Afrikaner political recovery which resulted first in self-government for the Transvaal (1907) and then in an Afrikaner-led Union of South Africa under white minority rule but within the British Empire (1910). During World War I he assisted in the seizure of South West Africa from Germany (1915) and was then put in command of the British forces which pursued General Lettow Vorbeck in German East Africa. In March 1917 he arrived in London to represent South Africa at the Imperial War Conference. His formidable energy and intelligence led Lloyd George to appoint him to the War Cabinet and send him on missions to France, Switzerland (to explore a separate peace with Austria-Hungary), Egypt and Palestine. At the Paris conference (1919) Smuts worked for a conciliatory peace with Germany. He led delegations to Budapest and

Prague in addition to his work, alongside President Woodrow Wilson, for the establishment of the League of Nations – whose mandates system he invented. His first term as Prime Minister of South Africa was from 1919 to 1924.

In a seminal speech in 1917 Smuts argued the case for a British Commonwealth of autonomous, self-governing nations, and in June 1921 he presented a memorandum to the Imperial Conference which anticipated all that the Balfour Declaration (1926) and Statute of Westminster (1931) were later to effect. In 1921 he recommended dominion status for Ireland and personally urged Eamon de Valera to accept this 'other form of freedom'. The failure of the League of Nations to stop Italy from annexing Abyssinia shocked him profoundly but he supported 'a resolute policy of appeasement' by Britain towards Germany until March 1939. When war broke out Smuts succeeded, by a narrow parliamentary majority, in bringing a deeply divided South Africa into the war and was appointed Prime Minister for the second time. During the war he consistently advocated a military strategy based upon the Middle East and North Africa. He participated in the Cairo conference (1942) and played an active part in restoring the Greek monarchy and establishing the United Nations. His BBC broadcasts made him widely known to the British public. In 1948 he lost office to the Nationalist Party; he was also elected Chancellor of Cambridge University.

Both an intellectual and a man of action, Smuts read widely throughout his life and was himself the author of several books, including a philosophical treatise on holism. His voluminous correspondence reveals one of the most cultivated minds of any political leader in the twentieth century.

FURTHER READING

Hancock, W. K., *Smuts*, 2 vols. (Cambridge: Cambridge University Press, 1962, 1968).

Hancock, W. K. and Van der Poel, J. (eds.), *Selections from the Smuts Papers*, 7 vols. (Cambridge: Cambridge University Press, 1966–73).

Ingham, K., *Jan Christian Smuts* (London: Weidenfeld and Nicolson, 1986).

IAIN R. SMITH

Snowden, Philip [Viscount Snowden of Ickornshaw] (*b*. Ickornshaw, Yorkshire, 18 July 1864; *d*. Tilford, Surrey, 15 May 1937). Labour Chancellor of the Exchequer. Snowden occupied a central place in the development of both the Independent Labour Party and the Labour Party. Like Ramsay MacDonald, he was never forgiven within the Labour movement for his decision to break with the majority of his colleagues over the policies judged to be necessary in the financial crisis of August 1931. That decision has also coloured the view of him taken by many Labour historians. As a consequence, Snowden's centrality to the growth and practice of independent Labour politics has been unduly neglected.

Snowden was born in the hamlet of Ickornshaw in the village of Cowling, high on the Pennine moors of the West Riding of Yorkshire, the only son of John and Martha Snowden. His father possessed the characteristics typical of the independent-minded weavers of that area: a memory of the Chartist movement; a fierce commitment to Liberal Radicalism in general and to Gladstone in particular; an active involvement in evangelical Methodism; and a love of the classics of English literature, evident in the possession of the works of Burns, Byron, Milton and Shakespeare and the Bible. It was this background which provided Snowden with the values which governed his whole life. As he noted in his autobiography, 'I imbibed the political and social principles which I have had ever since.'

The family circumstances of the Snowdens were such that, rather than entering the mill where his parents worked, Philip was able to become a pupil teacher at the Board school in Cowling. However, when in 1879 the mill closed, the family moved to Nelson, where Philip worked as a clerk in an insurance office. In 1886 he was successful in the examination for entry into the Excise Department of the Board of Inland Revenue. This appointment took him the length and breadth of the country, but more importantly introduced him to a wider cultural world, in particular that of the theatre, where the styles of the leading actors provided an object of study for him. In 1891 Snowden's life was changed when he contracted an infection of the spine, possibly spinal tuberculosis, which left him a severe cripple for the rest of his life. It was during the two years that he spent recovering with his mother in Cowling that he first read the works of contemporary socialists. On his own account, preparing a lecture for the Cowling Liberal Club convinced him of the force of the arguments in favour of socialism, though he insisted that, while he had read Carpenter, Hyndman and other modern authors as well as Owenite and Chartist writers, it was his own independent reasoning which made him a socialist. That insistence on the logical and moral superiority of his own arguments was to mark his political career.

For Snowden socialism was essentially a moral creed which actually applied the principles of Christianity to social and economic life, in contrast to the formal Christianity of the official churches. A speech on these lines at Keighley in 1894 launched him on a career as a propagandist for the newly formed ILP. For the next decade he engaged in peripatetic propaganda work, developing a relationship with the branches of the party second only to that of Keir Hardie himself. The influence of evangelical Methodism was evident not only in the Biblical imagery which informed his speeches but also in his practice of ending a long speech with a call to those who wished to bear witness to come forward and sign a membership form, a technique known throughout the ILP as 'Philip's come to Jesus'. Snowden's platform style and use of language, often based upon the study of local dialect, was carefully crafted to appeal to the respectable, self-improving members of the working and lower-middle class who provided the basis of ILP support. His most famous talk, *The Christ that Is to Be*, provided the classic statement of that ethical socialism which constituted the ideology of the party. In his appeal and his practice, Snowden was typical of the upwardly mobile autodidacts, possessed of highly developed rhetorical and literary skills, who throughout socialist parties in Europe and the USA came to live for and on socialism. Like others who had chosen socialist politics as a vocation, Snowden worked as a journalist, editing with great success the *Keighley Labour Journal*, and served both on local government bodies and the central administrative body of the party, on which he held the post of chairman between 1903 and 1906.

Snowden's life altered in March 1905 when he married a fellow socialist lecturer, Ethel Annikan, who provided not only the companionship and emotional security which he had previously lacked, but also a greater degree of financial security through her own earnings as a lecturer, writer and, increasingly, a public figure in her own right. Her views appear to have influenced Snowden on various occasions, as, for example, in his almost immediate conversion to the cause of women's suffrage, even if on the basis of a property qualification. The following year brought a second fundamental change in Snowden's position when he was elected an MP in the two-member constituency of Blackburn. It had been Snowden's campaign in 1900 in this centre of 'clog Toryism' which had first brought him a degree of national attention through the reporting of the Liberal journalist A. G. Gardiner, who presented Snowden as the embodiment of a new religious movement. Gardiner's account of his speeches, which combined the preaching of socialism with a remarkable command of factual material, great clarity and lucidity of expression, controlled and at times biting sarcasm, all expressed in a 'fierce and implacable' language, led many to see him as the epitome of implacable socialist enmity to the existing order – a Labour Robespierre. The extent of this misjudgement, based more upon his physical appearance and mode of expression – which reflected that vehemence in expression often characteristic of Yorkshiremen – became clear once Snowden entered parliament. His commitment to the staples of Liberal Radicalism was especially evident in his speeches and his writings on the drink question and on financial policy, where he was quickly established as the party's leading expert. That same commitment was equally evident in his open criticism of the industrial conflict of 1911–14 and of syndicalist ideas, expressed most fully in his *Socialism and Syndicalism* (1913). Whatever the issue, one constant was the power of invective on which Snowden would draw.

Philip Snowden arriving at 10 Downing Street for a cabinet meeting, September 1924

When war broke out in 1914 Snowden and his wife had already left Britain for a temperance crusade in Australia and New Zealand. On their return in 1915, Snowden made clear his outright opposition to the war. Although himself a pacificist rather than a pacifist, he became the foremost champion in parliament of the rights of conscientious objectors of all kinds, and viewed the Conscription Act as a violation of the most basic civil liberties. At the same time he was at the forefront of demands in the House of Commons for the opening of peace negotiations and for a fiscal policy based not on borrowing but on taxation. To this end he proposed a capital levy on all holdings of capital above £1,000, and demanded that the government should 'extend the conscription of life to the conscription of wealth'. His stance on these issues was widely publicized through his weekly front-page column in the *Labour Leader* and through the extensive series of meetings which he addres-

sed across the country. While the Labour Party was now the subject of his invective – 'the most craven and supine working-class party in the belligerent countries' – the ILP became once more the focus of his hopes. In 1915 he returned to the National Executive Committee from which he had resigned in 1909, and in 1917 and 1918 was elected chairman. The loss of his seat at Blackburn in 1918 only increased his standing within the party. Snowden had not, however, moved to the left in any significant way. His opposition to the war sprang from a Liberal Radical rather than a socialist analysis. The next decade was to reveal the tenacity with which he held to many of the assumptions of Liberal Radicalism.

By the time of his return to parliament as member for Colne Valley in the general election of 1922, Snowden had once more severed many of his links with the ILP. As before, conflicts developed with younger men over the future direction of the party, but on this occasion they were given a much sharper edge by the critical response to Ethel Snowden's account of her visit to Russia, *Through Bolshevik Russia*. Finally, in 1927 Snowden declined to renew his membership, ostensibly as a protest at the decision of the party to break the habit of 15 years by refusing to nominate MacDonald for the treasurership of the Labour Party. Although the personal relations between the two men continued to be difficult and distant throughout the 1920s, they were at one in their approach to political mobilization, believing that only moderate policies would bring electoral success. That approach was clearly demonstrated by the 1924 Labour Government, where Snowden as Chancellor of the Exchequer eschewed any idea of a radical, 'soak the rich' budget. Instead he produced, to great acclaim, a free trade, tax cutting budget, 'vindictive against no class and no interest', designed to appeal to progressive opinion. During the following five years of opposition, neither Snowden nor his colleagues gave any real thought to the economic policies necessary to tackle mass unemployment. When MacDonald formed his second administration, Snowden's return to the Exchequer was automatic.

The economic record of the second Labour Government has occasioned great historiographical debate. How far proto-Keynesian policies were an option and their likely effects remain open questions. What is clear is the continued unwillingness of Snowden to depart significantly from his long-held views. For him, socialism was conceived primarily in moral rather than in economic terms. But if his economic assumptions were Liberal, on questions of taxation and the distribution of wealth they were new Liberal rather than Gladstonian. Only his absolute commitment to free trade could plausibly be described as Gladstonian. Neither offered any guidance in the crisis of August 1931. Snowden was convinced of the need for cuts in government expenditure until there was an improvement in the economic climate. When the cabinet split over the proposed ten per cent reduction in unemployment benefit, Snowden accepted MacDonald's invitation to retain his position in the new National Government. In the subsequent election

Snowden's conviction of the rectitude of his own position led him to turn his formidable powers of invective against his former colleagues, most notably in his claim that the Labour programme was 'Bolshevism run mad'. After the election Snowden went to the House of Lords, becoming Lord Privy Seal in the reconstituted government. Nine months later, however, he resigned, since he would no more accept the protectionist policy of his new colleagues than he would the proposal for a revenue tariff of his old.

After his resignation Snowden gave full vent to the pent-up resentment of 30 years as he attacked MacDonald with unrestrained bitterness, notably in his autobiography, which still remains a valuable source for the history of Labour politics. In his last five years Snowden drew increasingly close to Lloyd George, his Surrey neighbour, coming out in support of his 'New Deal' in 1935. This support did not, however, represent any fundamental change in Snowden's views. He remained 'an unrepentant free trader only more so', but believed that, in contrast to 1929–31, cheap money and low business investment provided the opportunity for the state to bring forward major schemes of public works to effect 'a big forward push in national reconstruction'. While supporting the Liberals in the 1935 election, Snowden still looked to a moderate Labour Party, led perhaps by Herbert Morrison, as the best vehicle to unite progressive opinion against the government. In his last years, with his health waning, he grew increasingly depressed at his alienation 'from the movement served so long and loved so deeply'. Despite its rejection of him, his centrality to the early history of the Labour Party is clear. Better than any of his contemporaries, he expressed in himself that fusion of Liberal Radicalism and ethical socialism which gave a distinctive identity to the party in its formative period.

WRITINGS

An Autobiography, 2 vols. (London: Ivor Nicholson and Watson, 1934).

FURTHER READING

Cross, C., *Philip Snowden* (London: Barrie and Rockliff, 1966).

Laybourn, K. and James, D. (eds.), *Philip Snow-den* (Bradford: Bradford Libraries and Information Service, 1987).

J. S. ROWETT

Soper, Donald (Oliver) [Lord Soper of Kingsway] (*b.* London, 31 January 1903). Methodist minister. He was Methodist Superintendent of the Kingsway Central Hall, London, from 1936 to 1978. He achieved fame by open-air speaking at Tower Hill from 1926 and later at Hyde Park Corner. A staunch pacifist and Christian Socialist, he was created a life peer in 1965.

Brought up by middle-class Wesleyan parents in Streatham, Soper went as an exhibitioner to read history at St Catharine's College, Cambridge, in 1921. Ambitious and extrovert, he won university colours in five sports and spent two additional years at Cambridge training for the Wesleyan ministry. He served at the South London Mission (1926–9) and the Central London Mission (1929–36), and both married and completed a doctorate in 1929. At Kingsway Hall from 1936 he combined a liberal theology, a sacramental churchmanship and a dedication to organized social concern. His skills as a public speaker made him an effective radio broadcaster from 1934. After the war he travelled the world as a Methodist preacher and in 1953 was President of Conference.

Drawn by Dick Sheppard of St Martin's-in-the-Fields into the Peace Pledge Union in the 1930s, Soper did not modify his pacifism in wartime. He was afterwards thought to be a communist fellow-traveller, especially when in 1950 he declared a Russian occupation preferable to a third world war. He chaired the short-lived Hydrogen Bomb National Campaign in 1954 and led the first Aldermaston March of the Campaign for Nuclear Disarmament in 1958. A member of the Labour Party from 1926, he saw socialism as the expression in time of the kingdom of God. For 20 years from 1953 he contributed a weekly column to *Tribune*, often chiding Labour for inadequate commitment to socialist principle. From 1960 he was Chairman of the Christian Socialist Movement. In the House of Lords from 1965 he favoured liberalizing legislation on homosexuality and abortion. Nevertheless, his lifelong hostility to alcohol and gambling marked him as a continuing representative of the social gospel tradition.

WRITINGS

Calling for Action (London: Robson, 1984).

FURTHER READING

Purcell, W., *Odd Man Out* (London: Mowbray, 1983).
Thompson, D., *Donald Soper* (Nutfield, Surrey: Denholm House, 1971).

D. W. BEBBINGTON

Steadman, Ralph (*b.* Wallasey, Cheshire, 15 May 1936). Cartoonist and caricaturist. Steadman is one of Britain's most prolific satirical artists. A controversial observer of the British political and social scene, his caustic, and decidedly violent, pen-and-ink work has appeared in various publications – among them *Punch*, the *Daily Telegraph*, the *New Statesman* and the *New York Times*. Like his contemporary Gerald Scarfe, he is a caricaturist from the school nurtured by the anarchic magazine *Private Eye*. He began writing and illustrating books in 1964 and many commissions have followed. It is notable that in recent years his political work has had a slightly mercenary quality to it and it is because of this that he is now better known as an illustrator than a cartoonist.

Steadman was educated at Abergele Grammar School and learnt his draughtsmanship by studying part-time at the London School of Printing and Graphic Arts. His first cartooning job, drawing for the *Sunday Chronicle*, lasted three years. It was the cartoonist Leslie Illingworth who encouraged him to become freelance. Books by Steadman have appeared throughout the world. His fascination with Lewis Carroll led him to illustrate *Alice's Adventures in Wonderland*, for which he was awarded the Francis Williams Prize in 1967. A growing affinity with Leonardo da Vinci resulted in another much-fêted book – the biography *I, Leonardo* (1983). His most recently published work underlines the sustained power of his graphic invention: called *The Big, I Am*, it is an imagined conversation that God might have with himself.

Steadman's style is a highly disciplined one with an inventive use of colour that emphasizes the mastery of his technique. His work is a combination of incisive lines and areas of dense texture. Every scratch and blot is intended. His experiments with new media, particularly photography, have given yet another dimension to his creations – 'Paranoids' are a series of Polaroid portraits that are manipulated and turned into caricatures. The sureness of line in all his work is the key to his success.

WRITINGS

Between the Eyes (London: Jonathan Cape, 1984).

LIZ OTTAWAY

Steel, David (Martin Scott) (*b.* Kirkcaldy, Fife, 31 March 1938). Liberal leader. Of the four Liberal leaders since 1945, the first three affected the course of British politics, if at all, by keeping the Liberal Party in being and thereby influencing the electoral fortunes of the other two parties; only David Steel used the Liberal Party as an instrument to change the course of politics, and his use of it ended its separate existence. By entering the Lib-Lab Pact in 1977, Steel delayed a general election by two years, which Margaret Thatcher used to shape the Conservative Party for her style of government. By encouraging the formation of the Social Democratic Party in 1981 and then leading his own party into the Liberal/SDP Alliance, Steel created a force which came close to breaking the mould of British politics and administered such a shock to the Labour Party that Neil Kinnock was able to impose reforms upon it which had defeated abler Labour leaders for 30 years. After the 1987 general election, Steel created a situation in which he was able to force a merger of the two Alliance parties and the creation of the Social and Liberal Democrats; but in doing so he destroyed his own leadership and left a situation in which the new British liberal party (which is what the new party was on the spec-trum of Western European politics) appeared weaker than the old Liberal Party at the lowest ebb of its postwar fortunes. A politician of courage and vision to a degree unusual in British politics, a year after Steel gave up the joint leadership of the Social and Liberal Democrats, it appeared that the beneficiaries of the policy which he had pursued over 12 years to reshape British politics might be his opponents.

Steel became the baby of the House when he won the Roxburgh by-election in 1965. He had been an active Liberal in student politics at Edinburgh University, where he studied law, and had worked (1962–4) for the Scottish Liberal Party and for the BBC. In the 1966–7 session he made a significant contribution to Roy Jenkins's campaign to liberalize British society by taking a Private Member's Bill through the Commons to allow abortion in certain circumstances (see also JENKINS, ROY). He was a strong enough Liberal to take the risk, and a good enough politician to calculate correctly that the risk was not too great. He showed the same qualities in his outspoken support for the Anti-Apartheid movement, to which he was strongly committed by his childhood experience in Kenya (where his father, Moderator of the General Assembly in 1974–5, had served as a Church of Scotland Minister). In 1975 he again worked closely with Roy Jenkins in the European Referendum Campaign.

As Chief Whip (1970–5) Steel tried to edge the party towards his idea of radical realignment: the essential feature was that the party must be ready to work with politicians in other parties who were willing to advance Liberal causes. The logical conclusion of this policy was that the party must be prepared, if the terms were right, to enter coalition. Once he had become leader, after a bruising election contest with John Pardoe in which the Liberal membership at large formed the electorate (conducted under rules of such exquisite fairness that even the Liberals were baffled), Steel was able to press his case more strongly. At the 1976 Joint Assembly he faced a demonstration from a Young Liberal minority, and won an enthusiastic response from the majority of the audience for the general idea of coalition in certain circumstances. But the actuality of the

Lib-Lab Pact was much less palatable to the party in the constituencies, and every extension had to be fought through the Liberal Assembly. The best that could be said of the pact was that it had secured some improvements in the quality of government rather than that it had won the adoption of specifically Liberal measures. The failure of the Labour Government to pass through the Commons a limited scheme of proportional representation for the European elections due in 1979 intensified opposition in the party to its continuation into the 1978/9 session. Steel withdrew his support for the pact in May 1978 and had a year to distance himself from the Labour Party before the general election.

The 1979 election reminded the party of the dangers of coalition. The Conservatives tarred the Liberals with the socialist brush: the party's vote dropped by one million (from 18.3% to 13.8%) and the MPs were cut from 13 to 11 (although Thorpe's defeat in North Devon was for other reasons). Yet almost at once the party was faced with another coalition prospect: the Social Democrats who were emerging from the Labour Party led by Roy Jenkins. Steel could safely have accepted Jenkins's offer to join the Liberal Party. Instead he encouraged Jenkins to establish a separate party and then, like a Borders shepherd, coaxed and harried his nervous and excited flock into the Alliance.

In early 1982 the government was extremely shaky; the Labour Party was in chaos; and with Jenkins back in Parliament it seemed possible that Steel's calculated high-risk strategy would succeed. The Argentine invasion of the Falkland Islands and Mrs Thatcher's response to it (and her success in allowing Lord Carrington to take all the blame for the invasion happening in the first place) blunted the Alliance attack. In the general election Steel spear-headed the Alliance campaign (despite Jenkins's designation as the Alliance candidate for the premiership), which resulted in a vote that fell short of Labour by only two percentage points but secured about one-tenth of Labour's seats. The press concluded that the Alliance had failed.

Jenkins's precipitate resignation as leader of the SDP immediately after the election, at the virtual insistence of DAVID OWEN who suc-

ceeded him, created enormous difficulties for Steel in the 1983–7 Parliament. Steel and Jenkins had understood that the Alliance was a 'partnership of principle' which could not be allowed to stagnate. But Owen blocked the two essential developments. Under the seat-sharing arrangements, in half the constituencies Liberals had no say in the choice of the candidate that they were expected to support; they wanted 'joint open selection', which Owen would not allow. Liberals also attached enormous importance to the right of the Joint Assembly to 'make policy' (even though they had no means of making the Liberal leader abide by the policy thus made); under the Alliance arrangements, Alliance policy was made in small negotiating groups in which the very much smaller SDP had equal standing with the Liberal team. Above all Liberals were frustrated by the fact that Steel had so linked their party's fortunes to the Alliance that they had repeatedly to give way to SDP demands or face the 'collapse of the Alliance'.

There was a strong feeling in the Liberal Party that after the general election the mould of the Alliance would have to be broken: either the partnership would become very much closer, with joint selection and a democratic system for making policy, or else the two parties would have to go their separate ways. This feeling was heightened by what Liberals perceived as Owen's disruptive and disloyal conduct during the election. The election itself was a disappointment rather than a disaster for the Alliance (the vote fell from 7.7 to 7.4 million, 25.4% to 22.6%) and, although the SDP lost three leading MPs, including Jenkins, the Scottish Liberal Party made two gains. Without consulting any of his leading colleagues in either Alliance party, or the elected office-bearers of the Liberal parties (the Scottish, Welsh and English parties were autonomous, though the English party thought of itself as British), Steel called for the two parties to be merged.

This was a major error. It allowed Owen to denounce the proposal as a take-over bid and wrong-footed those Social Democrats, such as Jenkins, who believed that merger was desirable or inevitable. Jenkins himself had intended to raise the issue of merger within the SDP and had wished the Liberals to wait for the proposal to come from his own party. Steel compounded the initial error by standing aloof from the details of the merger negotiations, which were protracted and difficult. His third, and fatal, mistake was to leave the drafting of the new party's initial policy declaration in the hands of Robert Maclennan of the SDP. The draft was highly speculative and totally unacceptable to the Liberal Party. With great courage Steel salvaged the negotiations by accepting shared responsibility for the draft and allowing his parliamentary colleagues to repudiate it and, by implication, him. Steel acted as joint leader of the new party until elections were held. Although there was speculation that he would offer himself as leader, it was certain that, if he did so, Ashdown would stand against him, and very possible that he would lose.

Steel's final errors owed something to the bad impression he had formed of the Liberal Party's organization when he was Chief Whip, and which his subsequent experiences as leader had done little to alter. They stand against, but they do not overshadow, the considerable achievements of his leadership. He had made changes in British politics and he had not diluted the essential liberal quality of the Liberal Party as it had been distilled by Grimond. There were 17 Liberal MPs on the Social and Liberal Democrat benches in 1989 compared with the 11 elected in 1979. Key Liberal issues, such as electoral reform, European unity, civil liberties and the environment, were more firmly on the political agenda than they had been when he became leader. In 1989 Steel addressed himself to the old Liberal cause of Scottish Home Rule when he accepted the joint chairmanship of the Scottish Constitutional Convention.

WRITINGS

A House Divided: the Lib-Lab Pact and the Future of British Politics (London: Weidenfeld and Nicolson, 1980).

Against Goliath (London: Weidenfeld and Nicolson, 1989).

FURTHER READING

Bartram, Peter, *David Steel: his Life and Politics* (London: W. H. Allen, 1981).

C. M. MASON

Stewart, (Robert) Michael (Maitland) [Lord Stewart of Fulham] (*b.* Bromley, Kent, 6 November 1906). Labour Foreign Secretary. He was a member of Harold Wilson's cabinets throughout the Labour governments of 1964–70, serving as Foreign Secretary in 1965–6 and again from 1968 to 1970. He sat in the Commons from 1945 to 1979, thereafter becoming an active Labour life peer.

Stewart, a middle-class teenage convert to socialism, attended Christ's Hospital and St John's College, Oxford, where he became President of the Oxford Union. He taught, first at Merchant Taylors' School and then for the Workers' Educational Association, founded the Association for Education in Citizenship, and contested West Lewisham unsuccessfully for Labour in 1931 and 1935. During the war he was in Army Intelligence and the Army Educational Corps. After becoming MP for Fulham East in 1945 he was immediately appointed a Government Whip, and later became Under Secretary to Emmanuel Shinwell at the War Office. In opposition in the 1950s, Stewart was first an Education spokesman, then from 1959 charged with Housing and Local Government. Thus it was somewhat surprising that, when Labour came into office in October 1964, Harold Wilson gave him rather than Richard Crossman the Education portfolio. Here his proposals for phasing in comprehensive schooling, which included sanctions against recalcitrant local authorities, were rejected by cabinet. Meanwhile Labour's Foreign Secretary, Patrick Gordon Walker, was defeated first in his own seat and then in a by-election, leaving the post vacant. Stewart was promoted to it in January 1965.

At the Foreign Office Stewart was a strong supporter of Britain's entry into the European Community, on which Wilson appeared hesitant. He was also responsible (more fully so after the Foreign and Commonwealth Offices merged in October 1968) for Britain's reaction to the unilateral establishment of Ian Smith's white minority regime in Rhodesia. Stewart opposed the use of force by Britain, but had retrospectively to recognize that negotiations and economic sanctions had been ineffectual in dislodging Smith. Perhaps most controversial was Stewart's role in relations with the USA.

He became closely identified with Britain's support – albeit never wholly uncritical – for the US intervention in Vietnam, for which he was sharply attacked by the left and by many Labour backbenchers.

Stewart's Foreign Office career was broken by an odd interlude, characteristic of Wilson's sometimes ill-judged institutional experimentation. He was put in charge of the new and ill-fated Department of Economic Affairs, largely because Wilson's deputy George Brown threatened to leave the government unless he was given the foreign secretaryship. Brown and Stewart thus swapped jobs in August 1966, rather as Stewart and Crossman had done in 1964: but this left each man in a post for which he was ill-equipped. In March 1968 Brown finally did resign. Stewart returned to the Foreign Office, having extracted a promise that he would not be moved again. He was happier there, though his second stint was dominated by the crises over Rhodesia, military rule in Greece, the comic British 'invasion' of Anguilla, the more tragic Soviet invasion of Czechoslovakia, the Middle East conflict and the Nigerian Civil War. After 1970, failing to be elected to the shadow cabinet, Stewart returned to the back benches. He did so apparently without great regrets. When Labour returned to power in 1974 he was, at 67, too old to dream of office. He led the British Labour Group at the European Parliament in 1974–5, and became a life peer in 1979. His wife, Mary, whom he had met through the WEA in 1934 and married in 1941, had preceded him to the Lords as Baroness Stewart of Alvechurch in 1975. She died in 1984.

WRITINGS

Life and Labour: an Autobiography (London: Sidgwick and Jackson, 1980).

FURTHER READING

Crossman, R. H. S., *The Diaries of a Cabinet Minister*, 3 vols. (London: Hamish Hamilton and Jonathan Cape, 1975, 1976, 1977).

STEPHEN HOWE

Swinton, Lord [Lloyd-Graeme, Philip; Cunliffe-Lister, Philip] (*b.* East Ayton, York-shire, 1 May 1884; *d.* Masham, Yorkshire, 27 July 1972). Conservative politician. Despite an exceptionally long ministerial càreer, Swinton was little known to the general public. This was partly due to a triple name change. Born Lloyd-Graeme he became Cunliffe-Lister in 1924 to enable his wife to inherit the extensive Swinton estate near Masham in Yorkshire; and then in 1935 he took a peerage as Lord Swinton. In addition, he never held one of the major offices. Nevertheless, his tenure of the Air Ministry from 1935 to 1938 was crucial in preparing the RAF to fight the Battle of Britain.

After Winchester and University College, Oxford, Swinton embarked on a successful career at the London Bar. He was soon involved in Conservative politics and secured adoption for a Yorkshire constituency in 1911. The advent of war, however, postponed the realization of his parliamentary ambitions. He joined up immediately but in September 1916 was invalided home from the Somme, where he won the MC. The following year saw the young major in the surprising role of chief civil service adviser to Auckland Geddes, Minister of National Service. For his services Swinton was created KBE.

While still a temporary senior civil servant he was adopted for the new Hendon constituency, which he won easily in the 1918 election (and retained until his elevation to the Lords). In 1920 he gained office in Lloyd George's coalition, as Parliamentary Secretary to the Board of Trade, where he was to remain (apart from the brief Labour Government interlude in 1924) for the next nine years: first as a junior minister and then, with the break-up of the coalition in 1922, as President. This was a time when Britain was reversing its traditional commitment to free trade and Swinton, an ardent protectionist, had a major part in its implementation, culminating in the permanent system of protective tariffs and imperial preferences established in 1932. By then he had become a member of the National Government, briefly as President of the Board of Trade and then as Colonial Secretary. In that office he took a particular interest in economic questions and initiated the first comprehensive collection of colonial trade and production statistics. He was unable, however, to make much impact on the continuing problems of poverty and disease.

In June 1935 Swinton was appointed Secretary of State for Air, at a time when the government was under increasing attack for Britain's lack of air preparedness in face of the growing German menace. Here Swinton's undoubted administrative talents were given full scope. The capacity of the aircraft industry was greatly developed, the revolutionary new Hurricane and Spitfire fighters were ordered and the vital radar system was installed. Nevertheless, parliamentary criticism continued and Swinton, having gone to the Lords five months after his appointment, was in a poor position to meet it. The Prime Minister, Chamberlain, bowed to the pressure and obtained Swinton's resignation. This seemed at the time a confession of failure, but the Battle of Britain two years later provided Swinton's vindication.

The rest of his long career was something of an anticlimax. During the war Swinton had secondary posts as Minister Resident in West Africa and as the first Minister of Civil Aviation. In 1951 he joined Churchill's peacetime government and in the following year entered the cabinet once again as Commonwealth Secretary. He retired with Churchill in April 1955. Thereafter he remained close to Conservative politics, as confidant of the party's leaders and genial host on the Swinton grouse moors.

WRITINGS

I Remember (London: Hutchinson, 1948).

FURTHER READING

Cross, J. A., *Lord Swinton* (Oxford: Oxford University Press, 1982).

J. A. CROSS

T

Tawney, R(ichard) H(enry) (*b.* Calcutta, India, 30 November 1880; *d.* London, 16 January 1962). Social philosopher and economic historian. He exercised a major influence on socialist thought in Britain through his books, his teaching, his work for the Labour movement, adult education and the Church, and through the moral force of his personal example. Beatrice Webb's verdict in 1935 stands for others: 'A scholar, a saint and a social reformer, R. H. Tawney is loved and respected by all who know him.'

Born in India, where his father served Church and Empire as a notable Sanskrit scholar and principal of Presidency College in Calcutta, Tawney returned to England with his family when he was still very young. After Rugby, he went to Balliol College, Oxford, and was influenced by its turn-of-the-century ethos of scholarship linked to social duty. This was combined with his own profound religious faith, already seeking a social expression, to shape the course of his subsequent life. From Oxford he went to Toynbee Hall, the university settlement in the East End of London, where he combined educational social work with social investigation and reform, and supported this voluntary work by running the Children's Country Holiday Fund. There then followed a brief spell lecturing in economics at Glasgow University, until – in 1908 – he became the first tutorial class teacher under an arrangement made between the Workers' Educational Association and Oxford University.

Tawney's tutorial classes in the North of England have become a legend in the history of adult education. They were also very important to Tawney, not only in making him an economic historian but in their fusion of education and social commitment. Tawney always referred to these classes as the place where his real education had taken place. They continued in some form right up to the arrival of war in 1914. Tawney joined the Manchester Regiment, declining a commission, and was hit by a shell on the first day of the Battle of the Somme and almost killed. By the time he was discharged in 1917, his education was complete. He was a Christian moralist, socialist reformer and economic historian, with a mission to educate and persuade. The rest of his life was a working out of this mission.

In a trio of influential books, Tawney indicted the moral inadequacy of a society based only upon possessive individualism (*The Acquisitive Society*, 1921), charted the historical genesis of such a moral abdication (*Religion and the Rise of Capitalism*, 1926), and outlined the basis for a society of moral order and social unity (*Equality*, 1931). These works came to exercise an immense influence on social thinking and continue to provide the reason for Tawney's durable reputation.

However, he combined social thought with social action, on several fronts. He was centrally involved in initiatives during the 1920s to remind the Church of its social mission, and remained the uncompromising voice of Anglican socialism. His commitment to workers' adult education was profound and lifelong. On educational matters generally (on which he wrote more than anything else, much of it anonymously for the *Manchester Guardian*) he had a wide influence in the long period between the Fisher Act of 1918 and the Butler Act of 1944, contributing to several important reports and writing the statement on *Secondary Education For All* (1922) which became the basis of the Labour Party's approach to education for a generation. He also served the Labour Party and the trade-union movement in many other ways, having accepted a Balliol Fellowship in 1918 only on condition that he could stand as a Labour parliamentary candidate (which he did, unsuccessfully, on four occasions). He represented the trade-union side, to impressive effect, on the Sankey Commission on the coal industry in 1919; Labour's

1928 policy statement *Labour and the Nation* was but one product of Tawney's elegant pen.

He was in every sense a party man. Yet he was also a pioneering economic historian (appointed to the London School of Economics in 1919 and remaining there, after 1931 as Professor of Economic History, until retirement in 1949) who opened up major scholarly – and political – controversies with his work on the century before the Civil War. This work, too, was part of his larger mission to understand, explain and change. That mission was so successful that, on his eightieth birthday in 1960, *The Times* could write: 'No man alive has put more people into his spiritual and intellectual debt than has Richard Henry Tawney.'

FURTHER READING

Terrill, R., *R. H. Tawney and his Times* (London: André Deutsch, 1973).

Wright, A. W., *R. H. Tawney* (Manchester: Manchester University Press, 1987).

ANTHONY WRIGHT

Taylor, A(lan) J(ohn) P(ercivale) (*b*. Birkdale, Lancashire, 25 March 1906). Historian. Taylor's prolific writings on central topics in modern history have made him one of the most well-known English historians of his generation. He has combined scholarship, an incisive style and an iconoclastic disposition in a fashion that has excited and infuriated many thousands of readers. Always an active and vigorous journalist, he was the first historian to realize that television offered an opportunity to communicate with millions of people who would not read even his best-selling books. He lectured on the small screen with the same facility that had enthralled undergraduates at Oxford in his hey-day. British political life, past and present, came under his regular public scrutiny on such television shows as *In the News* and *Free Speech*. It was apparent that he inhabited no ivory tower, but his public activities did not entail any lessening of his commitment to 'serious' historical writing.

Taylor was the only child of a cotton merchant who worked in Manchester. Business and a somewhat attenuated nonconformity surrounded him in his childhood. He took it for granted that a lift and a billiards room were normal domestic equipment. Between 1919 and 1924 he attended Bootham School, York, a Quaker establishment, where he claimed to have preached anarchy for the school and communism for the country. At Oxford, he gained a First at Oriel in 1927. More importantly, it seems, he had developed an enthusiasm for the British working class and wished to devote his life to its emancipation. A visit to Russia in 1925 offered some clues. A spell in Vienna was followed by eight years at Manchester University before Taylor returned to provincial Oxford in 1938 as a Fellow of Magdalen. He wrestled with the complexities of the Habsburg Monarchy.

During the war Taylor continued teaching, but also did some work for the Political Warfare Executive. A contribution to a German handbook being prepared under its auspices failed to find the right note, but it was transformed into *The Course of German History* and became his first best-seller. He was also busy giving radio talks in London. He supposed that a Labour victory would bring about some fundamental change in British society, though he did not anticipate the victory that occurred in 1945. He saw no reason for there to be a cold war, and said so, frequently. His view, expressed in a broadcast in November 1945, was that 'private enterprise' would have no more future than the Jacobites in England after 1688. He excoriated the 'American way of life' – about which he knew little.

The pattern of Taylor's postwar activities was early established. He fitted in a vast number of talks, articles and lectures and worked on a severe study of European diplomacy, *The Struggle for Mastery in Europe 1848–1918*. He was clearly not merely a public entertainer, though even that book did not lack entertaining aspects. He then turned his attention to writing a biography of Bismarck. An invitation to give the Ford Lectures at Oxford produced a brilliant treatment of men, like himself, who had invariably found themselves dissenting from official British foreign policy, *The Troublemakers*. British Government policy in the 1956 Suez Crisis gave Taylor an opportunity both in print and on the public platform to prove that that tradition was both alive and relevant. On the other hand, his conscience was not troubled by Soviet intervention in Hungary.

By this juncture Taylor had a secure eminence in several fields normally considered quite distinct. He was the only Fellow of the British Academy to write regularly in the *Sunday Express*. However, neither in Oxford nor in London did he gain further academic promotion. He remained both prolific and pro-vocative. He played a major campaigning role in the Campaign for Nuclear Disarmament, and his *Origins of the Second World War* caused a comparable stir in the academic world. His devotion to Lord Beaverbrook was expressed in a biography. Taylor continued as a writer and broadcaster long after his career as a college tutor came to an end, and *English History 1914–1945* became one of his best-known works. He was among the best historians of his generation and was certainly the best known. His devotion to paradox perhaps sprang from the many private and public 'ups and downs' which he experienced in his life. One of the final ironies was that he lived long enough to witness the vigorous revival of that 'private enterprise' which he had so confidently dismissed 40 years earlier.

WRITINGS

A Personal History (London: Hamish Hamilton, 1983).
An Old Man's Diary (London: Hamish Hamilton, 1984).

FURTHER READING

Wrigley, C. J., *A. J. P. Taylor: a Complete Annotated Bibliography and Guide to His Historical Writing* (Brighton: Harvester, 1980).

KEITH ROBBINS

Tebbit, Norman (Beresford) (*b.* London, 29 March 1931). Secretary of State for Employment and Chairman of the Conservative Party. Norman Tebbit is arguably the politician who, of his generation, had the greatest rapport with that mythical man in the Clapham omnibus. When he uttered his classic advice to the unemployed to 'get on their bikes' and find

work, he was voicing a sentiment that rings true to millions of British voters of all social classes. But there is more to it than that. The earthy, brutal way that Norman Tebbit says these things is deliberate, and the purpose behind them is to discredit a generation of what he sees as woolly idealists, fostering the notion that the whole community should feel guilty – about unemployment, about the special difficulties of racial minorities, about social problems sup-posed to cause crime, about the special prob-lems of the regions.

In other words Tebbit is rejecting the so-called postwar consensus whereby both main parties for years accepted governmental responsibility for such things: he is the rude child saying the emperor has no clothes – indeed shouting it, and jeering at those who pretend to see the clothes. And of course – this is what made him an effective politician – he is not by any means unique in believing that the postwar consensus has actually been counter-productive, by discouraging individual responsibility, by encouraging excuses from those who can't find jobs, those who break the law, those who can't manage their finances. It is the wisdom of the saloon bar transported to the corridors of power, or at least the wisdom of the saloon bars patronized by those who *are* employed, who are not members of minority groups, and who live largely in the south-east of the country.

Tebbit's background was the lower-middle-class environment of the north-east London suburbs (his constituency is in Chingford, Essex, in east London suburbia). He has never aped the manners or style of speech that make for the difference between Essex and, say, Surrey suburbia. The Tebbit family knew all about the toughness of the high unemployment of the 1930s, and his father did indeed get on his bike to look for work. The boy got to a grammar school, and as a national serviceman was commissioned in the RAF and qualified as a pilot.

Tebbit's civil career started in journalism and advertising, which presumably enhanced a natural feel for the importance of picking the right word. Then he qualified as a BOAC pilot: the steadiness of nerves required there was no bad training for politics. He began work for the

Norman Tebbit, Chairman
of the Conservative Party,
during the general election
campaign, May 1987

Conservative Party when he was a teenager, but his introduction to public life really came (as did Ronald Reagan's) as an office holder in a middle-class union: in Reagan's case it was the Screen Actors' Guild; in Tebbit's it was the pilots' association BALPA. He was not popular with the bureaucrats of BOAC.

Tebbit entered Parliament in 1970, at the start of Edward Heath's government. He disliked various elements of Heath's policy, such as prices and incomes policy, and it was when Margaret Thatcher ousted Heath as party leader, after the Tories had been defeated in two general elections in quick succession in 1974, that Tebbit became a major Commons figure.

The Tories were in an uneasy state. Their policy was in flux, to say the least, and it was unclear how best to attack the Labour Government, led by a Prime Minister, Harold Wilson, skilled at exploiting every chink in an enemy's armour. The Tories' gentlemanly traditions,

391

moreover, had always made them more effective performers on the government than on the opposition benches. Into this vacuum, Tebbit advanced with a sure step. He did not suffer from 'gentlemanly' inhibitions. He could take on, and score points off, that wily old parliamentarian Michael Foot (who dubbed him 'a semi-house-trained polecat').

Tebbit took up the cause of employees penalized by the closed shop, and knew how to present the union bosses in a light that made sense to an important working-class constituency: 'The voice and common sense of the mass of ordinary British workers will be drowned by the carefully orchestrated shouts of the destructive, hateful doctrines of the red fascists who have seized control of our trade union movement.' His style grieved some old-fashioned Tories; newcomers to the party were simply delighted that he so obviously drew blood.

When Mrs Thatcher came to power he was a natural part of her Praetorian guard. Not only Labour but the Tory 'Wets' had reason to fear his tongue. He rose up the ministerial hierarchy, and when he joined the cabinet as Employment Secretary in 1981 it seemed that at last the unions were going to be taken on. Tebbit did indeed toughen the laws on strikes, but in one sense there was anticlimax: union militancy had already been largely tamed by the grim unemployment figures of the early Thatcher years.

After two years at Trade and Industry (1983–5) Tebbit took over what seemed to be the natural job for him, as Mrs Thatcher's choice as chairman of the party: he was to be the man who would, so to speak, wring out the last of Tory 'Wetness'. In fact he proved not to be an ideal chairman. Even in a Thatcherite Tory Party, the post calls for a lightness of touch he did not have. And ironically, when the 1987 election came along, those natural allies Thatcher and Tebbit found themselves on opposite sides on an important matter of tactics. The issue was the party's image. Tebbit had worked out what he saw as a forward-looking advertising theme which, so it seemed to her, played down the style of the Thatcher years. The Prime Minister did not like it, and brought in her own advertising team. Tebbit

did not serve long after the election was out of the way.

He had, even before this, various reasons for reconsidering his career. He had suffered the appalling experience of the Brighton bomb, which injured him and left his wife crippled. Apart from that, he may well have decided that he had got as far as he was going to get in politics. Moreover, he had the consolation of various fairly lucrative offers from the private sector.

JULIAN CRITCHLEY

Temple, William (*b.* Exeter, 15 October 1881; *d.* Westgate, Durham, 26 October 1944). Archbishop of Canterbury, theologian and ecumenical statesman. He was Archbishop from 1942 until his death. He is commonly regarded as twentieth-century England's greatest churchman.

Temple was much influenced by his father, Frederick, who was himself Archbishop of Canterbury from 1897 to 1902. Following education at Rugby and Balliol College he became a lecturer in philosophy at Queen's College, Oxford (1904). He was ordained in 1909, became Headmaster of Repton in 1910, Rector of St James's, Piccadilly, in 1914 and married in 1916. In 1918 he resigned his living to lead the recently created 'Life and Liberty' movement. His official ecclesiastical standing was acknowledged in 1919 with a Westminster Canonry and, in 1921, with the Bishopric of Manchester. Subsequent moves to the Archbishopric of York (1928) and to Canterbury recognized his national and international reputation.

This reputation rested on important contributions in several spheres. Firstly, he was a notable philosopher and theologian. The 1934 Gifford lectures, 'Nature, Man and God', were recognized as a substantial contribution to Christian philosophical thought. Equally, his part in preparing the official report *Doctrine in the Church of England* (1938) and his own wartime *Readings in St John's Gospel* (1939 and 1940) significantly influenced theological reflection.

Secondly, Temple was an evidently impressive spiritual leader. This was acknowledged, for example, by those who experienced University Missions over which he presided in the 1920s and 1930s. Subsequently important figures, in Church and state, testified to the lasting impact then made by Temple's personality.

Thirdly, his contribution to 'Life and Liberty' marked him out as a significant Church reformer. This group's activities paved the way for the 1919 Enabling Act which, by creating the 'Church Assembly', empowered to enact ecclesiastical legislation, allowed for greater Anglican self-government and initiated the process which, in 1970, led to the creation of synodical government.

Fourthly, his leadership of the nascent ecumenical movement confirmed him as a major international figure. In the 1930s he took the lead in drawing together the movement's initially separate wings respectively devoted to the Church's 'Faith and Order' and its socially orientated 'Life and Work'. Their merger (1938) entailed the creation, under Temple's chairmanship, of the Provisional Committee of the World Council of Churches – the postwar World Council's immediate precursor. Similarly, Temple became the British Council of Churches' first president (1943).

Finally, Temple had a uniquely significant influence on public debate. His socially critical attitudes owed something to friendship with R. H. Tawney, and found expression in brief Labour Party membership and his presidency (1908–24) of the Workers' Education Association. Through meetings like the 'Christian Conference on Politics, Economics and Citizenship' (1924) and such widely read books as *Christianity and Social Order* (1942) he later took the lead in re-asserting Christianity's claim to have a relevant prophetic function within the public domain. For example, his wartime contributions to debates about the nature of postwar national and international society stressed the need to work for a change of structures as well as of individuals.

Specific political interventions gave him additional prominence. Thus he incurred official displeasure by involvement in attempts to settle the 1926 miners' strike and by his recommendation to Neville Chamberlain (1934) that

William Temple,
Archbishop of Canterbury
(right), arriving at the church
of St Mary Woolnoth,
London, May 1942

393

budgetary surpluses should be used to restore expenditure cuts rather than to reduce taxes. Similar concerns underlay his part in preparing the influential report *Men Without Work* (1938). His continuing educational concerns were revealed while negotiating the Church–State 'Concordat' embodied in the 1944 Butler Education Act.

Such activities contributed to the formation of that climate of opinion which lay behind the election of the 1945–50 Labour Government. Their direct impact on future Anglican leaders also partially explains the criticisms levelled by some Church spokesmen against the ascendant 'free market' policies of the 1980s.

FURTHER READING

Baker, A. E. (ed.), *William Temple and his Message* (Harmondsworth: Penguin, 1946).
Iremonger, F. A., *William Temple: Archbishop of Canterbury* (Oxford: Oxford University Press, 1948).
Suggate, A. M., *William Temple and Christian Social Ethics Today* (Edinburgh: T. and T. Clark, 1987).

K. N. MEDHURST

Tewson, (Harold) Vincent (*b.* Bradford, Yorkshire, 4 February 1898; *d.* Letchworth, Hertfordshire, 4 February 1981). Trade-union leader. Tewson was General Secretary of the TUC from 1946 to 1960. Like most men who have held this post, his roots lay in the North of England. His father was a gardener in West Yorkshire. Tewson's involvement with the Labour movement began at a very early stage. He worked as an office boy for the Amalgamated Society of Dyers in Bradford on leaving school at the age of 14. Four years later he was fighting in France and won a Military Cross. After the war he returned to Bradford and immersed himself again in the problems of the textile industry and of local politics. In 1925, however, he moved south to become secretary of the organization department of the TUC. In 1931 he was appointed assistant secretary to Citrine and served loyally under him until 1946, when he in turn became General Secretary.

It was a novel experience for a General Secretary to have to advise the trade-union movement during a period of majority Labour government. Tewson sought to persuade trade-union leaders that it was in their interest to cooperate, in a general way, with 'their' government's policies. His ideas were not very popular on the left, particularly because of the prominent stance he took in international trade-union issues as the cold war became more intense. In 1945 he went to Greece at a time of acute internal conflict between communist and non-communist groups of trade unionists and devised what came to be known as the 'Tewson agreement' designed, without much success, to facilitate cooperation. There was no doubt, however, that Tewson was acutely suspicious of the communists. He had great anxieties about the World Federation of Trade Unions, and he played a leading part in setting up the alternative 'Western' International Confederation of Free Trade Unions at its organizing conference in Geneva in 1949. He served as its president from 1951 to 1953 and was very active on its behalf in Africa and Asia. He was knighted in 1950. The left accused Tewson of collaborating with capitalism and the right rejoiced at this rejection of the communist embrace. The issue dominated his general secretaryship. Tewson stood down in 1960 but kept himself active in retirement by sitting on numerous 'Productivity Councils'.

FURTHER READING

Weiler, P., *British Labour and the Cold War* (Stanford: Stanford University Press, 1988).

KEITH ROBBINS

Thatcher [née Roberts], **Margaret (Hilda)** (*b.* Grantham, Lincolnshire, 13 October 1925). Conservative Prime Minister. Thatcher has been Prime Minister since her general election victory of May 1979. The bare details of her record are remarkable. She has won three consecutive election victories. She has remained Prime Minister longer than any other twentieth-century British leader. She is the first woman Prime Minister in British history. She is the first Oxford science graduate to gain the highest office. She is still only approximately at an age when Attlee, Chamberlain,

Churchill or Macmillan first reached 10 Downing Street. Her staying power in itself entitles her to a unique place in twentieth-century British political life.

There was little in her background or early career to suggest such an achievement was possible. Her father, Alfred Roberts, was a grocer and a keen Methodist local preacher who also served the local community in a multitude of ways. Before her marriage, her mother had her own dress-making business. The family lived above the shop. Margaret won a scholarship to Kesteven and Grantham Girls School. The values of hard work, self-reliance and self-discipline and a concern for the community, instilled in her from an early age, carried her forward. She knew nothing about Oxford University before she went up to Somerville College in 1943 to read chemistry. The possibility of a political career was lurking in her mind but it did not seem feasible at this stage. She joined the University Conservative Association and became its president in 1946, but reading chemistry did not give her much spare time. Her first job was as a research chemist, but she successfully applied to become the candidate for Dartford, a safe Labour seat, in 1949. In the general elections of 1950 and 1951 she succeeded in reducing the Labour majority, but Dartford remained a safe Labour seat.

After the October 1951 election she married Denis Thatcher at Wesley's Chapel in City Road, East London, and two years later her twins, Carol and Mark, were born. During these years she read for the Bar, specializing in taxation law. She was called in 1954. The general election of 1955 passed her by, but in 1957 she was adopted for Finchley, a safe Conservative seat, and came to Westminster in 1959 at the age of 34. Within two years she was given her first ministerial job as Joint Parliamentary Secretary to the Ministry of Pensions and National Insurance. She early displayed her grasp of facts and figures. However, the prospects of further steady advance were dashed by the Labour victories of 1964 and 1966. In opposition, she initially shadowed on Pensions, but under EDWARD HEATH was given Housing and Land. In 1966 came promotion when she seconded Iain

Macleod, the Shadow Chancellor, on Treasury matters. In subsequent years she became, successively, Shadow Minister for Fuel and Power and for Transport. In 1970 she was Shadow Minister of Education, and Heath asked her to fill that office in government.

Thatcher was Secretary of State for Education throughout the Heath government. Women had held this post before; it was not likely to lead to higher things. She never became a member of the inner core of the cabinet and seemed to have her hands sufficiently full with the problems of her own ministry. One of her first steps was to issue a new circular advising that local authorities were no longer under pressure to go comprehensive, though they could still do so. She later announced that there would no longer be free milk for seven- to eleven-year-olds, leading to the cry that she was 'Thatcher the Milk-Snatcher'. In 1974 few commentators supposed that she would be the next Conservative Prime Minister. She had handled herself well in parliament but her national reputation seemed to be largely unfavourable.

By October 1974 Heath had led the Conservative Party for nearly ten years and had achieved one election victory and three defeats. The executive of the 1922 Committee wanted an election for the leadership. There was a general, though not unanimous, belief that Heath's personality did not go down well in the country. Heath himself, on the other hand, could argue that he had recently prevented the Labour landslide which many people had been predicting. His critics had to agree on a candidate, and it became clear that neither Keith Joseph nor Edward du Cann, whose names had been bandied about, was prepared to stand. In the event, the nominations received in January 1975 were Heath, Thatcher and Hugh Fraser. Only the first two were serious contenders. Thatcher knew that the stakes were high. If she failed, Heath and his supporters were not likely to forget her temerity. The initial odds still seemed to suggest that Heath would win; the weight of the shadow cabinet remained with him. Airey Neave, who had shared chambers with Thatcher in her barrister days, masterminded her campaign. Thatcher was speaking with considerable authority in the debates on

Margaret Thatcher with the
Soviet leader Mikhail
Gorbachev at RAF Brize
Norton, December 1987

the 1975 Finance Bill. She defeated Heath by 130 votes to 119 in the first ballot but lacked an overall majority. Heath withdrew, but other candidates came forward for the second round – WILLIAM WHITELAW, James Prior, GEOFFREY HOWE and John Peyton. Only Whitelaw polled respectably, but Thatcher had her overall majority and there was no need for a third ballot.

It was not clear at the time what the victory represented. Fundamentally, it was a matter of personality rather than ideology. Heath and Thatcher were both 'self-made' Conservatives who owed nothing to background, connection or wealth, but, for all his tenacity, Heath was judged to have failed. It was time somebody else had a go, and Thatcher gained the reward of her courage. Even so, her position was precarious. There were large gaps in her political experience, particularly as regards foreign policy and the economy. The Conservative Party was in an unhappy condition. She seems to have felt that if she failed at the first general election hurdle she would not survive. Even as Opposition Leader she was far from secure and she made few changes in the shadow cabinet. Heath, however, had declined to serve and, while it was unfortunate that continuing division was therefore public knowledge, his presence in the shadow cabinet would have made life very difficult. Whitelaw was a more conciliatory figure, but tensions between the 'old guard' and the incisive new leader did not disappear overnight.

'Thatcherism' was slow to surface, but, as it did so, it became apparent that the new leader was bent on something more than a modest adjustment of postwar Conservative orthodoxies. She was the first Conservative leader to have come of age in the kind of society fashioned by Labour after 1945. She had no part in formulating a political response to that administration and had become convinced that the Macmillanite 'middle way' was no longer an option, or at least not in the form Heath had attempted in the last couple of years of his government. The country and its economy seemed in disarray. Thatcher was prepared to press the logic further and faster than Labour could possibly contemplate. Monetary controls and public-spending discipline were the way to tackle inflation, not the elaborate setting of norms and targets together with accompanying monitoring commissions. In these years there was wide-ranging argument within the party as the sacred cows of a quarter of a century were brought under review. Heath still stood stoutly and publicly for an incomes policy; Thatcher pledged to restore free collective bargaining. It was not clear that she had gained sufficient authority to get her way, and the division of opinion was held to be making a Labour victory possible. Then came the 'Winter of Discontent' in 1978–9 which gave Thatcher an opportunity to urge major trade-union reform. She seized it eagerly, too eagerly for some of her colleagues. She would set the people free in a way no Conservative leader had done since 1945. She would restore to them their primary responsibility for their own affairs. There was a radical and evangelical ring about her approach which carried her through to victory in May 1979.

The gravity of the problems facing the country did not daunt Thatcher. The control of inflation and trade-union reform were high priorities. Her victory enhanced her standing within the party, but she was still not in a position to have the kind of 'conviction cabinet'

of which she talked. Many of the so-called 'Wets' in the cabinet supposed that their strength in its ranks would enable them to moderate or sabotage her radical initiatives. They were to find that this was not the case. The 1979 budget introduced by Sir Geoffrey Howe had as its keynotes the need to restore incentives and personal responsibility. Opposition politicians soon began to look for 'U-turns', only to find that they were not forthcoming. Dissent within the government was still vocal, particularly when the shape of the 1981 budget was known. In trade-union matters the replacement of Prior by Tebbit in September 1981 was an indication that Thatcher wanted to go further, as she put it, in restoring unions to their members, or, as her opponents described it, in emasculating trade-union power. But 1981 was a bad year, as the new Social Democratic Party in particular gained spectacular by-election victories. The medicine administered by the government was unpalatable and probably to no avail as unemployment climbed.

Two years later, when the Conservatives won their largest number of seats since 1945, it was easy to overlook this trough. In between came the Falklands War of 1982 – an episode which no commentator had predicted. It remains difficult to assess its ultimate significance, but it remains true that Thatcher displayed courage and determination of a high order.

The second Thatcher administration was less dramatic than the first, partly because her own ascendancy was inevitably more assured. One of her first acts was to dismiss her previous Foreign Secretary, Francis Pym. It was a sign of her determination. The general tone of the cabinet was now more to her liking. Even so, the administration seemed curiously to lack direction and was hampered by personal issues such as the private life of Cecil Parkinson. Then came the bitter and protracted coal dispute of 1984–5 which came to dominate all other issues. The 1972 and 1974 strikes lingered in Conservative memories. Another victory for the National Union of Miners would be catastrophic for the government. Thatcher was determined that she would win and was aided from the outset by the manner in which the dispute began. IAN MACGREGOR, who had already slimmed down British Steel, became chairman of the National Coal Board in September 1983 and had substantial coal stocks in hand to sustain him in any protracted dispute. Eventually, in March 1985, Arthur Scargill was forced to call off the strike, bitterly complaining about the inadequate support he had received from the trade-union movement and the Labour Party. The costs had been heavy, but from the government's view the 'right to manage' had been asserted successfully. The opposition argued that Thatcher's policies were eroding Britain's industrial base. Her answer was that only drastic overhaul and exposure to the reality of competition would engender the qualities and capacities necessary for survival.

It seemed almost by accident that the Prime Minister stumbled into what fast emerged as a major theme of government policy: privatization. British Telecom was transferred from the public to the private sector in November 1984 and other substantial sales followed. Here was popular capitalism at work. The government also claimed that efficiency and performance improved. Sceptics suggested that in most cases private monopolies were replacing public monopolies. There were, in addition, 'little local difficulties' which threatened the government's survival in 1986: the future of the Westland helicopter company, the acquiescence in American bombing of Libya and the *Spycatcher* affair among them. Even so, in June 1987 Thatcher attained her third electoral victory. The continuing difficulties of the Labour Party and the post-election problems of the erstwhile 'Alliance' parties ensured her parliamentary dominance, but by October 1989, in the wake of Lawson's resignation as Chancellor of the Exchequer, the cry for a return to 'Cabinet Government' was heard, and her public standing fell.

Few political leaders in modern British history have evoked such strong and contrasting responses as Margaret Thatcher. It is the Conservative Party under her leadership which has broken the mould in which postwar British politics appeared to be set. Her chief distinguishing characteristic is her belief in getting things done. Her zest for problems remains

formidable. Perhaps she has derived benefit from operating in what is still fundamentally a man's world. She has contributed to a revival of British self-esteem, and her political longevity, together with her capacity to master information, has resulted in a role for Britain internationally which seasoned observers believed had disappeared for ever. No record of success, however, can be achieved without a price being paid. Thatcher can be accused of philistinism in her pursuit of excellence, of parochialism in her pursuit of patriotism, of authoritarianism in her pursuit of liberty, of meanness in her pursuit of self-reliance, of materialism in her pursuit of increased living standards and of ruthlessness in her pursuit of realism. The justice or otherwise of these charges can be assessed only when the record is complete; the work is still in progress.

For further illustration, see HEATH, EDWARD.

FURTHER READING

Harris, Kenneth, *Thatcher* (London: Weidenfeld and Nicolson, 1988).
Jenkins, Peter, *Mrs Thatcher's Revolution: the Ending of the Socialist Era* (London: Jonathan Cape, 1987).
Minogue, Kenneth and Biddiss, Michael, *Thatcherism: Personality and Politics* (London: Macmillan, 1987).
Young, Hugo and Sloman, Anne, *The Thatcher Phenomenon* (London: BBC Publications, 1986).

KEITH ROBBINS

Thompson, E(dward) P(almer) (*b*. Oxford, 3 February 1924). Historian, polemicist, and prominent peace and human rights activist. He has been distinguished in three separate but inter-related fields. As a professional historian he has been the most eminent and influential of the postwar school of English Marxist historians; as a political polemicist he has produced a series of substantial writings over three decades advocating 'socialist humanism'; and as a political activist he has been a leading figure in the New Left and in the peace movement.

His professional work has dealt mainly with

eighteenth- and nineteenth-century England. In 1963 he published *The Making of the English Working Class*, the seminal work which analysed the creation of the new urban working class at the outset of the industrial revolution, and revolutionized our view of the process of industrialization and the nature of the working class. Other major historical works have included *William Morris: Romantic to Revolutionary* (1955, revised 1977) and *Whigs and Hunters* (1975). Thompson's political polemics have been wide-ranging, devastating and often of intellectual as well as political significance: for example, 'The Peculiarities of the English' (1965), a *tour de force* extolling the virtues of English radicalism, and the intricate and savage demolition of Althusserian Marxism in *The Poverty of Theory* (1978). In all these contexts Thompson has written with passion and intensity. He is probably the finest socialist *writer* of the late twentieth century in the English-speaking world.

Thompson was educated at Cambridge and, after war service in Italy, was appointed lecturer in the (then) Department of Extramural Studies at the University of Leeds, a post he held, latterly as Reader, from 1948 to 1965. His extramural teaching and research in labour history in the West Riding of Yorkshire provided the foundation of *The Making of the English Working Class*. In 1965 Thompson left Leeds for the University of Warwick. However, he was soon embroiled in student agitation over 'secret files' and the more general protest against Warwick's perceived role as the 'business university'. (He subsequently edited *Warwick University Ltd*, 1970.) Since his resignation from Warwick, Thompson has lived as a full-time writer and peace activist.

In one sense Thompson's political commitments have remained unchanged. His is a passionate, romantic and human-centred socialism, emphasizing always the importance of human agency and distrustful of party orthodoxies and bureaucracies. For Thompson, socialism, democracy and civic freedoms are indivisible. Until 1955/6 he was an active member of the Communist Party. The increasing rigidity of the party's 'democratic centralism', and the tensions within the intellectual movement following

Khruschev's denunciation of Stalin at the 20th Congress of the CPSU in 1956, led Thompson and his fellow historian and party colleague John Saville to produce a discussion journal, *The Reasoner*. After the suppression of the Hungarian uprising in the autumn of 1956, and the CP's support for the USSR's actions, Thompson and Saville refused the instruction to abandon their journal and resigned from the party. The journal, now renamed *The New Reasoner*, formed the basis of the first New Left. Dissident ex-CP members joined with the young radicals of the *Universities and Left Review* to create a network of 'New Left Clubs' throughout England. In 1960 the two groupings merged to produce *New Left Review*.

The New Left politics of this period and the traumatic events of 1956 have remained for Thompson *the* political watershed and the reference point for his subsequent political activity. The New Left stood for a fully democratic and socialist system: in essence, a socialized economic structure with a strong emphasis upon workers' control and organizational decentralization, and a free and democratic political system where civic and cultural freedoms would be greatly increased and diversified.

The peace movement and the demand for nuclear disarmament have focused and symbolized this ideological stance. Not only has nuclear disarmament been the humanistic demand *par excellence*: the cold war itself and the accompanying arms race have drawn attention to the dangers and absurdities of super-power confrontation. Moreover, the movement itself was precisely the popular, extra-parliamentary, quasi-libertarian and democratic mass movement that has best represented Thompson's vision of a socialist future. In the revivified peace movement of the 1980s Thompson's has been a powerful voice. It was his polemical pamphlet *Protest and Survive* (1980) which acted as the rallying point for the new movement, and it was Thompson's initiative which created the influential European Nuclear Disarmament (END) organization.

In his emphasis upon the necessary connections between peace and civil freedoms – in the Eastern bloc as much as in the West –

Thompson speaks authentically not only for humanistic Marxism but also for English radical politics, the 'Liberty Tree' so vividly described in *The Making of the English Working Class*.

Thompson's reputation and influence as an historian are not in doubt. In trying to extend, through his own political activity, the traditions of English radicalism with which he identifies so closely, he has also had a significant influence on progressive political thinking in Europe and the USA and contributed to the re-assertion and revitalization of the humanistic Marxist perspective.

FURTHER READING

Anderson, Perry, *Arguments Within English Marxism* (London: Verso, 1980).
Barker, Rodney, *Political Ideas in Modern Britain* (London: Methuen, 1981).
Inglis, Fred, *Radical Earnestness* (London: Martin Robertson, 1983).

RICHARD TAYLOR

Thomson, Roy (Herbert) [Baron Thomson of Fleet] (*b.* Toronto, 5 June 1894; *d.* London, 4 August 1976). Newspaper proprietor. If he had died at the age of 60, Thomson would have been remembered (but only by Canadians) as a very successful businessman. His origins in Ontario were humble, and in the 1920s he tried, without success, to be a farmer, a motor-supplies dealer and a radio-set salesman. His luck changed in the 1930s, when he turned his attention to radio stations and then to newspapers. By the end of World War II he was a wealthy man. He contemplated a career in Canadian federal politics but that did not come off. Then the death of his wife and certain other setbacks led him to contemplate a completely new area of operations. He bought *The Scotsman* in Edinburgh and was awarded the independent television franchise for Scotland. His great-grandfather had emigrated from Scotland and Thomson for a short time lived in Edinburgh, but he continued to have major Canadian interests.

Thomson's impact on British public life came after his acquisition of the Kemsley newspaper group in 1959. That brought him

the *Sunday Times* and many other titles. He made many organizational and printing changes and in 1962 the *Sunday Times* launched the first newspaper colour magazine. He was raised to the peerage in 1964. Three years later he acquired *The Times*, which was then in grave financial difficulty. Thomson and his son were willing to put substantial amounts of their own money into keeping the paper afloat. Not that *The Times* became an all-engrossing preoccupation: publishing houses were acquired, a travel service was launched and Thomson shrewdly and profitably invested in oil exploration in the North Sea. It is his ownership of *The Times*, however, which gives him a place in British public life. Without his commitment, the paper might well not have survived. Thomson was genuinely proud of his ownership, but did not see it as a vehicle for the expression of his own political views, which were, in any case, not well developed. He was fundamentally a businessman who liked to make things work efficiently and to generate as much money as possible in the process. He mingled with the great men of politics but had too many other enterprises to aspire to join their ranks. He remained a puzzled outsider in a country which had given him such an unexpectedly profitable and enjoyable last 20 years of life.

WRITINGS

After I was Sixty: a Chapter of Autobiography (London: Hamish Hamilton, 1976).

FURTHER READING

Braddon, Russell, *Roy Thomson of Fleet Street* (London: Collins, 1965).

KEITH ROBBINS

Thorneycroft, (George Edward) Peter [Lord Thorneycroft of Dunston in the County of Stafford] (*b.* Dunston, Staffordshire, 26 July 1909). Chancellor of the Exchequer and Chairman of the Conservative Party. Thorneycroft has enjoyed a professional and political career of considerable variety. He was once considered to be a possible leader of the Conservative Party and judged to have the capacity to be a Prime Minister of merit. However, having been Chancellor of the Exchequer for precisely one year (January 1957 to January 1958), and having subsequently lost his seat in the House of Commons in the general election of April 1966, he seemed set for political obscurity. On 12 February 1975, however, he was invited to become Chairman of the Conservative Party by Margaret Thatcher. 'I have been discovered again', he observed, 'and with this lady we will all have to hang on to our hats.' His last political appointment was owing principally to the fact that he had been the first guest speaker of Margaret Thatcher (then Margaret Roberts) when she was President of the Oxford University Conservative Association in 1946: she vividly remembered the doctrine of financial and monetary stringency which he had preached to his undergraduate audience, a doctrine subsequently associated more with her name than with his.

Thorneycroft is remembered principally for his resignation in 1958 from the post of Chancellor of the Exchequer in the government headed by Harold Macmillan (along with his juniors Nigel Birch and ENOCH POWELL). The Chancellor had presented to the cabinet a programme for the reduction of public expenditure, a programme which he believed to be essential to ward off inflation. There was a difference of opinion between himself and the other cabinet ministers of the day over how much should be cut. The difference amounted to some £50 million. He could not get his way and so gave up his office. 'If only', he said in 1975, when he was pulling together a party somewhat shocked to find itself led by a woman who took a like view of national financial exigency, 'we had taken fifty million off then, we would not now have the problem of taking off hundreds of millions.' In his mid-sixties, however, he did sterling service to the political cause in which he believed by rallying Conservatives behind Mrs Thatcher's banner until the Autumn of 1981, when he finally retired from public life.

A varied past, however, preceded his greatest moments in politics. He became a barrister in 1934, and served in the Royal Artillery Regiment during World War II. He served as MP for Stafford from 1938 to 1945, and for Monmouth from 1945 to 1966; in the general election of the latter year he lost his seat, and presumed his political career to be over. During his time in the House of Commons he had been Parliamentary Secretary to the Ministry of War between May and July 1945 and President of the Board of Trade (with a seat in the cabinet) between 1951 and 1957. Having been Chancellor of the Exchequer for a shorter period than anybody in the twentieth century except Stanley Baldwin and Iain Macleod he returned to government, as Minister of Aviation from July 1960 to July 1962, and as Minister of Defence from the latter date until October 1964, when the Labour Party returned to office. (He had been made Secretary of State for Defence by Sir Alec Douglas-Home in April 1964.)

In opposition between 1964 and 1966, Thorneycroft was Shadow Home Secretary. As he had striven to persuade the Macmillan government to pursue an austere policy in relation to national finance, so he strove to persuade Home, and Home's successor, Edward Heath, to put forward measures for the restriction of immigration into Britain from the New Commonwealth, in which efforts he was continually supported by Enoch Powell.

If Thorneycroft's public persona suggested a figure of rigour, in private he has ever been gregarious, agreeable, and possessed of a sense of fun. He was married twice: first to Sheila Page of Wolverhampton and then, after his divorce in 1949, to the daughter of a noble Italian Family, Carla Roberti. He is a painter (particularly in watercolours) of some distinction, though an unsuspected shyness prevented him from exhibiting until his later years. Future historians will, however, concentrate above all on his role as a prophet of the new – and, to some, harsh – economic policies introduced in 1979. The vicissitudes of political fortune ordained that he did not have the opportunity himself to administer the policies he supported for so long.

FURTHER READING

Cosgrave, Patrick, *Thatcher: the First Term* (London: Bodley Head, 1985).
Jenkins, Peter, *Mrs Thatcher's Revolution: the End-*

ing of the Socialist Era (London: Jonathan Cape, 1987).

PATRICK COSGRAVE

Thorpe, (John) Jeremy (*b.* London, 29 April 1929). Liberal leader. Thorpe was the first leader of the Liberal Party since Lloyd George to be driven by a single-minded political ambition and to cultivate deliberately the political skills needed to satisfy it. He sought successfully the presidency of the Oxford Union (1951) and although called to the Bar in 1954 he did not regard law as anything more than an interim occupation. He fought a winnable seat (North Devon) at the earliest opportunity (the 1955 general election) and won it in 1959. His principal gifts were his debating skills and wit, his talent for fund-raising and picking political organizers, and an extraordinary ability to remember by face, name and family history thousands of constituents and party members. He served as party treasurer from 1965 to January 1967, when he was elected by the parliamentary party as leader.

The son and grandson of Conservative MPs, Thorpe's political inclinations were radical and progressive, but he was hardly a radical thinker (nor was he liked by the radical sections of the party, who distrusted his cleverness and superficiality). He saw correctly that Harold Wilson's sanctions policy would take years rather than months to break the illegal regime in Rhodesia, and scandalized conservative opinion by advocating the bombing of Rhodesia's rail links with South Africa. But he left it to David Steel to continue to work out Jo Grimond's ideas on a radical realignment in British politics.

Thorpe's grandiose strategy for the 1970 general election (launched in 1968 as the 'Great Crusade') could not prevent the Liberal Party losing half its seats (though its share of the national vote dropped by no more than one percentage point). The party's luck turned in the latter half of the Heath Parliament. A run of by-election victories brought it back into prominence and the appeal for 'partnership', devised by David Steel, with Thorpe's campaign planning and brilliant presentation of the Liberal case in the February 1974 general election won over 6 million votes (more than at

any election since 1928) but only 14 seats. Heath's offer to go into coalition with the Liberals was refused because he could not promise his party's support for proportional representation.

Thorpe resigned the leadership on 10 May 1976 because of mounting allegations of homosexual conduct, which he denied. He was later charged with conspiracy to murder and other offences; shortly after he lost his seat in the 1979 general election he was acquitted on all charges at the Old Bailey. Although his Liberal colleagues shrank from him, the United Nations Association appointed him chairman of its Executive (1976–80) and of its Political Committee (1977–85). In 1987 the North Devon Liberal Association elected him as their president.

C. M. MASON

Trelford, Donald (Gilchrist) (*b.* Coventry, 9 November 1937). Editor of *The Observer*. He was appointed to the editorship of the venerable liberal Sunday paper in 1975, since when he and the paper have seldom been free of controversy. He joined *The Observer* in 1966, after three years as editor of the *Times of Malawi* in Central Africa. When David Astor retired nine years later, Trelford was chosen as editor after consultation with the paper's staff.

Almost immediately, he became involved in a dispute over *The Observer*'s ownership, when he campaigned determinedly against a proposal to sell it to Rupert Murdoch. Instead, it went to an American oil company, Arco. Under Trelford's editorship in the late 1970s it largely maintained its reputation as a vehicle for good writing, liberal comment and informed reporting about the Third World. However, it was always outsold by its powerful rival, the *Sunday Times*.

In 1981 came another ownership crisis, when Arco sold the paper to Lonrho, a company with considerable African interests which was run by the formidable 'Tiny' Rowland. Trelford and other staff members were openly opposed to the sale, in part because they believed the new ownership would taint their third-world coverage. After the sale went through Trelford had several public rows with

Rowland, notably one about his own reporting of a massacre by the army in Zimbabwe – a country whose goodwill Rowland was seeking to foster. From about that time, *The Observer* began to give increasing space to items that supported Lonrho's commercial interests, in particular the dispute over the sale of the House of Fraser department store group. Trelford came in for criticism for apparently allowing his paper to be used in this blatant manner, diverting attention from the less self-interested campaigns it was still conducting on issues such as press freedom and civil liberties.

FURTHER READING

Hall, Richard, *My Life with Tiny* (London: Faber and Faber, 1987).

MICHAEL H. LEAPMAN

Trenchard, Hugh (Montague) [Viscount Trenchard of Wolfeton] (*b.* Taunton, Somerset, 3 February 1873; *d.* London, 10 February 1956). Founder of the Royal Air Force. He was Commander of the Royal Flying Corps in France in the Great War, Chief of the Air Staff in the Royal Air Force in 1918 and from 1919 to 1929, and is known as 'the Father of the Royal Air Force'.

His early career in the army did not suggest that he was destined for great things. Though he served with some distinction in the Boer War, he was bored by peacetime army life. He spent some nine years in Nigeria after the South African war, but fell dangerously ill and had to be invalided home. In 1912, the year the Royal Flying Corps was formed, he was a 39-year-old major with little hope of advancement. He paid the air pioneer Tommy Sopwith to teach him to fly, and flew for just over an hour before finding himself one of only 17 officers in the armed forces 'qualified' as pilots at a time of rapid expansion of the RFC. At the outbreak of war, Trenchard was appointed Commandant of the Military Wing at Farnborough. He was soon out in France, however, commanding the 1st Wing. By 1915 he was in command of Britain's air effort on the Western Front, and had been made a Major General.

Trenchard soon earned himself a reputation as a relentlessly aggressive commander and an unswerving supporter of Sir Douglas Haig, the

Viscount Trenchard (seated) watching the fly past on Battle of Britain Day, Whitehall, September 1955

British Commander-in-Chief on the Western Front, in his fights with the political leaders on the direction of the war effort. Trenchard did not initially support the idea of amalgamating the RFC and the Royal Naval Air Service into a Royal Air Force. He felt that such an amalgamation was too large an administrative task to undertake in the middle of a war, and was worried that the RAF might be used primarily for long-range strategic operations at the expense of the immediate tactical needs of the army. Nevertheless, if long-range operations there had to be, Trenchard was prepared to command them, rather than leave the job to someone who did not have the confidence of Haig. He was appointed first Chief of the Air Staff in 1918, but resigned in a matter of months because he was unable to see eye to eye with the Air Secretary, Lord Rothermere. He then commanded the Independent Air Force, launching the RAF's first strategic raids, until the end of the war.

Once the RAF was formed, Trenchard responded with all the enthusiasm of the convert. When Winston Churchill combined the Air Ministry with the Colonial Office, he and Trenchard carved a place for the RAF in the permanent peacetime defence establishment in the 1920s, substituting cheap air power for expensive land power in the policing of the Empire. The army and the navy were convinced that the RAF should be wound up, but Trenchard, an enormously pugnacious and tenacious personality (known as 'Boom' for the power of his voice when roused), consistently fought them off, counter-attacking by demanding the further substitution of air power for other traditional roles of the army and navy.

Trenchard was appointed Commissioner of the Metropolitan Police in 1931, and undertook major organizational reforms in that post until he finally retired in 1935. The enormous respect he commanded in defence circles led to his being considered for a number of important posts in wartime, including Generalissimo in the event of invasion. He is buried in Westminster Abbey.

FURTHER READING

Boyle, A., *Trenchard: Man of Vision* (London: Collins, 1962).

Jones, N., *The Origins of Strategic Bombing* (London: William Kimber, 1973).

Smith, M., *British Air Strategy between the Wars* (London: Oxford University Press, 1984).

MALCOLM SMITH

Trog [Fawkes, Wally] (*b.* Vancouver, Canada, 21 June 1924). Cartoonist and caricaturist. Over the last 40 years the range of Wally Fawkes's work – his 'Flook' cartoon strip, political cartoons and brilliant *portraits chargés* – has established him as one of the most innovative caricaturists in the history of comic art. He

has worked for the *Daily Mail*, *The Spectator*, *Private Eye*, the *New Statesman* (where he pioneered Royal Family jokes), *The Observer* and *Punch*. He is also a talented jazz musician.

After emigrating with his parents from Canada to Britain in 1931, Fawkes studied at the Sidcup School of Art and Camberwell College of Art, where he was taught illustration by the painter John Minton. In 1945 he was talent-spotted by Leslie Illingworth, who secured for him a position as a graphic artist at the *Daily Mail* and became his artistic mentor. In 1949, at the behest of Lord Rothermere, Trog (he played clarinet with the Troglodytes jazz band) created a new cartoon strip. Ostensibly for children, it starred a boy (Rufus) and his magic pet Flook (the name was coined by Humphrey Lyttelton). Initially the graphic style was more unusual than the plots; later political satire and social comment became major features. A succession of scriptwriters (among them George Melly) ensured that a highly contemporary line of comment ran through the plots, although it was never the case that Trog was merely the illustrator. Trog's editorial cartoons have appeared in a succession of publications. Since 1971 he has been principal political cartoonist at *The Observer* while designing full-colour covers for *Punch*.

Trog has a strong, tight style bordering on the self-conscious, which underlines his belief that the political cartoon is uniquely dependent on caricature, and that caricature depends on highly developed graphic skills. His work is always cleanly designed with well-controlled distributions of solid black, textured and white areas. He uses a variety of media, including watercolour and gouache.

FURTHER READING

Lyttelton, Humphrey, *I Play as I Please: the Memoirs of an Old Etonian Trumpeter* (London: MacGibbon and Kee, 1954).

Melly, George, *Owning Up* (London: Weidenfeld and Nicolson, 1965).

Whitford, Frank, *Trog: Forty Graphic Years – the Art of Wally Fawkes* (London: Fourth Estate, 1987).

LIZ OTTAWAY

Tweedsmuir, Lord. See BUCHAN, JOHN.

V

Vansittart, Sir **Robert (Gilbert)** [Baron Vansittart] (*b.* Farnham, Surrey, 25 June 1881; *d.* Denham, Buckinghamshire, 14 February 1957). Permanent Under-Secretary at the Foreign Office. Descended from a family of considerable public distinction, he was the son of a cavalry officer who had inherited large estates in Kent, subsequently lost through injudicious financial ventures. These difficulties resulted in Vansittart's decision, after a distinguished career at Eton as captain of the Oppidans and winner of both the French and German Prince Consort prizes, to enter the Diplomatic Service in 1903 rather than to follow a literary career. Throughout his life he produced a stream of literary works, including verse, plays and novels. Even as a lowly Third Secretary in Paris, he had the distinction of having a play in French run for four months, much to the embarrassment of his ambassador. This literary flair was reflected in later Foreign Office memoranda, to the annoyance of colleagues, who found his prolix, often allegorical and obscure compositions too long and difficult to read, and tedious rather than informative. His minutes, on the other hand, could be brief, direct and pungent. Vansittart came top of the Diplomatic Service examination; he had three appointments abroad but thereafter, except for short official missions, spent his professional career in London.

The young diplomat returned to London in 1911 and worked under Eyre Crowe, a man whose views and integrity he deeply respected but from whom the flamboyant and socially expansive Vansittart differed in almost every other personal respect. After serving in the Contraband and Prisoners-of-War Department during the Great War, he went to Paris as a member of the Foreign Office delegation to the peace conference. It was through a series of private secretaryships, first to Lord Curzon (1920–4) and then to the successive Prime Ministers Stanley Baldwin and Ramsay Mac-Donald, that he made his way to the top position in the Foreign Office. Appointed Permanent Under-Secretary on 1 January 1930, Vansittart remained in this influential post for eight years until removed to the newly created position of Chief Diplomatic Adviser, to be replaced by ALEXANDER CADOGAN.

Vansittart firmly believed that his major function was to advise the Foreign Secretary and contribute to the formulation of British foreign policy. Though he was subsequently identified as a strong opponent of the policy of appeasing Nazi Germany, the advice which he gave his respective chiefs suggests that he was neither as consistent nor as clear in outlining an alternative policy towards Nazi Germany as his subsequent autobiography *The Mist Procession* (1958) suggests. In a series of 'old Adam' memoranda, written between 1930 and 1940, Vansittart repeatedly called attention to the dangers of the German challenge, the deep-rooted military instincts and innate barbarism of the German people, and the inevitability of another European war. But Vansittart's black view of Germany did not exclude the possibility of seeking a negotiated settlement with Hitler, such as an air pact or colonial arrangement, at least until Britain was strong enough to face the German threat. Vansittart did press for agreements with France and for a drastic increase in the pace of British re-armament, above all in the air, for he was haunted by the vision of the 'knock-out blow' which would crush Britain at the very start of the war. His increasingly shrill warnings about the Nazi menace were fuelled by intelligence gathered from his own private sources in Germany, which included Group Captain Malcolm Christie and Hans Ritter of the German Embassy in Paris, who provided Luftwaffe information, as well as such leaders of the German conservative opposition as Carl Goerdeler, the anti-Nazi burgomaster of Leipzig. This information, not always accurate, in addition to official intelligence coming to the

Foreign Office, gave substance to Vansittart's warnings about German air re-armament and imminent aggression in 1938–9, even when he no longer enjoyed the influence he exercised during the foreign secretaryships of Sir John Simon (1931–5) and Sir Samuel Hoare (1935).

Once Anthony Eden succeeded Hoare, it was inevitable that Vansittart would lose some of that influence. His Cassandra-like warnings and 'keep Germany lean' proposals but, above all, his trial of strength with a slow-moving Air Ministry, made powerful enemies in ministerial circles. Nor, apart from with a small group of Foreign Office intimates, was he a popular Permanent Under-Secretary – his isolation from his colleagues magnified by his lavish life style in London and at his splendid country home in Dedham. The Hoare–Laval pact was a crucial turning point in his loss of power. In Vansittart's anxiety to maintain the Stresa Front to isolate Hitler, he encouraged Hoare to make this agreement with the French at the expense of Ethiopia. It was almost immediately repudiated by the British Cabinet and led to Hoare's resignation. Eden wanted a less dramatic and more compliant Permanent Under-Secretary; the Foreign Secretary's hopes for a new appointment were fulfilled when Neville Chamberlain, prepared to take a new initiative in the search for an agreement with Germany, acted against the increasingly pessimistic Vansittart, who was publicly opposed to the Prime Minister's diplomatic interventions.

Vansittart's new title, Chief Diplomatic Adviser (1938–41), was far more impressive than his actual role. He kept his former room at the Foreign Office and, through his political, diplomatic and intelligence contacts, continued his efforts to influence policy. But he was now a marginalized figure and his criticism of the government's actions during the Austrian and Czechoslovakian crises had little effect on Downing Street. Though the war he had so long prophesied broke out in 1939, Vansittart remained an outsider. His views on Germany hardened; in a series of BBC talks, *Black Record: Germans Past and Present* (1941), he argued that Hitler was no accident but the natural product of a predatory and bellicose people, whose redemption would depend on a massive, and partly self-administered, spiritual cure. 'Vansittartism', an extreme and obsessive anti-Germanism, provoked considerable public controversy in wartime Britain and Vansittart's public campaign for a harsh peace was not without importance in shaping British surrender policies. During the last years of his life Vansittart took an equally passionate anti-Soviet line and became a major supporter of an integrated Western Europe as the best means of containing the Soviet Union.

WRITINGS

Lessons of My Life (London: Hutchinson, 1943).
The Mist Procession (London: Hutchinson, 1958).

FURTHER READING

Rose, Norman, *Vansittart: Study of a Diplomat* (London: Heinemann, 1978).

ZARA STEINER

Vaz, (Nigel) Keith (Anthony Standish) (*b.* Aden, 26 November 1956). Labour politician. With his winning of the Leicester East parliamentary seat from the Conservative Party in June 1987, Vaz became Britain's first MP of Asian origin since the 1920s – and, at the age of 30, one of the youngest members of the Commons.

A solicitor by training, educated at Latymer Upper School and Cambridge, Vaz had worked before entering Parliament for Islington Borough Council and for a law centre in Sheffield. His was a highly political family, and his sister Valerie is prominent in Labour local politics in London. He stood unsuccessfully for Labour in the 1983 general election and the 1984 elections to the European Parliament. Once in the Commons, he specialized in Home Office affairs, and also became treasurer of the new parliamentary Black Caucus: unlike many British citizens of Asian origin, he publicly identified himself as 'black' and argued for a commonality of interests between Asian and Afro-Caribbean communities. He also, though himself of Catholic background, developed close links with Britain's Muslims. During 1989 he took their side in the bitter controversy over Salman Rushdie's novel *The Satanic Verses*, which many Muslims thought blasphemous. Vaz's endorsement of Muslim leaders' calls for the book to be withdrawn or banned brought him sharp criticism from civil liberties campaigners.

STEPHEN HOWE

Vicky [Weisz, Victor] (*b*. Berlin, 25 April 1913; *d*. London, 23 February 1966). Cartoonist and caricaturist. He built a reputation as Fleet Street's leading political cartoonist in the 1950s and 1960s. His drawing expressed an intensity of feeling likely to exasperate people who did not share his brand of humanitarian socialism, but he was capable equally of inspiring warm affection. His prolific output appeared mainly in the *News Chronicle* (1939–53), the *Daily Mirror* (1953–8) and the *Evening Standard* (1958–66), where he was widely regarded as natural heir to David Low. 'The greatest worrier of his generation', as one of his editors described him, he suffered from depression, insomnia, overwork and the groundless fear of running dry of ideas. At the age of 52 and at the height of his fame, he died from an overdose of barbiturates.

Vicky's parents were Hungarian Jews living in Berlin. The youngest of three children, he began to make a living from sporting and theatrical cartoons for the *12 Uhr Blatt* after his father's death obliged him to leave school at the age of 15. His political drawings made Berlin unsafe for him after the Nazis came to power, and his Hungarian passport probably saved him from the concentration camps. He reached London via Paris in 1935, allegedly knowing the names of only three British politicians – Baldwin, Chamberlain and Churchill.

After several years of freelance work, the turning point came when Vicky met Gerald Barry, editor of the middlebrow Liberal mass-circulation daily the *News Chronicle*. Barry set him to learn systematically about the English by immersion in literature and popular culture, from Shakespeare and Dickens to greyhound racing and football. In 1941 he became staff cartoonist. His confidence and range grew steadily, and by 1947 he was drawing pocket cartoons, caricatures and column-breakers as well as the main daily cartoon. Barry's successor in 1950 handled him less well, and in 1953, impatient at the rejection of cartoons opposing the paper's policy, he joined the

Labour *Daily Mirror*. This was arguably a mistake. The tabloid style, geared to a circulation of four and a half million, suited neither his penmanship nor his outlook; and he disliked preaching largely to the converted. He was much more comfortable at the *Evening Standard* from 1958. From 1954 he delighted also in contributing weekly to the *New Statesman*. In addition, for a time in the 1950s he drew for *L'Express*, initially under the pseudonym Pierrot, agreeing the subject of each week's cartoon on the phone to Paris.

Vicky 'felt politics'; his socialism was emotional. Although many of his friends were on the Tribune wing of the Labour movement (Aneurin Bevan was a hero), he never joined the party. But he was active in pressure groups, especially those working for colonial independence, nuclear disarmament (he was an Aldermaston marcher) and against the growing gap between rich and poor nations. His 'Oxfam' style, reminiscent of *Simplicissimus* artists of his youth, depicted gaunt and shadowy images of human wretchedness often thought too grim by editors for publication. Mistrustful of the USA (John Foster Dulles was a favourite butt), he belied accusations of being 'soft' on Russia by the strength of his cartoons against the invasion of Hungary in 1956.

Vicky outgrew the early and almost inescapable influence of Low over format and style. His drawings, made with a pen, became increasingly economical, with fewer figures and less depth of detail within the frame. His use of the cartoonist's traditional armoury of techniques was inventive. Typical of his images – and most enduring – was the depiction of Prime Minister Harold Macmillan as 'Supermac'.

Vicky married four times – another facet of his restless private life. He had no children.

WRITINGS

Vicky's World (London: Secker and Warburg, 1959).

FURTHER READING

Cameron, J. (ed.), *Vicky: a Memorial Volume* (London: Allen Lane, 1967).

Davies, R. and Ottaway, L., *Vicky* (London: Secker and Warburg, 1987).

COLIN K. SEYMOUR-URE

W

Walker, Peter (Edward) (*b.* London, 25 March 1932). Senior Conservative minister. Peter Walker is the great survivor. When all the other Tory 'Wets' had long departed, he was still there in Margaret Thatcher's cabinet, admittedly not at the heart of the mainstream – but in the eyes of the zealots who out-Thatcher Thatcher it was an offence to political decency for him to be kept on, even in such a remote responsibility as Secretary of State for Wales.

Indeed, Wales under Walker since 1987 has actually been organized, to a substantial extent, according to the economic philosophy of traditional, paternalistic Tory ministers before the Thatcher revolution. With a network of consultative committees and the like to foster government partnership with private enterprise – and with characteristic skill in extracting money from the Treasury – Walker has presided over impressive economic recovery in the valleys. His more orthodox colleagues would say that Welsh prosperity simply shows how economic rectitude, as set out in monetarist decrees from Downing Street, eventually brings benefits throughout the whole of the United Kingdom.

Walker is what his critics would call a corporate-state man. He established that reputation in the Heath government of 1970–4 as Industry Secretary (1972–4), when he arranged injections of taxpayers' money into 'lame-duck' companies and encouraged his officials to forge contacts with the world of business (they would get better lunches in the City than in Whitehall, he explained affably). Under his aegis there was a massive expansion of the British steel industry – unjustified, as it emerged, by the way the market was moving.

Small wonder that, when the Tories' palace revolution came, and the party replaced Heath with Thatcher, Peter Walker – staunchly loyal to Heath – should have disappeared to the back benches. His reputation as a corporate-state man actually dated back before he was Industry

Secretary. As Environment Secretary (1970–2) he had been the man who changed the county boundaries – an operation which made enemies in practically every corner of British society (except among the bureaucrats who found that they suddenly increased their powers, salaries and numbers). The local government reorganization came to be seen in retrospect as marking a high point of the faith of the politicians of the 1960s and 1970s that they could bring untold benefits to their fellow citizens by administrative manipulation.

During the mid-1970s, when the intellectual battle raged within the Conservative Party, monetarists against old-fashioned paternalists, Walker was largely responsible for establishing the Tory Reform Group to present pre-Thatcher values.

In due course, in 1979, Mrs Thatcher arrived in Downing Street, and to everyone's surprise, including his own, Walker was invited to join her cabinet. The job he was offered represented a step down, but it was to take charge of an important enough Department: Agriculture. He was not invited to provide, and did not try to insist in providing, input on general strategy. Agriculture was not in fact an area where there was a great ideological gap betwen Thatcher and Walker. He might be upset when he returned from some EEC meeting in Brussels to be told: 'Ah, Peter, I hear you let the French walk over you again', but on the whole the Prime Minister seems to have accepted, when she saw taxpayers' money going to the British farmer, that this fitted in with her own rather chauvinistic inclination, provided there was some limit on the taxpayers' bill.

In 1981, when Thatcher purged her cabinet of Wets, Walker remained. She respected him as an efficient departmental minister, well able to fight his corner. There was also perhaps an instinct that in Walker – in contrast to the other Wets, public-school-educated and patrician –

Peter Walker

the Prime Minister could see one of her own kind. Like Norman Tebbit, he talks in the unpatrician accents of the London suburbs. And, as in Mrs Thatcher's case, Walker's parents were small shopkeepers. Like her, he grew up with a burning ambition to get to the top.

The story goes that, as a teenager in the bleak days just after the war, Walker looked up and down the road where he lived and noted that there was only one family with a car: the insurance man's family. Leaving school at the age of 16, he went into insurance. He speedily became a successful salesman, established his own broking business, and by his mid-twenties had joined Edward du Cann in launching a unit-trust-linked insurance scheme which fitted in with the fashionable ideas of the time on property-owning democracy. Financial success was important to him, but largely as a means of getting into politics: financial independence was more important then than now in getting anywhere in the Conservative Party. He had joined the Young Conservatives at 14, at 23 stood at the 1955 election as youngest candidate in the country and at 29 he was in Parliament.

As a minister in the Thatcher government he offset some of his Wetness when in 1983 he was moved from Agriculture to the Depart-

ment of Energy, where he was at the centre of the miners' dispute. At about this time – the Prime Minister was going through a bad patch in the opinion polls – there was much sage talk that the clever thing might be for the Tories to get rid of her, and that Walker, the survivor, might actually be the man to succeed her and pull the different strands together. Such talk did not last long. Incidentally, it emerged later from Ian MacGregor's memoirs that MacGregor did not regard him as being as tough with the miners as he had seemed to be (see also MACGREGOR, IAN).

On and off through the Thatcher years, Walker has taken opportunities to make fairly outspoken attacks on the philosophy of Thatcherism. His theme has been that capitalism – and he is unusual among senior Conservatives in having been a practising capitalist – is the way to create wealth, but that it must be caring capitalism – and the implication as it related to Mrs Thatcher was always clear. By the standards she applies to colleagues, she would have been well justified in getting rid of him. The ultimate reason why she didn't is probably that here is one Wet she thinks might just be able to be really troublesome on the back benches, in the way that none of the other sacked Wets ever were: perhaps, to use the famously eloquent imagery of President Lyndon Johnson, 'she would rather have him inside the tent pissing out than outside pissing in.'

JULIAN CRITCHLEY

Wavell, Archibald (Percival) [Earl Wavell of Cyrenaica] (*b.* Colchester, Essex, 5 May 1883; *d.* London, 24 May 1950). General, Commander-in-Chief and Viceroy of India. Known as 'Archie' to his friends and as 'The Chief' to his admirers, Wavell was an untypical soldier. Largely pressed into a military career by his father – a Major-General – Wavell never lost the interest in literature cultivated when he was a schoolboy at Winchester and is almost as well known for his poetry anthology, *Other Men's Flowers*, as he is as a wartime commander. Indeed, he was a frequent writer on military subjects and might well have been appointed Chichele Professor of the History of

War at Oxford but for the outbreak of World War II, which saw him serve successively as Commander-in-Chief in the Middle East and India. He ended his career as Viceroy of India.

Unfortunately, Wavell's considerable intellectual abilities were undermined by what a recent biographer has described as his 'shrouded personality', the general impression he created being one of grave taciturnity. The near impenetrable mask could arouse suspicion and hostility, especially among politicians. Indeed, there can have been few more disastrous initial meetings between two men than that between Wavell and Churchill in August 1940.

By 1940 Wavell had already enjoyed a distinguished career. Commissioned in his father's regiment, the Black Watch, in May 1901, he had served in the latter stages of the South African War and on the North-West Frontier. After attending Staff College he had been chosen to observe the Imperial Russian Army in 1911 and subsequently served in the Russian section of the War Office's Directorate of Military Operations. He began the Great War in intelligence appointments but became Brigade-Major of 9th Infantry Brigade in November 1914. After losing his left eye to a shell splinter in June 1915, the remainder of his war was spent in staff appointments, ending in 1918 as chief staff officer to XX Corps in Palestine.

Promotion prospects were not good in the inter-war army, but Wavell won a reputation as an imaginative trainer of troops as GSO 1 to 3rd Division in 1926, commander of 6th Infantry Brigade from 1930 to 1934 and of 2nd Division from 1935 to 1937. He declined the offer of being Director of Military Training in 1936 and, instead, was appointed GOC in Palestine in the following year. In April 1938 he became GOC of Southern Command; he delivered the Lees Knowles lectures of 1939 at Cambridge before being knighted and promoted to full General as GOC, Middle East, in July 1939.

Wavell's responsibilities were wide and his command was threatened by seemingly overwhelming Italian forces in Libya and Abyssinia. It was in journeying to London to ask for more resources in August 1940 that Wavell clashed with Churchill, neither man appreciating the other's difficulties. Wavell's near total silence in face of Churchill's demands for action had the worst possible impact. Wavell declined subsequently to remove the British commander overwhelmed by the Italian advance into British Somaliland in August 1940, and he ignored pressure from London in directing preparations for the Western Desert Force to attack into Libya at what he regarded as the appropriate moment. The British advance in December was immediately successful but Wavell was compelled to divert resources to Greece, which had been attacked by Italy in October 1940. Another complication was the need to defeat Italian forces in East Africa.

Wavell had few doubts of the need to assist the Greeks, but it was a hopeless venture once the Germans intervened themselves in April 1941. This also coincided with the arrival of the 'Afrika Korps' at Tripoli, and Rommel overran the weakened Western Desert force in that same month. The loss of both Greece and Crete to the Germans, Wavell's reluctance to become involved in campaigns against the pro-German regime in Iraq and the Vichy French authorities in Syria, and the failure of counter-attacks to throw back the 'Afrika Korps' brought Wavell's dismissal on 22 June 1941.

To avoid embarrassing the government Wavell was appointed to the Indian Command, but this became of vital importance with the entry of the Japanese into the war. Moreover, in December 1941 the Americans insisted that Wavell be appointed Supreme Allied Commander for the South-West Pacific theatre (ABDA Command). There could be little effective cooperation over such a large area and the command was dissolved in February 1942. Wavell could not have saved the situation but he did manage to put some inspiration into the defence of Singapore and briefly contemplated conducting the actual battle himself. Unfortunately, he generally underestimated the capability of the Japanese and this contributed to the loss of Burma by May 1942, but he also showed courage in beginning to plan for the British return to that country as early as April 1942. However, the offensive Wavell launched into the Arakan between December 1942 and May 1943 was not successful, although it yielded valuable lessons for the future. He again lost the confidence of Churchill.

Wavell, who had been promoted to Field Marshal at his own request in January 1943 to help him in his dealings with allies, was accordingly offered the appointment of Viceroy on 14 June 1943 and raised to the peerage as a Viscount. It was an appointment of pure Churchillian expediency: Wavell was no better suited to dealing with Indian politicians than with their British counterparts. He recognized the strength of Muslim opinion and attempted to create a genuine coalition administration, but was summarily dismissed by Attlee on one month's notice on 4 February 1947. His successor, Mountbatten, who had far wider powers, ironically endorsed Wavell's belief that only a timetable for British withdrawal and partition would solve the impasse.

An earldom was something of a consolation for the manner of his dismissal which, not for the first time in Wavell's career, had been unworthy. It was ever his fate to wage what his most recent biographer has called the 'poor man's war'.

FURTHER READING

Connell, John, *Wavell: Scholar and Soldier* (London: Collins, 1964).

Connell, John (ed. and completed by M. Roberts), *Wavell: Supreme Commander* (London: Collins, 1969).

Lewin, Ronald, *The Chief* (London: Hutchinson, 1980).

Moon, Penderel, *Wavell: the Viceroy's Journal* (Oxford: Oxford University Press, 1973).

I. F. W. BECKETT

Webb, Sidney (James) [Baron Passfield] (*b.* London, 13 July 1859; *d.* near Liphook, Hampshire, 13 October 1947).
Webb [née Potter], **(Martha) Beatrice** [Mrs Sidney Webb] (*b.* Standish House, near Gloucester, 22 January 1858; *d.* near Liphook, Hampshire, 30 April 1943). Socialist intellectuals and activists. Sidney Webb's parliamentary career began when he was in his sixth decade. He was elected to represent Seaham Harbour in 1920, and in 1924 was appoin-

ted President of the Board of Trade in the first Labour government. Although he did not contest the seat in 1929, the second Labour government needed him: he accepted a peerage and served as Secretary for the Colonies and Dominions until 1931. His chief contribution to British political life was not in Parliament, but in his earlier work as a social theorist and leading intellectual socialist. He followed this career in partnership with his wife, and 'the Webbs' acquired a collective identity.

The marriage, on 23 July 1892, of Sidney Webb and Beatrice Potter seemed a spectacular misalliance. Beatrice's father, Richard Potter, was a timber magnate and director of several railway companies, and the family moved in the highest social circles. Beatrice was the seventh of eight daughters, and the last to marry; her sisters took suitable husbands from the worlds of politics, business and the professions. Sidney Webb was unmistakably of the lower middle class: his father was a poorly paid accountant, and his mother ran a hairdressing and millinery business. The class difference between the Webbs was accentuated by their physical disparity: she, a tall, strikingly handsome woman, he, short and plain, with a large head and a tapering body that Beatrice unkindly likened to that of a tadpole.

Nevertheless, the pair were already travelling in the same intellectual direction. Both were largely self-educated; both early rejected formal religion and sought a social philosophy to replace it. At the age of 17 Sidney became a clerk in a colonial broker's office, and in 1878 he joined the Civil Service, where he moved through competitive examinations to a first-division clerkship in the Colonial Office. In the evenings he studied, gaining many prizes and an LL B from the University of London. He joined several of the transient radical societies proliferating in late nineteenth-century London, and encountered British socialism in its confusing variety of forms. In 1885 he joined the Fabian Society, which, with his friends George Bernard Shaw and Graham Wallas, he developed into the intellectual forum and research centre of the socialist movement. Rejecting Marxism, the Fabians developed a pragmatic socialist theory. They repudiated forcible expropriation of private property: Webb emphasized collective action by the state through control of large public enterprises and progressive taxation. A slow revolution by education and persuasion would result from gradual 'permeation' of political life at all levels. In a contribution to *Fabian Essays in Socialism* (1889), Webb claimed that collectivism, rooted in local government, was now an irreversible process. His own practical commitment came with his election to the London County Council in 1892.

Beatrice Potter also saw socialism as a moral issue. A strong sense of social guilt led her to stifle a romantic passion for Joseph Chamberlain, who made it plain that he was seeking a submissive wife. Unlike Sidney, she had first-hand experience of working-class life, acting as rent collector in one of Octavia Hill's model dwellings and assisting Charles Booth's research for *Life and Labour of the People in London* (1891–1903). She investigated dock labour, unemployment and the sweated trades, and gave evidence to the House of Lords Select Committee on the Sweating System in 1888. She wrote a short account of the Cooperative movement which brought her into contact with trade-union and labour leaders. In 1890 she admitted, with the fervour of religious conviction, 'I am a Socialist.'

Their marriage united Sidney's gift for abstract theory and attention to detail with Beatrice's intuitive insights and practical skill as a social investigator. Both possessed prodigious energy. Her private means, around £1,000 a year, enabled him to leave the Civil Service, and the pair engaged in full-time social research and political activity. One of their first joint creations was the London School of Economics, founded in 1894 from a small legacy and nurtured carefully into a major college within the University of London. By this action, the Webbs hoped to provide for the scientific study of society, and to educate enlightened administrators for the new order. Although they took a keen interest in the fortunes of the LSE, they avoided forcing it into any ideological mould. Its combative staff-

Sidney and Beatrice Webb at their home in Liphook, Hampshire, 1941

room was to contain social scientists of every shade of opinion.

The Webbs' own research bore fruit in a series of massive volumes both historical and polemical. *The History of Trade Unionism* (1894) and *Industrial Democracy* (1897) grappled with the significance of organized labour in democratic societies. The history of trade unionism had scarcely been treated seriously before, since economists often saw it as a futile effort to interfere with the 'wages fund' which was regarded as a fixed element in economic activity. Beatrice Webb had already abandoned the older Liberal view of a society based on individual contracts, and used the phrase 'collective bargaining' to describe the unions' role. *Industrial Democracy* argued that it was time for the unions to move from mere wage issues towards the demand for a national minimum, 'the deliberate enforcement, by an elaborate Labor Code, of a definite quota of education, sanitation, leisure, and wages for every grade of workers in every industry.'

Although the Webbs believed that trade unions represented only one of several social interests, they accepted that the unions were the most stable base for representing the labour movement in politics. Nevertheless, for several years the Webbs did not take the emerging Labour Party seriously. At first, they hoped the established political parties would prove permeable to Fabian ideas. Sidney, strongly interested in educational reform, negotiated with leading Conservatives and supported R. L. Morant's Education Act of 1902. After 1906, as political interest turned towards social reform, the 'New Liberals' seemed a more likely prospect.

In the interests of permeation, the Webbs held their famous dinners, where politicians and intellectuals met for an evening of serious conversation sustained by the plainest of fare and very little alcohol. The 'salon politics', lampooned by H. G. Wells in *The New Machiavelli* (1911), caused many to distrust the Webbs as intriguers. The Webbs appreciated intellectual capacity more than political ability, and hence underestimated such Labour leaders as Hardie and MacDonald.

Research provided more tangible results. Between 1903 and 1929 the Webbs published

11 volumes on the history of English local government. They employed a secretary and research assistants, but their own grasp of an enormous range of documentation, together with personal knowledge of the intricacies of local government, produced lasting works of reference. Beatrice undertook most of the travelling and interviews; Sidney tackled the official literature at great speed, and wrote rapidly, if not elegantly. There was also a steady flow of tracts and journalism. In 1913 they gave intellectual socialism its distinctive voice by founding the *New Statesman*.

The culmination of the Webbs' prewar labours came with Beatrice's membership of the Royal Commission on the Poor Laws and Relief of Distress. The commission's bulky report in 1909 was backed by several volumes of evidence, but although the Webbs hoped to 'capture' its findings, they were overborne by the majority. The Webbs produced their own Minority Report, signed by Beatrice, George Lansbury and two other commissioners. The two reports had much in common: both wished to replace the small Poor Law unions with more coherent local government, and to provide specialized institutions rather than workhouses; but whereas the majority wished to keep the Poor Law as a back-stop for organized charity, the Webbs pressed for its abolition, and for new ministries of state to provide a variety of social services. They emphasized the need for prevention, rather than amelioration, of social problems. The minority's unemployment programme also seemed radical at the time, with emphasis on compulsory labour exchanges, ending of casual labour, modest investment in public works during times of slump, and incarceration of the workshy in labour colonies.

The Webbs backed the Minority Report with a vigorous but unsuccessful public campaign: they were effectively 'dished' by Lloyd George's alternative strategy for old-age pensions and contributory insurance for health and unemployment. Their own theories appeared, by contrast, both expensive and coercive: but the government's reforms left many people unprotected.

Disillusionment with the Liberals finally drove the Webbs towards Labour; Beatrice joined the Independent Labour Party in 1912, and during the war she and Sidney were drawn into closer cooperation with Arthur Henderson. In 1916 Sidney became a member of the Labour Party executive, to assist in formulating policy for the postwar period. He is usually credited with drafting much of the 1918 constitution of the Labour Party, with its aim 'to secure for the producers by hand or brain the full fruits of their industry and the most equitable distribution thereof that may be possible upon the basis of common ownership of the Means of Production . . .' The constitution embodied the Webbs' notion of the 'National Minimum', based on progressive taxation and public expenditure. The Labour Party had at last accepted a cautious socialist goal, aimed as much at radical members of the middle class as at the workers.

After this, Sidney Webb's parliamentary career was an anticlimax. His short spell at the Board of Trade was uneventful, while as Colonial Secretary he was faced with the intractable problems of the demands of white Kenyans for absolute control of their Legislative Council and Jewish demands for increased immigration to Palestine. Since he was inclined to oppose both these demands in the interests of communal harmony, he made many enemies. The 1931 political crisis reinforced the Webbs' old suspicions of MacDonald, and Sidney would not serve in the coalition.

In their last years, the Webbs' country home at Passfield Corner continued to attract the intellectual élite. The pair were 'Sacred Monsters' to the younger generation of socialists, but all acknowledged their kindliness and the enduring happiness of their marriage. Their reputation at the end was clouded by Beatrice's conversion to communism and their joint infatuation with Stalinist Russia, which they visited in 1932. *Soviet Communism: a New Civilization* (1935) has been seen either as the product of gullible senility or as ultimate proof of the Webbs' undemocratic fondness for the rule of bureaucracy. Their views were not uncommon among the left in the 1930s: they believed that capitalism was disintegrating and clung to Russia, despite all contrary evidence, as the successful example of a workers' state.

The Webbs are among the best known of modern political figures. Their huge collection of papers, in the British Library of Political and Economic Science, is an important historical source. Most of their joint writing came from Sidney's hand, but from youth to old age Beatrice wrote the diary in which the Webbs and their wide circle are revealed through her acute observation. Her character was complex and introspective, and the diaries and her autobiography speak with a living voice. Sidney, whose correspondence was more mundane, is presented mainly through her eyes as a serene, uncomplicated man. Their precise influence is still a matter for debate. They, and the Fabians generally, have been seen as dilettantes whose woolly-mindedness exemplifies the failings of the Labour Party; alternatively, they have been applauded for developing a pragmatic socialism suited to the British political climate. They undoubtedly helped to establish the social sciences as a serious field of study and were among the architects of the welfare state, which broke up the Poor Law but also fragmented the social services among competing bureaucracies. The issues they addressed are still relevant. They engaged in politics through a sense of moral responsibility and regarded wealth as the means to a just society: in these respects they may now appear out of date.

WRITINGS

Webb, B., *My Apprenticeship* (London: Longman, 1926).
——, *Our Partnership* (London: Longman, 1948).

FURTHER READING

Mackenzie, N. and J., *The First Fabians* (London: Weidenfeld and Nicolson, 1977).
Mackenzie, N. (ed.), *The Letters of Sidney and Beatrice Webb*, 3 vols. (Cambridge: Cambridge University Press, 1978).
Mackenzie, N. and J. (eds.), *The Diaries of Beatrice Webb*, 4 vols. (London: Virago, 1982–5).
Radice, L., *Beatrice and Sidney Webb: Fabian Socialists* (London: Macmillan, 1984).

M. A. CROWTHER

Weinstock, Sir **Arnold** [Baron Weinstock of Bowden] (*b.* London, 29 July 1924). Industrialist and creator of the modern firm GEC. As a highly successful businessman and head of the largest manufacturing concern in Britain, he became involved in the industrial policies of the 1960s and an important commentator on matters concerning industry.

Weinstock was the second son of Polish emigrés, Simon and Golda Weinstock, who came to Britain at the turn of the century. His father worked in the London rag trade. Both Weinstock's parents died when he was young, his father when he was five, his mother when he was nine. Thereafter Weinstock lived with his brother, a hairdresser, until World War II, when he was evacuated to Withybrook, Warwickshire. In 1941 he left his state school to undertake a statistics degree at the London School of Economics, then based in Cambridge to avoid German bombing. He achieved a second class degree in 1944 and was drafted into the Admiralty as an administration officer until his demobilization in 1947.

Weinstock's first postwar job was found for him by his brother, who cut the hair of a Mayfair estate agent, Louise Scott; the latter employed him as a junior assistant. During Weinstock's six years with this firm Scott rendered him one major service: she introduced him to Netta Sobell, whom he married in 1949.

Netta's father, Michael Sobell, was a producer of television sets. In 1953 he had retired and sold his business to EMI for £300,000, but in 1954 he bought it back and started producing televisions again with Weinstock. Their firm, Radio and Allied Industries, had remarkable success and soon attracted the attention of the electrical group GEC, which in the late 1950s had badly underperformed. GEC's solution was to buy RAI and its management team, and the Weinstock and Sobell families received a 14 per cent stake in GEC, making them the largest shareholders. Weinstock became a director in January 1960 and managing director in 1963; in only nine years in the electrical industry he had become the head of one of its three biggest firms.

Weinstock, together with his financial adviser from RAI, Kenneth Bond, rapidly improved GEC's position. They made the executives more competitive by using a system of decentralization, causing managers to be responsible for the financial success of their

Sir Arnold Weinstock, November 1968

operation. Weinstock was sometimes seen as ruthless, however, especially after a purge of management at the Osram subsidiary.

This success put GEC at the centre of plans to rationalize the electrical industry, especially its heavy generating side, which was seen as too decentralized and having too much capacity. In the spring of 1967 the Labour Government's Industrial Reorganization Corporation tried to sponsor the merger of GEC and one of its two main rivals, AEI, using the offer of loans as bait. This initiative ended when the IRC became aware that AEI would resist. In late 1967 Weinstock went for a full take-over bid. He asked for and received IRC public support to help win over the stock-market and to head off any worries in the Post Office and the CEGB, who were two major clients. The IRC provided no cash but did encourage the Scottish Electricity Board to make an early payment to GEC to help its cash flow. GEC won the bid battle despite criticism in the House of Commons of the power of faceless managers. GEC agreed to discuss the rationalization of the two companies with the IRC.

Within a year the electrical industry was stunned again by another proposed take-over:

415

Plessey were bidding for the larger English Electric. Plessey were interested in EE's electronics operations and its stake in ICL, the computer firm sponsored by Tony Benn's Ministry of Technology, which would make Plessey the largest shareholder. EE were not pleased; nor were the company's government customers. EE had also aided government industrial policy, especially in the formation of ICL and BAC. Such a merger would do nothing for the IRC plans to rationalize the heavy sector of the industry. Weinstock was therefore seen as a white knight and proposed a GEC–EE merger; he again received IRC backing, in return offering them a seat on the board. To ensure the firm was run in a 'statesmanlike manner', the IRC was to help stop a monopolies enquiry. Weinstock and the chairman of EE, Lord Nelson, were viewed more favourably than most industrialists by the government, so the enquiry was prevented.

Weinstock was knighted in 1970 and was now the managing director of one of Europe's major electrical companies. The management techniques advocated by GEC have received much attention: both the company and Weinstock's leadership have been criticized for using a system which leads to excessively short-term decision-making. GEC has been seen as unwilling to invest funds in long-term projects or to commit themselves to large R. & D. proposals, unless it involves a safe market such as military electronics. It is claimed that the firm has failed to exploit its position in commercial electronics markets, despite being the largest British electronics company. The massive cash surplus built up in the 1980s was often seen as owing to lack of initiative.

In the early 1970s Weinstock continued to be important in government industrial plans. He was a director of the newly nationalized Rolls-Royce and had a major influence over nuclear power provision via GEC's 50 per cent stake in the government-created National Nuclear Corporation. In the latter role he was an advocate of abandoning the commercially and technically unsuccessful advanced gas-cooled reactor programme in favour of building the proven US pressurized water reactor.

From the mid 1970s Weinstock displayed a strong interest in the direction of educational policy. He was critical of the lack of basic skills shown by school-leavers, which made them unsuitable for skilled employment. Through the *Times Educational Supplement* and conferences he condemned authorities for their inefficiency, especially for employing more administrators than teachers, and teachers for not teaching basic skills. He also believed the whole system put more emphasis on encouraging people into 'non-wealth-creating' careers such as banking and the civil service, leaving 'wealth-creating' industry with what was left over.

He used similar themes when commenting on the economy. Lord Weinstock, having been made a peer in 1980, criticized the Conservative Government in the early 1980s, and in 1985, together with the Chairman of ICI, Sir John Harvey-Jones, he gave evidence to the Lords Select Committee on Overseas Trade, disparaging government industrial policy. He ridiculed the theory that the decline of manufacturing industry was unimportant as service industry would replace it. He questioned how this would be able to create adequate exports, since it was industry that created wealth, and he speculated whether Wigan was to become a tourist attraction.

Lord Weinstock continues to run one of the major companies in Britain and is at the centre of high technology industry.

FURTHER READING

Hague, D. and Wilkinson, G., *The IRC: An Experiment in Industrial Intervention* (London: George Allen, 1983).

Jones, R. and Marriot, O., *Anatomy of a Merger* (London: Jonathan Cape, 1970).

Williams, K. et al., *Why are the British Bad at Manufacturing* (London: Routledge, 1983).

ANTHONY GANDY

Weir, Sir **William (Douglas)** [Viscount Weir of Eastwood] (*b.* Glasgow, 12 May 1877; *d.* Giffnock, Renfrewshire, 2 July 1959). Industrialist and first Secretary of State for Air. He started his career as an industrialist but became better known for his public service, especially his tenure of office as Secretary of State for Air at the end of World War I.

Weir was the son of James Weir and Mary Douglas. He had one step-brother on his mother's side, (Sir) John Richmond. James Weir and his brother George entered the business of marine engineering, based on the developments patented by James during his experience as a sea-going engineer. The family firm, G. & J. Weir, established in Cathcart near Glasgow, supplied ancillary machinery for the engine rooms of steam ships. Weir joined the company board in 1898 at the age of 21, having left Glasgow High School at 16 to be apprenticed within the firm. In 1902 he was made the managing director, following his father's desire to retire early. In 1904 he married Alice Blanch, daughter of a Glasgow lawyer. They had two sons and one daughter.

Weir was a confident leader, and he found it easy to communicate with prestigious clients. The company prospered as the world's navies expanded in the pre-1914 period; the navies wanted the new generation of large armoured capital ships, and G. & J. Weir were happy to supply ancillary machinery for them. The company was operated in a conservative manner. The only diversification before World War I was into the growing motor vehicle industry, but two ventures into this market were both short-lived and unprofitable.

The war saw Weir becoming an active if background figure in public service. He resigned as managing director of Weirs but remained its chairman. The company entered many new fields of war production at an early stage, especially the manufacture of the desperately scarce artillery shells, constructing a factory for this purpose. Both in his private capacity and as a member of Lloyd George's Central Advisory Committee on Munitions responsible for the West of Scotland, Weir actively supported the process of 'dilution'. This was the practice of replacing skilled workers, who were often in the front line, with the unskilled and women. This was resisted by the craft unions, who feared it would be an irreversible process and a prerequisite of automation. Weir received notoriety for this campaign, especially after helping to break a strike on the Clyde. He was often viewed suspiciously by craft unions: they were upset by the form of payment by performance which his factories used before the war.

A specific task to which Weir turned his attention, and the area for which he was most remembered, was the problem of military aircraft production. Under his urging Lloyd George created the Air Board and in March 1917 made Weir its Controller of Aeronautical Supplies. Weir's own company started production to aid output, and by the end of the war had produced 1,100 machines to Royal Aircraft Factory (Establishment) designs. Nationally Weir presided over a massive increase in output: in 1916 deliveries were 6,099, and in 1917, 14,168. In 1917 Weir was knighted.

The formation of the RAF and Air Ministry saw Weir appointed Director General of Aircraft Production. In April 1918 he was made Secretary of State for Air and a member of the Privy Council, becoming Lord Weir of Eastwood. He was a major influence on the formation of the RAF and as Minister he started work on a long-range bombing force. He resigned in December 1918, but first made recommendations to support civil air transport.

Weir continued to hold many positions with influence over aeronautical policy. He defended the separate identity of the RAF twice, as Chairman of the Sub-committee on Service Costs in 1922–4 and as a member of the Committee for Defence Policy and Requirements in the mid- and late 1930s. He was also an adviser to the Principal Supply Officers Committee from 1933 and to the Secretary of State for Air. He supported Churchill's calls for re-armament following the rise of the Nazis, and it was his plans which allowed aircraft production to be accelerated as the threat grew. Before the war started, however, he resigned, following the sacking from government of Cunliffe-Lister. During this period he was given public recognition by being made a GCB in 1934 and a Viscount in 1938.

In the inter-period Weir also concerned himself with industrial policy. He chaired the committee which recommended the formation of the National Grid and the Central Electricity Board, which was established by the Conservative Government in 1926; he lent support to the subsidizing of the sugar-beet industry after

World War I because of its importance in time of war; he became involved in the merger of the North Atlantic passenger lines and the subsidy of the *Queen Mary* and *Queen Elizabeth*; and he joined the board of the new firm ICI after supporting Alfred Mond's rationalization of the chemical industry. Although a Conservative, he supported intervention when required.

His own company maintained its previous conservative policies in the inter-war years. The company, like so many others, was severely cut back in this period. At the time the most important positive move was to acquire Drysdales of Yoker, a firm with expertise in centrifugal pumps. One new activity undertaken in the 1920s was to be of more importance to the firm in the long run. This was the development of a steel house which could be assembled by unskilled labour, thus being useful in reducing unemployment and easing the housing situation. Yet again Weir was challenging vested union and, this time, trade interests. Authorities therefore refused to take up the process. However the needs of the post-1945 housing crisis meant the idea was resurrected and Weirs provided 10 per cent of the house building in Scotland in the 1950s. Weir and his company also played a part in the short history of the autogiro and supported some of Frank Whittle's pre-1939 research into jet engines.

World War II again saw the company's products in strong demand as the Royal Navy expanded, and they diversified into other products of war. In 1939 Weir was Director General of Explosives and in 1942 Chairman of the Tank Board. In the 1950s demand was much healthier than it had been after the first war, helped by the Korean War and the replacement of war losses. In 1946 the firm had been floated as a public company, with Weir as its chairman. Weir resigned this position in 1953, leaving a healthy company, but warned that the future of their chosen market, shipping equipment, looked bleak.

FURTHER READING

Obituary, *The Times* (3 July 1959).
Reader, William J., *Architect of Air Power: the Life of the First Viscount Weir* (London: Collins, 1968).

——, *The Weir Group: a Centenary History* (London: Weidenfeld and Nicolson, 1971).
Thompson, Elizabeth, 'Weir, William Douglas', *Dictionary of Business Biography*, ed. David J. Jeremy and Christine Shaw, 6 vols. (London: Butterworths, 1984–6).

ANTHONY GANDY

Weisz, Victor. See VICKY.

Wells, H(erbert) G(eorge) (*b*. Bromley, Kent, 21 September 1866; *d*. London, 13 August 1946). Writer and Utopian socialist. His origins, although sufficiently elevated to be termed lower middle class, were bleakly penurious. Initially apprenticed to a firm of drapers, he had larger ambitions and applied himself to study. In 1890, a student of T. H. Huxley, he graduated from the Normal School of Science, Kensington. He found sudden recognition with *Anticipations of the Reaction of Mechanical and Scientific Progress Upon Human Life and Thought* (1901), which led to his adoption by the Fabians (he already knew Graham Wallas), to whose society he belonged from February 1903 to September 1908. Significant publications of this period include *A Modern Utopia* (1905), *The Faults of the Fabian* (1906) and *This Misery of Boots* (1907).

In 1914 Wells published *The War That Will End War*, associating himself with the jingoist faction, and, incidentally, creating a national slogan. During 1918 he served briefly in the Ministry of Information. His early involvement in efforts to create a League of Nations was short-lived: the League's ideals proved incompatible with his own notions of a world state and world citizenship. Wells visited Russia to meet Lenin in 1920, as he did to meet Stalin in 1934 (he met F. D. Roosevelt also that year). He twice fought, without success, the London University parliamentary seat for Labour (1921, 1922). Practical politics and the minute gradualism of committee work were not his *métier*. His true political vocation was as a polemicist and a 'prophet', whether proposing mankind's salvation through history, by means of such works as *The Outline of History* (1920), or foretelling its doom, as in *Mind at the End of its Tether* (1945). Like Bennett and Galsworthy, Wells, as a novelist, was a 'materialist'. Social criticism colours almost all and dominates much of his fiction (as does autobiography), none of which should be overlooked by students of the socio-political history of the post-Victorian period.

WRITINGS

Experiment in Autobiography: Discoveries and Conclusions of a Very Ordinary Brain – Since 1866 (London: Gollancz and Cresset Press, 1934).

FURTHER READING

Mackenzie, Norman and Jeanne, *The Time Traveller: the Life of H. G. Wells* (London: Weidenfeld and Nicolson, 1973).

ANDREW MCNEILLIE

Whitehouse, Mary (*b.* Shrewsbury, 13 June 1910). Moral crusader and political campaigner. She is president of the National Viewers and Listeners Association (NVALA). She was educated at the Chester City Grammar School and the Cheshire County Training College, and from 1932 until 1964 she was a Midlands schoolteacher. She was married in 1940 and has three sons.

Mrs Whitehouse did not come into public prominence until 1964, when she acted as co-founder of the 'Clean Up TV Campaign'. This was followed, in 1965, by the creation of NVALA, of which she remained Honorary General Secretary until, in 1980, she became its president. Also in 1980, she was publicly recognized with the award of a CBE.

NVALA's emergence and activities represent a reaction against the moral 'permissiveness' perceived by Mrs Whitehouse and her allies as a characteristic feature of the post-1945 era and, in particular, of the 1960s. The broadcasting media's challenging of some traditional values or taboos, most notably in the sexual domain, was viewed as an especially serious sign of a more general national moral decline. NVALA's specific task has been to monitor the content of radio and, above all, television, with a view to bringing public pressure to bear on those responsible for programme making. A particular aim has been to guard against the portrayal of what those concerned have perceived as offensive or gratuitous sex and violence. The campaign in question has been pursued on the assumption, regarded by some authorities as unproven, that the broadcasting media not only reflect but also help to foment anti-social or pathological behaviour.

The notion of 'moral decline' underlying NVALA's work assumes the previous existence of a stable society, based on traditional Christian values, which finds itself under threat because of the corrosive effects of secular humanism. Blame for this situation was attributed to the dominant influence of a liberal intelligentsia which had largely abandoned traditional values, and to official Church leaders who, it is alleged, had failed to defend them. The impact of these influences on national life is particularly seen to have been at work in legislation of the 1960s, or later, that relaxed literary and theatrical censorship and liberalized measures governing such sexually related matters as homosexuality, abortion and divorce. The abandonment of capital punishment is perceived as part of the same trend. Thus Mrs Whitehouse's work with NVALA has frequently broadened out to embrace crusades of a more obviously political kind. She campaigned, for example, on behalf of the Private Member's Bill promoted by Graham Bright which, in 1984, resulted in the Video Recordings Act that provides for the official classification of videos.

Underlying Mrs Whitehouse's own commitment exists the influence of 'Moral Rearmament' and, most fundamentally, of John Wesley and Evangelical Christianity. Her wider importance lies in the significant part she played in catalyzing and articulating strong currents of opinion which arose out of popular reactions to rapid changes in postwar Britain's moral climate. Within the political domain she has generally been allied with Conservatives, and can be seen as fostering those demands for the rehabilitation of traditional moral values which have apparently constituted part of the popular appeal of Mrs Thatcher's brand of Conservatism. Critics accuse her of being unduly simplistic, authoritarian and individualistic in her approach. Allies perceive her as a major figure in the struggle to restore Christian-based moral standards to British society.

WRITINGS

Mightier than the Sword (Eastbourne: Kingsway Publications, 1985).

FURTHER READING

Sutton, N. (ed.), *Christianity and Change* (London: SPCK, 1971).

K. N. MEDHURST

Whitelaw, William (Stephen Ian) [Viscount Whitelaw of Penrith] (**'Willie'**) (*b.* Nairn, Scotland, 28 June 1918). Conservative Home Secretary and Leader of the House of Lords. He was among the most generally respected Conservative politicians of his day, and his party's sheet-anchor through almost three decades of political storms.

Born into an upper-middle-class Scottish family – his father died of wounds from World War I when he was still an infant – Whitelaw was educated at Winchester and Trinity College, Cambridge. Commissioned into the Scots Guards in 1939, he had a distinguished war record. He commanded a tank squadron in the invasion of Normandy, was awarded the Military Cross and served in Palestine as a Regular before resigning his commission in 1947 to run the family's property interests. Loyalty to his old regiment remained, with his passion for golf and his family (he married Celia Sprot in 1943 and they have four daughters) among his major non-political interests.

Whitelaw was elected to Parliament for the safe Cumberland Conservative seat of Penrith and the Border in 1955. He was Parliamentary Private Secretary to Peter Thorneycroft at the Treasury (1957–8), an Assistant Government Whip (1959–61) and a junior minister successively at the Treasury and the Ministry of Labour. In opposition from 1964, he acted as Conservative Chief Whip. It was a job he was 'delighted' to hold, a 'great parliamentary opportunity'; but under Alec Douglas-Home he confessed to being 'torn' between the dictates of what were, then and later, two of his most distinctive political traits: personal loyalty to his leader and instinct for the party's best interests. He was considerably happier under Edward Heath's leadership after 1965.

In 1970, in Heath's Conservative administration, Whitelaw became Leader of the House of Commons and Lord President of the Council – the latter a post he held again as a peer after 1983. Two years later he took charge of the Northern Ireland Office, responsible for introducing British Direct Rule in the province. His tenure coincided with the most intense phase of sectarian murder in the entire 'Troubles'; and, as his memoirs confessed, Whitelaw found the strain considerable. He succeeded, however, in retaining the reputation for urbane unflappability which increased his standing within his party, though the power-sharing executive for Northern Ireland over whose formation he presided was virtually stillborn. He moved at the end of 1973 to the Employment portfolio. This proved almost equally stormy, for he was faced with a mineworkers' dispute, an energy crisis and a state of emergency. This in turn provoked the February 1974 general election, in which the Conservatives lost power.

In opposition, Whitelaw took on what he called the 'unenviable' and 'difficult' task of Party Chairman. There was great bitterness and dissension within the parliamentary party, much of it directed against Heath. It was, Whitelaw said, 'the worst time of my political life'. He remained loyal to the leader; but when Heath, having been challenged by Margaret Thatcher for the leadership, withdrew after the first ballot, Whitelaw too decided to enter the contest. He gained 79 of the 274 MPs' votes cast. Many observers believed that, had he stood from the first rather than waiting for Heath's withdrawal, he might have emerged as leader instead of Mrs Thatcher. However, he characteristically offered to serve Thatcher in any capacity she chose. She immediately asked him to become Deputy Leader of the party, and he was soon her most indispensable lieutenant.

In 1976 he took on also the job of Shadow Home Secretary. This was, as so often in the Conservative Party, an especially delicate post; for Whitelaw's instincts on law and order and

William Whitelaw (centre) leaving 10 Downing Street with (left) Paul Channon and Norman Fowler

immigration were more conciliatory, perhaps more liberal than those of his leader or of the party majority. In government at the Home Office from 1979 to 1983 he often faced the ire of Conservative activists for supposedly insufficient stringency in fighting crime and for his opposition to re-introducing capital punishment. It was one of the very few issues on which he disagreed publicly with Mrs Thatcher, though privately there was a significant gulf between her radical aims and his more traditional, consensual brand of Conservatism. He came to 'dread and dislike' the annual law and order debate at party conference, and recognized that it damaged his standing as Home Secretary. His efforts to reform the Official Secrets Act and to solve the problem of Britain's overcrowded prisons were, he also recognized, unsuccessful. On top of this Whitelaw faced recurrent crises caused by terrorism, and by the urban disturbances in Bristol, Brixton, Liverpool and elsewhere in 1980 and 1981. As a member of the Overseas

Defence Committee, South Atlantic, or 'War Cabinet', he was further intimately involved in the conduct of the Falklands campaign in 1982.

Soon after the 1983 election Whitelaw was asked to go to the Lords as Leader, receiving one of the first two hereditary peerages (with that of former Speaker George Thomas, Viscount Tonypandy) since 1964. He had strong private doubts about this arrangement, though the fact that neither he nor Tonypandy had sons somewhat lessened the importance of the revival of hereditary peerages. Here he presided over the introduction of television coverage for Lords' debates, and as Lord President of the Council chaired the committee setting targets on departmental expenditure, the so-called Star Chamber. Less happily for him, this was also a period when the peers with increasing frequency rejected his government's legislation, making management of the Lords' business a task which yet once more tested his negotiating and conciliating skills.

At the end of 1987 Lord Whitelaw suffered a stroke which, although he made a good recovery, necessitated his resigning governmental office early the following year. Patrick Cosgrave's summation of his character, though harsh-sounding, may be accepted as broadly accurate: 'Whitelaw was not a man of ideas; he was no thinker; he was a man of instincts and attitudes . . . He was bluff, gregarious, humorous, charming and kindly.' Yet he was also one of the most quietly formidable Conservative politicians of the postwar era.

WRITINGS

The Whitelaw Memoirs (London: Aurum, 1989).

FURTHER READING

Behrens, R., *The Conservative Party from Heath to Thatcher* (London: Saxon House, 1980).
Cosgrave, P., *The Lives of Enoch Powell* (London: Bodley Head, 1989).
Young, H., *One of Us* (London: Macmillan, 1989).

STEPHEN HOWE

Wilkinson, Ellen (Cicely) ('Red Ellen') (*b.* Ardwick, Chorlton-on-Medlock, Lancashire, 8 October 1891; *d.* London, 6 February 1947). Left-wing activist and Labour minister. She was Minister of Education in the Attlee Government between 1945 and 1947, an unlikely conclusion to the career of a Labour militant who had more usually been a vociferous critic of the party leadership.

Born to a Conservative, Methodist working-class family, she was a suffragist and Independent Labour Party member in her teens. Academic flair and personal ambition gained her a scholarship to read history at Manchester University in 1910. Here she developed contacts with the Fabian Society and served on the executive of the University Socialist Federation. Subsequently, she became full-time organizer for the National Union of Women's Suffrage Societies and then, in 1915, the national woman organizer for the Amalgamated Union of Cooperative Employees. In the postwar years she sharpened her speaking skills in flirtations with most left-wing organizations, including the National Unemployed Workers Movement and the Communist Party, to which she belonged until 1924.

Women and the unemployed were her main concerns as a member, briefly, of the Manchester City Council. She was elected as Labour MP for Middlesbrough in 1924. As Parliamentary Secretary to the Minister of Health from 1929 she distrusted the party leadership, particularly Ramsay MacDonald. She opposed his solutions to the economic crisis of 1931 and, like other leading left wingers, lost her seat in the ensuing general election. In 1935 she won Jarrow. Her participation in the famous hunger march and her book *The Town that was Murdered* did much to ensure that her constituency became synonymous with the worst deprivation of the interwar depression. Both reflected her sympathy for the socially oppressed. So, too, did her practical work on behalf of Spanish Republican refugees, and the passage of her Hire Purchase Bill in 1938, which brought much needed protection to consumers.

As international issues came more to the centre of political debate Wilkinson became progressively more sympathetic to official Labour Party policy and in 1939 she resigned from the board of *Tribune*, which she had helped to found. Despite her pacifism she served successively in the wartime coalition as Parliamentary Secretary first at the Ministry of Pensions and then at the Home Office. With particular responsibility for civil defence, she dispensed hygiene and cheer with considerable warmth and energy. The progressive moderation of her political views probably owed something to her relationship with Home Secretary Herbert Morrison. While discrete, it was certainly more than merely official and she was a constant intriguer on his behalf for the Labour leadership.

As Minister of Education from 1945, Wilkinson was limited in her achievements both by her short tenure of office and by the general economic constraints of the postwar period. Nevertheless, a commitment to raising the school-leaving age, the widespread provision of milk and dinners, and the training of emergency teachers all stood to her credit when she died in February 1947. Although there was some talk of suicide, the official verdict was that she had accidentally taken an overdose of the drugs prescribed for her chronic and deteriorating bronchial asthma.

Despite her university training, sharp tongue, dynamic oratory and acerbic prose Ellen Wilkinson remained intellectually muddled and personally disorganized. Highly ambitious, politics were her life and she never married. Her socialist convictions were rooted in experience rather than in ideology and she did much to articulate the humanitarian concern of the Labour left in the interwar years.

WRITINGS

The Town that was Murdered (London: Gollancz, 1939).

FURTHER READING

Vernon, B. D., *Ellen Wilkinson* (London: Croom Helm, 1982).

KENNETH D. BROWN

Williams, Raymond (Henry) (*b.* Pandy, Monmouthshire, 31 August 1921; *d.* Saffron Walden, Essex, 26 January 1988). Cultural historian, literary critic and novelist. The bare facts of Williams's life – his Welsh origins, his father's trade unionism, his schooling – partly explain why he became an intellectual hero of the left, but they are important because they offer more than causal explanation. The facts became symbols – functioning as stable points of reference of almost mythic significance both for himself and for those who were attracted by his thinking.

Williams was the son of a railway signalman. After grammar school in Abergavenny he went to Cambridge to read English. From 1946 until 1961 he held a position as a staff tutor in adult education for the Oxford Delegacy. He was then appointed university lecturer in English at Cambridge and was Professor of Drama there from 1974 until 1983.

The publication of *Culture and Society, 1780–1950* (1958) established Williams's reputation. Whereas literary critical studies had previously sought to analyse the relation-

ship between literature and its social 'background', Williams showed that the literature which was the object of academic study and from which moral values were extracted was itself a social construct and, more specifically, a consequence of the alienation of artistic producers from the thrust of economic change in industrial Britain. *The Long Revolution* (1961) continued the argument to insist that values should be acquired through engagement with the processes of social change rather than be derived from an inherited culture that was detached from them. Williams's first novel of this period – *Border Country* (1960) – dramatized the tension experienced by a grammar-school boy in seeking to reconcile the values of a Welsh upbringing with those encountered at university. Williams's intellectual attempt to contextualize 'high' culture reflected a personal need to accommodate emotionally his social and cultural origins.

While continuing to maintain his political orientation in the practice of cultural criticism – in relation to drama and mass communications – he was active in the 1960s in constructing the 'New Left' in order to advance a socialist critique of Labour policies. He helped to found the *New Left Review* and was mainly responsible for the 'May Day Manifesto, 1968'.

In his short study of Orwell (1971), Williams analysed the way in which Eric Blair adopted an authorial persona. Constrained, perhaps, by his institutional position, Williams gradually made himself into a 'thinker'. He became the Coleridge of contemporary radicalism, self-consciously seeking to affirm and integrate the opposing social forces which he experienced. As in *The Country and the City* (1973), these opposites were indeed conceptualized in Romantic terms. By oscillating physically between Wales and Cambridge, he sought personally to hold in balance the claims of family, soil and tradition and those of technological modernity – expressed in fiction in *The Fight for Manod* (1979). In numerous articles in newspapers and journals, on television, and in public appearances, he unfalteringly and optimistically presented the case for a humane socialism which would neither deny its roots nor reject progress.

It is no denigration of his life's effort to say

that his sudden death was experienced as the loss of a symbolic presence more than of an active political force. The symbolism was potent in ways which cannot be quantified. His private myth no longer, perhaps, has public currency and socialism may not need to be so identified with his form of cultural materialism, but Williams's sustained intellectual contribution to postwar political life should not be underestimated. Among the posthumous collections of his essays are *Resources of Hope: Culture, Democracy, Socialism* (1989) and *What I Came to Say* (1989), both of which contain work spanning the whole of his career.

DEREK ROBBINS

Williams [née Catlin], **Shirley (Vivien Teresa Brittain)** (*b.* London, 27 July 1930). Labour cabinet minister and co-founder of the Social Democratic Party. She stood out as the foremost representative of the social democratic wing of the Labour Party in the late 1970s and played a notable part in establishing the Social Democratic Party. As president of the SDP, she led its majority faction into a merger with the Liberal Party in 1987–8.

Both her parents, the political scientist Professor Sir George Catlin and the feminist writer Vera Brittain, were left-wing intellectuals. After a wartime schooling, spent partly in the USA, she became a scholar of Somerville College, Oxford, where she was remembered as much for her dramatic as her academic activities. She married the philosopher Bernard Williams in 1955 (marriage dissolved, 1974) and there was one daughter. She was three times a Labour parliamentary candidate before she was 30 and achieved national recognition as General Secretary of the Fabian Society (1960–4). From 1964 she served as Labour MP for Hitchin, and after redistribution in 1974 chose the part of the constituency which included the new town of Stevenage, which she held until 1979. Williams carved out a useful career as a junior minister in the first Wilson government: her academic background singled her out for prominence at Education, and her Roman Catholicism made her highly acceptable at the Home Office, with its growing

responsibilities for Northern Ireland. She became one of the representatives of the women's section on Labour's National Executive Committee from 1970. Her progress to cabinet office was assured on Labour's return to government in 1974 and she soon became a controversial Secretary of State for Education and Science, identified with the implementation of a major move towards comprehensive schools.

Williams was by this stage a leading figure in social democratic politics and, following Labour's shift to the left in 1979–80, her decision to work in concert with DAVID OWEN and William Rodgers was indispensable in rallying solid support from within Labour ranks for what became the SDP. Indeed, many saw her as the natural leader for the new party, but she did not press this claim and became instead its most charismatic presence, notably in the sensational by-election victory which she achieved at Crosby in November 1981. She was also the author of two original books on policy issues. Serving as president of the SDP from 1982, Williams worked effectively for closer cooperation with the Liberals, to whom she was latterly a much more sympathetic figure than the new leader Owen. The disappointing performance of the Alliance in the general election of 1987 (when Williams herself came second in Cambridge) brought suppressed differences to the surface and she now voiced the wish of most SDP members for a full merger with the Liberals. For a second time she played a crucial role in forming a new party (the Social and Liberal Democrats), though personally abstaining from any candidature in its initial elections in 1988 following her second marriage, to the American political scientist Richard Neustadt.

For illustration, see JENKINS, ROY.

P. F. CLARKE

Willis, Norman (David) (*b.* Ashford, Middlesex, 21 January 1933). Trade-union leader. As General Secretary of the TUC from 1984, he presided over a period of decline and uncertainty for the union movement which overwhelmed his limited powers of consensus and organization.

A large, cheerful, untidy man, he was an unexpected choice for the post, having started as an office worker with the Transport and General Workers' Union and later become an assistant to its powerful general secretaries FRANK COUSINS and JACK JONES, for whom he helped organize campaigns. Unexpectedly selected as an assistant general secretary of the TUC, partly as a protest against the automatic promotion of internal candidates, he became general secretary in 1984 after the early retirement of LEN MURRAY. Again it was a surprise – the result of the inability of factions to agree on an outside candidate, the resentment of insiders, and a wish among some union general secretaries to weaken the power of the centre. It was a most difficult time: the mid-point of the 1984–5 Miners' Strike, which split the movement. Willis spent long hours keeping all sides talking. He saw a noose dangled above his head when he bravely condemned picket-line violence at a miners' rally, but ultimately failed to promote a TUC formula for settling the dispute.

In spite of a series of disastrous conference performances, his patient efforts managed to keep the TUC together through a series of crises, mostly involving the right-wing Electrical, Electronics, Telecommunications and Plumbing Union, over taking government money for union ballots, no-strike agreements and the printing dispute at Wapping. But Willis's lack of authority and jokey, tangential style could not hold an increasingly frustrated movement for long. In 1988, he first failed to win unanimity for a single-union agreement for an important new Ford factory, which was subsequently lost abroad, and then saw the movement split disastrously, suspending the EEPTU for not renouncing two single-union deals. It was potentially the biggest rift of the century.

MARTIN ADENEY

Wilson, (James) Harold [Baron Wilson of Rievaulx] (*b.* Huddersfield, Yorkshire, 11 March 1916). Labour Prime Minister. Wilson was leader of the Labour Party from 1963 to 1976. He was Prime Minister from 1964 to 1970 and again from 1974 to 1976. His deci-

sion to stand down from the office when he reached the age of 60 came as a surprise to the country at large. He claimed that he had arrived at the decision to take this step after the result of the February 1974 election had become known. He had noted, it seems, that in diplomacy and the economy things tended to repeat themselves. You could either decide in the same way because things had subsequently worked well or take a different decision because they had not. Wilson claimed that his major anxiety was that he would grow stale in high office. This explanation has not invariably been found conclusive but, despite speculation, no alternative has been adequately documented. Wilson had always shown great pride in pointing out how youthful he had been when he achieved certain offices; to have retired early completed the story.

Wilson was initially brought up in the Huddersfield area but moved to the Wirral at the age of 16 when his father, an industrial chemist, changed his job. The Wilsons were Congregationalists. They were not prosperous but neither were they poor. Harold went to London in his father's motorcycle sidecar when he was seven and was photographed standing outside 10 Downing Street. He went up to Jesus College, Oxford, in 1934 with an exhibition in history, but transferred to read politics, philosophy and economics. He graduated with a distinguished First and various university prizes. He had already told his future wife (the daughter of a Congregational minister) that he intended to be Prime Minister, but his decision to join the university Liberals was not perhaps the best first step. He was put off the Labour Club by public schoolboys spouting Marxism. After graduation he earned a living in Oxford from teaching and as Beveridge's assistant. It was G. D. H. Cole who pointed him in the direction of the Labour Party.

In April 1940 Wilson was summoned to London to work in the economics section of the War Cabinet Secretariat under Professor John Jewkes. Their immediate task was to work on forward estimates of industrial manpower requirements. Later in his job he had to tell innumerate coal owners some uncomfortable statistical facts about their industry. He also began drawing up a new plan for a Ministry of

Harold Wilson

Fuel and Power. In 1943 he was appointed a joint secretary of a sub-committee of the Anglo-American Combined Chiefs of Staff concerned with energy requirements. That responsibility took him for a while to the USA. Before he had reached the age of 30, therefore, he believed he had an intimate knowledge of how Britain was governed. He applied himself to becoming a Labour candidate and was adopted for Ormskirk in Lancashire. It is conceivable that his first book, *New Deal for Coal*, published on election day, played a part in securing his victory. He immediately received preferment and became the Parliamentary Secretary at the Ministry of Works. One of his most pressing immediate problems was housing. He was also sent out by the Prime Minister on special negotiating missions to the USA and the USSR. In the late autumn of 1947, at the age of 31, he became President of the Board of Trade. Such an elevation suggested that Wilson had a bright future. He threw himself energetically into various foreign trade negotiations, particularly with the Russians. A little later it became increasingly difficult to hold the exchange rate of $4.03 to the pound. Wilson

was generous in his advice to his superiors on how the devaluation should be handled.

In the early 1950s the succession to Attlee occupied many minds. HUGH GAITSKELL, the new Chancellor, and Aneurin Bevan, the Minister of Health, were rivals. The focus of their conflict was the proposed expenditure cut in the National Health Service arising out of the re-armament programme. Wilson had diagnosed that Gaitskell was ambitious and an economist. His sympathies appeared to veer towards Bevan, but when he resigned in 1951 he was careful to point out that his grounds for doing so were not the same as the Health Minister's. Wilson simply believed that a great deal of money would be wasted in too rapid a re-armament programme. His resignation earned him the reputation of being a left-winger, and in the early 1950s he moved up steadily in the voting for the National Executive Committee. He tried to keep open his links with other sections of the party and was regarded with suspicion by some who considered themselves true Bevanites. Wilson supplemented his income considerably by acting as a foreign trade consultant for Montague

Meyer, an international timber merchant. He travelled a good deal and let it be known that he was meeting very important people. There was press speculation that he was grooming himself for 'Bevanism without Bevan'. In the autumn of 1954, when Bevan was not standing because he was challenging Gaitskell for the party treasurership, Wilson topped the poll for the constituency section and then came twelfth in the ballot for 12 seats on the shadow cabinet for the forthcoming parliamentary session. This was the period of stormy internal party debate on German re-armament, but Wilson kept a low profile. His distance from Bevan grew and he talked more and more about party unity. When Labour failed again in the 1955 general election Wilson was appointed Chairman of an NEC sub-committee to examine party organization, and in the elections for the shadow cabinet he moved up to fifth place ahead of Bevan, who was seventh. Here was the emerging new left-wing leader consolidating his position?

Gaitskell gained the leadership of the Labour Party in December 1955 and appointed Wilson Shadow Chancellor in the following month. His opposite number was Harold Macmillan. The two men enjoyed their sparring. Wilson's debating style lightened and he seemed to revel in his new role as a House of Commons comedian. With Gaitskell his relationship was uneasy, partly because of all that had passed over the previous few years, but also because there remained a certain latent professional rivalry. Certainly, Wilson's economic mastery allowed Gaitskell to concentrate on other topics, and in the year of Suez there was plenty to engage his attention. Failure to regain power in 1959 was a great disappointment to both men, but they reacted to it in very different fashion.

Gaitskell addressed the November party conference in a wide-ranging speech which claimed to expose the reasons for the recent defeat. He called into question Clause IV of the party constitution with its commitment to the nationalization of the means of production, distribution and exchange. Wilson was angered by this speech and the influence of the 'Hampstead set' which he detected behind it. Bevan died in July 1960 and it looked as though

the mantle was descending upon Wilson. When the Labour conference was held in the autumn Gaitskell resolved to 'fight, fight and fight again' to reverse the vote in favour of unilateral nuclear disarmament. Wilson was finally persuaded to be the standard-bearer in the battle against the way in which Gaitskell was trying to lead the party. Reluctant to be again identified solely with the left, Wilson tried to argue that his opposition was based on the need for unity. He was defeated by more than two to one. Even so, he became Shadow Foreign Secretary and endeavoured to have some fun at the expense of Lord Home, then Foreign Secretary. The issue of membership of the EEC moved to the fore, requiring once again from Wilson some consummate fence-sitting in the interests of party unity, though on this matter he was not far away from his party leader.

Gaitskell's death occurred when Wilson was lecturing in the USA. In the second round of voting for the leadership Wilson defeated George Brown by a considerable majority. There could not be more than 18 months to go before a general election and Wilson lost little time in enunciating his 'technology' theme; he was thinking about the administrative changes that would be necessary to marry 'national planning' and 'technological progress'. He launched this programme with great panache; its great advantage was that it by-passed many of the rifts within the Labour Party. It was inconceivable that clever Harold Wilson could allow himself to be defeated by a Douglas-Home, though in the event, in 1964, the election produced an overall Labour majority of only four.

In the early stages such a small majority, combined with the fact that the party had been out of office for so long, gave Labour greater cohesion than it had known for years. Wilson seemed in his element. Even though his government could collapse at any time, he appeared remarkably fertile in his ideas and suggestions. He made much capital out of the balance of payments deficit which he inherited. He gave the feeling that he knew where he was going and blurred the internal divisions on defence policy effectively. He could with justice claim that his own artful leadership was responsible for the more comfortable general election victory which he gained in March 1966. He needed all his resilience as the difficulties mounted in the years immediately ahead. The pound, on which Wilson had set great store for many months, was devalued in November 1967, and assurances that nothing much would change were not altogether believed. Wilson's self-confidence appeared not to be dented, but his verbal dexterity could not disguise a growing bewilderment about what, if anything, he was now seeking to achieve. His ability to alienate theoretically opposed sections of the party simultaneously no doubt enhanced a reputation for judicious impartiality, but it indicated a loss of direction. The abortive attempt to tackle trade-union reform through Barbara Castle's 'In Place of Strife' legislation was a case in point (see also CASTLE, BARBARA). Even so, Wilson was shocked when he was defeated by Heath in June 1970.

It is very revealing that he should immediately have set about compiling an extensive chronicle of his government's fortunes, which was published in 1971. He was not a man to sit back and reflect. Detail, once again, was everything. He had to put the record straight, as he saw it. There was no question of resignation and in opposition he battled hard for an opportunity to try again. However, Labour's quarrels did not disappear during the early 1970s. The issue of membership of the Common Market again proved divisive. Heath's economic and industrial difficulties multiplied, but the Labour victory in February 1974 was scarcely adequate and the result in October hardly an improvement. It is not easy to evaluate Wilson's final two years in office without being conscious of the reasons he himself advanced for his retirement. The referendum in 1975, as a means of settling Common Market membership, proved a masterstroke despite the tension it generated. The fact that cabinet divisions were openly displayed was somehow cathartic. However, the issue of relations between party and trade unions proved less amenable to such resolution. The appointment of Michael Foot seemed to be a signal that Wilson had learnt his lesson within the party, but it also gave further ammunition to the opposition. Despite the

Prime Minister's apparent buoyancy, the will to govern was apparently draining away. He was now surrounded by seasoned and experienced colleagues. His position was not secure, or so he felt. The bounce which had launched the 'Hundred Days' a decade earlier was no longer present. Problems of inflation and employment which he had approached for years with the confidence of a clever undergraduate now seemed somewhat formidable.

Surprisingly quickly after his retirement it became difficult to believe that Wilson had ever been the dominant figure he had once appeared in the 1960s. Cabinet diaries published by his erstwhile colleagues did not enhance his reputation, nor did his final Honours List. He remained in the Commons for a further seven years before taking a life peerage, but made little contribution. He became a Knight of the Garter. Once again he busied himself with a massive account of his last administration, which was published in 1979. It could appear that his remarkable memory, which had helped him to shine when he was young, had in the end proved a curse. He remembered so much that would have been better forgotten. In a curious way, he had failed to 'grow with the job'. He remained fundamentally a very clever grammar-school boy whose desire to shine had once impressed, then amused, and finally bored his colleagues and the nation at large.

WRITINGS

The Making of a Prime Minister 1916–64 (London: Michael Joseph with Weidenfeld and Nicolson, 1986).

The Labour Government 1964–70 (London: Michael Joseph with Weidenfeld and Nicolson, 1971).

Final Term: the Labour Government 1974–76 (London: Michael Joseph with Weidenfeld and Nicolson, 1979).

KEITH ROBBINS

Wilson, Sir **Henry (Hughes)** (*b.* Currygrane, Co. Longford, Ireland, 5 May 1854; *d.* London, 22 June 1922). Anglo-Irish general, political intriguer and Unionist MP. Wilson, who was Chief of the Imperial General Staff

(CIGS) from February 1918 until February 1922, was one of the ablest staff officers ever to serve in the British army and the most explicitly political soldier of his generation. Before and during World War I he worked tirelessly to secure a close Anglo-French alliance, and he sided with Lloyd George in the politician's conflict with Haig and Robertson. An Irish Protestant, his strong Unionist sympathies emerged particularly during the 'Ulster Crisis' of 1914 and the Anglo-Irish War of 1919–21. After retiring from the War Office in 1922, he entered the House of Commons, serving as Unionist MP for North Down for four months before his death.

Wilson was born into a moderately well-off land-owning family whose forbears had been Ulster-Scots merchants. He was sent to school in England – Marlborough College – where he excelled only at games. He failed the entrance examinations for the army several times and in the end entered the service through the Militia. In 1884 he obtained a regular commission in the Rifle Brigade. Most of Wilson's career, like that of his great rival Sir WILLIAM ROBERTSON, was spent in staff appointments. In the 1890s he served in the Intelligence Department of the War Office as the youngest staff officer in the army. During the South African War of 1899–1902 he worked for the Commander-in-Chief, Lord Roberts, who proved to be a most valuable patron. Wilson, for his part, gave Roberts help with his campaign for conscription in Britain. On his return from South Africa Wilson also began to enjoy increasing contacts within the wider world of Conservative and Unionist politics. An articulate and stimulating speaker, he was flattered by the attention paid to his views by politicians. They were impressed by his alertness and breadth of vision.

From 1907 to 1910 Wilson was an inspiring and notably successful Commandant of the Staff College. One of his highest priorities, as he saw it, was to prepare the British army for what he regarded as the inevitable war between France and Germany. A lifelong Francophile, Wilson believed – like many other soldiers – that Britain's place was at France's side in this conflict and he laboured, often rather in advance of any political commitment to a French alliance, to ensure that this came to

pass. His unusually close personal friendship with Ferdinand Foch did much to facilitate Anglo-French military cooperation before, during and after World War I.

Wilson's concern for the future of the Union between Great Britain and Ireland took him into a leading, if equivocal, role during the Ulster Crisis of 1914. He kept his Unionist politician friends well informed of developments within the War Office and he encouraged fellow officers to threaten resignation while seeming to hold back from taking such a drastic step himself. He emerged from the affair with a deserved reputation for intrigue which blackened him in the eyes both of colleagues and some Liberal politicians. Yet, despite his die-hard Unionist sympathies, Home Rulers such as Lloyd George and Churchill continued to respect Wilson's strategic and military opinions, and as many brother officers admired his ability to communicate with politicians as deplored his penchant for doing so.

As Director of Military Operations between 1910 and 1914 Wilson was responsible for making the detailed arrangements to deploy the British Expeditionary Force (BEF) in Northern France. In the event the successful movement of the BEF across the Channel was a triumph for Wilson and his colleagues. But the very precision of the arrangements, and the lack of any feasible alternative, limited the options open to the politicians in August 1914, thus giving Wilson's work a very important decision-making dimension. For most of the war, however, he was denied a similar influence on policy. Distrusting him, Asquith and Kitchener kept him out of the most important jobs, and he did not gain any position of real influence until after Lloyd George became Prime Minister at the end of 1916. Lloyd George thought Wilson had 'undoubtedly the nimblest intelligence amongst the soldiers of high degree'; he enjoyed discussing policy with him and used him as an alternative source of military advice to either the gruff and inarticulate Robertson or the dour and uncompromising Haig.

In February 1918 Lloyd George succeeded in manoeuvring Robertson out of the CIGS-ship and replacing him with Wilson, whose position as a close prime ministerial adviser for the next year or so was matched only by that of the Cabinet Secretary, Sir Maurice Hankey. But kitchen-cabinet decision-making of this sort could not very long survive the end of the war. Once Lloyd George turned to wider questions of domestic and foreign reconstruction, Wilson's value as an adviser began to decline. Wilson, too, for all his 'political' instincts, was not a man much given to compromise in any particular situation. Faced with an overextended empire in the aftermath of the war, and an upsurge of internal discontent, all Wilson could advise was a blunt 'govern or get out'. He was particularly intransigent regarding Ireland, where he would contemplate no policy beyond the forcible crushing of Sinn Fein and the IRA. So the 'frock' (politician) and the 'brasshat' (soldier) fell out, and Wilson simply refused to speak to Lloyd George after the Prime Minister had opened negotiations with the Irish nationalists in 1921.

During the war, when he felt that the nation was not properly utilizing his manifold talents, Wilson had toyed with – and rejected – the idea of entering Parliament. In 1922 he finally accepted an Ulster Unionist offer of a Northern Ireland Westminster constituency – unopposed – but his parliamentary career was abruptly cut short when he was assassinated on his doorstep in Belgravia by two Irish republicans, both British ex-servicemen, one with a wooden leg. One of Wilson's biographers – Bernard Ash – has suggested that Wilson was 'the lost dictator', that he might have become leader of the Conservative Party and even gone on to be a British Mussolini or Hitler. There is no evidence to support this contention, even in Wilson's wildest fantasies. There were two reasons why Wilson became an MP: one practical and one emotional. In the first place he needed the money and hoped that a seat in the Commons might bring him a directorship or two. Secondly, apart from his undoubted desire to serve the cause of Unionism, he was seduced by the activity of politics itself. Sir Sam Fay, an admirer of Robertson, reported the cruel jibe of a senior soldier that 'whenever Wilson came within a mile of prominent politicians he suffered from a sexual disturbance.' Wilson dearly enjoyed the company of politicians and the illusion of sharing their power, but he never

himself exercised any power. In the sphere of politics, as in that of battle, he was only a spectator, never a player.

FURTHER READING

Ash, Bernard, *The Lost Dictator* (London: Cassell, 1968).
Callwell, Sir C. E., *Field Marshal Sir Henry Wilson: his Life and Diaries*, 2 vols. (London: Cassell, 1927).
Fay, Sir Sam, *The War Office at War* (London: Hutchinson, 1937).
Jeffery, Keith (ed.), *The Military Correspondence of Field Marshal Sir Henry Wilson, 1918–1922* (London: Army Records Society/Bodley Head, 1985).

KEITH JEFFERY

Wood, (Howard) Kingsley (*b.* Hull, Yorkshire, 19 August 1881; *d.* London, 21 September 1943). Conservative Chancellor of the Exchequer. He was prominent in Conservative politics between the wars and, despite the fact that he had been close to Neville Chamberlain, Churchill made him Chancellor of the Exchequer in 1940. He retained that office until his sudden death in 1943 and played a central part in the early discussions on how the war should be financed. The advice he received from Keynes and other economists can be seen reflected in the system of postwar credits which he introduced. He also accepted the PAYE system, introduced shortly after his death. Naturally, too, he wrestled with particular problems produced by war and accepted the responsibility of the state to compensate for damage to property. His important role was unexpected because he was neither a financial expert nor a crony of the Prime Minister. His appointment was nevertheless testimony to the fact that he had obtained a reputation for getting things done.

Wood was the son of a Wesleyan Methodist minister and in due time he became treasurer of Wesley's Chapel in the City Road, where his father latterly ministered. Wood remained a prominent Methodist throughout his life. Early articled to a solicitor, he set up his own practice subsequently in the City and became active on the London County Council. He was knighted in 1918, chiefly for his work in connection with health insurance, and later that year became Conservative MP for West Woolwich – the constituency he represented until his death. He worked closely with Neville Chamberlain as his Parliamentary Secretary at the Ministry of Health throughout the second Baldwin administration. In 1930 he became chairman of the executive committee of the National Union of Conservative and Unionist Associations. After the 1931 general election, which confirmed the National Government in office, Wood became Postmaster-General. He played a significant role in the expansion of the telephone service and was rewarded by a seat in the cabinet in 1933. In 1935 he was transferred to the Ministry of Health, where his previous experience under Chamberlain was put to good use. In May 1938 the new Prime Minister, who retained his high opinion of Wood, transferred him to the Air Ministry. He had no previous service background but there was a belief that he might be able to accelerate the supply of aeroplanes with the same skill as he had shown in increasing the number of telephones. There can be no doubt that he was very energetic and his efforts tend now to be regarded with more respect than was once the case. He became Lord Privy Seal in April 1940 and his advice to Chamberlain in that month that he should resign as Prime Minister may have been of considerable importance in persuading the latter to go.

Despite the fact that his mother was related to Sarah Siddons, Wood never excelled on the public platform. He had a squeaky voice. That he was plump and a Methodist was held against him in some Conservative circles, but his contribution to the flavour and achievements of the National Governments in the 1930s was substantial in more than a physical sense.

KEITH ROBBINS

Woodcock, George (*b.* Walton le Dale, Lancashire, 20 October 1904; *d.* Epsom, Surrey, 30 October 1979). Trade-union leader. Woodcock was General Secretary of the TUC from 1960 to 1969. His combination of practical experience and intellectual ability is so far unique among holders of this office. His father

was a cotton weaver and George initially followed him into the mill, though he apparently hankered after a career as a professional footballer. He was a self-disciplined young man who took his Catholicism and Labour politics seriously. However, he did not play a major role in local activities. His spare time was devoted largely to study, which took him on a TUC scholarship to Ruskin College, Oxford. From there, unusually, he moved to New College and took a First in philosophy, politics and economics in 1933. He then spent two years in the Civil Service before joining the TUC as head of the research and economic department. Woodcock retained this post for a decade until 1947, when he became Assistant General Secretary. It gave him an opportunity to share in the discussions and debates about 'full employment' after the war was over. He was not a major figure in these deliberations, but after 1945 he began to wrestle with the role of trade unions in a Labour – and then a Conservative – Britain. Trade unions had been outside the 'system'. Their leaders were formed in a culture of opposition. Woodcock knew what that meant from his own boyhood but believed that trade unions had to exercise their new power, in changed circumstances, 'responsibly'. The management of the economy entailed partnership between government and both sides of industry.

It was almost inevitable that Woodcock should succeed Tewson in 1960 – the tradition of internal promotion was well established. It was by no means the case, however, that all trade-union leaders accepted either Woodcock's analysis of industrial realities or the paths of cooperation he advocated. It was with difficulty that the TUC was persuaded in 1962 to take part in the National Economic Development Council set up by a Conservative Chancellor. Woodcock also was able to persuade his colleagues to accept a prices and incomes policy under Labour and supposed that the TUC could effectively 'vet' the wage claims of individual unions. It was a role the TUC had never previously espoused and a measure of Woodcock's influence that it could even be attempted. He was an intelligent man but not a dry intellectual. He passionately believed in the close inter-meshing of unions and government, as he saw it, in the interests of preserving full employment. He was the obvious person to be appointed first chairman of the Commission on Industrial Relations by Wilson in 1969, and he remained in this post under Heath until his resignation in 1971 in opposition to the government's wish to give the commission a legal role.

Woodcock was one of the major public figures of the 1960s. His bushy eyebrows became familiar to a television audience in his hey-day. However, in his last years he was a disappointed man as he watched the collapse both of the ideas and the institutions he had played a major part in creating, within and beyond the trade-union movement.

KEITH ROBBINS

Woolf, Leonard (Sidney) (*b.* London, 25 November 1880; *d.* Rodmell, Sussex, 14 August 1969). Socialist writer and Labour Party worker. A member of the Fabian Society and the Labour Party, who also belonged, as did J. M. Keynes, to the so-called Bloomsbury Group, Woolf was an authority in two political fields: international affairs and cooperation. After reading classics at Cambridge, he joined the Colonial Service in 1904 and was posted to Ceylon, but resigned in 1912 to marry the future novelist Virginia Stephen. By this time his political outlook had begun to mature. He joined the Fabians, became involved in the cooperative movement (not least in the activities of the Women's Cooperative Guild) and began to specialize in international politics. British proposals for the formation of the League of Nations drew considerably on his *International Government* (1916), but in *Empire and Commerce in Africa* (1920) he produced a withering account of colonial exploitation hardly calculated to attract similar state approval. Woolf's writings on cooperation include *Co-operation and the Future of Industry* (1919) and *Socialism and Co-operation* (1921).

In 1917 Woolf and his wife founded the Hogarth Press which, in time, developed a strong political list, publishing, among others, G. D. H. Cole, R. H. S. Crossman, J. M. Keynes and H. G. Wells. Woolf unsuccessfully contested the Combined Universities seat for

Labour in 1922. His capacity for self-effacing committee work seemed unlimited, and he served as secretary to the Labour Party's committees on International Questions (1918–40) and Imperial Affairs (1924–46). He was also joint editor of the *Political Quarterly* (1931–59).

During the 1930s Woolf wrote in passionate opposition to totalitarianism, notably in *Quack, Quack!* (1935) and *Barbarians at the Gate* (1939). His larger ambitions as a political thinker, resulting in *After the Deluge* (1931, 1939) and *Principia Politica* (1953), were to pass unsatisfied. An excessively pessimistic estimate of his political career may be found in his autobiography, itself a masterpiece.

WRITINGS

Autobiography, 5 vols. (London: Hogarth Press, 1960–9).

FURTHER READING

Wilson, Duncan: *Leonard Woolf: a Political Biography* (London: Hogarth Press, 1978).

ANDREW MCNEILLIE

Woolton, Lord. See MARQUIS, FREDERICK.

Worsthorne, Peregrine (Gerard) (*b.* London, 22 December 1923). Journalist. He was for three decades Britain's leading right-wing polemical journalist, writing for the *Sunday Telegraph.* He held a number of senior positions on the paper but his promotion to the editorship, which many felt long overdue, did not come until 1986, when he was already 62. The reason for the delay was that he had achieved notoriety by using an indecent word in a live television discussion – and the proprietor, Lord Hartwell, never forgave him. Only when Hartwell sold the paper to the Canadian Conrad Black was the way left clear for Worsthorne's appointment. One of his first acts was to replace the leading articles with an essay, signed by him, on the main issue of the week, vesting the piece with authority and impact.

Apart from five years on *The Times*, from 1948 to 1953, Worsthorne has spent his entire Fleet Street career with the *Telegraph* group.

He is an old-fashioned Conservative of the right, with an unashamed belief in privilege and a distaste for populism. If his support for the Conservative governments of the 1980s was less than absolute, it was because he had little stomach for the brash entrepreneurial style of many of Mrs Thatcher's ministers. He was nostalgic for a more elegant and gentlemanly age of politics that reflected his sensibilities.

Worsthorne remained editor of the *Sunday Telegraph* for only three years. Although circulation originally rose when he took over, it quickly began to slip as a result of powerful competition from the more bulky *Sunday Times*. In 1989 the proprietors decided to bring the Sunday and daily editions closer together under a single editor, Max Hastings. Worsthorne became editor of and a contributor to four pages of comment inside the paper.

MICHAEL H. LEAPMAN

433

INDEX

Page references to the major entries on persons in the dictionary are in bold type.